Studies and reports in hydrology 28

Recent titles in this series

20. Hydrological maps. *Co-édition Unesco-WMO.*
21 * World catalogue of very large floods/Répertoire mondial des très fortes crues.
22. Floodflow computation. Methods compiled from world experience.
23. Water quality surveys.
24. Effects of urbanization and industrialization on the hydrological regime and on water quality. Proceedings of the Amsterdam Symposium, October 1977/Effets de l'urbanisation et de l'industrialisation sur le régime hydrologique et sur la qualité de l'eau. Actes du Colloque d'Amsterdam, octobre 1977. *Co-edition IAHS-Unesco/Coédition AISH-Unesco.*
25. World water balance and water resources of the earth. *(English edition).*
26. Impact of urbanization and industrialization on water resources planning and management.
27. Socio-economic aspects of urban hydrology.
28. Casebook of methods of computation of quantitative changes in the hydrological régime of river basins due to human activities

* Quadrilingual publication : English — French — Spanish — Russian.

For details of the complete series please see the list printed at the end of this work.

Casebook of methods of computation of quantitative changes in the hydrological régime of river basins due to human activities

Project 5.1 of the
International Hydrological
Programme

Prepared under the
chairmanship of
H. J. Colenbrander

unesco

The designations employed and the presentation of material throughout the publication
do not imply the expression of any opinion whatsoever on the part of Unesco concerning the legal
status of any country, territory, city or area or of its authorities, or concerning
the delimitation of its frontiers or boundaries.

Published in 1980 by the United Nations
Educational, Scientific and Cultural Organization,
7, place de Fontenoy, 75700 Paris
Printed by
Imprimerie de la Manutention, Mayenne
ISBN 92-3-101798-5

© Unesco 1980

Printed in France

Preface

The "Studies and Reports in Hydrology" series, like the related collection of "Technical Papers in Hydrology", was started in 1965 when the International Hydrological Decade was launched by the General Conference of UNESCO at its thirteenth session. The aim of this undertaking was to promote hydrological science through the development of international co-operation and the training of specialists and technicians.

Population growth and industrial and agricultural development are leading to constantly increasing demands for water, hence all countries are endeavouring to improve the evaluation of their water resources and to make more rational use of them. The IHD was instrumental in promoting this general effort. When the Decade ended in 1974, IHD National Committees had been formed in 107 of UNESCO's 135 Member States to carry out national activities and participate in regional and international activities within the IHD programme.

UNESCO was conscious of the need to continue the efforts initiated during the International Hydrological Decade and, following the recommendations of Member States, the Organization decided at its seventeenth session to launch a new long-term intergovernmental programme, the International Hydrological Programme (IHP), to follow the decade. The basic objectives of the IHP were defined as follows:
(a) to provide a scientific framework for the general development of hydrological activities;
(b) to improve the study of the hydrological cycle and the scientific methodology for the assessment of water resources throughout the world, thus contributing to their rational use;
(c) to evaluate the influence of man's activities on the water cycle, considered in relation to environmental conditions as a whole;
(d) to promote the exchange of information on hydrological research and on new developments in hydrology;
(e) to promote education and training in hydrology;
(f) to assist Member States in the organization and development of their national hydrological activities.

The International Hydrological Programme became operational on 1 January 1975 and is to be executed through successive phases of six years' duration. IHP activities are co-ordinated at the international level by an intergovernmental council composed of thirty Member States. The members are periodically elected by the General Conference and their representatives are chosen by national committees.

The purpose of the continuing series "Studies and Reports in Hydrology" is to present data collected and the main results of hydrological studies undertaken within the framework of the decade and the new International Hydrological Programme, as well as to provide information on the hydrological research techniques used. The proceedings of symposia will also be included. It is hoped that these volumes will furnish material of both practical and theoretical interest to hydrologists and governments and meet the needs of technicians and scientists concerned with water problems in all countries.

Contents

Foreword

PART 1 INTERNATIONAL SUMMARY

1.1	Introduction	13
2.1	Observational Requirements for Changes in the Hydrological Regime	21
2.2	Operational Aspects of Water Resources Management Schemes	32
2.3	Experimental Methods, Water Balance Methods, Experimental Basins	33
2.4	Hydrological Analogy	44
2.5	The Correlation between Cause and Effect	48
2.6	Statistical Analysis	51
2.7	Mathematical and Physical Modelling	53

PART 2 CASE STUDIES

3.1	Introduction	65
3.2	The Impact of Irrigation	66
3.2.1	Study of Man's Influence on the Hydrological Cycle in the Basin of the River Ebro	71
3.2.2	Modification of the Chu River Runoff due to Irrigation	79
3.2.3	The Greater Mussayeb Project in the Central Mesopotamian Plain	89
3.3	Drainage	99
3.3.1	Impact of Drainage on Stream Flow	103
3.3.2	The Hydrological Effects of Forest Drainage	108
3.3.3	The Effects of Arterial Drainage on Flood Magnitude	116
3.4	Stream Flow Regulation	127
3.4.1	Quantitative Changes in the Hydrological Regime in the Damodar Valley due to Stream Flow Regulation	131
3.4.2	Some Possibilities for Reconstructing the Data Corresponding to Natural Hydrological Conditions	154
3.4.3	Study Showing Man's Influence on the Hydrological Cycle in the River Tajo Basin	170
3.5	Land use cases	184
3.5.1	Estimation of Streamflow changes of the Tobol River up to Kustanai due to Agrotechnical Measures	187
3.5.2	The Quantitative Influence of Forests upon Floods	194
3.5.3	Inventory of Finnish Basin Characteristics using Landsat Digital Data, Topographic Maps and Aerial Photographs	200
3.5.4	Effect of the Cultivation of a Tropical Basin on its Hydrological Regime (Korhogo, Ivory Coast, 1962-1972)	206
3.5.5	The Effect of Land Use on Flood Flow Peaks from small East African Basins	227
3.6	The Effects of Urbanization and Industrialization	240
3.6.1	Changes in the Physical Conditions of Aquifers due to withdrawal of Large Volumes of Groundwater	242

3.6.2	Application of the Model for Groundwater Flow and Evapotranspiration to an Area around a Pumping Station used for Public Water Supply	254
3.6.3	Deep Open Pit Mining and Groundwater Problems in the Rhenish Lignite District	274
3.6.4	A Parallel Cascades Model to Predict the Effects of Urbanization on Watershed Response	291
3.7	The Integrated Influence of Various Human Activities	303
3.7.1	Streamflow Changes due to Man's Activity	307
3.7.2	Integrated Human Activities in the Upper Basin of the Paraiba do Sul River, Brazil	318

PART 3   CONCLUSIONS

4	Conclusions	327
5	Selected Bibliography	329

Foreword

This casebook on "Methods of computation of quantitative changes in the hydrological regime of river basins due to human activities" emanates from the International Hydrological Programme (IHP) Intergovernmental Council which, in 1975, appointed a special IHP Working Group under Project 5.1.

The Working Group, which was specifically assigned the task of preparing the casebook met in three sessions, 5-9 April 1976, 28 February-4 March 1977 and 16-19 May 1978. It was composed of the following experts:

- Mr H J Colenbrander (Netherlands), Chairman
- Mr Goh Kiam Seng (Malaysia)
- Mr V Kriz (Czechoslovakia)
- Mr J M Martin Mendiluce (Spain), later replaced by Mr R L Garcia Fresca (Spain)
- Mr B N Murthy (India)
- Mr H Niini (Finland)
- Mr I A Shiklomanov (USSR)
- Mr V A Stanescu (Romania)
- Mr O Starosolszky (Hungary)
- Mr K Uehara (Brazil)

The following international organizations were represented: the Food and Agriculture Organization (FAO), the World Meteorological Organization (WMO), the International Association of Hydrological Sciences (IAHS), the Scientific Committee on Water Research (COWAR) of the International Council of Scientific Unions (ICSU), and the United Nations Educational, Scientific and Cultural Organization (UNESCO), the last body being represented by Messrs F Verhoog and A Pinilla.

Following the preparation of a first draft of the manuscript, a panel of editors consisting of Messrs H J Colenbrander (Netherlands) and O Starosolszky (Hungary) prepared a second draft. The final editing was carried out by Mr J C Rodda (United Kingdom).

Part 1 International summary

by the IHP/UNESCO Working Group on the
Assessment of Quantitative Changes in
the Hydrological Regime of River Basins
Due to Human Activities (Project 5.1)

Contents of Part 1

1.1 Introduction
by H J Colenbrander, Committee for Hydrological Research TNO
Prinses Beatrixlaan 7, P.O. Box 297, 2501 BD, The Hague, Netherlands. ... 13

2.1 Observational Requirements for Changes in the Hydrological Regime
by R Bremond, Ministere de l'Environment et due Cadre de Vie,
14 Boulevade du Generale Leclerc, 92521 Neuilly sur Seine, Cedex,
France, with the assistance of Messrs Loriferne, Cheron, Chevassus,
Coste, Lafosse, Michel and Oberlin on behalf of the World Meteorological
Organization. ... 21

2.2 Operational Aspects of Water Resources Management Schemes
by V A Stanescu, Institute of Meteorology and Hydrology, Soseava
Bucuresti-Ploiesti No 97, Bucarest, Romania. ... 32

2.3 Experimental Methods, Water Balance Methods, Experimental Basins
by I A Shiklomanov, State Hydrological Institute, 2, Linija 23,
Leningrad V-53, USSR. ... 33

2.4 Hydrological Analogy
by V Kriz, PHMU, 70800 Ostrava-Poruba, Kmyslivne 1, Czechoslovakia. ... 44

2.5 The Correlation Between Cause and Effect - Human Activities and the
Hydrological Regime
by I A Shiklomanov, State Hydrological Institute, 2, Linija 23,
Leningrad V-53, USSR. ... 48

2.6 Statistical Analysis
by J M Martin Mendiluce, c/o Spanish National Committee for the IHP,
P Bajo de la Virgen del Puerto 3, Madrid 5, Spain. ... 51

2.7 Mathematical and Physical Modelling
by V A Stanescu, Institute of Meteorology and Hydrology, Soseava
Bucuresti-Ploiesti No 97, Bucarest, Romania. ... 53

Chapter 1

1.1 INTRODUCTION

1.1.1 Purpose and scope of the casebook

The first session of the IHP-Council in April 1975 adopted as Project 5: "Investigations of the Hydrological and Ecological Effects of Man's Activities and their Assessment".
A Working Group under Project 5.1 was established with the following terms of reference: "to prepare a casebook on methods of computation of quantitative changes in the hydrological regime of river basins due to human activities. The casebook is to contain examples representative of different climatological regions and of different levels of basin development, of methods of computation which have been effectively used to predict or to evaluate changes in the hydrological regime due to human activities".
The group, as such, was to continue, at least in part, the work of the former IHD Working Group on the Influence of Man on the Hydrological Cycle. The main difference in the work is that the present activities concentrate on methods of computing the hydrological consequences of human influences, rather than on a description of the possible hydrological effects. Human influences are to be evaluated quantitatively using recently developed models and the most relevant parameters; also due attention is to be paid to cause/effect relations.
The casebook is intended for hydrologists and other scientists, water resources engineers. and planners in general. It is not intended for decision-makers who maybe more interested in the actual extent of changes in the hydrological regime due to human activities and their significance in relation to the economy of the country concerned. It is felt that facts of this type have already been well documented. The human influences to be discussed in the casebook are those resulting from:
- irrigation schemes;
- drainage and reclamation projects;
- river engineering works (eg construction of reservoirs and dams; streamflow regulations);
- changes in land use (agricultural activities; forestry, etc);
- urbanization and industrialization;
- the totality of human activities and their integrated consequences.

However, as has been pointed out in the terms of reference, the casebook does not cover water quality aspects. This means that the hydrological and ecological consequences of the disposal of waste water and waste heat will not be discussed.
The hydrological phenomena and systems to be considered are:
- the overall water balance of an area;
- the surface water system (the maximum and minimum levels and flows; the temperature etc);
- the subsurface water system (ie the ground water and soil moisture subsystems);
- the sedimentation process;
- the salt/fresh water balances.

In particular, the effect of human activity on the water balance and on surface and subsurface water systems are to be elucidated.
The present Working Group is not the only group continuing the work of the former IHD Working Group on Human Influences on the Hydrological Cycle.
Under the same IHP Project - Project 5, there are also working groups set up for the Sub-projects 5.3, 5.4, 5.6 and 5.7. Besides these projects there are also several other

Introduction

IHP-projects which are directly or indirectly dealing with the problem of human influences.
These are Project 4.1 on representative and experimental basin research, Project 7 on effects of urbanization on the hydrological regime and Project 8.1 on models for investigations and predicting the changes in groundwater regimes due to human activities.
The interrelationship of all these projects calls for an effective co-ordination.

1.1.2 The role of water and its impact

From the beginning of time man has been using water and has also been fighting it. Water is not only a primary necessity of life; from time to time it also threatens life. This means water "shows two faces": one an aimiable one and one a malicious one. Using water and fighting it, man, in one way or another, influences the hydrological system.

People protected their habitats against floods by building hillocks to live upon and, later, by building sea dikes, embankments and barrages. Initially these man-made devices were of minor importance, but gradually their number and inherent effects grew.

As the population increased, more land was needed for the production of food. Marshes and waste land were reclaimed, and other areas were deforested. These measures had a significant effect on the conditions of water management of such areas.

At first, drinking water was not a great problem because the surface waters were not polluted. As urbanization and industrialization progressed however, the problem become more serious. Many surface streams became heavily polluted, and today in many parts of the world water cannot be used directly for domestic and industrial water supply. Large storage reservoirs have been built and huge quantities of groundwater extracted to meet human needs. All in all, human interference in the hydrological cycle has increased considerably.

It has, meanwhile, become clear that the various sub-systems are closely interrelated. Any intervention in one of these may affect others; for instance, extraction of ground water often affects the surface water system. These interrelationships have not been given proper attention in the past. The surface water system is probably the first sub-system that was influenced by man. The building of river and sea dikes, dams and other regulation works, was started in more or less pre-historic times. Other regulation works are, for example, the straightening and lining of channels, the construction of levees, weirs and other hydraulic structures. Many of these reduce the water level gradients and, consequently, the flow velocity thereby preventing erosion. Sand traps have also been built in order to concentrate the deposition of the remaining sediment. Many flood reduction works have also been constructed. These are mainly reservoirs in which water is temporarily stored during high floods.

Another very early influence of man on the flow behaviour of a river is the reclamation of waste land, especially for agriculture. As a consequence the existing drainage system has to be enlarged and usually intensified. The run-off from undrained land is generally smaller than that from reclaimed land, because under natural conditions much water is stored in depressions etc and this evaporates before reaching the river.

Other changes in land use often have a considerable effect on run-off. The most striking example is the deforestation of large areas. Besides a considerably increased run-off and higher peak flows, this run-off often causes severe erosion. Therefore, during the last few decades large areas have been reforested. But even a rather minor change in land use, eg from grassland into arable land or vice versa may have a significant effect on stream flow.

In many cases weirs and dams are installed to raise the water level in certain drainage channels and subsequently they raise the water table in the adjacent soils. The higher water table increases the amount of water available for transpiration by capillary rise from the groundwater. This will generate not only a higher production of agricultural crops, but may also change the natural vegetation. Plants, typical of dry conditions, may be replaced by water-loving vegetation. A comparable effect occurs where a network of irrigation canals is constructed in areas with a very deep water table and where infiltration of water from the canals may alter the vegetation. Obviously, the opposite effect may also be brought about. An artificial lowering of the original water levels in the drainage channels increases the drainage to these channels and the water table drops. The soil becomes drier and vegetation changes are likely to occur.

In certain areas, mining activities have a great influence on the original channel network. In these areas enormous quantities of ground water are often extracted and drained elsewhere, changing the run-off situation. As a consequence of mining, land subsidence often occurs, affecting the gradient of the drainage system.

Introduction

Another human activity which influences the channel system is the process of urbanization and industrialization. Large areas of formerly vegetated soil are now paved and have houses, factories, etc built upon them. The percentage of the fast run-off consequently increases markedly, and the base-flow component decreases. Higher peak flows occur. The total volume of run-off increases because, generally speaking, the evapotranspiration of an urbanized area is smaller than that of vegetated soil.

To sum up, the human activities discussed tend to alter river characteristics such as the run-off volume, the shape of the run-off hydrograph and the height of flood peaks, the frequency distribution of river flows, the water level gradients of flow velocities, the bed roughness, the amount of penetrating light, the sediment transport, the water quality and the water temperature.

Man-made lakes or reservoirs are used to store water for power generation, irrigation, domestic and industrial use and recreation. The USSR IHP Committee (1978) has published data concerning the number and size of the existing reservoirs (see Table 1). Man-made lakes superimpose an aquatic ecosystem on a terrestrial one. The immediate result is an unstable situation that cannot easily be defined. In the past the changes due to the construction of lakes have very often not been given enough attention in the planning stage of a project.

A quite different effect of man-made lakes arises because they impose new stresses on the earth's crust and these may generate landslides and even seismic movements. Large reservoirs will moreover affect the micro-climate. Up to now, however, not much detail is known about these effects.

Not only the surface water but also the sub-surface water is influenced by man's activities. Sometimes this occurs in an indirect way as a consequence of manipulations of the surface water system. However, the groundwater system is also influenced in a very direct way. The point is that groundwater has several properties which make it very attractive for domestic and industrial use. First, the quality of groundwater is mostly far better than that of surface water and second, the temperature is relatively constant. Hence large volumes of groundwater are extracted over the world. Preferably, groundwater should be extracted from (semi) confined aquifers below impermeable layers, so that the phreatic water table is not, or is only slightly, affected. However, due to the considerably increased water need, extraction nowadays also takes place in areas where the situation is less favourable. Consequently, the phreatic water table often drops steeply, and this affects the soil moisture zone. When the land is used for agriculture, the drawdown of the water table causes a reduction of evapotranspiration which means a smaller crop yield.

Other human activities which influence the soil moisture system are land treatment and such farm practices as levelling, deep ploughing and terracing. These activities lower the depression storage and overland flow and will, in general, increase the infiltration capacity. The various measures also strongly influence soil erosion and sediment transport.

As discussed above, an artificial drawdown of the water table may also affect the surface waters. This means a reduced flow and lower levels in the water courses, which may even dry out completely. This of course affects the aquatic ecosystem and the users of the surface water downstream of the point of extraction.

One special aspect that must be mentioned briefly is the increase in salt-water intrusion because of groundwater extraction. In many coastal areas, the fresh water body lies upon the salt water. By extraction of fresh water the boundary between the fresh and the salt water rises rapidly and salinity increases. Therefore, in coastal areas it is necessary to be very careful with groundwater extraction. Surface water from elsewhere may be used for recharging an underground barrier against saline penetration.

In order to determine as precisely as possible to what degree the quantitative changes in the hydrological regime are due to different human activities, these various activities must be quantitatively measured or assessed. To this end the various activities can be grouped in different ways. Two of these possibilities will be elucidated.

These activities of man are of 3 kinds:

(1) primary,
(2) secondary,
(3) inadvertent.

(1) The 'primary' activities include any activities (operations), the very purpose of which is, or means, a certain change in the hydrological regime, like irrigation, dam construction, streamflow and water level regulation, drainage, water supply and partly also waste water

15

Table 1 Larger reservoirs of the world

Continent	Total number of reservoirs	Total volume km³	Number of reservoirs missing	Surface area km²	Number of reservoirs missing
Europe	22	336,84	1	48.721	2
Asia	48	1447,97	0	72.476	12
Africa	12	1064,47	0	100.292	1
North America	42	835,18	2	55.578,5	15
South America	10	286,1	0	8.525	3
Australia and Oceania	3	37,7	0	361	0
World	137	4008,26	3	285.953,5	33

(Source: USSR IHP Committee)

disposal. The quantitative influence on the hydrological regime of the very activity can, and should, then be both measured and controlled simply by managing the operation itself.
(2) The 'secondary' activities include works which in themselves are not a hydrological change but which are known to be directly dependent on the hydrological regime. Examples of these activities are canal, bridge, and embankment construction, water traffic, timber floating, fishing industries, water recreation, and waste water disposal in part. Because of their dependence on the water regime, these activities often bring about an endeavour to 'improve' the water regime to meet the special requirements of the activity in question. However, their influence on the hydrological regime is often indirect and very complicated and to assess their effects both measurements of the historical extent of these activities and the determination of their basic physical characteristics are needed.
(3) The inadvertent activities at first might be seen to be independent from the hydrological regime, but may, in reality, affect it considerably in an indirect way. The effects are often very complex. Many human activities related to agriculture and forestry, urbanization, and industrialization belong to this group. In order to assess quantitatively their influence on the hydrological regime, it is not sufficient to observe the entire activity as a fixed entity, but the basic constituents of the activity should be appropriately separated and their chronological evolution as well as their physical nature should be determined. The final purpose of such determinations is to minimise the inadvertent effects of these activities by appropriate control measures.

As to the observational requirements, a different classification of the several human activities affecting the hydrological regime is more useful:

(4) sudden,
(5) gradual, or
(6) irregular activities.

(4) The first category comprises a sudden (or relatively abrupt) change, like building a dam, a reservoir, a canal, an embankment etc. The start of any regular activity like water supply or water traffic may be a sudden change. Such a sudden activity may over a short space of time cause a permanent change in the environmental conditions.
(5) Activities termed gradual comprise continuous operations like peat extraction, mining, and many other industrial as well as urban activities including long-lasting construction activities. It is obvious that the hydrological effects of these activities will gradually increase.
(6) Irregular activities include many forestry and agricultural practices like clear-cutting and thinning of forests, soil improvement measures, and the extraction of water, eg for irrigation. Naturally many human activities are more or less intermediate between these basic groups. This fact further emphasizes the needs of detailed measurement and analysis in future of the various human 'cause' activities.

1.1.3 Research developments

As an introduction to Chapter 2 where various computational methods are discussed, this section elucidates the developments in research in the field of human influences while the work of some previous commissions and working parties is also mentioned.

Depending on the availability of reference data, the physical and geographical characteristics of the catchment areas, the type of economic activity and the extent of its development, a very varied range of methods is applied in evaluating the influence of human factors on the hydrological regime. These may be grouped in two categories:
- methods based on the investigation of run-off variations over many years at hydrological research sites, combined with analysis of the change in natural meteorological factors and the development of economic activity in the basin;
- water balance methods, involving separate calculations of the water drawn off and of changes in the components of the water and heat balances in the river basin resulting from the effects of each type of economic activity.

The approach adopted for the first group is to study the long-term variations in the hydrological characteristics at the outfalls from the basins as influenced by natural factors, and on this basis to elucidate the influence of man's activities.

The nature of these methods is such that they can be used to evaluate the influence on the hydrological regime of a whole series of economic activities affecting a catchment area.

Introduction

However, they can also be successfully used to elucidate the role of individual activities. Methods of various kinds for reconstructing the natural hydrological characteristics of a river under observation using rivers with similar characteristics, or the use of so-called control catchment areas with undisturbed regimes, have been employed as means for evaluating the influence of various activities.

For this purpose, use is usually made of a simple correlation, or graphs are plotted of the relationship of the integral run-off values (the so-called double mass curve). In the latter instance, the effect of man's activity is judged by the change in the gradient of the relationship, although this in individual cases may also be caused by natural changes in the meteorological conditions of one of the basins under comparison. However, the reconstruction of hydrological characteristics by this means is not a sufficiently effective method, and in most cases, it is difficult to make a reliable quantitative evaluation of the influence of human factors.

It is possible to take account of a large number of factors (natural and human) acting on the run-off by using various mathematical methods, particularly the method of linear multiple correlation which uses experimental data to establish a multifactoral mathematical model of changes in hydrological characteristics. The theory of this method is well known and is described in texts on mathematical statistics. Hydrologists all over the world have adopted this technique as the chief method of hydrological analysis. It is widely used, for example, in calculating changes in hydrological characteristics brought about by changes in land use and cultivation. The multiple linear correlation method is used in two ways for evaluating the influence of economic activity on run-off. It is used first of all for research into run-off variations in time at the outfall from the catchment area over the greatest possible number of years, and second for studying the spatial variation of average run-off values over one and the same period of observation on the greatest possible number of basins of a given region with differing physical and geographical characteristics and levels of economic development.

A word is also clearly in order about the experimental method which is widely used for evaluating the influence on the hydrological regime of various kinds of land use, eg forest clearance and afforestation, changes in the crops grown in a catchment area, etc. On the basis of the difference between the components of the water balance before and after the changes in the basin, one can judge what effect the changes have had on the various hydrological characteristics. The setting up of an experiment to measure changes in the water balance in a catchment is the most effective method of elucidating the role of land-surface factors in a particular basin. However, substantial deficiences are inherent in it, such as the high cost involved and the large number of years with varying meteorological conditions necessary to arrive at reliable conclusions. Therefore this method cannot be considered as the principal method for evaluating the influence of human activities on a hydrological regime.

For evaluating man's influence on the hydrological regime, use must therefore be made of the approach based on a study of the changes which occur in the components of the water, heat and saline balances in certain portions of the catchment areas and in the water course, as the result of a change in natural conditions induced by economic activity (land taken for urban development, irrigated and drained areas, areas flooded by reservoirs, etc). On the basis of an analysis of experimental data concerning the hydrological regime and the water and heat balances, methods have to date been worked out for evaluating the influence of various activities.

Evaluation methods based on the mathematical modelling of processes occurring in the basin or in various parts of it can be regarded as one variant of balance methods. Mathematical modelling methods have considerable merit in the sense that, in a short time and without great expense, they make it possible to evaluate in quantitative terms the effects of even the most heterogeneous combination of natural and human factors and so allow prediction of the future hydrological regime and water balance of basins, should this or that alternative type of regional development plan be adopted. The chief drawback of evaluation methods which use mathematical modelling is that their conclusions depend not only on the reliability of the initial data, but also on the completeness and validity of the equations adopted for the calculations and, to an equal degree, on the extent to which the process itself can be studied.

The techniques mentioned have been used by various committees and working groups. One of these was the Working Group on the Influence of Man on the Hydrological Cycle. The

Table 2 Relations between type of human activity, climate, basin size and country concerned in the case studies reported in Chapter 3

HUMAN ACTIVITIES	TEMPERATE			ARID			TROPICAL		
	Small	Medium	Large	Small	Medium	Large	Small	Medium	Large
					Catchment				
3.2. Irrigation			Spain		Iraq	USSR			
3.3. Drainage	Finland	USSR Ireland							
3.4. Streamflow regulation		Spain Rumania						India	
3.5. Land use	Finland Rumania				USSR		Africa East Africa		
3.6. {Urbanization Industrialization	FRG	Netherlands Hungary FRG							
3.7. Integrated						USSR		Brazil	

19

References

first report of this Working Group was published by Pereira (1972) as a contribution to the report: Status and Trends of Research in Hydrology (1965-1974). As recommended by this Working Group a second report on this topic was written by Dooge, Costin and Finkel (1973).

Many international symposia and workshops have dealt with the subject of human influences such as the symposium of the International Geographical Union on: Man made Transformation of Water Balance (USSR, July 1976) and a Speciality Conference of the American Society of Civil Engineers on Environmental Aspects of Irrigation and Drainage (Ottawa, July 1976).

1.1.4 Contents of the Casebook

Besides this introductory chapter and the case studies (Chapter 3), the book contains a methodological chapter. This chapter, Chapter 2, describes the methods of computing the changes of the hydrological regime due to man's activities. It also discusses the observational aspects related to the study of human influences.

Special emphasis is given to observations on experimental basins and to water balance investigations. Relationships are presented between two sets of variables characterising, on the one side the hydrological regime, and on the other the human activities. In this connection, the use of some recently developed statistical methods are discussed as well as some promising conceptual and physical catchment and river models.

The third chapter contains the case studies. For their selection various criteria were used such as: the type of human activity, the physiographical region, basin size, etc. (see Table 2).

Of the 20 case studies presented, three of these deal with experiences gained in Asia, two in Africa and one in South America. The others are from Europe. Relatively few case studies have become available from arid and tropical regions, notwithstanding the efforts made to obtain them by the Working Group. Because most of the developing countries are located in these regions and especially as these countries can benefit from the experiences gained, more attention should be paid to these regions in future studies. Certain experiences can be transferred directly to different areas but the utilization of other experiences will need local investigations, especially in the case of numerical parameters.

In Chapter 4 some conclusions are presented and, in addition to the bibliographies given with each chapter and case study, a selected general bibliography of a comprehensive character has been compiled and concludes this casebook.

REFERENCES

Dooge, J.C.I., Costin, A.B., and Finkel, H.J. 1973. 'Man's influence on the hydrological cycle'. *FAO Irrigation and Drainage Paper*, No 17, 71 pp.

Pereira, H.C. 1972. The influence of man on the hydrological cycle - Guide lines to policies for the save development of land and water resources in Status and Trends of Research in Hydrology, UNESCO, *Studies and Reports in Hydrology*, No 10.

USSR IHP Committee, 1978. World water balance and water resources of the earth, UNESCO, *Studies and Reports in Hydrology*, No 25.

Chapter 2

2.1 OBSERVATIONAL REQUIREMENTS FOR CHANGES IN THE HYDROLOGICAL REGIME

2.1.1 Introduction

The changes in the hydrological regime due to human activities can be observed either by national hydrological networks or by specialized monitoring stations. Since the need for these specialized stations was recognized but recently, long-term trends can be detected only by studying the hydrological time series. When improving or establishing new networks, consideration should be given to those aspects of the hydrological regime necessary to detect future changes.

Generally two basic problems should be solved:
(1) For assessing changes in the hydrological elements much higher observational accuracy is needed, because the changes are differential values.
(2) For determining the cause and effect interrelationships, besides observation of the hydrological elements simultaneous observation of the several human activities, whenever possible, in numerical form, is necessary. Thus the observational programme should be greatly enlarged and the various observations should be co-ordinated.

Both problems are more economic than technical because the means and methods are available but the costs of the enlarged observational programme can be so high that the available limited financial sources are insufficient.

Most countries of the world should now consider the priority of the required investments and therefore it is of primary importance to call to their attention this change in the basic concept of network improvement and establishment.

The relevant human activities may be classified as:
(a) water management (eg intakes, outlets, reservoirs etc); and as
(b) other human impacts (land use, urbanization, mining etc).
In category (a) impact data are usually available in well-formulated dimensions and their observation is well organized. In (b) often no systematic data collection was previously necessary so no historical data are available and continuous and regular observations have not been organized.

Different hydraulic structures may change the water regime in their vicinity and the gauging stations used under natural conditions are not suitable for characterizing the flow under artificial conditions. New methods for gauging are necessary or corrections of the data should be made. As a most pertinent example, reference may be made to the backwater effect where no constant rating curve (stage-discharge relationship) can be applied. On the other hand, the hydraulic structures may give new measuring sites. Calibrated weirs or gates are sufficient tools for discharge measurement at artificially-affected reaches. As a consequence of human activities, the traditional hydrological network is improved.

In this manner a "feed-back" system may characterize the interrelationship between the network and changes in the hydrological regime due to human activities.

Observational requirements

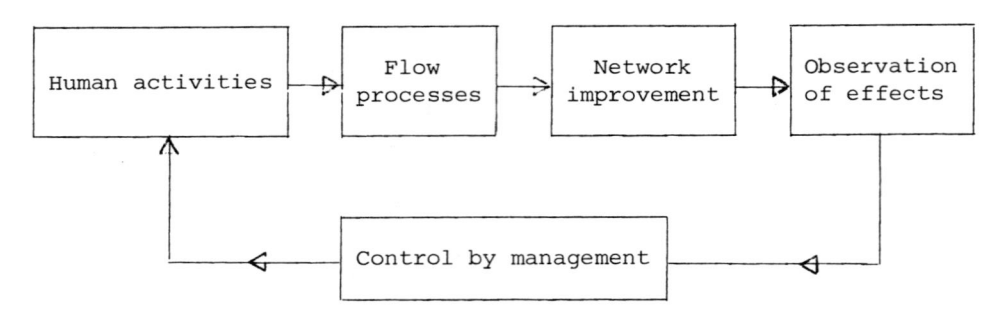

```
┌─────────────────┐   ┌──────────┐   ┌─────────────┐   ┌─────────────┐
│ Human activities│──▷│   Flow   │──▷│   Network   │──▷│ Observation │
│                 │   │processes │   │ improvement │   │  of effects │
└─────────────────┘   └──────────┘   └─────────────┘   └─────────────┘
         ▲                                                     │
         │              ┌──────────────────────┐               │
         └──────────────┤ Control by management├───────────────┘
                    ◁   └──────────────────────┘   ◁
```

2.1.2 <u>Difficulties encountered in measuring changes in the hydrological regime</u>

Certain human activities have a pronounced effect on the hydrological regime. These include urbanization, major projects such as the construction of motorways, industrial complexes or new towns, deforestation under severe physiographical and climatic conditions or the creation of reservoirs. The influence of other activities, however, such as irrigation, drainage, the regrouping of farmland, or changes in crops or agricultural techniques is less marked, if not minimal, particularly in temperate climates and on flat land.

Changes may also occur suddenly or in a short period of time, as in the case of forest fires or the building of dams, for example, or, on the contrary, they may take place slowly and over a long period as with small-scale irrigation using water drawn from rivers or groundwater reserves, drainage etc. Other changes may be foreseen or planned, for example by a statutory framework which provides for co-ordination on the part of the various authorities so that the consequences can be properly calculated. In many cases, however, it is not known that changes are going to occur until too late or until they have begun to take place.

All these different situations have a decisive influence on arrangements for measuring changes in the hydrological regime. The problem is comparatively easy to solve when the human activities in question have a pronounced impact, develop rapidly and are foreseen well in advance. When these activities are diffuse or gradual, the changes which they lead to are smaller or lie within the accepted margin of error of conventional instruments and methods of observation. In such cases, more accurate means are required to detect significant variations in the hydrological regime.

When observations are made for only a limited number of years before a man-induced change occurs, the series of measurements so obtained is insufficient to permit any direct comparison with the series obtained after the change. Other arrangements have to be made in that case, particularly for the measurement of rainfall, whose sensitivity to human activities is much less marked. In certain cases, it may suffice to make measurements on a very similar basin where there has been no human intervention of any kind. But comparison of the discharge with the rainfall or discharge of the analogous basin introduces a further source of inaccuracy into the results.

Interest in <u>a posteriori</u> quantitative data concerning modifications produced by human activity is often not great enough for funds to be made available for a network specifically for the measurement of such modifications. By sufficient interest we would mean a hope that with such data, it would be possible to predict the changes that planned developments would bring about. Such predictions can, however, very rarely be quantified. It will, therefore, often be necessary either simply to detect changes from existing data gathered from the water resources monitoring networks, or to seek other objectives which would justify - more than the mere measurement of change - the creation, for example, of an experimental basin.

2.1.3 <u>General principles</u>

As a general rule, the degree of accuracy, density and complexity required of any observation network designed to detect the influence of human activity must be all the greater as that influence is slight, gradual, not foreseen or not understood.

Arrangements for more accurate measurement may be made in that range of situations where the influence is the most interesting. When water is pumped from the alluvial aquifer for irrigation purposes, for example, instruments may be installed for the precise measurement of the lowering of the groundwater level. Changes in the hydrological regime may be measured

Observational requirements

directly or indirectly:
- direct measurements may be made of streamflow, and, where appropriate, of rainfall and groundwater levels before and after human intervention.
- changes in the hydrological regime may be measured indirectly through measurement of the causes of change (eg amounts of water drawn from or fed back into rivers) or through estimates based, for example, on a survey of surface areas under irrigation, or a study of crops and the monthly rates of water consumption per hectare. The indirect method may lack accuracy, but it sometimes produces better results than direct measurement of changes in the rate of flow although it may be difficult to apply in certain cases of feedback. Indirect measurements may be made by different methods, ranging from field surveys to remote sensing.

Measurements of changes in the hydrological regime may be made:
- on the scale of a relatively extensive basin. In such a case, several types of human activity come into play in a complex way. It is impossible to distinguish between individual influences, but the total result can be followed and monitored. The oldest established observation points are generally situated in such areas so that data covering long periods are available;
- on the scale of a small basin where there is virtually only one human activity. This provides data that can more easily be transferred to other situations.

Certain of these basins may be used as representative or experimental basins.

2.1.4 Networks

Most governments have set up national networks of hydrological instruments and are conducting studies to discover the distribution in space and time of their countries' water resources. Some of the stations in these networks have been providing information for a considerable time, ie a century or more, particularly rainfall and river flow stations and groundwater observation wells. Networks for the measurement of the water equivalent of snow, evaporation, soil moisture and water quality are of much more recent origin, however. The criteria applied in planning a countrywide network can vary from one country to another, but most networks have been developed in response to national requirements, the greatest attention being devoted to the large basins in the most developed areas of the country concerned, where there is the greatest pressure on resources.

Such networks are well adapted to the purposes for which they were created but they are frequently ill-equipped to measure changes in the hydrological regime due to human activities. Despite the fact that their standards of accuracy and the homogeneity of the results obtained are often insufficient to reveal the impact of such activities on their measurements, the existence of these networks, and more particularly the length of time over which they have been taking measurements, are of very considerable interest. Their ability to detect changes due to human activities can, in fact, be enhanced by improvements in the study of low water levels. When levels are low, the level-outflow correlation often gives poor results, and in such cases it is frequently better to replace this correlation by periodic interpolations between measurements. In this case, the sole function of the limnograph is to check that there have been no sudden increases (eg minor floods due to rainstorms during the dry season) in the period between gauging measurements. If such floods occur, this interpolation brings into play a Q(H) rating curve limited to that range of levels which have in actual fact to be translated into discharge. This procedure necessitates frequent gauging (every 1-3 weeks). If such frequent measurements are impossible, the rating curve is adjusted at seasonal or monthly intervals. Systematic adjustments may be introduced on the basis of a "level/date correction" curve identical from one year to the next.

One objective of these networks that must be mentioned concerns the forecasting of floods and the issue of flood-warnings. Although they were not initially established specifically to assess the impact of human activities on the natural outflow, these networks inevitably reveal some of the beneficial or harmful effects produced on flood control by development projects in certain catchment areas.

Measurements made at the observation stations are vital for estimating the effect of human activities on runoff, particularly as far as the forecasting and advance warning of floods are concerned. These measurements should thus be collected, classified, verified, inventoried and even published. This involves problems of three sorts:
- Information gathering *in situ*, which involves frequent limnometric and pluviometric readings.

Observational requirements

- Information transmission. Depending on the circumstances, this is done by paid or voluntary observers, and is tending to make increasing use of automatic devices. These include telephone answering machines which, in reply to an ordinary telephone call, record the measurements dictated. The recording is then transmitted to the correspondent. It is possible to direct a transmission to a pre-arranged number. Telemetry is also used. Under this system the measurements are put into digital form and memorized, the information then being relayed to a central telemetry station by cable or by radio.

The measurement of discharge by the calibrated hydraulic structures is one way to solve the problems associated with the backwater effect and/or the daily unsteady regime due to structures.

At structures composed of several parts (spillway, weir, movable gate, power station, etc) and especially when sudden changes may occur in the operation, measurement of the discharge needs continuous measurement of upstream and downstream water stages, gate openings, output of turbines etc.

The interrelationships amongst stage/water level difference/operational parameter/gate, opening, output/and the discharge should be determined by field measurement (calibration) or by model tests. The measurements should cover the complete range of operation and so they are cumbersome and time consuming, therefore, in many cases, scale model tests are the basis of the calibration. Computation of the discharges needs graphs or tables.

Recent development of ultrasonic discharge measurement techniques enable the operators to apply continuous direct measurement and recording. The high investment costs of this instrument limits its applicability to large structures. The establishment of new water quality monitoring stations can be combined with the application of the ultrasonic discharge measurement in order to lessen the costs by combining the two stations.

In certain regions and for certain water-courses, the prediction of floods and the issue of warnings are not concerned simply with previous precipitation as measured by raingauges. They also take future precipitation into account, sometimes a determining feature, which has either to be predicted or deduced from earlier measurements.

Forecasting rainfall can sometimes be done with meteorological radar able to track distant atmospheric disturbances. The radar has to be calibrated during a good climatological year in order to establish a correlation between the weakening of the echo (in decibels) and the intensity of the disturbance (in millimetres per hour). Meteorological radar is being used in the Dordogne region, and an experiment is under way at the French National Meteorological Office.

The networks of many countries also include small and medium-sized basins in the general survey of water resources, and this permits the observation of hydrological regimes close to the natural state. The techniques of measurement and data processing are also becoming surer and clearer. When the regimes of these basins are affected as a result of human activities, observations can continue, providing measurements of the changes occurring in the hydrological regime. Measuring stations provide results of greater or lesser precision and completeness according to the quality, accuracy and length of experience. To give an example, measuring the influence of drainage on the form of hydrographs and the lag-time of floods calls for faithful and accurately-timed limnometric recordings. A station may be capable of revealing the influence of human activity on low-level discharge or on groundwater reserves.

When one or more rainfall measurement stations representative of a basin have been in operation for a sufficiently long period of time before human activity begins to cause any change, it is generally possible to make better use of the data measured on the hydrometric or piezometric network, by distinguishing between variations in the hydrological regime due to modifications in the pattern of rainfall and those due to human activities.

The hydrometric network of small catchment areas also permits the transposal of data between analogous basins. If human activity influences a basin for which no earlier hydrometric data are available, but whose regime is well correlated with that of a known basin untouched by human activity, changes in the regime of the first basin can be shown by comparison with the reference basin.

Management of flow regulation systems needs operational manuals which are usually computed by the designers. The checking of these operational manuals should be based on real observations. Therefore, on the river reaches where the water regime is affected by man-made structures, the need for a hydrological network is greater, ie a denser network is necessary. If the observations do not support the conditions predicted by the designers, the operational manuals should be modified in order to ensure a good fit between the computed and observed data.

This is the feed-back in the complex process by which Nature reflects human activity and hydrological networks should be improved so that these differences between predicted and observed values can be a good basis for the proper operation of schemes.

Since the human activity changes the hydrological regime the forecast of its elements is also affected. Forecasting methods, especially the flood warnings and forecasts, should be up-dated when new structures are commissioned. The data supply for the forecasts should be carefully studied in order to enable the forecasting centre to issue the forecasts only after reviewing the changes due to operation of structure.

Without this feed-back, major accidents may occur and therefore the observations are basic to the operation of water management systems. The feed-back for other human activities may be not so direct, but control by the management system can provide the basic support for the increasing costs of the observations.

The case studies in this book demonstrate the great economic-social importance of the changes in the hydrological regime due to human activities. Certain studies reflect the observational problems of quantifying the changes and correlated human interferences.

In this chapter, due references will be made to the hydrological network requirements for observing "causes and effects" simultaneously in the water regime and certain comments will be made on the observations of other impacts. As far as the measuring networks are concerned, therefore, observation requirements may be summarized as follows:

- National networks should include an adequate number of stations covering small and medium-sized basins whose hydrological regimes are as "natural" as possible and which are representative of a wide range of geographical types. Networks covering large basins should be planned for the close monitoring of lowest water levels.
- Important changes in human activity should be foreseen as far in advance as possible, and specific measuring stations then installed without delay. The accuracy of these stations at the different phases of the hydrological regime should be adapted to the type of influence and their intensity.
- The climatological network should be sufficiently dense and representative for its measurements to be correlated with those of the hydrometric network. Supplementary pluviometric stations should be installed where appropriate at the same time as the specific hydrometric stations.
- If human activities have a pronounced influence on groundwater reserves, piezometric stations representative of those reserves should be added to the specific hydrometric stations.

2.1.5 Representative and experimental basins

Representative and experimental basins provide a very useful means for understanding the elements of the hydrological regime, both individually and as they interact, either under natural conditions or under the modifying influence of human activity.

During the International Hydrological Decade, a large number of basins were investigated with the aim of establishing quantitative and qualitative water budgets and developing new techniques and instruments for measurement and analysis. The results were extrapolated, compared and evaluated.

The objectives pursued in those basins were extremely varied, and serve very usefully for a study of the impact of human activities, to the extent that these activities can be accurately defined. Experimental basins have thus been developed to provide basic information for the preparation of hydroelectric and hydro-agricultural projects, or civil engineering water projects related to urban development.

The creation of an experimental basin depends on a certain number of basic operations:

2.1.5.1 Selection of the experimental basin. The choice of experimental basin (or basins) should be made in the light of the intended research activities. An accurate description is thus needed of the goals to be attained, the observations to be made and the materials to be used, the criteria for selection of the experimental catchment area then being laid down in consequence. The calculation of the discharge of exceptional floods on the basis of data obtained from experimental basins of an area of less than 50 km^2 requires these basins to be organized in a way which is scarcely different from that required for determining the discharge from rainfall over urbanized catchment areas measuring from 2 km^2 to 20 km^2.

Surveys are often made by questionnaire, one or more of which are sent out. If several questionnaires are sent, the questions in them are made increasingly precise so that a

Observational requirements

choice has to be made between a limited number of alternatives. A study carried out in French-speaking Africa, designed to determine exceptional discharge on the basis of results from experimental basins with an area of less than 50 km^2, involved some fifty such basins, while a study in France designed to determine the discharge from rainfall on urbanized areas measuring from 2 km^2 - 20 km^2, involved a dozen basins distributed throughout 3 pluviometric regions.

2.1.5.2 Methodology. The basin, or basins, selected are rarely representative of all the climatic, physical, geological or other features of the country or region concerned. Very frequently, too, and particularly in the case of hydrological studies required for an understanding of phenomena related to the expansion of existing communities or the creation of new towns, the measuring instruments have to be adapted to the point on the basin where they will be used, whilst the siting of these points must be done in such a way as to ensure their maximum representativity.

As experience is accumulated, studies are often extended to cover sites which present different characteristics, eg a greater or lesser amount of forest cover, steeper or gentler gradients, different geological structures with numerous runoff and infiltration phenomena, etc. It is also possible to proceed in two stages. The first, lasting one or two years, involves the adaptation and testing of instrumentation at the measurement points, the search for the greatest representativity in the information and the determining of final operating conditions. The second, definitive phase involves the installation of more complex instruments for more precise measurements.

2.1.5.3 Conditions for success
(a) Continuity:
A certain degree of continuity is required in the measurement of data in order to account for the different conditions produced by climatological variations. Time-spans are difficult to determine, but should be established in the light of:
- the degree of risk which it is agreed to run should the planned installations fail;
- the threshold of acceptability of damage due to failure of the installations; the increase in the cost of the work should be lower than the total of the damage caused;
- no figure can be put on the psychological aspect of damage, but this aspect must be taken into account.
(b) Uniformity and sound positioning of instruments:
Stations for taking hydrometric, pluviometric, piezometric or other readings should be carefully distributed over the catchment area so as to cover all the required aspects; uniformity of equipment makes for economy and produces homogeneous and consistent results. There is sometimes a case for simple but reliable measurement stations in preference to sophisticated stations that are less reliable and have to be more thinly spread because of the cost of equipping and operating them.
(c) Staff:
A permanent and motivated specialist staff is required. It is very often necessary for them - at least those engaged on taking readings - to live near the catchment areas since their work involves the supervision and maintenance of the equipment, taking manual measurements (eg stream gauging), reading record sheets, etc. Although the centralized sifting, processing and exploitation of results is desirable and actually achieved in most cases, it is important that there should be contact between the people taking measurements in the field and those sitting in an office doing the calculations, with continuous liaison between the two groups.
(d) Synchronization of operations:
The individual nature of the operative factors, ie the rainfall (hyetographs), the characteristics of the catchment area, and the frequently random nature of their occurrence, make it necessary to measure them every time they appear. The brief duration of the precipitation often calls for the measurement of the induced parameters, ie the water levels in the piezometers or pipes (limnographs) and the rates of flow (hydrographs), over very brief periods of time. This necessitates the irksome but essential chore of synchronizing all these measurements.

2.1.6 <u>Aids of use in observing changes in the hydrological regime</u>

We shall merely draw attention very briefly to two aids that have already been tried out in practice and appear promising for observation of changes in the hydrological regime, namely, detailed topographical survey indexes, and remote sensing from the air and from space.

2.1.6.1 Detailed topographical survey indexes. In many countries there is a government department that produces a land register in the form of maps of the country, periodically brought up to date and showing details of land use.

A detailed topographical and land-plot survey index is produced by processing information of a cadastral and topographical nature. It has two aspects:
- A numerical or quantitative aspect, in that the information is expressed in the form of co-ordinates (X,Y,Z) in relation to a frame of reference;
- A descriptive or qualitative aspect, in that the information contributes to the definition of administrative areas (the boundaries of departments, communes, villages, etc), physical features (islands, plots of land, buildings, etc), individual topographical points and linear or surface topographical features (such as embankments, walls, etc), and place names.

This information, which is stored electronically and brought up to date periodically, gives hydrologists a picture of the situation at any given time, which enables them to assess or even to keep track of developments and changes occurring in time.

Reference to this index for the Paris area made it possible to calculate land use coefficients in various ways and runoff coefficients as related to the density of urban development, and to pinpoint plots of land with the same runoff coefficient, determine the areas of those plots, calculate the dimensioning of the sewage networks, etc.

2.1.6.2 Remote sensing from the air and from space. The operational application of satellites for hydrological and water management purposes is expanding, especially in the United States. The possibilities are much wider than the recent applications. The publication "The role of satellites in the WMO programmes in the 1980s" (WMO - No 494) contains satellite observational requirements for hydrology. The desired resolution, accuracy and frequency of observation for each hydrological element is indicated both from the operational viewpoint and for the needs of specific hydrological research work. The possibility of meeting these needs with data from meteorological satellites in the 1980s is given. The details of some of the hydrological elements contained in WMO publication No 494 are reproduced in Table 1.

In the future, faster expansion of the application of remote-sensing techniques can be expected; however, because remote sensing usually requires land-located reference stations, its reliability depends primarily upon the accuracy of the measurement of the reference stations.

In the context of application of remote sensing to the study of human activities, the main advantage is the observation of the areal distribution of the phenomena such as land use, urbanization, soil erosion, cultivation and crops. Since the areal distribution of such large-scale human activities cannot be observed practically without using remote sensing techniques, their importance will grow with increasing demands for regular observations.

Among the several satellites, the LANDSAT (previously ERTS) family seems to fulfill the requirements with their return period of 18 days. However, this return period in many cases, especially on smaller catchments, permits very limited hydrological observations, and for remote sensing of human activities annual or monthly observations are often quite satisfactory. Generally speaking, the LANDSAT satellite is used for broad surveys and the observation of changes. The provision of data by satellite required ground-based co-ordination in order to localize, code and classify the information. This ground reference operation, carried out by taking measurements on the ground, may be supplemented by aerial photography producing black and white, colour and infra-red pictures. If a satellite is not available remote sensing can also be accomplished by aerial photographic reconnaissance.

The using of photographs or satellite data always has to be worked out to permit their interpretation for the purposes of analysing the desired information. It is possible to pinpoint a situation at a given moment in time and to follow its evolution as regards landscape patterns and particularly land use; the description of catchment areas from the physical, hydrological and other points of view, forest fires, etc.

TABLE I

Satellite observational requirements for hydrology*

Main category	Parameter and its definition	Scale**	Resolution	Frequency	Accuracy	Expected 1980s	Remarks
Main category	Flood extent: surface covered by water during flood	A	10 m	1 hour (3,4)	5%	–	Same as Snowline
		B	30 m	12 hours (3,4)	5%	Possible (but not daily) over limited areas only	
		C	100 m	1 day (3,4)	5%	Possible over limited areas	
RUNOFF, FLOOD MANAGEMENT	Flood plain boundaries: lines which separate flood-prone from non-flood-prone areas	A	10 m	5 years (3) and after every major flood	5%		(May be mapped with horizontal resolution of 100 m (present), 40 m (1977), and 30 m (beyond 1980).)
		B	10 m		5%		
		C	10 m		5%		
	Lake or river stage: elevation of the water surface of a lake or a river relative to a datum	A	–	10' (3); 30' (5)	± 1 cm	Not possible	In-situ measurement with satellite data collection provides the only way of meeting the requirement in the foreseeable future.
		B	–	15' (3); 1 hr (5)	± 1 cm	Not possible	
		C	–	1 hr (3); 4 hrs (5)	± 1 cm	Not possible	
	Saturated soil area: surface of soil not capable of significant infiltration or percolation	A	10 m	Daily (3)	5%	–	An inventory of soil type can be taken by satellite imaging devices within the limitations of horizontal resolution of 100 m (present), 40 m (1977), and 30 m (beyond 1980).
		B	30 m	Daily (3)	5%	May be possible (but not daily) over limited areas only	
		C	100 m	4 days (3)	5%	May be possible over limited areas only	
	Drainage area: whole area having a common outlet for its surface runoff	A, B	30 m	Every 10 years	± 1% of watershed area	Possible	
		C	100 m				
	Channel dimensions and patterns length, number, order and pattern of stream-channel networks must be outlined, even into the headwater reaches, to define the channel pattern. Channel order or number values can then be assigned to channel branches according to a variety of geomorphic quantification techniques	A, B	30 m	Every 5 years or after major flood event	± 5% of length	Possible	
		C	100 m				
	Overland flow length: average horizontal distance that water must flow over the ground before it enters a definite channel	A, B	30 m	Every 5 years	± 5% of length	Possible	
		C	100 m				
	Surface slope: the average slope between a divide and the stream channel over which water must run to reach the stream channel	A, B	30 m	Every 5 years	± 5% hor. ± 5 cm vert.	Not possible	
		C	100 m				
	Land cover type: natural vegetation or soil or artificial surface, expressed as a percentage of watershed area	A,B,C	100 m	Every year	± 1% of watershed area	Possible	Can be met on a limited area basis at present. Requires large-scale digital processing.

(3) Time interval between measurements
(4) During a flood event only
(5) Time interval for transmission by DCP
* From "The role of satellites in the WMO programmes in the 1980's" WMO-No. 494, Annex, Table III
** Figures are given for the following sizes of drainage basin:
  A $< 100 km^2$
  B $\geq 100 km^2, < 1000 km^2$
  C $> 1000 km^2$

TABLE 2

Satellite observational requirements for hydrology

Main category	Parameter and its definition	Scale	Resolution	Frequency	Accuracy	Expected 1980s	Remarks
SNOW AND ICE	**SNOW ON THE LAND** <u>Snowline</u>: line separating a region of less than 50% snow cover from a region with more than 50% snow cover	A	30 m	Daily	–	Possible (but not daily) over limited areas only	
		B	100 m	Daily	–	Possible (but not daily) over limited areas only	Current experimental: horizontal resolution 100 m for limited areas. Frequency twice per 18 days for cloud-free areas.
		C	1000 m	Daily	–	Possible over limited areas only	In 1980s horizontal resolution expected 30-40 m. Coverage will remain twice per 18 days.
	<u>Snow cover</u>: percentage of a basin or other specific area, in horizontal projection, covered by snow	A	300 m	Daily	± 5% of snow area	Possible for cloud-free areas	
		B	1000 m	Daily	± 5% of snow area	Possible for cloud-free areas	
		C	10000 m	Daily	± 5% of snow area	Possible for cloud-free areas	
	<u>Water equivalent</u>: depth of water that would result if a vertical column of the snowpack of unit cross-section were melted	A	100 m	Daily	± 2 mm if < 2 cm ± 10% if > 2 cm	Not possible	There are no presently known techniques. In-situ measurements can be made and collected via satellite data-collection systems, either continuously within the regions covered by geostationary satellites, or up to four times per day from any location on the earth.
	<u>Free water content</u>: equivalent depth of all the water in the liquid phase contained in a vertical column of the snowpack of unit cross-section	B	300 m	Daily	± 2 mm if < 2 cm ± 10% if > 2 cm	Not possible	
	<u>Continuous ice cover</u>: percentage of a lake or river area covered by continuous land-fast ice	A	300 m	Daily	± 2%	Possible over limited areas only	
		B	1000 m	Daily	± 2%	Possible over limited areas only	
		C	10000 m	Daily	± 2%	Possible over limited areas only	
	<u>Ice concentration</u>: fraction of an area within a lake or river that is covered by free-floating ice	A	10 m [1]	Daily [2]	–	Not possible	The resolution of foreseeable operational satellite sensors is not great enough to provide useful measurements, at least until after 1984. Can be done every 9 days in cloud-free areas on an experimental basis.
		B	30 m [1]	Daily [2]	–	Not possible	
		C	300 m [1]	Daily [2]	–	Not possible	
	<u>Thickness</u>: vertical depth of ice which may include snow cover on the ice	A	30 m	Daily	± 2 cm if < 20 cm ± 10% if > 20 cm	Not possible	
		B	100 m	Daily		Not possible	
		C	1000 m	Daily		Not possible	

(1) Mean concentration values averaged over larger areas are useful.

(2) During melt season only

TABLE 3

Satellite observational requirements for hydrology

Main category	Parameter and its definition	Scale	Resolution	Frequency	Accuracy	Expected 1980s	Remarks
WATER BALANCE	Precipitation: liquid or solid products of the condensation of water vapour falling from clouds or deposited from air on the ground	A	100 m	6-hourly [10]	± 2 mm if < 40 mm ± 5% if > 40 mm	Experimental	In-situ measurement with geo-stationary satellite data collection is currently operational in a few locations in the western hemisphere. Coverage can be greatly expanded in the western hemisphere as rapidly as platforms can be put in place, and can be extended to the rest of the world in 1978-1980. Precipitation measurement by satellite with useful accuracy may be possible on an experimental basis before 1985. The prospects for operational measurements over land areas are not promising for the foreseeable future. Stated resolution cannot be met.
		B	1000 m	6-hourly [10]	± 2 mm if < 40 mm ± 5% if > 40 mm	Experimental	
		C	5000 m	6-hourly [10]	± 2 mm if < 40 mm ± 5% if > 40 mm	Experimental	
	Evaporation: quantity of water evaporated from an open water surface or from ground	A	100 m	Daily	± 0.5 mm	Not possible	No potential for the direct measurement of this parameter by satellite exists at the present time. Related variables can be measured. These will exist in computations.
		B	1000 m	Daily	± 0.5 mm	Not possible	
		C	5000 m	Daily	± 0.5 mm	Not possible	
SUBSURFACE WATER	Aquifer mapping: indication of the area where groundwater is found	A	100 m	5 years	–	Not possible	No remote sensing techniques are known at present. In-situ measurements of some of the desired parameters can be made via satellite data-collection.
		B	100 m	5 years	–	Not possible	
		C	100 m	5 years	–	Not possible	
	Location of springs: same as Discharge to rivers	A	30 m	5 years	–	Not possible	
		B	30 m	5 years	–	Not possible	
		C	30 m	5 years	–	Not possible	
	Groundwater level: elevation, at a certain location and time, of the piezometric surface of an aquifer	A	300 m	Daily	1 cm	Not possible	
		B	1000 m	Daily	1 cm	Not possible	
		C	1000 m	Daily	1 cm	Not possible	
	Soil type: classification of loose deposits on Earth's surface	A	100 m	5 years	–	Possible over limited areas only	An inventory of soil type can be made by satellite imaging devices within the limitations of horizontal resolution of 100 m (present), 40 m (1977), and 30 m (beyond 1980).
		B	1000 m	5 years	–		
		C	1000 m	5 years	–		
	Moisture content profile[7]	A	100 m	Daily	10% of field capacity	Not possible	
		B	300 m	Daily		Not possible	
		C	1000 m	Daily		Not possible	
	Temperature profile[7]	A	100 m	Daily	0.5°C	Not possible	
		B	300 m	Daily	0.5°C	Not possible	
		C	1000 m	Daily	0.5°C	Not possible	
	Infiltration: flow of water from the soil surface into the soil	A	100 m	Daily	10%	Not possible	
		B	300 m	Daily	10%	Not possible	
		C	1000 m	Daily	10%	Not possible	
	Percolation: flow of water through a porous medium, mainly downward gravity flow	A	100 m	Daily	10%	Not possible	
		B	300 m	Daily	10%	Not possible	
		C	1000 m	Daily	10%	Not possible	
	Depth of seasonal frost: distance from the ground surface to the freezing level (0°C)	A	100 m	Weekly	10%	Not possible	
		B	300 m	Weekly	10%	Not possible	
		C	1000 m	Weekly	10%	Not possible	

(7) At depths of 5, 10, 20, 50 and 100 cm
(10) Should be measured during 5-minute intervals for basins of sizes A and B, and during 30-minute intervals for basins of size C; these measurements should be transmitted by a data-collection system at intervals of 1 hour for basins of size A, 2 hours for size B, and 6 hours for size C.

TABLE 4

Satellite observational requirements for hydrology

Main category	Parameter and its definition	Scale	Resolution	Frequency	Accuracy	Expected 1980s	Remarks
WATER QUALITY	Suspended sediment: sediment which remains in suspension in flowing water for a long time without settling on the streambed	A	30 m	Daily	± 10 ppm	Not possible	Some information about turbidity can be derived from multi-spectral imaging such as those obtained experimentally from "LANDSAT" and "METEOR" and expected from the Coastal Zone Colour Scanner to be flown on Nimbus-G.
		B	100 m	Daily	± 10 ppm	Not possible	
		C	1000 m	Daily	± 10 ppm	Possible over limited areas only	
	Colour: deviation from the aspect of pure transparent water	A	30 m	Daily (8)	± 10 mg Pt/l**	Not possible	
		B	100 m	Daily (8)	± 10 mg Pt/l**	Not possible	
		C	1000 m	Daily (8)	± 10 mg Pt/l**	Possible over limited areas only	
	Algae bloom: a large number of a particular algae species, often amounting to 0.5 to 1 million cells per litre	A	30 m	2-3 days	-	Not possible	
		B	100 m	2-3 days	-	Not possible	
		C	1000 m	2-3 days	-	Possible over limited areas only	
	Surface film: layer of oil or another fluid distinct from water spread over an area of the water and having molecular dimension	A	30 m	Daily (8)	-	Not possible	Limited capability has been demonstrated experimentally using multi-spectral high-resolution sensors. Operationally useful systems not yet assured.
		B	100 m	Daily (8)	-	Not possible	
		C	1000 m	Daily (8)	-	Not possible	
	Surface water temperature: temperature of the water in the top mm layer	A	30 m	6 hours	± 0.03°C in 0-1° range, ± 0.1°C in 1-4° range otherwise ± 1°C	Not possible	1 to 1.5°C absolute and 0.5°C relative temperature accuracy can be achieved. 0.03 to 0.1°C not feasible.
		B	100 m	6 hours		Not possible	
		C	1000 m	6 hours		Not possible	
	Temperature profile: temperature variation in depth	A	-	2-3 days	± 0.25°C	Not possible	Cannot be measured by satellite in the foreseeable future, but could be transmitted using satellite data-collection system.
		B	1000 m	2-3 days	± 0.25°C	Not possible	
		C	10000 m	2-3 days	± 0.25°C	Not possible	
	DRAINAGE BASIN CHARACTERISTICS						

(8) Six hours for pollution monitoring for rivers and small lakes

** Range of measurements is 1-50mg Pt/l; (mg Pt/l = mg og Platinum per litre), i.e., accuracy listed in the Table corresponds to 20% of the range.

Operational aspects

2.1.7 Conclusions

From the foregoing, two main conclusions can be derived:
- the investment and operational costs of hydrological networks are higher because of man-made structures and improvement of the network should be linked with the construction of the structures;
- in order to detect the effect of the human activities on the hydrological cycle, human activities should also be observed and quantified, simultaneously with the hydrological observations.

2.2 OPERATIONAL ASPECTS OF WATER RESOURCES MANAGEMENT SCHEMES

2.2.1 Data concerning the manner of operation of water management installations

Man's influence upon the hydrological regime of rivers leads to modifications in the natural values of the flow. The same may be also said about man's influence on groundwater as pumping and irrigation can modify the underground flow both in the saturated and unsaturated zones as well as the level of the water table. Hydrologists work with natural, unaltered values of flow which are considered samples picked out from statistical populations and they are studied on the basis of the distribution laws. Only the natural values of a characteristic can be considered as random variables and hence fitted for statistical study. If man's influence is manifest, then the altered values no longer form a homogeneous statistical series. Hence a modified regime appears as an overlapping of two regimes: one of the natural water resources and one of intakes and releases caused by man. To get back to the natural regime, it is necessary to subtract from the modified regime the residuals which represent man's influence. For this, it is necessary to know the amount of water either abstracted from a river or discharged to it; hence a supplementary hydrological network needs to be set up. But often there is no hydrological monitoring of the users, although it is necessary to appreciate, at least approximately, the values of the intake or release.

One method is to use the available hydraulic installations to measure the water discharges. For instance, dam spillways can be used to measure the water discharge if the spilled water depth is measured. If the spillway equation has been previously established, then the discharge with the free spillway depends only on the depth of the spilled water (h) and the contraction coefficient (ψ). Integrating the discharge values for the period provides the total amount of water discharged which is then considered in the water balance equation. But in other cases, the spillways are provided with gates of different types which are handled according to the management rules for the reservoir when the water level is high. To compute the discharge over these spillways it is necessary to know the discharge as a function of the flashboard control orifice and of the number of flashboards if more than one is in use.

Water intakes for use in hydropower stations also disturb the natural regime. Hydropower stations, especially the medium power ones, are peak-load stations and thus their water consumption varies greatly in time. The water amounts are estimated on the basis of records of energy released or from the dispatcher diagrams of the hydropower stations.

As the variation of the hydraulic turbine efficiency η the discharge Q and the head H are known, the water discharge through the hydropower station is:

$$P = 9.8 \, \eta \, Q \, H$$

where: P is the turbine power.

The above equation is applied to each turbine separately because it is possible that their running may differ according to their management plan. If this is known, the intake amounts from the river can easily be determined.

Another case of water spillage is provided by irrigation canals. If no measuring devices are installed along these canals, the water discharge is determined from knowledge of the watering diagram, ie the canal's gate orifice at any moment. The discharge is computed by considering a drowned broad crested weir, on which the gate is located. If this method cannot be applied, the pumping station management scheme can be examined and, in this case, the discharge computation is similar to that for the hydropower station.

If floods are alleviated by opening the gates of an "on-site-detention" works, then, if the manner of operation is known, the discharges in the "on-site-detention" works can be determined using a hydraulic computation.

2.2.2 Impact on the manner of operation on the hydrological regime

The effects of incorrect operations of river management cause further problems. Unreasonable or late operation of the gates of weirs during floods may bring about the flooding of a downstream river reach. For instance if, at the beginning of a flood, water is kept in a reservoir and then is suddenly released, the river reach downstream can be seriously affected by artificial flooding, often worse than the natural one would have been.

Another example is illustrated in Figures 1 and 2. Assume that a flood A is alleviated in a reservoir resulting in the flood given by discharge curve A. Consider further a flood B over the rest of the basin (area B in Figure 1), assumed to be formed under natural, uninfluenced conditions. Adding the floods A and B on the one hand and the floods A_1 and B on the other, gives floods C and C_1 respectively. Figure 1 shows that if the gates are so operated that they alleviate flood A, the resulting flood C_1 at the outlet of the basin might exceed that one, C, considered under natural conditions.

Another further example is when the over-irrigation of a particular area causes the water table to be raised to the point where the soil becomes saline. Many examples of this could be cited.

In order to prevent undesirable side effects caused by incorrect manipulation of management installations, accurate and timely streamflow forecasting is required combined with adequate operating rules.

2.3 EXPERIMENTAL METHODS, WATER BALANCE METHODS, EXPERIMENTAL BASINS

2.3.1 Introduction

According to the nature of their impact, the components of man's influence on streamflow may be classified into two groups:
- impacts caused by channel regulation and direct water withdrawal from the channel network for economic purposes (construction and operation of reservoirs, large water intakes and discharges, diversion of streamflow, etc);
- impacts not connected with water intake directly but which change the conditions of streamflow formation and of other water balance components in river basins (agricultural practices, forest reclamation, urbanization, drainage of marsh-ridden areas, etc).

In every large river basin in populated areas, a great number of impacts are experienced and these may be related to either or both of the above groups. The effect of the impacts on the water regime may vary with natural cyclic variations of hydrometeorological elements, with the nature of the use of the transformed terrain, with the local physiography and with the character of the underlying surface.

A quantitative evaluation of the effect of man's activity on streamflow is complicated because of numerous factors acting simultaneously. Moreover, anthropogenic factors, usually directed, overlap with the natural streamflow variations, the amplitude of which considerably exceeds the magnitude of the cultural changes.

Different design methods are usually applied to the study and quantitative evaluation of anthropogenic changes of streamflow, such as have occurred and are expected:
- methods based on investigation of long-term fluctuations of streamflow at benchmark gauging stations in combination with analysis of changes of natural meteorological factors and development of man's activity in the basin;
- water balance methods which provide individual accounts of water intakes and changes of water balance components in the river basin as a result of each type of man's activity.

According to their nature, the methods of the first group evaluate the whole complex of man's activity acting in the basin without separation into individual components.

The water balance methods are based on the study of changes of components of the water balance occurring on basin plots and channel reaches where a change of natural conditions occurs under the effect of man's activity (irrigated and drained terrain, ploughed areas, urban territories, areas inundated by man-made lakes, etc). Detailed experiments elucidate the physical nature of the processes occurring under different economic arrangements; they allow the evaluation of the importance, and the role of, each anthropogenic factor individually and the computation of the characteristic hydrological changes both past and

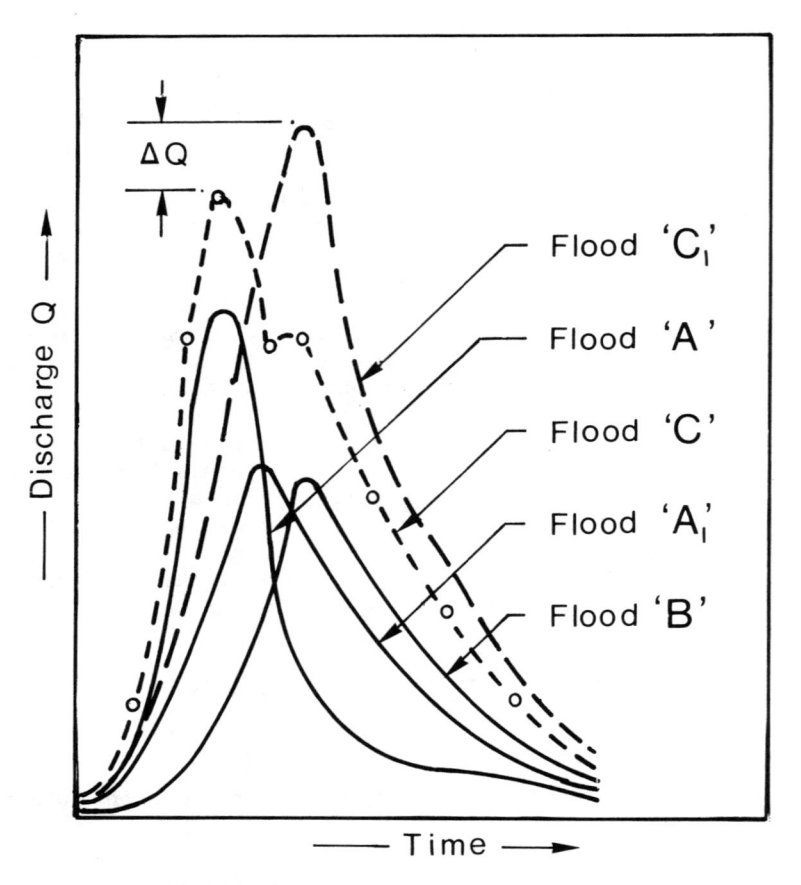

Figure 1   Flood hydrographs

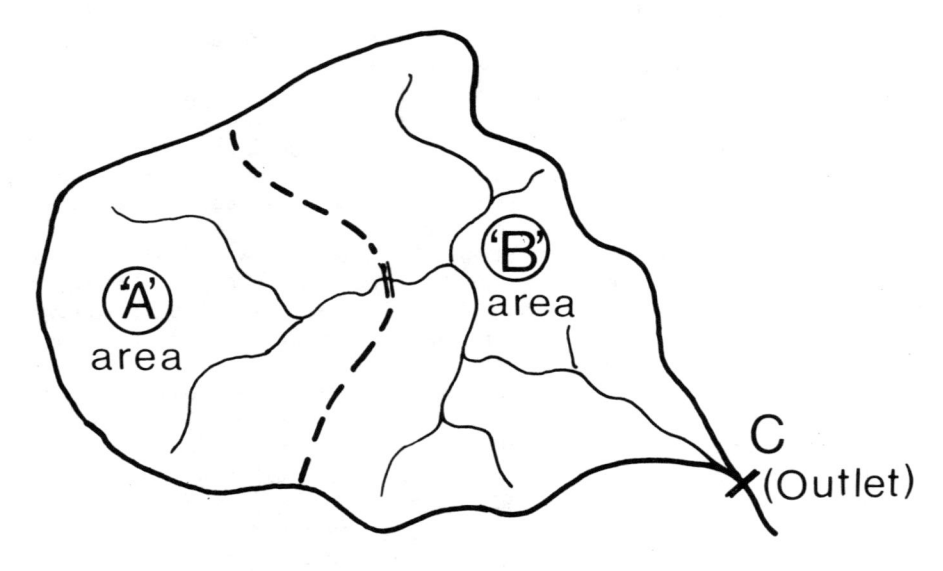

Figure 2   The basin generating the floods in Figure 1

future. Experimental methods are used to estimate the influence of different types of man's activity on runoff.

Computation methods based on physical and mathematical modelling of the processes observed in the drainage basin or its parts may be regarded as a variant of water balance methods (see sub-chapter 2.7). For example, the description of some methods is given below, based on the use of experimental data and water balances to evaluate the impact of irrigation and drainage improvements for farming arid lands and the effect of channel control on streamflow.

2.3.2 Use of experimental methods for the evaluation of the effect of irrigation and drainage improvements

2.3.2.1 Irrigation. Irrigation, and engineering works providing irrigation, influence water resources and the hydrological regime most importantly by irretrievable water consumption. The creation of large irrigated areas in arid regions results in time-and-space changes and redistribution of many elements of the water, energy and salt balances, productive and non-productive evaporation, overland flow, temperature, humidity, etc, which occur not only within the limits of irrigated terrain but on the adjacent areas as well. All these processes are to a certain extent reflected in changes in different characteristics of the streamflow at the outlets.

Changes in streamflow and in the hydrological regime of river basins developed for irrigation occur under the influence of several, sometimes contradictory, processes. There are some principal processes, such as additional evaporation from irrigated areas (irretrievable water loss), increase in infiltration to groundwater and in drainage returned to the river, decrease in non-productive losses of river water following the elimination of water-loving plants, accumulation of water and salts in the zone of aeration, salt discharge out of the soil and salt inflow into the river network, etc. Water, salt and energy balances of typical irrigated areas and fields are studied with an account of the time dynamics of the processes and their areal changes to make a quantitative evaluation of these elements; thus streamflow and water balance changes in river basins under the effect of irrigation can be computed. The use of balance methods is made possible (Karchenko, 1975) by multi-purpose research and by systems analysis of the distribution of observational bodies and points.

The multi-purpose research consists of:
- a simultaneous study of changes in hydrological, hydrogeological, hydrochemical, soil-chemical and other processes according to a co-ordinated programme;
- a territorial combination of the principal types of observations and works within an agricultural field, an irrigated area or the whole irrigated region.

A systems approach to the research is made by separating individual bodies or sub-systems (agricultural fields, irrigation areas), each independent but together comprising a system (irrigation region) as a whole. Equations describing water, salt-water and energy balances are used as mathematical models; they are already fully developed and can analyse the data for every moment of time and at many points on the surface. A general water balance equation for irrigated areas is given in the international guide for water balance computations (Sokolov and Chapman, 1974), while in Karchenko (1975) the equations of water, salt and energy balances of irrigated areas are given with specific values for all the basic elements for individual irrigated areas located in different environments.

Inevitably field experiments cannot cover all the variety of natural peculiarities of the terrain under study; therefore selection of research areas should be preceded by a careful analysis of the landscape and hydrogeological regionalization of irrigated areas. Experimental areas should be located on terrain with geomorphological and hydrogeological characteristics such as debris cones, piedmont plains, river valleys, watersheds, typical of the basin under study.

Field observations of water, salt and energy balance components are made on the most typical agricultural fields on farm lands with a variety of groundwater tables.

When the results of experimental observations on irrigated areas are available as well as information on future planning, a preliminary computation of the magnitude of streamflow changes under the effect of irrigation may be made.

For any reach of the river channel within the irrigated zone the water balance equation may be presented as follows:

Experimental methods

$$Q_{S_1} - Q_{S_2} + Q_{M_1} - Q_{M_2} + Q_{SY} - Q_\alpha + Q_{uY} - Q_{uO} + Q_\beta + P - E_1 - E_2 + S_S + Q_{MG} = 0 \qquad (1)$$

where: Q_{S_1} and Q_{S_2} are channel (surface) flow at the upper and lower gauging stations respectively; Q_{M_1} and Q_{M_2} are sub-channel flow at the upper and lower gauging stations; Q_{SY} is lateral inflow; Q_α is water withdrawal; Q_{uY} is groundwater inflow into the channel from the contour; Q_{uO} is groundwater outflow from the channel in the direction to the contour; Q_β is total returned water; P is precipitation; E_1, E_2 are evaporation from the water surface and evapotranspiration from adjacent plots of the flood plain and semi-submerged water-loving plants; S_S is accumulation of water in micro-depressions in the flood plain; Q_{MG} is water exchange between groundwater and deep aquifers.

Future discharge at the lower gauging station may be evaluated from equation (1).

$$Q_{S_2} = Q_{S_1} + Q_{M_1} - Q_{M_2} + Q_{SY} - Q_\alpha + Q_{uY} - Q_{uO} + Q_\beta + P - E_1 - E_2 + S_S + Q_{MG} \qquad (2)$$

This equation may be presented in a simplified form:

$$Q_{S_2} = Q_O + X \qquad (3)$$

where

$$Q_O = Q_{S_1} + Q_{SY} - Q_\alpha + Q_\beta + P - E_1 - E_2 + S_S \qquad (4)$$

$$X = Q_{M_1} - Q_{M_2} + Q_{uY} - Q_{uO} + Q_{MG} \qquad (5)$$

If a graph $Q_{S_2} = f(Q_O)$ is plotted from equation (3), the quantity X is simply the intercept of the curve on the ordinate axis. Its value depends on the lithological structure of the underlying rocks and is determined individually for every stream or channel reach. In this case $Q_{M_1} - Q_{M_2} = 0$ and $Q_{MG} = 0$, parameter $X = Q_{uY} - Q_{uO}$. Hence if parameter X is positive, groundwater inflow is predominant in the reach under study, whilst a negative sign shows losses from the river to the groundwater in the direction of the surrounding contour. On this basis, equation (3) may be written:

$$Q_{S_2} = Q_{S_1} + Q_{SY} - Q_\alpha + Q_\beta + P - E_1 - E_2 + S_S + X \qquad (6)$$

In the above equation, the components characterizing channel inflow, lateral inflow, water intake, precipitation, evaporation and accumulation of water in the flood plain are capable of instrumental measurement quite reliably.

It is very difficult to determine hydrogeological parameters of natural inflow Q_{uY}, Q_{M_1} and outflow Q_{uO}, Q_{M_2} of groundwater, or the irrigation component of runoff from irrigated areas (drainage). When observations of groundwater levels are available as well as data on coefficients of infiltration and of water yield of water-bearing rocks, hydrogeological parameters may be determined by existing methods. In the case of inadequate observational data, as often happens, parameter X which characterizes the mean difference between inflow and outflow of groundwater as well as water exchange with deep aquifers may be approximated from the graph $Q_{S_2} = f(Q_O)$ on the basis of hydrometeorological information. For example, preliminary computations suggest that $X \simeq +7.0$ m^3/s for the Chu River in the reach from Chen-Kemin up to Milianfan; this means that in this reach groundwater drains into the Chu River.

Equation (2) enables future runoff values for the Syrdaria River to be computed in the lower reaches as well as its discharge into the Aral Sea. The results show that at the planned rates of irrigation development the discharge in the lower reaches will be decreased by 12-14 km^3/year by 1990; in practice this means total elimination of runoff except for water returned to the lower reaches which may be re-used for irrigation. This would lead to considerable changes in the water balance of the Aral Sea and might result in a considerable decrease in its surface area.

To obtain more reliable conclusions, the results of runoff changes which have occurred under the effect of irrigation, obtained through experimental observations of the water balance on irrigated areas should be verified in all possible cases with long-term observations at benchmark stations, within the principal irrigation areas.

2.3.2.2 *Drainage of swamps and marsh-ridden areas.* To evaluate streamflow under the effect of drainage, methods of analogy or of control basins are widely used. The water balance method is also widespread; it is based on special experimental observations at stations located in regions of extensive swamp drainage in marsh-ridden areas and in areas with water surplus. Such programmes include observations of precipitation, evaporation, streamflow, swamp and groundwater levels, soil moisture, energy balance elements, meteorological elements, temperature and freeze-up of soils and sub-soils, phenology of plants, as well as studies of hydrophysical properties of peats and mineral soils and sub-soils. These observations should be made simultaneously on natural (undrained) and drained and cultivated swamp areas, marsh-ridden and water-surplus areas. To distribute point results to the whole river basin, water balance investigations are organized on individual plots in agricultural fields, in drainage improvement systems, swamp areas and river basins.

In the evaluation of the effect of drainage improvement on components of the water regime, experimental water balance investigations are used in two ways: for direct comparison of experimental data on individual components of the regime obtained from improved and unimproved plots for the same period; to establish the dependence of individual components of the water regime on the controlling factors under natural and improved conditions.

The water balance method is used mainly to evaluate streamflow changes from drained areas (swamp areas, plots with water surplus, river basins) and especially in preparation of predictions of the changes of this characteristic. In this case computation of streamflow changes ΔQ is made by difference before (Q) and Q^1):

$$\Delta Q = Q^1 - Q \tag{7}$$

For a swamp area (with waterlogged soil) equation (7) becomes:

$$\Delta Q = (P - E_1 + \Delta M^1)^1 - (P - E + \Delta M) \tag{8}$$

where: P is precipitation; E, E_1 are evaporation from the area of initial swamp before and after drainage respectively; ΔM, ΔM^1 are changes in water storages in the top soil for a design period before and after drainage.

For a drained river basin equation (7) may be presented as follows:

$$\Delta Q = (P - E.a - E_1.a_1 - E_2 a_2 + \Delta M_T^1)^1 - (P - E_a - E_2.a_2 + \Delta M_T) \tag{9}$$

where: E_2 is evaporation from dry valleys of area a_2 expressed as a function of the whole basin area, a_1, a_2 are fractional areas of swamps and drained swamps; ΔM_T, ΔM_T^1 are changes of water storage over the basin for a design period before and after drainage. Since precipitation is not affected by drainage works, equations (8) and (9) for periods with equal amounts of precipitation may be presented as follows:

$$\Delta Q = (-E + \Delta M^1)^1 - (-E + \Delta M) \tag{10}$$

$$\Delta Q = (-E.a - E_1.a_1 - E_2.a_2 + \Delta M_T^1)^1 - (-E.a - E_2.a_2 + \Delta M_T) \tag{11}$$

If the minor effects of drainage of swamps and lands with water surplus on evaporation from adjacent areas is neglected then only changes in evaporation and water storage need be considered. The effect of drainage on the change of evaporation and of water storage is determined from experimental data.

In case of inadequate observational data on evaporation for the conditions of mineral lands of water surplus (drained and non-drained) it may be computed from the observational data on other components of the water and energy regime using the following approximation:

$$E = \beta E_o \qquad \text{if } \frac{M_1 + M_2}{2} \geqslant \gamma \tag{12}$$

$$E = \beta E_o \frac{M_1 + M_2}{2\gamma} \qquad \text{if } \frac{M_1 + M_2}{2} < \gamma \tag{13}$$

where: E is evapotranspiration; β is a parameter depending on the conditions of the underlying surface; E_o is potential evaporation; M_1, M_2 are storages of available moisture in the soil layer 1 m deep at the beginning and end of the design period; $\gamma = M_3 - M_4$ is the difference

Experimental methods

between the field capacity and wilting point in the top layer 1 m deep.
    In the evaluation of the effect of drainage on evaporation from swamps the latter may be computed by ratio in (Romanov, 1962):

E - CR   (14)

where: R is the radiation balance and C is an empirical coefficient. C depends on the rate of moistening of the top soils and the phase of plant development. Values of C may be determined experimentally and correlated with swamp water level on natural undrained swamps and moisture content at the top soil drained peats (Schebeko, 1965). On the basis of such relations for different swamp micro-landscapes and for different agricultural crops on drained areas, equation (13) may be used to forecast changes of evaporation from swamps under the effect of their drainage and cultivation, and using equation (11) it is possible to predict changes of runoff from drained river basins.

2.3.3 Experimental basins in the evaluation of the effect of dry farming agricultural practices on runoff

The basic objective of experimental basins is the study of the effect of cultural changes of the underlying surface on the hydrological regime and water balance. The selection of experimental basins including the evaluation of the effect of land use on river runoff and other problems are described in detail in a special international guide 'Representative and experimental basins' published by UNESCO in 1970 within the framework of the IHD programme (Toebes and Ouryvaev, 1970).
    In the USSR multi-purpose investigations on experimental basins are made by 16 water balance stations covering the basic physiographic zones of the country. Relative to the evaluation of the effect of land use on overland flow and river runoff the following observations are made at every station:
- Observations of the overland flow from different types of surfaces (virgin land, fallow, meadow, different types of ploughing, forest and shelter belts) taking into account the effect of precipitation, soil moisture content and its rate of freezing, steepness of slopes, difference in the mechanical composition of soils etc;
- Observations of runoff from ravines with smoothed slopes, from temporary water courses and from river basins with different ploughed and forested areas;
- Observations of groundwater regime over the network of observational boreholes located within the above lands combined with measurements of the hydro-physical characteristics of soils and sub-soils in the unsaturated zone;
- Observations of moisture content in soils and sub-soils from the surface to the groundwater table;
- Observations of evaporation from soil and from snow on different farmlands and under the canopy of tall vegetation using snow and soil evaporimeters and lysimeters of different designs;
- Meteorological observations;
- Phenological observations on fields and determination of taxonomic characteristics of forest and shelter belts.

Evaluation of the effect of agricultural and forestry reclamation practices is based on the comparison of measurements of components of the water balance of basins containing ploughed or forested slopes with those for basins containing unploughed and non-forested slopes. Moreover, the equality of all the other basic factors affecting the components of the water balance of the basins under study is assumed.
    Naturally observations made at water balance stations cannot cover all the variety and the range of all possible changes of meteorological conditions, topography, hydrogeology, soils and sub-soils and their combinations observed in land use practice.
    Special design methods based on the generalization of results from experimental basins have been developed to solve practical problems of the effect of agricultural practices for dry farming on the components of the water balance of individual territories, river and lake basins. This method for evaluation of the effect of agricultural practices on annual river runoff has recently been developed at the State Hydrological Institute; a detailed description with appropriate case studies is published in special 'Methodological Recommendations' (Anon, 1975).
    This method envisages a differentiated evaluation of the effect of agricultural

afforestation on overland flow, on groundwater flow and on evaporation from land on individual farms and on the entire basin.

Evaluation of overland flow changes is made by plotting and analysis of the following dependence:

$$K_{Q_{ov}} = f(C_M, i) \tag{15}$$

where: $K_{Q_{ov}}$ is a coefficient of overland flow on the farm lands being compared; C_M is an index characterizing the moisture content in the layer 1 m deep and the rate of soils and sub-soils freeze-up during the period preceding runoff; i the slope steepness.

Index C_M is related to the permeability to water of soils and sub-soils, the greater the index, the greater the runoff coefficient.

The correlation coefficient (non-linear) of equation (15) is 0.80-0.90, and the relative root mean square error does not exceed 17%.

The results of the research show a decrease in overland flow on ploughed and forested slopes; moreover, the magnitude of the decrease depends on the total moisture content of the zone, on annual precipitation, on soils and sub-soils, on steepness of slopes and on depth of ploughing.

Changes in the groundwater component of runoff have been evaluated by plotting and analysis of the dependence:

$$K_{Q_{up}} = f(h) \tag{16}$$

where: $K_{Q_{up}}$ is the coefficient of infiltration of precipitation to groundwater on the farms being compared; h is the depth of the groundwater table (thickness of the unsaturated zone).

This dependence shows that the coefficient of groundwater recharge decreases with increasing depth of the groundwater table.

The linear correlation coefficient in equation (16) is 0.85-0.95; the relative mean square root error does not exceed 12%.

Within all the physiographic zones the coefficient $K_{Q_{up}}$ increases on agricultural fields, in the forest and in shelter belts as compared to virgin plots.

The effect of agricultural practices on annual river runoff is evaluated according to formulae of the following types:

$$\Delta Q = (\sum_{i}^{n} \Delta \overline{Q}_{ov1,2} \cdot a_{1,2} + \sum_{i}^{n} \Delta \overline{Q}_{up1,2} \cdot a_{1,2})_{I,II} \tag{17}$$

$$\Delta Q = (\sum_{i}^{n} \Delta \overline{E}_{1,2} \cdot a_{1,2})_{I,II} \tag{18}$$

where: ΔQ is the change of total river runoff comprising an algebraic sum of changes of the overland flow and groundwater flow or changes of evapotranspiration of "n" individual plots (farm lands); $\Delta \overline{Q}_{ov1,2}$ is the mean decrease in overland flow from ploughed land taking into account the effect of additional accumulation of snow in the hydrographic network and in shelter belts (Anon, 1975); $\Delta \overline{Q}_{up1,2}$ is the mean increase of groundwater flow or groundwater recharge by precipitation on different farm lands; $\Delta E_{1,2}$ is the difference in evapotranspiration from different farm lands; $a_{1,2}$ are areas of individual farm lands within sandy loam (light loamy) soils - (I) and loamy soils (clay loamy soils) - (II) and sub-soils expressed as fractions of the total basin area.

The computation according to equation (18) can be used to check the results obtained from equation (17). The evaluation of the effect of agricultural practices on runoff by computing the changes in evapotranspiration in the basin is made by comparing experimental data on evaporation from different farm lands (fallow, fields with spring crops, winter and row crops) with that from virgin and meadow slopes.

The effect of forest belts on evaporation is determined by comparison of evaporation data computed by equation:

$$\frac{E_{3.2}}{E_O} = f\left(\frac{R}{LP}\right) \tag{19}$$

where: $\frac{E_{3.2}}{E_O}$ is the ratio of evapotranspiration from virgin land (Sokolov and Chapman, 1974) and from shelter belts (Anon, 1975) to the potential evaporation from the farm lands being

Experimental methods

compared; $\frac{R}{LP}$ is an index of radiation (ratio of radiation balance to precipitation).

The methodology presented has been used in the evaluation of changes of river runoff caused by afforestation practice in many small and medium-sized river basins located in different physiographic zones in the USSR (Shiklomanov, 1976). Ploughing of 70-80% of the basin area has not been found to decrease annual runoff in the forest zone, while in the forest-steppe zone runoff may decrease by 0-15%, and in the steppe zone - by 8-25%.

The effect of shelter belts is different. In river basins with 6-12% of forest area, with slopes of $30^0/_{00}$ and groundwater table < 10 m deep the increase in annual runoff is from 1.5-5%. For basins with slopes of $30^0/_{00}$ and groundwater table > 10 m deep, annual runoff decreases by 1-4%.

In evaluating the effects of different types of land use on streamflow from analysis of data from experimental basins special attention should be paid to the method of active experiment.

The idea of this method is the following: in a basin with sufficiently reliable long-time observations of the hydrological regime and of the meteorological elements controlling the water regime, an artificial change of one of the factors of the underlying surface is made (the forest is cut or planted, the agricultural practice is changed, etc); the effect of this factor on the water regime is quantified using several years' subsequent observations of all the elements of the water balance including years of different meteorological conditions. The difference in these elements before and after the changes is a measure of the effect of these changes on particular hydrological characteristics. The method is often used on small basins and the results obtained are not always representative for medium-sized and large rivers.

In some cases a hydrological experiment is not the end in itself; it is undertaken in regions where fundamental changes in land use are planned over vast territories. For example, gross cultivation of virgin areas of North Kazakhstan in 1955-1960 (ploughing, construction of reservoirs, ponds, etc) which resulted in a great change of streamflow conditions in large river basins, may be considered from the hydrological point of view as an experiment, and the results may be used to draw a reliable conclusion on the effect of man's multi-purpose activity on the characteristics of streamflow in the area under study.

2.3.4 Evaluation by the water balance method of the effect of reservoirs on annual river runoff

The construction of reservoirs usually causes fundamental changes in the time distribution of streamflow and increases the water resources available during low water periods and dry years. Moreover, the reservoirs inundate substantial areas and increase the evaporation from the water surface especially in arid zones, thus being one of the principal users of water resources.

In this connection a reliable quantitative evaluation of the effect of channel regulation on streamflow is very important for research into changes in water resources as a result of man's activity.

The construction of reservoirs on rivers usually decreases the discharge volume at the outlet ΔQ due to water losses through evapotranspiration in the basin $F_{\Delta E}$ as well as through the filling of the reservoir basin and through the increase of groundwater storage $F_{\Delta S_u G}$:

$$\Delta Q = F_{\Delta E} + F_{\Delta S_u G} \qquad (20)$$

The first component of equation (20), $F_{\Delta E}$ acts constantly during the whole life of the reservoir. The value of $F_{\Delta S_u G}$ indicates temporary losses from the moment of the reservoir filling up to the stabilization of groundwater regime (provided that there is no permanent groundwater outflow from the reservoir beyond the watershed); for large reservoirs in the plain this period is long and may last for 15 years. The values of $F_{\Delta E}$ and $F_{\Delta S_u G}$ are usually greatest during the construction of reservoirs in zones of water deficit: the former is caused by the great difference between evaporation from an open water surface and from land while the latter reflects the deeper position of groundwater table under natural conditions in the area of the construction of reservoirs.

The water loss due to the change of evaporation in the basin is composed of the three components:

$$F_{\Delta E} = F_1 + F_2 + F_3 \qquad (21)$$

where: F_1 is the volume of losses from the zone of inundation; F_2 is the volume of water losses from the area around the inundated zone with a high groundwater table; F_3 is the volume of losses due to the change of inundation rate in the lower pools of reservoirs.

The first component F_1 is most important in equation (21); it is determined by the following design ratios obtained by comparison of the water balance equation for the territory before and after the construction of the reservoir (Shiklomanov, 1973).

$$F_1 = F_1^1 \cdot A_1 \cdot 10^{-6}$$
$$A_1^1 = A_L - A \qquad (22)$$
$$A = f(Q_{SY})$$

where:

$$F_1^1 = E_L - P - Q_{S_1}^1 \qquad (23)$$

In equations (22) and (23) F_1^1 indicates losses from the inundated zone in mm; A_1 is the additional area of inundation, km^2; A_L and A respectively indicate water surface area of the reservoir and water surface area before the construction of the reservoir, ie under natural conditions; E_L is evaporation from the open water surface of the reservoir, mm; P is precipitation on to the water surface, mm; Q_{S_1} is inflow to the reservoir, km.

The value of A is a function of inflow and is subject to considerable changes over a single year and during a long-term period. For lake-type reservoirs the value of A may be neglected since it is very small; for river reservoirs A will be quite considerable especially in the case of great amplitudes of water level fluctuations in river under natural conditions.

For example, for the Kuibyshev reservoir during the low water period when mean monthly discharges are 2000-3000 m^3/sec, the area of the channel under natural conditions, A, was about 1200 km^2 (19% of the area of the reservoir at the normal backwater level); at high water with discharges of 40,000 m^3/sec (1.5% frequency) the area, A, increased to 5000 km^2 some 80% of the area of the Kuibyshev reservoir surface.

At high groundwater level losses from the area around the reservoir, F_2, are determined by the difference in evaporation before and after the construction of the reservoir ΔE_2, times the area A_2 stipulated by the high level of groundwater:

$$F_2 = \Delta E_2 \cdot A_2 \cdot 10^{-6} \qquad (24)$$

In practice ΔE_2 is determined from evaporation of groundwater E_M which may be calculated approximately from the equations given in Shiklomanov and Kozhevaikov (1974).

The effect on evaporation of large reservoirs is evident not only within the zone of inundation, but also on the lower reaches due to the change of regime and to the areas of flood plain inundation. Under unchanged meteorological conditions the value of water losses of F_3 is proportional to the parameter of inundation rate ΔA_T showing the change of the maximum inundation area and the duration of water stay in the flood plain as a result of decrease of maximum discharge and volumes of spring snowmelt flood stipulated by the construction of reservoirs. For example, in the basin of the Volga, the largest river in Europe, the value of F_3 is most significant for the river reaches downstream of Volgograd - ie for the Volga Akhtuba flood plain and the Volga delta. Special investigations (Shiklomanov and Kozhevnikov, 1974) estimated the annual runoff losses of the Volga by evaporation downstream of Volgograd and the effect of regulation in the basin. In particular, the following reliable design equations have been obtained:

$$\frac{E_3^1}{du} = f(\Delta A_T) \qquad (25)$$

$$\Delta A_T = f(V)$$

where: E_3^1 is evaporation during the Volga flood downstream of Volgograd, mm; d and u indicate respectively air humidity deficit and wind velocity; ΔA_T is the parameter of inundation rate being the product of the maximum inundation rate in parts of the whole area and the resistance time of water in the flood plain, in days; V is the volume of spring runoff of the Volga at Volgograd, km^3. If the volume of spring runoff at Volgograd is known as a result of regulation, the change of runoff depth E_3^1 and the volume of water losses by evaporation F_3 may be calculated from equation (25).

During the construction of reservoirs, runoff tends to decrease at the outlet due to accumulation of water in the reservoir basin ΔS_u and to groundwater recharge G

$$F_{S_u G} = \Delta S_u + G \qquad (26)$$

The total water resources in the basin do not decrease; only their redistribution takes place coupled with the transformation of one of the water resources into another. The determination of ΔS_u is easy if data on the water balances of reservoirs are available. The value of G is composed of water losses by saturation of the aeration zone of the reservoir bottom G_1 and volumes of water penetrating the shores G_2. The first value is determined for every reservoir from the following equation:

$$G_1 = A_1 \cdot h_1 \cdot V_{uz_1} \cdot 10^{-3} \qquad (27)$$

where: h_1 is depth of the zone of aeration at the bottom of the reservoir before its construction, m; V_{uz_1} is the soil moisture deficit.

Saturation of the zone of aeration usually occurs during the first 10-20 days after the filling of the reservoir basin. The recharge of groundwater storage in regions adjacent to reservoirs for different reservoirs occurs over many years after their filling and is a very significant amount; this should be taken into account in the multi-purpose evaluation of the effect of reservoirs on river runoff.

For example, the groundwater table in the zone of the Kuibyshev reservoir has risen since 1955 (the start of filling) until 1964 and expanded in a zone up to 20 km wide. During this time the total volume of water discharging out of the Kuibyshev reservoir into underground horizons was approximately 15 km^3. Where detailed hydrogeological data are available, the value of G_2 for every reservoir may be determined (Anon, 1974); thus the change in exploitable water resources and in ground water storage resulting from channel regulation may be quantified.

The analysis of data available shows that volumes G_2 depend mainly on backwater in reservoirs, their lengths and volumes as well as on the depth of groundwater tables and on the soil characteristics in the surrounding terrain.

For large plain reservoirs the value of G_2 may be approximated from the following empirical formula obtained by generalization of available (though not numerous) materials

$$G_2 \sim 0{,}5 \, K \cdot S_u \cdot h_2^{0.6} \cdot V_{uz_2} \qquad (28)$$

where: $h_2^{0.6}$ is the mean depth, m, of the groundwater table in the areas adjacent to the reservoir before its construction; V_{uz_2} is water coefficient of soils in the adjacent terrain, S_u is the total volume of the reservoir, km^3; K is the coefficient of filling.

Using the above method, a multi-purpose evaluation of the effect of existing and projected reservoirs on the Volga streamflow has been made for the period 1936-2000. For the period 1936-1973 the evaluation has been made for individual years using the extensive hydro-meteorological and hydrogeological information available as well as project data on every large reservoir. For the period 1973-2000 the values of changes averaged for 5-year periods have been computed taking into account the planned commissioning of reservoirs of volume in excess of 50 million m^3 and the project data on every reservoir. Necessary meteorological data were taken from the nearest meteorological stations or from maps of isolines.

Computation of water losses from the zones of inundation F_1 requires data on monthly water balances for the Volga-Kama series of reservoirs since their construction, data on the hydrological river regime under natural conditions and the curves of the reservoir areas (Shiklomanov, 1973). The values of Q_{S_1} were computed by the method of analogy, and the basins used as analogues are located in the area of the reservoir; the physiographic features of these basins correspond closely to the characteristics of the inundated territory. The areas around the inundated zones with high groundwater tables are taken from project data and from the results of actual surveys made for the main reservoirs in the series. The values of

G_2 are computed by equation (28).

The analysis shows that at present the volumes of temporary losses implied by the accumulation of water in reservoirs and by the recharge of groundwater are the most important factors decreasing runoff in the Volga. These volumes amounted to about 173 km^3 or 11.5 km^3/year during 1956-1970; this was explained by the construction of the largest reservoirs during that period. Since the majority of potential reservoirs in the Volga basin have now been constructed, the volumes of water used for accumulation and for groundwater recharge will average only 2.5 km^3/year for the period 1976-2000. Losses from additional evaporation from reservoirs and ponds at present are 4.7 km^3/year, including 3.5 km^3/year from the Volga-Kama series of reservoirs; for the period 1990-2000 these values will increase slightly to 6.7 and 4.6 km^3/year respectively. Additional evaporation from the areas with high groundwater tables around the zones of inundation is not great; at present it is evaluated as 0.5 km^3/year and for the future, 0.6 km^3/year.

On the other hand, due to the regulation of the runoff of the Volga, water losses in the downstream reaches of the river have decreased, as compared to the period of natural streamflow, by 1.4 km^3/year, $F_3 = -1.4$ km^3/year). This value exceeds the volume of the additional losses by evaporation from the Kuibyshev reservoir which is the largest in Europe.

On the whole, the construction of reservoirs and ponds in the basin substantially decreased the total runoff of the Volga into the Caspian Sea; during 1956-1970 the average reduction was 14.5 km^3/year (6% less than the normal runoff at the mouth); up to the year 2000 this value will decrease and on the average it will be about 9 km^3/year for 1976-2000.

REFERENCES

Anon 1974. *Metodicheskie rekomendatsii po otsenke vliania vodokhranilishch na resursy i zapasy podzemnykh vod (Methodological recommendations on the evaluation of the effect of reservoirs on groundwater resources and storage)*, VSEGINGEO Press, Moscow, 24 pp.

Anon 1975. *Metodicheskie rekomendatsii po otsenke i uchetu vliania agrolesomeliorativnykh meropriatiy na stok rek (Methodological recommendations on the evaluation and account of the effect of agricultural afforestation on streamflow)*, Girdrometeoizdat, 110 pp.

Kharchenko, S.I. 1975. *Hydrologia oroshaemykh zemel (Hydrology of irrigated areas)*. Gidrometeoizdat, Leningrad, 373 pp.

Romanov, V.V. 1962. *Isparenie s bolot Evropeiskoi territorii SSSR (Evaporation from swamps in the European territory of the USSR)*. Gidrometeoizdat, Leningrad, 288 pp.

Shebeko, V.F. 1965. *Isparenie s bolot i balans pochvennoi vlagi (Evaporation from swamps and soil moisture balance)*. Urozhai Press, Minsk, 394 pp.

Shiklomanov, I.A., and Veretennikova, G.M. 1973. Bezvozvratnye poteri stoka r. Volgi za schet isparenia s vodokhranilishch Volzheno-Kamskogo kaskada (Irretrievable streamflow losses of the Volga due to evaporation from the surface of the Volga-Kama series of reservoirs). *Trans. GGI*, 206, 22-52.

Shiklomanov, I.A. and Koshevnikov, V.P. 1974. Poteri stoka v Volgo-Akhtubinskoi poime i delte Volgi i ikh izmenemie pod vlianiem khoziaistvennoi deatelnosti (Runoff losses in the Volga-Akhtuba flood plain and in the Volga delta and their changes under the effect of man's activity). *Trans. GGI*, 221, 3-47.

Shiklomanov, I.A. 1976. *Vlianie khoziaistvennoi deatelnosti na vodnye resursy i hydrologicheski rezhim (Impact of man's activity on water resources and hydrological regime)*. Survey, VNIIGMI - Obninsk, 111 pp.

Sokolov, A.A. and Chapman, T.G. (Eds) 1974. *Methods for water balance computations: An International guide for research and practice*. Studies and Reports in Hydrology 17, The UNESCO Press, 127 pp.

Toebes, C. and Ouryvaev, V. (Eds) 1970. *Representative and experimental basins: An international guide for research and practice*. Studies and Reports in Hydrology No 4, The UNESCO Press, 348 pp.

2.4 HYDROLOGICAL ANALOGY

2.4.1 Introduction

Analogy is not specific to hydrology (Kobar and Stransky, 1962): this brief survey suggests that hydrological analogy represents a method of indirect determination of hydrological data by comparison with an analogous gauged water body, hydrologically similar. It involves assumption of similarity or correspondence of two phenomena on the basis of similarity or correspondence of their properties. Hydrological analogy presumes, in accordance with genetic analysis and empirical verification, that corresponding properties of catchment areas give rise to analogous hydrological phenomena and thus also to analogous quantitative demonstrations. Analogy may be applied in hydrological calculations, in the determination of the hydrological characteristics of water bodies for which there are insufficient hydrological data, and also in hydrological forecasts. Recently the use of hydrological analogy for indirect quantification of the changes in the hydrological regime of river basins caused by human activity has grown in importance.

2.4.2 Hydrological analogy: the concept

Hydrological analogy is a method of estimation of the characteristics of hydrological regimes of ungauged or little gauged water bodies on the basis of:
- the choice of a gauged object (analogue), the physical and geographical conditions of which correspond to those of the ungauged object;
- the extension of the hydrological characteristics of the gauged object to the ungauged object (Chebotarev, 1964).

Fundamental to the successful use of hydrological analogy is the suitability of the gauged water body selected as an analogue. This selection is based on comparison and analysis of processes in the hydrological regime in respect of:
- correspondence of climatic conditions;
- synchronism of hydrological phenomena;
- similarity of environmental conditions in terms of relief, geology; hydrogeology and pedology, areal and generic representation of vegetation, exploitation of the catchment areas, etc;
- adequate correspondence of hydrographic parameters;
- high quality of observations over a sufficiently long period on the analogue adopted.

The selection of a suitable analogue enables derivation of the necessary hydrological characteristics for the water body for which observations are either not available or where observations have been made for only a short period which usually coincides with part of the long term record for the analogous catchment. Hydrological analogy (Dub, 1963, WMO, 1965, Anon, 1969, Anon 1973) serves the purposes of:
- estimation of hydrological characteristics for a little gauged water body;
- extension of the data and characteristics obtained from short-term observations to a longer or long-term period;
- verification of results obtained indirectly (eg by use of empirical formulae).
  Further, analogy is used:
- in systematic elaboration of hydrological characteristics in regional detail (for a greater number of river profiles, localities, etc, than there are sites suitable for direct measurement;
- for assessing indirect determinations of characteristics of the hydrological regime (detailed comparison of catchment areas and water bodies according to the principles of hydrological analogy makes it easier to select a suitable model in respect of the influence of possible partial differences in causitive factors).

The desired data to be derived by analogy usually comprise the basic characteristics of the hydrological regime, ie average values of hydrological elements, extreme values of quantities characterizing hydrological phenomena and the characteristics of the temporal courses of hydrological phenomena. Other data are required for special purposes such as the extension of values of some quantities (eg average annual discharges) for periods exceeding those of the short-term observations on a little gauged water body.

The process of derivation depends on the desired datum (characteristic), on the extent of information obtained about the little gauged water body and on the extent and generalization of hydrological knowledge on the gauged water bodies usable for analogy in the

broader area of interest. Besides direct extension of hydrological characteristics from the
gauged water body to the ungauged one, it is possible to use graphic dependance of corresponding quantities from the period of synchronous observation (for interpolation or
extrapolation of data), interpolation of values of the hydrological quantities between
measurement points, cartographic representation of various hydrological quantities and
auxiliary parameters, calculations based on correlative methods and regional dependances of
hydrological quantities on catchment area parameters, etc. These problems are dealt with
in greater detail in specialized treatises or in internal instructions of hydrological
services (WMO, 1969, Anon, 1969, Anon, 1972, Anon, 1973)

2.4.3 The use of hydrological analogy for the quantification of changes in the hydrological regime caused by human activity

Hydrological analogy may be used to evaluate changes in hydrological regimes due to human
activity by:
- use of parallel analogous catchment areas to assess the influence of certain kinds of
  human activity;
- use of observations on the influenced water body and on the uninfluenced analogue;
- extension to other analogous catchment areas of the data quantifying changes in the
  hydrological regime.

2.4.4 Parallel analogous catchment areas

Changes in the hydrological regimes of rivers are evaluated by parallel hydrological
observations in two catchment areas chosen according to the principles of hydrological
analogy according to the objective of the study. The two catchment areas are selected so
that the basic natural conditions (climatic, geological, geomorphological) affecting the
hydrological regimes are similar; the hydrographical characteristics of the two catchment
areas show minimum differences. The catchments, however, differ in terms of the various
forms of human activity resulting in different exploitation of the catchment area (afforested
catchment areas, agriculturally exploited catchment areas, etc). With this parameter
("human activity"), usually substantial differences between the two catchment areas are
selected on purpose. At the same time it is profitable if these differences concern only one
factor influencing the hydrological regime. Therefore, on the basis of detailed long-term
observations of the two catchment areas' hydrological regimes and evaluation of the
hydrological characteristics, the differences resulting from the comparison of the data are
attributed to the influence of man in the catchment area and its effect on the hydrological
regimes of the rivers.

This approach is illustrated by an example from the study of two parallel catchments
established in 1927 in the CSSR (Valez, 1935). The catchment areas are situated on the
territory of one geomorphological whole (the Maple Mountains, the system of the Outer West
Carpathians) and they are only 8 km distant apart. The catchment of the Kychová river
measures 4.09 sq km and is 93.2% forested; the catchment of the Zdechovka river is 4.04 sq km
and is 4.7% forested, 95.3% farmed with fields, pastures and meadows. The mean elevation
of the Kychová catchment is 718 metres, of the Zdechovka catchment 618 metres. The results
of the measurements show (Cermak, 1954) that the average long-term runoff is almost identical
in the two catchment areas; the average runoffs in individual years of observation, however,
differ in the two catchment areas. In terms of streamflow, the driest and wettest years
do not occur simultaneously in the two catchment areas; the wooded catchment area smoothes
and delays the extremes of the average annual runoffs. The distribution of the runoffs
within the year in the two catchment areas is similar (the greatest runoff in March, the
lowest runoff in September). The minimum discharges from the agricultural catchment are
only 50-57% of those from the wooded catchment. At times of flood there are also
considerable differences in the runoffs from the two catchments in that runoff from the
wooded catchment is substantially lower than that from the farmed catchment (thus eg the
evaluated annual discharge with a probability of exceedence of 1% is more than twice as high
in the agricultural catchment area (Kriz, 1965). If runoff relations in the two catchment
areas are evaluated according to runoff losses (the difference between the average
precipitation falling in the catchment area and the runoff) then the wooded catchment area
shows somewhat higher losses than the farmed one.

The above example utilizes:

Hydrological analogy

- the principles of hydrological analogy in the selection of the comparative catchment areas (with only the factor under study varying);
- mathematical statistical elaboration of the observations;
- the comparative method based on the assumptions of hydrological analogy;
- hydrological analogy in extending data (characteristics) to evaluate the hydrological regimes of other catchment areas.

2.4.5 <u>The use of observations on the treated water body and on the control analogue</u>

The evaluation of changes in the hydrological regime is based on:
- hydrological data for the particular water body in the period prior to a significant anthropogenic influence;
- data derived for the treated water formation after conditions had changed using the analogue;
- comparison of data derived by analogy with data obtained in the treatment period (comparison of derived untreated data with measured treated "influenced" data).

The use of this procedure presupposes:
- hydrological observations on the particular water body before the effects of change occurred;
- continuation of these observations after conditions changed;
- selection of a suitable analogue for which simultaneous observations are available for the periods both before and after the changes on the particular water body; with two water bodies the observations in the period before the application of the treatment to one of them have to cover a sufficiently long time interval and to show close correlation.

Where initial data are sparse, it is practical although less reliable, the control data can be derived as for an ungauged water body (by transformation of the analogue data etc); or even the treated data may have to be extended to a longer period by hydrological analogy. If the impact of man on the hydrological regime occurred gradually, the evaluation of the extent and nature of the anthropogenic influence must be based on the study of observations of both water bodies over the whole, preferentially long-term, period.

To clarify the possibilities of application of the procedure described there follows a brief outline of the problem of characterising discharges in areas where man's influence is significant (Kritz and Schneider, 1975).

Together with the temporal prolongation of discharge sequences and with a gradual, often difficult to quantify, anthropogenic influence upon the runoff process, there arises a question of homogeneity of the basic discharge data, representativeness of the observed hydrological characteristics and their interpretation for practical application in water management. The changes in discharge caused by human activity are caused mainly by locally determined water management (water management objects) but also by influences occurring in particular areas (agriculture, forestry, urbanization, etc). There arises a demand for quantification of at least the more important influences upon discharge caused mostly by accumulation, extraction, release and consumption of water. One of the possibilities of such an evaluation of artificial changes of discharges is provided by the method of balancing these changes on the basis of direct detailed measurements of both the manipulation of water and its distribution. This presupposes good organization of reliable and usually extensive measurements, and analysis and systematic evaluation of the results together with other data about river discharges. Its use is directed to the parallel evaluation of actual, really occurring and therefore influenced discharges (discharge characteristics) in the channel network and of so called uninfluenced discharges (characteristics) modified by the more significant changes brought forth by human activity (it is above all the average values - average monthly and annual discharges - the utilization of which is expected).

For the same purpose, hydrological analogy can be utilized to derive "uninfluenced" discharge characteristics and to evaluate the character and extent of the effect of the hydrological regime. The proper derivation (extension) of the uninfluenced discharge characteristics results from the graphic relations of mutually corresponding discharge values (in the observed and analogue catchment areas or profiles, respectively) and the calculation of correlations. Sometimes double mass analysis can illustrate the relationship between the cumulative values of quantities of the two series (the explored and analogue ones, respectively). From the changes in these relations it is possible to deduce the extent and kind of anthropogenic influence, or even to find a way of naturalizing the influenced hydrological characteristics and thus to determine the uninfluenced characteristics (Dyck et al, 1976).

2.4.6 The extension of data quantifying changes

Hydrological analogy is an indirect way of determining hydrological data by comparison with an analogous water body. Also in the case of hydrological data on the influence of human activity, the correspondence not only of the natural factors, but also the factors expressing the anthropogenic influences (kind, extent, character of activity, temporal and spatial distribution, etc), on both water bodies must be assessed. In this way analogy contributes to the extrapolation of data obtained on the changes in the hydrological regime to other water bodies, and, if need be, also to the direction both of possible changes in the hydrological regime and of the consequence of a notional application of a certain activity.

2.4.7 Conditions limiting the use of hydrological analogy

Conditions limiting the use of hydrological analogy result from the description of its conception and the outline of its application.

In quantitative evaluation of changes of the hydrological regime due to human activity the use of hydrological analogy represents an indirect solution. Where there are available enough hydrological data as well as analytical facts from a broader area of interest, this indirect way can lead to sufficiently reliable information. Hydrological analogy, however, is most appropriate in the provision of preliminary, approximate data for basic orientation.

Hydrological analogy requires the similarity of all factors affecting the hydrological regimes in the gauged and analogue catchment areas, respectively; this condition is generally better fulfilled with basins of small to medium size, situated near to each other. Within larger areas there is often because of the low density of the network of stations difficulties in using this method.

When extending hydrological data to unexplored catchment areas it is necessary to respect the consequences of the influence of zonal and azonal character (UNESCO/WMO/IAHS, 1973). This is connected also with the choice of methods of detecting these influences.

The use of hydrological analogy to evaluate changes in the hydrological reg me caused by human activity provides satisfactory results especially when:
- the two catchment areas (the gauged and analogue ones respectively) show the highest possible correspondence of their basic characteristics;
- the two catchment areas differ from each other only in the application of human activity;
- human activity interferes with the least possible number of factors influencing the hydrological regime but shows considerably in the changes of the hydrological regime.

Hydrological analogy concentrated on the changes of hydrological regime caused by anthropogenic influences can offer very useful information especially in the initial phase of the operation of these new influences, provided that sufficiently reliable information is available in the explored and analogous catchment areas. Data should be collected from the period before the start of those influences (in the gauged catchment area) and during their operation. Good results, but only after long-term observation, are gained from paired catchment areas with synchronous observations selected according to the principles of hydrological analogy with respect to the object of the study. The use of hydrological analogy is not convenient in those cases where changes in the hydrological regime are due to a number of factors influencing the hydrological regime and for large areas.

REFERENCES

Anon 1969. Zasady obliczania najwiekszych przeplywów recoznych o okreslonym prawdopodobieństwie pojawania sie (Principles of calculation of the greatest annual discharges with determined probability of occurrence). *WTP-H1, Wydawnictwo katalogów i cenników*, Warszawa, 40 pp.

Anon 1972. Ukazaniya po opredeleniyu raschotnykh ghidrologhicheskikh kharakteristik (Instructions for determination of hydrological characteristics). *Ghidrometeorologhicheskoye izdathelstvo*, Leningrad, 20 pp.

Anon 1973. *Rukovodstvo po opredeleniyu raschotnykh ghidrologhicheskikh kharakteristik (Handbook of determination of hydrological characteristics)*. Ghidrometeorologhicheskoya izzdathelstvo, Leningrad, 111 pp.

The correlation between cause and effect

Cermák, M. 1954. Odtokové pomery malého povodi (The runoff relations of a small catchment area). *Vodni hospodárstvi (Water Management)*, Prague, 1 9-12, 2 41-44.

Chebotarev, A.Y. 1964. *Ghidrologhichesky slovar (Hydrological dictionary)*. Ghidrometeorologhicheskoye izdathelstvo, Leningrad, 222 pp.

Dub, O. 1963. *Hydrológia, hydrografia, hydrometria (Hydrology, hydrography, hydrometry)*. SVTL, SNTL, Prague, 526 pp.

Dyck, S. et al 1976. *Angewandte Hydrologie*, T.1. Dresden, 512 pp.

Korbar, T. and Stránský, A. (Eds) 1962. *Technický naucný slovnik (Technical Encyclopaedia Dictionary)*, SNTL, SVTL, Prague, 1, 653 pp.

Kriz, V. 1965. *Hydrologická vyhodnoceni povodnových prùtokù a jejich zpracování pro hrazeni bystrin (Hydrological evaluations of flood discharges and their elaboration for the stemming of torrents)*. Vysoká skola zemedelská (College of Agriculture), Brno, 207 pp.

Kriz, V. and Schneider, B. 1975. Nástin problematiky ovlivnených prùtokù (The outline of the problems of influenced discharges). *Vodní hospodárství (Water Management)*, Prague, 8:201-203.

UNESCO/WMO/IAHS 1973. *Proceedings of symposium on the design of water resources projects with inadequate data*, Madrid, 1, 442 pp and 2, 643 pp.

Válek, Z. 1935. Výzkum a výsledky pozorování vlivu porostu na odtok srázkových vod v bystrinných povodich Kychové a Zdechovky za léta 1928-1934 (The research and results of observation of the influence of vegetation upon the runoff of discharge waters in the catchment areas of the Kychová and Zdechovka torrents in the period 1928-1934). *Sborník Výzkumných ústavù zemedelských (Miscellanies of the Research Institutes of Agriculture)*, Prague, 114, 130 pp.

World Meteorological Organisation 1969. Estimation of Maximum Floods. *WMO Technical Note No 98*, Geneva, 288 pp.

World Meteorological Organisation 1965. *Guide to Hydrometeorological Practices*, Geneva, 513 pp.

2.5   THE CORRELATION BETWEEN CAUSE AND EFFECT - HUMAN ACTIVITIES AND THE HYDROLOGICAL REGIME

2.5.1   Introduction

Man's activities may cause considerable changes in various characteristics of the hydrological regime and in natural water quality. Such changes inevitably lead to the modification of all the rest of the elements of the hydrological regime of river basins. Computation of such hydrological characteristics as annual or seasonal streamflow which characterize the water content of a certain region is of great scientific and practical value.

Anthropogenic changes of streamflow may be estimated quantitatively from a knowledge of the long-term variations of runoff at "benchmark" gauging stations in combination with analyses of the natural fluctuations of meteorological factors and of the economic development of the watershed. Such an approach has certain advantages since it allows some results to be obtained from the study of available hydrometeorological data without collecting new data and performing costly experiments. Investigations of this kind are important in helping to estimate the integrated influence of all anthropogenic factors within the basin and may serve as a basis for objective evaluation of water resources within large regions. However, a considerable drawback to the above approach is the limited choice of sites with the required long observational periods covering the various stages of economic development within the basin. Besides, this approach does not reveal the physical nature of the processes and thus there is no way to distinguish the influence of each economic factor separately. There is no possibility of estimating the role of those anthropogenic factors which are not sufficiently marked in the basin for their influence upon streamflow to exceed the margin of error of the hydrological measurements at the outlet.

Quantitative estimation of man's influence upon streamflow, even if reliable long-term observational series on the hydrometeorological regime are available, is rather a difficult task because anthropogenic modifications are superimposed on natural runoff variations which exceed the magnitude of the artificial changes. To solve this problem, one must develop a long-term correlation between runoff and the natural runoff formation factors and the indices which characterize quantitatively the degree of the economic development of the basin. Taking into account the regional physiography, the economic development and the extent of the utilization of water resources, one may choose various efficient approaches to determine the role of the anthropogenic factors in several groups of river basins.

2.5.2 Mountainous river basins with zones of runoff formation and utilization

This group of basins includes first of all the watersheds of the traditionally irrigated regions. streamflow of these watersheds is formed in the mountains and is utilized in plains and lowlands[1]. Within the basins of such rivers one can easily distinguish the runoff formation zone where seasonal and annual runoff depends only on changes in meteorological factors and thus exhibits only natural variations within the whole long-term observational period, and the runoff utilization zone of intensive consumption of the basin water resources for non-productive evaporation and economic needs.

There is no reason to consider a trend towards a reduction in total water resources in the studied group of basins since the magnitude of water resources usually estimated from runoff values in the formation zone (in the mountains) has not changed quantitatively under the influence of man's activities and remains natural. Neither is there reason to think that it may be reduced in future. However, in many regions, runoff at the outlet has already changed substantially because of economic activities in the zone of runoff utilization and this process is going to accelerate in future.

Research results (Shiklomanov and Smirnova, 1973; Shiklomanov, 1970) show that it is most convenient to use the following multi-factorial relationships for estimation of the changes in the annual runoff and the runoff values of the vegetation period under the influence of the economic activities:

$$Q = f(\Sigma Q_{SY}, P, d) \tag{1}$$

$$Q = f(\Sigma Q_{SY}, P, d, F) \tag{2}$$

where: ΣQ_{SY} is the characteristic of the inflow from the mountainous part of the basin estimated from the gauging stations within the zone of formation; P and d are precipitation and air humidity deficit (Q is air temperature, as an alternative) in the zone of runoff utilization; F is complex anthropogenic factor quantitatively characterizing runoff losses for economic needs; for the irrigated areas it is most frequently accepted as the area of irrigated levels or the volume of water diverted for irrigation.

The above relationships, (1) and (2), are analysed by multiple linear correlation with the help of computers. Observational series used for this purpose should cover no less than 30-40 years. Equation (1) appears to be more suitable for computation. In such cases, the main task is to restore runoff values at the outlet during the whole period of runoff distortion with the help of the function interrelating runoff and the main natural factors during the period of the natural runoff. The runoff change ΔQ due to the influence of all economic factors during the period of runoff distortion is the difference between the computed annual Q_c and the actual observed Q_{obs} runoff:

$$\Delta Q = Q_c - Q_{obs} \tag{3}$$

The random error of computing runoff changes $\delta_{\Delta Q}$ may be approximated from the following equation:

---

[1] In the USSR streamflow of such rivers provides water for about 80% of the total irrigated area.

$$\delta_{\Delta Q} = \frac{1}{\sqrt{n}} \sqrt{\delta_{Q_C}^2 + \delta_{Q_{obs}}^2} \qquad (4)$$

where: n is the number of years in the period for which ΔQ was computed. The computation error of the restored runoff values Q_C estimated by the multiple regression equation with the total correlation coefficient R, is calculated by a well-known equation:

$$\delta_{Q_C} = \delta_Q \sqrt{1-R^2} \qquad (5)$$

where: δ_{Q_C} is the mean square deviation of the Q variable.

While using the multi-factorial relationship (2), the complex economic factor F, usually indicating the area of irrigated land is included directly in the multiple regression equation; its role in the change of runoff during the whole period of study is estimated quantitatively by the usual statistical methods (Rakhmanov, 1973; Shiklomanov and Smirnova, 1973).

To obtain approximate estimates of restored runoff for the given group of river basins, one may plot for the whole, long-term, observational period a simpler relationship using the usual binary correlation $Q = f(\Sigma Q_{SY})$ or the double mass curves $\Sigma Q = f\Sigma(\Sigma Q_{SY})$.

2.5.3 Flat watersheds of middle-size rivers

The estimation of the runoff changes due to the economic activities within the basins of this large group of rivers is particularly difficult since runoff formation and utilization occurs over the whole basin area. In this case, estimation of restored runoff values at the outlet is made only with the help of the interrelationship of runoff with meteorological factors since their regime may be regarded as natural and independent of the economic development of the basin.

In the zones of moisture excess restored runoff values at the outlet may be estimated with sufficient accuracy by means of annual runoff-precipitation curves which are closely correlated ($\Gamma_{QP} = 0.80 - 0.95$).

In the regions of insufficient or variable moisture (for instance, forest-steppe and steppe zones of the USSR), the correlation between annual and spring runoff and any single meteorological factor proved to be unreliable (the coefficient of correlation between annual runoff and precipitation, for instance, does not exceed $\Gamma_{QP} = 0.50$). Therefore, one must use complex multi-factorial relationships to restore runoff values. Quantitative estimation of anthropogenic modifications of water resources is still more difficult because of the natural variability of annual and spring runoff of rivers.

Investigations and numerous computations have shown that good estimates of restored spring runoff Q_S of the central flat watersheds within forest steppe and steppe zones of the European USSR and Northern Khazakhstan may be obtained using relationships of the following type:

$$Q_S = f(S_{sn}, C_M, d, \theta) \qquad (6)$$

where: S_{sn} is maximum snow storage in the basin at the end of the winter; C_M is the characteristic of the amount of moisture available in the basin during the autumn period (October-November of the antecedent year); d is the average basin air humidity deficit during June-September of the antecedent year; θ is the mean air temperature during snowmelt.

In equation (6) the variables are ranked in accordance with their contribution to the multiple regression equation. In all watersheds the maximum contribution is due to the first variable - maximum snow storage. The majority of studies may be limited to analysis of the first three variables in the right-hand side of the equation (6).

The meteorological variables in equation (6) makes it possible, as a rule, to derive runoff multiple regression equations for long-term natural periods with correlation coefficients $\Gamma \geq 0.80$. These equations may be used for estimating the restored average runoff values and for evaluating the complex anthropogenic effect in the basin ΔQ as the difference between the estimated restored values and the observed runoff (3). The computation error is approximately estimated by formulae of the type (4) and (5).

In some cases, given a reliable quantitative index of the dynamics of the economic development of the basin in the long-term (the area of the ploughed land, crop yields, etc) it may be useful to include this index directly in the multiple regression equation (6) for estimating anthropogenic runoff changes at the outlet (Rakhmanov, 1973, Anon, 1965, Lull and Sopper, 1966).

REFERENCES

Anon 1965. Elektronnye vychislitelnye mashiny v gidrologii (Electronic computers in hydrology). *Gidrometeoizdat*, Leningrad, 220 pp. (Collection of articles translated from English).

Lull, H.W. and Sopper, W.E. 1966. Factors that influence streamflow in the northeast. *Water Resources Research*, 1966, 2, (3).

Rakhmanov, V.V. 1973. Rechnoi stok i agrotekhnika (Streamflow and agrotechnical practice). *Trudy GMI SSSR,* 114, 200.

Shiklomanov, I.A. and Smirnova, L.E. 1973. Otsenka vliania khozyaistvennoi deyatelnosti na stok krupnykh rek Kavkaza (Kura, Terek, Kuban) (Estimation of the influence of the economic activities upon streamflow of large Caucasian rivers (Kura, Terek, Kuban). *Trans. GGI*, 206, 92-122.

Shiklomanov, I.A. 1976. Gidrologisheskie aspekty problemy Kaspiyskogo morya (Hydrological aspects of the Caspian Sea problem). *Gidrometeoizdat,* Leningrad, 77 pp.

2.6   STATISTICAL ANALYSIS

2.6.1   Generalities

The value of runoff at a given place and within a given period of time (a day, a month, a year) evidently depends on the volume of water which has fallen during that period of time and in preceding periods; also it depends on the amount of water transferred from the given basin to a neighbouring one or vice versa, and transferred from each period of time to a later period, and on the losses of precipitation due to evaporation, evapotranspiration, etc. One can imagine the existence of a stochastic function defining the dependence of runoff on precipitation. This function is influenced by the precipitation regime by physical characteristics, geographic and geologic features of the basin, and by climatic conditions In other words, given the function representing the precipitation regime the topographic features of the basin and the hydrological conditions of the basin in the present and preceding periods, it should be possible hypothetically to calculate the runoff of a watercourse at a given place within the prescribed period of time.
    To predict water resources, we might choose one of two possibilities: either to admit a cyclic or random repetition of the known precipitation (or directly operating through the known runoffs), or to make a statistical study of the whole phenomenon, taking advantage of the fact that random variables also conform to laws.

2.6.2   Hydrological data processing

The methods of descriptive statistics can be applied to the set of recorded runoffs to find the estimates of several statistics (such as expectation, median, variance, assymetry and other moments, etc) - applicable to the distribution function of a random variable defining the runoff. The estimates can be identified as the parameters of a distribution function chosen as appropriate for representing the phenomenon. However, before accepting the choice as being right, the selected function and available set of data must be subjected to a fitness test method, eg the one based on the chi-square distribution of Pearson.

2.6.3   Auto-regression

Hydrological studies must be based on sample data. The majority of hydrological phenomena in nature are stochastic processes. Therefore, sample data must depend on stochastic processes and to a lesser degree on purely deterministic processes. Data may be treated either by a deterministic approach, by a stochastic approach, or by both simultaneously. Future progress of hydrology may depend on how these two approaches are combined for discovering and understanding hydrological regularities.

Hydrological data are mainly chronological. But it is convenient to treat other types of observations in the same way as hydrological phenomena, for example, depths of groundwater, sediment characteristics etc. One can think of two or more random variables that may be treated so as to obtain some relationship. The main purpose should be to transfer statistical information between them.

Study of the quality of the data is necessary. One must consider the possibility of errors and non-homogeneity. Random errors are always present in data. If errors are approximately symmetrically distributed about the true value and follow a normal distribution, then the standard deviation can be used for detecting major discrepancies due to real mistakes.

Correlation applied to several sets of data is a further aid to the task of treating hydrological data. By establishing the regression equation between the random variable and the remaining variables (random or not) it is possible to fill gaps in the data series. By estimation of the correlation coefficient the degree of relationship between the variables represented in the data sets can be shown. But although the correlation coefficient may differ from zero this does not necessarily indicate that the variables are correlated. It is necessary to establish significantly the difference from zero of this correlation coefficient (by means, for example, of Student's distribution, or more rigorously the F.distribution or the Snedecor distribution). Where two variables are serially dependent a greater degree of confidence can be obtained in the correlation coefficient by making use of the autocorrelation coefficients of the series involved.

Spurious correlation can be obtained especially if the series of data are not reasonably homogeneous.

Auto-regression processing has been very frequently made without a previous study of the random variables to which that process was applied. Certain hypotheses must be applicable to those variables, otherwise the results obtained will be meaningless. For example, when studying the regression between two variables the first variable must always be assumed to show the same distribution function for any given value of the second variable; only its expectation can vary and this will define the corresponding regression line.

Likewise, in the case of the auto-regression processing the acceptance of the necessary hypotheses must be realized. For example, there might be a different distribution function for small runoffs. When compared with the one corresponding to large runoffs, the auto-regression processing would not be correct unless the pertinent change in variable were made.

2.6.4 Periodicities

Periodicities do evidently exist, at least annual periodicities which arise neatly when the chosen period of time equals, eg a month. Repeatedly, attempts have been made to discover the existence of periodicities hidden among sets of recorded data. Had such periodicities existed they would have been obvious; if they are not, then a large sample would be needed to establish their existence.

On the other hand, even should such periodicities exist, an excessive size of sample may also show the influence of a possible evolution of, or modifications in the hydrological characteristics of the watercourse being studied; this would help to disguise those possible periodicities even more. It would be better to explore deeper into a more aprioristic study of the phenomenon. Precautions must be taken in applying serial correlations between separated members of the series of data showing cyclic movement. This cyclic movement should first be removed.

2.6.5 Study of a distribution function

From now on all previous opinions regarding the law ruling the succession of runoffs are going to be disregarded. Given only a continuous random variable, its probability density function must be discovered.

The criterion for adoption of specific distribution functions have normally been based on common empirical considerations. The probability distribution function should resemble the histogram of the sample in question. As the histograms usually present an asymmetrical bell shape, with a given minimum value, possible subjectively acceptable probability density functions have been derived from the normal distribution, or similar structure functions.

The following distributions can be mentioned:
Goodrich's distribution
Galton's distribution
The different curves of Pearson
The gamma distribution

The curve type selected may be adjusted in various ways. One method is graphic data plotting using single logarithmic or double logarithmic, Gumbel type paper. Another process uses statistics: the mean, variance and successive moments, which can be computed from the sample data, will define the distribution of the chosen type.

2.6.6 Trend analysis

This method can also be used to define the runoff distribution to study its possible evolution. To do so, the available sample need merely be broken down, taking sub-samples and advancing chronologically. Trends or alterations can be detected as in the case of correlations by analysis of variance.

Statistics such as the mean value and standard deviation applied to sub-series can be used to detect non-homogeneity, due to accidents, or to evolution in nature or to human activities. These changes in hydrological data are investigated by detecting the magnitudes of random errors.

2.7 MATHEMATICAL AND PHYSICAL MODELLING

2.7.1 The use of mathematical models for the estimation of changes in the hydrological regime of river basins due to human activities

2.7.1.1 Methodological aspects. During the last decade, mathematical models have been used a great deal for the assessment of quantitative changes in the hydrological regime of rivers due to human activities.

The development of mathematical models starting with the first version of the Stanford Model in 1960 (Crawford and Linsley, 1960), and the possibilities of solving sophisticated algorithms using computers, have offered hydrologists an invaluable tool to assess the impact of anthropic factors on runoff formation.

Lately, a series of symposia and workshops have been devoted to this subject (IAHS, 1975, IAHS/UNESCO, 1976, Anon, 1971, UNESCO, 1976, IAHS/UNESCO, 1974, IAHS/UNESCO/WMO, 1969).

This chapter considers only analytical and conceptual models for the estimation of changes induced by man. The methodology for the assessment of changes in the hydrological regime due to human activities depends on the hydrological data available in the basin under study.

2.7.1.1.1 Streamflow data are available on a long enough period before the event when the impact has been significant. In this case the main steps are:
(a) Selection of the most adequate model for the basin studied. The concept on runoff formation assumed by the model must be matched to the characteristic features of the basin. If, for instance, the basin is a small one and of a mountainous type, a Dawdy, Lichty and Bergman model (1970) or a SSARR Model (Rockwood, 1974) may be selected. Procedures for selecting the most adequate model depending on the type of the basin, the existing data and the availability of the computation techniques have been published (Dawdy and O'Donnell, 1965, Roche, 1971, Stanescu and Serban, 1974, Fleming, 1975).
(b) The calibration of the model using recorded and simulated streamflow data corresponding to natural hydrological conditions.
(c) The simulation of the streamflow data during the period in which the influence of human activities becomes significant. The simulation leads to the assessment of the streamflow corresponding to natural hydrological conditions as though no human activity has occurred. (The model parameters derived from the previous step reflect the natural conditions of runoff formation).
(d) The comparison of simulated streamflow over the period during which the human influence was active with the recorded streamflow over the same period.
(e) Drawing up the conclusions concerning the amount of changes induced by human activities in the hydrological regime.

2.7.1.1.2 Inadequate streamflow records prior to significant human impact. In this case the determination of the parameters of the model to simulate the streamflow in natural conditions, should be made as follows:
- If the model selected has parameters of a physical character which depend on the physiographic characteristics of the basin, the values of such parameters would be usually found in graphs, tables or by field investigations. Under this category fall the models of the "Kinematic Wave type" (or analytical models) which are derived from the Saint Venant's continuity and motion equations.
- If the selected model is of a conceptual type, each parameter depends on the characteristics of the basin. Such a model should be calibrated using hydrological records from a basin which is physiographically analogous to the basin under study.

   The parameters derived from an analogous basin can be used for streamflow simulation of natural hydrological conditions for the period in which human activities were made evident. The better the analogy between the basin under study and the one used for calibration the higher the reliability of the simulated streamflow.
- If there are records available during the period consecutive to the moment of human impact, the comparison should be made as described in 2.7.1.1.1.

   If there are no records during the mentioned period, it is recommended that the initial values (ie in natural hydrological conditions) of those parameters which are directly related to the human impacture changed.

   The procedure of changing the initial estimates of the parameters takes into account the results obtained in experimental and/or representative basins. Further, some examples concerning general methodological aspects are given. These examples will refer both to the types of human activities which influence the hydrological regime of river basins significantly and to the main types of models used.

2.7.1.2   Main types of deterministic models.

2.7.1.2.1 Analytical models. Under this category fall the models which are based on the so called "Theory of Kinematic Wave".

   As a rule, the model considers the basin to have its slopes in two plane surfaces to which the following system of equations is confined:

$$\frac{\partial h}{\partial t} + \frac{\partial q}{\partial x} = r_e(t)$$
$$h = K q^p \qquad K = (N/\sqrt{\sin\theta})^p \tag{1}$$

where: h is the depth of flow, q is the discharge per unit width of the slope, $r_e(t)$ is the intensity of effective rainfall, x is the distance, t is the time, $\sin\theta$ is the slope, N is the roughness coefficient and p is a parameter which is a function of the slope canopy (Stanescu, 1972, Toyokuni, 1975, Befani, 1959, Wooding 1965 and 1966). The function q(t) is found by integrating the system (1) using either the characteristics method or a numerical method of a "grid type".

   The discharge q(t) enters the rivercourse and then the following system is written:

$$\frac{\partial A}{\partial t} + \frac{\partial Q}{\partial x} = q(t)$$
$$A = K \times Q^P \tag{2}$$

where: A represents the cross sectional area of the river, Q is the discharge of the river in the moment t and the distance x, K and P are channel constants or the parameters of the rating curve.

   There are many versions of models of this type but all of them are derived from equations (1) and (2).

   This type of model could be applied successfully to estimating the effect of urbanization on the formation of runoff in small basins.

   As a rule, the shape of the small basins is more complicated than having merely two planes so that it is quite usual to resort to a procedure of modulating the basin. Each module should equate to a plane surface (Toyokuni, 1975, Machmeir and Larson, 1967).

The roughness coefficient N is estimated using isotopes (Diaconu and Craciun, 1971) on experimental plots on slopes covered with grass or cultivated plants. For quasi-impermeable urban areas such as streets, roofs, etc, the N value can be assessed using special tables.

In investigating the effect of urbanization, these models are used first to simulate the natural hydrological conditions and then by predicting an increase in the area of the city, the effect of human impact can be evaluated.

Equation (2) can also be used to assess the change in flood hydrographs due to river embankments. Application of the model (2) is useful in determining the height of the dikes or/and the dimensions of the "on-site-detention" works. As regards the mathematical models of groundwater movement, it can be said that the most general and rigorous approach of the problem uses a single equation to model the saturated and unsaturated subsurface flow (Rubin, 1968, Neuman, 1970, Vachaud, Vauclin and Hoverkamp, 1975, Freeze, 1971). Though efficient computation techniques (Pikul et al, 1974) have been proposed, linking Boussinesq's equation for the vertical unsaturated flow, the non-linearity in the equation for the unsaturated flow still raises difficulties.

The transient vertical flow has been solved lately by means of a succession of steady state conditions combined with the continuity principle (Pikul et al, 1974). The boundary condition at the soil surface is described by a flow resulting from evapotranspiration and the water inflow from precipitation. The equation of the model for the saturated zone is:

$$\frac{\partial}{\partial x}\left(T \frac{\partial \phi}{\partial x}\right) + \frac{\partial}{\partial y}\left(T \frac{\partial \phi}{\partial y}\right) = S \frac{\partial \phi}{\partial t}$$

where: ϕ is the hydraulic head; T is the transmissivity of the aquifer; S is the specific yield; t is the time.

A supplementary function W is added to take into consideration recharge or discharges from the unsaturated zone, as well as pumping and the rivers supply. The equation is solved by using a finite element technique.

The following equation results from Darcy's law for the unsaturated zone:

$$z = -\int_0^h \frac{k(h)}{q_c + k(h)} \, dh$$

where: z is the vertical co-ordinate; k is the hydraulic conductivity; h is the pressure head, negative above the ground water surface.

Darcy's equation written for the unsaturated zone gives the amount of air in the root-zone S_r and in the subsoil S_s.

The computation of the evapotranspiration is carried out using Penman's formula adapted for cropped surfaces by Rijtema. These equations are used to solve the model by iteration.

If the ultimate conditions for the saturated zone include pumping, deep drainage canals, or for the unsaturated zone irrigation or surface drainages, then the influence of these human activities on the underground flow balance and its movement can be determined.

An interesting application is made by De Laat et al (1975) for the determination of the consequences of underground water extraction on evapotranspiration and on water movement in the saturated as well as the unsaturated zone.

2.7.1.2.2 Conceptual models. The most frequently used conceptual models are of the "reservoir type". A very complete and overall description of their algorithms and parameters is given in Fleming (1975); most of the models are derived from the main physical scheme drawn up by Ven Te Chow (1964).

The derivation of their parameters consists in general in applying a dynamic programming method to optimize an objection function defined by:

$$F_c = \sum_{i=1}^{n} (Q_i - Q_o)^2 \qquad (3)$$

where: Q_i and Q_o are, respectively, the simulated and recorded hydrograph discharge over the time interval $i = 1, \ldots n$.

In some particular cases the objective function is of a more complicated form while another hydrological element enters its structure (Dawdy et al, 1970). The conceptual models contain two main structures.

In the first one (the so-called "production function") the effective precipitation is determined and in the second one (the so-called "modulation function") the integration of the basin water yield is performed using the unit hydrograph or the isochrones method (Ven Te Chow, 1964).

Further, a method such as that of Muskingum (Ven Te Chow, 1964) or Kalinin (Manoliv, 1972) is applied to route the hydrograph along the river channel.

Derivation of parameters for the production function raises two special problems if for the basin under study there are available data both prior and subsequent to human intervention. But where there is a lack of recorded data, the results obtained in experimental and/or representative basins should be considered.

For example, the use of a HSP model (Hydrocopm Inc, 1969 and 1972) to assess different effects on the flood hydrograph of several alternatives of a reservoir scheme in a basin in Brazil, needed first a model calibration performed in an analogue basin; afterwards the model was applied to simulate the streamflow in the basin studied.

The use of the results obtained in an experimental basin could be applied successfully with "in situ" determination of some of the model parameters which characterise a given process subject to modification due to human activity.

For example, using a Stanford IV model (HSP version) for assessing the effect of the basin deforestation due to fire on the streamflow hydrograph (Fleming, 1971), the K3 and EPXM parameters, which reflect respectively the evapotranspiration of the interception by the forest, have been determined experimentally.

These parameters could be determined experimentally as shown by Leaf and Brink (1972) varying the input data and the parameters of the basin cover in a calibrated model.

Conceptual models are also largely used to assess the influence of urbanization particularly for basins, a significant part of which is not subject to urban works. For the "undisturbed" part of the catchment area a model of the reservoir type is recommended (Tank, Stanford IV, HSP, etc).

Many of the papers contained in the publications (IAHS, 1975, Anon, 1971) concern the impact of urbanization on the river basin hydrological regime.

Specialised models as for example the USDAHL-Model (Holtan and Lopez, 1971) are used in determining (Corps of Engineers, 1960) the changes in the water yield of the basin due to the combined effect of irrigation and natural streamflow. Besides the reservoir production function these types of models contain an additional structure which describes the soil moisture phase of the hydrological cycle.

All the above mentioned examples refer to the assessment of the changes in the hydrological regime of river basins due to human activities on the sloping catchment. These lead to changes in water balance of the sloping catchment and therefore modify the production function parameters.

The modulation function parameters do not change because in general, the integration of the runoff over the basin and the routing in the channel are not modified.

Therefore, if the human activities do not modify the water balance but act upon the runoff integration and/or upon the streamflow routing, a model of which the parameters of the production function are constant while those of the modulation function are modified, should be adopted.

Among the most used models for the modulation functions are the unit hydrograph of the effective precipitation of a given duration, Muskingum models, the isochrone method and the storage function method.

These models could be linear or non-linear according to the nature of the relationships between the storage and the output from the system.

In the Muskingum models the storage output function is linear while in the storage-function method the storage-output function is non-linear but the routing along the channel is performed according to a linear function (Kikkawa et al, 1975).

$$S(t) = I(t) - O(t)$$
$$S(t) = K[O(t)]^p \qquad (4)$$
$$O(t) = O(t + T)$$

where: I, O, S are the input, output and storage respectively; K and T are parameters. The unit hydrographs are frequently applied in urban hydrology for basins for which there are no measurements prior to urbanization but there are data after urbanization.

In such cases, the synthetic unit hydrograph is determined from the morphological characteristics of the basin (Ven Te Chow, 1964, Snyder, 1938, Serban, 1975). Further, flood hydrographs are simulated in natural conditions and are then compared with the hydrographs recorded over the urbanization period.

The Muskingum model and storage-function method are largely used to assess the changes in the river streamflow due to river training works and/or embankment works. These models require either recorded data prior to and after the moment of human impact or that the model parameters can be determined synthetically as functions of the river bed features (Baciu, 1973).

Usually the models which express the modulation function have two parameters, one of them representing the lag-time of the flow through the river channel and the other one the storage process in the river reach. For example, in the Muskingum method, the K parameter is the lag-time of the flow and the x parameter ($0 < x < 0.5$) expresses the flood alleviation process (total < partial < nil) along the river reach. Thus for $x_{max} = 0.5$ there is no alleviation but merely a shifting of the hydrograph with a mean velocity corresponding to the K parameter estimate.

In view of the physical meaning of these parameters, the hydrologist could establish relationships between their values and the morphological characteristics of the channels for which recorded streamflow data are available; such relations could then be used to assess synthetically the model parameters for rivers for which hydrometric measurements are lacking.

In general, the modulation function is considered to be linear. Quite recent researches (Amorocho, 1962, Prasas, 1967) have shown that the linearity hypothesis is not fully acceptable for small basins. In such cases, therefore, it is appropriate to adopt a model, having a non-linear response of the basin given by the equation:

$$K_2 \frac{d^2Q}{dt^2} + K_1 \, mQ^{m-1} \frac{dQ}{dt} + Q = I \tag{5}$$

where: the Q is the runoff, I is the intensity of the effective precipitation and K_1, K_2, m are parameters of the model.

This equation can be solved by dynamic programming. In small catchments, the hydrological response is very rapid; therefore as the basin area decreases, the importance of the intensity of the rain in the peak streamflow formation increases.

That is why, such non-linear models are usually used for the assessment of the changes in maximum runoff of small basins, particularly due to urbanization.

The conceptual models of the "global runoff coefficient type" (SSARR, API models) are seldom applied to determining the changes due to the influence of man on rivers because of the difficulty of predicting the global runoff coefficient under such circumstances.

2.7.1.2.3 The significance of the results and the limits of applying the mathematical models. In applying mathematical models to the assessment of changes in the hydrological regime due to human activity, there are some difficulties concerning the availability of and reliability of hydrological records prior to and after river basin management as well as to information on the manner in which the operation was conducted.

These important aspects have been analysed in detail in Sections 2.1 and 2.2.

Even if these data are available, their accuracy is likely to range between limits of ±20%.

If therefore the changes induced by human activities fall within these limits, the results of applying such models however sophisticated should be treated with caution. Thus the results obtained by several authors concerning the effect of human impact on the hydrological cycle, are sometimes different or even contradictory.

Finally the application of models to assess the changes in the natural regime of rivers can sometimes lead to results which cannot be generalized, because they depend strictly on the type of management scheme, its rules of operation as well as on its complexity which can act upon the hydrological regime in contradictory modes. Hence, the following principles for selective application of the models are:

(a) If records are available prior to and after river basin management, it is necessary to trust those comparative results which can make obvious the significant changes.

In this case, the changes should be:

- considerably more significant than the accuracy limits of the hydrological data, and in this respect a careful analysis on these limits should be undertaken;
- logical point of the runoff formation process under the circumstances of human activites.

With respect to this last requirement it should be noticed that the logics of the results are not always reliable if the process exhibits contradictory sides.

For example, the deforestation of a basin results, on the one side, in a reduction in the maximum runoff due to the absence of interception and to lower soil humidity and on the other side, in an increase of streamflow peaks because of increased velocity of overland flow.

In such cases the analysis of the logical agreement became difficult so that the modelling should be corroborated with the results obtained in experimental and representative basins.

(b) If the recorded data are partially available and the parameters have a precise physical meaning and they are synthetically derived, a sensitivity analysis of the model parameters should be undertaken.

This analysis determines the influence on the final results of the modelling of the errors in evaluating the parameters.

(c) If the data are not or are only partially available and the model calibration is made using an analogue basin, the sensitivity analysis should be corroborated with a careful study of the degree of analogy between the basins.

Often, to ensure a satisfactory analogy a network of representative basins should be proposed.

In this respect, the proposals made by Ogigevski (1970), Diaconu (1965), van der Made (1976), Courewitch (1969 show the importance of the use of "microhydrology" in the improvement of the modelling results.

(d) If the model is of a "routing type" or if it is based on the Saint Venant (kinematic wave) the results can be considered sound provided that the model has been calibrated using measurements in the period prior to the river basin management.

2.7.2 The use of physical models for the estimation of changes in the hydrological regime of river basins due to human activities

2.7.2.1 Methodological aspects. Physical modelling is similar to mathematical modelling. This method is based on hydrology and hydraulics and it has some advantages as compared to field investigations (Grace and Eagleson, 1960, Nemec and Mondry, 1969, Amorocho and Hart, 1963, Cherry, 1966, Yian Zhu et al, 1959, Nemeth, 1965, Ven Te Chow, 1967).

Whereas in nature the runoff factors are merely recorded, they could be created in any combination on a physical model. Such investigations however require similarity criteria, ie the conditions ensuring similarity between the model and the prototype.

On the basis of π theorem and dimensional analysis criteria for storm runoff at constant rainfall intensity could be obtained.

The hydrograph yielded by the prototype could be obtained by multiplying model runoff characteristics q_m (discharge in the model), W_m (runoff volume), $t_{n,M}$ (rise time) by scale coefficients:

$Q_H = q_M \cdot M_Q$

$W_n = W_M \cdot M_M$

$T_n = t_{n,M} \cdot M_t$

where: Q_H, W_n and T_n are the discharge, volume and rise time of the prototype, respectively.

Scale coefficients are derived from formulae. For example $M_Q = M_F \cdot M_a$ where $M_F = F_n/F_M$ and $M_a = a_n/a_M$.

F_r, F_M are the areas of the basin model and basin prototype, and a_n, a_M are similarity parameters.

The use of the physical models for the assessment of the changes in the hydrological regime of river basins due to man's activity is made in two directions.

A first one is referred to those basin models which, on the basis of a rain simulator, provide estimates of the changes due to the changes in conditions of runoff integration over slopes. Such a models does not consider any soil conditions; it assumes an impermeable surface and therefore the effective rainfall is that produced by the rain simulator itself. Such physical models could be successfully applied when determining the influence of urbanization on the storm runoff. In fact, the model is first calibrated for natural conditions and then the urban constructions are built. Then, rainfall of several intensities and durations are consecutively applied and the changes are determined.

A second direction of research is referred to those models which are more "hydraulic" than "hydrological" and they are used to assess, for particular conditions of water flow in channels, the impact of some constructions in these river courses.

For example, in cases where the use of kinematic wave equations (Saint Venant) is difficult due to the water flow not being parallel, then a physical model is more suitable for the assessment of the changes induced by constructions in the hydrological regime of the rivers. Such an example could be referred to the assessment of the changes due to a partial embankment of a river, the effect of which is difficult to estimate because of transverse flow of the water in the flood plain of the river which is not embanked (Hibcu and Duma, 1969, Hibcu and Stanescu, 1967).

2.7.2.2 Accuracy of the physical modelling. In general, it is practically impossible to satisfy all the criteria of similarity. That is why, usually, we resort to consecutive modelling corresponding to several criteria (Nemec and Mondry, 1969).

Also, the experimental studies can answer merely "to what extent the modelling criteria can be violated and yet still give results that are valid to a prescribed accuracy" (Amorocho and Hart, 1963).

The mathematical and physical modelling to assess changes in the hydrological regime of river basins due to human activities represents an invaluable tool of the hydrologist. However, to ensure reliable results, the mathematical and physical modelling should be corroborated by the other methods presented earlier.

REFERENCES

Amorocho, J. 1962. On the Analysis of Watersheds as Non-Linear Systems, *J Geophys Res*, 67, 9, 3531.

Amorocho, J. and Hart, W.E. 1965. The use of Laboratory Catchments in the Study of Hydrologic Systems. *J Hydrology*, 3, 106-123.

Anon 1971. Proceedings of a Seminar on Computer Applications in Hydrology. *The Hydrologic Engineering Center*, Corp of Engineers, US Army, Davis, California.

Baciu, N. Stefan 1973. Aplicarea metodei Muskingum de calcul a prognozei undelor de viitura in cazul riului Somes. *Studii de hidrologie*, Bucuresti, 43.

Befani, A.N. 1959. Teoria protesov rechnovo stoka i obosnovani metodov rascheta elementov vodnovorejima. *Trui vseso znovo ghidrologhiceskovo siezde*, Leningrad, Tom II.

Cherry, D.L. Jr. 1966. A Review of Rainfall-Runoff Physical Models as developed by dimensional analysis and other methods, *Hydrology Symposium*, American Geophysical Union, 47th Annual Meeting, Washington DC.

Corps of Engineers 1960. Routing of floods through river channels manual. *US Army EM* 1110-2-1408.

Crawford, N.H. and Linsley, R.K. 1960. Computation of a synthetic streamflow record on a digital computer, *Bull IAHS*, 51, 526.

Dawdy, D.R. and O'Donnell, T. 1965. Mathematical models of catchment behaviour. *J Hydraulic Division*, Am Soc Civil Engrs 91, HY4, 123-137.

Dawdy, D.R., Lichty, R.W. and Bergman, I.M. 1970. A rainfall-runoff simulation model for estimation of flood peaks on small drainage basin - A progress report. *Open file report, Menlo Park, Calif, US Geological Survey*.

De Laat, P.J.M. and van den Akker, C. and van de Nes, Th.J. 1975. Consequences of Groundwater Extraction on Evapotranspiration and Saturated-Unsaturated Flow. *Application of Mathematical models in Hydrology and Water Resource Systems, IAHS Publication No 115*, Proceedings of the

References

Bratislava Symposium, 67-76.

Diaconu, C. 1965. Aplications des résultats des recherches de microhydrologie aux problèmes de prévision de l'écoulement dans les bassins versants. *Raport élaboré dans le cadre de la convention conclue entre l'Organisation Météorologique Mondiale et l'Institut de Météorologie et Hydrologie de Bucarest,* No 3369/A/CNOS de l'OMM.

Diaconu, C. and Craciun, S. 1971. Results obtained in the study of runoff formation using isotopes. *Studii de Hidrologie,* Bucharest, 30.

Fleming, G. 1971. Simulation of water yield from devegetated basins, *J Irrigation and Drainage Division,* Amer Soc Civ Engrs, 91, IR 2, 249.

Fleming, G. 1975. *Computer Simulation Techniques,* Environmental Sciences Series, 333 pp.

Freeze, R.A. 1971. Three-dimensional, Transient, Saturated-Unsaturated Flow in a Groundwater Basin, *Water Resources Research,* 7(2), 347-366.

Gourevitch, M.I. 1969. The estimation of runoff of large and medium rivers proceeding from the runoff of minor rivers. Floods and their Computation, *Proceedings of the Leningrad Symposium,* 2, 708-714.

Grace, R.A. and Eagleson, P.S. 1966. The Modelling of Overland Flow. *Water Resources Research,* 2, 3, 393-403.

Hibcu, S. and Stanescu, V. 1967. Probleme der Hochwasservorhersage im ausgehauten Teil des rumanischen Donauabschnittes. *Deutsche Gewasserkdl,* N Deilgn, Sonderheft.

Hibcu, S. and Duma, D. 1969. Hydraulic Problems and Works of Hydrotechnical Development within the Danube Delta. Hydrology of Deltas. *IAHS Publication* No 9, *Proceedings of the Bucharest Symposium,* 453-467.

Holtan, H.N. and Lopez, N.C. 1971. USDAHL - 70 Model of Watershed Hydrology, *USDA Tech Bull No 1435,* Agricultural Research Service, Washington DC.

Hydrocomp Inc 1969. *Operations Manual 2nd ed,* Palo Alto, Hydrocomp.

Hydrocomp Inc 1972. Probable Maximum Precipitation Floods in the Paranaiba Watershed, Brazil. *Report prepared for the International Engineering Co,* Palo Alto.

IAHS 1975. The hydrological characteristics of river basins and the effects of these characteristics on better water management, *IAHS Publication No 117, Symposium of Tokyo,* 882 pp.

IAHS/UNESCO 1968. The use of analoge and digital computers in hydrology, *Proceedings of the Tucson Symposium, IAHS Publication Nos 80 and 81,* Tuscon, 755 pp.

IAHS/UNESCO/WMO 1969. Floods and their comparison, *IAHS Publication Nos 84 and 85, Proceedings of the Leningrad Symposium,* 985 pp.

IAHS/UNESCO 1974. Mathematical models in hydrology, *IAHS Publication Nos 100, 101 and 102, Proceedings of the Warsaw Symposium,* 1357 pp.

Kikkawa, H., Taurara, T. and Ishizaki, K. 1975. Change of runoff characteristics due to river improvement, *IAHS Publication No 117, Symposium on the Hydrological Characteristics of River Basins, Tokyo,* 549-550.

Leaf, C.F. and Bink. G.E. 1972. Simulating watershed management practices in Colorado subalpine forest. Amer Soc Civ Engrs, *Proc Annual Environmental Engineering Meeting,* Houston, Texas.

Machmeir, R.E. and Larson, C.L. 1967. A mathematical watershed routing model. *Proc of the*

International Hydrology Symposium, Fort Collins.

Manoliu, M. 1972. Prognoza hidrografului undei de viitura pe Dunare privind de la metoda Kalinin-Miliukov. *Studii de hidrologie,* Bucharest, 17.

Nemec, I. and Mondry, M. 1969. Peak discharge and time of concentration relation to rain intensity investigated by physical models of watersheds. *Floods and the Computation, Proceedings of the Leningrad Symposium,* 1967, 1, 510-517.

Nemeth, E. 1965. Etude sur modèle reduit du ruissellement s'accomplissant dans un bassin versant, *IAHS Publication No 66, Representative and experimental areas,* Proceedings of the Budapest Symposium, 2, 122-130.

Neuman, S.P. 1970. Galerkin approach to saturated-unsaturated flow in porous media. In: *Finite Elements in Fluids,* vol 1, John Wiley and Sons, London, 201-217.

Ogijevsky, A.W. 1970. Indicator basins, *Trudi GMS,* series IV, 26.

Pikul, M.F., Street, R.L. and Remson. I. 1974. A numerical model based on coupled one-dimensional Richards and Boussinesq equations. *Water Resources Research,* 10 (2), 295-302.

Prasad, R. 1967. A non-linear hydrologic system response model. *J Hydraulics Div,* Amer Soc Civ Engrs, 93, no HY 4, 201-221

Roche, M. 1971. Les divers types de modèles déterministes. *La Houille Blanche,* 111-129.

Rockwood, D.M. 1964. Streamflow synthesis and reservoir regulation. *Engineering Studies Project 171, Tech Bull No 22,* US Army Engineer Division, North Pacific Portland, Oregon.

Rubin, I. 1968. Theoretical analysis of two-dimensional, transient flow of water in unsaturated and partly unsaturated soils, *Proc Soil Sci Amer,* 32, 607.

Serban, Petru 1975. Méthode de détermination de l'hydrogramme unitaire synthétique. *Meteorology and Hydrology,* Bucharest, 2.

Snyder, F.F. 1938. Synthetic unitgraphs, Trans Amer Geophys Union, 19, Part 1, 447-458.

Stanescu, Al. V. 1972. Mathematical models for the determination of the critical flood waves - *Studii de Hidrologie,* IMH, Bucharest, 34.

Stanescu, Al. V. and Serban, P. 1974. Mathematical models applied in hydrology and problems of their testing. *Studii de hidrologie,* Bucharest, 42.

Toyokuni, E. 1975. Some considerations on modelling of urban drainage basin on storm water runoff, *IAHS Publ No 117, Proceeding of the Tokyo Symposium on the Hydrological Characteristics of River Basin,* 405-414.

UNESCO 1976. Workshop on the water balance on Europe, Varna, 178 pp.

Vachaud, G. Vauclin, M. and Hoverkamp, R. 1975. Towards a comprehensive simulation of transient water table flow problems. In: *Computer Simulation of Water Resources Systems,* North Holland Publishing Company, Amsterdam, 103-119.

Van der Made, J. 1976. Computation and improvement of the water balance of the Rhine basin. *UNESCO-WMO Workshop on the Water Balance of Europe,* Varna.

Ven Te Chow 1964. *Handbook of Applied Hydrology.* McGraw Hill, Book Comp Inc, New York.

Ven Te Chow 1967. Laboratory study on watershed hydrology. *Hydraulic Eng Series No 14,* Dept of Civil Engineering, University of Illinois.

References

Wooding, R.A. 1965 and 1966. A hydaulic model for the catchment-stream problem, I, II and III. *Journal of Hydrology,* 3,254; 3,268, 4, 21.

Yian Zhu et al 1959. Basic assumptions on unit graph method as checked by hydrological scale model experiments. *Shnili Xuebao,* Pekin, 3, 1959.

Bibliography

Becerril, Enrique 1959. *La regulacion de los rios.* Alfonso El Sabio Award, 1946. Superior Board of Scientific Research, Madrid.

López, R.M. and Fresca, G. 1976. *Estudio de la Distribution de una Variable Aleatoria Aplicable las Aportaciones Anuales de un rio* (Study of the Distribution of an Aleatory Variable applied on the annual contributions of a river). Operative Research and Statistics, College of Madrid University.

Roche, M. 1963. *Hidrologie de Surface,* Gauthier-Villars, Paris.

Yevjevich, Vujica 1972. *Probability and Statistics in Hydrology.* Water Resources Publications, Fort Collins, Colorado.

Part 2 Case studies

Chapter 3.1

3.1   INTRODUCTION
      by H J Colenbrander[1]

In accordance with the terms of reference of the Working Group, the greatest part of the case studies which have been selected deal with methods of computation which have been used effectively to predict or evaluate quantitative changes in the hydrological regime. In particular, effects on the surface water system are discussed.

For the selection of the case studies various criteria have been used, such as:
- the type of human activity;
- the climatic region;
- the size of the research basin.

Besides these aspects others have also been taken into account:
- the type of influence on the hydrological cycle;
- the level of basin development;
- the degree of knowledge within the country concerning the problems under discussion.

Table 2 in the Introduction gives a review of the case studies which are presented.

As discussed in 1.1.4 relatively few case studies were available from arid and tropical areas. Therefore the regional distribution of the case studies is not optimal.

The case studies are in part related to other studies carried out under the same IHP-project 5. The case studies on irrigation, presented in Sub-chapter 3.2, can be considered as an example of the detailed research on this subject which is being carried out by the Working Group on Sub-project 5.4. The case studies in Section 3.3 are related to Sub-projects 5.2 and 5.3. However, not only studies within the same IHP-project are related to the present work, other studies within IHP-projects and projects of other organizations such as FAO and ICID are also closely linked to them.

For example, there is a link between some of the case studies presented in this case book and the technical report prepared by the Working Group on Representative and Experimental Basins (Project 4.1). Research on experimental basins is very important for the study of human influences on the hydrological cycle. In addition, the case studies presented in Sub-Chapter 3.6 on the effect of urbanization and industrialization can be considered as examples of the studies carried out under IHP-Project 7.

Finally, some case studies presented in this chapter deal with man's influence on the groundwater regime and a close relationship exists to IHP-Project 8 where these influences are studied thoroughly.

While considering the effects of man on the hydrological regime, the influence of various natural phenomena on this regime cannot be neglected. Such natural phenomena include land subsidence, land slides, avalanches and earthquakes. Although these phenomena will very often have a great impact on the hydrological regime, according to the terms of reference of the present group these will not be discussed in the selected case studies.

The case studies presented are successively dealing with the effects of:
- irrigation;
- drainage;
- river engineering works (ie lining of channels, construction of weirs, dams and reservoirs);
- changes in land use;
- urbanization and industrialization;
- the complexity of human activities and their integrated consequences.

---

[1] Committee for Hydrological Research TNO, Prinses Beatrixlaan 7, PO Box 297, 2501 BD, The Hague, Netherlands

Chapter 3.2

3.2 THE IMPACT OF IRRIGATION
by O Starosolszky[1]

Irrigation is practised in order to enhance agricultural production, or simply to make it possible at all. It plays an increasingly important role in meeting the growing demand for food and the irrigated area is expanding steadily.

The areal extent of irrigation from 1900 and a prediction of the future trends are shown in Table 1.

Table 1. Irrigated area in the World (million hectares) (USSR 1974)

	1900	1940	1950	1960	1970	1985	2000
Europe	3.5	8	10	15	21	30	45
Asia	30	50	65	135	170	220	300
Africa	2.5	4	5	7	9	12	18
North America	4	9	13	17	25	32	35
South America	0.5	1.5	3	5	7	10	15
Australia and Pacific	0	0.3	0.5	1.0	1.6	2.2	3
Total rounded	40	73	96	180	234	310	420

An estimate by FAO, by regions, of areas suitable for irrigation is given in Figure 1, which also shows a tentative projection of the growth of these areas. In 1975 the total world irrigated area amounted to 223 million hectares, which included 92 million hectares in the developed countries. By 1990, it is estimated that these figures will have risen to 273 million and 119 million hectares respectively.

Cropping intensity is a key element in deciding the value of irrigation and the benefits to be derived from the investment. Where arable land is scarce, the intensity of its use, together with crop yields, represent the major factors determining the physical limits to agricultural production. Under differing conditions of climate and land availability, cropping intensity varies widely. In Table 2, present values range between less than 80% to 135% (with two harvests in some countries). The same table shows the progressive improvements necessary to expand cropped areas and to meet production targets.

This objective, to provide food and crop products for domestic use and for export, calls for more than the construction of major dams, diversions and canales to deliver water to the

---

[1] Vizgazdalkosi Tudemanjos, Kutato Kozport, Vituki, 105 Bp Kuassy Jeno ut 1, Budapest, Hungary

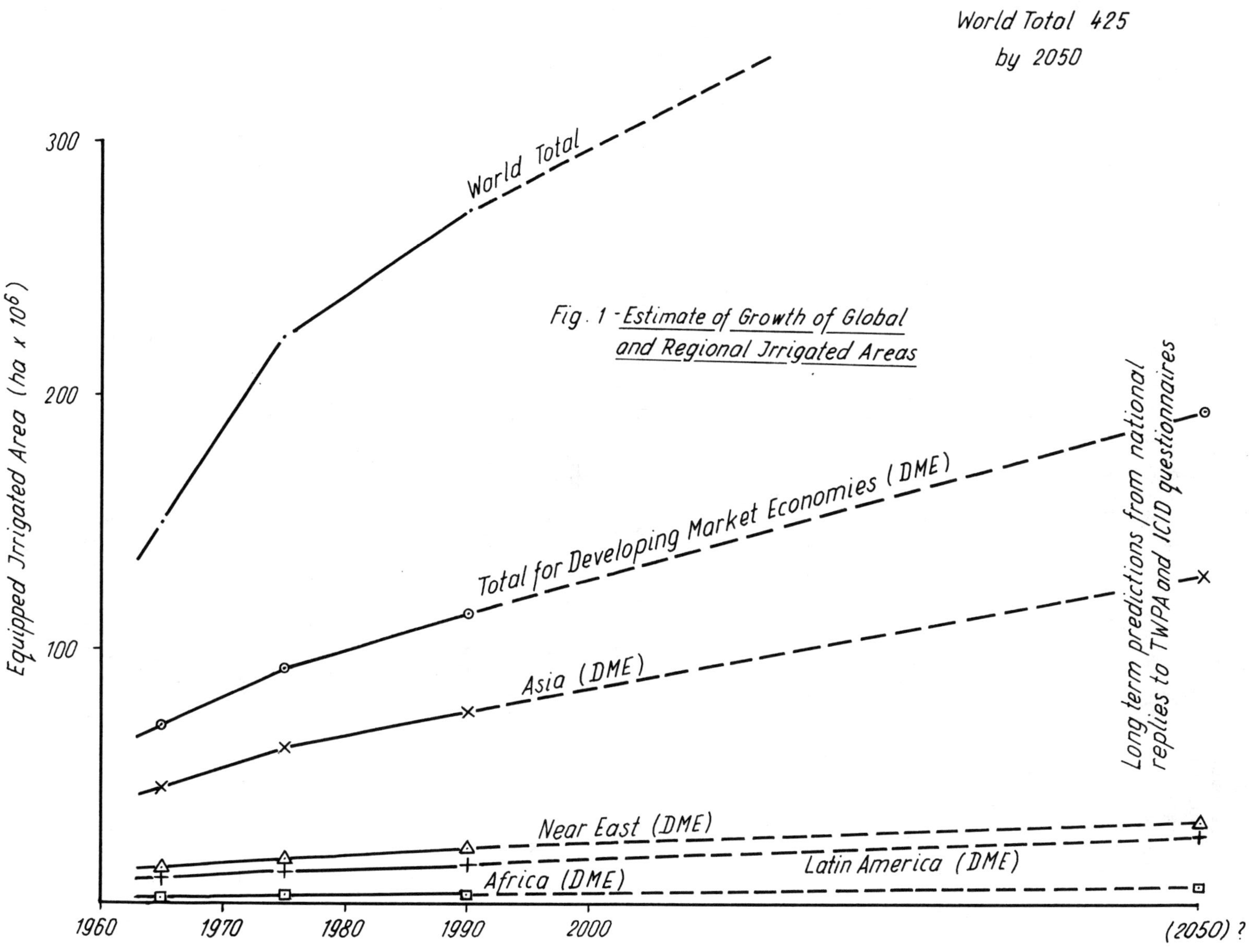

Figure 1 Estimate of growth of global and regional irrigated area

head of the extensive schemes. Such an approach has indeed been followed in many areas and in many regions in the past. It has become associated with failures to plan for the real needs of agriculture and of the farmer; neglect of the services essential to ensure proper operation and maintenance, and operation of training, research and extension facilities without which there can be little hope of any advance in the level of irrigated agriculture.

Table 2 Actual and Projected Irrigated Areas {IA} (1000 hectares) and Cropping Intensities {CI} (% utilization of cultivated area)

Region	1965 IA	1965 CI	1975 IA	1975 CI	1990 IA	1990 CI
Africa	1 882	104	2 610	107	3 570	121
Latin America	9 623	77	11 749	89	14 850	95
Near East	13 329	80	17 105	95	21 400	106
Asia	45 691	119	60 522	129	74 370	142

This is the background against which the World Food Conference established the need for rehabilitation of irrigation as a top priority. It is a situation which, if allowed to contrinue, threatens to cancel out a major part of the efforts and investments to increase crop production, and at the same time, to waste vast quantities of the ever-scarcer water resource.

It would be unrealistic to attempt an accurate evaluation of the total volume of water needed for the expansion of irrigated agriculture. Present day irrigation calls for 1200 to 1300 x $10^9 m^3$ each year, which is utilized at various levels of efficiency. Improvements in irrigation will raise the efficiency of water use, with consequent savings, but measures aimed at increasing inadequate water supplies and extending cropped areas in existing schemes will create added demands, as of course will all new developments. The increase in gross demand for water from all sources, to meet the tentative 1975-1990 programme for irrigation in the developing market economies is estimated at almost 440 x $10^9 m^3$. Thus by 1990 the annual demand will be approaching 1700 cubic kilometres.

This then is the magnitude of the programme to be executed by 1990 in the developing countries:

    22   million hectares of new irrigation
    45   million hectares of improved irrigation
    78   million hectares of drainage
    440   thousand million cubic metres of additional irrigation water
    97   thousand million dollars of investment, at 1975 prices.

The terrestrial cycle of water is greatly modified by irrigation, in that major water volumes are transferred in both space and time to meet the demands of irrigation. The impact of irrigation is especially important in regions where no plant growth would otherwise be possible, such as the arid desert areas, but it is considerable even in temperate climates, where irrigation is of supplementary character. The aim of irrigation is to meet the actual water demand of the plants in an optimal manner and increasingly successful steps are made towards this aim (eg, by drip irrigation).

The principal impacts of irrigation on water resources are as follows:
- Water for irrigation purposes is diverted from surface, or subsurface resources and the natural runoff process is modified. The rate of diversion may approximate the natural low-water flow in minor streams, or may even exceed it in the case of storage. As a consequence some stream sections may run dry in low-water periods, or only the obligatory flow may remain in the bed. Discharge hydrographs are modified accordingly, but even the volume of runoff to the oceans may be changed.
- Water diverted for irrigation is conveyed to the fields in networks of open canals, or closed pipes. Some of this water is lost by evaporation depending on the climatic

characteristics, while another part may be lost by seepage, depending on subsoil conditions. This conveyance loss remains unutilized by the plants, but it changes the micro-climate, as well as the groundwater conditions. The greater part of such conveyance losses is returned directly, or indirectly through the soil to the atmosphere, the part appearing as runoff in natural channels being insignificant. On the other hand, the excess water used for irrigation is mostly returned to the recipients.
- The water conveyed to the fields is distributed by appropriate methods. Depending on the means of distribution, losses may occur in this process, eg evaporation may be an important factor in sprinkler irrigation and some water is evaporated from the foliage of the plants. The water that is most useful to the plant percolates downto the root zone, where it is absorbed by the plant together with the nutrients and returned to the atmosphere by evapotranspiration. In the case of over irrigation, the water entering the soil percolates down to the groundwater and may be lost to the plant. Surface runoff may result from excess water, which is returned by way of drainage canals into the recipients.
- Irrigation, supplying a great amount of surplus water to groundwater over large areas is one of the most important human activities and recharging the groundwater may cause a considerable rise in the water table. The effects can be divided into two main groups. The first includes the infiltration from the new - generally temporary - surface waters, which are parts of the distribution system of the irrigation schemes, while the top-soil overlying the water table remains unsaturated in those areas where the effects pertaining to the second group are acting, only the hydrological balance of this zone is altered by irrigation (surface or sprinkler type).
- Far from the canals and reservoirs, where the top layer of soil remains unsaturated, irrigation also influences the regime of groundwater. Irrigation water is not supplied continuously, but periodically and the aim is to fill to field capacity on each occasion the layer above the water table. The amount of water cannot be, however, regulated very accurately and therefore, over irrigation may occur temporarily and locally. This means that surplus water runs through the unsaturated zone and reaches the groundwater. Since irrigation aims to keep soil moisture near field capacity, there is only a very limited empty storage capacity in the layer to retard the infiltrating part of the summer rains, thus natural recharge will be increased in the growing season.
In contrast to the increase of evapotranspiration, the amount of water used from the gravitational groundwater is, however, decreased because the largest part of evaporation is supplied by irrigation.
- The water balance of the unsaturated zone in winter is also affected by irrigation. The infiltration in this period is higher than the original one as a consequence of the higher soil moisture content at the end of the growing season.
- The accumulation of salt, which is a consequence of irrigation and a high groundwater table, is very dangerous because the productivity of agriculture is lowered considerably by the presence of salts, especially sodium. The high salt content degrades the structure of soils. Other effects of the accumulation of sodium ions are: the higher swelling and wilting point as well as the lower permeability and available water content of soils. These effects, together with the high water table, cause rapid water-logging, the soil becomes saturated and the final result is deterioration of the cultivated crops.
The natural runoff process is thus modified by irrigation in three ways, namely
  - by reducing the natural runoff to a noticeable extent, mainly in the low-water period,
  - by increasing evaporation from canals and the fields in general, and
  - occasionally by raising the groundwater table.
- Irrigation development does not always lead to an increase in evaporation such as in areas which originally had abundant aquatic vegetation (marshlands, deltas).
- Diversion of water from river channels is inevitable in the interests of irrigation, at best, attempts may be made to reduce floods but dry-weather flows are adversely affected. Unnecessary evaporation and the raising of the groundwater table can be minimized by the proper technical equipment and by proper operation of the scheme. The effect of increasing evaporation is mostly favourable, while that of raising the water table is usually adverse.

In order to identify the effects of irrigation, the elements outlined previously must be observed continuously. The observations must be extended to
- the stream discharges,
- the water volumes diverted for irrigation and returned as excess water,
- evaporation

References

- groundwater stages.

Since the water content of the top soil layer is utilised by the plant cover, observations are needed of the soil moisture content and evapotranspiration. Where records of sufficient length are available prior to irrigation or investigations can be made in the planning stage, the impact of irrigation can be demonstrated and even the statistical characteristics of the change can be determined.

Great care must be exercised, however, in the generalization of such results, since differences in climate, soil conditions and agricultural techniques may greatly affect these phenomena. Secondary effects are also conceivable, thus the conductivity of the soil may be changed by irrigation, with subsequent effects on infiltration conditions, or changes in the crop pattern may modify the water demands. Difficulties may also be encountered by comparison with natural conditions. This is because irrigation farming calls for more intensive cultivation (eg, deep ploughing and fertilizers) and this alone is sufficient to change runoff conditions in the area irrigated, especially outside the irrigation season. A higher rainfall-runoff ratio may be expected within the growing season, since the soil is often saturated before major storms. Land improvement in the irrigated areas moderates contour, at the same time filling the depressions which tend to collect runoff.

In modern times, irrigation in flood plains must be accompanied by flood control works and almost invariably by drainage. For this reason in the majority of cases the combined effect of irrigation and drainage must be considered, irrigation being one element of advanced agricultural water management.

The impact of irrigation on the water regime, or on the hydrological cycle may thus be analysed as both a micro- and macro-process, as well as an element of a complex process. In practic the impact is analysed on the scale of irrigated plots, irrigation farms, irrigation sections, catchment arease and in the country as a whole. Whereas on the small scale, information is obtained from observations in experimental catchments, on major areas one of the water balance (or water budget) methods may prove successful.

Irrigation is an important factor in the economic development of tropical, arid and moderate climates alike. For this reason attempts will be made at selecting examples from each of the climatic belts in the following case studies. The examples will include areas of different size.

In planning large irrigation schemes, consideration must be given invariably to the impacts which irrigation will have on the water balance and these impacts must be modified, enhanced, or moderated as dictated by the interests of mankind and the environment.

REFERENCES

ICID 1969. Irrigation and drainage in the World - a global review *International Commission on Irrigation and Drainage* New Delhi

ICID 1976. Irrigation and Salinity - a world-wide survey *International Commission on Irrigation and Drainage* New Delhi

Shiklomanov, I.A. 1976. Impact of economic activities on water resources and hydrological regime (in Russian) *Obzor VNIIGMN-MID* Obnunsk.

USSR National Committee for the International Hydrological Decade, 1978. World water balance and water resources of the earth, *UNESCO Studies and Reports in Hydrology,* No 25.

3.2.1 STUDY OF MAN'S INFLUENCE ON THE HYDROLOGICAL CYCLE IN THE BASIN OF THE RIVER EBRO
by Jose Maria Martin Mendiluce and Jesus Cirugeda Guardiola[1]

3.2.1.1 Introduction

The River Ebro flows across the Iberian Peninsula almost completely within Spain: out of its basin of about 85,000 km^2, only the catchment of the Valira (530 km^2) and that of the Segre (with its tributaries the Eftahiya, Rahus and Carol) (430 km^2), lie outside and are in Andorra and France respectively. The characteristics of the Ebro Basin above the lowest gauging station (Number 27) at Tortosa are given below.

Longitude of station	0°31'30"W
Latitude of station	40°48'50"N
Area of basin above station	84,230 km^2
Altitude of station	8 m
Length of river	910 km
Mean annual discharge	18,747 x m^{3}x10^6 (over 51 years)
Mean runoff	222.6 mm
Mean precipitation	607.9 mm
Runoff coefficient	0.36
Mean evaporation	385.3 mm

3.2.1.2 Method of study

To investigate the effect of man on the hydrological cycle, a study has been made of the availability of water in the basin under the natural regime, its present state and its state at a point in the future. The future state takes into account the reservoirs that have been built and those that are planned; their possible impact on the hydraulic regime of the river is deduced.

The study is based on the 'Hydraulic Resources Inventory' published by the Hydrographic Studies Centre in 1970, where there are to be found historic series of monthly and annual river flows for the natural regime. These data are from official hydrometric stations of the Ministry of Public Works and Urbanism and with them it has been possible to obtain the complete 51 year series for the water years from 1912-13 to 1962-63. These data have been compared and, where necessary, corrected to the natural flow regime in the cases where stations have been affected by upstream developments which may be: regulation, losses, use of water by consumers and the return of water to the river by discharges.

To determine the availability of water, a computer program has been developed for use in the Hydraulic Resources Inventory. This allows updating of the reservoirs for their present and future states and the program allows the effects of regulation to be studied. These studies have followed the method used for the River Tajo and explanations will be avoided here.

---

[1] C/o Spanish National Committee for the IHP, P. Bajo de la Virgen del Puerto 3, Madrid 5, Spain

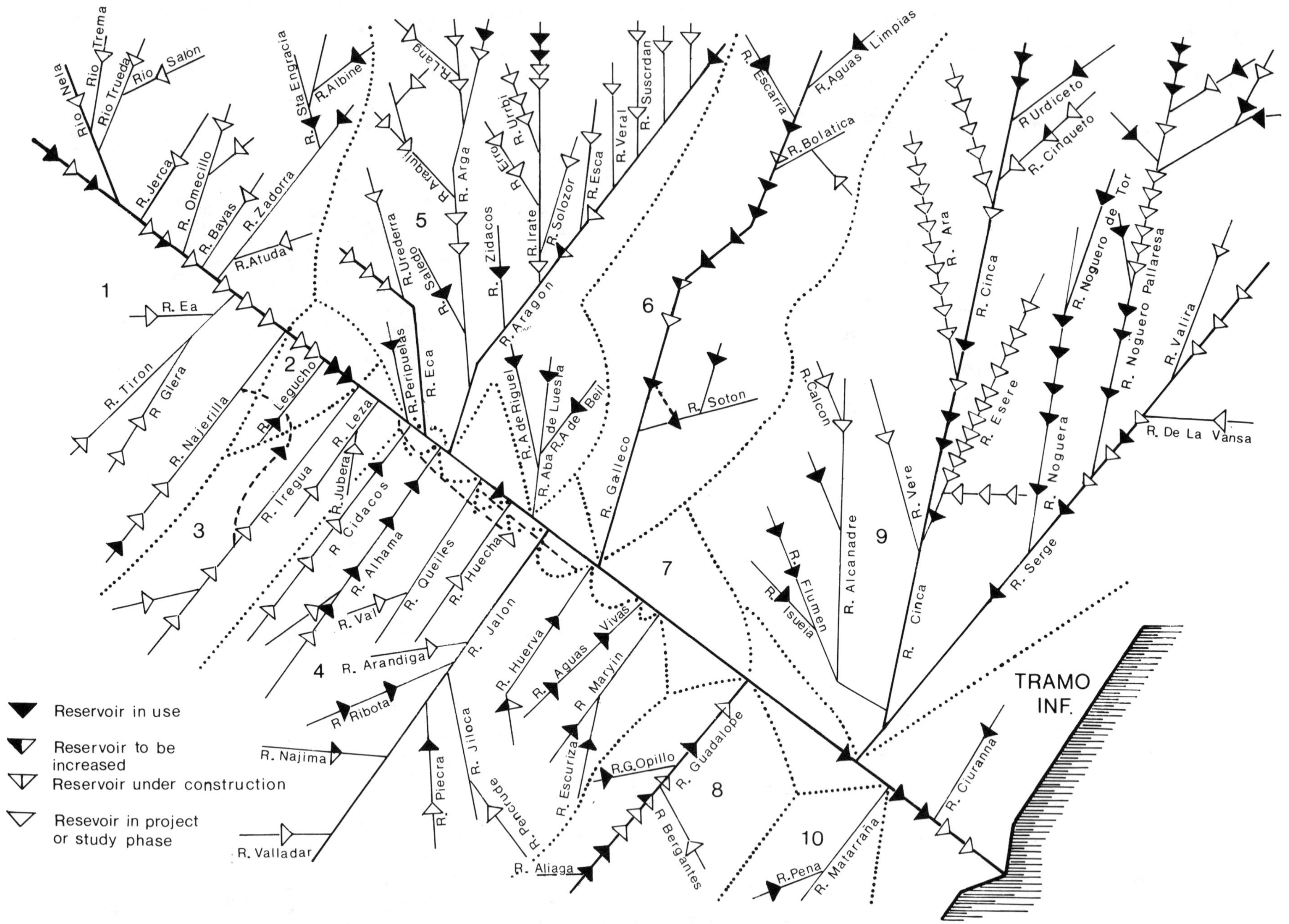

Figure 1 Schematic site plan of section division and location of reservoirs in the Ebro basin

3.2.1.3 Sections of the Ebro chosen for the study

To make the study, the Ebro River has been divided up into the following sections:
1 - From the head of the Ebro River until it meets the River Najerilla, including the latter in this section.
2 - River Ebro between the confluences of the Najerilla and the Iregua, but not including these tributaries.
3 - River Ebro between the confluences of the Iregua and Cidacos not including the latter, but with the Iregua and Lez.
4 - Basins of the rivers on the right bank, between the Cidacos and the Martin, namely the Cidacos, Alhama, Queiles, Huecha, Jalon, Juerva, Aguas Vivas and Martin.
5 - Basins of the rivers on the left bank between the Peripuelas (Linares) and Arba de Luesia, namely both the Ega and Aragon.
6 - The Gallego basin.
7 - River Ebro between the Cidacos and the Guadalupejo, not including the latter and the intermediate tributaries.
8 - The Guadalupejo basin.
9 - The basins of the Segre and Cinca
10 - The Matarrana basin.
11 - The total of the middle and upper section (namely all the above basins)
12 - The lower section, namely the Ebro basin up to its outfall, discounting the middle and upper sections.

The following table shows the basic characteristics of the sections under study:

Table 1. Basic characteristics of the sections under study

Section No.	Basin area(s) km²	Mean annual discharge m³x10⁶	Precipitation m³x10⁶	mm	Runoff coefficient
1	10,030.4	2,999.6	7,948.8	792.5	0.38
2	430.5	115.8	268.9	625.3	0.43
3	2,013.6	367.7	844.9	419.6	0.44
4	17,050.6	1,231.3	7,289.1	427.5	0.17
5	12,547.3	4,110.7	10,293.8	820.4	0.40
6	4,008.8	952.3	2,719.6	678.4	0.35
7	6,104.9	576.7	2,569.6	420.9	0.22
8	3,892.3	285.4	1,698.2	436.3	0.17
9	22,578.7	7,580.9	15,084.8	668.1	0.50
10	1,727.4	206.3	759.7	439.8	0.27
11	80,384.5	18,435.7	49,477.4	589.6	0.37
12	4,616.3	406.3	2,192.7	475.0	0.19
TOTAL	85,000.8	18.842.0	51,670.1	607.9	0.36

3.2.1.4 Application of the method

The above method has been applied to the Ebro basin, to determine the availabilities or regulated volumes in the three situations: 'Natural Regime', 'Actual State' and 'Future State' and this application has been made at variable flows.

The computer outputs are omitted to avoid making this description too length but the results are summarized in Table 2.

3.2.1.5 Analysis of results

Figure 1 shows a reservoir site diagram and Table 2 summarizes the data obtained by computer, applying the method of successive regularizations. In Table 2, the mean contributions of the sections are given, along with the availabilities or regularized volumes in the three states compared. An analysis of these results makes obvious the considerable influence man has on the river's regime.

The total availability of water (regularized volume) at the outfall of the Ebro is 1,392 m³x10⁶/year in the case of 'Natural Regime' and is 11,380 m³x10⁶/year in the 'Actual State' (8.2 times the 'Natural Regime), and 16,001 m³x10⁶/year in the 'Future State' which is 11.5 times the 'Natural Regime'. Section Nos. 3, 8 and 10 have practically no regulating

Table 2 Availabilities in Hm³/year with 96% guarantee and variable flow in the Ebro Basin
(Hm³ = m³ x 10⁶)

SECTIONS	NATURAL REGIME					ACTUAL STATE				FUTURE STATE			
	Area of basin		Capa-city	Regularized volume		Capa-city	Regularized volume		Capa-city	Regularized volume	
	Partial	Total		Partial	Total		Partial	Total		Partial	Total
1. Head Ebro – Conf Najerilla	2999.6	2999.6	0	59.5	59.5	841.3	640.3	640.3	3973.6	3090.6	3090.6
2. Conf Najerilla – Conf Iregua	115.8	3115.4	0	53.7	113.2	14.7	92.0	732.3	33.6	69.8	3160.4
3. Conf Iregua – Conf Cidacos	376.7	3492.1	0	1.2	114.4	32.2	34.9	767.2	697.2	234.6	3395.0
4. Basins from the Cidacos to the Martin	1231.3	4723.4	0	2.6	117.0	142.2	116.5	883.7	420.3	249.9	3644.9
5. Basins from the Linares to the Arba	4110.7	8834.1	0	36.1	153.1	607.8	709.2	1592.9	7333.0	3030.6	6675.5
6. Gallego Basin	952.3	9786.4	0	40.2	193.3	327.6	495.0	2087.9	733.6	676.1	7351.6
7. Ebro between Cidacos and Guadalope	576.7	10363.1	0	215.9	409.2	1.0	220.0	2307.9	1.0	62.0	7413.6
8. Guadalope Basin	285.4	10648.5	0	0.1	409.3	68.9	53.2	2361.1	357.9	218.8	7632.4
9. Basins of the Segre and Cinca	7580.9	18229.4	0	562.2	971.5	2703.1	3667.4	6028.5	7992.3	5360.5	12992.9
10. Basin of the Matarrana	206.3	18435.7	0	0	971.5	18.5	10.9	6039.4	18.5	10.9	13003.8
11. Total, middle and lower section	–	18435.7	0	–	971.5	4757.4	–	6039.4	21561.0	–	13003.9
12. Lower section	406.3	18842.0	0	420.5	1392.0	1778.9	5341.3	11380.7	1820.9	2997.2	16001.0
Total Ebro Basin	–	18842.0	0	–	1392.0	6536.3	–	11380.7	23381.9	–	16001.0

capacity in the 'Natural Regime'; in No. 3, the basins of the Iregua and Leza stand out, as they have moved from 1.2 m^{3}x10^6/year to 34.9 m^{3}x10^6 and in future will reach 234.6 m^{3}x10^6/year (196 times the 'Natural Regime'). As regards the other sections, No. 5 stands out, namely the basins of the rivers Linares, Ega, Aragon and Arba de Luesia, where in the 'Natural Regime' the availability of water is 36.1 m^{3}x10^6/year; the present state is 19.6 times greater and in the future the demand will be 84 times more.

Finally, it should be noted that the availability of the Ebro basin is 11,380.7 m^{3}x10^6/year, representing 60% of the natural resources and in future will reach 85% with 16,001.0 m^{3}x10^6/year.

3.2.1.6 Demands and balances

Demands for both supply to towns and for irrigation can be seen in Table 2, where the partial and total balances are established by basins, based on the availabilities, for variable flow, for the 'Actual State' and the 'Future State'. The surpluses for the lower sections have been calculated allowing an 80% recovery of the demands in supplies and 20% in irrigations.

For the 'Actual State' several sections give a negative balance. In No. 4, all the regulated waters are used and no returns are considered due to the great difference between available water and the demand for irrigation already established. In No. 5, the difference is not so noticeable, the available water is 79.8% of the total demands; the regulated sources are used and returns are available for other sections. In No. 6 the regulated resources are used; civil engineering works on the Cinca River allow water to be used for irrigation. In No. 8, the regulated resources are used and returns are not considered; the works at Calanda are in progress to meet these irrigation demands. In No. 10 all the resources and are used and no returns are considered.

The total balance of the Ebro basin is positive, with 11,380.7 m^{3}x10^6 of water per year available to meet a demand of 445 m^{3}x10^6/year, for supply and 6,536.9 m^{3}x10^6/year for irrigating 674,649 hectares. It has therefore been necessary to build reservoirs with a total capacity of 6,536 m^{3}x10^6.

For the 'Future State', sections 2 and 3 that were previously positive, have a negative balance, but demands are practically covered as the water available is 98% and 80% of the respective demands. The basins of the sections numbered 4 and 10 are in deficit, and a solution is being studied for these.

The total balance of the Ebro basin is positive, bearing in mind the surpluses and the available water totalling 16,001.0 m^{3}x10^6/year to meet a demand of 1,964.0 m^{3}x10^6/year for supplies and 15,361.5 m^{3}x10^6/year for irrigating 1,577,291 hectares. The total storage capacity foreseen to reach this situation is 23,281 m^{3}x10^6.

After studying the above results, one can realise that present and future demands could not be covered without man's influence on the hydrological cycle and management of it.

3.2.1.7 The Ebro - East Pyrenees transfer

The transfer of water from the Ebro river to the basin of the East Pyrenees (both Mediterranean) has been studied; in future 1,400 m^{3}x10^6/year are going to be diverted and this will affect the lower section of the Ebro. This diversion could be made in two stages: the first one for a maximum flow of 840 m^{3}x10^6/year and the second for a flow of 560 m^{3}x10^6/year.

The water situation at present is:
Water available in the lower section .... 5,431 m^{3}x10^6/year
Surpluses and returns from the middle and
upper sections   .... 1,859 m^{3}x10^6/year
TOTAL   .... 7,200 m^{3}x10^6/year

The future situation will be:
Water available in the lower section.......... 2,997 m^{3}x10^6/year
Surpluses and returns from the middle and
upper sections   .... 2,577 m^{3}x10^6/year
TOTAL   .... 5,574 m^{3}x10^6/year

The amount of water in the 'Natural Regime' are 420.5 m^{3}x10^6/year for the lower section and at the moment there is 12.9 times more available, not counting the surpluses and 17.1 times more if these are included. Compared with the future situation, there will be 7.1 times more not counting the surpluses and returns from the middle and upper sections and 13.2 times more if these are included. This clearly shows man's influence on the

Table 3 Partial balances of the Ebro Basin in 'Future State'

SECTIONS	AVAILABILITIES (Hm³/year) Own section	Upstream	Total	Irrigated Area (Hec)	DEMANDS (Hm³/year) Supply	Irrigation	Total	Balance	Surplus for lower sections
1. Head Ebro-Conf Najerilla	2927,7[1]	–	2927,7	35578	290,0	270,5	560,5	+	2653,3
2. Conf Najerilla – Conf Iregua	69,8	2653,3	2723,1	276913	98,0	2684,9	2782,9	–	78,4 + 525
3. Conf Iregua – Conf Cidacos	234,6	78,4[2]	313,0	46314	21,0	370,5	391,5	–	75,2
4. Basins from the Cidacos to the Martín	249,9	–	249,9	92357	96,0	912,8	1008,8	–	0
5. Basins from the Linares to the Arba	3030,6	–	3030,6	292553	274,0	2534,2	2808,2	+	222,4 + 726
6. Gállego basin	676,1	1150,7[3]	1826,8	209012	52,0	2090,1	2142,1	–	396,5
7. Ebro between Cidacos and Guadalope	62,0	1722,7[4]	1784,7	67271	788,0	667,1	1455,1	+	1093,4
8. Guadalope basin	218,8	–	218,8	19569	9,0	195,7	204,7	+	60,4
9. Basins of the Segre and Cinca	5360,5	–	5360,5	343179	284,0	3690,3	3974,3	+	1423,1[5]
10. Matarraña basin	10,9	–	10,9	3350	4,0	33,5	37,5	–	0
11. Total medium and upper section	13003,8			1386096	1916,0	13449,6	15365,6		
12. Lower section	2997,2	2576,9[6]	5574,1	191195	48,0	1911,9	1959,9	+	4035,0
Total Ebro basin	16001,0			1577291	1964,0	15361,5	17325,5		

1 Deducting 162,9 Hm³ of the transfer to Bilbao
2 Coming from supply returns of section no 2
3 Coming 222,4 Hm³ from section no 5 and 928,3 Hm³ from section no 9
4 Coming from sections nos 2, 3, 5 and 6
5 Deducting 928,3 Hm³ transferred to section no 6 (Alto Aragon irrigations)
6 Coming from sections nos 7, 8, 9 and 10

Table 4 Partial balances of the Ebro Basin in 'Actual State'

SECTIONS	AVAILABILITIES (Hm³/year) Own section	AVAILABILITIES (Hm³/year) Upstream	AVAILABILITIES (Hm³/year) Total	Irrigated Area (Hec)	DEMANDS (Hm³/year) Supply	DEMANDS (Hm³/year) Irri-gation	DEMANDS (Hm³/year) Total	Balance	Surplus for lower sections
1. Head Ebro-Conf Najerilla	477,4[1]	–	477,4	13620	53	104,5	157,5	+	383,2
2. Conf Najerilla – Conf Iregua	92,0	383,2	475,2	650	30	5,2	35,2	+	465,0
3. Conf Iregua – Conf Cidacos	34,9	465,0	499,9	39488	9	315,9	324,9	+	245,4
4. Basins from the Cidacos to the Martín	116,5	–	116,5	90236[2]	38	891,6	929,6	–	0
5. Basins from the Linares to the Arba	709,2	–	709,2	91640	54	835,2	889,2	–	174,2[3]
6. Gállego basin	495,0	–	495,0	82579	6	825,8	831,8	–	102,6[3]
7. Ebro between Cidacos and Guadalope	220,0	522,2[4]	742,2	57198	162	566,4	728,4	+	256,7
8. Guadalope basin	53,2	–	53,2	11933	5	119,3	124,3	–	0
9. Basins of the Segre and Cinca	3667,4	–	3667,4	256392	72	2563,9	2635,9	+	1601,8
10. Matarraña basin	10,9	–	10,9	3350	2	33,5	35,5	–	0
11. Total medium and upper section	6039,4			647086	431	6261,3	6692,3		
12. Lower section	5341,3	1858,5[5]	7199,8	27563	14	275,6	289,6	+	6976,5
Total Ebro basin	11380,7			674649	445	6536,9	6981,9		

1 Deducting 162 Hm³ of the transfer to Bilbao
2 Most of the irrigations are eventual
3 All the regularized resources are used
4 Coming from sections nos 3, 4, 5 and 6
5 Coming from sections nos 7, 8, 9 and 10

hydraulic regime of the River Ebro.

The demands in the lower section, affected by the Ebro-East Pyrenees transfer are at present 14 m^{3}x10^6/year for supplies and 275.6 m^{3}x10^6/year for irrigation of 27,563 hectares which represents a total demand of 289.6 m^{3}x10^6/year that is widely covered by the present amount of water which is available, which is 5,200 m^{3}x10^6/year, even discounting the 1,400 m^{3}x10^6/year diverted to the East Pyrenees and 600 m^{3}x10^6/year in respect of the Jucar basin that is today under construction (Ebro-Mijares transfer).

The future demands of the lower section are virtually covered by the 3,574 m^{3}x10^6/year available after deducting the 2,000 m^{3}x10^6/year for the transfers to the East Pyrenees and Jucar.

Finally, it should be noted that the influence of man is to be felt in the evolution of the delta and the reduction in the amount of silt deposited that the construction of reservoirs has caused as well as the soil conservation policy being followed in the basin.

3.2.2 MODIFICATION OF THE CHU RIVER RUNOFF DUE TO IRRIGATION
by S Kharchenko, K Tsytsenko, V. Sumarokova and T. Kann[1]

3.2.2.1 Physiographical characteristic of the Chu River Basin

The Chu river basin occupies the territory in the north of the Tien Shan mountain system. Its drainage area is about 67,500 km^2 including endorheic areas and the adjacent deserts in the lower reaches. Two hydrological areas may be distinguished in the basin, the area of runoff formation and that of runoff dispersion. The mountainous part of the territory is the area of runoff formation; it is about 25% of the total drainage area (approximately 17,000 km^2). This is the most elevated part of the basin with differences in altitudes from 4,800 m to 1,300 - 1,500 m. The glacier area is 597 km^2 and the mean weighted slope of the channel of the Chu river up to its outflow from Boomskoye Gorge is 8.8%. The water balance here is characterized by a predominance of precipitation compared to water losses by evaporation; this explains the relatively high amount of runoff from the territory.

The discharge of the main stream into the Chu valley is 1.61 km^3/year; the tributaries discharging from the mountains contribute 2.98 km^3/year of surface water.

Within the area of runoff dispersion, the slope of the Chu river falls suddenly to 0.85% on average. Irrigation canals, ponds and reservoirs serve as an essential element of the territory. The majority of rivers, discharging into the Chu valley from the adjacent mountains do not reach the main stream since their water is almost completely used for irrigation.

The Chu valley is characterized by the formation of the so-called 'Karasu'[2], ie, groundwater seepage on debris cones and the inflow of returned water from the irrigated fields.

Vast fertile areas available in the Chu valley in combination with favourable climatic conditions cause a large-scale development of farming based on irrigation, mainly using surface waters. The municipal and industrial water supply is based on the use of groundwater.

At present hundreds of wells are bored in the Chu valley; more than 50% of them are used for urban municipal and rural supply; while about 40% of the wells are used for industrial needs. The rest of the wells provide water for irrigation. Intensive surface water withdrawal for irrigation needs and the intake of groundwater for municipal and industrial needs could not help changing the regime, the quantitative and qualitative characteristics of surface and subsurface water resources. A substantial part of the present report comprises an estimation of the changes to surface water quality and quantity as well as a consideration of possible changes of surface waters in the future under the influence of man.

3.2.2.2 History of irrigation development in the Chu river basin

Various literary and archaeological sources testify that the Chu valley has been cultivated since ancient times. The development of agriculture and settlements in the Chu valley date from the 4th century AD. The maximum rise in the prosperity of the economy of the Chu valley,

---

[1] State Hydrological Institute, 2 Linija 23, Leningrad V 53, USSR

[2] 'Karasu' means stream produced by groundwater seepage

however, was observed during the 9th-12th centuries, ie the period of feudal development. At that time irrigation systems were used for production of cereal crops. The Mongolian invasion in 1259 caused the economic decay.

Subsequent alterations before the 19th century left no reliable data on the scales and nature of man's activity. Despite systematic wars and devastations irrigation farming was nevertheless in progress; this is illustrated by the remnants of ancient irrigation systems found by Russian Archaeologists during the second half of the 19th century and at the beginning of the 20th century.

Activity in the Chu valley was stimulated by the reunion of Kirghizia with Russia in 1863. The Hydrotechnical Department was organised in 1898 and this resulted in the irrigation of about 5,000 hectares of arable lands. Further work resulted in the extension of irrigated lands to 50,000 hectares in the Chu valley at the beginning of the 20th century.

In 1910 the Department of Land Reclamation of the Ministry of Agriculture organised a special team to discover areas suitable for irrigation and to supply them with water. It was headed by V.A. Vasiliev, later known as professor and honoured irrigator of the Kirghiz SSR, who initiated the multi-purpose research and development of irrigation practices in the Chu valley.

V.A. Vasiliev envisaged an extension of the irrigated areas by 90,000 hectares on the basis of the water resources of the Chu river without any regulation and by 220,000 hectares with control of streamflow by the projected Ortotokoisk Reservoir. Simultaneously, projects have been developed for a dam at Chumysh rocks on the Chu river, for Atbashinski, Georgievski and some other irrigation canals. Stages for the reconstruction and development of the irrigation systems based on runoff from the mountain rivers (tributaries of the Chu) were proposed. In 1915 about 130,000-150,000 hectares of land were irrigated in the Chu valley, including 20,000 hectares irrigated from the Chu river. The implementation of V.A. Vasiliev's project was realised only after the Great October Socialist Revolution.

By the end of the twenties the Krasnorechenskaya and Samsonovskaya irrigation systems were put into operation and the irrigation network supplied by the tributaries was partially reconstructed. The above arrangements results in irrigation of 186,000 hectares by the beginning of thirties.

During the thirties the rate of construction in reclamation and water management was very high. The Chumysh power plant and the Atbashinski and Georgievski canals were put into operation at that time and the construction of the Tashutkul power plant was completed just before the war of 1941. By 1940 the irrigated areas occupied 195,000 hectares.

During the Great Patriotic War of 1941-1945, irrigation development was slowed down. During the war, the construction of the Great Western Chu Canal was undertaken (in 1943). Water from the canal was diverted from the Krasnaya river and then from the Chu river. The most significant transformation in irrigation farming occurred during the post-war period. The construction of the Great Western Chu Canal was completed. Its length exceeds 200 km. The canal contributes to the water supply of the territory of Kirghizia and to the irrigation of some portions of the Chu valley in the territory of Kazakhstan. At present, the total area irrigated by the Great Western Chu Canal exceeds 80,000 hectares. Simultaneously, the construction of another long canal, the Great Eastern Chu Canal was started; the first stage of the canal was put into operation in 1958.

In 1957 the construction of the Ortokoisk Reservoir, with a capacity of 475,000,000 m^3, was completed. In the middle of the sixties a system for the control of the Alamedin was put into operation: numerous reservoirs were constructed which are supplied by local runoff due to groundwater seepage and runoff during the spring snow melt period.

Much work was done on the modification of the irrigation systems of the Chu tributaries. This provided for the expansion of the irrigated areas in the Chu valley to 280,000 hectares in 1970 and to 400,000 hectares in 1975.

During the seventies a new stage in water management practice of the Chu valley was initiated. A new large irrigation system based on the Great South Chu Canal (155 km long) is under construction. The Tashutkul Reservoir with capacity of 600,000,000 m^3 has been completed to provide the lower reaches of the Chu with water. Much work has been done on the improvement of irrigated lands. During the last 10 or 15 years a network of drains has been constructed with a total length within the left-bank area of the Chu river of 4,700 km.

At present the total irrigated area is 400,000 hectares. 260,000 hectares are irrigated by waters from the Chu river (in 1915 the area was 20,000 hectares), 120,000 hectares are supplied with water from tributaries, and about 20,000 hectares are irrigated by local runoff.

The development of irrigation farming in the Chu valley was accompanied by fundamental changes in the structure of the crop rotation. At the beginning of the present century, the irrigated lands were mainly occupied by cereal crops (67%), grass, vegetables and melon fields. Today cereal crops occupy about 30% of the total irrigated area, sugar beet occupies about 20% of the area and more than 40% of the area is occupied by fodder grass.

The irrigated area occupied by orchards and vineyards has increased 2 or 2.5 times. The major portion of the groundwater abstracted is for municipal water supply.

3.2.2.3 Water resources of the Chu river basin

The surface water resources are the main source of irrigation farming, therefore the present and future development of irrigation in the Chu valley depends greatly on the reliable assessment of surface water resources.

Surface water discharges into the Chu valley from the three main runoff-producing areas, namely the upper reaches of the Chu river, the northern slope of the Kirghiz ridge and the southern slopes of the Chu-Ili mountains. Runoff occurs in drains and collecting channels in the plains due to the excess of irrigation water and precipitation. Surface water resources are therefore divided into primary (stream flow) and secondary resources (runoff in the network of drains, collecting channels and 'karasu'). It should be noted that the latter is not assessed with sufficient accuracy.

Surface runoff from the upper reaches is produced by the inflow to the Chu and Chon-Kemin rivers. The mean long-term discharges of these rivers is 51.1 m^3/s for the period from 1930 to 1975.

The Kirghiz ridge acts as a natural accumulator of moisture in the form of glaciers and snow patches which give rise to several rivers.

The total discharge of left-bank tributaries averages 66.5 m^3/s, including 62.9 m^3/s from gauged rivers and 2.6 m^3/s from ungauged rivers.

There are four right-bank tributaries of the Chu river and the total discharge averages 11.8 m^3/s. The total surface runoff produced in the valley at present is 17.8 m^3/s. Besides the runoff from collecting channels and drains, the runoff produced by seepage of groundwater as karasu and springs may be related to the secondary surface resources with an average discharge of 26.9 m^3/s.

The total volume of water released by industrial enterprises, power plants and by irrigation canals was 29 m^3/s for the 5-year period of 1971-1975. Thus, the natural surface resources of the Chu basin are about 130 m^3/s, the secondary surface water resources are 74 m^3/s at present, and the total volume is 204 m^3/s.

In order to compute the total water resources of the basin, it is necessary to add groundwater resources. The natural groundwater resources of the Chu valley are 71 m^3/s while there is an additional 49 m^3/s which is abstracted for use.

3.2.2.4 Abstractions from the Chu river and its tributaries; groundwater withdrawal

Data on total abstraction from the Chu river and its tributaries are given in Table 1. Since the 1920s abstractions have increased from 60 or 70 m^3/s to 151 m^3/s (in 1971-1975); this is explained by the increase in irrigation. Abstractions from the Chu river have increased almost four times (from 25 m^3/s to 100 m^3/s). Data available show, that during the second half of the 1940s, the natural discharge of the Chu river into the valley (50 m^3/s) was completely used for irrigation. With the re-use of returned water and other sources of groundwater during recent years, the total water withdrawn in the Chu valley exceeded natural water resources of the particular region by 25-30%.

At present, groundwater use is as follows: 7.0 m^3/s are used for water supply, 4.8 m^3/s are used for technical needs and 3.3 m^3/s for irrigation. By 1980 it is planned to use about 30 m^3/s of groundwater in the Chu valley including 12 m^3/s for irrigation.

3.2.2.5 Change in the water exchange between the Chu river and adjacent areas

The development of irrigation introduces fundamental changes in the structure of the water balance and streamflow regime. These changes are displayed by the changes in the regime of exchange between the river channel and adjacent areas (seepage of groundwater into the channel and channel water losses for infiltration), which should be taken into account in the compilation of water balances for water management and in the computation of runoff.

The characteristics of losses and seepages were determined from hydrometric data by computing the hydrometric balance of the Chu using the following equation:

Table 1. Abstractions from the Chu river and its tributaries, in m^3/s.

	1910-15	1926-27	1941-45	1946-50	1951-55	1956-60	1961-65	1966-70	1971-75
Total water abstracted	-	(60-70)	93.7	115	128	143	149	166	151
From the Chu river	(25-30)	(35-40)	46.4	63.5	84	98.3	106	111	100
From tributaries	-	(25-30)	47.3	51.5	44	44.7	44.4	55.1	50.5
Water abstracted for irrigation needs			76.1	85.8	95.7	102	112	130	123

Notes:
1. The water withdrawn for irrigation has been obtained from the difference between total water intake and idle discharges by hydroelectric power plants and industrial enterprises.
2. Data for the period 1941-45 should be considered quite reliable since they were obtained from systematic measurements.

$$\Delta Q = Q_1 - Q_u + Q_{with} - Q_{in} - \Delta Q_{(X-E)}$$

where, Q_1 and Q_u are the discharges at the lower and upper gauging sites of the design reach; Q_{with} indicates water abstracted for irrigation and for industrial and municipal water supply; Q_{in} is total inflow to the river over the surface; $Q_{(X-E)}$ is a resulting characteristic of the effect of precipitation and evporation on the channel and flood-plain.

To discover trends in the exchange between the channel and the adjacent areas, it was necessary to divide the Chu river into several reaches, firstly, according to the principle of runoff genesis, ie in such a way that the boundaries of the reaches coincided with the location of zones of seepage and losses of water, and secondly, taking account of the site of large hydraulic structures causing fundamental changes in runoff. Within the zone of intensive irrigation development, the river was divided into the following reaches.

Reach I is the zone of runoff losses. The reach is 60 km long. The river flows along its alluvial cone, composed of coarse fragments. The groundwater table is deep (25-100 m). Losses are 19-33 m^3/s and have tended to decrease.

Reach II is 67 km long; it is characterized by intensive groundwater seepage. The upper end of the reach corresponds to the point of the break in the longitudinal slope of the Chu river which explains the slowing down of the groundwater flow. A change of composition of the water-bearing rocks is also observed, ie gravel and pebbles occur instead of sand, fine earth and loams. The underground channel is full and groundwater appears at the surface. About 20-30 m^3/s of water appear at the surface and flows out into the Chu channel at the particular reach. The amount of water seepage tends to increase with the irrigation development. During the last five years the discharge of such waters decreased from 30 m^3/s to 20 m^3/s due to the re-use of returned water for irrigation because of the dry period.

Reach III is 149 km long; it differs from the above reaches because of a dense network of collecting channels and drains facilitating groundwater outflow over the surface. In general the reach is characterized by groundwater inflow into the river channel increasing discharge by 15-20 m^3/s on average for the period from 1941 to 1975. Quite evident trends of groundwater seepage increase are observed here with the cultivation of new irrigated areas. The increase of ΔQ from 6 m^3/s in 1941-45 to 24-27 m^3/s in 1951-60 has been observed. At present, groundwater inflow to the channel has become stable and is equal to 13 m^3/s.

Reach IV is 183 km long; it resembles the previous reach III but groundwater seepage is less intensive. The amount of groundwater seepage is 6 m^3/s.

3.2.2.6 Returned water from the irrigated areas of the Chu valley

Irrigation is the most intensive water-using part of the economy in the Chu valley. Its present and future development, however, depends to a great extent on the accuracy of the inventory of water resources. When water resources are determined, it is very important to make a quantitative evaluation of returned water from irrigated areas.

Returned water means irrigation runoff of surface and groundwater after their discharge into the receiving channel. It is suitable for re-use for economic purposes.

The water balance method is used for the quantitative evaluation of the returned water volume; the method is based on a combined solution of water balance equations of the study basins during the period of irrigation and during the period before irrigation.

The design equation (Kha chenko, 1975) is:

$$B_r = (X-X^*) + (Y_{si} - Y_{si}^*) + (Y_{gi} - Y_{gi}^*) - (Y_s - Y_s^*) - (E - E^*) + (\Delta U - \Delta U^*) + Q$$

where:

B_r = total amount of returned water from the irrigated fields;

X = precipitation;

Y_{si}, Y_{gi} = surface and groundwater inflow;

Y_s = outflow of surface water;

E = evapotranspiration;

ΔU = change of groundwater storage;

Q = water withdrawal for irrigation.

An asterisk indicates the same water balance components during the period before irrigation development.

Because of historically stable climatic and geological conditions, significant changes ie $Y_{si} - Y_{si}^*$ and $Y_{gi} - Y_{gi}^* = 0$, have not been observed in the values of surface and groundwater flow.

Groundwater storage, ie $\Delta U^* = 0$, did not suffer great changes during the pre-irrigation period. It is also possible to assume that surface outflow from the reaches of the Chu river has not been changed and $Y_s - Y_s^* = 0$.

The difference, $E - E^*$ corresponds to the value of water losses by evaporation from irrigated areas (ΔE) where E^* is evaporation from wild plants.

The difference in the level of the groundwater table over a vast area is assumed numerically equal to the precipitation change over the same period. The change in precipitation, $X - X^*$ is assumed to be 10% of the B_t value during the present period on the basis of recommendations made by Soviet climatologists.

As a result, the calculation of the returned water of the Chu valley was made from the following equation:

$$B_r = 0.1X + Q - \Delta E - \Delta U.$$

This equation provides a quantitative determination of returned water draining from irrigated fields. During flow to the Chu river, some of the returning water evaporates.

Estimation of the amount of returned water in the Chu valley discharging into the receiving channel (B_r^*) has been made from the following equation:

$$B_r' = 0.1X + Q' - \Delta E' - \Delta U$$

The amount of precipitation was computed from data from stations situated within the study area. Groundwater storage changes were evaluated from the equation:

$$\Delta U = \mu \cdot \Delta H$$

where, μ = water yield coefficient,

ΔH = change in position of mean annual groundwater table.

The calculation of ΔU are altered according to the different hydrogeological zones.

Evapotranspiration from irrigated fields was computed by the energy and water balance (Kharchenko, 1975).Evaporation was computed for the agricultural crops predominant in the Chu valley. The calculated evaporation was interpolated over the area taking account of the structure of the farm lands and the depth of the groundwater table as it affected the conditions of vertical moisture exchange in the aeration zone and in the aquifer.

The value of B_r' consists of two components, ie groundwater (B_g) reaching the river channel by the subsurface route and surface water (B_s) in the form of surface discharges of excess irrigation water and inflow into the network of receiving channels and drains. B_s is evaluated by means of separating the hydrographs of the receiving channels. Thus, B_g was computed from the difference between B_r' and B_s.

On average, during the period 1941-75, the actual irrigated area in the Chu valley exceeded 400,000 hectares, and the water intake for irrigation needs for the same period was 103 m^3/s or 729 mm. Irretrievable water losses were assessed at 500 mm. In the case of mean annual precipiation, X = 347 mm, B_r was 451 mm or about 45% of the total water intake. B_r' was assessed as 37 m^3/s or 34% of the water intake. Thus, water losses by evaporation from the transit zone and from areas not irrigated made up 190 mm or 44% of the initial returned water volume. Out of the total amount of returned water discharges in the Chu river (B_r') the groundwater component makes up 31 m^3/s (86% from the total value of B_r'), 5.2 m^3/s or 14% of the water reaching the receiving channel over the surface. During the initial period, returned water made up 18% of the total amount of water intake; in 1971-75, that amount increased to 32-43%.

In the upper part of the Chu valley B_r' on average equals 42% of the total water intake. Since the network of collecting channels and drains is not very dense, the returned water reaches the river channel almost completely in the form of groundwater outflow and only 6-10% discharges into the Chu river as surface flow.

In the central part of the Chu valley, the amount of returned water averaged 36% of the total water intake over 35 years. In 1960-65, the period of the intensive development of the network of receiving channels and drains, the increase of the surface component of the returned water was from 1-2 m^3/s to 5-6 m^3/s.

In the reaches of the Chu river the returned water makes up 30% of the total water intake and this portion reaches the Chu river almost completely in the form of subsurface flow.

Comparison of the groundwater component of returned water with the values of groundwater seepage into the Chur river, determined from the channel water balance, showed that groundwater seepage downstream from the Chumysh Dam is almost completely caused by man, ie water returned after irrigation. In the upper valley (upstream of the Chumysh gauging station) 60-70% of groundwater seepage is caused by natural factors.

A considerable portion of returned water in the Chu valley (35%) is caused by hydrogeological and soil conditions, ie highly permeable rocks and a high infiltration rate.

3.2.2.7 Evaluation of up-to-date changes in the Chu river runoff

It has been mentioned that irrigation farming is an important user of the water resources. The arid zone and the zone of water deficit are usually supplied with much more energy resources than with precipitation, which is the only source of water in these zones. Irrigation causes the increase of evaporation and is an irretrievable water loss which results in a considerable change in water resources amounts. On the other hand, irrigation of agricultural fields is almost always accompanied by an increase of infiltration of irrigation water into the soil and by additional recharge of groundwater. The latter stimulates groundwater outflow and the formation of the so-called returned water. Thus, irretrievable water losses and returned water are the principal factors; their values and interrelations determine the changes in water balance and river runoff in the basins with highly developed irrigation. It is very important to note that the different hydraulic structures (dams, reservoirs, canals, networks of collecting channels and drains) affecting river runoff also provide the development and operation of irrigated systems.

According to up-to-date opinion, there are two types of irrigation influence on river runoff: (1) direct water withdrawal out of the river, with its subsequent use for irrigation and other economic needs; (2) runoff losses in the process of irrigation, due to additional evaporation of irrigation water and its accumulation in the unsaturated zone.

The first type of water loss is determined quite easily, ie runoff losses equal water intake; the second type of water loss is determined by different methods.

In essence to determine the effect of irrigation farming on river runoff consists of the solution of the two following problems:

(1) the development of methods for up-to-date assessment of changes of runoff;
(2) the development of methods for the computation of runoff changes in the future.

Evaluation of up-to-date runoff changes may be made by two main methods:

(1) The comparative analysis of long-term runoff series.
(2) The computation and analysis of the water balance of a drainage basin.

The application of the above methods depends on the avilability of data such as the physiographic peculiarities of the basin, types of activity and the rate of development. For example, the first method is based on sufficiently reliable hydrometric data, but it does not take into account the main factors, producing changes of the water balance and river runoff (water intakes, water losses, returned water, etc). In turn the advantage of the balance method is in the possibility of independent determination of returned water and irretrievable losses, and its use for the prediction of runoff changes in the future. The use of the water balance method, however, is restricted in some cases because of inadequate data. It follows that the most reliable results for the evaluation of the effect of irrigation on runoff should be expected by the simultaneous application of both methods.

The method of comparative analysis of runoff series is widely applied at present for the quantitative evaluation of the effect of irrigation on runoff and on the river regime. It is based on the comparison of runoff values (annual or seasonal runoff) for synchronous periods at base hydrometric stations in the zone of runoff use.

Runoff changes are usually computed for the period with the natural or nearly natural hydrological regime. The term 'nearly natural regime' is introduced for river basins where irrigation has been developed for a long period and river runoff was distored long before systematic hydrometric measurements were organized. Data on water levels in reservoirs stable for a long time serve as an indicate of the relative constancy of the hydrological river regime.

The runoff changes determined from hydrometric data contain not only the effects of irrigation but also the effects of the change in the hydraulic character of the zone of runoff formation. In order to separate the evaluation of hydraulic effects from the effect of irrigation farming, the relationship $Y_u = f(\Sigma Y_f)$ should be plotted, where Y_u is the runoff at the gauging site situated in the zone of runoff use; ΣY_f is the runoff in the zone of runoff formation.

Runoff changes in the zone of runoff formation are automatically taken into account by the position of ΣY_f values on the axis. The effects of man's activity and the hydraulic effects on runoff are computed from the difference between the total decrease obtained from the hydrometric series and the decrease determined from the graphs:

$$Y_u = f(\Sigma Y_f)$$

The evaluation of runoff changes by the water balance method is made on the basis of a combined solution of the equations of the water balance of the channel reach in the zone of runoff use and the water balance of the irrigated areas adjacent to the study reach.

The design equation of the water balance is as follows:

$$Y_u - Y_l + Y_{uc} - Y_{lc} + Y_{tr} - Y_w + Y_{in} - Y_{out} + B_r + X - E - \Delta W + \Delta q \pm \Delta = 0$$

where:
Y_u, Y_l = channel (surface) flow at the upper and lower gauging sites;
Y_{uc}, Y_{lc} = runoff of sub-channel water at the upper and lower gauging sites;
Y_{tr} = runoff from tributaries;
Y_w = withdrawal of water from the river within the reach;
Y_{in} = inflow (seepage) of natural groundwater;
Y_{out} = outflow (or filtration losses) from the channel by subsurface routes;
B_r = water returned from the irrigated fields;
X = precipitation on the surface of rivers;

E = evaporation from water surface, from semi-submerged weeds and inundated areas in the flood plain;
ΔW = regulation and accumulation of the channel water in the flood plain;
Δq = exchange between groundwater and deep aquifers;
Δ = the water balance discrepancy;

The value of B_r is computed from the water balance equation for the irrigated area adjacent to the study reach of the channel. On the basis of computations of the above equations irretrievable water losses and returned water are determined. The two factors in combination with data on water abstracted from the river, data on sub-channel runoff, seepage and losses of channel water provide the evaluation of their effect on the change of river runoff at the study site (Y_1).

The study of the history of irrigation in the Chu valley shows that the runoff of the main stream was to a certain extent distorted by man's activity long ago. During the last 60 years, fundamental changes of runoff are observed. Runoff in the reach of the Chu river from Buruldai to Miliafan has reduced considerably for the period while from Miliafan to Tashutkul an increase is observed, but the changes discovered are of a qualitative nature.

In order to determine quantitative runoff changes under the influence of irrigation it is essential first of all to evaluate the nature of runoff variations in the zone of runoff formation and the climatic factors causing those variations.

Results of research show that during the last 50 or 60 years no consistent changes of air temperature and precipitation have been observed in the mountains, and consequently, no changes in the volume of the Juanaryk and Kochkor rivers (the confluence of those rivers form the Chu river), as well as of water courses flowing down the northern slope of the Kirghiz ridge and southern slope of the Chu-Ili mountains. This fact made it possible to perform a combined analysis of runoff changes under natural conditions and of runoff data for sites where the effect of man may not be neglected.

Three sites have been selected on the Chur river; they are: Miliafan, Tashutkul and Furmanovka; they gauge three large areas of irrigation in the eastern, central and western parts of the valley respectively.

For the analysis of the Chu runoff at the three gauging sites, the following methods were applied: plotting of combined integral curves of annual values of runoff in the zone of runoff formation and at sites with a distorted hydrological regime; plotting of the correlations between culturally changed discharges and natural discharges from the mountains; comparison (in tabular form) of averaged values of annual and seasonal runoff in the zone of runoff formation with similar characteristics at sites where river runoff is intensively used for irrigation needs.

The results of the quantitative evaluation of the Chu runoff changes can be summarised as follows. The most considerable changes occur at Miliafan where annual runoff decreases for the period 1962-75 were 65% compared with the Chu runoff during 1930-42. Similar decreases are observed for seasonal values.

Annual runoff of the Chu at the other sites has suffered practically no change; at Tashutkul the runoff decease does not go beyond the limits of measurement accuracy and runoff computation, while at Furmanovka no changes have also been observed.

Despite relatively stable annual values of discharges at the above two sites, a fundamental transformation of stream flow distribution has occurred during the year caused by the effects of man. These changes consist in the reduction of runoff during the growing season (by 20-25%) and an increase in the volume of water in the river during the autumn-winter period by 6-20%.

It should be noted that the above changes occurred against a background of stable runoff amounts for the growing and non-growing seasons of the year in the zone of runoff formation. The decrease of flow in summer occurs due to an increase of water withdrawal for irrigation while its increase in winter is explained by the greater discharge of water into the Chu from the network of collecting channels and drains, or by subsurface outflow. In particular, an increase of inflow from the Aksu river is observed; at present it is 2 or 2.5 times the volume of runoff in 1930.

Considerable changes occurred in the mechanism of exchange between surface and groundwaters. For example, in the reach from Chumysh to Tashutkul where runoff losses were previously observed, groundwater seepage takes place which is caused by the water returned from irrigated fields. The change of discharge to the Chu inevitably caused a quality change in namely increased minearlization. Thus, the apparent constancy of the Chu conceals important processes which, to a certain extent, compensate for the water withdrawn for irrigation.

In 1910-15, the flood plain of the Chu river from Chumysh to Tashutkul was occupied by 30,000 hectares of thick reed-beds. At present, reclamation and runoff control has resulted in a complete elimination of water-weeds in the Chu valley.

Data show that the compensating ability of the Chu valley at the beginning of the seventies should have been exhausted. If natural water losses were 25-30% during the period 1942-45 (the other 70-75% contributed to irrigation), total irretrievable losses in 1971-75 were completely determined by runoff losses for the different economic needs. Therefore, the start of the operation of the Tashutkul reservoir disturbed the existing equilibrium causing a great decease in the Chu runoff after 1973.

It should be noted that the redistribution of the Chu runoff to the lower reaches of the Chu valley by the Eastern and Western Great Chu Canals played an important role in the process of runoff reduction. This caused about 80% of the total runoff reduction while the remaining 20% was cuased by the increase of water losses from the irrigated fields occupying the western part of the Chu valley.

3.2.2.8 Evaluation of future runoff changes

According to Kharchenko (1975) and Kharchenko and Tsytsenko (1976), runoff at the outlet of a river for $\Delta q. = 0$ may be determined from equation:

$$Y_l = Y_u + Y_{ue} - Y_{lc} + Y_{tz} - Y_w + Y_{in} - Y_{out} + B_r + X - E + \Delta W \pm \Delta$$

The above equation may be presented in a simpler way:

$$Y_l = D + a$$

where

$$D = Y_u + Y_{tr} - Y_u + B_t + X - E + \Delta W; \qquad a = Y_{uc} - Y_{lc} + Y_{in} - Y_{out}$$

Parameter 'a' is an integral characteristic of the interrelations between the channel and groundwaters. In the case of the required data being available, 'a' is determined, for example, from hydrodynamic equations (finite difference). In the case of inadequate data on the hydrogeology, parameter 'a' is approximately computed from the graph.

To evaluate the future changes of the Chu runoff from the above equation, the parameter 'a' was accepted from the data for the previous period. Returned water was computed from the increase of water losses associated with irrigation development. Abstractions of water were computed according to the planned expansion of the irrigation areas.

In addition to the water losses from irrigated fields, water losses from the surface of reservoirs were computed (ΔE_{res}) as well as the diversion of some portion of runoff along the canals to other areas of the Chu valley (T).

Evaluation of runoff changes by the above method was made relative to the mean amount of water in the river; therefore mean long-term runoff values for the zone of runoff formation (ΣY_f) were used for the computation.

The maximum reduction in runoff is assumed to occur at Furmanovka in the lower reaches where it is 78% relative to the present amount of water in the Chu river at that site. In absolute values, runoff reduction in the future will be 3-4 m^3/s in the middle reaches, 28 m^3/s at Tashutkul and 48 m^3/s at Furmanovka.

Reduction in runoff by diversions to other areas plays an important role in determining the future total runoff losses; at Miliafan the portion of the diverted water will be about 70%.

In future, the runoff in the Chu will be to a certain extent supplied by returned waters. It should be noted that the computed decrease of runoff reduction in the Chu river is based on the most rational water resources development, ie, the introduction of a scientifically planned irrigation regime and the increase of the level of water management.

It is possible to expect that in connection with the development of irrigation, municipal water supply and other types of water resources development, runoff in the Chu river and groundwater discharge will decrease more rapidly than at the present time.

References

REFERENCES

Kharchenko, S.I. 1975. *Hydrologia oroshaemykh zemel* (Hydrology of irrigated areas). Gidrometeoiżdat, Leningrad, 373 pp.

Kharchenko, S.I., and Tsytsenko, K.V. 1976. Otsenka vliania irrigatsyonnykh meropriatiy na rechnoi stok (na primere r. Chu) (Evaluation of irrigation effects on river runoff (illustrated by the Chu river)). *Trans. GGI.*, Gidrometeoizdat, Leningrad, 230, 6-24.

3.2.3 THE GREATER MUSSAYEB PROJECT IN THE CENTRAL MESOPOTAMIAN PLAIN
by Faruk Y El Yussif[1]

3.2.3.1 Introduction

The Greater Mussayeb Project is located in the centre of the Mesopotamian Plain (Figure 1). The main canal with an operational capacity of 40 m^3/sec takes off from the Euphrates river 9 km upstream of an existing barrage (Figure 2). The main canal is 49.5 kms long and irrigates a gross area of 84,000 hectares. The project was started in 1953 and completed in 1956. In keeping with the practices in 1957, the first settlers were moved to the agricultural lands, and by 1960 about 1775 farm units which formed about 30% of the total were occupied. The pace of agricultural development was however slow. By 1969 the main canal was run to its operational capacity of 40 m^3/sec. The population in the area in the meantime rose from 1000 in 1952 to nearly 25,000 in 1969.

The soils in the region had a high salinity and therefore the cropping pattern needed to be adjusted accordingly. To facilitate this a semi-detailed soil survey and some hydrological investigations were completed in 1974. Efficient maintenance of the drainage network already constructed, and adequate leaching of the soils yielded satisfactory results. The main canal however showed a tendancy to draw a high charge of sediment which eventually has started depositing in the bed of the canal. Comparison of the actual cross sections with those of the designed sections indicate raising of the bed by nearly 1 m. Measures to reduce the entry of silt into the canal have therefore been considered essential.

3.2.3.2 Description of the project

3.2.3.2.1 Location. The project is located in the central Mesopotamina Plain about 90 km south of Baghdad city and 20 km north of Babylon between latitudes 32°32' - 32°52' north and longitudes 44°30'-44°55'. The canal takes off from the left bank of the Euphrates, about 9 km upstream of the existing Hindiyah Barrage.

3.2.3.2.2 Elevation. The project area lies between contours 24 and 31 m above mean sea level. The average slope of the land is 0.1 m per km.

3.2.3.2.3 Geology. The formations outcropping in the area are predominantly limestones. Additional sulphates in the form of gypsum or gypsiferous marls were deposited around the beginning of the Alpine orogeny. The presence of these minerals has resulted in a high concentration of calcium sulphate ions in the valley sediments which consist predominantly of fine grains of silt and clay.

3.2.3.2.4 Geomorphology. The project area is characterised by sand dunes, mobile masses of sand consisting of salt cemented by clay and silt pellets. A characteristic feature is the presence of ancient relics of early human settlements.

3.2.3.2.5 Irrigation and drainage network. The irrigation network consists of a main canal

---

[1] Ministry of Irrigation, Baghdad, Iraq

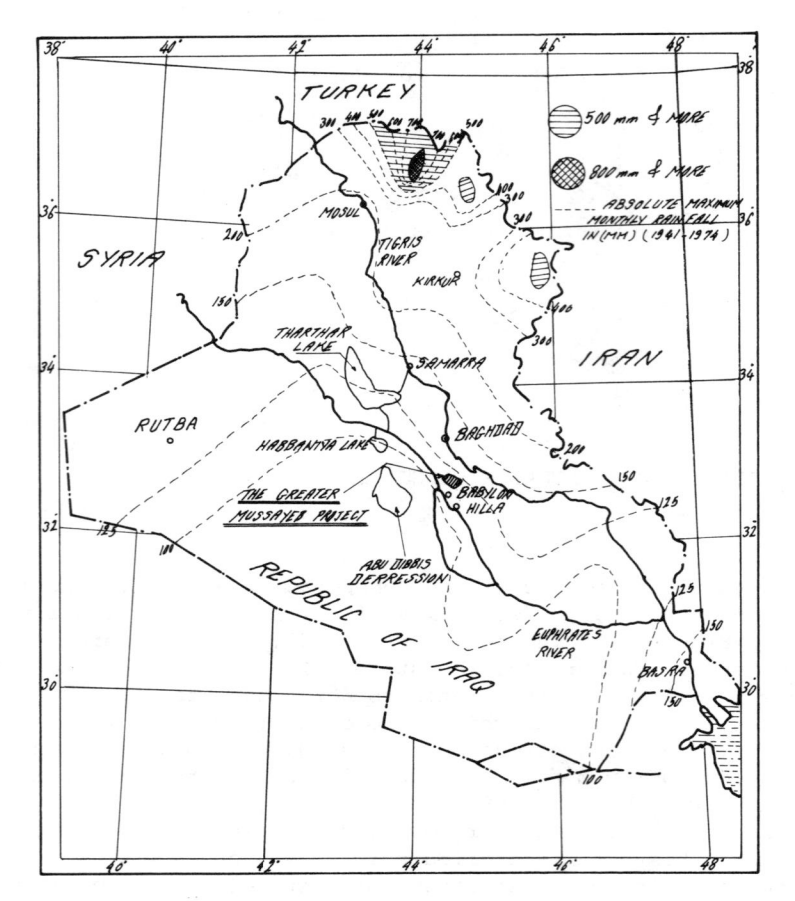

Figure 1   General location map

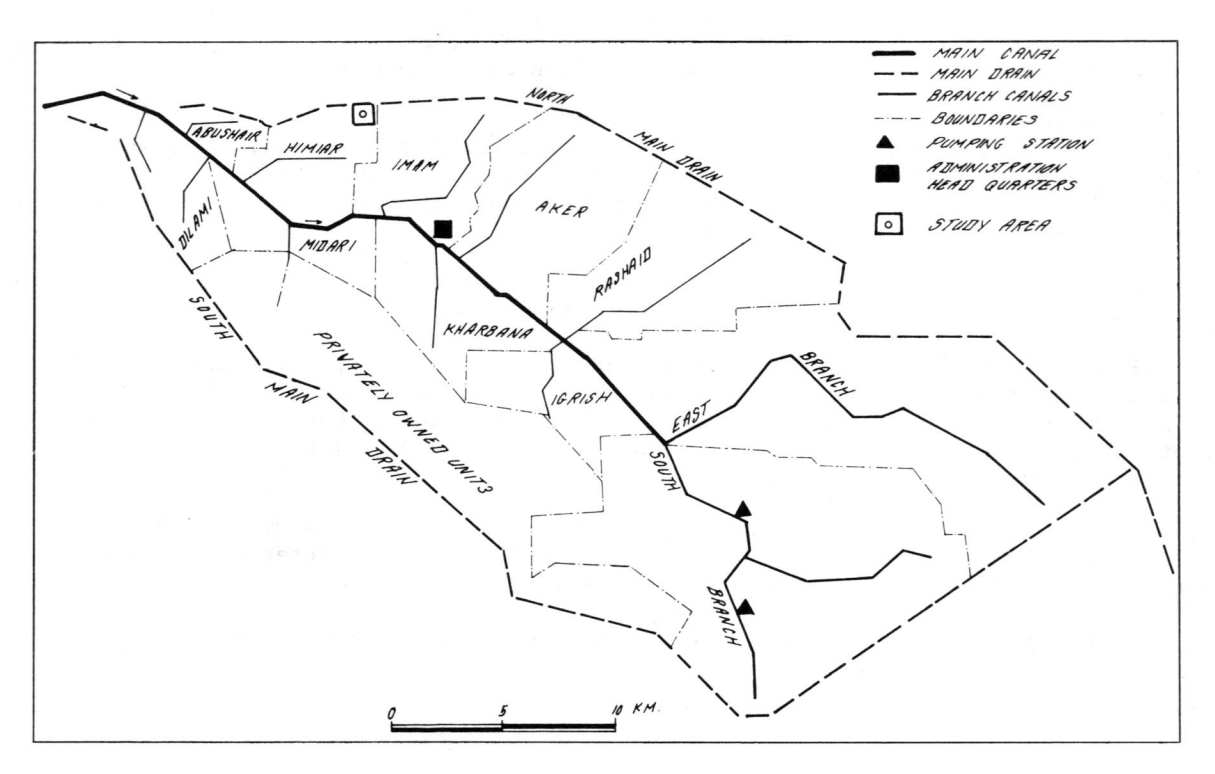

Figure 2   Irrigation and drainage network

49.5 km long, 13 branch canals and 7 parallels, in addition to a large number of laterals. The total length of the canal system is 710 km.

The head regulator of the main canal is a reinforced concrete structure of 4 openings each 5 m wide fitted with 4 radial gates 2.9 m high. The maximum design discharge is 60 m^3/sec and the operational discharge is 40 m^3/sec.

The drainage network consists of 170 km of main drains, 120 km of branch drains, 970 km of collector drains and 1050 km of field drains, the total length of the drainage network is thus about 1710 km.

3.2.3.2.6 Climate. The climate of the project area is one of hot and dry summers and cool winters. A meteorological station was established in the project area in 1972, and the data collected so far is presented in the following tables:

Table 1   Annual rainfall (in mm)

Year	mm
1972	81.8
1973	64.7
1974	209.7
1975	225.0
1976	146.5
1977	125.9

Table 2   Mean monthly rainfall (in mm)

1972-1977

Jan	Feb	Mar	Apr	May	June	July	Aug	Sept	Oct	Nov	Dec
36.0	23.2	33.5	11.7	-	-	-	-	-	1.0	5.0	23.0

The above data would show that the average rainfall is 142.26 mm, with a highest recorded rainfall of 36 mm in January. No rain occurs in summer months. The highest mean monthly maximum temperature is 42.55°C in August, while the corresponding minimum is 3.3°C in January. The highest mean monthly relative humidity occurs in December, this being 67% the lowest being 19.5% in July.

3.2.3.2.7 Hydrology. As stated earlier the canal takes off from the river Euphrates. The river has a catchment area of 274,100 sq kms at the project site. Systematic hydrological data are available at the Hit and Ramadi discharge sites which are upstream and at Hindiyah Barrage downstream.

Some data on the discharge of the main canal since 1958 is presented in Table 3.

It would be seen from the table that the canal has been run throughout at a very low capacity for most of the months. This has perhaps been the main cause of siltation.

The Greater Mussayeb Project

Table 3 Discharges in the Mussayeb canals

	Average Discharge in 1958	Capacity factor	Average Discharge in 1978	Capacity factor
January	12.36	0.20	28.08	0.46
February	11.91	0.19	29.22	0.49
March	9.01	0.15	29.28	0.49
April	30.14	0.50	25.39	0.42
May	35.66	0.59	34.77	0.58
June	30.20	0.50	35.48	0.59
July	31.91	0.53	42.05	0.70
August	15.71	0.26	40.83	0.68
September	22.02	0.36	42.43	0.70
October	27.54	0.46	-	-
November	-	-	-	-
December	-	-	-	-

Max Discharge 60 m^3/sec

3.2.3.3 Actual performance of the project

3.2.3.3.1 *Project objective.* The project was designed for irrigating a gross area of 84,000 hectares and 80% of the gross area was taken as the cultivable area. The project was completed in 1956, and by 1960 the cultivable area covered for irrigation was estimated at 15,000 hectares. This figure rose to 20,000 hectares, in 1969 and to 35,000 hectares in 1971.

The main crops grown in the project area are:
In winter: Wheat, Barley, Beans
In summer: Green gram, Cotton, Sesame and Vegetables
Perennial crops: Orchard crops including dates

3.2.3.3.2 *Drainage conditions.* It would be interesting to note that prior to the construction of the project, the depth of groundwater in the area was around 40 cms below ground level. With the construction of the drainage network with two main collector systems (North Mussayeb collector 20 cum/sec capacity and South Mussayeb collector 12 cum/sec capacity), it has been possible to lower this level to 2 metres below the ground level.

3.2.3.3.3 *Salinity.* Soil salinity was one of the main problems in achieving full development of the project. Salt and lime content in the soil are high while the gypsum content is low. The groundwater salinity is also high due to practicing fallow system of irrigation since centuries.

Experiments conducted during the period 1960-64 confirmed that leaching the salts from the soils presented no difficulty, provided a sufficient quantity of water was used and an efficient drainage system could be ensured.

It has also been observed (Thamer and Joher, 1974) that in order to keep the soil salinity within permissible limits, proper and efficient maintenance of the existing drainage network is needed. Construction of more drains in some areas of the project and certain other measures like land levelling, leaching etc were also considered essential. These have since been implemented and the problem solved.

3.2.3.4 Sediment control study

3.2.3.4.1 *The problem.* As stated earlier the canal system in general and the main canal in particular have shown an increasing tendency to silting. The head regulator of the main canal is located on the outer side of a curve on the river Euphrates which should normally

The Greater Mussayeb Project

be considered as a suitable location. The regulator is however 9 km upstream of the Hindiyah Barrage whose backwater effect extends to a distance of nearly 55 km. It is noticed that the higher velocity layers of water at the top of the water surface of the Euphrates are deflected away from the intake while the bottom layers which are heavily charged with silt are drawn into the main canal. Another striking feature is that deposition of sediment has taken place on the left side of the leading channel which indicates that the intake is not ideally oriented. Consequently a considerable part of the sediment entering the main canal is transferred to smaller branches which have relatively smaller discharge capacities. This in turn leads to loading these branches with a sediment load which is out of proportion to their design capacities. This also leads to deposition of silt in the branches.

Costly dredging works are reported to have invariably been resorted to for proper maintenance of the water system as a temporary solution. Construction of the Hadita Dam in the upper reaches of the Euphrates is expected to arrest the flow of sediment to a great extent. Therefore completion of this dam is going to considerably improve the functioning of this canal.

3.2.3.4.2 The options. Although construction of this dam on the Euphrates will reduce the flow of sediment some further remedial measures will also be necessary. These are:
(1) Running the canal to its full capacity by adjusting the canal irrigation supplies by rotation.
(2) Remodelling and regrading the main canal branches and distributaries in accordance with the design criteria.
(3) Continuous dredging of the canals.
(4) Construction of a raised sill 1.20 m high, 50 m long between the river and the forebay of the head regulator in order to skim only the upper layer of water from the river flow.
(5) Construction of a settling basin between the road and railway bridges in the upper reaches of the river and the periodic dredging of the accumulated silt.

Another study (Hekket, 1972) recommends the construction of some river training works on the basis of model experiments. These experiments were carried out for various combinations on a model having a horizontal scale of 1:200 and vertical scale of 1:50. The model was run for the following discharge conditions:

(a) Low discharges: River Euphrates   210 cum/sec
                        Mussayeb Canal   30 cum/sec
(b) Average discharges: River Euphrates   1508 cum/sec
                        Mussayeb Canal   40 cum/sec
(c) High discharges: River Euphrates   2894 cum/sec
                        Mussayeb Canal   60 cum/sec

For each of the above discharge conditions, tests were carried out to study the surface currents, velocity distribution, bed currents, and efficiency of the proposals in reducing the sediment entry, with respect to the existing conditions.

3.2.3.4.3 The results. Results of the experiments are illustrated with the aid of the following figures:

Figure 3: Behaviour of the bed load with sheet piles driven in the Euphrates river near the head of the leading channel, as determined by model experiments.
It is seen that in this proposal the bed load enters the canal from the right side of the opening and turns to the left. A small portion of the bed load enters the Mussayeb Canal through the left side gate and the rest of the charge gets deposited upstream of the head regulator.
The percentage reduction in sediment entry in this case is:
- at average discharge   76
- at high discharge   54

Figure 4: A curved divide wall was tried on the right side of the leading channel under the same conditions of flow as above. It was seen that a greater concentration of the bed load moves under the curved wall for a certain distance downstream of the intake and a larger percentage comparatively enters the canal. A small portion of the load entered the canal from the left side gate and the rest was deposited upstream of the regulator.

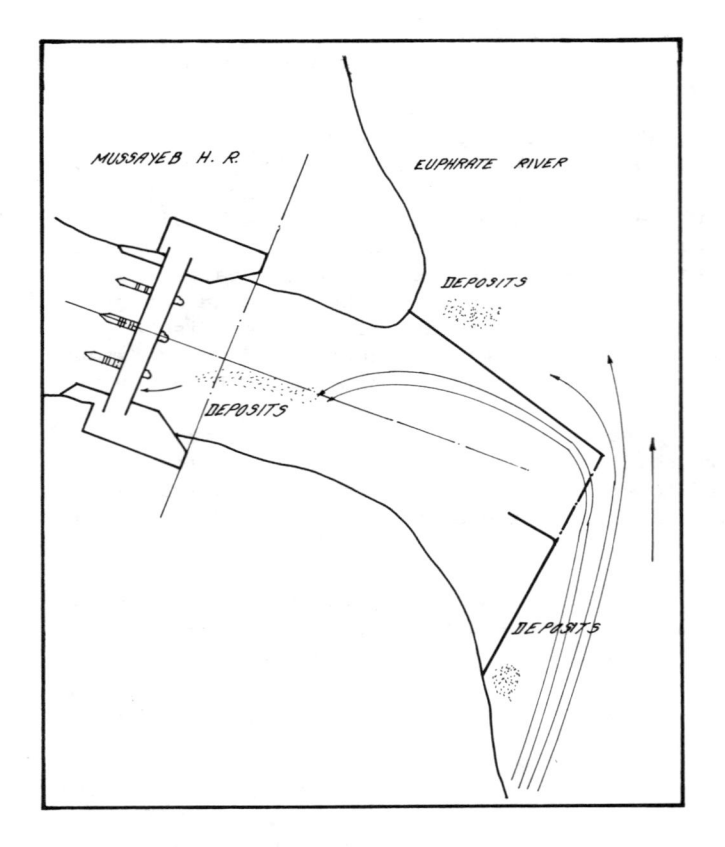

Figure 3   Behaviour of bed loads
         - case of sheet pile

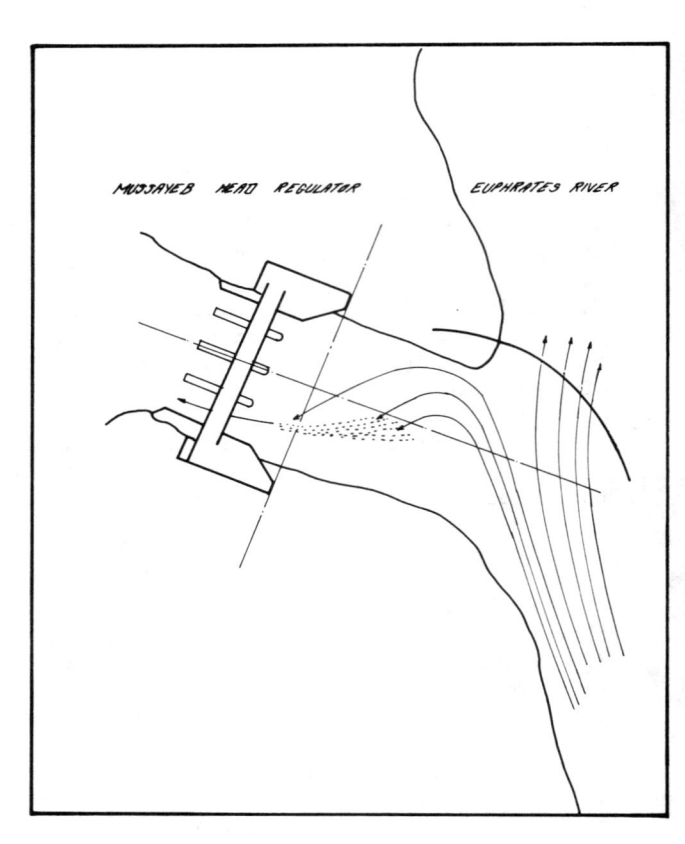

Figure 4   Behaviour of bed loads
         - case of curved divide wall

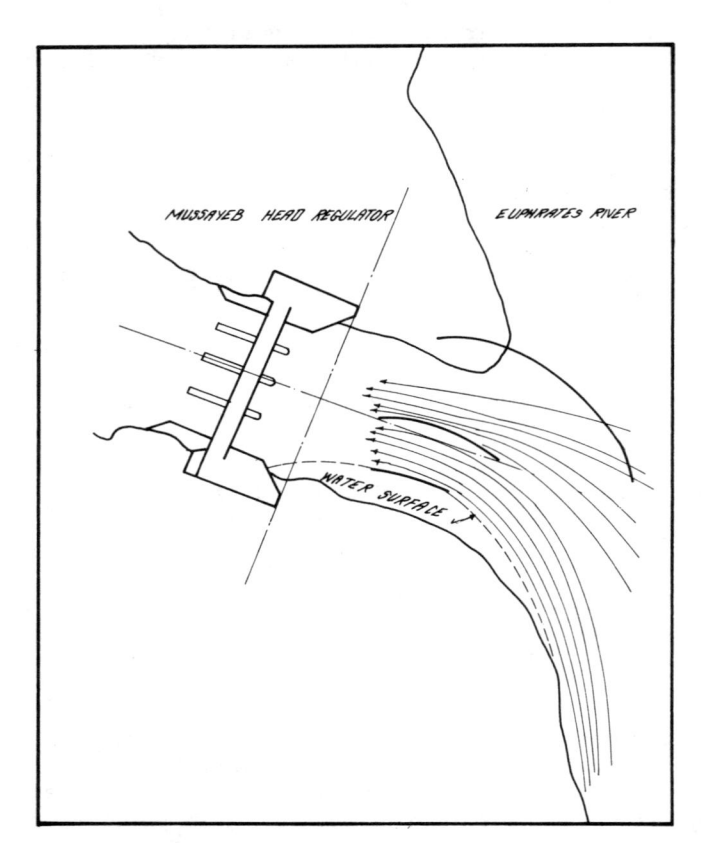

Figure 5   Stream lines of bed currents
         - case of curved divide wall
           and vanes

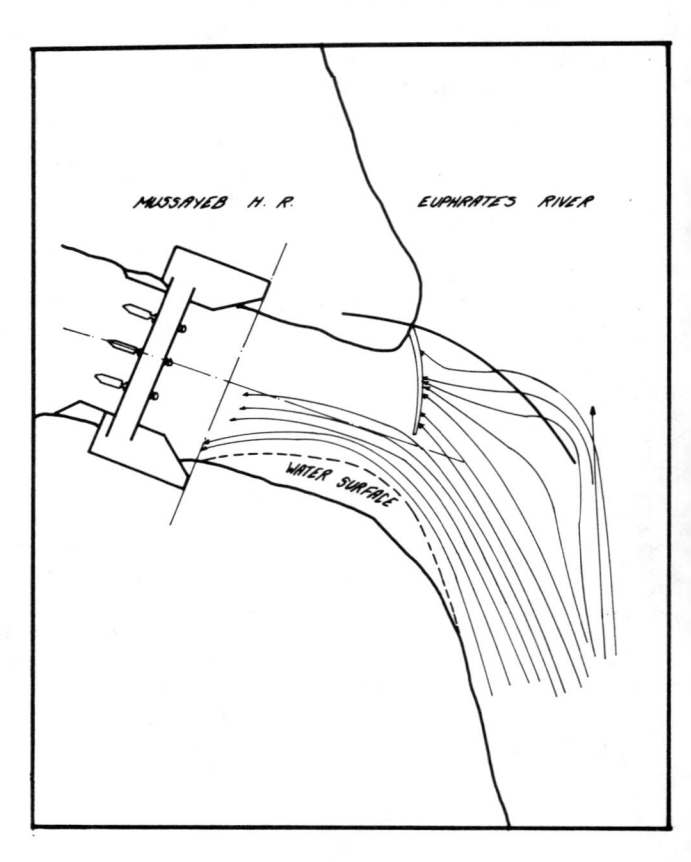

Figure 6   Stream lines of bed currents
         - case of curved divide wall
           and super elevated sill

The Greater Mussayeb Project

Figure 5:
      The best results were obtained when the length of the divide was 40 m. The percentage reduction in sediment entry was:
- for average discharge   57.5
- for high discharge   56.5

Another combination tried was the curved divide wall as above and in addition two vanes placed in the central portion of the leading channel. It was seen in this case that most of the bed load moved under the curved divide wall and the rest turned to the intake where part was deposited in between the vanes and part entered the canal. The percentage reduction in sediment entry was:
- for average discharge   70
- for high discharge   62

Figure 6: In this, a combination of a curved divide wall and super elevated sill in the head of the leading channel was made and conditions of flow tested. It was seen that most of the bed load passed under the curved divide wall, the balance indicated a tendency to enter the intake either by crossing over the sill or being deposited upstream of the sill on the right side. Unlike other cases entry of the silt from the left side was considerably less.

      The percentage reduction in sediment entry was:
- for average discharge   61
- for high discharge   62

A comparison of the reduction in sediment entry under the various conditions tested is given in Table 4 below.

Table 4

Reference to Figure No	Type of lay-out tested	Reduction in sediment entry %	
		For average discharge 40 m^3/sec	For maximum discharge 60 m^3/sec
3	Sheet piles at the head of leading channel	76	54
4	Curved divide wall	57.5	56.5
5	Curved divide wall and vanes	70	62
6	Curved divide wall and super elevated sill	61	62

It can be seen from the above table that, while the curved divide wall or its combination with the super elevated sill is the best proposal for the maximum discharge condition, that with the sheet pile gives the best results for average discharge conditions corresponding to 40 m.cu/sec. The operational discharge capacity of the canal was also the same. Hence from these considerations the proposal of the sheet piles in the leading channel appears to be the best solution.

3.2.3.5 <u>Causes and hydrological effects</u>

3.2.3.5.1 Introduction. The filling of the canal beds is due to a variety of causes, some of which are natural while others are induced by the structures. These are discussed below in a very brief way.

3.2.3.5.2 The sediment charge in Euphrates. There have been varying estimates of the sediment discharge of the river. It was estimated by Ionides (Knappen et al) that the rate of sediment production in the Euphrates basin above Ramadi (which is upstream of the canal

under study) is of the order of 100 cubic metres per sq km per year. The area of the Euphrates basin at certain places is given below.
- At Hit   264,120 sq kms
- At Ramadi   267,300 sq kms
- At Mussayeb 274,100 sq kms

Applying the rate indicated by Ionides, to the area at Mussayeb the average amount of sediment at Mussayeb will be of the order of 27,410,000 cubic metres. This rate is however expected to decrease after the construction of the Haditha dam.

3.2.3.5.3 Positioning of the off-take. The leading channel and the head regulator do not have proper upstream orientation. In the pool conditions with the Hindiyah Barrage gates closed the coarse sediment is deposited in the head of the canal and when the flow commences sudden change of direction of flow causes eddies which throw up coarser bed load into suspension.

3.2.3.5.4 Role of desert sand. Dust and sand storms of severe magnitude are a common feature in central and southern Iraq. Fortunately the menace of this desert sand is localised in only a few areas of the project.

3.2.3.5.5 Sinuosity of alignment of main canal. The alignment of the main canal is extremely sinuous particularly in the head reaches. This is obviously dictated by practical considerations. Nevertheless, this has contributed largely to alternate silting and scouring of the canal bed and banks respectively.

3.2.3.5.6 Effect of Hindiya Barrage. As stated earlier this barrage is located 9 km downstream and its effect extends to a distance of nearly 55 km. The regulation by the Hindiyah Barrage is presently dictated by the requirements of the Hilla Canal System (the biggest system in Euphrates taking off immediately upstream of the barrage) and the downstream releases required to be made. The maximum releases made are of the order of 2500 cum/sec. No detailed study with regard to the pond regulation at this barrage appears to have been carried out so far. Whether the method of "Still Pond" or "Semi-Open Flow" regulation would be advantageous from over all considerations needs to be examined urgently in the near future.

It would be interesting to note that silt concentration samples were collected from the Euphrates river and in the canal reach in April 1975, when maximum discharge conditions occurred in the year.

Silt concentrations in ppm at various places in Euphrates river and Mussayeb Canal are given in Table 5 which indicates that with the conditions as they exist now the silt concentration in the canal is practically the same as in the river. In other words, effective silt control measures are all the more necessary.

Table 5   Silt concentration for Euphrates river and Mussayeb Canal

Table 5(a) Cross section for Euphrates river U.S. of Mussayeb Canal - Date 6.4.75

S No	Depth of sample cms	Distance of sample along C.S.	Sediment concentration ppm
1	75	75 m from LB	277.3
2	150	75 m from LB	228.2
3	225	75 m from LB	293.0
4	50	150 m from LB	273.7
5	100	150 m from LB	205.2
6	60	60 m from right	209.1

Table 5 (continued)

Table 5(b) Cross section in Mussayeb Canal U.S. of Mussayeb Head Regulator - Date 12.4.75

S No	Depth of sample cms	Distance of sample along C.S.	Sediment concentration ppm
1	50	6 m	262.7
2	100	6 m	222.2
3	50	12 m	201.1
4	100	12 m	285.2
5	150	12 m	362.6
6	50	18 m	307.1
7	100	18 m	263.7
8	150	18 m	201.8

Table 5(c) Cross section on Musseyab Canal D.S. of Head Regulator

9	80	8 m	191.6
10	160	8 m	211.5
11	240	8 m	277.8
12	60	16 m	205.2
13	120	16 m	256.9
14	180	16 m	254.1
15	60	24 m	234.0
16	120	24 m	196.1
17	180	24 m	266.4

3.2.3.6 Main conclusions

After the completion of the project in 1956, settlements in the area have been increasing at an average rate of 1500 persons per year. Along with this the pace of agricultural development has also been increasing. The cultivable area covered was 15,000 hectares in 1960, 20,000 hectares in 1969 and 35,000 hectares in 1971.

The problem of soil salinity has been successfully solved by proper leaching of soils and an extensive drainage network, while that of sediment entry is still under study. Lack of proper orientation of the canal intake, inadequacy of river training works and the ponding effect of the Hindiyah Barrage are considered to be the main factors. A broad study of this problem with the aid of model experiments gives an indication that the driving of sheet piles in to the head of the leading channel and proper regulation techniques will reduce the sediment entry by nearly 76%. This, if accomplished, would be of great help in the rapid development of the project area.

REFERENCES

Hekket, H. 1972. Sedimentation of the Irrigation System of the Greater Mussayeb Project. *Technical Note* No 9, Greater Mussayeb Project Authority and FAO, Baghdad.

Knappen Tippetts Abbett McCarthy (USA), 1952. *Report on development of Tigris and Euphrates rivers*.

Hakeem Thames and Tahseen Joher, 1974. Report on soil and hydrological investigations for Greater Mussayeb Project. *State Organisation for Soils and Land Reclamation*, Baghdad.

References

Bibliography

Al-Hardan, Dhari, 1971. *Greater Mussayeb Project Development,* Ministry of Agrarian Reform Baghdad.

Amer, M.H. and Fakhri, W.A., 1975. Cost analysis of execution of a tile drainage network on the pilot project area, *Technical Note No 33,* Greater Mussayeb Project, Ministry of Agriculture and Agrarian Reform and FAO, Baghdad.

Anon, 1975. Final report on sediment control study on the Greater Mussayeb Canal intake. *Ministry of Irrigation,* Baghdad.

Dougrameji, J.S. and Clor, M.A., 1977. Case study on desertification Greater Mussayeb Project. *United Nations Conference on Desertification,* Nairobi.

Nedeco, 1969. Report on irrigation problems of the Greater Mussayeb Project, *Nedeco Consultant Engineering Services,* Baghdad.

Nugteren, J, 1966. *Report on the design of the Greater Mussayeb Project,* Directorate-General of Irrigation, Baghdad.

Rouse, Hunter, and Ince, Simon, 1963. *History of Hydraulics,* Dover Publications, Inc, New York.

Sumanovac, P. 1972. Farm management studies and machinery requirements, *Technical Note No 13,* Ministry of Agriculture and Agrarian Reform and FAO, Baghdad.

Chapter 3.3

3.3 DRAINAGE
   by H Niini[1]

Drainage - as undertaken by man for different purposes - means the removal of excess water from the land by surface or subsurface means. Drainage is mainly used as a method of improving soil conditions in wet and waterlogged areas, in order to increase agricultural or silvicultural production. Drainage, together with irrigation, was regarded in the Mar del Plata Action Plan (UN Water Conference, 1977) as a major programme component of the Action Programme on Water for Agriculture, which the Conference recommended to be implemented with high priority in a co-ordinated manner at the national and international level.

It has been estimated (Bulavko, 1971) that there are over 3.5 million km^2 of marshland and other waterlogged lands in the world, ie 2.9% of the total land area. Almost 60% of the marshes are in the Soviet Union, where over 9% of the land is marshy. Large areas of marshland are also found in North America and central and northern Europe. For instance, in Finland 30% of the land area is covered with peat. A large part of these areas with excess water has been, or will be, drained for agriculture or forestry (Mustonen, 1976).

Surface drainage removes water promptly from natural, treated and artificial surfaces, often increasing the leaching of the surface layers of the soil at the same time. For agricultural purposes drainage is also carried out by the use of subsurface drainage, which allows the penetration of fertilizers and the improvement of soil texture without additional leaching of the surface.

In tropical areas, drainage works are frequently undertaken in order to eliminate conditions conducive to the spread of certain diseases that seriously hamper any activities (Dooge et al, 1973). Well over 100 million ha in Asia are used to grow rice under submerged or partly submerged conditions during rainy seasons. The rice fields are enclosed by water-detaining bunds, and excess water from rain, or from irrigation, flows from one field to the next one at lower elevation. The main problem of drainage then is to limit the depth of submersion and to provide adequate outflow from the lowest-lying fields (FAO, 1972).

In dry areas, where agriculture is possible only by means of irrigation, drainage is a costly but essential measure to prevent certain drawbacks (as, for example, salting) caused by irrigation of long duration.

Drainage works for another purpose and often on a larger scale are represented by river improvement works aimed at improving water traffic conditions or at preventing overbank flows during flood periods.

In urban areas, drainage is undertaken in order to decrease the damage caused by storm waters to property, traffic and recreational activities as well as to construction sites. Urban drainage thus includes surface facilities such as gutters, culverts, and storm sewers, as well as the slopes of highways, streets, railways, etc. Also mining and underground construction in general (tunnels, rock stores etc) need or cause effective and deep-reaching drainage of the surrounding ground. Drainage of these kinds and the resulting hydrological

---

[1] Koukkusaarentie 7 C 329, SF-00980, Helsinki 98, Finland

Drainage

effects will be dealt with in connection with urbanization and industrialization studies (in sub-chapter 3.6).

The effect of drainage on the water regime and water balance is displayed immediately in the areas adjacent to the drainage systems, and in the river basin as a whole. Due to changes in the groundwater table, soil moisture content and the vegetative cover, the construction of a drainage system has a great influence upon the evaporation and transpiration regimes of swamps. This influence depends on the meteorological conditions, the nature of man's activity and on the level of the soil moisture content and its regulation in the drained lands.

In man's long history of engineering development, methods of drainage have developed faster than those of the study of the effects of drainage on soils, vegetation, water cycles, and the whole environment, so that costly mistakes still occur (Pereira, 1972). For example, the consolidation of organic residues after drainage causes land subsidence, oxidation of ferrous sulphide and other salts in the dried soils may give toxic levels of soil acidity, and the changed water use of the vegetation adapted to the new drainage conditions may result in large-scale changes in the water regime of the area. Because several unfavourable effects of drainage are slow-acting and are discovered only in the course of time, the importance of the adequate investigation of the hydrological effects of drainage has increased in importance (UNESCO-IAHS, 1975).

Changes in water balance of swamps and marsh-ridden areas, under the effect of drainage determines the change of hydrological characteristics of river basins (normal runoff, maximum spring snow melt and rainfall runoff, minimum flow, the streamflow distribution during a year etc) which should be taken into account in the evaluation of water resources and their development. Of course the effect of drainage on river regimes due to the difference in their capacities may vary greatly. In the case of small rivers, the depth of erosion is often compatible with the depth of the drainage network, and small rivers are subject to greater changes in regime than large rivers. Therefore, it is quite possible that because of the transfer of the major portion of surface flow into subsurface flow, the runoff of large rivers may be unchanged or slightly increased whereas the mean runoff in small rivers would decrease. Even in the case of basins similar, areas of drainage may affect the water regime in different ways according to the climatic, pedologic and hydrographic features of the basin, the percentage swamp, the types of swamps, and the extent of swamp drainage. In some areas the effect of drainage is considerable, in others it is significant (Shiklomanov, 1976).

The essential hydrological changes aimed at in ordinary drainage works are the lowering of the water table and the origination of a considerable zone of unsaturated soil-moisture storage in areas where none or little existed earlier. The primary and practical hydrological effect of these changes is that the volume of infiltration into the unsaturated soil is increased. For an irrigated area, drainage enables irrigation to be practised successfully. It relieves water logging, accumulation of harmful salts, deterioration of the soil structure, and flood damage to the project or other properties.

In the drained areas, the following quantitative consequences of the drainage measures are common:
(1) The groundwater table drops rapidly depending on the depth of the ditches. In conditions typical of northern temperate-climate areas the drop is commonly as much as 1-1.5 m and in forest drainage 0.3-0.5 m (Mustonen, 1976).
(2) Surface evaporation immediately decreases. The gradual decay or destruction of the former vegetative cover may reduce transpiration, decreasing in addition evaporation. In extreme cases, evaporation can be reduced by more than 50% (Mustonen, 1976). On the other hand, the gradual development of a new type of plant cover suitable to the new moisture conditions increases evaporation and transpiration.
(3) Infiltration, groundwater flow to the channels, and runoff increase, corresponding to the decrease in evaporation and transpiration.
(4) The drying soil layers consolidate causing subsidence of the ground surface. The subsidence is biggest close to the channels. This helps surface water to flow into them. In flat-lying highly organic soils a considerable amount of subsidence, however, tends to negate the original purpose of the drainage. The maintenance of a controlled water table contributes to arresting the rate of subsidence of the land.
(5) The better hydraulic conditions due to drainage make the flood peaks come earlier and contribute to a general increase in flood flows. Both contribute to an additional small

decrease in evaporation and transpiration.
(6) Due to increased groundwater flow, even low flows are usually increased after drainage.
(7) Due to the disappearance of surface water storage, the total water storage capacity of the drained marshland decreases. Also, the capacity of the area to trap sediments carried down from upper areas decreases.
(8) There is also an increase in runoff corresponding to the reduction in the water storage in the area.
(9) Changes in the water regime, especially in water storage, also cause changes in the soil temperature regime.

The hydrological effects of drainage are most obvious when the drained area is left as it is after the drainage. Such is the case in peat extraction and often in timber production. The agricultural use of drained areas usually comprise a series of other reclamation and cultivation measures, which even out some of the changes mentioned. In forestry the effects listed gradually become less significant after the stand or trees has developed and has started to evaporate effectively.

<u>In the downstream reaches</u> of a river basin, the effect of drainage on the flow regime varies, depending on the location of the drained area within the whole basin.

The draining of the upper reaches of the basin tends to cumulatively increase peak flows downstream, sometimes contributing to the creation of severe floods even in areas where flooding was formerly unknown or rare. Then also the effects of erosion in the river channel are accentuated and the sediments are carried further downstream where they may have damaging effects. Especially the draining of swamps formed behind natural barriers like bedrock thresholds etc, which act as temporary reservoirs, will cause a serious flood hazard to the downstream reaches. Therefore, careful attention is necessary before such marshy areas are drained.

When drainage is carried out only in the lower reaches, the flood flow of the basin is even decreased. Then the flood peak from the drained downstream areas comes earlier than it would without the draining, making the hydrograph for the whole river basin flatter.

To assess the quantitative hydrological influence of drainage, the water balance elements outlined previously must be observed continuously. Thus, observations must be made of stream discharges in the upstream reaches, the drained areas proper, and the downstream reaches of the basin and groundwater stages, infiltration, evaporation, transpiration, soil-moisture conditions, as well as the subsidence of the land surface in the area concerned.

In order to demonstrate positively the impacts of drainage and to determine the statistical characteristics of the changes observed, records of sufficient length are needed prior to drainage. In the planning of the drainage, investigations should be extended to all the elements mentioned. Great care should always be exercised in generalisation of the results, since differences in weather and soil conditions as well as in agricultural and silvicultural techniques greatly affect these phenomena. Also, secondary effects should always be considered, eg the increased volume of infiltration may affect the conductivity of the soil, subsequently affecting the groundwater flow, etc.

Some kind of drainage is almost regularly connected with modern irrigation. In order to prevent possible floods caused by any drainage it is essential that the effects of drainage are also considered in close connection with those of the other measures concerned (irrigation, flood control, etc). The impact of drainage on the hydrological regime may thus be analysed as a separate or a complex process on any scale. Suitable units to be analysed are drained plots or sections of minor catchments, small river basins, other physiographic units, and whole large basins. At the small scale, information is obtained mainly from observations in well-equipped experimental or research basins - usually using the method of analogy - in large areas the water-balance or water-budget methods might prove successful.

REFERENCES

Bulavko, A.G. 1971. The hydrology of marshes and marsh-ridden lands. UNESCO. *Nature and Resources,* Vol VII, No 1.

Dooge, James C.I., Costin, A.B. and Finkel, Herman J. 1973. Man's influence on the hydrological cycle. *FAO, Irrigation and Drainage Paper,* No 17, Special Issue.

References

FAO, 1972. Design criteria for drainage at the farm level in Asia and the Far East (by Water Resources Development Division, United Nations ECAFE Secretariat, Bangkok, Thailand). *FAO Irrigation and Drainage Papers,* 12.

Mustonen, S.E. 1976. Water balance transformation of meliorated areas. General report. *Proceedings of the Symposium on the Man-Made Transformation of the Water Balance* (prel ed), Leningrad, July 1976. Albert-Ludwigs-Univ Freiburg i Br, FR Germany.

Pereira, H.C. 1972. The influence of man on the hydrological cycle: guidelines to the policies for safe development of land and water resources. In: Status and trends of research in hydrology. *Studies and Reports in Hydrology,* Vol 10, pp 31-70.

Shiklomanov, I.A. 1976. Vlianie khoziaistvennoi deatelnosti no vodnye resursy i hydrologicheski rezhim (Impact of man's activity on water resources and hydrological regime). Survey, *VNIIGMI* - Obninsk, 111 pp.

UN Water Conference, 1977. *Mar del Plata Action Plan.* Report of the United Nations Water Conference, Extract 1.

UNESCO-IAHS, 1975. *Hydrology of marsh-ridden areas.* Proceedings of the Minsk Symposium, June 1972. Studies and Reports in Hydrology, Vol 19.

3.3.1   IMPACT OF DRAINAGE ON STREAM FLOW (the Oressa River up to Andreevka)
by S M Novikov and Yu N Pokumeiko[1]

3.3.1.1 Introduction
The basic characteristics of the reclaimed basin are as follows: drainage area 3580 km^2, mean basin elevation 147 m, lake area 1%, the total swamp area 25%, reclaimed lands 22%, area of the swamp before reclamation was 47% of the basin area.

The basin occupies the northern part of Byelorussian Polessje and it lies in a north-south-east direction, its shape is asymmetric (Figure 1). The basin's surface is a flat plain with extremely smooth watersheds. Its upper part is hilly, and smooth rises alternate with narrow and wide marsh-ridden depressions. Downstream of Lyuban there is a considerable depression and the number of swamps increases (flood-plain marshes are predominant).

Peat-bog soils and peat lands prevail in the basin, they occupy 65% of the total basin area, podzolic sandy soils cover 17% of the basin, podzolic boggy soils occupy 12% of the area and strongly podzolized sandy loam soils occupy 6% of the area.

The river valley is not clearly defined over a considerable distance. The slopes are low (5 or 8 m), gentle and crossed by the tributary valleys and marsh-ridden depressions. The valley varies from 300 m to 3 km in width.

The flood plain of the river varies from 100 m to 1 or 2 km in width and it is intersected by drains and flood plain lakes.

3.3.1.2 The reclamation of the basin
The drainage of swamps was started by a special expeditionary party during the last quarter of the 19th century. By 1896 about 194 km of trunk and minor canals had been dug, about 33 km being concentrated in the upper reaches while the rest of the canals were constructed in the lower reaches. When the work of the team was over in 1896, the drainage canals were neglected and were subject to silting and destruction. The result was that the major portion of the reclaimed swamps had turned to the former state by the 1930s. In 1926 the drainage of the swamps and marsh-ridden areas in the Oressa basin was resumed according to the following steps.

During 1926-1935 extensive reclamation was undertaken in the south of the basin where large swamps occupied 650 km^2 on both river banks. During that period control works of the channel of the Oressa river and its tributaries were constructed.

From 1936-1941 the drainage of swamp areas proceeded, as well as straightening and dredging operations in the middle and lower reaches of the Oressa river and cultivation of the reclaimed areas was started.

During the period 1941-1945 a major portion of the canals and reclamation structures were destroyed, the drained areas became waterlogged once more. The reconstruction of all the drainage systems and additional drainage of swamps were undertaken from 1948 to 1970. In 1962-1966 the Lyuban man-made lake was built upstream of Addreevka and by 1973 28.8% of the basin area was drained.

[1] State Hydrological Institute, 2 Linija 23, Leningrad V 53, USSR

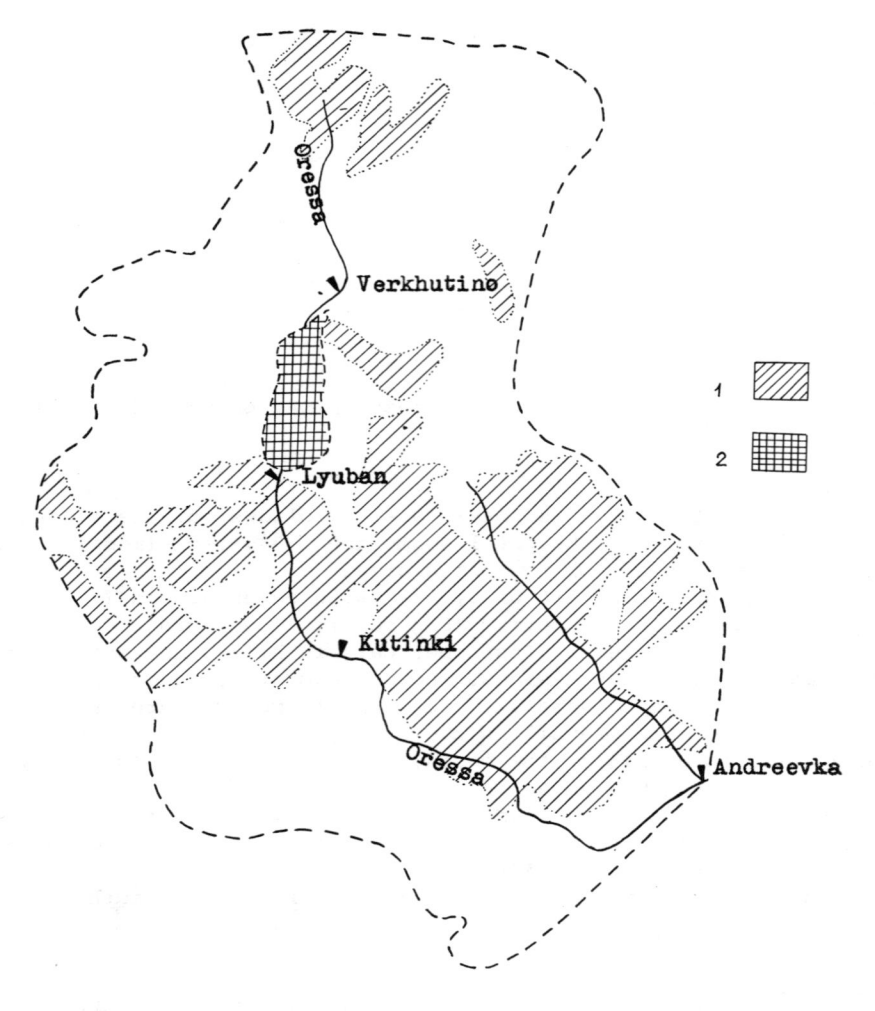

Figure 1   The Oressa Basin

1. Reclaimed areas
2. Reservoirs

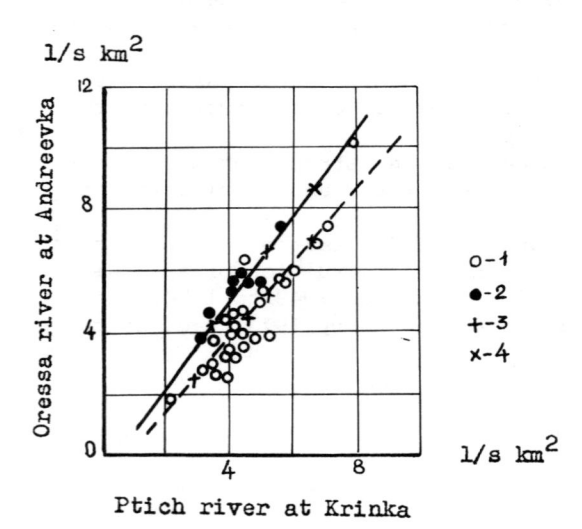

Fig.2. Graph of mean annual specific discharges from reclaimed(Oressa river)and control (Ptich river)watersheds
1-before reclamation
2-after reclamation
3-mean runoff during the period of simultaneous observations
4-values of equal frequencies

The improvements to the basin are presented in Table 1. The changes in the reclaimed area are shown in Table 2.

The drained areas usually occupy flood plains and terraces but they are distributed over the basin; the large drained areas are close to Andreevka. Reclaimed areas are usually low marshes and bogs composed of sedge-Bryales peats of medium age. The peat layer is usually 0.4-1.2 m deep.

The reclaimed basin area, ie 28.8% of the total drainage area, is used for agriculture, and it is 89.6% of the total reclaimed area and is distributed in the following way: ploughed fields occupy 58.0% of the area, improved grasslands used for hay require 20.1% of the area, improved pastures cover 10.8% of the area, and private plots and long-term planting occupy 0.7%

The rest of the reclaimed area is occupied as follows: canals and ditches - 2.1%; roads - 0.6%; forest - 3.9%; peat excavation - 0.7% other economic uses - 3.1%.

The total length of ditches is 16,972 km consisting of 6,350 km of open ditches and 10,622 km of closed drains. The distance between the ditches is 100-200 m, the drains are spaced 15-40 m from each other. The ditches are 0.9-1.5 m deep; the drains are at a depth of 0.9-1.2 m.

3.3.1.3 The basic information and methods for the evaluation of the effects of drainage
Data from the observational network of the Hydrometeorological Services were used as a basis for the evaluation of the effect of drainage on stream flow. The period of stream flow observations prior to drainage was 35 years long (1926-1940, 1945-1964), and stream flow was observed for 9 years after drainage (1965-1973).

Precipitation was measured at 7 stations and the observation period at the different meteorological stations was 46 years (1925-1941, 1945-1973).

The evaluation of the changes of the hydrological regime caused by multi-purpose reclamation measures was made from the relations between the annual runoff of the study basin for the period before and after reclamation and the appropriate data from the control basin.

The basin of the Ptich river at Krinka where no reclamation had been carried out was selected as the control basin for the Oressa river at Andreevka. The area of the Ptich basin is 2010 km^2, the mean basin elevation is 186 m, marsh-ridden forest occupies 15% of the basin, the lake area is 1% and the total swamp area is 23% of the drainage area. The relations between annual runoff values are given in Figure 2, and this graph allows the evaluation of the changes in the river regime. Mean long-term runoff characteristics for the undisturbed regime and the coefficients of runoff under the effects of drainage of the Oressa river are given in Table 3. In the case of the reclaimed basin of the Oressa normal annual runoff is determined directly from the observations as well as the coefficients of variation and skewness.

3.3.1.4 The effect of drainage on annual runoff
The annual runoff of the Oressa river at Andreevka is affected by the drainage and cultivation of the areas. After reclamation annual runoffs increased by 28%; the increase of annual runoff for the 95% frequency reaches 40% (Table 3).

The basic reason for the changes in annual runoff (increase) are as follows:
(1) During reclamation the factors governing the formation of runoff are subject to considerable changes due to river control works as well as due to canalization of tributaries.
(2) When reclamation is undertaken in the basin runoff tends to increase because of the following factors:
    (a) due to dredging operations in river channels and in tributaries their rate of erosion increases, thus raising the drainage capacity of the channels;
    (b) a dense network of ditches and drains in the basin creates favourable conditions for the diversion of groundwater into rivers;
    (c) the reduction of the period of high groundwater levels in the basin contributes to the decrease of groundwater losses by evaporation.

The decrease of river water temperature also indicates a greater groundwater contribution to the rivers in the study basin after reclamation.
(3) The increase of stream flow after reclamation is to a certain extent explained by the discharge of groundwater storage accumulated in the peatlands in the marsh areas and in the adjacent mineral soils of the basins.

These reasons, for change of annual runoff are common for every basin, but the effect is different for various basins, since it depends on the physiography of the basin, the rate

Impact of drainage on stream flow

Table 1 Improvements to the Oressa Basin on 1 January 1973

		Open drainage	Closed drainage	Total
Drained area %	From the basin area	16.7	12.1	28.8
	From the total area of swamps and marsh-ridden areas	35.5	25.8	61.3
Drainage network density $H = \frac{L}{A}$, km/km^2		$\frac{1.77}{6.15}$	$\frac{2.97}{10.3}$	$\frac{4.74}{16.4}$
Rate of canalisation $a = \frac{h\,L}{A} 10^3$		$\frac{2.12}{7.38}$	$\frac{3.27}{11.3}$	$\frac{5.39}{18.7}$
Accumulation capacity of the drained area $W = h\,A$, km^3		0.718	0.477	1.20

Note: The drainage density and canalisation rate are referred to the basin area in the numerator and to the total area of the reclaimed lands over the basin in the denominator.

Table 2 Changes in the areas reclaimed (in % from total basin area)

Year	Drained area, % Total	By closed drainage
1928-1940	(6.7)	
1949-1953	(6.7)	
1954	8.6	
1955	10.1	
1956	11.1	
1957	13.2	
1958	14.1	0.04
1959	14.8	0.2
1960	15.6	0.5
1961	15.7	0.8
1962	16.0	1.2
1963	17.2	1.8
1964	19.1	2.7
1965	22.5	2.9
1966	24.4	3.9
1967	26.3	5.1
1968	27.0	6.6
1969	27.5	8.5
1970	27.9	8.7
1971	28.4	10.8
1972	28.8	12.1

and nature of drainage and the method of cultivation of the reclaimed soils.

Table 3 Characteristics of Long-Term Annual Runoff of the Oressa River at Andreevka

Characteristics	Mean long-term	Frequency %						C_v	C_s
		5	25	50	75	90	95		
Runoff before reclamation (M)	4.3	7.01	5.22	4.15	3.22	2.49	2.12	0.35	0.60
Transformation coefficient (K)	1.28	1.24	1.26	1.28	1.32	1.36	1.39	0.91	1.00

Notes: M - annual specific discharge, $1/a\ km^2$;

K - transformation coefficient of runoff characteristics, equal to the ratio of runoff characteristics after reclamation to runoff value before reclamation.

Bibliography

Alexeev, G.A. 1960. Grafoanaliticheskie sposouy spredelenia raspredelenia (Graphic and analytic methods of determining and reducing to a long-term observation period the parameters of distribution curves). *Trans GGI*, 73, 50-140.

Klibashev, K.P. and Goroshkov, I.F. 1970. *Hydrologicheskie reachety* (Hydrological computations). Leningrad, 460 pp.

Klyueva, K.A. 1973. Vlianie osushitelnoi melioratsil na hydrologicheskiy reshim riada rek Byelorussii (The effect of drainage reclamation on the hydrological regime of some rivers in Byelorussii). *Trans GGI*, 208, 187-212.

Klyusva, K.A., and Pokumaiko, Yu M. 1978. Resultaty otsenki vliania osushitclynykh melioratsiy na vodny rezhim rek Byelorussii (The results of evaluation of the effect of drainage reclamation on the water regime of rivers of Byelorussie). *Complete set of papers on hydrology No 15.*

3.3.2   THE HYDROLOGICAL EFFECTS OF FOREST DRAINAGE
        by Seppo E Mustonen and Pertti Seuna[1]

3.3.2.1 Introduction

The total area of peatlands in the world has been estimated at about 100 million hectares. A considerable part of this area is to be found within regions where intensive forestry is practised. Draining peatlands for forestry is a way of increasing timber production that has been used in various countries.

In Finland there are 10 million hectares of peatland. Of this area approximately 7 million hectares are suitable for draining. By the end of 1976, some 5 million hectares has been drained and about 200 000 ha per year has been added to this total in the last few years. This means that by 1980 approximately one fifth of the land area of Finland will be treated in a manner and this has considerable hydrological significance.

This paper discusses the methodology used in studying the hydrological effects of forest drainage and the results of an experiment.

3.3.2.2 Research basins

The two research basins covered by this case study are shown in Figure 1. In 1935 various hydrological observations were started in two adjacent natural drainage basins in south-eastern Finland. The location of the basins is $61°N$ and $29°E$. The altitude of the control basin (Latosuo) various from 80 to 130 m and that of the experimental basin (Huhtisuo) from 100 to 125 m above the sea level. Table 1 shows certain of the physical characteristics of the two basins.

Table 1   Data on the research basins of Huhtisuo and Latosue

Basin	Drainage area km²	Peatland %	Cultivated land %	Mean slope %	Tree stand 1958 m³/ha	Tree stand 1970 m³/ha
Huhtisuo	5.03	44	0	5.0	58	39
Latosuo	5.34	15	19	8.2	58	74

In the control basin (Latosuo) there are pine and spruce swamps comprising 15% of the drainage area, and a large cultivated area (19%), which was long ago reclaimed from peatland. In the experimental basin (Huhtisuo) there are no cultivated areas. Open bogs and swamps with a poor growth comprise about 45% of the basin.

---

[1] Water Research Institute, National Board of Waters, Helsinki, Finland

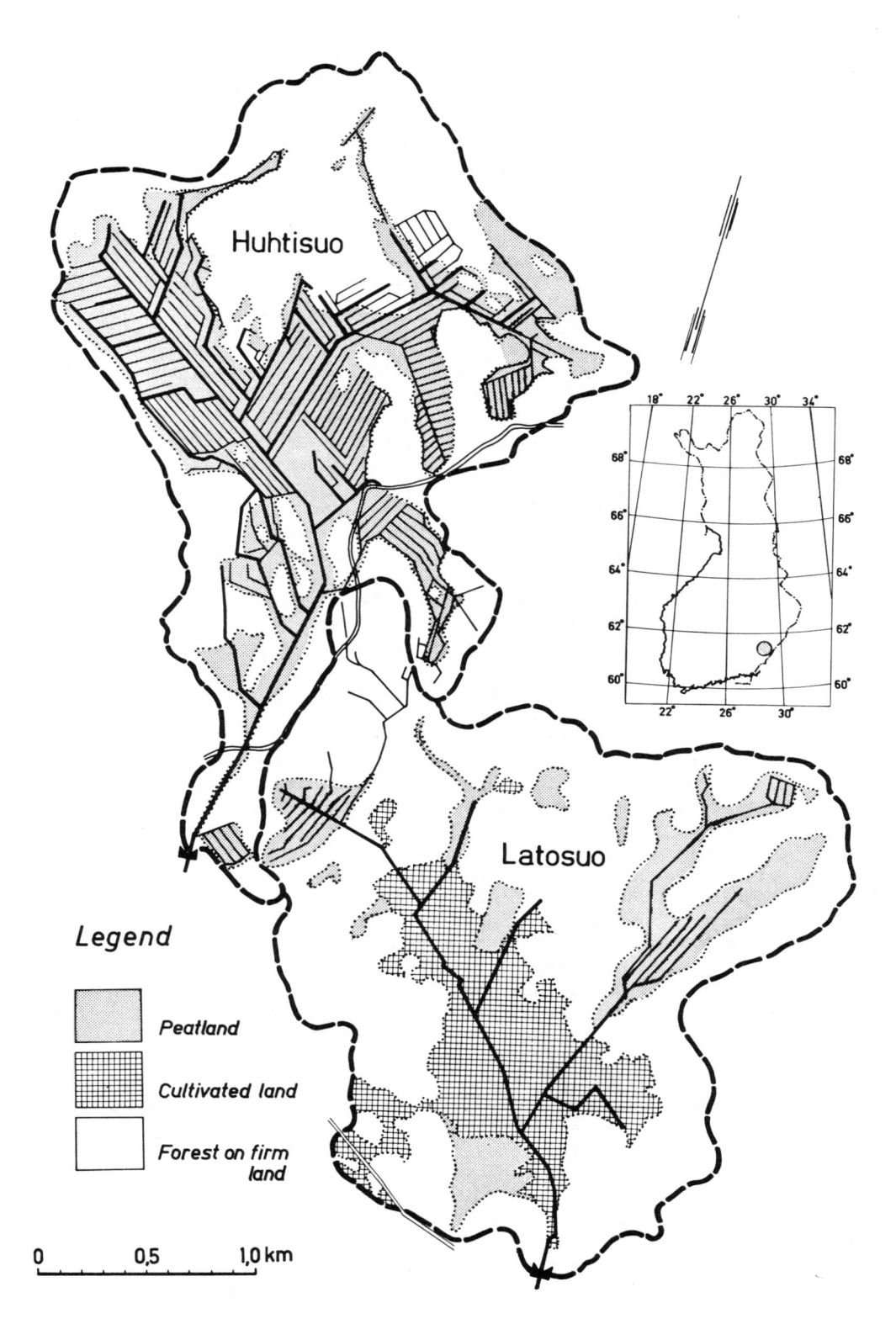

Figure 1 Huhtisuo and Latosuo research basins
(Heavy lines show main ditches, thin lines forest ditches)

The hydrological effects of forest drainage

Before drainage, the peat layer was about 1.5 m thick. The mineral soil below the peat is mostly sand and gravel. Some sandy soils (12%) also exist in the control basin. Both basins are uninhabited.

The climate in the region is humid. Mean annual precipitation is about 700 mm with a range of 500 to 850 mm. Of the total precipitation approximately 250 mm is discharged and 450 mm is evaporated as a long-term average. A large part of precipitation occurs as snow. The average water equivalent of snow on March 15 is about 120 mm. Thus spring runoff forms a considerable part, about 50% of the total annual runoff. Precipitation is fairly evenly distributed throughout the year so that most of the rain falls in August (about 80 mm) and least in March (about 40 mm). Mean annual temperature is 4^0C with a range of +1 to +6^0C. The warmest month is July with a mean temperature of 17^0C, and the coldest is February, with a mean of -9^0C.

3.3.2.3 Methodology and treatment of basins

The analyses of observations were based on the control basin method, the research basins being kept in their natural state for a calibration period. After the calibration period, the experimental basin was treated and the other basin was kept in its natural state. Regression equations are then calculated for the desired variables measured in the treated and control basins for the calibration period. These equations are then used after the treatment for the computation of what the quantity of the variable in the treatment basin would have been if the treatment had not been performed. In this experiment the variable was the runoff and the treatment was drainage. The difference between the computed and measured runoff from the treated basin is then calculated. If no treatments, except the one under investigation, have been given during the whole research period, then the difference shows the change in the quantity of runoff caused by the treatment investigated. The statistical significance of the change can be determined using the t-test.

In this study the aim was to investigate the effects of draining the forest. For this purpose, main ditches, 130 cm deep, were dug in the Huhtisuo basin in 1958. The drainage was completed by digging small forest ditches, 60 cm deep in 1960. The drained area comprised about 40% of the Huhtisuo basin. Drainage density was 80 m of main ditch and 225 m of forest ditch per drained hectare. The calibration period extended from 1936 to 1957. There were data covering the three-year period when there were only main ditches. However, this is too short a period to be studied separately. Therefore only the years from 1961 were considered a treatment period. The results are based mainly on the period 1961-1969, but some findings are also available from years after 1969.

When the control basin method is used, the aim is to keep both basins unchanged throughout the research period , except for the treatment of the experimental area. In this case this was not quite possible. Before 1956 changes in the basins were insignificant but in 1956 some forest drainage and clear-cutting were carried out on both basins. The area drained in the Huhtisuo basin was 4% and in Latosuo 7%. Clear-cutting percentages were 12 and 9, respectively. Both draining and clear-cutting increase runoff (Mustonen and Seuna, 1971, Mustonen, 1965) but considering how small these percentages are it is concluded that the effects of these treatments can be largely eliminated. That is why they have not been taken into account in the computation of the runoff changes.

During the period from 1958 to 1970 the volume of growing stock increased in the Latosuo basin and decreased in Huhtisuo basin because of the differences in silvicultural treatment (Table 1). Because of these changes, the volumes of growing stock differed by 35 m^3/ha in 1970 compared with 1958. Felling in 1960-1961 formed 60% of the total felling in Huhtisuo after 1958 and the rest of the felling is evenly distributed during the period 1962-1970. Hence the average difference in tree stands were 28 m^3/ha during 1961-1969. It has been shown (Mustonen, 1965) that the decrease of 10 m^3/ha in growing stock causes an increase of 7.7 mm in annual runoff. So, for this reason, the average increase in annual runoff has been 22 mm.

I has not been possible to take the changes in the growing timber stock into account in any of the runoff quantities except annual runoff. However, there may be a slight effect eg in maximum spring runoff because of the changes in melting conditions.

The amount of water stored in the soil varies and the observed changes in runoff may be "too small" or "too big" in different years. However, it is impossible to make corrections in this respect due to the lack of soil moisture observations. On the other hand groundwater level and laboratory tests on the air space of the peat are available and also the settling of peat surface has been measured. The total settling during 1961-1969

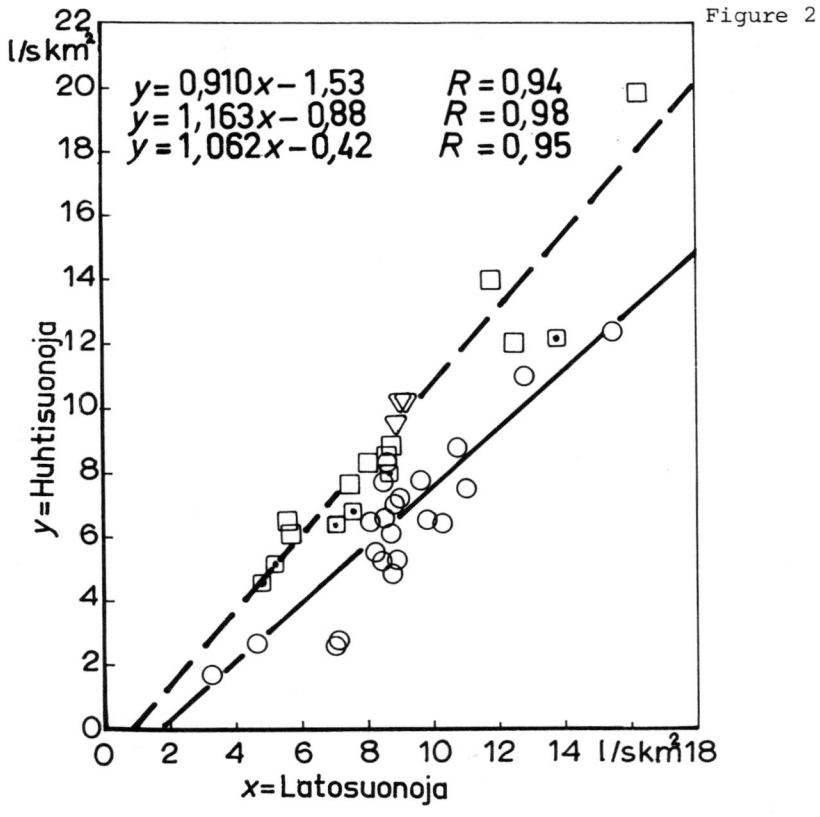

Figure 2 Correlation of mean annual runoff of research basins 1936-1957 (circles and full line) and in 1961-1969 (squares and broken line). Triangles indicate years 1958-1960, squares with dots years 1970-75. Equation 1: 1936-1957, 2: 1961-1969, 3: 1961-75.

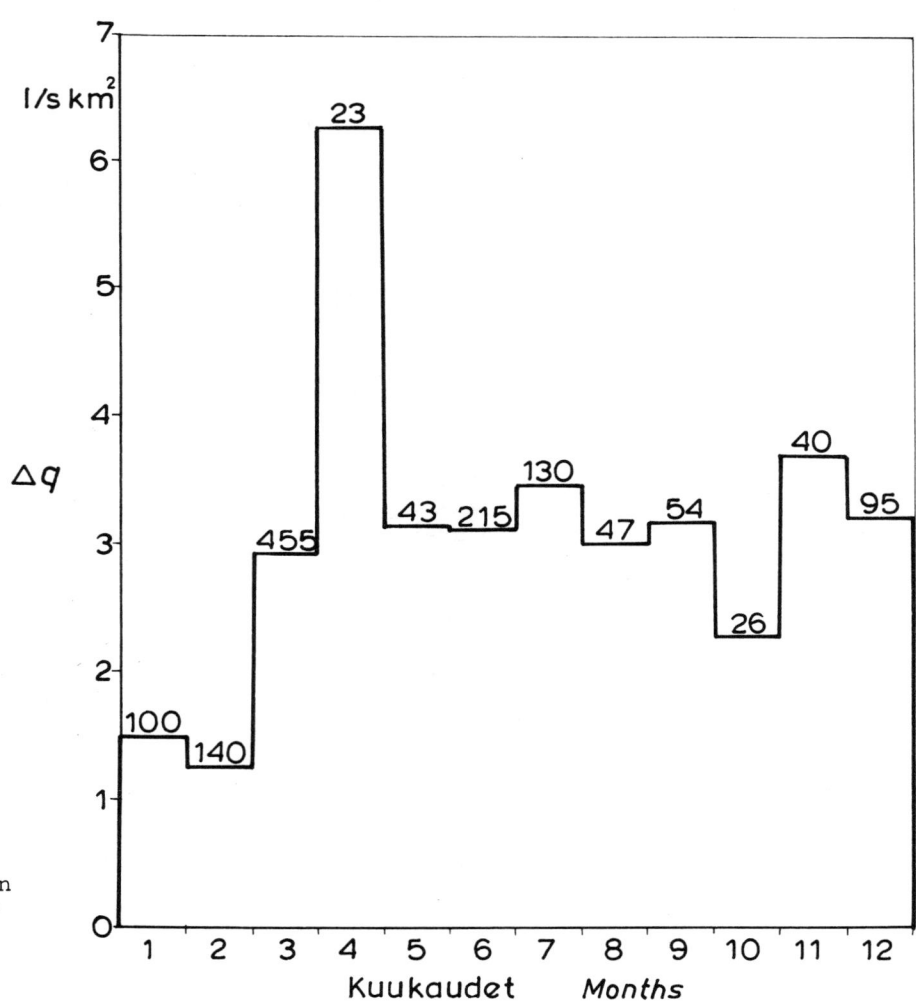

Figure 3 Increment of mean monthly runoff Δq caused by drainage in Huhtisuonoja. Figures above the columns indicate the increment in %

The hydrological effects of forest drainage

was 120 mm and the increase in the air space of the peat was 50 mm. So the total decrease in the water storage of the peatland has been 170 mm. Calculated for the whole catchment area and for one single year the depletion of the water storage contributed

$$\frac{0.40 \cdot 170}{9} = 8 \text{ mm to the annual runoff.}$$

As for the changes in the tree stands the effects of the soil water depletion have been taken into account only in the computation of annual runoff.

3.3.2.4 Results

3.3.2.4.1 Annual runoff. As a result of the draining of the forest all runoff quantities increased the variations in annual runoff being shown in Figure 2. The probable undrained runoff (y) in each year after drainage was estimated by entering the control basin runoff (x) of the year into the calibration period regression equation (y = 0.910 x - 1.53). The difference between the calculated undrained runoff and the actual measured runoff indicates the change in runoff. The average increase in 1961-1969 was 3.02 l/s km^2 or 95 mm/year. Thus the observed mean annual runoff was 43% greater than it would have been without draining (7.04 l/s km^2) and the increase is highly significant statistically. The effects of changes in growing stock and the depletion of soil water storage were discussed earlier. Taking these into account the net increase in runoff due to the decrease in the evaporation and transpiration was 95 - 8 - 22 = 65 mm/year on average. This is 29% of the mean "undrained" annual runoff during the treatment period. The decrease in evaporation and transpiration is obviously caused by the drop in the groundwater table and the drying of the upper part of the peat.

Later, when a new tree stand has grown on drained peatland, runoff begins to decrease again. According to preliminary studies the decrease in annual runoff will reach the level of statistical significance 15 years after drainage. However, such studies need to be continued for some years before the trend can be confirmed.

3.3.2.4.2 Monthly runoff. The runoff increased in all months due to drainage (Figure 3). A relatively large increase could be observed during low flow months in both winter and summer. The monthly runoff was statistically significant (at the 0,1% level) in February, March, June, July and August, and significant (at the 1% level) in January, May, September, November and December and almost significant (at the 5% level) in April and October.

3.3.2.4.3 Maximum runoff. Both spring and summer maximum runoff increased as a result of drainage (Figures 4 and 5). The increase was statistically significant in both cases. The spring maximum increased by 31% and the summer maximum by 131%, on average, as compared with "undrained" runoff. The increase in maximum runoffs was largely due to the ditches accelerating the flow. The flood lakes that normally formed on the natural peatland of the Huhtisuo type also disappeared and their buffering effect on runoff was eliminated. The increase in infiltration caused by drying of the surface layer of the peatland was rather slight. During heavy summer rains, in particular, the moisture deficit of the peat was filled at very early stages and the runoff peak was not reduced by increased infiltration. Thus the runoff caused by heavy rains increased most, in relative terms.

There was proof that during the drainage period spring runoff came 1 to 5 days earlier on average than before. This may be partly due to clear-cutting but it is mainly due to the drainage works. When a drained area is situated on the upper part of a river-basin it increases the flood peak for the reason mentioned above.

After 1969 the spring maximum runoff decreased to some extent compared with the control basin. This may be due to the coverage of young pines which may delay the melting of the snow, but the maximum runoff can vary greatly for other reasons, too. This decrease, however, has so far not become statistically significant.

3.3.2.4.4 Minimum runoff. The minimum runoff for both winter and summer increased markedly (Figure 6). The increase in both cases was statistically highly significant. Drainage made the Huhtisuo basin similar to some extent to the control basin, in terms of minimum runoff. This was largely because the ditches made flow possible in all seasons of the year. Before drainage there was only a short shallow natural channel on the lower part of the Huhtisuo basin. In addition, the main ditches reached the pervious mineral soil which improved

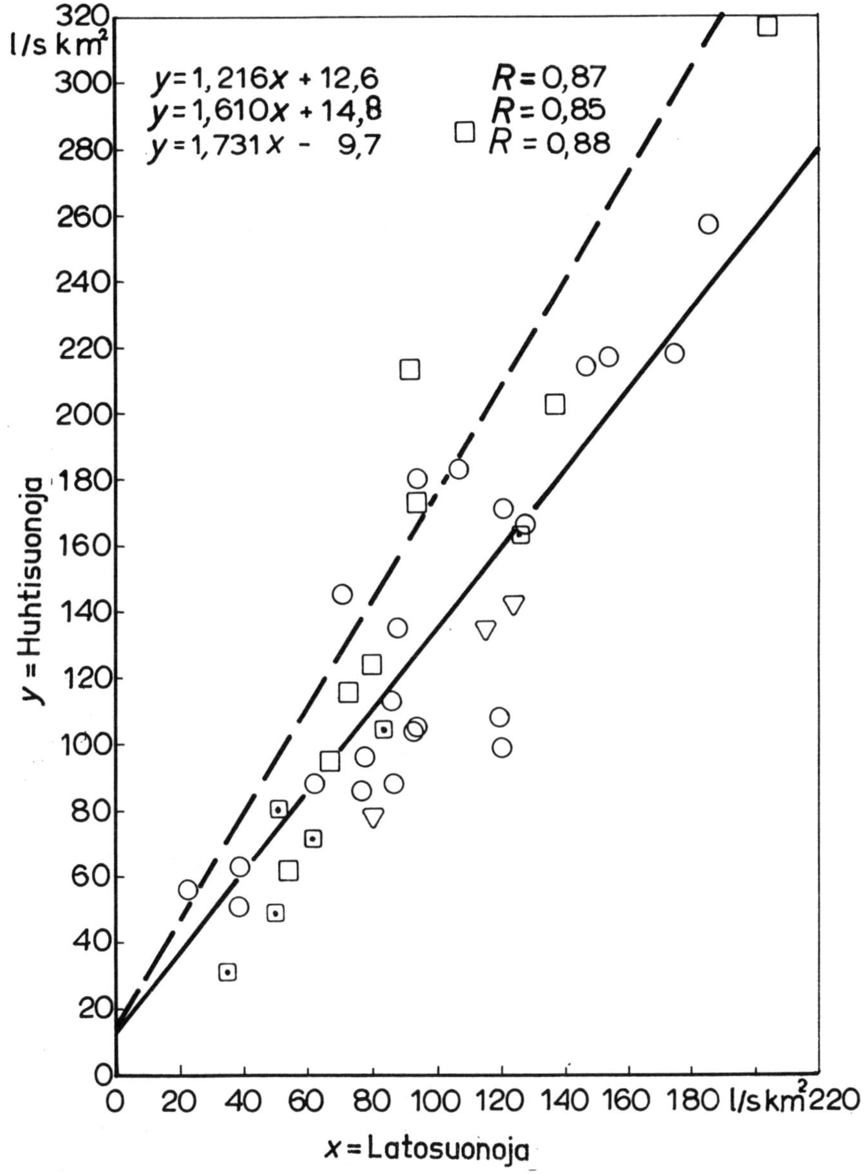

Figure 4 Correlation of spring maximum runoff Hq_w of research basins in 1936-1957 (circles and full line) and in 1961-1969 (squares and broken line). Triangles indicate years 1958-1960 and squares with dots years 1970-1975. Equation 1: 1936-1957, 2: 1961-69, 3: 1961-1975

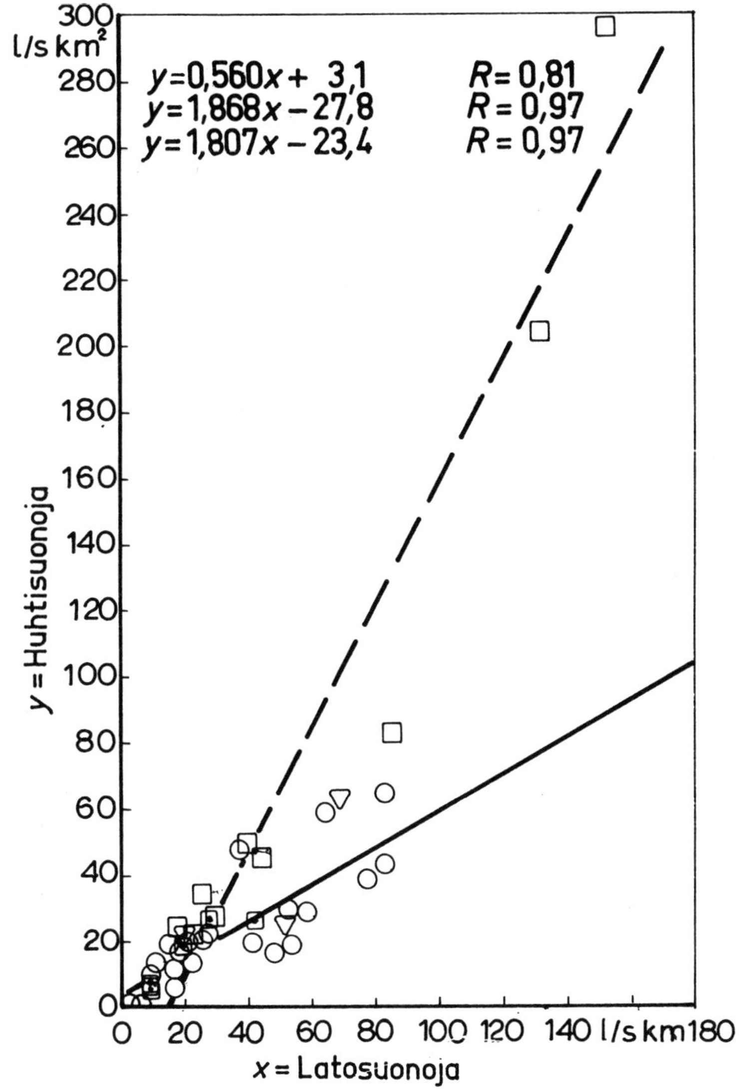

Figure 5 Correlation of summer maximum runoff Hq_s of research basins in 1936-1957 (circles and full line) and in 1961-1969 (squares and broken line). Triangles indicate years 1958-1960 and squares with dots years 1970-1975. Equation 1: 1936-1957, 2: 1961-1969, 3: 1961-1975

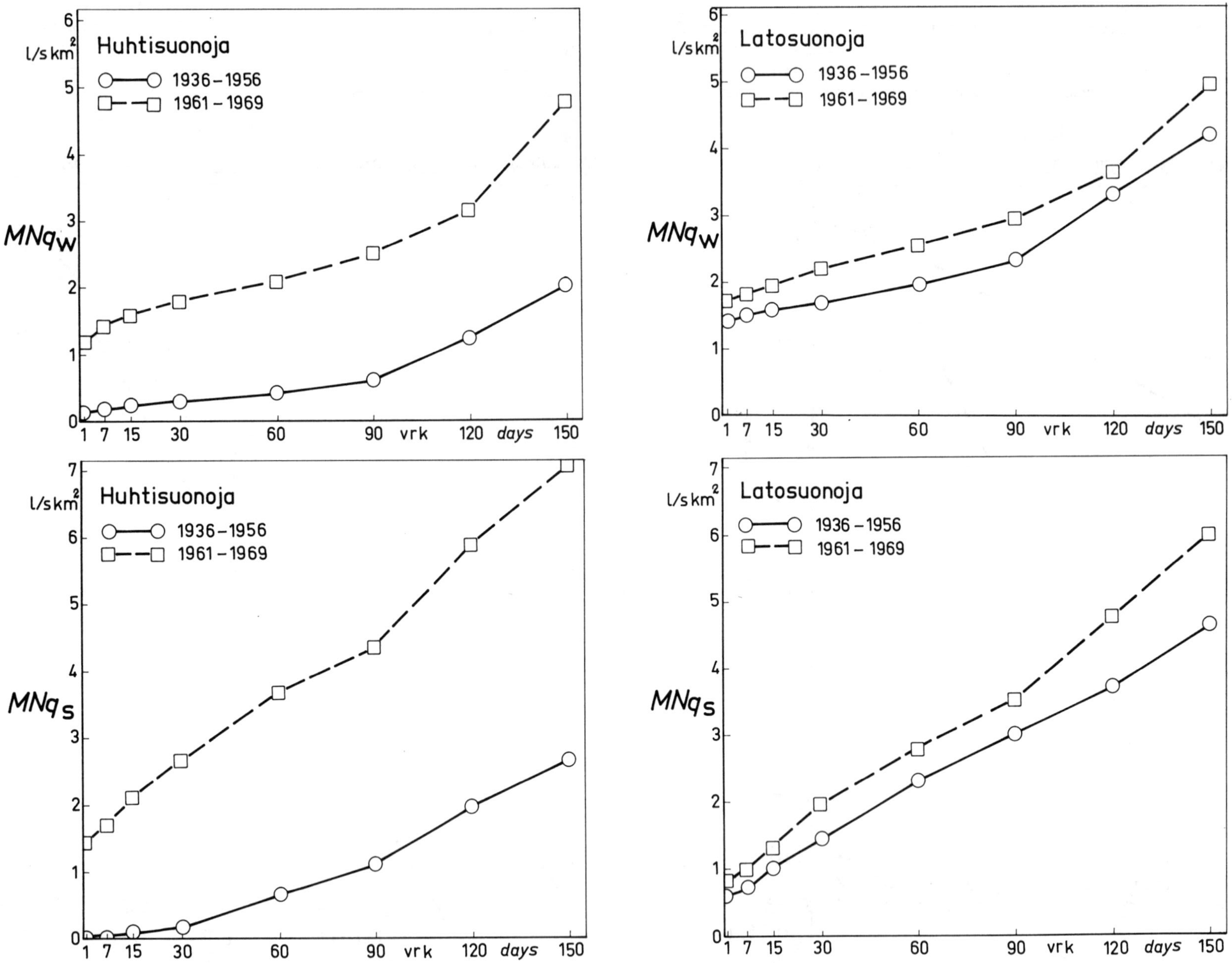

Figure 6 1-150 days winter (MNq$_w$) and summer (MNq$_s$) mean minimum runoff in research basins in 1936-1956 and 1961-1969

underground drainage and intensified the effect of the drains.

In the last few years the summer minimum runoff of Huhtisuo has been somewhat smaller than the "drained values" predicted from the regression curve. This may be due to increased evaporation and transpiration caused by the growth and coverage of the young tree stand mentioned above.

3.3.2.5 The representativeness of the results

In the light of the research carried out, it seems justified to suppose that same kind of influences can be expected after draining similar wet open bogs to the ones described in this investigation. Basic changes, (a) decrease in evaporation and transpiration due to the fall of the water table and the drying of the peat surface and (b) an acceleration of the flow caused by the drainage network are obvious in similar conditions. As a consequence annual runoff and maximum runoff can be expected to increase due to forest draining. However, in some cases the acceleration of the flow may result in a decrease in maximum runoff, if the drained area is situated in the downstream parts of the basin.

The observed increase in minimum runoff may be partly due to local circumstances. A coarse mineral soil under the peat layer was reached by ditches and a kind of underground drainage could have been caused. So in a basin with thick peat layers the effects may be different.

On wooded peat lands the situation appears different from open bog. The tree stand continues to transpire after drainage and the rate may even increase as soil moisture conditions become more favourable to tree growth. On wooded peat lands evaporation caused by interception is also an important form of water loss, and drainage does not, of course, influence interception. The increase in annual runoff from forested peat may, therefore, be smaller than from an open bog. Because snow melt is delayed due to the presence of the tree stand, the increase in spring maximum runoff from a wooded peat land may be smaller than from an open bog.

3.3.2.6 Accuracy

In this study the basin characteristics were determined by using maps and a point-line survey. The point-line survey comprised about 150 points in one basin. At each point the terrain type, bog type, soil type, land slope. ditches and the volume, distribution and coverage of the growing tree stock were surveyed. Every point represented 0,7% of the whole basin and because lines and points are fixed, statistical sampling was possible. It is impossible, however, to demonstrate the representativeness of the measuring points for the whole basin in all respects but no systematic errors are likely to be found in this method.

Regarding hydrological and meteorological observations, runoff was measured using weirs equipped with water level recorders. The accuracy of observation was ±2,5 mm, which means in terms of runoff ±5-8% for low flow periods, ±2-5% during average water levels and ±1-2% during floods. The rating curves were determined from measurements made with current meters, plastic bags and metal containers. Precipitation was observed by using 4 raingauges and 4 pluviographs. The water equivalent of snow was measured using 2 km snow courses with 50 points in the basin.

Groundwater level was measured by using about 50 groundwater tubes, and the tubes were levelled yearly. No soil moisture observations were available, giving rise to some doubts which were discussed earlier.

REFERENCES

Kovner, J.L. and Evans, T.C. 1954. A method for determining the minimum duration of watershed experiments. *Transactions American Geophysical Union,* 35, 608-612.

Mustonen, S.E. 1965. Effects of meteorologic and basin characteristics on runoff. English abstract. *Soil and Hydrotechnical Investigations 12,* Helsinki.

Mustonen, S.E. and Seuna, P. 1971. Influence of forest draining on the hydrology of peatlands. *Publications of the Water Research Institute 2,* Helsinki.

Mustonen, S.E. and Seuna, P. 1972. Influence of forest draining on the hydrology of open bog in Finland. The Hydrology of marsh-ridden areas. *IAHS Publication No 105 Proceedings of the Minsk Symposium,* 519-530.

The effect of arterial drainage on flood magnitude

3.3.3 THE EFFECT OF ARTERIAL DRAINAGE ON FLOOD MAGNITUDE
by T Bree and C Cunnane[1]

3.3.3.1 Introduction

The main purpose of an arterial drainage scheme is to improve main drainage channels so that overland flooding can be alleviated, thus bringing more land into agricultural production, as well as lessening inconvenience and hardship to the people affected by flooding. Arterial drainage schemes in Ireland are designed on a catchment basis. This means that the channel downstream of the points of major relief must be adequate, or be made adequate, to cater for the increased peak flow rates resulting from flood alleviation.

The works are designed so that the main channel capacity in agricultural areas is normally equal to a peak flow of a one to three year return period; the need to provide adequately for field drainage and water table management usually implies a higher standard in the flood carrying capacity of the minor channels. Works so designed not only reduce the frequency of flooding but also its extent and duration. Typically the duration of flooding and waterlogging may be reduced from periods of months to a matter of just a few days per year.

The physical works can be described as both intensive and extensive; intensive in that the channel cross-section may be increased in area by up to 100%, usually achieved by an increase in both width and depth, and extensive in that several hundred kilometres of channel in a large catchment may be involved, exclusive of minor field drains. As an example the River Maigue drainage scheme which was commenced in 1973 involves a total area of 100 000 ha of which 12 000 ha will benefit from the drainage works. The total length of channel being improved is 730 km and this involves the removal of $4,3 \times 10^6 m^3$ of material. About 1 300 bridges are affected by this work, some of them needing reconstruction, the remainder being underpinned. The duration of work is 8 years carried out by a workforce of about 300 men and 20 excavators. The total cost is about nine million pounds (sterling) expressed in 1978 terms.

Because of the elimination of flooded areas and the general improvement in the hydraulic efficiency of the channels, the response of a catchment is substantially modified by the drainage works. Therefore the pre-drainage hydrometric record cannot be used without modification as the basis for channel design. For this purpose O Kelly (1955) studied the flood producing characteristics of a number of Irish catchments which were relatively free of overland flooding, and design procedures based on his results have been developed. In this paper the effect of drainage works on the flood peak - return period (Q-T) relation is examined, while the effect of drainage works on the unit hydrograph is described later in another paper (Bree and Cunnane, 1979).

3.3.3.2 Climatic and hydrological regime

Ireland is an island lying off Western Europe between latitude $51\frac{1}{2}°$ and $55\frac{1}{2}°N$ and longitude $5\frac{1}{2}°$ and $10\frac{1}{2}°W$ and has an area of 84 000 square kilometres. Physically the country is saucer

---

[1] Office of Public Works, Dublin, Ireland

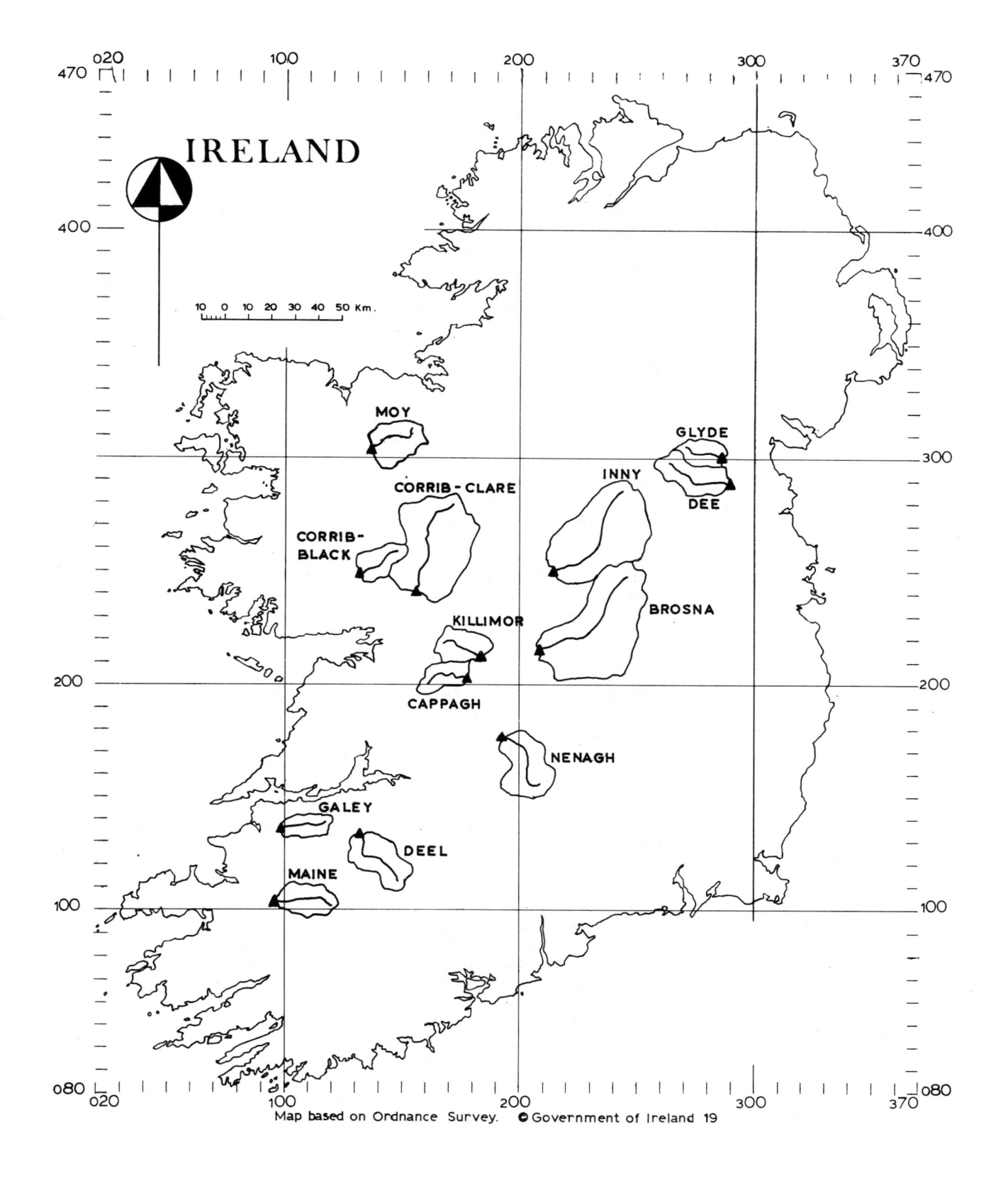

Figure 1   Location of study catchments

shaped with a raised maritime rim surrounding a flat interior central plain, a combination of factors which cause most rivers to have poor gradients frequently intercepted by lakes. This results in sluggish flow and poor channel conditions giving rise to prolonged flooding over wide areas.

The two major factors affecting the climate are the westerly atmospheric circulation of the middle latitudes and the proximity of the North Atlantic Ocean. Frontal systems and depressions are a feature of this westerly circulation and give a very variable climate. Although variable, the climate is not extreme; summer temperatures rarely exceed 30^{0}C while prolonged spells of sub zero temperatures are also rare; average annual rainfalls vary between 800 and 2 500 mm depending on location, but with an almost uniform distribution throughout the year. Flooding occurs mainly during November to March, although summer flooding is not unknown.

3.3.3.3 Hydrometric data and data on catchment characteristics

Since the enactment of legislation in 1945 (Government of Ireland, 1945) drainage works are carried out on a comprehensive catchment basis and the drainage authority (Office of Public Works) has been charged with the task of setting up hydrometric stations to provide data for design. While arterial drainage works have been executed in Ireland since 1842 none of the schemes prior to 1945 have supplied data suitable for this study. Catchments with suitable pre- and post-drainage data are shown on Figure 1 and listed in Table 1 where their main drainage characteristics are summarised. Table 2 gives the physical and climatic catchment characteristics and the years of hydrometric records available at the stations selected.

The catchment characteristics are defined in the Glossary at the end of this chapter. Note that the catchment area to the gauging point is usually less than that of the entire drainage area. In three cases the position of the gauging station was changed to a nearby but better location for the post-drainage record and in these cases two sets of catchment characteristic values are shown.

3.3.3.4 Flood frequency analysis

For this the partial duration series model, also known as the peaks over a threshold model, was used. The model considers a series of flood peaks in excess of an arbitrary threshold q_o. The peaks are considered to be statistically independent and identically distributed. The exponential distribution:

$$PR(Q \leqslant q) = F(q) = 1 - \exp\left|-(q-q_o)/\beta\right| \tag{1}$$

has been found satisfactory for Irish rivers. If λ is the average number of peaks exceeding q_o per year then the T year flood is

$$Q_T = q_o + \beta \log_e (\lambda T) \tag{2}$$

In this study flood peaks were extracted from the hydrometric records to provide a series of length $M = 2N$ where N is the number of years of record. This procedure fixes $\lambda = M/N = 2$ in such samples while q_o and β have to be estimated from the sample. Larger samples corresponding to a larger λ could be used, but the exponential assumption has been found to be violated in such samples.

Arbitrary but consistent rules were used to eliminate from the series peaks which occur very close together in time. Thus both of a pair of neighbouring peaks are included only if (a) they are separated by more than $3t_p$, where t_p is an average time to peak value, and (b) the flow between them drops to below 0.66 q_p, where q_p is the value of the first peak.

The unbiassed, maximum likelihood estimators of q_o and β are expressed in terms of $\bar{q}$, the mean of the series of M values, and q_{min} the minimum of the series

$$\hat{\beta} = M(\bar{q} - q_{min})/(M-1) \tag{3}$$

$$\hat{q}_o = q_{min} - \hat{\beta}/M \tag{4}$$

These, along with the fixed value of $\lambda = M/N$, are used in equation (2) to estimate Q_T. The derivation of these estimators is given in Flood Studies Report (1975) where the standard error of estimate is also derived

Table 1 Drainage characteristics of study catchments

ARTERIAL DRAINAGE SCHEME			AREA OF BENEFITTED LAND km²	LENGTH OF CHANNEL		LENGTH OF EMBANKMENTS FORMED km	QUANTITY OF MATERIAL REMOVED m³
RIVER	COMMENCED	COMPLETED	CATCHMENT AREA km²	MAIN km	TRIB. km		
BROSNA	MAY '48	DEC '55	1252·1	348·8	144·8	498·9	95·0	4 250 000
GLYDE / DEE	JUN '50	NOV '57	736·9	106·3	87·7	338·8	13·8	2 500 000
CORRIB-CLARE	APR '54	DEC '64	1044·0	303·3	257·5	611·5	—	6 000 000
NENAGH	APR '55	DEC '60	323·7	27·0	59·5	86·9	2·0	1 100 000
MAINE	FEB '59	DEC '63	344·7	47·1	32·2	193·1	90·1	3 265 250
INNY	JUN '60	DEC '68	1173·5	202·8	74·0	737·1	11·3	5 750 000
BROADMEADOW	JUN '61	DEC '64	173·2	29·7	45·9	109·4	—	1 100 000
KILLIMOR / CAPPAGH	JUN '62	DEC '68	390·5	51·1	50·2	264·2	3·62	2 057 000
DEEL	DEC '62	DEC '68	493·3	48·1	56·3	246·2	—	2 341 750
MOY	APR '60	JUL '71	2088·1	239·1	83·0	1118·5	—	11 230 000
CORRIB-BLACK	JUN '67	DEC '72	983·3	78·7	60·7	164·6	—	944 500

Table 2 Catchment characteristics

RIVER	GAUGING STATION LOCATION	NUMBER	HYDROMETRIC RECORDS Pre-drainage	Post-drainage	Remarks	Area km²	Main Stream Length km	Channel Slope m/km	Median Overland Slope ᵐ/₀₀	Stream Frequency j/km²	Soil Index	R smd mm	Annual Average Rainfall mm	Lake Index
DEEL	GRANGE	2412	1954-61	1967-76		359	45·3	1·70	97	1·35	0·470	40·6	1230	1·0
NENAGH	ANNABEG (pre)	2529	1950-55	1957-76		318	33·7	5·20	253	1·17	0·302	36·50	1043	1·0
	CLARIANNA (post)					301	29·0	5·20	253	1·21	0·302	36·50	1043	1·0
INNY	BALLYMAHON	2621	1954-60	1968-74	Gauge not operating in 1974/75.	1067	86·9	0·23	71	0·73	0·274	32·80	916	1·706
CLARE	COROFIN	3004	1951-58	1964-72 & 1975-76		695	57·9	0·99	32	0·43	0·225	37·14	1200	1·0
DEE	DRUMGOOLESTOWN	0623	1939-51	1958-76	Daily read gauge to 1947.	30·2	41·8	2·72	180	1·04	0·327	31·90	924	1·288
GLYDE	MANSFIELDSTOWN	0621	1940-50	1955-76	Daily read gauge to 1955.	314	38·6	1·84	168	0·23	0·327	31·90	924	1·650
BROSNA	FERBANE	2506	1939-49	1955-75		1027	56·9	0·89	50	0·87	0·382	30·50	919	1·168
MOY	CLOONACANNANA	3410	1952-65	1972-76		488	34·2	2·58	102	0·82	0·440	39·10	1317	1·021
BLACK	OWER	3002	1952-66	1974-76	Only 2yrs post dr.	178	22·7	1·20	58	0·30	0·150	43·53	1100	1·0
MAINE	RIVERVILLE	2203	1953-60	1962-76	1947/52 record omitted because of rating. Also 3yrs omitted post dr. because of water level faults.	272	16·5	6·28	473	1·83	0·457	36·20	1252	1·0
KILLIMOR	MOAT (pre)	2520	1955-63	1968-76		206	24·1	1·69	65	0·51	0·232	33·40	980	1·0
	KILLEEN (post)					197	23·0	2·43	65	0·54	0·232	33·40	980	1·0
CAPPAGH	CAPPAGH (pre)	2519	1955-62	1966-76		131	17·7	9·19	183	1·18	0·150	35·70	1103	1·0
	CONICAR (post)					125	15·0	9·85	183	0·86	0·150	35·70	1103	1·0
GALEY	INCH	2301	Available but bad rating.	1959-76	Pre dn over-bank flow in all floods, rating extends only to bank full.	196	34·2	4·76	189	1·59	0·454	33·02	1100	1·0

The effect of arterial drainage on flood magnitude

$$\text{se }(Q_T) = \frac{\hat{\beta}}{M} \left(\frac{(1 - \log_e \lambda T)^2}{M - 1} + (\log_e \lambda T)^2 \right)^{\frac{1}{2}} \tag{5}$$

Table 3 gives estimated β and Q_3 values for pre- and post-drainage samples, all with $\lambda = 2$. The latter are included because Q_3 is a commonly used channel design value. Probability plots were also prepared from each sample. Ranked sample values

$$q_{(1)} \leq q_{(2)} \leq \ldots q_{(i)} \ldots \leq q_{(M)} \tag{6}$$

were associated with plotting positions

$$y_{(1)} \leq y_{(2)} \leq \ldots y_{(i)} \ldots \leq y_{(M)} \tag{7}$$

expressed as values of the exponential distribution reduced variate. This variate has a distribution function given by equation (1) with

$$q_o = 0 \quad \text{and} \quad \beta = 1$$

The ith plotting position is

$$y_i = E(y_{(i)}) = \sum_{j=1}^{i} \frac{1}{M + 1 - j} \tag{8}$$

which is the expected value of the ith order statistic in samples of size M from the exponential reduced variate, (Cunnane, 1978). These plotting positions correspond in principal with those expressed as probability values and derived by the Gringorten (1963) formula:

$$F_i = \frac{i - 0.44}{N + 0.12} \tag{9}$$

although the correspondence is not numerically exact, as these F_i values are but an approximation to the probability values $F = 1 - \exp(-y_i)$ obtained via equation (8).

An example of such a probability plot for the River Nenagh is shown in Figure 2, in which the fitted line is given by equation (2) in expanded form

$$Q_T = (q_o + \beta \log_e \lambda) + \beta \log_e T \tag{10}$$

In all cases the post-drainage Q-T relation lies above its pre-drainage counterpart. This is also seen in Table 3 in respect of Q_3 values.

3.3.3.5   Testing the statistical significance of the increases
It is possible that the pre- and post-drainage records on the same catchments could differ because of the random nature of the data, rather than because of any causitive effect of the arterial drainage works. The hypothesis of no difference was tested in three ways (a) using $\hat{Q}_3$ values alone, (b) using β values, the slope of the probability plot and (c) using the entire sample in a likelihood ratio test.

3.3.3.5.1   (a) $\hat{Q}_3$ values. The differences $\hat{Q}_3' - \hat{Q}_3$ for each of the 12 records available were tested to see if their mean differed significantly from zero. These have a mean value 30.4 and a standard deviation s = 23.1. The test statistic is $t = (\hat{Q}_3' - \hat{Q}_3)\sqrt{12}/s = 4.55$ which is significantly large at the 1% significance level. This test is equivalent to a two-way analysis of variance test where the intercatchment effect is removed.

However, the effect of catchment size is not entirely removed from this comparison because the differences themselves also reflect catchment size. This can be removed by considering the percentage increase. Testing the mean% increase against zero in a one sided test gives a critical region $\{t_{11} \geq 4.0\}$ at the 1% significance level. In this case $t_{11} = 6.48$ as shown in Table 3 and this firmly rejects the hypothesis of no difference.

3.3.3.5.2   (b) $\hat{\beta}$ values. The mean of the differences in the estimated $\hat{\beta}$ values is 5.34 with a standard deviation of 6.96. The test statistic for the hypothesis of no difference is $t = 2.66$ which is not significant at the 1% level. The change in the relation $Q_T = q_o + \beta \log_e \lambda T$ after drainage is therefore due to a change in q_o rather than β. This means that

RIVER	GAUGING STATION	Pre-drainage m³/s	Post-drainage m³/s	Increase $Q_3 - Q'_3$	% Increase	Pre-drainage β	Post-drainage β'	Differences	% $\frac{\beta_{post}}{\beta_{pre}}$
Deel	Grange	81.3	134.3	53.0	65	8.16	19.12	10.96	234
Nenagh	Clarianna/Annabeg	28.5	62.0	33.5	118	6.67	12.40	5.73	186
Inny	Ballymahon	62.9	64.7	1.8	3	15.88	11.95	-3.93	75
Corrib-Clare	Corofin	61.0	96.7	35.7	59	14.07	12.62	-1.45	90
Dee	Drumgoolestown	25.9	40.6	14.7	57	4.06	7.08	3.02	174
Glyde	Mansfieldstown	21.4	25.9	4.5	21	3.59	4.93	1.34	137
Brosna	Ferbane	73.3	100.2	26.9	37	14.79	13.80	-0.99	93
Moy	Cloonacannana	141.1	221.7	80.6	57	29.39	38.66	9.27	132
Corrib-Black	Ower	17.9	28.5	10.6	59	3.51	10.05	6.54	286
Maine	Riverville	95.2	149.0	53.8	57	10.18	29.91	19.73	294
Killmor	Killeen/Moat	28.6	58.3	29.7	104	5.09	18.29	13.20	359
Cappagh	Conicar/Cappagh	32.2	51.8	19.6	61	8.40	9.11	0.71	108

Mean: 30.4, 58, 5.34
Standard deviation: 23.1, 31, 6.96
Test statistic t_{11}:
$\frac{30.4 - 0.0}{23.1/\sqrt{12}} = 4.55$
$\frac{58 - 0.0}{31/\sqrt{12}} = 6.48$
$\frac{5.34 - 0.0}{6.96/\sqrt{12}} = 2.66$

Table 3 Flood characteristics

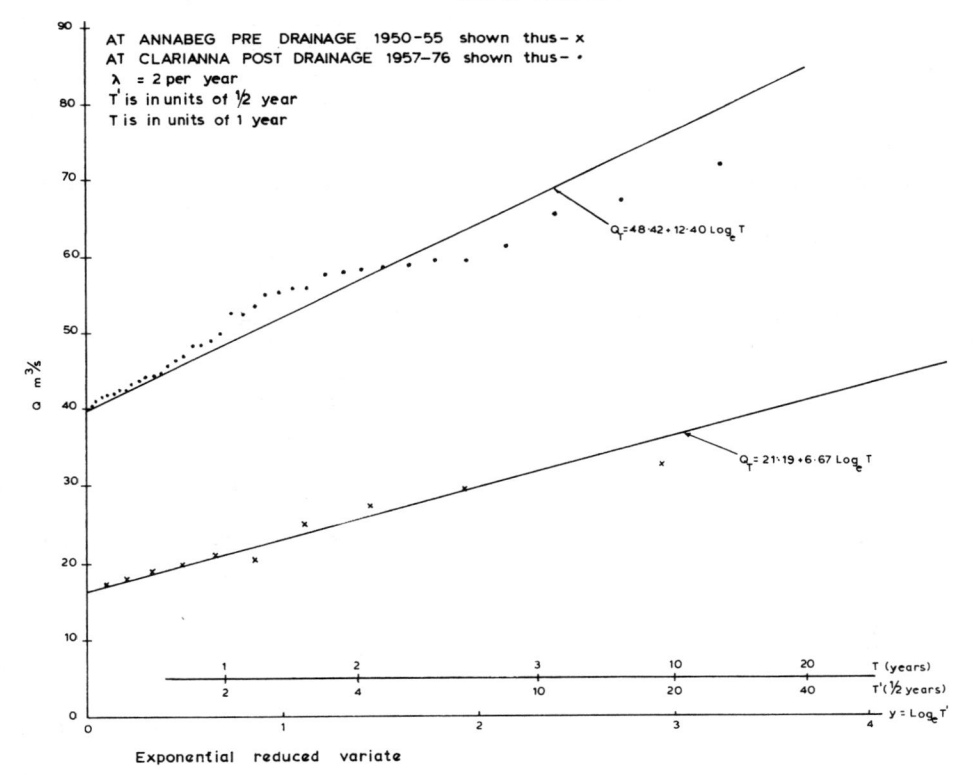

Figure 2 Probability plot for River Nenagh before and after drainage

although the flood peaks are increased, their variance is not changed from pre- to post-drainage.

3.3.3.5.3 (c) Entire record. Let x_i ($i = 1, M_1$) be the pre-drainage flood peaks from the exponential distribution (q_0, β) and let z_i ($i = 1, M_2$) be the post-drainage peaks with parameters q_0' and β'. The hypothesis to be tested, denoted H_0, is that $q_0' = q_0$ and $\beta' = \beta$. The likelihood ratio test is based on a statistic C which is the ratio of the likelihood of the sample under the alternative hypothesis H_1 to the likelihood under the null hypothesis H_0. The critical region will be denoted by $\{C \geq c\}$ where c is some numerical value. As no particular values of the parameters are specified a priori, the likelihood function values used in the ratio are taken as the maximum values over all possible values of parameters. Then the critical region is

$$C = \frac{\max_{H_1} L(x_i, z_i \mid q_0, \beta, q_0', \beta')}{\max_{H_0} L(x_i, z_i \mid q_0, \beta, q_0', \beta')} \geq c$$

This expression can be simplified to

$$C' = (M_1 + M_2) \log_e \left| \frac{M_1 \bar{x} + M_2 \bar{z}}{M_1 + M_2} - \min(x_{min}, z_{min}) \right| - M_1 \log_e (\bar{x} - x_{min})$$

$$- M_2 \log_e (\bar{z} - z_{min}) \geq c' \tag{11}$$

In order to find c' the distribution of C' must be known. It has been found that this depends on M_1 and M_2 only but in a manner which is not easily handled analytically. The distribution of C' was therefore obtained by Monto Carlo methods and the critical value c' was found separately for each catchment being tested, based in each case on the appropriate values of M_1 and M_2, the length of the pre- and post-drainage series respectively. These values of c' for $\alpha = 0.01$ and the calculated values for each catchment are shown in Table 4, where it is seen that in all but one case the null hypothesis is rejected, showing that the difference between pre- and post-drainage Q-T relations really is statistically significant. In the case where H_0 is not rejected, it should be noted that the post-drainage record is only two years long.

3.3.3.5.4 (d) Split record tests. The results of the last section show that post-drainage flood peaks of a given return period exceed their pre-drainage counterparts by an amount which is significantly large in comparison to the random variation inherent in the values themselves. There may be a cause for this, other than arterial drainage effects, and an obvious one is that of climate, ie increased post-drainage flood peaks might be due to wetter, more flood producing weather having occurred in the post-drainage than in the pre-drainage period.

One method of assessing this on any catchment is to split the record of an adjoining catchment, which was in an unaltered condition throughout the period in question, into two portions corresponding to the pre- and post-drainage portions respectively of the drained catchment. This has been done for a small number of cases, one of which is shown in Figure 3. One is on the Brosna at Ferbane whose post-drainage record is split into two parts corresponding to the pre- and post-drainage records on the Killimor river. It can be seen that the later period actually gives a lower Q-T relation than the earlier one in contrast to the increase observed on the Killimor.

3.3.3.6 Flood prediction from catchment characteristics

Relations between mean annual flood, $\bar{Q}$, and catchment characteristics were published in the Flood Studies Report (1975). Two six variable formulas were given

$$\bar{Q} = a.X \tag{12}$$

Where: $X = A^{0.94} F_s^{0.27} G^{1.23} R_{smd}^{1.03} S^{0.16} W^{-0.85}$

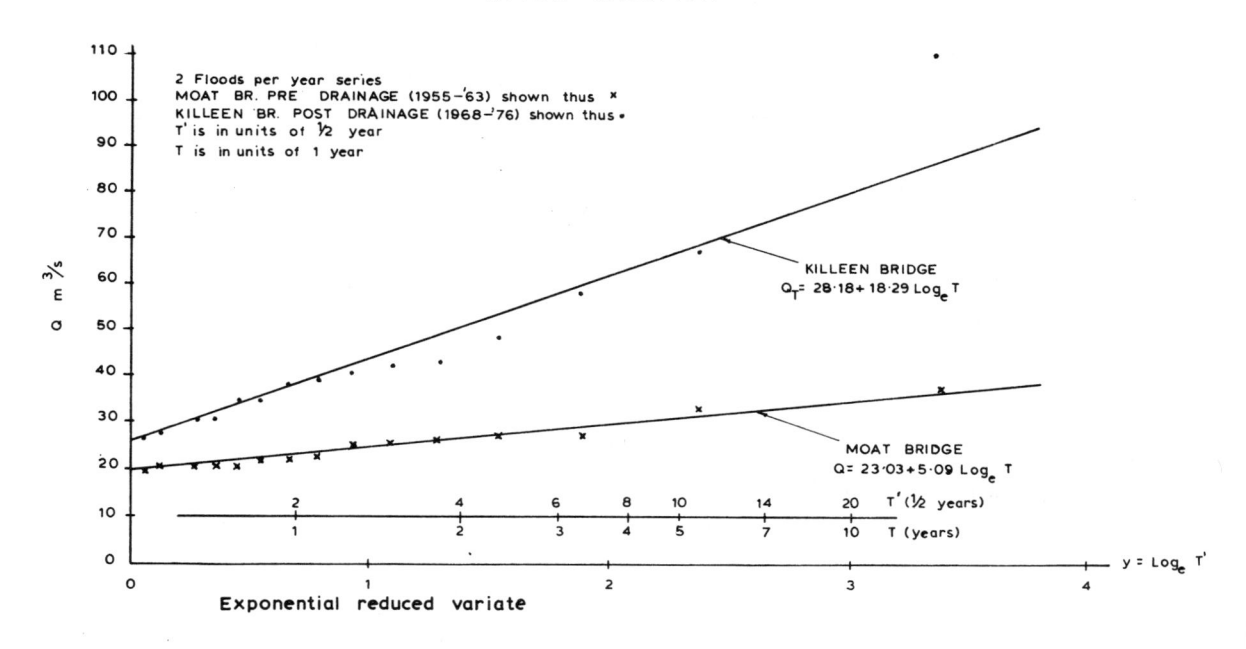

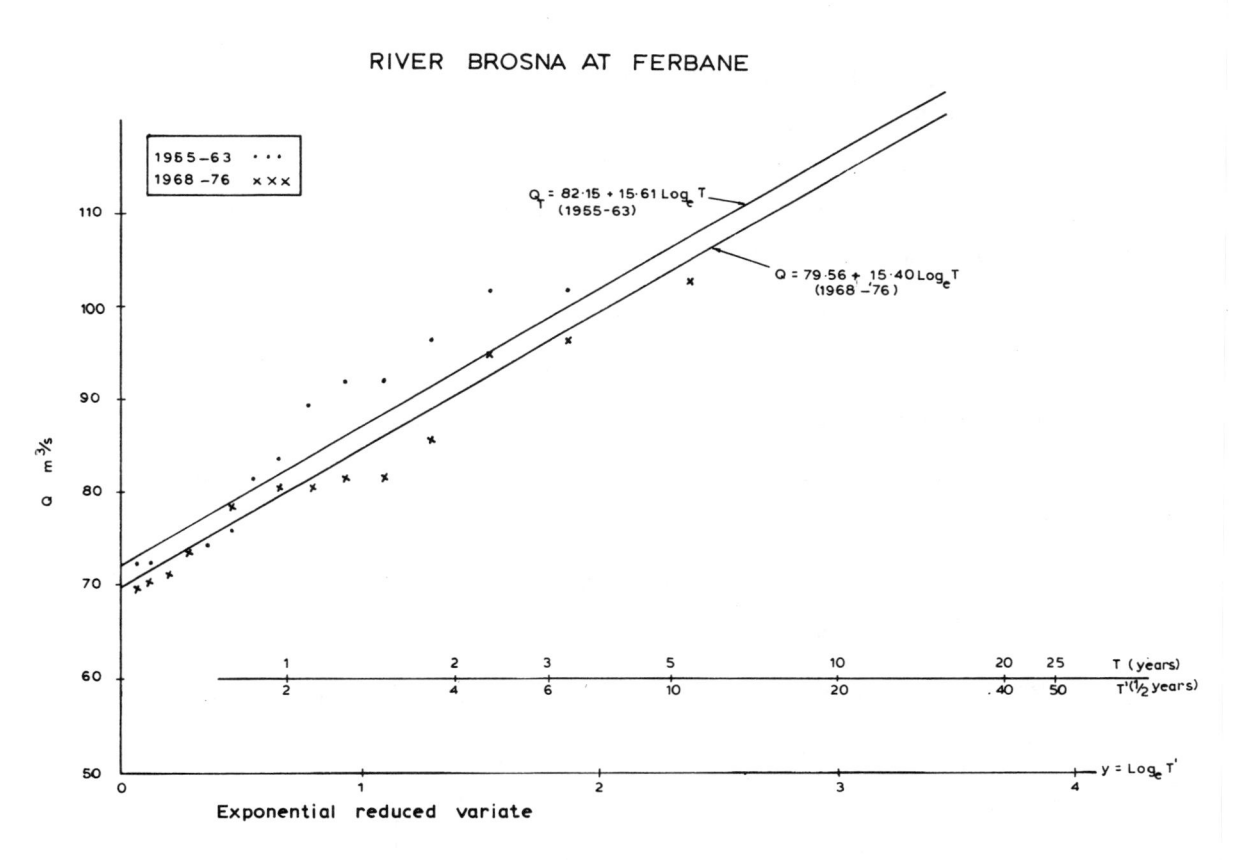

Figure 3   Split record test results

Table 4 Critical values of statistic C at 1% significance level and observed values of C in likelihood ratio test of difference between entire pre- and post-drainage Q-T relations

River	Gauging Station	M = No of pre-drainage peaks	M = No of post-drainage peaks	1% Rejection region C > c	Observed value of C
Deel	Grange Br	14	18	6.2	30.94
Nenagh	Clarianna/Annabeg	10	38	5.7	48.95
Inny	Ballymahon	12	12	6.2	7.15
Clare	Corofin	14	18	5.9	32.07
Dee	Drumgoolestown	24	36	6.1	43.42
Glyde	Mansfieldstown	20	42	5.9	17.70
Brosna	Ferbane	20	40	6.1	52.01
Moy	Cloonacannana	26	8	5.9	14.74
Black	Ower Br	28	4	7.1	2.64
Maine	Riverville	14	22	6.8	20.42
Killimor	Killeen Br/Moat Br	16	16	6.0	14.81
Cappagh	Conicar/Cappagh Br	14	20	6.2	28.19

Split records

Brosna	Ferbane	16	16	6.0	2.60
Feale	Listowel	8	30	6.0	5.67

Table 5 Pre-drainage and post drainage $\bar{Q}$, Y and X values for the study catchments

RIVER	GAUGING STATION	PRE-DRAINAGE $\bar{Q}_{pre}$	Y by 10^5	X by 10^{-3}	POST-DRAINAGE $\bar{Q}_{post}$	Y by 10^{-5}	X by 10^{-3}
1	2	3	4	5	6	7	8
Deel	Grange	77.1	2.277	5.337	124.3	2.277	5.337
Nenagh	Annabeg/Clarianna	25.0	1.124	2.671	55.6	1.097	2.606
Inny	Ballymahon	54.7	0.904	2.399	58.5	0.904	2.399
Clare	Corofin	53.7	1.224	2.470	90.1	1.224	2.470
Dee	Drumgoolestown	23.8	0.741	1.795	36.9	0.741	1.795
Glyde	Mansfieldstown	19.5	0.477	1.202	23.3	0.477	1.202
Brosna	Ferbane	65.5	2.886	6.758	93.0	2.886	6.758
Moy	Cloonacannana	125.8	2.882	5.799	201.5	2.882	5.799
Black	Ower	16.1	0.182	0.458	23.3	0.182	0.458
Maine	Riverville	89.9	2.442	4.723	133.4	2.442	4.723
Killimor	Moat/Killeen	26.0	0.402	0.893	48.7	0.386	0.861
Cappagh	Cappagh/Conicar	27.8	0.271	0.561	47.0	0.245	0.499
Galey	Inch	—	—	—	153.1	1.378	2.884
ΣY_i^2 or ΣX_i^2 / $\Sigma Y_i \bar{Q}_i$ or $\Sigma X_i \bar{Q}_i$		32.38 x 10^{10} / 1159.18 x 10^5 / b=0.00036	155.46 x 10^6 / 2451.31 x 10^3 / a=0.0158		34.19 x 10^{10} / 1965.46 x 10^5 / b=0.00057	162.93 x 10^6 / 4210.27 x 10^3 / a=0.0258	

and

$$\overline{Q} = b.Y \qquad (13)$$

Where: $Y = A^{0.95} F_s^{0.22} G^{1.18} R^{-1.05} S^{0.19} W^{-0.93}$

The multipliers a and b included in that Report were estimated for Ireland from the data of 112 catchments, about 10% of which had been drained. The values a = 0.0172 and b = 0.00042 were found. These equations were recalibrated for pre- and post-drainage conditions by finding new values for a and b. These were obtained by least squares by solving

$$\frac{\partial}{\partial a} \left\{ \sum_{i=1} (\overline{Q}_i - ax_i)^2 \right\} = 0$$

which gives

$$a = \Sigma \, \overline{Q} x_i / \Sigma x_i^2$$

and similarly for b. The summation was over 12 catchments pre-drainage and 13 catchments post-drainage. The values so obtained, see Table 5, are

a = 0.0158, b = 0.00036; Pre-drainage   (14)

a = 0.0258, b = 0.00057; Post-drainage   (15)

These show increases in a and b of 63% and 58% respectively.

3.3.3.7 Discussion of results

Study of pre- and post-drainage records on 12 catchments show that drainage works cause an increase in Q_T; the value of Q_3 being increased by approximately 60%. The change in the Q-T relation appears as a shift in the origin of the discharge values with no change in the variance of the flood peaks. Statistical tests show that these increases are significantly large in comparison with the random variation inherent in the data themselves. In addition split record tests, although neither extensive or exhaustive, show that the increase noted could not reasonably be accounted for by changes in the flood producing characteristics of the weather.

Seven of the catchments show a percentage increase in $\hat{Q}_3$ of between 57% and 65% with a mean of 59% for these seven, while two give increases of over 100% and three give increases of considerably less than 59%, being 3, 21 and 37%. These latter three, the Inny, the Glyde and the Brosna, all have lakes in their catchments, with the percentage of their catchments draining through them being 70.6%, 65% and 16.8% respectively. These percentages are inversely proportional to the percentage increase observed in $\hat{Q}_3$. However, there is an anomaly among these lakey catchments because 28.8% of the Dee's catchment flows through a lake, but nevertheless it shows a 57% increase in $\hat{Q}_3$. The two catchments which gave high percentage increases, Nenagh and Killimor, are not very similar and certainly prior to drainage, there was no evidence to suggest that they would produce similar results. The Nenagh, while quite steep, had a very sluggish flow before drainage, while the Killimor which is quite flat, had a fairly bouncy pre-drainage hydrograph.

Acknowledgement

This contribution is presented with the permission of the Chief Engineer and the Commissioners of Public Works, Dublin, Ireland.

REFERENCES

Bree, T. and Cunnane, C. 1979. Effect of arterial drainage works on the unit hydrograph. *Paper submitted to Leningrad Symposium*.

Cunnane, C. 1978. Unbiassed plotting positions - a review. *J of Hydrology*, 37, 205-22.

References

Flood Studies Report 1975. Natural Environment Research Council, London. Vol I, Chapter 4.

Government of Ireland 1945. "Arterial Drainage Act", Government Publications Office.

Gringorten, I.I. 1963. A plotting rule for extreme probability paper. *Trans Am Geophys Union*, 68, 813-814.

O Kelly, J.J. 1955. The employment of unit hydrographs to determine the flows of Irish arterial drainage channels. Proc Instn Civ Eng, 4, 365-412.

Glossary - symbol definitions

A	catchment area, km^2
C'	likelihood ratio test statistic
F_i ($i = 1, 2, \ldots m$)	plotting position as probability value
F_s	stream frequency, junctions/km^2 as measured on 1:25000 map
G	runoff coefficient ($0.10 \leq G \leq 0.50$) based on soil type
L	main stream length, km
M	number of peaks in series
N	number of years in series
Q	flood peak variate
q	flood peak value
q_o	threshold value
$\bar{Q}$	mean of annual maximum flood series
$\bar{R}$	average annual rainfall, mm
R_{smd}	1 day rainfall of 5 year return period, corrected for average soil moisture deficit
S	channel slope between points at 10% and 85% of stream length from the gauging station
T	return period, years
t	student test statistic
W	Lake index = 1 + fraction of catchment draining through a lake
y	exponential reduced variate
y_i ($i = 1, 2, \ldots m$)	plotting position as reduced variate value
β	parameter of exponential distribution
λ	average number of peaks exceeding q_o per year

Chapter 3.4

3.4 STREAM FLOW REGULATION
   by B N Murthy[1]

Man's development of water resources has resulted in great economic and social benefits by providing a favourable environment for agriculture, for industry and for housing. These development schemes interfere in some way or other with the natural balance, and become potential sources of various problems. There has been increased use of river water and groundwater and their regulation brings forth general changes in the environment at a much faster rate than hitherto envisaged (IHP, 1975).

The changes in hydrological regime of river basins are primarily caused by reservoirs and dams, irrigation and drainage and changes in the land use practices and river bed modifications (IHP, 1975). In order to even out the vagaries of nature, reservoirs are built to impound water so that excess water available at certain times is stored and utilised at other times when natural flows become insufficient.

The natural hydrological regime of river basins is becoming more and more transformed into a man-influenced and controlled regime.

Stream channel control and regulation provide deep water in the river channel for navigation, increase the runoff of flood waters, or confine them with the restricted limits in the channel. Impounding dams or reservoirs contribute to stream channel control by restricting the size of the flood flows and increasing low water flows. A large portion of the major rivers are now extensively affected by channel control works of one type or another. The principal channel control methods are canalization of natural rivers by barrages, dams, with locks to pass boats or barges, open channel regulation by training dykes, jetties, or wing dams to deflect the channel into a more desirable alignment.

River regulation by means of dams will alter the frequency and magnitude of flood flows and also the mean flows. It is estimated that the increased regulation will result in a slight decrease in the total stream flow of about 3 to 5 per cent and may have a significant long term influence on the global hydrological and the related geophysical system. Further, the flow regulation influences the climatic conditions by transformation of air masses over the reservoir and such changes may be expected within 10 to 15 km around the reservoir depending on its size. In the case of large lakes, all meteorological conditions including atmospheric precipitation are changed to some extent locally (Butorini, 1971).

Reduction of flood damage may benefit downstream regions remote from a reservoir as well as its adjacent areas. The impoundment has economic effects on downstream agriculture, fisheries and public health. Due to control, there will be no longer flood irrigation and the availability of nutrient sediment to the fields. Lacking perennial irrigation, the fields may now require additional use of fertilizer. The increased use of artificial fertilizers may in turn pollute the water and soil (Murthy, 1976).

The reservoirs often disturb the regime of groundwater levels along its periphery and in surrounding areas by infiltration etc. Such newly created or augmented groundwater can provide for supplementary irrigation on the lands bordering the reservoirs. The rise in

---

[1] Damodar Valley Corporation, PO Maithon Dam, Dist Dhanbad (Bihar), India

water level along the shore line would affect the shore soil ecosystem. It is possible that the process of gleying and swamping might also develop and such alteration of the soils affects the development of forests.

Impounding dams or reservoirs contribute to channel control by restricting the size of the flood flows and increasing low flows. Sometimes, flood control is also done by constructing an embankment or levees.

As levees or embankments have been used extensively since the start of history, they certainly have a few inherent merits that cannot be surpassed by other methods of flood protection. For example, embankments with proper drainage are only the answer for protecting low lands along the river course which may be very valuable commercially. Other drastic measures like flood detention, channel improvements etc in most cases are beyond consideration. The principles involved in flood protection by embankments are easily understood by lay-men and the construction of embankments may be carried out by unskilled labour which may be reasily available. The embankments can be easily designed according to the material available along the channel. The skill for the maintenance of such embankments can be easily acquired. Unlike detention basins and channel improvements, levee construction is a more or less flexible proposal that may suit the local financial conditions. As levees can be built piece-meal the effect of breaches can be much localised.

As levees confine flood waters, they increase stage heights, and such an increase in stage height from 6 to 15 feet has been observed on the Mississippi at various points of measurement (Stafford, 1960).

The levees do not control all the floods and there are frequent occurrences of breaches whenever large floods occur. When breaches occur in embankments, the flood waters transform large areas into ponds, and such areas are lost to irrigation on account of heavy coarse sediment brought by the flood waters. Thus, a large portion along the river turns out to be a swampy region, with the consequent mosquito hazard.

Due to the meandering tendency of some rivers, the bed gets aggraded thereby raising the flood levels. The raising of the river bed higher than the adjacent land would often make it an elevated canal and seepage water through levees often accumulates chemical deposits after evaporation and this results in alkaline lands along the river course (Shih-Ta, 1952). Further, the water table in the areas behind the embankment is also raised.

Whenever the water resources available in a particular area are inadequate to meet the needs, either the rate of supply is retarded, or water must be imported from another catchment into the particular area to meet the pressing demands. Such water transfers create complex problems. While diverting water from one basin to another, the region along the transfer canal also develops and its developmental needs for irrigation, drainage, industrial and domestic water supply will create further hydrological problems. Major water transfers may also offer opportunities for reducing the flood levels in the rivers from which flow is diverted thus increasing the flood safety in the protected plains (Nagy, 1975).

Impoundment of water in a reservoir causes changes in the quality of water due to the hydro-dynamic action of the reservoir. Due to evaporation losses from the reservoir, the salinity of the impounded water increases. In most of the bigger reservoirs, high water temperatures increase the metabolic activities. Further impoundment also causes thermal and chemical stratification in water together with vertical mixing. In some cases, the presence of hydrogen sulphide has been observed in the tail race waters, consequent on the vegetation and other favourable deposits left in the bed of the reservoir (Elliot, 1971, Murth, 1976).

Impoundment has its effects on the surroundings, while periodical fluctuations in the river down stream forces substantial changes in the natural systems. With the development activities there is an assured supply of water and consequently industrial and urban development takes place. Urbanisation represents one of the major human interferences with the hydrological cycle. With the growth of an industrial complex, considerable amounts of industrial effluents and other effluents, mine drainage and other waste materials are discharged into the river, creating pollution problems making water unfit for human consumption and also for use in industries.

With the creation of man-made lakes the development of a delta takes place in the upstream reaches of the reservoir. The building up of a delta gradually raises the bed level (Murthy, 1968). The rise is river bed level in Lake Mead, USA, was accompanied by a rise in the groundwater level on adjacent land making it unfit for cultivation. Land has been lost year after year, and cultivation of the river valley has been abandoned for a distance of about 15 miles above the upper limits of the reservoir (Lagles, 1969). Such building up is particularly serious around the developing areas and needs constant surveillance. The town of San Marcial, on the Riogrande in the USA, was buried under sand, consequent on the rise of the bed level in the delta region and flooding (Harrison, 1952). Due to the availability of nutrient material in the delta deposit, brush wood and other vegetation would grow luxuriously. This vegetation causes loss of water from the reservoir. For example (Murthy, 1968), at the head of Elephant Butte Reservoir, USA, this non-beneficial consumptive use has been estimated to be equal to about 37 per cent of the evaporation losses from the lake surface. In the case of Lake Mead, the evaporation losses amount to about 17 million cubic metres annually. To reduce this non-beneficial use, levees and channels had to be constructed costing about 2.5 million dollars (Lane, 1953).

Initially, at the dam site, the river section will retain its ability to transport sediment at certain flow stages. With the creation of a reservoir, the input of sediment at this section becomes zero and erosion will commence which, in turn, will reduce the slope of the channel, reduce the bed sheer stress and increase the average size of the bed sediment. The rate and the extent of down stream erosion will depend on the nature of the alluvial material, the slope of the channel, the imposed flow regime and the activities of tributary channels. The silt free water escaping from the dam has capacity to pick-up silt and tries to establish a new equilibrium condition. The degradation below the dam may initiate a new cycle of head-water erosion in tributary basins. In severe cases, this may also lower the groundwater table with resulting damage to agricultural land. If the channel bed is highly resistant compared to the banks, then bank erosion takes place with consequent meandering to provide a natural balance between the flow and the sediment load.

Quantitative estimation of the hydrological changes brought out by human activities are based on methods ranging from simple graphs of time series before and after change and double mass curves to deterministic and stochastic models for predicting the results. The success of these methods, however, depends on the reliability of data.

Statistical correlation and regression still provide useful means for the analysis of past behaviour and prediction of future consequences. This type of analysis is essentially empirical but it should be based on a rational understanding of the impact of the relevant associated factors. These methods have several advantages over graphical analysis, the most important ones being the ability to consider multi-variable problems and the ability to provide a mathematical measure for the reliability of estimate.

Analysis of time series before and after the change in the regime provides an understanding of the corresponding changes in the various statistical elements of the system. This includes the analysis of the deterministic and stochastic components on which to base the future predictions.

Parameter optimisation has been recognised as an important and powerful tool to understand cause and effect relations. Its application is limited by the need to make use of a computer, barring some simple cases with small computational requirements.

REFERENCES

Butorin, N.V. 1971. The Rybinsk man-made lake and its impact on environment. *Symposium on Man-made Lakes,* Knoxville, Tennessee.

Elliot, Reed A. 1971. The TVA Experience, *Symposium on man-made lakes.* Knoxville, Tennessee.

Happ, Stafford C. 1960. Stream channel control, Corps of Engineers. *Applied sedimentation.* (Ed) P.D. Trask, John Wiley, New York.

Harrison, Alfred S. 1952. Deposition at the heads of reservoirs, Corps of Engineers, Omaha, Nebraska. Proceedings of the Fifth Hydraulic Research, June 9-11, 1952.

IHP, 1975. International Hydrological Programme, *Final Report,* First Session of the Intergovernmental Council, UNESCO, Paris, 9-17 April 1975.

Lagler, K.F. 1969. Man-made lakes - planning and development. *FAO Publication,* Rome.

Lane, E.W. 1953. Some aspects of reservoir sedimentation, *Central Board of Irrigation and Power Journal,* New Delhi.

Murthy, B.N. 1968. Capacity survey of storage reservoirs, *Central Board of Irrigation and Power Journal 89,* India, February.

References

Murthy, Y.K. 1976. Environmental impacts of water development projects, *Central Board of Irrigation and Power Journal,* India, February.

Nagy, La'szlo S. 1975. Water management engineering system for large size water transfer, *Water/SEM, 4/R.5/COM 4,* Hungary, December.

Shih-Ta, Hsu 1952. The use of embankments for floods control, their merits and demerits, *Proceedings of the Regional Technical Conference on Flood Control in Asia and the Far East. Flood Control Series No 3* - United Nations, Bangkok.

Bibliography

Dale, A. Hoffman and Jonez, Al.R. 1971. Lake Mead, USA. *Symposium on man-made lakes,* Knoxville, Tennessee.

Dooge, J.C.I., Costin, A.B. and Finke, C.H.J. 1973. Man's influence on the hydrological cycle: *Irrigation and Drainage Paper No 17, Special Issue.* FAO Rome.

Pereira, H.C. 1972. The influence of man on the hydrological cycle, guide lines to policies for the safe development of land and water resources in *Status and Trends of Research in Hydrology,* UNESCO. Studies and Reports in Hydrology No 10.

TVA, 1968. Sedimentation in TVA Reservoirs, TVA, Division of water control planning, Knoxville, *Tennessee Report No 6693,* Feb 1968.

3.4.1 QUANTITATIVE CHANGES IN THE HYDROLOGICAL REGIME IN THE DAMODAR VALLEY DUE TO STREAM FLOW REGULATION
by B N Murthy[1]

3.4.1.1 Introduction

The Damodar Valley, in Eastern India, covering an area of about 22,000 km^2 is characterised by heavy monsoon rains and a hot humid climate. The flat deltaic plains are subjected to annual floods of devastating magnitude. For the purposes of flood control, irrigation and power, multi-purpose reservoirs have been built and they are in operation for the last two decades.

This case-study evaluates changes in the various hydrological elements such as rainfall, runoff, water balance, as well as changes in river regime, and reservoir capacity brought about by reservoir regulation. The quantitative evaluation is based on methods ranging from simple graphical analysis and double mass-curves, to statistical correlation and regression.

3.4.1.2 General features

The Damodar Valley (Figure 1) is located approximately within latitude 22^0 to 24^0-30' and longitude 84^0-45' to 88^0-30'. The River Damodar, after a south-easterly course of about 560 km, falls into the River Hooghly just above the ill famed "James and Mary" sands.

The catchment area of the river is about 22,000 km^2. Its source is about 310 m above the mean sea level. The general slope for the first 240 km is about 3.4 m/km, which flattens out to 0.6 m/km for the next 160 km and then for the last 160 km, to less than 0.2 m/km. In the upper reaches, the slope varies from 7.6 to 7.2 m/km.

The topography of the valley ranges from rough hilly sections in the upper reaches, to the flat deltaic plains of the lower region. The catchment is generally denuded of forests and vegetative cover. Land management being poor, the soil is exposed, and consequently, the heavy down-pour of the monsoon rains causes a high rate of land erosion and sediment inflow into the river.

The geological formations of the valley consist mainly of metamorphic granite-gneisses with associated schists. These are overlain by sedimentary rocks (sandstones and shales) containing large coal fields. There has been considerable disturbance in the area and the rocks are much folded and jointed. Intrusions and faults are numerous. The gneiss is the hardest rock within the area, but on the hill sides it is decayed for a considerable depth. The type of soil derived from these granite gneisses is a light sandy loam which has just enough clay to make it set very hard when dried and soft and greasy when wet.

The area is rich in minerals and contains a large percentage of India's copper reserves and kyanite, iron ore, coal, mica, chromite, fire clay and china clay.

3.4.1.3 Hydrometeorology

The area is in a humid region characterised by a long, hot summer. The highest recorded maximum temperature is 46^{0}C, which occurred over a large part of the lower valley and the lowest minimum is about 2^{0}C, which was recorded in the upper region. The mean annual range

---

[1] Damodar Valley Corporation, PO Maithon Dam, Dist Dhanbad (Bihar), India

132

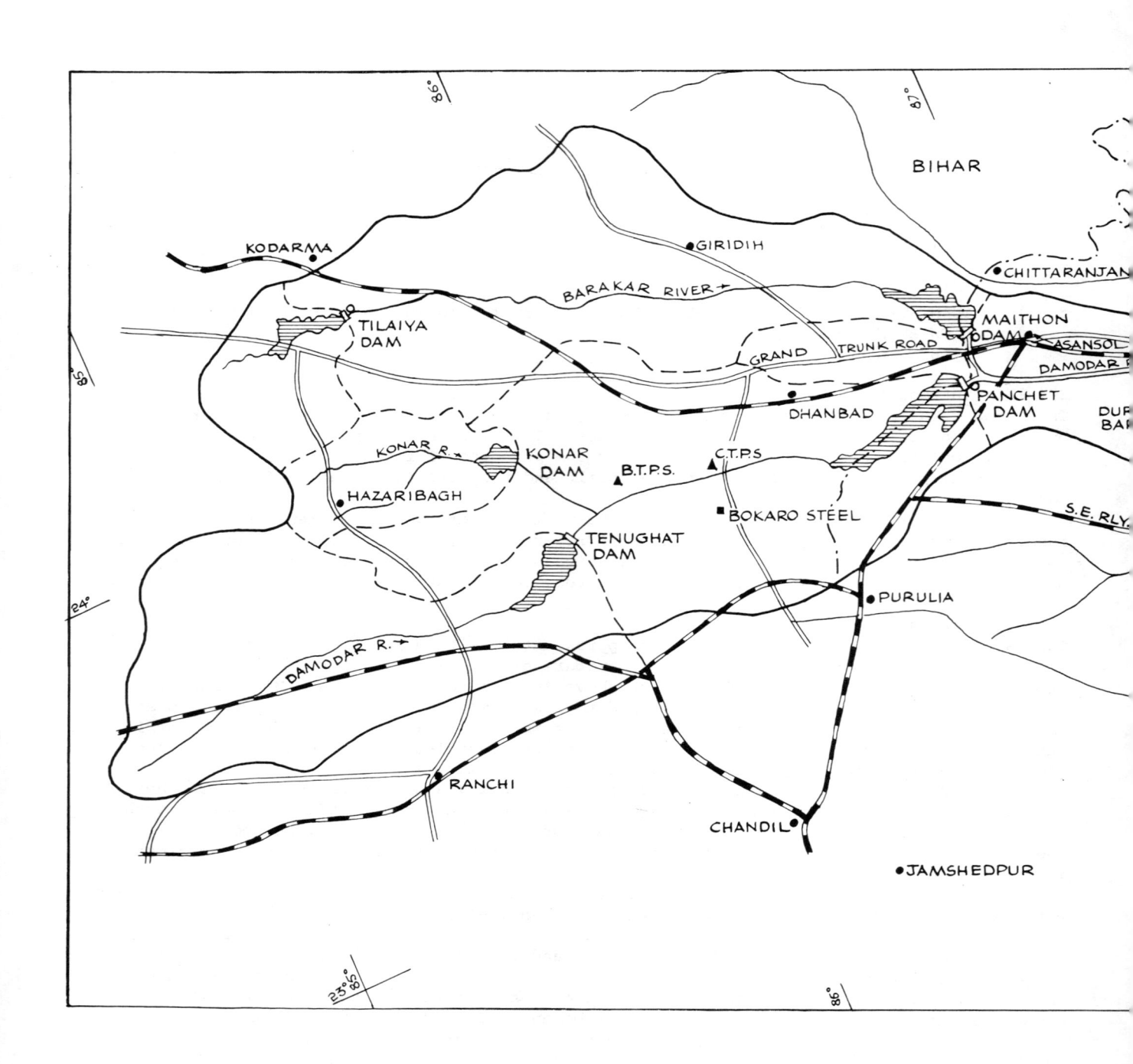

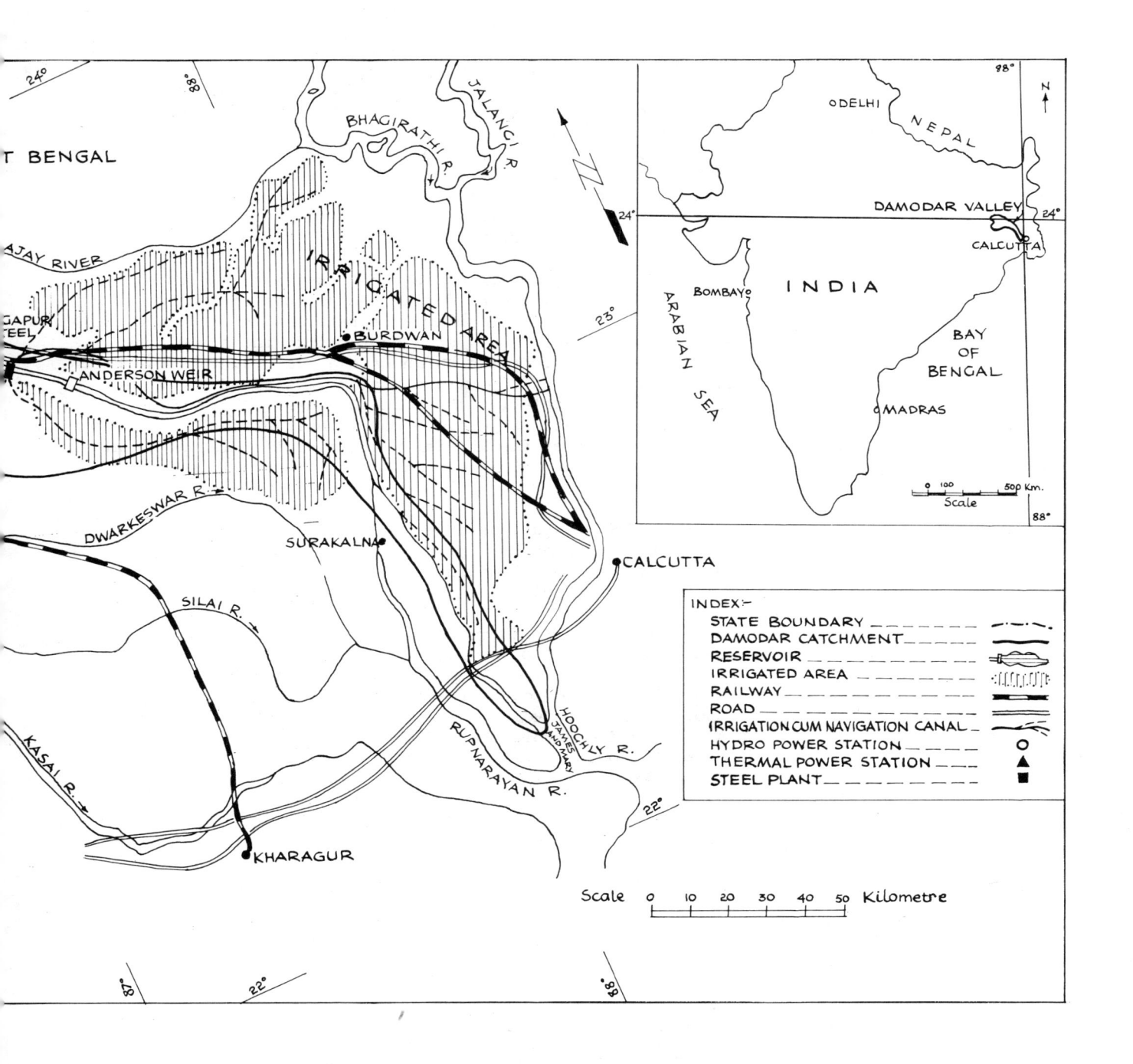

Figure 1   Damodar basin - India

of temperature is 10-12°C for the entire area. The mean annual humidity is about 65 per cent for the morning and about 50 per cent for the evening.

The valley experiences a well defined monsoon which is normally confined to the period from the middle of June to early October. The annual rainfall in the basin averages between 1270 and 1320 mm with a maximum of 1960 mm and a minimum of 790 mm. About 80 to 95 per cent of the rain falls during the monsoon when all major floods occur. The peak floods occur after the middle of July by which time the ground storage is nearly saturated. The maximum observed flow is 18,406 m^3/sec at Rhondia (drainage area 20,616 km^2) and this occurred during 1913, 1935 and 1941 but was reported to have been considerably exceeded during the flood of August 1823. During the dry period (November to May) there are extended periods of little or no flow in the main river as well as in the tributaries. The runoff averages about 510 mm on the catchment during the monsoon with a variation from 255 to 840 mm. Monsoon flow accounts for over 90 per cent of the total annual yield.

Heavy rainfall in this region is generally caused during the passage of cyclonic depressions which form at the head of the Bay of Bengal during the monsoon months, June to October, and travel in a north-westerly direction. Sometimes depressions which form over land also cause heavy precipitation. On average 3 to 4 such storms form in each of the monsoon months. The worst storm that occurred over the basin gave a mean rainfall of about 300 mm in 5 days in August 1913, with a runoff of 270 mm and a peak flow of 18,400 m^3/sec.

Rainfall records for the valley are available for the last 80 years. There are, at present, about 63 raingauge stations, ie 3 stations per 1000 km^2. Observations in the past with non-recording gauges gave no information on the intensity of rainfall. The difficulty has been overcome with the installation of some self-recording raingauge stations.

3.4.1.4 The project and its operation

As the lower areas of the basin have suffered widespread damage from time to time from recurring floods, major flood protection works became inescapable. A system of multipurpose reservoirs was designed not only with a view to providing adequate flood control for the threatened region, but also for generation of power for the expanding industry and for irrigation of cultivable lands.

The first phase of this scheme consisting of four dams (Tilaiya, Konar, Maithon and Panchet Hill) with a total reservoir capacity of 0.36 million ha m has been completed (Figure 1). Out of the total capacity, 0.18 million ha m is reserved for flood control. Maithon and Panchet Hill flood control dams are together able to control the highest observed flood of 18,400 m^3/sec with a runoff of 270 mm (volume 0.47 million ha m with 7 days duration) to 7100 m^3/sec at Durgapur. Besides flood control, these dams provide water for irrigation and power. About 0.39 million ha of the most fertile land on both the banks of the Damodar in the lower valley will be irrigated by means of networks of canals. Main cultivation is paddy with a water requirement of about 1020 mm. Within these two decades, irrigation has developed over 0.4 million ha.

The reservoirs in the system are operated in an integrated manner and are allowed to impound during the monsoon, simultaneously meeting the irrigation demand and hydro-power needs of the system. When the reservoirs attain their normal levels, the excess flow is spilled depending upon the incoming floods and the condition of the valley downstream, so that the total discharge from the dams together with the discharge from the uncontrolled catchment does not exceed 7100 m^3/sec. This is the safe capacity of the downstream channels. Since the project went into operation, the previous observed maximum flood has been surpassed and this flood and several other major floods have been regulated so that they were within the channel capacity downstream.

Hydro-power and thermal power plants with the associated transmission and distribution systems have also been constructed. At Tilaiya, Maithon and Panchet Hill, hydro-power is generated while at Bokaro, Durgapur and Chandrapura thermal power is generated. The total installed capacity of both thermal and hydro-power for the present is of the order of 1200 mega-watts.

The other subsidiary objects include navigation, supply of industrial and domestic water, soil conservation, protection of public health, fisheries and tourism.

3.4.1.5 Watershed management

There has been large scale deforestation and the existing forests have not been allowed to grow to their full extent, particularly the Sal wood tree which has been in continuous demand for building. Indiscriminate felling of the trees has exposed the steep slopes of the forest, developing deep gullies and ravines in a short time and rendering the land unfit for further use. Forest fires have also been frequent in this region.

There is also a lot of coal mining activity and the mining debris has been left in a disorderly manner. These dumps erode under the intensity of the monsoon rains and they contribute a lot of sediment load to streams.

The crop under cultivation is mainly rice. The land holding of the average farmer in the area is less than one hectare and as such, over-grazing on his poor holding has led to severe erosion.

Soil erosion control and other watershed management practices are, therefore, urgent for the general socio-economic wellbeing of the valley and also to protect the large reservoirs from rapid silting.

The detailed analysis of the land use in the upper valley is shown in Table 1.

Table 1 Land use of the Upper Damodar valley

Description of various types of land	Areas in million hectares	Percentage of the total
1. Forest land	0.40	22.7
2. Paddy land	0.42	23.8
3. Agricultural upland	0.30	16.4
4. Current fallow	0.29	15.9
5. Cultivable waste land	0.19	10.5
6. Culturable waste land	0.08	4.6
7. Roads, buildings, ponds, etc	0.11	6.1
Total	1.79	100.0

The Damodar Valley Corporation has been carrying out soil conservation measures since 1950 over the basin. The entire Upper Damodar catchment has been divided into 39 sub-catchments. An integrated protection work plan has been drawn up and phased. This envisages the selective approach to rehabilitating the critical areas which contribute heavy sediment flow into the streams. The plan calls for various types of soil conservation treatment measures in the agricultural upland, waste land, denuded forest and also in the wooded forest.

Priority for the treatment of sub-catchments has been based on high silt load content and on those catchments which are directly draining into the reservoirs and also where the erosion index is very high. Out of the total area of 1.79 million ha, the problem areas requiring some immediate treatment total 0.59 million ha. The land treated by the different measures up to 1973 cover a total area of 0.26 million ha comprising 0.09 million ha under afforestation, 0.12 million ha under upland treatment and 0.06 million ha under engineering treatment. This is about 45 per cent of the problem areas, and the effects of such treatments are being slowly felt (Murthy, 1976).

3.4.1.6 Effect of water resources development
Basin development as discussed above has resulted in great economic and social benefit by providing a favourable environment for flood control, agriculture, power development, industries and living conditions. In turn, such development schemes also interfere in some way or other with the natural balance and themselves become potential sources of problems (Lagler, 1969). The effect of reservoir regulation will bring changes in the total volume of streamflow, evapotranspiration, climatic conditions, groundwater levels, water quality, alteration of river bed slope by aggradation, degradation and meandering etc.

3.4.1.7 Methodological aspects of the estimation of changes
The quantitative estimate of the hydrological changes brought about by human activities is based on methods ranging from simple graphs and double mass curves to deterministic and stochastic models for predicting the results. The success of these methods, however, depends

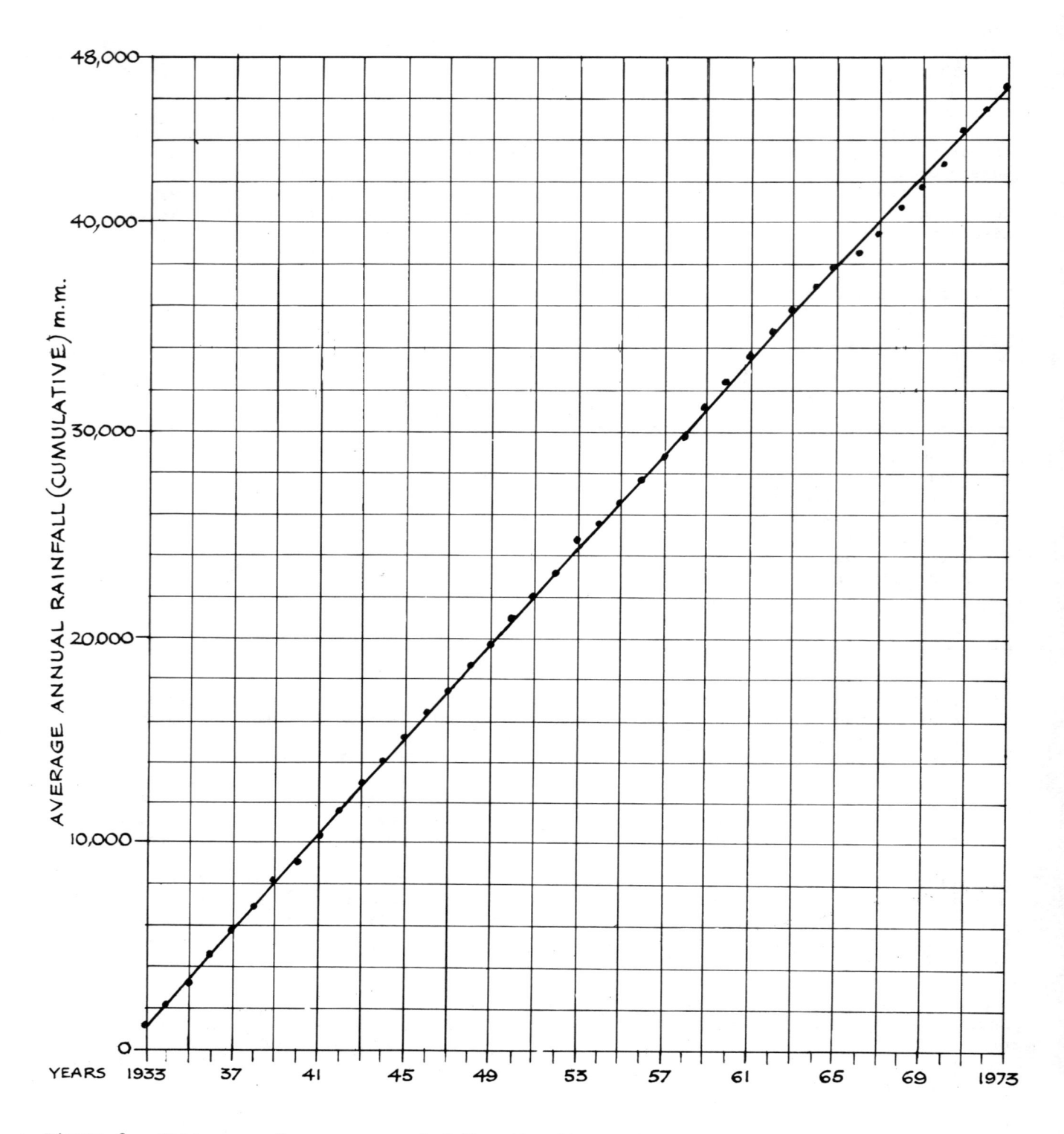

Figure 2   Mass curve for monsoon rainfall - Rhondia catchment

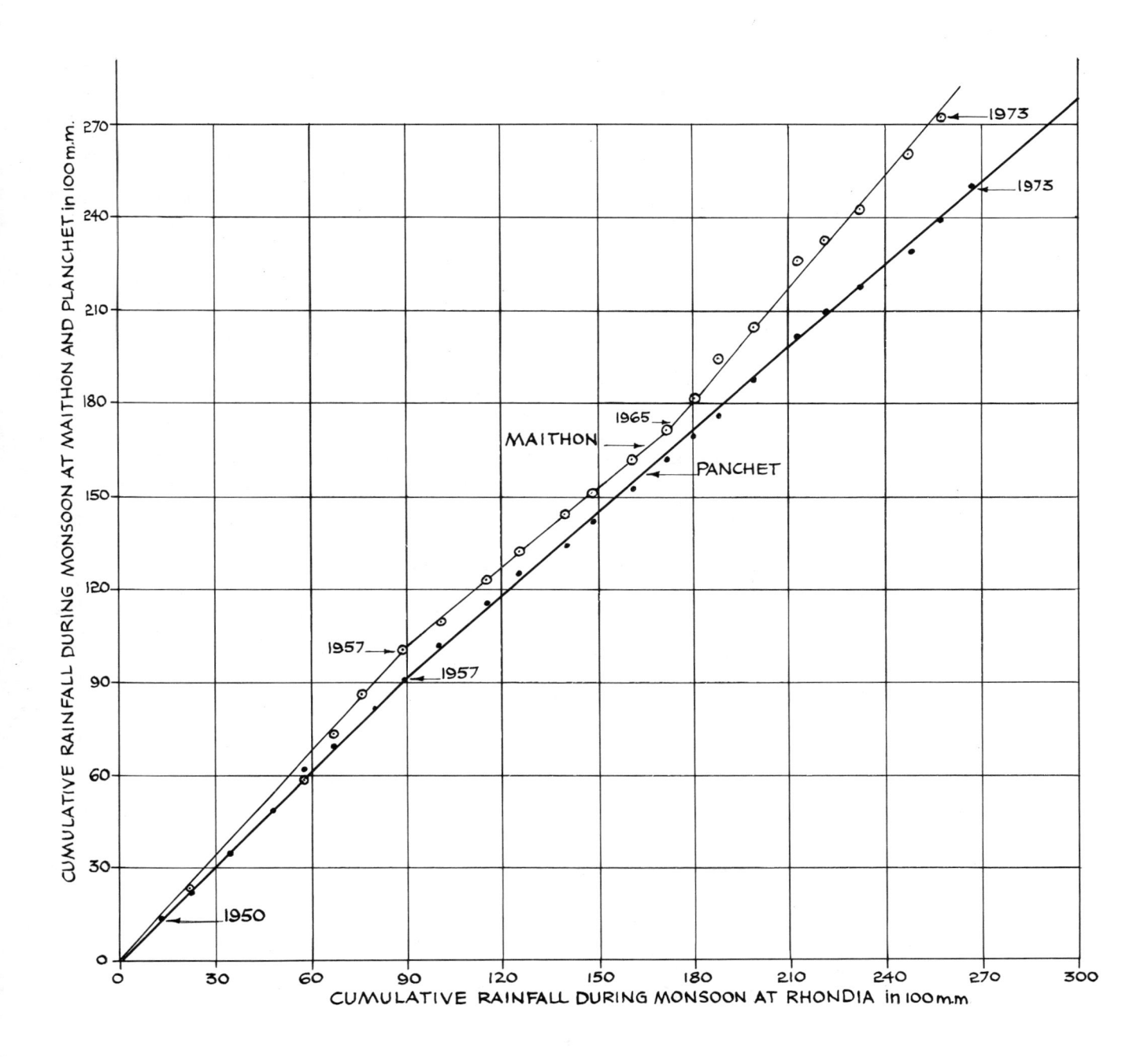

Figure 3   Double mass curve for monsoon rainfall

on the reliability of data.

Statistical correlation and regression still provide useful means of analysing past behaviour and for the prediction of future consequences. These types of analysis are essentially empirical, but they should be based on a rational understanding of the impact of the relevant and associated factors. These methods have several advantages over graphical analysis, the most important ones being the ability to consider multi variable problems and the availability of mathematical measures for the reliability of estimates.

Analysis of time series before and after the change in regime provides an understanding of the corresponding changes in the various statistical elements of the system. This includes the analysis of the deterministic and stochastic components on which to base the future predictions.

Parameter optimization has been recognised as an important and powerful tool to understand cause and effect relations. Its application is limited by the need to employ a computer, barring some simple cases with small computational requirements.

3.4.1.8   Various observed hydrological changes
3.4.1.8.1 Changes in the rainfall regime. Long term flow regulation through impounding reservoirs influences the climatic conditions by transformation of air-masses over the reservoir. Such changes may be expected within 10 to 15 km of the reservoir belt depending on its size. In the case of large lakes, all the meteorological conditions including atmospheric conditions are changed to some extent (Butorin, 1971). This aspect has been studied in this basin by using the double mass curve.

Rainfall data for the Damodar basin to Rhondia is available for more than 40 years. The average rainfall for the period 1933-77 is 1135 mm with the range of 686 to 5575 mm. Table 2 shows the average annual rainfall over the catchment to Rhondia.

The mass curve for annual rainfall in Figure 2 shows almost a straight line plot, suggesting that there has been little change in the rainfall regime on account of reservoir building in the catchment as a whole, while a slight variation is observed, as shown in Figure 3, in the individual stations at Maithon and Panchet Hill near the respective reservoirs.

Table 2   Average annual monsoon rainfall for the basin to Rhondia in millimetres

Year	Rainfall	Year	Rainfall	Year	Rainfall	Year	Rainfall
1933	1168	1943	1295	1953	1449	1963	1194
1934	991	1944	1092	1954	1016	1964	1092
1935	1092	1945	1092	1955	864	1965	940
1936	1397	1946	1245	1956	1194	1966	686
1937	1168	1947	1092	1957	991	1967	1067
1938	940	1948	1092	1958	1067	1968	1270
1939	1321	1949	1194	1959	1524	1969	914
1940	914	1950	1245	1960	1067	1970	1143
1941	1295	1951	991	1961	1372	1971	1575
1942	1372	1952	1143	1962	889	1972	1194
						1973	1194
						Average	- 1135

3.4.1.8.2 Changes in the runoff characteristics. For the period 1933-73 discharge data for the catchment Rhondia area available and are given in Table 3.

The average annual monsoon flow for the period 1933-73 is 0.90 million ha within the range 0.24-1.72 million ha m which shows extreme variability.

A double mass plot of monsoon rainfall and monsoon runoff shown in Figure 4, indicates a significant break in the trend around 1953 when the Damodar Valley Corporation reservoirs started impounding water. The shift in the trend suggests a lower availability of runoff for a certain amount of precipitation. This shows that changes are taking place in the basin due

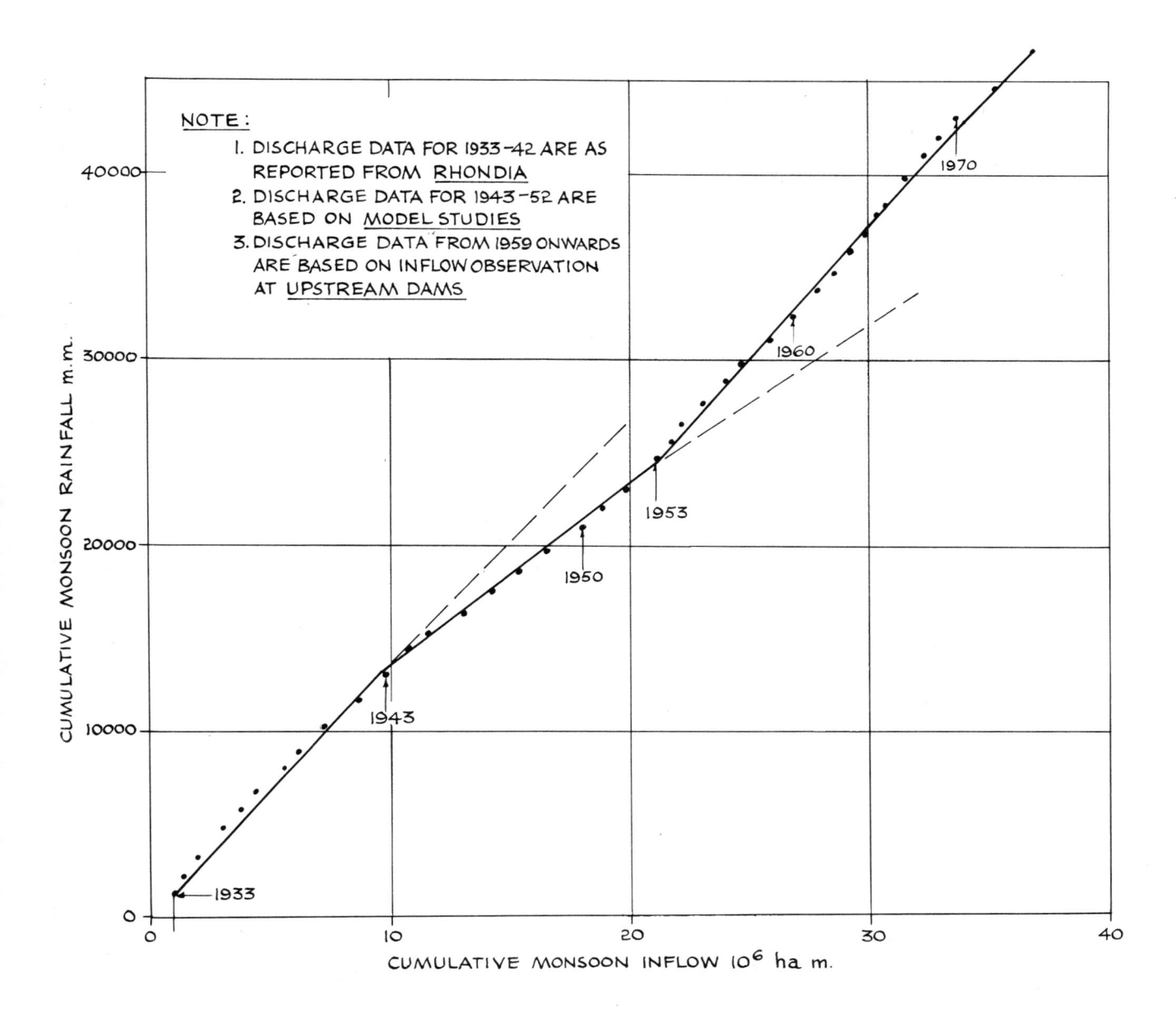

Figure 4   Double mass curve for monsoon rainfall and monsoon inflow - Rhondia (June-Oct)

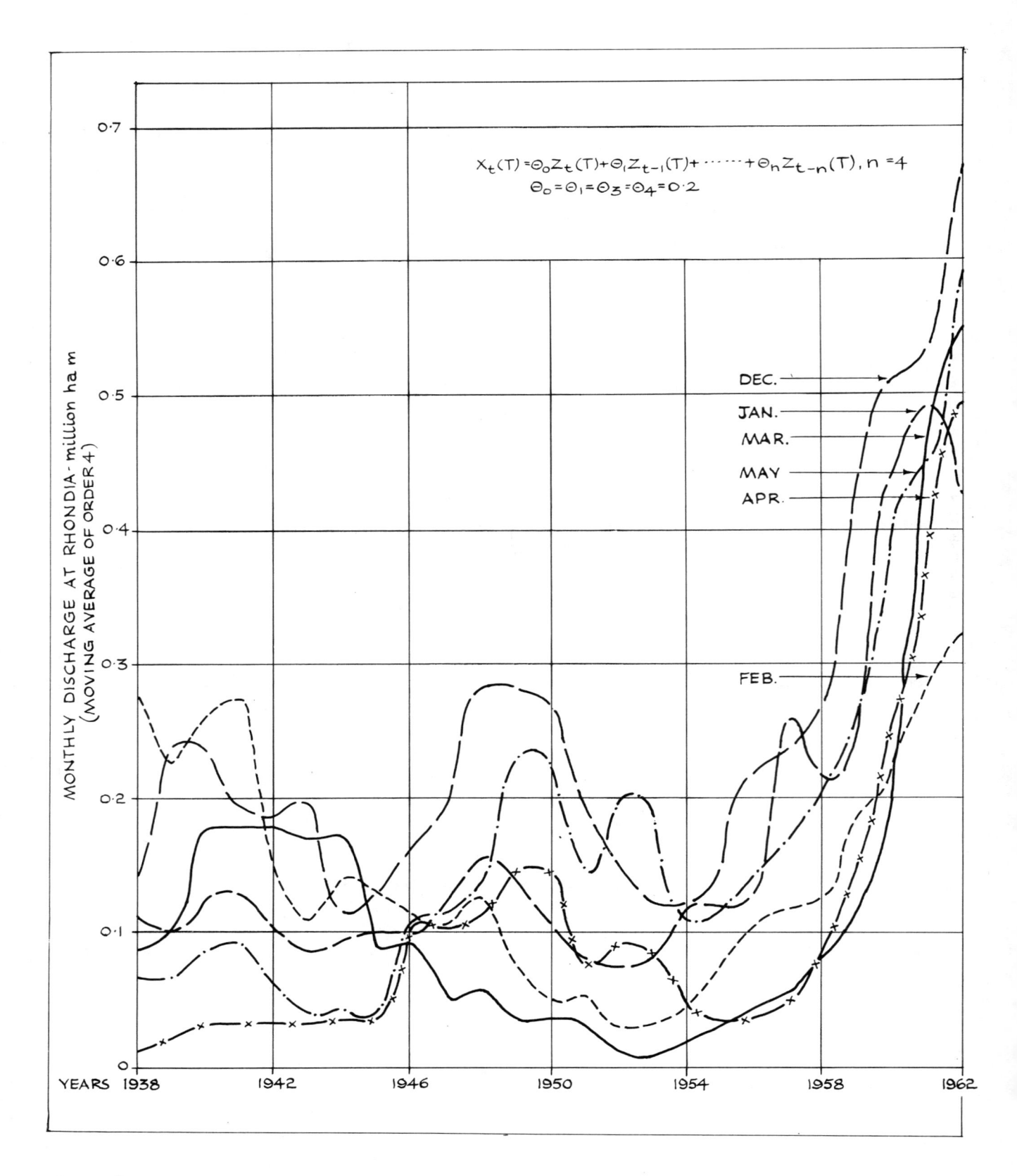

Figure 5   Trend of monthly flow at Rhondia - dry weather period

Quantitative changes in the hydrological regime

Table 3 Annual monsoon flow at Rhondia in million hectare metres

Year	Flow	Year	Flow	Year	Flow	Year	Flow
1933	0.86	1943	1.09	1953	1.20	1963	0.74
1934	0.52	1944	0.93	1954	0.59	1964	0.66
1935	0.62	1945	0.90	1955	0.63	1965	0.51
1936	1.00	1946	1.48	1956	0.89	1966	0.24
1937	0.78	1947	1.07	1957	0.80	1967	0.78
1938	0.67	1948	1.02	1958	0.69	1968	0.98
1939	1.16	1949	1.35	1959	1.30	1969	0.55
1940	0.59	1950	1.44	1960	0.78	1970	0.77
1941	1.09	1951	0.80	1961	1.23	1971	1.72
1942	1.48	1952	0.94	1962	0.49	1972	0.48
						1973	0.98

Average - 0.90

to development activities which intercept water upstream thereby reducing the availability of runoff at the point of measurement.

A previous break in the trend in 1943 is due to the improvement in the quality measurement at that point.

3.4.1.8.3 Variation in the monthly flows. The system is characterised by extreme variability in monthly flows. Precipitation is mainly limited to the monsoon season, June to October, with a very dry post monsoon winter and premonsoon summer. Table 4 shows the volume of monthly discharge at Rhondia for the period 1933 to 1962.

In order to study the trend of monthly flows, a moving average model of order 4 was fitted with a view to suppressing components other than the trend.

$$X_t(T) = \theta_0 Z_t(T) + \theta_1 Z_{t-1}(T) + \ldots + \theta_n Z_{t-n}(T)$$

with n = 4; and $\theta_0 = \theta_1 = \theta_2 = \theta_3 = \theta_4 = 0.2$
where: $X_t(T)$ = moving average value for year t, month T; $Z_t(T)$ = monthly discharge for the year t, month T; θ = constants.

Table 4 Monthly discharge at Rhondia in million hectare metres

	1933	1934	1935	1936	1937	1938	1939	1940	1941	1942
January		0.01	0.00	0.00	0.01	0.00	0.00	0.01	0.00	0.01
February		0.02	0.00	0.00	0.04	0.01	0.00	0.01	0.01	0.01
March		0.00	0.00	0.00	0.02	0.00	0.01	0.02	0.00	0.02
April		0.00	0.00	0.00	0.00	0.00	0.00	0.00	0.00	0.00
May		0.00	0.00	0.00	0.01	0.01	0.00	0.00	0.00	0.00
June		0.07	0.00	0.05	0.05	0.05	0.14	0.02	0.12	0.02
July	0.25	0.14	0.06	0.24	0.12	0.12	0.18	0.11	0.27	0.33
August	0.36	0.16	0.38	0.27	0.20	0.28	0.50	0.34	0.25	0.73
September	0.19	0.12	0.17	0.30	0.25	0.18	0.25	0.13	0.24	0.35
October	0.05	0.02	0.03	0.13	0.15	0.04	0.12	0.05	0.30	0.05
November	0.01	0.00	0.00	0.05	0.01	0.00	0.03	0.01	0.03	0.00
December	0.01	0.00	0.00	0.03	0.00	0.00	0.03	0.00	0.01	0.00

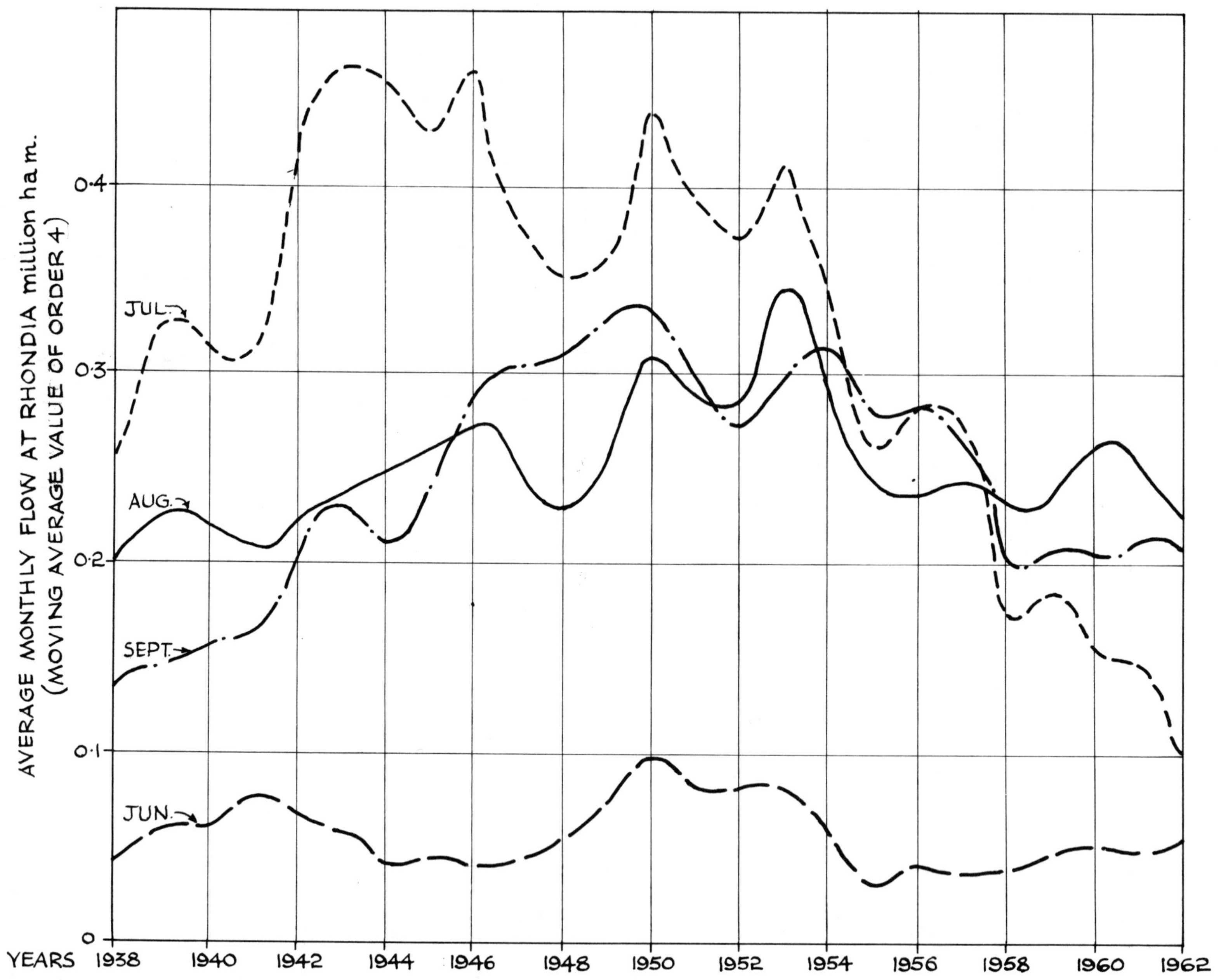

Figure 6 Trend of monthly flow at Rhondia - wet weather period

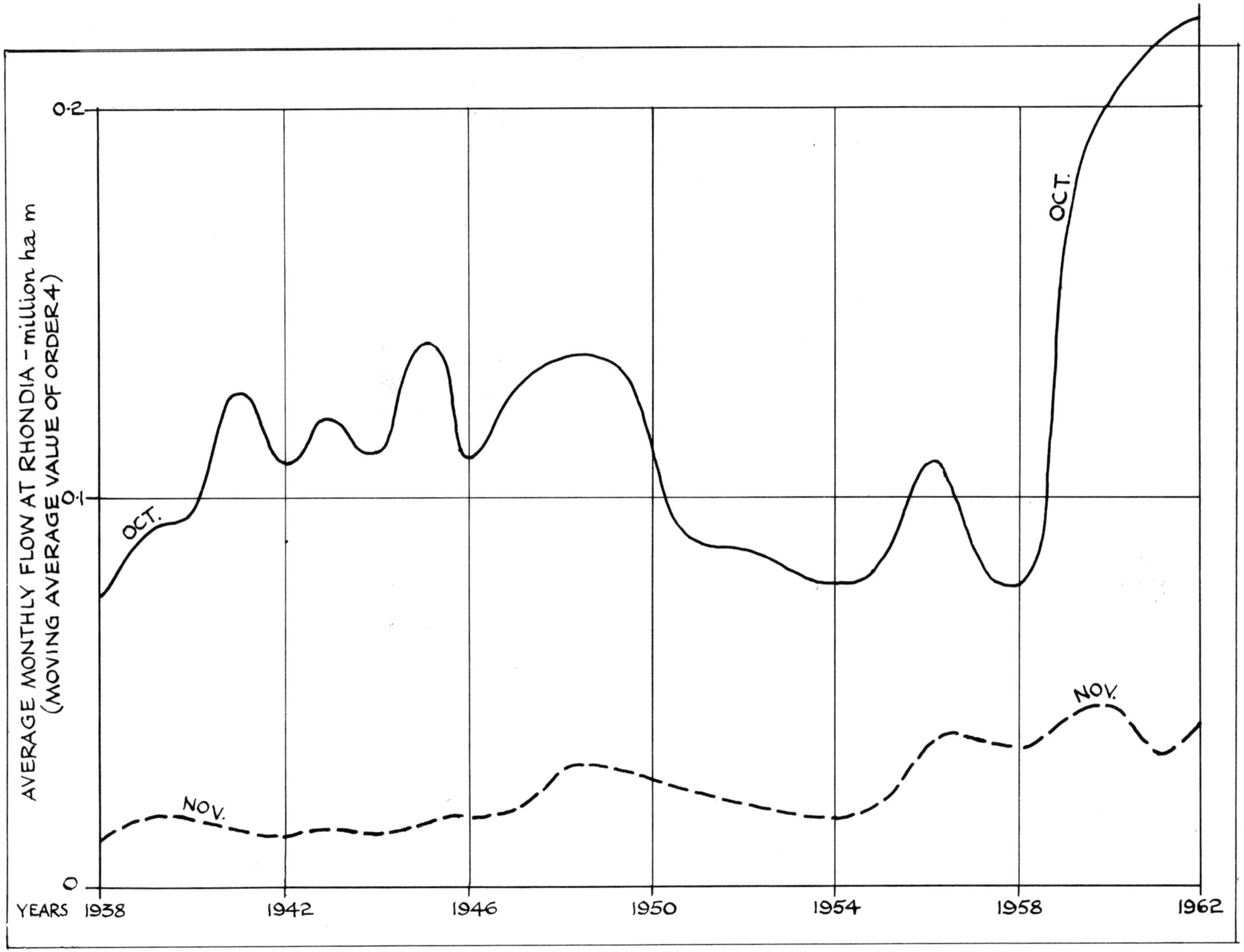

Figure 7   Trend of monthly flow at Rhondia – post-monsoon period

Quantitative changes in the hydrological regime

Table 4 Continued

	1943	1944	1945	1946	1947	1948	1949	1950	1951	1952
January	0.00	0.00	0.01	0.00	0.01	0.01	0.00	0.00	0.00	0.00
February	0.00	0.01	0.01	0.00	0.01	0.01	0.00	0.00	0.00	0.00
March	0.00	0.01	0.00	0.00	0.01	0.00	0.00	0.00	0.00	0.00
April	0.00	0.00	0.00	0.02	0.00	0.00	0.01	0.00	0.00	0.01
May	0.00	0.00	0.00	0.02	0.00	0.00	0.03	0.00	0.00	0.02
June	0.00	0.05	0.03	0.11	0.03	0.05	0.14	0.15	0.03	0.04
July	0.31	0.21	0.17	0.35	0.11	0.28	0.35	0.47	0.23	0.24
August	0.49	0.47	0.20	0.43	0.35	0.32	0.51	0.59	0.21	0.26
September	0.20	0.14	0.29	0.47	0.41	0.23	0.29	0.29	0.28	0.27
October	0.10	0.07	0.19	0.14	0.14	0.14	0.07	0.04	0.05	0.14
November	0.01	0.01	0.03	0.04	0.01	0.06	0.02	0.01	0.01	0.01
December	0.00	0.01	0.01	0.02	0.01	0.03	0.01	0.00	0.00	0.01

	1953	1954	1955	1956	1957	1958	1959	1960	1961	1962
January	0.01	0.01	0.00	0.01	0.03	0.01	0.01	0.05	0.02	0.01
February	0.01	0.00	0.01	0.01	0.00	0.01	0.02	0.02	0.03	0.01
March	0.00	0.00	0.00	0.00	0.00	0.01	0.01	0.02	0.07	0.02
April	0.00	0.00	0.00	0.00	0.01	0.01	0.01	0.03	0.04	0.04
May	0.00	0.00	0.00	0.01	0.01	0.03	0.02	0.04	0.02	0.04
June	0.04	0.04	0.02	0.07	0.03	0.03	0.09	0.04	0.06	0.06
July	0.46	0.12	0.21	0.18	0.29	0.10	0.16	0.07	0.14	0.06
August	0.51	0.18	0.22	0.24	0.15	0.12	0.23	0.19	0.32	0.11
September	0.38	0.31	0.08	0.37	0.21	0.17	0.33	0.25	0.30	0.08
October	0.10	0.05	0.05	0.19	0.02	0.06	0.54	0.19	0.28	0.05
November	0.04	0.02	0.02	0.11	0.01	0.01	0.06	0.04	0.04	0.06
December	0.01	0.01	0.01	0.02	0.01	0.02	0.05	0.03	0.03	0.05

Figures 5, 6 and 7 show moving average plots for dry weather months, wet weather months and post monsoon months respectively. The increasing trend in the dry weather flow after 1955 when the project come into operation and the falling trend in the wet weather flow around the same time can be readily appreciated. There is little change in the trend of flow just before and after the monsoon.

3.4.1.8.4 Mass balance for surface water. The presence of reservoirs causes evaporation loss from their surfaces, and seepage loss in the bed and the periphery. In some cases where vegetative growth has taken place in the delta region, evapotranspiration losses have been considerable.

For a seven year period beginning 1.6.1968 the surface water balance has been studied for the four reservoirs at Maithon, Panchet Hill, Tilaiya and Konar. For each reservoir the following equation was applied:

$$\Delta S = I - O - EL$$

where: ΔS = change in the volume of water held in storage during the period; I = total volume of inflow during the period; O = total volume of outflow during the period; EL = total volume of lake surface evaporation, seepage below reservoir and other losses.

Tables 5 and 6 show that for the Maithon reservoir the annual volume of surface water loss is about 14,432 ha m which is about 5 per cent of the average annual inflow. For the Panchet Hill reservoir, the water lost on account of storage is only 8,758 ha m (2 per cent of the average annual inflow) and this is consequent on its lower operating levels for most

Quantitative changes in the hydrological regime

of the period.

Table 5 Water balance for Maithon reservoir. Reservoir area at El. 146 m is 7.12 hectares.

Year	Reservoir level m	Capacity ha m	Change in storage ha m	Inflow ha m	Outflow ha m	Evaporation losses etc ha m
1.6.68	139.87	45,141				
			+ 492	398,274	385,359	12,423
1.6.69	139.97	45,633				
			-16,728	215,865	219,555	13,038
1.6.70	137.30	28,905				
			+ 5,904	225,951	205,164	14,883
1.6.71	138.91	34,809				
			-15,129	603,561	606,021	12,669
1.6.72	134.04	19,680				
			- 492	152,151	136,776	15,867
1.6.73	133.83	19,188				
			+ 2,337	322,137	305,040	14,760
1.6.74	134.76	21,525				
			+ 0	208,116	190,650	17,466
1.6.75	134.75	21,525				
1.6.1968 - 1.6.1975			-23,616	2,126,055	2048,565	101,106

Table 6 Water balance for Panchet Hill reservoir. Reservoir area at El. 125 m is 5.87 hectares

Year	Reservoir level m	Capacity ha m	Change in storage ha m	Inflow ha m	Outflow ha m	Evaporation losses etc ha m
1.6.68	121.79	25,830				
			- 5,658	423,366	422,874	6,150
1.6.69	120.16	20,172				
			- 984	261,990	256,701	6,273
1.6.70	120.15	19,188				
			+ 861	461,373	452,148	8,364
1.6.71	120.43	20,049				
			-16,236	893,349	893,226	16,359
1.6.72	111.37	3,813				
			+21,279	244,770	215,742	7,749
1.6.73	122.04	25,092				
			-17,466	523,488	532,098	8,856
1.6.74	114.85	7,626				
			+ 5,289	361,989	349,074	7,626
1.6.75	117.80	12,915				
1.6.1968 - 1.6.1975			-12,915	3170,325	3121,863	61,377

Quantitative changes in the hydrological regime

3.4.1.8.5 Changes in reservoir capacity and loss of nutrient sediments. Measurement of sedimentation in a reservoir by the capacity survey technique using electronic equipment and its computation by the 'Constant Factor' method shows that the two main multipurpose reservoirs, Maithon and Panchet Hill are losing storage capacity at a fast rate. With the loss of capacity due to sedimentation, there is also the loss of nutritive silts which would have otherwise gone to the area downstream. Table 7 shows data for the two reservoirs surveyed in different years.

Table 7 Sediment deposition and other data for Maithon and Panchet Hill reservoirs

		Maithon	Panchet Hill
1.	Catchment area effective km^2	5206	9920
2.	Capacity-inflow ratio	0.60	0.36
3.	Annual silt deposit in m^3/100 km^2 of catchment	1548 (1963) 1429 (1965) 1310 (1971)	1334 (1962) 1238 (1964) 1048 (1966) 1000 (1974)
4.	Loss of capacity (per cent): Dead storage Live storage Flood zone	22 10 Negligible	35 18 Negligible
5.	Overall per cent loss (up to top of gates)	8.0	9.0
6.	Rate of annual capacity loss	0.5	0.5
7.	Year survey	1971	1974
8.	Age - years	16	18

Tables 8 and 9 show the change in storage capacity in the two reservoirs and Tables 10 and 11 show the depthwise distribution of sediment. Table 12 shows the changes in bed profile of the two reservoirs.

Table 8 Capacity in 1000 ha m - Panchet Hill reservoir

Elevation above-MSL m	1956	1962	1964	1966	1974
98	0	0	0	0	0
101	0.1	0	0	0	0
104	0.5	1.1	0.1	0.1	0.1
107	1.5	0.7	0.7	0.7	0.6
110	3.3	2.3	2.2	2.3	2.1
113	7.3	5.1	4.9	5.0	4.5
116	13.2	9.6	9.2	9.2	8.2
119	21.3	16.5	15.4	15.4	13.6
122	32.5	26.2	24.9	24.6	22.1
125	48.7	41.1	39.7	39.1	36.0
128	70.5	62.7	61.1	60.3	56.7
131	98.6	90.7	89.0	88.1	84.1
136	157.6	149.8	148.0	147.1	143.2

Table 9 Capacity in 1000 ha m - Maithon reservoir

Elevation above-MSL m	1955	1963	1965	1971
107	0	0	0	0
110	0.1	0	0	0
113	0.7	0.2	0.2	0.1
116	1.6	0.9	0.9	0.7
119	3.1	1.9	1.9	1.6
122	5.2	3.7	3.4	3.1
125	7.8	5.9	5.6	5.3
128	11.6	9.2	8.9	8.5
131	16.9	13.9	13.5	13.0
134	24.3	20.6	20.0	19.2
137	33.8	29.4	28.4	27.2
140	46.0	40.7	39.6	37.8
143	61.6	55.4	54.2	52.0
146	81.1	74.5	73.2	70.4
149	105.2	98.6	97.6	94.1
151	119.2	113.0	111.9	108.4

Table 10 Distribution of sediment - Panchet Hill reservoir

Per cent depth	Per cent total deposit			
	1956-62	1956-64	1956-66	1956-74
0	0	0	0	0
11	1	1	1	1
22	6	5	4	3
33	11	10	8	7
44	14	12	10	10
56	30	26	24	22
67	49	47	43	40
78	63	66	62	61
89	82	85	83	82
100	100	100	100	100

Table 11 Distribution of sediment - Maithon reservoir

Per cent depth	Per cent total deposit		
	1955-63	1955-65	1955-71
0	0	0	0
8	2	2	1
16	7	6	5
24	11	10	9
31	18	15	14
40	23	21	18
47	29	28	23
54	37	35	29
62	45	45	37
77	66	68	61
85	79	82	75
92	92	94	88
100	100	100	100

Evaluation of loss of nutritive silts is to ascertain the amount of fines which are normally beneficial to plants. Sand particles are harmful to the plants and do not, by and large, have a nutritive value.

Table 12 Change of bed slope – Maithon and Panchet Hill

		Bed slope in m/km			Ratio	
Reservoir	Age Yrs	Forest S_f	Top set S_t	Original bed O_b	S_f/O_b	S_t/O_b
Maithon	8	4.9	1.1	1.9	2.6	0.59
	10	5.7	0.9	1.9	3.0	0.46
	16	6.4	0.8	1.9	3.4	0.43
Panchet Hill	6	2.5	0.5	0.9	2.6	0.54
	8	3.0	0.4	0.9	3.2	0.44
	10	3.0	0.6	0.9	3.2	0.62

Assuming that clay and silt form the nutritive silts, there has been a loss of about 100 million tonnes in a period of 10 years since impounding. The average composition of the deposited sediment in the reservoirs is given in Table 13.

Table 13 Composition of deposits – Maithon and Panchet Hill reservoirs

Material	Size	Load in million tonnes Maithon	Panchet Hill
Clay	2 microns and below	27.1	26.6
Silt	2 to 20 microns	15.5	33.8
Sand	20 microns and above	38.1	45.6
		80.7	106.0

3.4.1.9   *River bed variations – aggradation and degradation aspect*
3.4.1.9.1   Aggradation. Creation of man-made lakes cause development of deltas in their upstream reaches and the process would continue year after year raising the bed levels and becoming a catalyst to further deposition (Harrison, 1952). Consequent on the availability of nutrient materials in the delta deposit, brushwood and other vegetation grow luxuriously. This vegetation causes loss of water from the reservoir by evaporation. This vegetative screen also induces over land deposition of sediment far up the valley, resulting in swamp conditions and high groundwater levels in the adjacent fields.

Consequent on the formation of the delta, river bed changes are brought about in the upstream of the reservoir and the changes brought about in the Maithon and Panchet Hill reservoirs over the years is shown in Table 12. In the case of the Panchet Hill reservoir, the original slope of the river in the delta region which was of the order of 0.95 m/km has now been flattened to 0.475 m/km. In the case of the Maithon reservoir, the slope of the river in the delta portion which was about 1.9 m/km has been flattened to 0.95 m/km. The prediction of the occurrence of a delta region is necessary, not only from the aesthetic point of view for recreation etc, but also for predicting the region where the bed levels are likely to rise causing inundation at the time of high floods (Murthy, 1974).

3.4.1.9.1.1 A reservoir delta prediction technique. This has been based on the empirical procedure developed from the study of delta depositional patterns in reservoirs which have been surveyed and also by assuming certain values of slope for the formation of the delta in

Quantitative changes in the hydrological regime

terms of the original bed slope of the river, and fixing the pivot point between the topset and foreset slopes at half of the operating levels (normal and minimum). These levels are applied to the reservoir sections and the coarse quantity of sediment which is likely to deposit during the life time of the reservoir in the delta region is balanced by trial and error (Strand, 1970). Figure 8 shows an idealized reservoir delta profile.

Present knowledge and observational data are not enough to predict the slopes of the topset and foreset bed formations in the delta as the reservoirs are still in the formative stage, deltas with growth in their head reaches.

3.4.1.9.2 Degradation. The impounded, fairly silt free water passing over the dam has again the capacity for picking up the sediment load in the downstream reaches progressively lowering the bed of the channel. The scouring of the channel depends on the regulation of water from the dams and on the type of material making up the bed.

The quantitative aspects of the movement of river bed sand and the consequent change in river reaches below the Maithon and Panchet Hill dams is shown in Table 14. It is observed that there is a gradual increase in curvature as far as the backwater of the Durgapur Barrage. Within the barrage pond, there is a gradual accumulation of sediment. Below the barrage, there is again increase in volume. Table 15 shows the variations in bed slope in different reaches of the river downstream over a period of 10 years. The trend shows improvement in the channel regime.

Table 14 Volume of river reach below the dams in ha m

Year	A	B	C	D	E	F
1957	–	2,020	–	–	–	–
1958	–	–	–	–	–	–
1959	–	2,235	–	–	–	–
1960	–	2,364	–	–	–	–
1961	2,759	2,430	16,478	1,859	7,677	26,717
1962	2,859	2,440	17,650	1,792	8,137	27,181
1963	2,970	2,475	17,445	1,716	7,613	27,134
1964	3,072	2,512	18,074	1,498	7,889	28,238
1965	3,166	2,540	18,173	1,363	7,947	27,825
1966	3,242	2,598	18,337	–	8,114	28,433
1967	3,351	2,620	18,660	–	8,269	28,443
1968	3,396	2,735	19,054	1,406	8,002	28,847
1969	3,584	2,748	19,046	1,307	8,500	28,118
1970	3,605	2,740	19,335	1,149	8,414	28,014
1971	3,643	2,769	18,578	–	8,025	28,582

Reach A – Maithon Dam to confluence
Reach B – Panchet Dam to confluence
Reach C – Confluence to 8 km upstream of Durgapur
Reach D – 8 km upstream of Durgapur to Barrage
Reach E – Durgapur Barrage to Rhondia
Reach F – Rhondia to Surekalna

3.4.1.9.2.1 Factors for consideration. The main factors to be considered in analysing the degradation process are (1) the quantity and duration of the release below the dams and the sediment content, (2) hydraulic features of the channel including the bed form, (3) the inflow of water and sediment from the uncontrolled catchments, and (4) the grain size properties of the bed materials and their stratification in the river reach.

Quantitative changes in the hydrological regime

Table 15 Variation in bed slope in m/km

Reach	Original	1961	1971	Remarks
Maithon to confluence	1.1	0.7	0.5	Flattening
Panchet to confluence	0.6	0.4	0.2	Flattening
Confluence to Durgapur Pond	-	0.5	0.5	Status quo
Durgapur Barrage	-	0.5	0.7	Steepening
Durgapur Barrage to Rhondia	-	0.5	0.4	Flattening
Rhondia to Surekalna	-	0.4	0.4	Status quo

3.4.1.9.2.2 The technique for prediction of movement of the bed in the channel. Movement of river bed particles depends on the fluid properties and grain size properties. The most important fluid properties are the quantity and intensity of the flow and the most important grain properties are shape, size, roughness and bed formations such as ripples, dunes, plain bed, antidunes etc. Different theories have been put forward in the past to explain the initiation of particle motion and also the amount of movement. These procedures have limited applicability as the problem is very complex and the relevant parameters cannot easily be evaluated. It has, however, been generally appreciated that for a certain type of bed material the quantum of movement can be related to the water discharge as an exponential function, once incipient motion has taken place. For a river reach below dams to be stable, it is necessary to find out the conditions for the initiation of particle motion. This can be done through analysis of sand transport data along with the water discharge down the reach. A simple 3 parameter model of the following form can be studied to explain movement of sand from a certain river reach on account of water flow:

$$Q_s = K \left| \sum_{Q'} Q_i^n H_i \right|$$

where: Q_s = quantity of bed material moved during the period; Q_i = different rates of discharge, $L^3 T^{-1}$; Q' = discharge relating to the initiation of motion for the given reach with the existing bed material; H_i = duration of flow of intensity Q_i; n = index; k = constant for the given reach with the existing bed material.

The applicability of this model was tested in the important reach below Durgapur Barrage to Rhondia, a distance of 22 km. The bed material in this reach is fairly uniform to a considerable depth and consists of 90-100 per cent coarse sand of size 200-2000 microns. Survey data from year to year indicates the change in volume during the different years. The volume of sand movement for the years under study are given in Table 16.

Table 16 Volume of sand transported in the reach Durgapur Barrage to Rhondia in ha m

Year	A	B	C	D	E	F	G
1961	1285	401	884	(-)	67	818	461	1279
1962	(-) 59	401	(-)	(-)	76	(-)	526	0
1963	770	424	346	(-)	218	128	277	404
1964	222	439	(-)	(-)	136	(-)	58	58
1965	299	447	(-)		14	14	168	182

(-) indicates deposit

Reach A - Maithon Dam to confluence
Reach B - Panchet Dam to confluence
Reach C - Confluence to 8 km upstream of Durgapur
Reach D - 8 km upstream of Durgapur to barrage
Reach E - Durgapur Barrage to Rhondia
Reach F - Rhondia to Surekalna gauging station

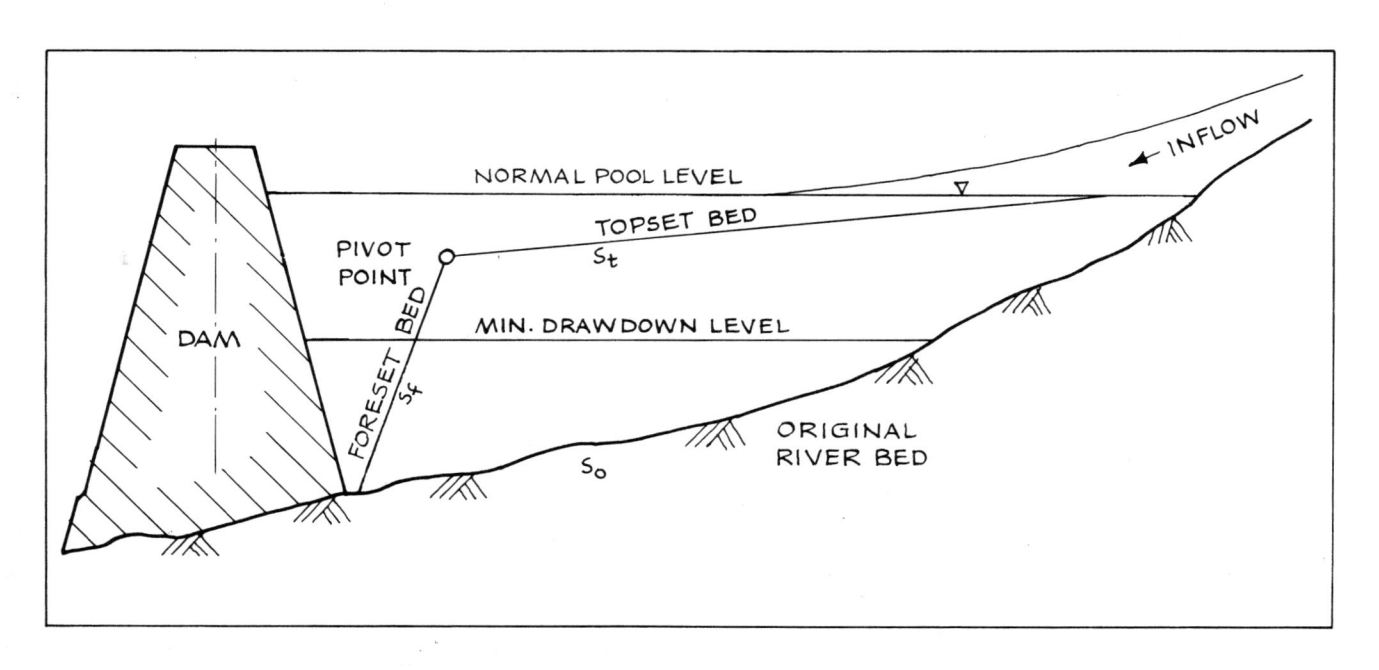

Figure 8   Idealised reservoir delta profile (not to scale)

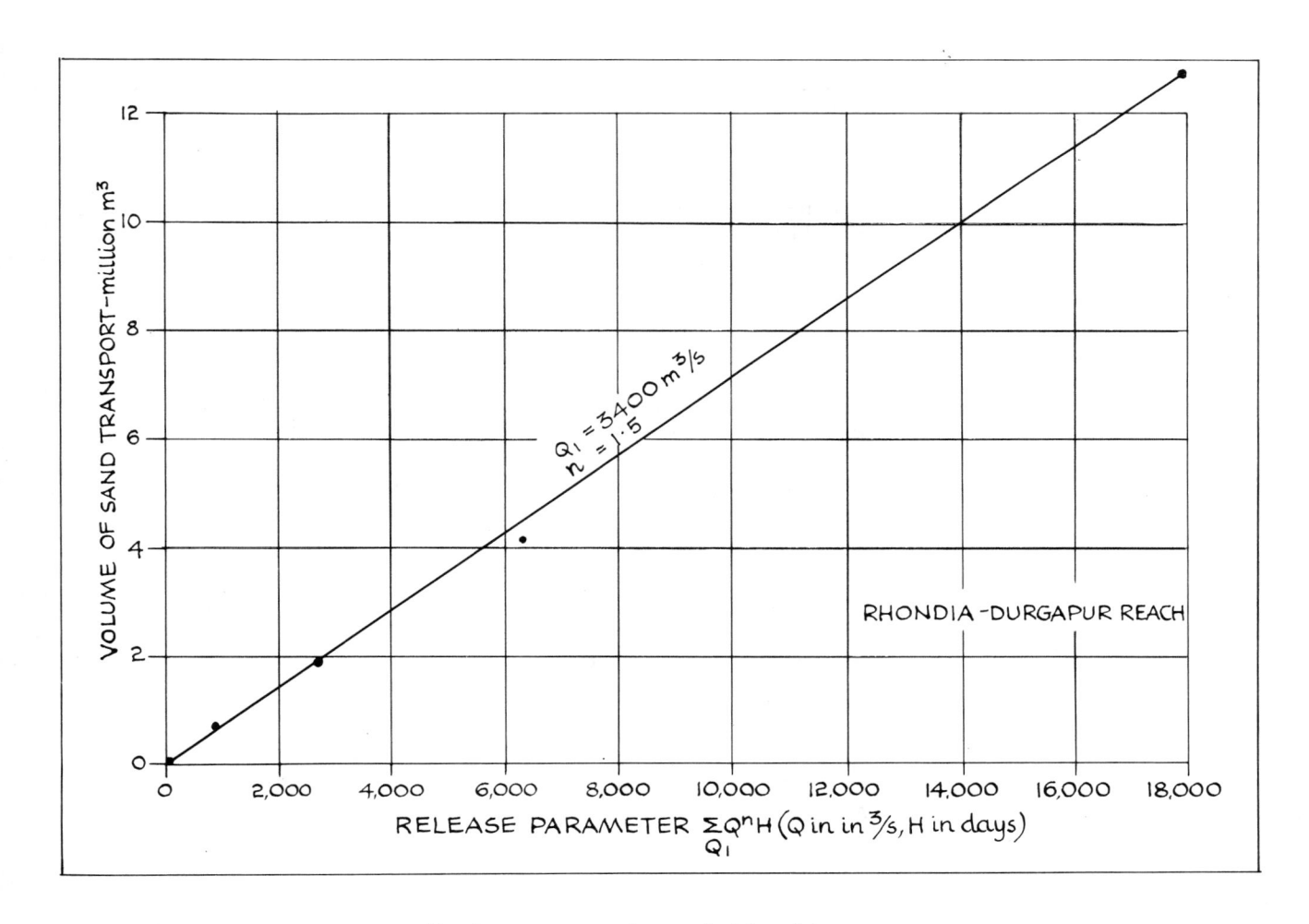

Figure 9   Sand transport - discharge parameter relationship

References

Water data for the corresponding years exists in the form of the release below the reach and the respective duration of the release. The model was developed on the basis of these data using an optimization process, the parameters n, k and Q' being fitted by the Rosenbrock optimization technique (Rosenbrock, 1960) with the following objectives:

$$F = \text{Min} \sum \left| (Q_{s\ oj} - Q_{s\ cj})^2 \right|$$

$$j = 1, 2, \ldots, N$$

where: $Q_{s\ oj}$ = observed quantity of sand movement during year j; $Q_{s\ cj}$ = computed quantity of sand movement during year j; N is the number of years of analysis.

Based on data relating to the period 1961-1965, the process of scouring in the reach below the Durgapur Barrage to Rhondia will be governed by the equation:

$$Q_s = 717 \sum \left| Q_i^{1.5} H_i \right|$$

$$Q' = 3400 \text{ m}^3/\text{sec}$$

where: Q_s = quantity of sand to be transported from the reach, m^3; Q_i = water flow below the reach, m^3/sec; H_i = no of days of water release of intensity Q_i.

It is apparent from this analysis that a flow of 3400 m^3/sec is the minimum required to initiate particle motion and transport of sand from the reach in question. Flow below this rate has no effect and does not figure in the sand-water discharge correlation. Prediction of sand movement during a certain period from this reach can be based on the discharge parameter $\Sigma_i^{1.5}$ relating to the same period. The minimum value of Q_i to be considered in this case is 3400 m^3/sec. Figure 9 presents a graphical plot valid for the reach and the existing sand grains.

Acknowledgements

The author gratefully acknowledges the assistance rendered by Mr B K Banerjee, Executive Engineer, and Mr K S Kundu, Draftsman, in preparing this report.

REFERENCES

Butorin, N.V. 1971. The Rybinsk man-made Lake and its impact on environment. *International Symposium on Man-made Lakes,* Knoxville, Tennessee, USA.

Harrison, A.S. 1952. Deposition at the heads of reservoirs, Corps of Engineers, Omaha, Nebraska, *Proceedings of the Fifth Hydraulic Research,* USA.

Lagler, K.F. 1969. *Man-made lakes - Planning and Development,* FAO Publication, Rome.

Murthy, B.N. 1974. River bed variations - aggradation and degradation, *International seminar on Hydraulics of Alluvial Streams* (Background papers), IAHR, New Delhi, India.

Murthy, B.N. 1976. Watershed management and soil conservation in the Damodar Valley, Hydrological Review, Vol 12, No 1 (a contribution to IHP), The Indian National Committee for the IHP, Council of Scientific and Industrial Research, New Delhi, India.

Rosenbrock, H.H. 1960. An automatic method of finding the greatest or least value of a function, *The Computer Journal,* 3, 175-184.

Strand, Robert I. 1970. Reservoir Sedimentation, Hydrology Section, United States Bureau of Reclamation, Denver, Colorado, USA.

Bibliography

Dale, A. Hoffman, and Jonez, Al.R. 1971. Lake Mead, USA, *International Symposium on Man-made Lakes,* Knoxville, Tennessee, USA.

References

Division of Water Control Planning, 1968. Sedimentation in reservoirs, *Report* No 6693, Knoxville, Tennesse.

IAHS/UNESCO, 1968. The use of analogue and digital computers in hydrology, *Proceedings of the Tucson Symposium, IAHS Publication Nos 80 and 81,* Tucson, 755 pp.

IAHS/UNESCO, 1970. Symposium on World Water Balance, *Proceedings of the Reading Symposium, IAHS Publication Nos 92 and 93,* 537 pp.

Influence of man on the hydrological cycle, Guidelines to policies for the safe development of land and water resources, Status and trends of Research on Hydrology, 1965-74, UNESCO.

Lane, E.W. 1953. Some aspects of reservoir sedimentation, *Central Board of Irrigation and Power Journal,* New Delhi, India.

Murthy, B.N. 1968. Capacity survey of storage reservoirs, *Central Board of Irrigation and Power Publication* 89, New Delhi, India.

Reed, A. Elliot, 1971. The TVA Experience, *Symposium on Man-made Lakes,* Knoxville, Tennessee, USA.

3.4.2 SOME POSSIBILITIES FOR RECONSTRUCTING THE DATA CORRESPONDING TO NATURAL
HYDROLOGICAL CONDITIONS
by C Diaconu, P Serban and V A L Stanescu[1]

3.4.2.1 General
The natural hydrological regime which is the basis for water management activities is modified as these activities develop. Thus the situation is reached that at a certain gauging station where once the natural runoff regime was measured, a substantially modified flow was gradually recorded. This new flow regime is no longer directly relevant for assessing the potential of the natural water resources. The further use of water resources should consider the natural hydrological regime as the only standard for assessing the water resources potential, in order to establish the characteristics of further development.

Knowledge of the long term natural hydrological regime in the case of rivers which are already utilized to a considerable extent should, on the one hand, improve the statistical basis for computation of hydrological characteristics and, on the other hand, allow for the knowledge of the temporal variations of water resources.

These requirements impose a need for reconstructing the natural hydrological regime of rivers which are already developed from the water resources point of view. This reconstruction of the natural runoff is defined as the computation procedures which, starting with the modified regime, delete or correct the modifying facts so as to yield final results reflecting the runoff irrespective of the water uses or the development of the region.

Modification of the natural regime can be caused by two main categories of water use:
- water consumption (or water use)
- activities which change runoff distribution in time.
These categories of use can occur either separately or together (in which case the effects are accumulated).

The types of water comsumption fall in turn into two groups:
- permanent ones (industrial)
- seasonal (agricultural)

Figures 1 and 2 show the way the water consumption, or the runoff redistribution in time, can modify the natural hydrological regime.

3.4.2.2 When is reconstruction to be performed?
A problem of utmost importance in reconstructing natural runoff is the determination of the discharge amount in comparison with required corrections marked ΔQ for which the following relation is valid:

$$Q_N = Q_M \pm \Delta Q \tag{1}$$

where: Q_N and Q_M are the natural and modified discharges respectively, at a given hydrometric station.

---

[1] Institut de Meteorologie et d'Hydrologie, Soseava Bucuresti-Ploiesti No 97, Bucarest, Romania

Figure 1   Modification of the natural pattern of runoff by man's use of water

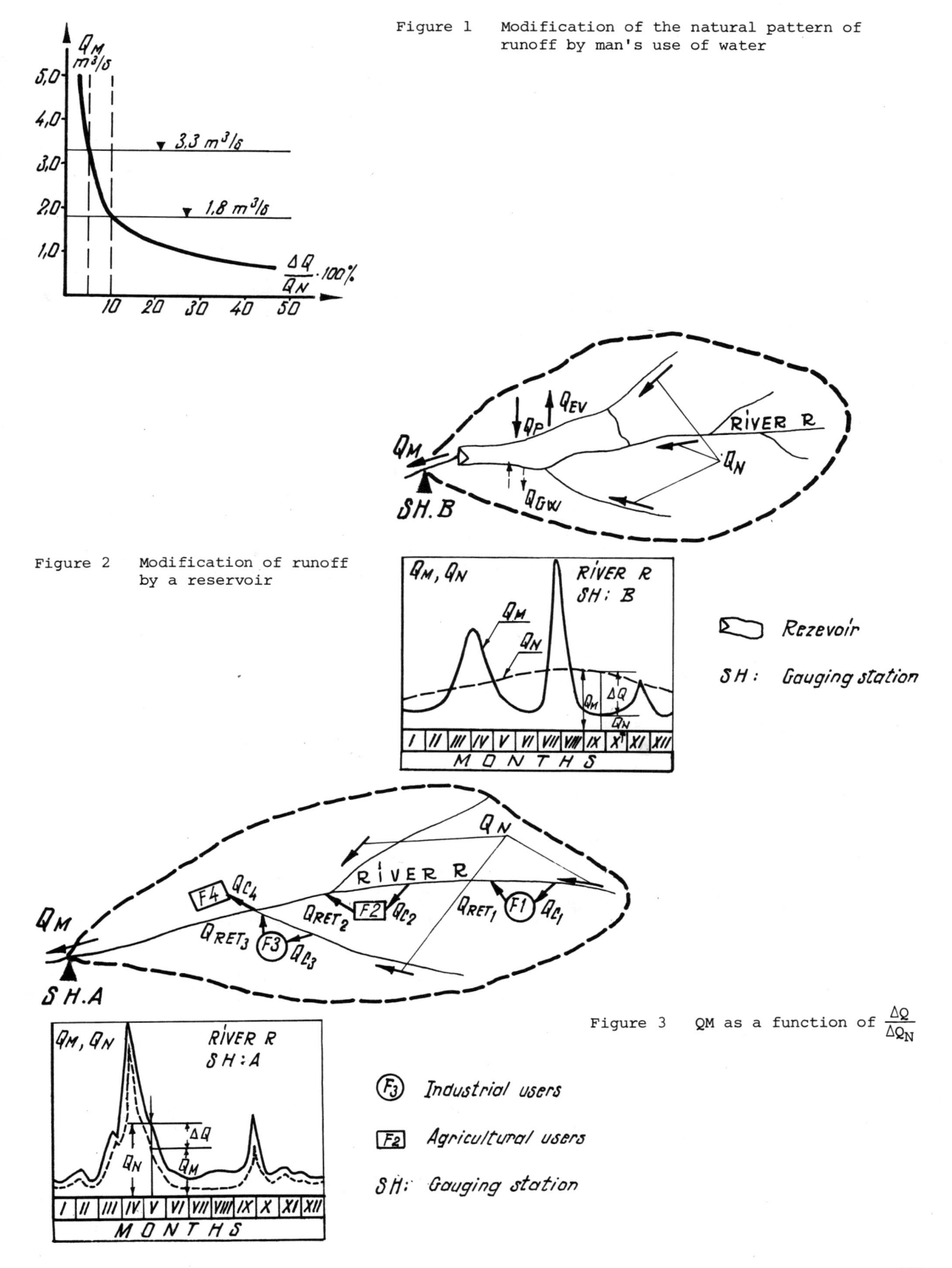

Figure 2   Modification of runoff by a reservoir

Figure 3   QM as a function of $\frac{\Delta Q}{\Delta Q_N}$

155

Possibilities for reconstructing the data

The reconstruction is justifiable only for a correction exceeding the accuracy ε% with which the natural discharge is measured, ie:

$$\left|\frac{Q_N - Q_M}{Q_N}\right| \cdot 100 > |\varepsilon\%| \qquad (2)$$

or

$$\left|\frac{\Delta Q}{Q_N}\right| \cdot 100 > |\varepsilon\%| \qquad (3)$$

Generally, the accuracy of measurement, ε, is of the order a ± (5-10)%.

When the correction ΔQ is between 5 and 10% or between -5 and -10%, then reconstruction is necessary. When the correction exceeds ± 10% reconstruction becomes absolutely necessary.

This criterion implies a correction which varies with the natural flow and with the modified discharge, respectively. That is:

$$\frac{Q_N - Q_M}{Q_N} \cdot 100 = f(Q_M) \qquad (4)$$

and

$$\frac{Q_N - Q_M}{Q_N} \cdot 100 = f(Q_N) \qquad (5)$$

This variation allows, in its turn, for the Q_N and Q_M discharges to be established, for which corrections are necessary or absolutely necessary.

Suppose that for a given period of time the modified discharge varies something between 0.500 m³/s and 7.5 m³/s and that ΔQ varies as a function of Q_M as shown in the table below. Making use of relation (1) one arrives at Q_N and $\frac{\Delta Q}{Q_N} \cdot 100$ as

Q_M	ΔQ	Q_N	$\frac{\Delta Q}{Q_N} \cdot 100\%$
0.500	0.220	0.280	78.5
1.000	0.200	0.800	25.0
2.000	0.180	1.320	13.6
3.000	0.160	1.840	8.7
4.000	0.150	2.850	5.3
5.000	0.150	4.850	3.1
7.000	0.150	6.850	2.2

The graphic representation of Q_M as a function of $\frac{\Delta Q}{Q_N}$ shows (Figure 3) that for $Q_M < 3.3$ m³/s the reconstruction is optional, (ε < ±10%) while for $Q_M < 1.8$ m³/s it is absolutely necessary (ε > ±10%).

3.4.2.3   **The theoretical basis for reconstructing the average monthly discharges**
3.4.2.3.1   Water balance equation. The basis of the average monthly discharge reconstruction lies in the water balance equation:

$$I = O + WU \qquad (6)$$

where: I is the input hydrological element to be found in the section under study and represents the natural runoff regime; O is the output element of the section under study either measured at a hydrometric station or computed as the discharge from a reservoir; WU represent the water use.

3.4.2.3.2   Derivation of the reconstruction equation for mean monthly discharges. The reconstruction equation can be established assuming the following hypotheses:

- there is water use only
- there is redistribution of usage of the runoff only
- there are both types of use.

3.4.2.3.2.1 Water use. Considering the example in Figure 1, the equation is:

$$Q_N = Q_M + Q_{C_1} - Q_{RET_1} + Q_{C_2} - Q_{RET_2} + Q_{C_3} - Q_{RET_3} + Q_{C_4} = Q_M + \sum_{i=1}^{4} Q_{C_i} - \sum_{j=1}^{3} Q_{RET_j} \qquad (7)$$

where: Q_N is the mean natural monthly discharge; Q_M is the mean modified monthly discharge; Q_{C_i} is the mean monthly discharge drawn off the river R through the use i; Q_{RET_j} = the monthly discharge restored to river R through use j.

Marking Q_{N_x} the mean natural monthly discharge in the x section and Q_{M_x} of the modified regime, we come to a general relationship:

$$Q_{N_x} = Q_{M_x} + Q_{U_x} \qquad (8)$$

where:

$$Q_U = \sum_{i=1}^{NC(x)} Q_{C_i} - \sum_{j=1}^{NRET(x)} Q_{RET_j} \qquad (9)$$

where: NC(x) is the number of abstractions upstream of the respective x section; $N_{RET}(x)$ is the number of discharges upstream of section x.

If a transfer is carried out from one river to another then (Q_C) is considered the amount of water abstracted from the river releasing water and (Q_{RET}) is the amount returned to the river receiving it.

3.4.2.3.2.2 The runoff redistribution use. The continuity equation (6) applied to a reservoir (Figure 2) is of the following form:

$$Q_N + Q_P = Q_T + Q_S + Q_E + Q_{AC} + Q_{EV} \pm Q_{GW} \qquad (10)$$

where: Q_N is the mean monthly rate of flow entering the reservoir; Q_P is the discharge equivalent to the mean depth of precipitation falling on to the surface of the reservoir; Q_T is the mean monthly turbine discharge of the hydro-electric power station; Q_S is the mean monthly discharge exceeding the turbine discharge; Q_E is the mean monthly discharge released as bottom water outlet; Q_{AC} is the mean monthly discharge stored in or released from the reservoir; Q_{EV} is the mean monthly loss caused by evaporation; Q_{GW} is the mean monthly change in the water table.

From the studies performed it is evident that generally Q_P, Q_{EV} and Q_{GV} can be neglected for most cases. If we take the outlet discharge (Q_M) to be:

$$Q_M = Q_T + Q_S + Q_E \qquad (11)$$

then (10) becomes:

$$Q_N = Q_M + Q_{AC} \qquad (12)$$

For a certain section x equation (12) generally becomes:

$$Q_{N_x} = Q_{M_x} + \sum_{k=1}^{NR(x)} Q_{AC_x} \qquad (13)$$

where: NR(x) is the number of reservoirs located upstream of the section x.

3.4.2.3.2.3 Water consumption redistributing the runoff. Applying the superposition principle of the effects we come to the mean monthly discharge in the natural regime in section x marked Q_{N_x} which is:

$$Q_{N_x} = Q_{M_x} + Q_{U_x} \qquad (14)$$

where:

Possibilities for reconstructing the data

$$Q_{U_x} = \sum_{i=1}^{NC(x)} Q_{C_i} - \sum_{j=1}^{NRET(x)} Q_{RET_j} + \sum_{k=1}^{NR(x)} Q_{AC_k} \qquad (15)$$

Q_{U_x} being the mean monthly discharge used upstream of section x.

3.4.2.4 Methodology for determining the elements required in reconstructing the natural regime

3.4.2.4.1 Turbine discharge determination

3.4.2.4.1.1 General. Determination of the discharges from hydro-electric stations reveal several shortcomings due to unsteady flow and to the difficulty of performing the measurements.

Anyway, the accuracy of discharge determination, making use of hydro-electric station installations, is greater than that obtained by normal means.

Hence the turbine discharge Q_T is determined as an outlet discharge from the relation below:

$$P_g = 9.81\, \eta_h(Q_T) \cdot \eta_t(Q_T) \cdot \eta_g(P_T(Q_T)) \cdot Q_T\, H_b \qquad (16)$$

where: P_g is the power yielded by the hydro-electric station in Kw; Q_T is the turbine discharge in m³/s; H_b is the gross head of the site in m; $\eta_h(Q_T)$, $\eta_t(Q_T)$ and $\eta_g(P_T(Q_T))$ are the hydraulic, turbine and general efficiencies respectively.

The conclusion can be drawn that the three efficiency types depend on the turbine discharge to be determined. In order to determine the turbine discharge when P_g and H_b are known, a method is suggested herein which is simplified but sufficiently accurate. Beforehand, each element in equation (16) is analysed.

3.4.2.4.1.1.1 The power yielded by the hydro-electric station. Generally a hydro-electric station is provided with several generators. In this case the overall power yielded by the stations is:

$$P_g = \sum_{i=1}^{N} P_{g_i} \qquad (17)$$

where: N is the number of generators; P_{g_i} is the power from the ith generator.

The P_{g_i} power can be determined either:
- directly, from the megawatt graph (Figure 4), or
- indirectly, from the E_i energy recording on the counter where P_{g_i} can be inferred from D the operating period:

$$P_{g_i} = \frac{E_i}{D} \qquad (18)$$

3.4.2.4.1.1.2 Gross head of a hydro-electric site. This is the difference between the holding level in the reservoir, Z_h and the water level in the energy dissipator Z_d:

$$H_b = Z_h - Z_d \qquad (19)$$

In the computations it is sufficiently precise to determine an average discharge for the operation period (d) of the station. Hence the power and gross head can be estimated as an average for the given duration.

From an analysis on several hydro-electric stations, the maximum error given by this method was found to be ± 7%.

3.4.2.4.1.1.3 The efficiency of power generator is given by:

$$\eta_g = \frac{P_g}{P_T} \qquad (20)$$

where P_T is the turbine power.

The generator efficiency appears as a curve in Figure 5.

3.4.2.4.1.1.4 Turbine efficiency is given by the relation below:

$$\eta_T = \frac{P_T}{P_{H_n}} \qquad (21)$$

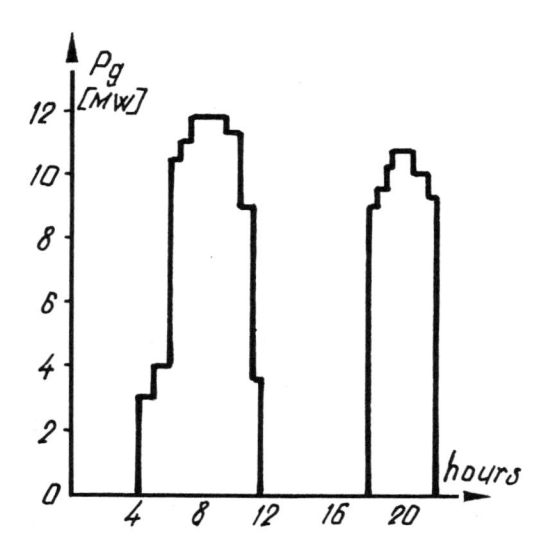

Figure 4 Power yielded by a hydro-electric power station

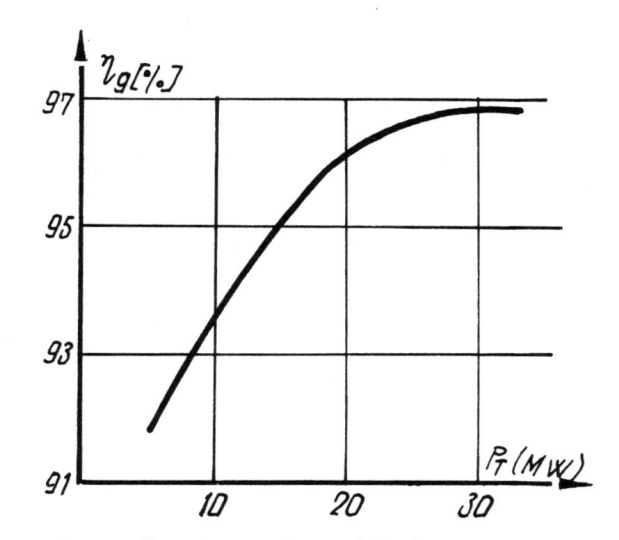

Figure 5 Generator efficiency

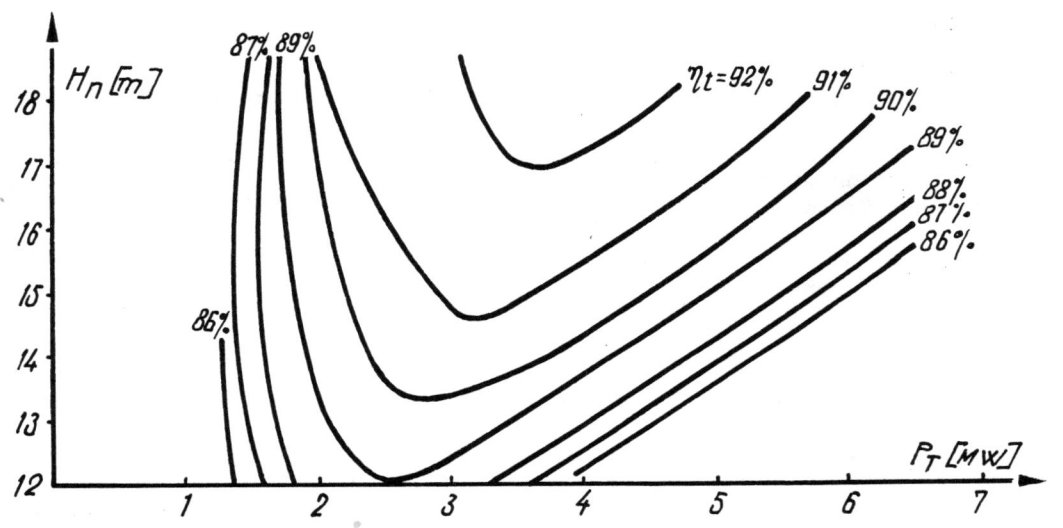

Figure 6 Turbine efficiency function in terms of turbine power (P_T) and net head (H_n)

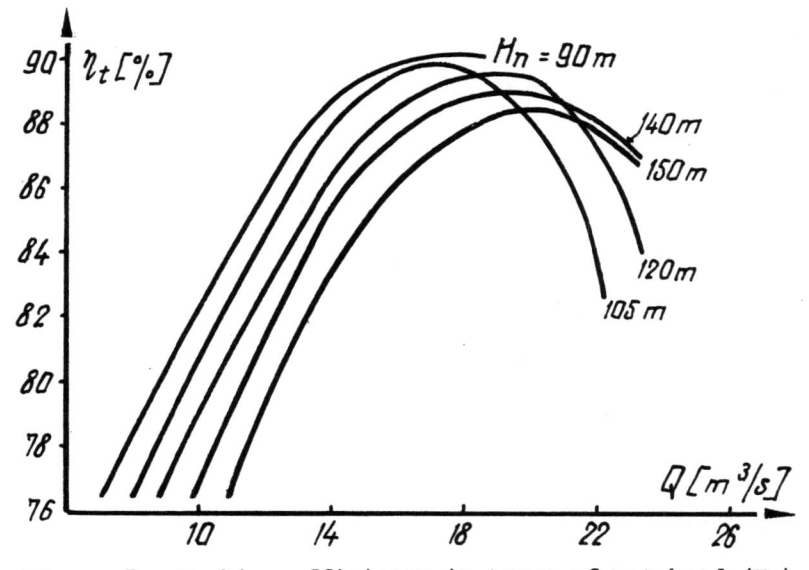

Figure 7 Turbine efficiency in terms of net head (H_n) and turbine discharge (Q_T)

Possibilities for reconstructing the data

where: P_{H_n} is the hydraulic power employed by the turbine.

The turbine efficiency can be determined on experimental grounds or as function of the curves of the turbine established by laboratory tests. These curves are also called topographs and occur as two types.

One of these types gives the turbine efficiency function of the turbine power P_T and the net head H_n (Figure 6) while the other gives the turbine efficiency in terms of turbine discharge (Q_T) and net head H_n (Figure 7).

3.4.2.4.1.1.5 Hydraulic efficiency. η is the ratio between the net head H_n and the gross head H_b.

$$\eta_h = \frac{H_n}{H_b} \tag{22}$$

The net head is:

$$H_n = H_b - \Delta h \tag{23}$$

where: Δh represents head loss. The head losses take place all the way from the reservoir to the turbine and the formula is as follows:

$$\Delta h = \frac{1}{g\pi^2 D^2} \left(\Sigma \lambda \frac{1}{D} + \Sigma \zeta \right) Q^2 \tag{24}$$

Particular attention should be paid to hydraulic efficiency in the case of hydro-electric stations with a large head.

3.4.2.4.1.2 Methods for turbine discharge computation. There are two methods for turbine discharge computation of the hydro-electric station, namely the exact method and the simplified one.

3.4.2.4.1.2.1 The exact method. The relation below is considered:

$$P_g = 9.81 \, \eta_T \, \eta_g \, Q_T \, H_n \tag{25}$$

where: η_T, η_g, H_n are initially unknown and dependent on the turbine discharge of the hydro-power plant

For computing Q_T use is made of an iterative method in which an initial value (Q_T) is chosen for the discharge and then the net head, the head losses and the turbine and generator efficiencies are computed. With their aid the Q_T value is again computed from (16) and compared to the initial value. If between the initially chosen value and the one computed from equation (16) there is a relative deviation of more than 2%, the iteration is resumed.

3.4.2.4.1.2.2 The simplified method. This method consists in drawing diagrams $Q_T = f(H_b \cdot P_g)$ for each hydro-electric station, taking into account the most probable versions of the turbine - generator sets. In order to achieve this N versions for the group supply, one for each pair of Q_T, H_b values.

Suppose, for instance, an A hydro-electric station having 6 turbines with Q_1, Q_2 ... Q_6 discharges.

Suppose that 4 of the turbines are connected to a forced conduct and the other two are connected to another forced conduct.

For some value Q_j of the discharge between the 0 and the final discharge as well as the distributed version of the discharge in the 6 turbines is determined as follows:
(1) Head loss per each group i (Δh_i) as a sum of head losses along headrace conducts.
(2) Net head per each i group (H_n) by means of formula (23).
(3) The turbine efficiency (η_{T_i}) results from its characteristics (Figure 7) as a function of Q_{T_i} discharge and the net head H_{n_i}.
(4) Turbine power P_{T_i} from the following formula

$$P_{T_i} = 9.81 \, \eta_{T_i} \, Q_{T_i} \, H_{n_i} \tag{26}$$

(5) Generator efficiency (η_{g_i}) resulting from the curve in Figure 5, is a function of the

Table 1 Power supplied by the hydro-electric power station

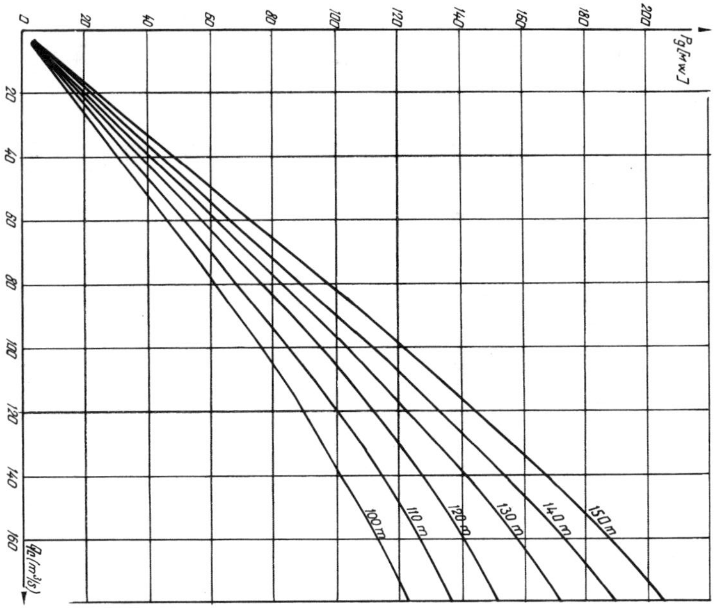

Figure 8 Power station curves

Possibilities for reconstructing the data

turbine power P_{Ti}.
(6) Generator power (P_{gi}) is obtained by means of formula (20).
(7) The overall power P_g supplied by the hydro-electric station is obtained from formula (17).

Finally we come to the power supplied by the hydro-electric station corresponding to each P_{gi} version. Calculating the arithmetic mean of these values the most probable P_y power results as given by the station for a Q_T, H_b pair of values.

Table 1 shows the method of computation for the power supplied P_{gj} by the hydro-electric station, where $H_b = 120$ m and $Q_T = 50$, 100 and 150 m^3/s.

Performing similar computations for other pairs of values (H_b, Q_T) for each pair (H_b, Q_T) there is a P_g value. Starting from these curves can be drawn such that $Q_T = f(H_b, P_g)$ in Figure (8) valid for a hydro-power station. Another method for $Q_T = f(H_b, P_g)$ curve drawing is presented in Figures (9) and (10) worked out for two other hydro-electric stations.

The determination of turbine discharges by means of the simplified method is to an accuracy of ± 8% if the following recommendations are considered:
- for the low head hydro-electric stations (H_b < 20 m) it is necessary that the turbine discharges were determined for the characteristic time interval Δt_i of quasi-stationary power and head.
- for the other types of hydro-electric stations (of medium and large head) the determination of turbine discharges is done at Δt_j time intervals when the power is quasi-stationary as the head varies little with these stations.

3.4.2.4.2 Determination of pumped discharges. Some hydro-electric stations are provided with pumps to move water from downstream to upstream.

The power P_m received by a pump from the electricity system (Kw), required to raise a certain water discharge for a given level difference H_b, is:

$$P_m = \frac{9.81 \, Q_p \, H_b}{\eta_m \, \eta_p \, \eta_h} \qquad (27)$$

where: Q_p is the pumped discharge in m^3/s; H_b is the pumping height (m); η_m is the efficiency of the electric motor received from the supplying works; η_p is the efficiency of the pump under the form of topographs similar to the turbine efficiency; η_h is the hydraulic efficiency of the pumping device.

The determination of the pumped discharges is similar to the turbine discharges of the hydro-electric station.

3.4.2.4.3 Spillway discharge determination. Waste water discharge determination is performed by means of the weir curve, knowing the depth of the water and the operating principle of the gates. The weir curve represents the relation between the discharge passing the weir and the depth of the water (H). Sometimes the weir curve $Q_s = f(H)$ is drawn after hydraulic laboratory tests.

3.4.2.4.4 Determination of discharges released by the bottom water outlet. The determination of discharges released by bottom water outlet, the depth of water above the release axis, is given by:

$$Q_s = m \, w \, \sqrt{2gH} \qquad (28)$$

where: w is the section area;

$$m = \frac{1}{\sqrt{1 + \lambda \frac{L}{D} + \Sigma \zeta}} \qquad (29)$$

λ and ζ coefficients refer to linear and local head losses, respectively.

3.4.2.4.5 Determination of stored or released discharges from storage reservoirs. The computation of the stored discharge Q_{AC} for a Δt period is by means of the formula below:

$$Q_{AC} = \pm \frac{\Delta W}{\Delta T} \qquad (30)$$

where:

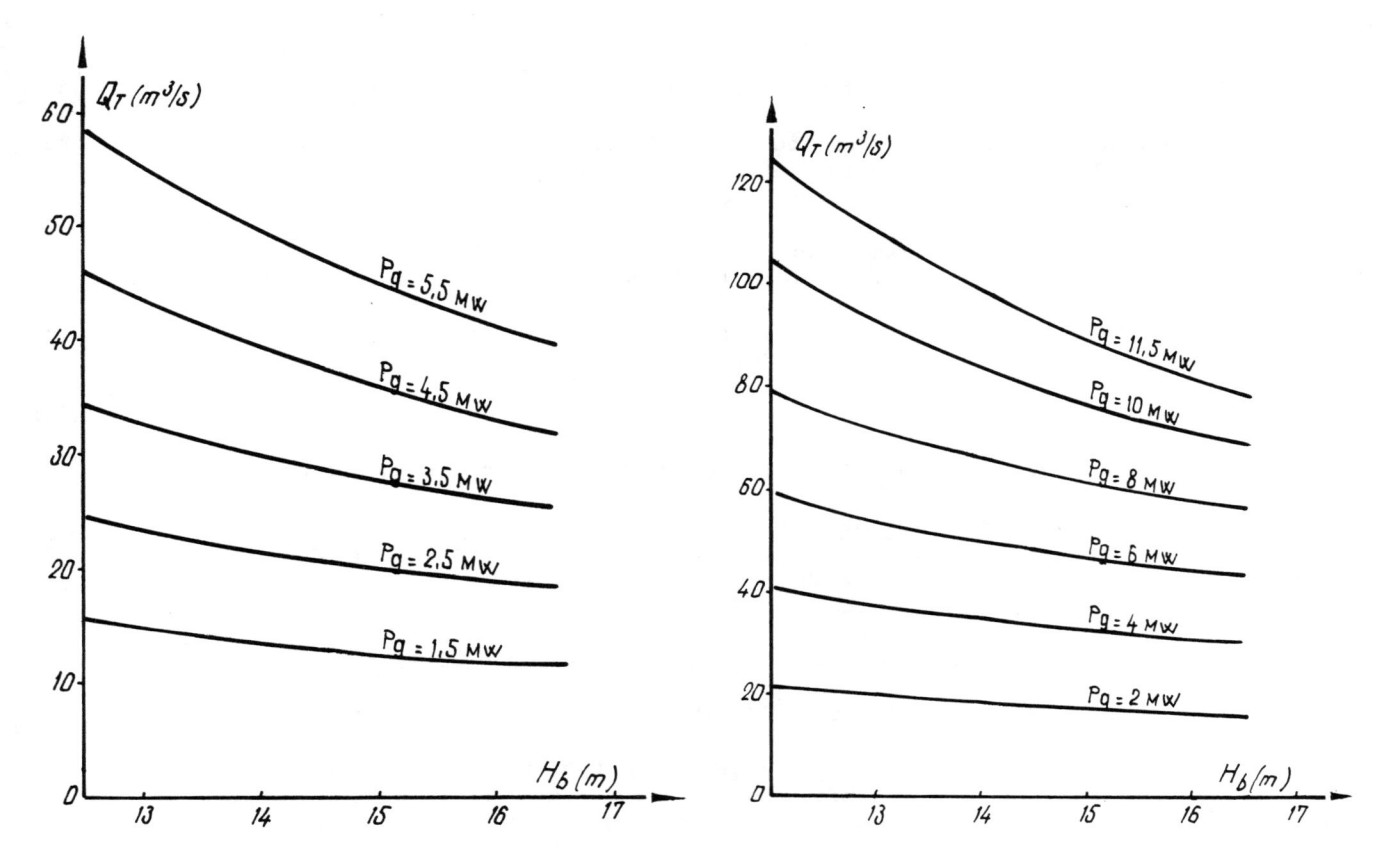

Figures 9 and 10   Alternative power station curves

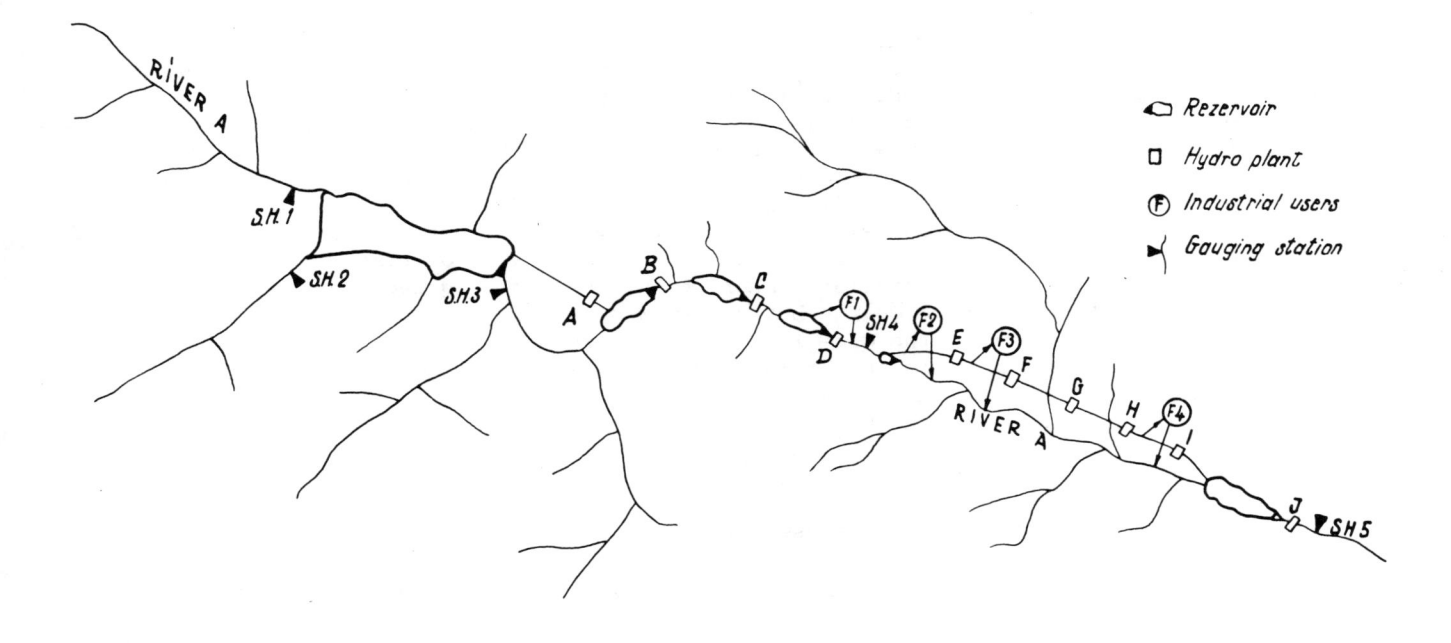

Figure 11   Design scheme for River A

Possibilities for reconstructing the data

$$\Delta W = W_2 - W_1 \tag{31}$$

where: W_1 and W_2 are the amounts of water in the storage reservoir at the beginning and end of the period ΔT.

These volumes are obtained from the reservoir capacity curve $W = f(H)$, the levels at the beginning and end of the time interval ΔT being known.

The values of the stored discharges are determined by formula (30) and can be affected by two types of errors, namely:
- errors of observing the reservoir levels
- errors caused by modification in time of the reservoir capacity curve due to siltation.

3.4.2.4.6 Reservoir discharge determination. Reservoir discharge can be determined from pump characteristics and hours of operation of the pumps as follows:

$$Q_{C(RET)} = \frac{\sum Q_{P_i} \Delta t}{T} \tag{32}$$

where: Q_{P_i} is the pump discharge; T is the hours of operation within one month.

3.4.2.5 **An example of average monthly discharge calculation**
Re-examining formulae (14) and (15) we come to the conclusion that all the elements of the balance equation can be computed by the procedures indicated under points 4.1 to 4.6.

In order to find the right method to do so, we shall choose a design scheme for the river A (Figure 11):
- five storage reservoirs, four of which (B; C; D; J) undergo daily regulation and another one (A);
- ten hydro-electric stations of which nine (B to J) have a low head and one (A) has a high head;
- four industrial supplies F_1; F_2; F_3; F_4 return part of their abstractions to the river.

Before any design or construction on river A, 5 hydro-metric stations existed on this river: SH_1; SH_2; SH_3; SH_4; SH_5. Out of these only SH_1 and SH_2 still exist (cf Figure 11) unaltered by human activities.

To provide a homogeneous statistical series it is necessary that reconstruction of the natural mean monthly discharges should be performed for stations SH_3; SH_4 and SH_5.

With this aim formulae (14) and (15) will be applied as follows:
- the turbine discharges of the (A; D and J) hydro-electric stations will be computed as they are situated upstream of the SH_3; SH_4; SH_5 stations.

The turbine discharge computation uses the diagrams in Figures 8 (for A); 9 and 10 (for D and J respectively). In this case the power (recorded megawatts) is necessary, for various time intervals as well as the gross head for the same period of time.

For each interval i considered a Q_{T_i} turbine discharge will result. The average monthly value Q_T is reached by means of a weighted average in the period of time considered:
- the spillway discharges from reservoirs A, D and J are computed. In order to do this both weir curves are drawn as shown in Figures 12, 13 and 14. The rising level of the canal intake above the weir peaks, as well as the water level, in the reservoirs being known, one can determine the constant runoff discharge for a given period of time. The mean monthly value Q_S can be obtained in a similar manner, by means of a weighted average:
- the released discharges due to $\overline{Q_E}$ the bottom water outlet are computed for the storage reservoir A as a function of the $Q_E = f(H)$ curve, shown in Figure 15.

The mean monthly value Q can be obtained by a similar weighting procedure taking into account the discharge periods in a month;
- The measured discharge is computed

$$\overline{Q}_M = \overline{Q}_T + \overline{Q}_S + \overline{Q}_E$$

- Function of the discharge recordings used by F_1, F_2 ... and F_5 their sum is determined as $\Sigma \overline{Q_F}$.
- The mean monthly stored discharges Q_{AC} are determined for each section S_3, S_4 and S_5, as follows.
- For section S_3 only reservoir A is considered (cf Figure 11) for which the capacity curve is given (Figure 16). Thus Q_{AC} is obtained in section 3 as a function of the levels recorded in reservoir A at the beginning and end of the month.

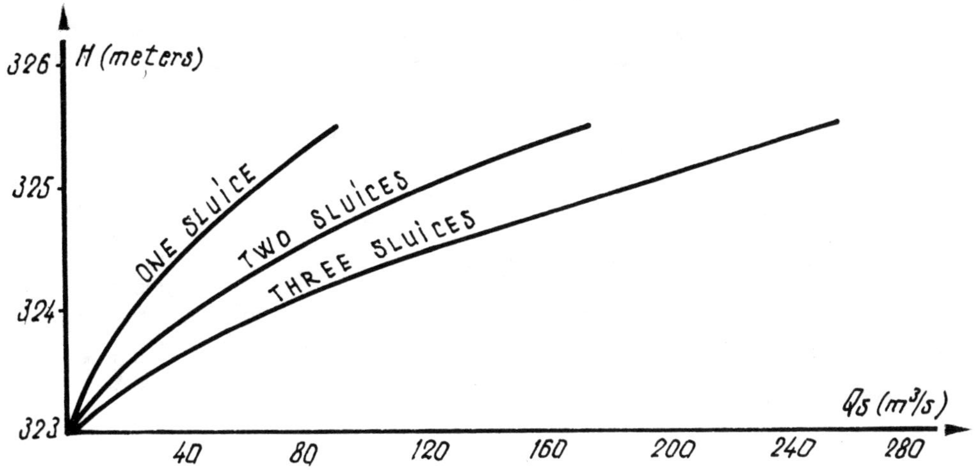

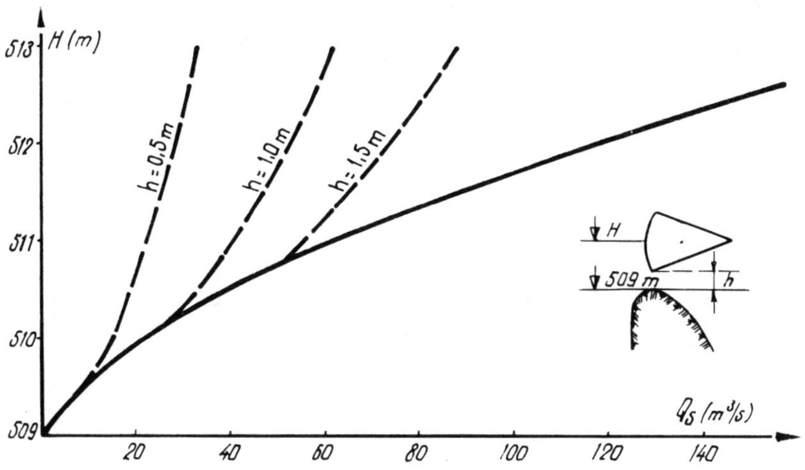

Figure 12   Weir curve

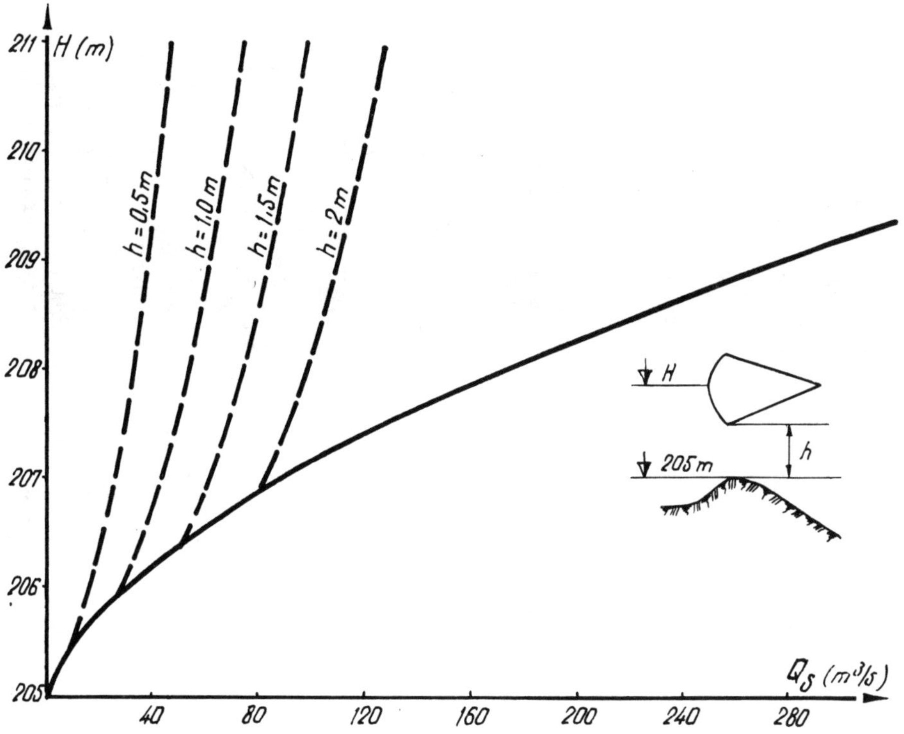

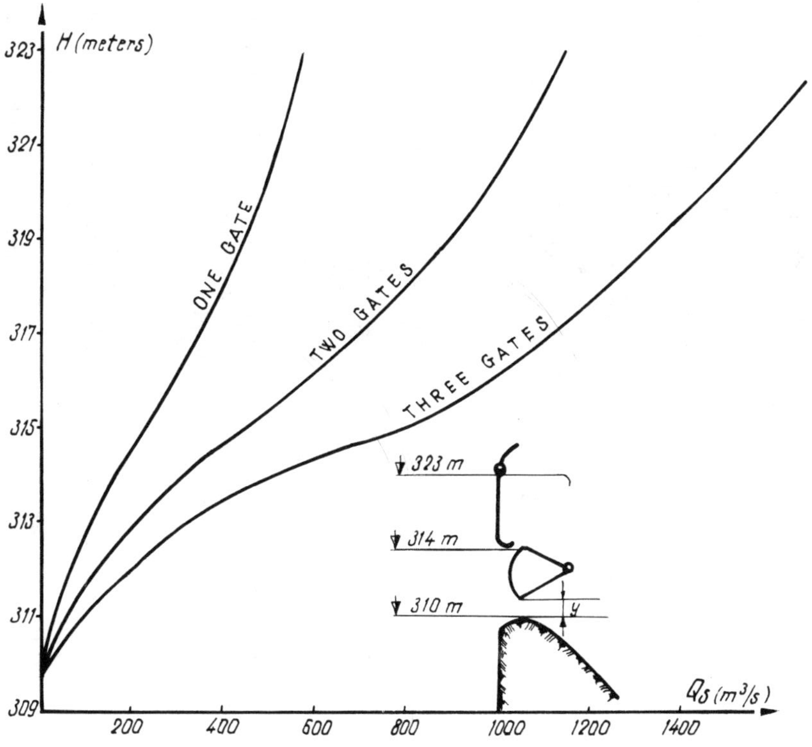

Figure 13a Weir curve

Figure 13b Weir curve

Figure 14   Weir curve

165

Possibilities for reconstructing the data

- For section S₄, reservoirs A, B, C and D will be considered, for which the capacity curves are given. Q_{AC} can be estimated in section 4 as the sum of stored discharges Q_{AC} in the four reservoirs (A, B, C and D). The capacity curves of the storage reservoirs in B, C, D and J are shown in Figure 17.
- For section S₅, all reservoirs are to be considered (A, B, C, D and J) so that $\sum_{1}^{5} Q_{AC}$ can be computed.
- The sum of "waste" discharges is computed $\overline{Q}_U = \Sigma \overline{Q}_F + \Sigma \overline{Q}_{AC}$ for each section.
- According to formula (14) the mean monthly reconstructed discharge is:

$$\overline{Q}_N = \overline{Q}_M + \overline{Q}_U$$

The outcome of these computations is shown in Table 2 for 1970, monthly values.

3.4.2.6 Possibilities of reconstructing flood waves

As is commonly known, flood waves undergo modifications when passing through storage reservoirs. Such modifications are larger, the larger the retention potential of the reservoir.

Where there is a certain number of storage reservoirs on a river, the measured discharges in the various sections do not reflect the natural potential of flood wave occurrence. Maximum discharges will be reduced.

Therefore, the conclusion can be drawn that it is necessary to reconstruct the flood wave.

Due to the small time unit used and to the various conditions existing in each river section, reconstruction of the flood waves cannot be performed but with computers.

In order to do that it is necessary that all conditions possibly existing on a given river section are established, namely:
(1) River sections with substantial lateral contributions without storage reservoirs;
(2) River sections with substantial lateral contributions and with storage reservoirs;
(3) River sections without substantial lateral contributions without storage reservoirs;
(4) River sections without substantial lateral contributions but with storage reservoirs;
(5) River sections with large discharges.

Figure 18 shows an example with 7 sections displaying all five possible conditions existing.

In order to reconstruct the flood wave at any point on the river the following procedure should be considered:
- For sections 1 and 2 the flood waves for the natural regime are recorded at stations A and B.
- For section 3 the relation below can be written:

$$I - O = \frac{dW}{dt} \tag{33}$$

where: I is the discharge into the reservoir; O is the discharge released from the reservoir; $\frac{dW}{dt}$ is the discharge variation in the reservoir for the given time interval (dt).

The flow from the reservoir (O) can be determined with the maximum accuracy from the weir and bottom outlet curves.

Hence I is to be determined as it represents the flood wave in the natural regime at the outlet from section 3 and relation (34) can be written:

$$\frac{Q_I^{(t)} + Q_I^{(t+\Delta t)}}{2} - \frac{Q_O^{(t)} + Q_O^{(t+\Delta t)}}{2} - \frac{W^{(t+\Delta t)} - W^{(t)}}{\Delta T} \tag{34}$$

In the first moment $Q_I^{(1)}$ is considered equal to $Q_O^{(1)}$ and $Q_I^{(t+\Delta t)}$ is computed. Then, $Q_I^{(t+2\Delta t)}$ and $Q_I^{(t+3\Delta t)}$ are successively calculated and the flood wave in natural regime determined.
- For Section 4 the flood wave has to be translated in the natural regime from the upstream end of section 4 to the downstream one. This operation employs a Muskingum procedure, the parameters of which (k and x) can be determined as follows:
  - the flood wave U₁ is computed unattenuated at the end of section 4. This is done by applying relation (34) above to the flood wave recorded on the second dam weir;
  - the flood wave U₂ recorded at the upstream end of section 4 is registered on the first dam weir. U₁ and U₂ being known, parameters k and c can be determined, afterwards the

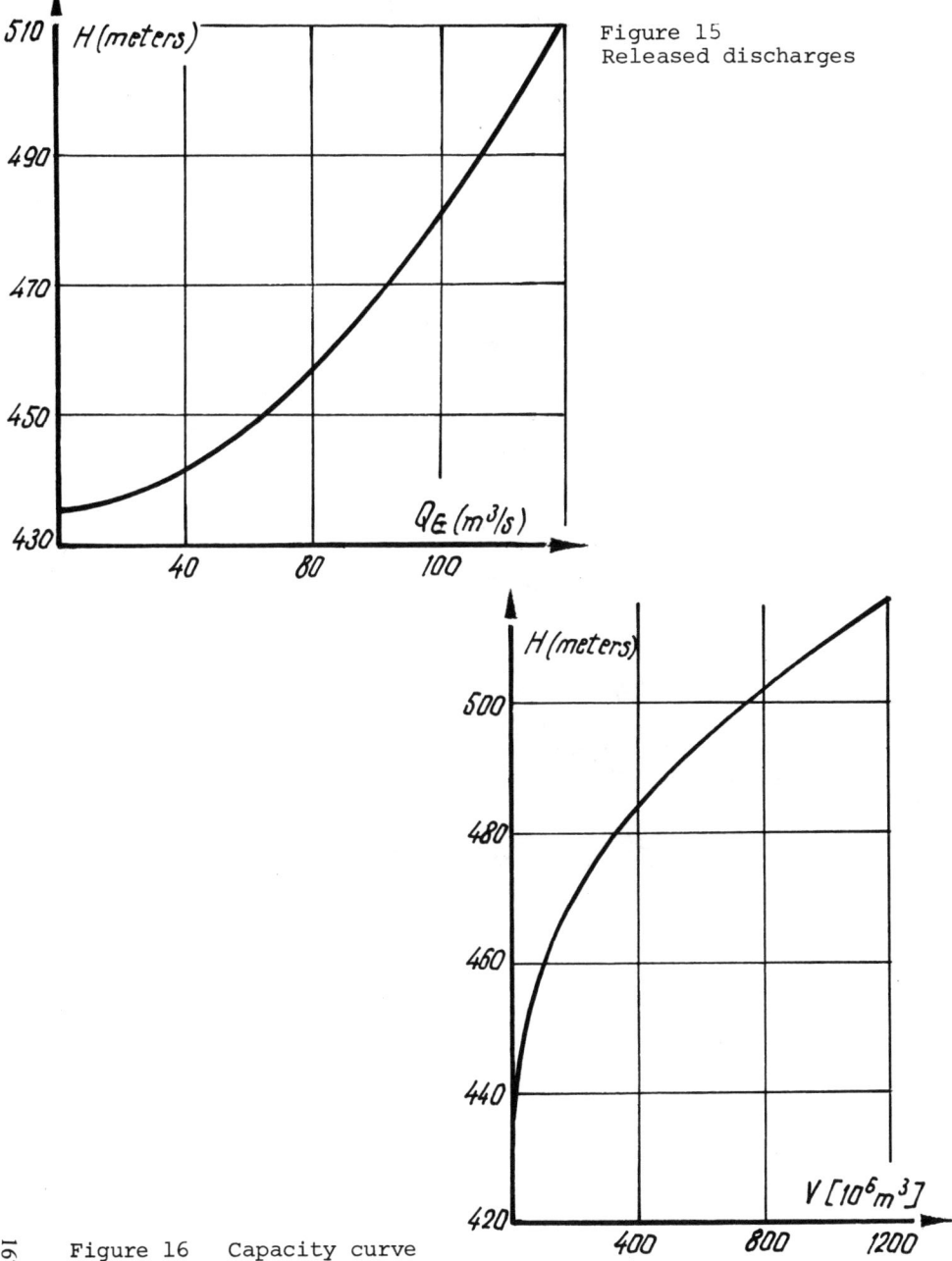

Table 2 Mean monthly reconstructed discharge

MONTH	SECTION	Q_T	Q_S	Q_E	Q_M	ΣQ_F	ΣQ_{AG}	Q_U	Q_N
	1	2	3	4	5	6	7	8	9
JAN	SH3	52.9	0	0	52.9	0	-35.6	-35.6	17.3
	SH4	54.3	0	0	54.3	2.0	-35.1	-33.1	21.2
	SH5	62.0	0	0	62.0	3.0	-35.1	-32.1	29.9
FEB	SH3	45.9	0	0	45.9	0	-22.6	-22.6	23.3
	SH4	48.8	0	0	48.8	2.0	-21.8	-19.8	29.0
	SH5	59.2	0	0	59.2	4.1	-22.2	-18.1	41.1
MARCH	SH3	35.3	0	0	35.3	0	+15.0	+15.0	50.3
	SH4	46.4	0	0	46.4	2.0	+14.6	+16.6	63.0
	SH5	67.9	0	0	67.9	4.6	+14.5	+19.1	87.0
APRIL	SH3	36.6	0	0	36.6	0	+127.6	+127.6	164.2
	SH4	67.2	0	0	67.2	2.0	+129.6	+131.6	198.8
	SH5	65.3	39	0	104.3	6.0	+130.0	+136	240.3
MAY	SH3	156.6	85.9	0	242.5	0	+31.7	+31.7	274.2
	SH4	65.9	361.7	0	328.6	2.0	+32.1	+34.1	362.7
	SH5	158.3	192.1	0	350.4	8.0	+32.5	+40.5	390.9
JUNE	SH3	129.4	5.1	0	134.5	0	-2.3	-2.3	132.2
	SH4	63.4	111.6	0	176.0	2.0	-2.8	-0.8	175.2
	SH5	151.8	39.4	0	191.2	8.0	-2.8	+5.2	196.4
JULY	SH3	66.9	0	0	66.9	0	-16.6	-16.6	50.3
	SH4	64.2	25.6	0	89.8	2.0	-18.6	-16.6	73.2
	SH5	111.3	3.6	0	114.9	5.0	-20.1	-15.1	99.8
AUGUST	SH3	38.5	0	0	38.5	0	-3.1	-3.1	35.4
	SH4	48.0	0	0	48.0	2.0	-3.5	-1.5	46.5
	SH5	30.9	24.4	0	55.3	7.0	-4.2	+2.8	58.1
SEPT	SH3	36.8	0	0	36.8	0	-.8	-8.0	28.8
	SH4	46.6	0	0	46.6	2.0	-8.5	-6.5	40.1
	SH5	0	49.0	0	49.0	7.0	-8.8	-1.8	47.2
OCT	SH3	33.3	0	0	33.3	0	-6.0	-6.0	27.3
	SH4	42.7	0	0	42.7	2.0	-7.5	-5.5	37.2
	SH5	43.2	0	0	43.2	8.0	-7.5	+0.5	43.7
NOV	SH3	46.8	0	0	46.8	0	-12.7	-12.7	34.1
	SH4	49.2	0	0	49.2	2.0	-13.7	-11.7	37.5
	SH5	60.0	0	0	60.0	8.2	-14.2	-6.0	54.0
DEC	SH3	54.5	0	0	54.5	0	-28.6	-28.6	25.9
	SH4	54.8	0	0	54.8	2.0	-28.0	-2.6	28.8
	SH5	58.4	0	0	58.4	9.0	-27.7	-18.7	39.7

Figure 15
Released discharges

Figure 16 Capacity curve

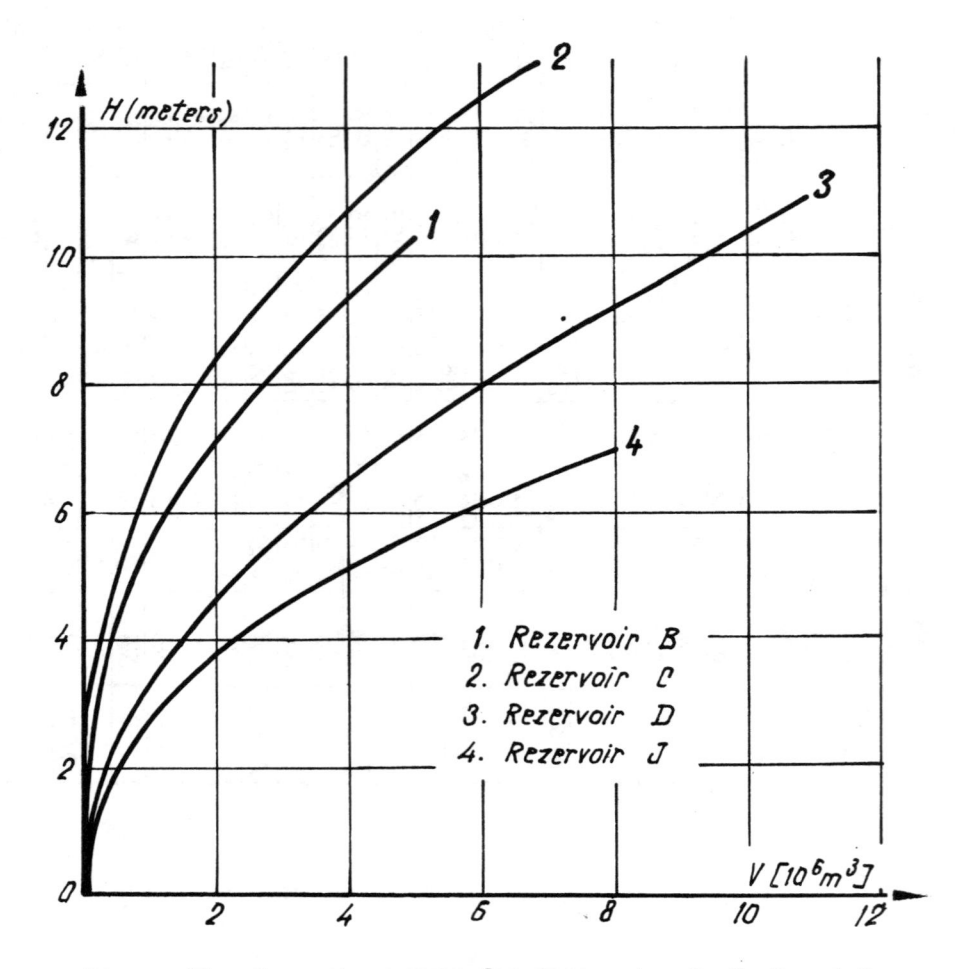

Figure 17   Capacity curves for reservoirs B, C, D and J

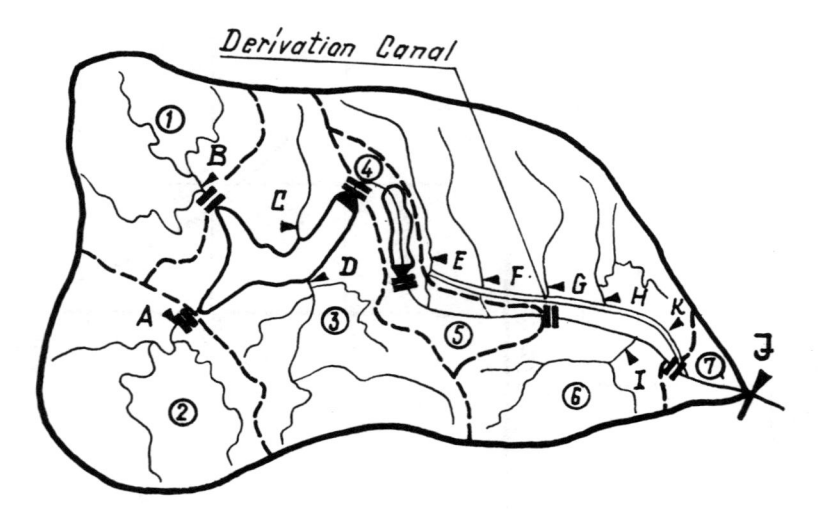

Figure 18   Hypothetical basin showing five possible conditions

Muskingum procedure can be easily applied.
- For section 5 a Muskingum translation procedure is applied and then the flood waves recorded at the gauging stations E, F and G are added.
- For section 6 a similar procedure is resorted to as in the case of section 5.
- For section 7 the wave coming from section 6 is translated by means of a Muskingum procedure, and afterwards the outlet flood wave coming from section 6 (U_6) is added to the one recorded on the canal at station k. The wave U_7 resulting from this addition is translated to section 7 having used the same Muskingum procedure, the result being compared to the wave recorded at station J. If the two waves U_7 and U_J are similar the results could be considered reliable.

3.4.3   STUDY SHOWING MAN'S INFLUENCE ON THE HYDROLOGICAL CYCLE IN THE RIVER TAJO BASIN
         by José Maria Martin Mendeluce and Jesus Cirugeda Guerdiola[1]

3.4.3.1   Introduction

The River Tajo flows across the Iberian Peninsula, mostly in Spanish territory, and reaches Portugal at its confluence with the River Erjas. It has a basin area of 52,384 km² in Spanish territory, and 53,549 km² including the area of the Erjas basin shared by Spain and Portugal. The Tajo River continues as the frontier between these countries until it meets the River Sever, with a basin area of 58,261 km² and 59,050 km², including the Sever, where it finally enters Portugal (Figure 1).

The basin characteristics of the hydrometric station number 19 of the Tajo River in Alcántara are set out below. This station is sited immediately downstream of the reservoir that bears the same name and very near to the first contact with Portugal, upstream from the River Ejas:

Longitude of station	6°53'18"W
Latitude of station	39°43'19"N
Area of basin above station	52,170 km²
Altitude of basin	110 m
Length of river	780 km
Mean annual discharge	9307 m³ x 10⁶ (over 51 years)
Mean runoff	178.4
Mean precipitation	659.2 mm (over 20 years)
Runoff coefficient	0.27
Mean evaporation	480.8 mm

3.4.3.2   Method of study

To investigate the effect of man on the hydrological cycle, a study has been made of the availability of water in the basin under the natural regime, its present state and its state at a point in the future. The future state takes into account the reservoirs that have been built and those that are planned; their possible impact on the hydraulic regime of the river is deduced.

The study is based on the 'Hydraulic Resources Inventory' published by the Hydrographic Studies Centre in 1970, where there are to be found historic series of monthly and annual river flows for the natural regime. These data are from official hydrometric stations of the Ministry of Public Works and Urbanism and with them it has been possible to obtain the complete 51 year series for the water years from 1912-13 to 1962-63. These data have been compared and, where necessary, corrected to the natural flow regime in the cases where stations have been affected by upstream developments which may be: regulation, losses, use of water by consumers and the return of water to the river by discharges.

To determine the availability of water, a computer program has been developed for use in

---

[1] C/o Spanish National Committee for the IHP, P Bajo de la Virgen del Puerto 3, Madrid 5, Spain

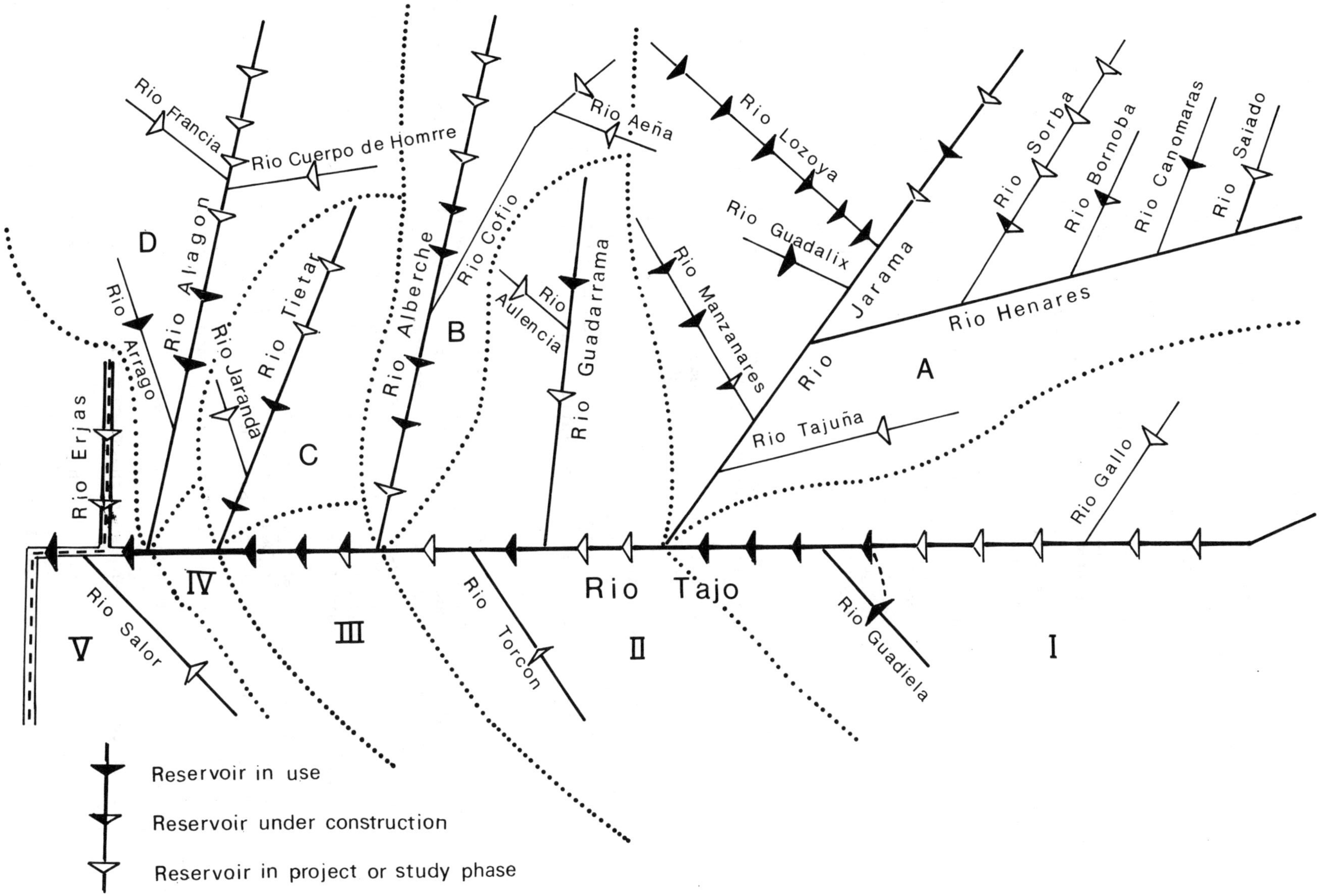

Figure 1 Tajo basin schematic site plan of reservoirs

the Hydraulic Resources Inventory. This allows updating of the reservoirs for their present and future states and the program allows the effects of regulation to be studied.

To determine the availability of water a computer program has been developed which may be used in the Hydraulic Resources Inventory, updating the reservoirs in their present and future states and studying:
(1) Regulation with an even demand.
(2) Regulation with a modulated demand.
(3) Successive regulation.

3.4.3.2.1 Regulation with an even demand. For all the monthly series for the 51 water year period, the curves that relate the continuous regulated flow with reservoir capacity have been calculated using the accumulated difference method, disregarding losses due to evaporation from the reservoirs. Calculations have been made removing the two driest years and assigning the regulation curves obtained a 96% probability, supposing that the historic series is representative. This type of demand can be considered representative of water and electric supplies.

3.4.3.2.2 Regulation with a modulated demand. For all the monthly series, the curves that relate the annual mean regulated volume with storage capacity have been calculated using the same procedure for a representative seasonal demand for irrigation. Losses due to evaporation from the reservoir have not been considered in this case either.

The modulation in the demand has been made in terms of the data obtained in the study on "Water Needs of Crops in Irrigation Plans", made by the Hydrographic Studies Centre. For each hydrometric station a mean demand is assigned to those relating to the irrigation. The calculations have been made, as in the above case, for a 96% probability.

3.4.3.2.3 Successive regulation. Applying the above processes to the data series from the hydrometric stations, for the regulation curves (regulated annual mean volume storage capacity) are obtained for the two demand types. The development locations do not always coincide with the hydrometric stations and it is consequently necessary to adopt certain assumptions that permit the regulation produced by a storage system to be determined in a sufficiently approximate way. The process followed to assess the maximum regulation (or availabilities) with the storage system is as follows:

"The capacity of each reservoir can be divided, using the partial capacities to regularize the contributions of its basin or that of the basins located upstream, choosing the gradient (of the curve: capacity-annual regulated volume) that is most convenient". In other words: "Given a reservoir system, the capacities can be redistributed, moving volumes from the downstream locations to other upstream ones, so that the sum of the regularized volumes in a maximum".

All this is supposing that the reservoir system is located in such a way that there is always a reservoir (even if it has zero capacity) through which the circulating flows pass to all the rest of the basin, and knowing the regulation curves in all the locations, regarding the contributions of the partial basins belonging to each reservoir.

The process indicated has been programmed for computer calculation and has been applied to the "Actual State" of reservoirs and "Future State", and also to the "Natural Regime", supposing that the reservoir capacity is zero. Thus the results obtained in the three locations are homogeneous and comparable.

3.4.3.3 <u>Sections of the Tajo River chosen in the study</u>
To make the study, the Tajo River has been divided up into the following sections:
I - Head of the Tajo until it meets the Jarama River.
A - Jarama River basin.
II - Tajo basin between the confluences of the Jarama and Alberche River.
B - Alberche River basin.
III - Tajo basin between the confluences of the Alberche and Tietar River.
C - Tietar basin.
IV - Tajo basin between the confluences of the Tietar and Alagón River.
D - Alagón basin.
V - Tajo basin between the confluences of the Alagón and Portuguese border.

Figure 2 shows the position of the basin hydrometric stations where the balances in the sections chosen and indicated above can be made. The characteristics of the stations are

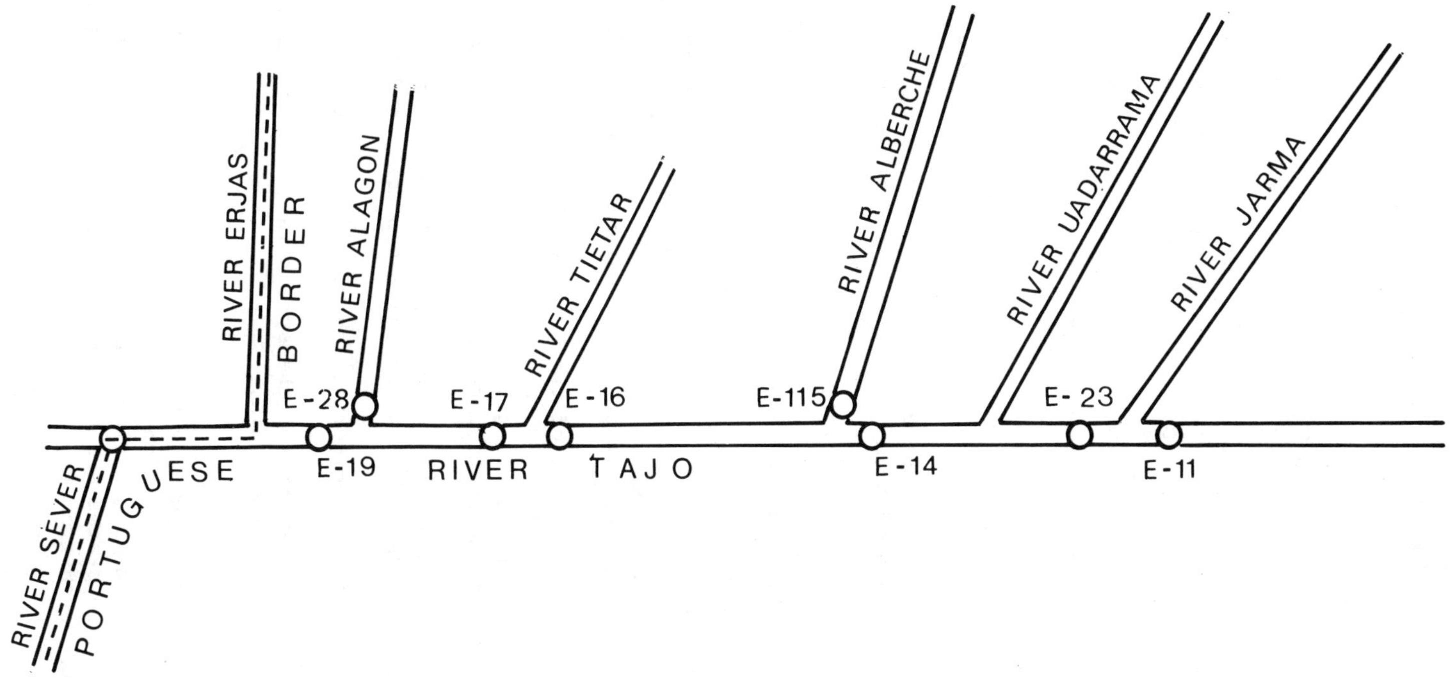

Figure 2 Site diagram of the basic hydrometric stations

Study showing man's influence on the hydrological cycle

given below:

No	River	Site	Basin area(s) km^2	Mean annual discharge m^3 x 10^6	Precipitation m^3 x 10^6	mm	Runoff coefficient
11	Tajo	Aranjuez	9,340	1478.2	5733.8	613.9	0.26
23	Tajo	La Flamenca	20,976	2322.3	13133.1	626.1	0.18
14	Tajo	Los Barrancos	29,632	3530.9	16715.4	564.1	0.21
115	Alberche	Cazalegas	3,993	917.9	2617.4	655.5	0.35
16	Tajo	Torrejon	37,094	4900.4	21581.3	581.8	0.23
17	Tajo	Villarreal	41,610	6490.6	25981.3	624.4	0.25
28	Alagón	Alcántara	3,373	2080.8	3068.1	909.6	0.68
19	Tajo	Alcántara	52,170	9307.7	34390.5	659.2	0.27

3.4.3.4   Method application

The above method has been applied in the Tajo River basin in the two cases of uniform flow and variable flow and for the following cases: "Natural Regime", "Present State" and "Future State".

By way of example, Table 1 shows the computer output for the "Actual State", with continuous flow regulation, preceded by a diagram in which the existing and planned reservoirs are shown (Figure 1).

The output data are composed of the following columns:
- River and order number; in this case the river is the Tajo. The order number refers to the point where the regulation is made and always goes from upstream to downstream, branches being treated the same way.
- Name of the reservoir; in this column the names of the reservoirs are shown; these are the ones built that are being exploited in the case of the "Natural Regime" and "Actual State"; in the "Future State", however, those that are foreseen are also shown. The numbers of the basic closure stations are also given.
- Capacity; the capacities are given, except in the natural regime situation that is taken as zero for all.
- C-V-T curve; in this column the number of the hydrometric station is shown; here the "strict storage capacity-annual mean regularized volume" curve has been used.
- Mean contribution of the basin; this is given in two columns for the partial and total basins.
- Annual regularized volume; of the partial basin (3 columns), for the reservoir (2 columns), for the system (2 columns).
. NO, with the order number of the partial basin by which the basin in regulated.
. Hm3, annual mean regulated volume of each partial basin for the duration indicated of the emptying period.
. T, duration in months of the emptying period regarding the curve segment used to calculate the regulated volume.
. The regulated volume of the reservoir and the system is given in Hm3 and the percentage rate of the mean contribution of the basin.

3.4.3.5   Analysis of results

The availability of water. The computer output data, obtained by applying the method, are summarized in Table 2, one with regulation at uniform flow and the other at variable flow. In both tables, apart from the mean contributions in the sections, the availabilities or volumes regulated in the three states are also shown. The influence of man can be noticed here, for if we observe the even flow regulation, we find: the total availability (regulated volume) at the Portuguese border is 275.7 Hm3/year for the "Natural Regime", and 7.043 Hm3/year for the "Actual State" (25.5 times that of the Natural Regime) and 8.420 Hm3/year in the "Future State", which is 30.5 times the natural regime. The section where man's influence is most marked is III. At the confluence of the Alberche with the Tietar, where the availability in natural regime of 19.8 Hm3/year become 57.6 times more for the "Actual State", whilst for the "Future State", the basin with most difference in B, Alberche basin, where the availabe water 8 Hm3/year becomes 60 times more.

Table 1 Successive regularization - even flow - actual state - 96% guarantee

River and Order No	Name of Reservoir	Capacity in Hm³	Curve C-V-T	Mean basin contribution Partial	Mean basin contribution Total	Of the partial basin No	Of the partial basin Hm³	T	ANNUAL REGULARIZED VOLUME By the reservoir Hm³	By the reservoir %	By the system Hm³	By the system %
21	Torcon	4.4	E-3	12.0	12.0	5	7.4	4	7.5	62.7	7.5	62.7
						20	1.5	5				
						19	11.8	5				
						20	7.4	6				
22	Estacion 14	0.0	E-3	96.4	3530.9	21	7.5	40	6.6	0.2	2164.7	61.3
						22	6.6	1				
23	Burguillo	208.0	E-111	452.7	452.7	23	227.5	30	227.5	50.3	227.6	50.3
24	Charco del Cura	3.0	E-111	0.0	452.8	24	0.0	30	1.2	0.3	228.9	50.5
						23	1.1	30				
25	San Juan	148.0	E-112	248.9	701.8	25	126.0	30	126.0	18.0	355.0	50.6
26	Picadas	15.0	E-112	1.0	702.9	26	0.6	30	6.2	0.9	361.3	51.4
						25	5.6	30				
27	Alberche	9.2	E-115	214.9	917.8	27	32.6	5	32.6	3.6	394.0	42.9
28	Estacion 115	0.0	E-115	0.0	917.9	28	0.0	1	0.0	0.0	394.1	42.9
29	Azutan	85.0	E-115	169.9	4618.8	29	1.9	1	199.7	4.3	2758.6	59.7
						22	3.7	1				
						28	0.0	1				
						29	9.1	2				
						22	15.5	2				
						28	0.0	2				
						29	1.0	3				
						28	0.0	3				
						29	3.3	4				
						28	0.0	4				
						29	24.3	5				
						22	0.4	5				
						28	0.0	5				
						27	17.7	5				
						29	9.1	6				
						22	13.0	6				
						20	37.7	6				
						19	62.1	6				

Table 1 (continued)

River and Order No	Name of Reservoir	Capacity in Hm³	Curve C-V-T	Mean basin contribution Partial	Mean basin contribution Total	Of the partial basin No	Of the partial basin Hm³	Of the partial basin T	ANNUAL REGULARIZED VOLUME By the reservoir Hm³	By the reservoir %	By the system Hm³	By the system %
30	Valdecanas		E-16	155.1	4774.0	30	64.1	6	831.5	17.4	3590.2	75.2
						19	72.0	6				
						5	10.5	6				
						12	0.2	6				
						28	0.0	6				
						27	11.6	6				
						30	10.3	7				
						22	8.6	7				
						20	30.0	7				
						19	63.5	7				
						12	1.5	7				
						30	20.3	17				
						12	0.6	17				
						29	9.4	18				
						12	1.0	18				
						17	7.3	18				
						28	0.0	18				
						27	11.9	18				
						22	11.3	19				
						20	39.2	19				
						19	95.1	20				
						5	9.0	22				
						3	1.7	22				
						5	5.6	23				
						4	0.8	23				
						3	2.0	23				
						12	5.9	28				
						30	8.1	29				
						5	2.3	29				
						4	0.3	29				
						3	0.8	29				
						13	1.7	29				
						17	7.2	29				
						16	0.9	29				
						15	1.6	29				
						29	37.2	30				
						22	0.4	30				

Table 1 (continued)

River and Order No	Name of Reservoir	Capacity in Hm³	Curve C-V-T	Mean basin contribution Partial	Mean basin contribution Total	Of the partial basin No	Of the partial basin Hm³	Of the partial basin T	ANNUAL REGULARIZED VOLUME By the reservoir Hm³	By the reservoir %	By the system Hm³	By the system %
						20	1.5	29				
						19	9.5	30				
						5	3.8	30				
						4	0.5	30				
						3	1.3	30				
						2	0.6	30				
						6	33.1	30				
						28	0.0	30				
						27	47.1	30				
						25	8.5	30				
						23	50.5	30				
						22	13.0	40				
						20	44.9	40				
						19	53.2	40				
31	Torrejon 1	166.0	E-16	125.7	4899.8	31	83.5	29	115.6	2.4	3705.9	75.6
						19	32.1	40				
32	Estacion 16	0.0	E-16	0.5	4900.4	32	0.0	1	0.0	0.0	3706.0	75.6
33	Rosarito	84.2	E-127	982.9	982.9	33	221.8	6	221.8	22.6	221.8	22.6
34	Torrejon-Tiétar	12.5	E-16	606.2	1589.2	34	127.1	2	127.1	8.0	349.1	22.0
35	Estacion 17	0.0	E-16	0.9	6490.6	35	0.0	1	0.0	0.0	4055.3	62.5
36	Gabriel y Galan	924.0	E-141	1155.5	1155.5	36	756.9	29	756.9	65.5	756.9	65.5
37	Valdeobispo	53.0	E-141	162.2	1317.8	37	74.5	29	74.5	5.7	831.6	63.1
38	Borbollon	84.0	E-148	149.2	149.2	38	82.8	29	82.8	55.6	82.9	55.6
39	Estacion 28	0.0	E-141	613.8	2080.8	39	−6.8	1	6.8	0.3	921.4	44.3
40	Alcantara	3162.0	E-19	735.6	9307.0	40	32.3	1	2019.5	21.7	6996.2	75.2
						35	0.0	1				
						32	0.0	1				
						39	7.4	1				
						40	12.2	2				
						35	0.1	2				

Table 1 (continued)

River and Order No	Name of Reservoir	Capacity in Hm³	Curve C-V-T	Mean basin contribution Partial	Mean basin contribution Total	ANNUAL REGULARIZED VOLUME Of the partial basin No	ANNUAL REGULARIZED VOLUME Of the partial basin Hm³	ANNUAL REGULARIZED VOLUME Of the partial basin T	By the reservoir Hm³	By the reservoir %	By the system Hm³	By the system %
						32	0.0	2				
						34	8.1	2				
						39	0.2	2				
						40	18.9	3				
						35	0.0	3				
						32	0.0	3				
						34	6.4	3				
						40	15.5	4				
						39	14.9	4				
						35	0.0	5				
						32	0.0	5				
						34	4.0	5				
						39	6.4	5				
						40	57.2	6				
						35	0.1	6				
						32	0.1	6				
						34	104.8	6				
						33	46.6	6				
						40	57.4	7				
						35	0.0	7				
						32	0.0	7				
						34	40.4	7				
						39	55.9	7				
						40	64.5	8				
						39	182.5	12				
						40	16.5	16				
						33	178.7	16				
						40	96.5	17				
						35	0.1	17				
						32	0.0	17				
						34	79.6	17				
						40	202.8	29				
						35	0.0	29				
						32	0.0	29				
						34	31.8	29				
						39	182.7	29				

Table 1 (continued)

River and Order No	Name of Reservoir	Capacity in Hm³	Curve C-V-T	Mean basin contribution Partial	Mean basin contribution Total	Of the partial basin No	Of the partial basin Hm³	Of the partial basin T	ANNUAL REGULARIZED VOLUME By the reservoir Hm³	ANNUAL REGULARIZED VOLUME By the reservoir %	ANNUAL REGULARIZED VOLUME By the system Hm³	ANNUAL REGULARIZED VOLUME By the system %
						37	46.3	29				
						36	103.6	29				
						38	27.2	29				
						40	35.3	30				
						39	28.6	30				
						37	7.5	30				
						36	53.9	30				
						38	7.2	30				
						33	182.9	32				
41	Estacion 19	0.0	E-19	0.6	9307.7	41	0.0	1	0.0	0.0	6996.3	75.2
42	Total regulado	0.0	E-19	1204.1	10511.9	42	46.6	1	46.6	0.4	7043.0	67.0

Table 2 Tajo Basin - Availabilities in Hm³/year with 96% guarantee and variable flow

SECTIONS	NATURAL REGIME					ACTUAL STATE					FUTURE STATE			
	Area of the basin		Capa-city	Regularized volume		Capa-city	Regularized volume		Capa-city	Regularized volume	
	Partial	Total Tajo		Partial	Total Tajo		Partial	Total Tajo		Partial	Total Tajo
I. Head Tajo - Conf Jarama	1478,2	1478,2	0	23,4	23,4	2433,9	1166,4	1166,4	2751,3	1194,5	1194,5
A. Jarama basin	844,1	2322,3	0	16,9	40,3	914,7	614,5	1780,9	1610,0	948,2	2142,7
II. Conf Jarama - Conf Alberche	1208,6	3530,9	0	10,9	51,4	45,4	117,5	1898,4	204,2	226,8	2369,5
B. Alberche basin	917,9	4448,8	0	3,1	54,3	383,2	333,9	2232,3	593,8	415,6	2785,1
III. Conf Alberche - Conf Tiétar	451,6	4900,4	0	7,2	61,5	1680,0	1178,5	3410,8	1680,0	943,7	3728,8
C. Tiétar basin	1590,2	6490,6	0	15,0	76,5	96,7	162,2	3573,0	1157,1	718,4	4447,2
IV. Conf Tiétar - Conf Alagón	736,3	7226,9	0	9,6	86,1	0	9,6	3582,6	0	9,6	4456,8
D. Alagón basin	2080,8	9307,7	0	7,8	93,9	1061,0	772,2	4355,2	1346,8	869,1	5325,9
V. Conf Alagón - portuguese border	1204,2	10511,9	0	15,5	109,4	3162,0	1883,5	6238,7	6002,0	2352,8	7678,7

Man's influence is felt most in the regulation at variable flow. We need merely glance at the data of the table corresponding to Table 2, where the availability of 109.4 Hm3/year (at the Portuguese border) is 57.0 times more in the "Actual State" and 70.2 times more in the "Future State", compared with 25.5 and 30.5 times that were deduced (at the same point) for uniform flow.

3.4.3.6 Demands and balances

Demands for both supply to towns and for irrigation can be seen in Table 3, where the balances are established for partial basins, based on the water availability of the "Actual State" and the "Future State" at variable flow at this is more unfavourable and when, in general, the demands for irrigation dominate. The surplus for inferior sections have been calculated assuming a recovery of 80% of the water put into supplies and 20% used for irrigation. For the "Actual State", it can be observed that all the partial balances have proved positive except section C, Tietar basin, where after supplying towns with 9.5 Hm3/year, there is a deficit of 24.5 Hm3/year compared with the 177.2 Hm3/year that are needed to meet the irrigation demands of the 21,001 hec. The total balance is positive, with a surplus at the Portuguese border of 5.146,1 Hm3/year after meeting a demand of 680,9 Hm3/year for supply and 1.220 Hm3/year for irrigation of 145.466 hec.

For the "Future State", all the partial balances including Section C, Tietar basin, that previously was in deficit have proved positive.

The total balance is also positive, with a surplus of 5001,0 Hm3/year at the Portuguese border, after covering a demand of 1.614 Hm3/year for supply and 3.014,0 Hm3/year for the irrigation of 366.393 hec.

Understandably, these demands could not have been covered had it not been for man's influence on the hydrological cycle, that has been possible thanks to the policy of building storage dams.

3.4.3.7 The Tajo-Segura transfer

The work of transferring the waters of the Tajo River (Atlantic basin) to the Segura (Mediterranean basin) are now almost concluded; in an initial phase, 600 Hm3/year are going to be diverted, increasing to 1000 Hm3/year proposed as the maximum and that will affect Section I - Head of the Tajo - Confluence with the Jarama. The water is taken from the Bolarque reservoir and as shown in Table 2, it has a mean contribution of 1,378.1 Hm3, with an availability of 37.7 Hm3/year in the nature regime with flow regulation and an availability of 1.209,8 Hm3/year in the actual state with flow regulation. Diverting the 1000 Hm3/year some 209.8 Hm3/year are therefore available, which is 5.6 times more than the volume of 37.7 Hm3/year available in the natural regime.

Demands in the "Actual State" are 10.2 Hm3/year for town supply and 113.9 Hm3/year for irrigating 14.456 hec (Table 3) giving a total of 124.1 Hm3/year, which is covered by the 209.8 Hm3/year available after deducting the transferred volume.

In the "Future State" there is 1.233,7 Hm3/year available and after diverting the 1000 Hm3/year in the transfer, 233.7 Hm3/year are left at even flow, which is 6.2 times more than the available 37.7 Hm3/year in the "Natural Regime". On the other hand, future demands are 17.9 Hm3/year for supplies and 126.9 Hm3/year for irrigating 16.174 hec, representing a total of 144,8 Hm3/year, which is 62% of the water available.

Man's influence on the hydrological cycle has also been noted earlier, since the minimum flows have been regulated and notably improved, in spite of the volumes that have been transferred. The minimum contribution at station No 11 of the Tajo in Aranjuez (which is at the end of the section) is actually 1.3 Hm3/month for the 51 year period of the historic series and four values of approximately 3 Hm3/month and various occasions of 5 Hm3/month are shown, whereas it is expected with a 96% probability that these amounts will not at present drop from 17.5 Hm3/month due to the regulation and 19.5 in the future. This section is the one that is most sensitive to the transfer. From its confluence with the Jarama, the situation is very similar to what would be obtained without the transfer, since the Madrid supply acts as a hydraulic re-arranged of the basin, by demanding about 900 Hm3/year of resources over from the west of the basin which, after being used and suitably treated, restores the balance that could have come about with the transfer from the Tajo with a similar volume.

Table 3 Partial balances of the Tajo Basin in "actual state"

| SECTIONS | AVAILABILITIES (Hm³/year) ||| Area irrigated (Hec) | DEMANDS (Hm³/year) |||| Surplus for lower sections |
	Own section	Upstream	Total		Supply	Irrigation	Total	Balance	
1. Tajo Head - Conf Jarama	1166,4	-	1166,4	14456	10,2	113,9	124,1	+	1073,2
A. Jarama Basin	734,5[1]	-	734,5	7435	591,3	55,4	646,7	+	571,9
II. Conf Jarama - Conf Alberche	117,5	1645,1	1762,6	31006	30,6	261,8	292,4	+	1547,0
B. Alberche Basin	213,9[2]	-	213,9	9972	5,7	80,0	85,7	+	148,8
III. Conf Alberche - Conf Tiétar	1178,5	1695,8	2874,3	2170	7,7	19,3	27,0	+	2857,4
C. Tiétar Basin	162,2	-	162,2	21001	9,5	177,2	186,7	-	38,1
IV. Conf Tiétar - Conf Alagón	9,6	2895,5	2905,1	229	8,6	2,0	10,6	+	2091,8
D. Alagón Basin	772,6	-	772,6	46603	11,9	400,4	412,3	+	449,9
V. Conf Alagón - Portuguese border	1883,5	3351,7	5235,2	114	5,4	1,0	6,4	+	5233,3
Interspersed irrigations of the INC	-	5233,3	5233,3	12480	-	109,0	109,0		5146,1
	6238,7			145466	680,9	1220,0	1900,8		

1 Including the Alberche transfer to Madrid (West system) with 120 Hm³/year
2 Deducting the 120 Hm³/year from the transfer to Madrid

Table 3 (Continued)

SECTIONS	AVAILABILITIES (Hm³/year)			Area irrigated (Hec)	DEMANDS (Hm³/year)				Balance	Surplus for lower sections
	Own section	Upstream	Total		Supply	Irrigation	Total			
I. Tajo head – Conf Jarama	1194,5	–	1194,5	16174	17,9	126,9	144,8	+	1089,4
A. Jarama basin	1894,4[1]	–	1894,4	45277	1398,5	342,0	1740,5	+	1341,1
II. Conf Jarama – Conf Alberche	126,8[2]	2430,5	2557,3	93006	78,1	741,0	819,1	+	1948,9[a]
B. Alberche basin	15,6[3]	455,4[b]	471,0	53700	8,3	462,7	471,0	+	99,2
III. Conf Alberche – Conf Tiétar	943,7	1592,7	2536,4	32755	30,6	270,0	300,6	+	2314,3
C. Tiétar basin	328,4[4]	–	328,4	36424	20,4	303,7	324,1	+	81,4
IV. Conf Tiétar – Conf Alagón	9,6	2395,7	2405,3	10229	16,1	88,0	104,1	+	2331,7
D. Alagón basin	869,1	–	869,1	66234	36,5	569,7	606,2	+	406,0
V. Conf Alagón – portuguese border	2352,8	2737,7	5090,5	114	7,7	1,0	8,7	+	5088,2
Interspersed irrigations of the INC	–	5088,2	5088,2	12480	–	109,0	109,0		5001,0
	7734,9			366393	1614,1	3014,0	4628,1		

[1] Including the transfer to Madrid from the west with 900 Hm³/year and taking the section's own availability with even flow regularization as the supply demand overrules
[2] Deducting 100 Hm³/year of the transfer of the Guadarrama to Madrid
[3] Deducting 400 Hm³/year of the transfer of the Alberche to Madrid
[4] Deducting 390 Hm³/year of the transfer of the Tiétar to Madrid
[a] From this surplus 455,4 Hm³/year are used to cover the demand of section B (low zone)
[b] Subtracting the surplus from section II to meet the irrigation demand of the Alberche

Chapter 3.5

3.5 LAND USE CASES
    by K S Goh[1]

Land use has a great impact on the hydrological regime of river basins. Although the effects are often of an indirect nature, they are still very pertinent. The following sub-systems of the hydrological cycle are influenced: overland flows, storage, infiltration, soil moisture and sedimentation. Because all the sub-systems are interrelated, it will be clear that the ultimate effect of a change in land use is not easy to determine, not to mention its prediction.

The effects of different types of vegetation and agricultural activities (type of farming and land management for example) and forest practices have been well documented as well as earlier in this volume (Pereira, 1972, Dooge et al, 1973, Boughton, 1970, Toebes and Goh, 1975).

It has been shown that because of its high infiltration capacity, forest exerts a regulatory effect on river regimes by reducing overland stormflow and usually by maintaining baseflow. Additionally, a forested basin produced clean water with little sediment load in it. Upon deforestation, flood peaks, peak flows, flow volumes and sediment load increase (for smaller catchments).

The evapotranspiration rate of a forest is usually larger than that of the arable crops or pastures which replace the trees. The greater the height and rougher the canopy the greater the rooting depth and sometimes the longer the season of transpiration of the trees and these factors all tend to decrease water yield. Additionally, if conditions are such that infiltration rates remain high upon deforestation, the low flows may increase and the water table rises. Overgrazing in semi-arid grassland, the uncontrolled expansion of subsistence farming and the population of arable crop-land in developing countries have given rise to soil erosion and flood problems.

An extreme case of land use is horticulture in glass houses: surface runoff is increased considerably and the effect on the flow regime is very similar to the effect of urbanization (see Chapter 3.6).

The early studies of the effects of land use on river flow were based on long-term comparisons, usually of a decade or more, which were continued until the flow from one valley could be confidently predicted from that of the other. A similar period after the land-use change was then needed to assess the magnitude of any resulting departure from this relationship. (This method remains useful, and, in fact, much of our slender store of knowledge is derived from it). The major practical disadvantage of these comparative methods is the length of time required for the results to be obtained. The period of preliminary comparisons or pre-treatment calibration usually amounts to seven or more years. The use of multiple watershed experiments overcome some of the difficulties of interpretation of paired basin experiments.

---

[1] Environment Division, Ministry of Science, Technology and Environment, Oriental Plaza, Parry Road, Kuala Lumpur, Malaysia

In the past two decades, much progress has been made in the study of energy relationships involved in evaporation and in transpiration. Similarly, combination of an energy budget with a water budget offers new possibilities for the study of land use changes. Using this method, there are now very good scientific prospects of measuring the main components of the water cycle in a basin directly as evaporation, soil moisture storage etc and thus predicting with much greater confidence the probable hydrological effects of changes in land use. In particular, the establishment of an energy budget as well as a water budget can give an approximation to the more elusive term in the latter, ie the amount of water lost to the system as deep-seepage.

Most of the experiments designed to study the impact of land use changes on the hydrological regime of river basins are conducted on small basins. This is necessarily so because of the high cost of the instrumentation and operation of such basins. Furthermore, it is very difficult to obtain accurate data on any one hydrological characteristic. Requirements for the proper installation and operation of instruments used in the experimental basins are given in detail in Toebes and Ouryvaev (1970). Hydrological methods necessarily involve sampling in space and time from infinite populations. Uncertainty as to the space and the time distribution of the various inflows and outflows of the hydrological cycle is still as obstacle to obtaining sufficiently accurate data for establishing firm physical laws governing this cycle thus facilitating the interpretation of experimental results. In experimental basins used for studying land use changes, the particular need to sample basin characteristics and to deal with the non-stationarity of basins due to natural evolution (erosion, climatic changes etc) makes sound statistical sampling essential to improve hydrological methods in general. For hydrological sampling in time, non-random sampling techniques are applicable, while for sampling in space, a purposive or stratified sampling is used (Toebes and Ouryvaev, 1970)

Analysis of data collected in experimental basins is aimed at:
(1) To define a basin by a set of quantitative parameters, thus permitting translation of research results to other basins.
(2) To define as accurately as possible the relevant basin and climatological characteristics.
(3) To determine mathematical models representing some or all of the hydrological processes on the experimental basins.
(4) To develop in some cases water balances for basins.

Although these objectives are worth aiming at, neither the development of satisfactory practical models, nor the derivation of a quantitative index for each physiographical element of the basin is easy (Toebes and Ouryvaev, 1970). It is always necessary to consider the ultimate translation of results to other basins and the hydrological effects of natural and cultural changes on hydrological prediction and translation of results to other areas. Research on experimental basins, is more and more directed to a description of hydrological processes by complex model systems. However, this does not preclude the use of relatively simple means, but, in such solutions, it is important that the scientist compare results with those obtained previously.

Simpler methods are useful but require a great deal of common sense. Finally, the translation of result results from one basin or group of basins to others is a prediction problem. A number of techniques may be applied. Some of these involve the use of the unit hydrograph method, others employ the general non-linear analysis, while the use of conceptual models is now becoming more and more common. The application of these methods is discussed in detail elsewhere.

The following case studies have been selected to illustrate the use of some of the methods outlined above in computing the quantitative changes to the hydrological regime due to land use changes.

REFERENCES

Boughton, W.C. 1970. Effects of land management on quantity and quality of available water. *Water Research Lab,* Report No 120, University of New South Wales, Australia.

Dooge, C.I., Costin, A.B. and Finkel, J. 1973. Man's Influence on the Hydrological Cycle. FAO, *Irrigation and Drainage Paper,* No 17, 71 pp.

References

Pereira, H.C. 1972. The influence of man on the hydrological cycle - Guidelines to the policies for the safe development of land and water resources. In: Studies and trends of Research in Hydrology, UNESCO, *Studies and Reports in Hydrology,* No 10.

Toebes, C. and Ouryvaev, V (Ed) 1970. *Representative and experimental basins :* An International Guide for Research and Practice, *Studies and Reports in Hydrology*, No 4, The UNESCO Press, 348 pp.

Toebes, C. and Goh, K.S. 1975. Notes on some hydrological effects of land use changes in Peninsula Malaysia. *Water Resources Publication,* No 4. Drainage and Irrigation Department, Ministry of Agriculture and Rural Development, Malaysia, 20 pp.

3.5.1 ESTIMATION OF STREAMFLOW CHANGES OF THE TOBOL RIVER UP TO KUSTANAI DUE TO
AGROTECHNICAL MEASURES
by V E Vodogretoki and L V Efimova[1]

3.5.1.1 Introduction

The Tobol River originates in the south-eastern Urals and discharges into the River Irtysh near the town of Tobolsk. The drainage area up to Kustanai is 44,800 km^2; the active area (total drainage area minus the area of inland drainage represents 28,224 km^2 (Figure 1).

The drainage network is developed mainly on the left-bank, elevated part of the basin which is crossed by the tributaries of the Tobol that originate on the eastern slopes of the Urals. The flat relief and lower elevation of the rest of the basin result in the poor development of the drainage network. The tributaries of the Tobol have a distinct flood period during the spring snowmelt when the major portion (90%) of the annual flow is discharged. During the rest of the year the flow of these rivers is very low, the rivers often being dry or turning into a series of separate pools. In winter the shallows freeze to the bottom. The Tobol has a fairly constant streamflow over the greater part of its length.

The Tobol drainage basin is typical of the steppe and dry steppe zones of Kazakhstan and lies in the region of insufficient moisture. The drainage area is predominantly flat, its western part being slightly hilly.

The south-western part of the basin is situated in the piedmont zone of the Urals in the most elevated area of the Tobol drainage basin; the elevation of this zone ranges from 300 m to 500 m above the sea level. Within the rest of the basin elevation varies from 120 m to 250 m.

The drainage basin is composed mainly of bedded rocks outcropping on the slopes of the hills and river valleys. The bedded rocks are covered by Quarternary clay loams. The basin is composed of Tertiary clays which are covered by brown clays. The average depths to the groundwater table in the open area and in the forests are 13 m and 20 m respectively.

Vegetation of non-cultivated areas is that typical of the steppes (spear-grass, sheep's fescue) while small birch groves occur in depressions.

Up to 1954 the cultivated area made up 18% of the drainage basin. Intensive ploughing of the basin since 1956 has increased this area so that by 1970 about 67% of the drainage basin was occupied by crops; forests and virgin lands made up 3% and 30% respectively. Within the drainage basin there exist numerous closed sub-basins substantially influencing the formation of the spring flood, particularly during dry years. These sub-basins appear mainly on the left-bank area of the drainage basin, their aggregate area being 16,576 km^2, or 37% of the total drainage basin up to the town of Kustanai. The entire runoff of this area is accumulated in basins without outlets. The mean value of slopes within the drainage basin in 10^0/$_{00}$, the mean slope of the ploughed land is 7-8^0/$_{00}$, and that of virgin land (long fallow) and forests - 12^0/$_{00}$.

---

[1] State Hydrological Institute, 2 Linya 23, Leningrad V 53, USSR

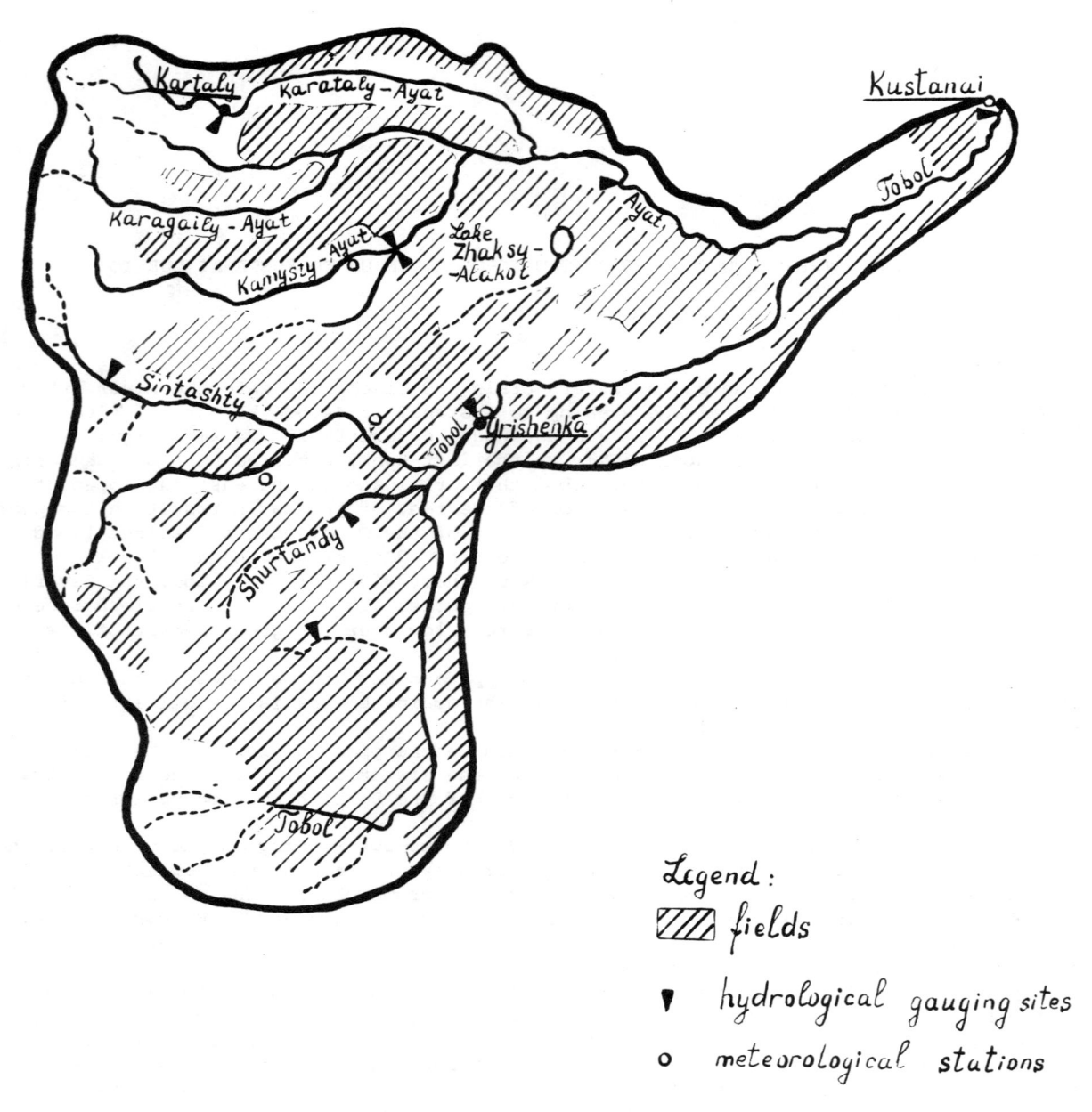

Figure 1 Scheme of the active area of the Tobol drainage basin up to Kustanai

Streamflow measurements on the Tobol near Kustanai were started in 1931. At present there are 9 hydrological stations and posts and 10 meteorological stations within the basin. Streamflow of the main river is measured at two points: at Grishenka village and at Kustanai. Meteorological stations are distributed evenly over the basin area.

Mean annual precipitation over the basin is 320 mm, snow storage - 77 mm, the mean annual discharge of the Tobol at Kustanai is 15.5 m^3/sec, and this is equivalent to an annual runoff depth of 17.3 mm.

The data being analysed cover the period from 1931 to 1970.

The volume of the surface runoff accumulated in artificial reservoirs (storage basins, ponds) within the given drainage basin makes about one million m^3, the water surface area being 16 km^2.

3.5.1.2 Techniques, methods and results

Using the pertinent technique (Chapter 2 of the present Casebook) and proceeding from the various items of data on the basin, it was possible to estimate the influence of agricultural and forest reclamation measures upon the average annual streamflow of the Tobol up to Kustanai.

The changes in the overland runoff due to ploughing and small groves have been computed in per cent by the following formula:

$$\Delta Q_{OV_{1,2}} = (\Delta \overline{Q}_{OV_{1,2}})_{I,II} \cdot a_{1,2} \cdot C_1 \tag{1}$$

where $\Delta \overline{Q}_{OV_{1,2}}$ is the average annual reduction of the overland runoff for the mean slope for the whole of the open area or forest (the value is computed from Tables 1 and 2); $a_{1,2}$ is the open area of the area of forest in parts of the total drainage area, taken as a unit; C_1 is the coefficient for the depth of the ploughing (the depth of ploughing being up to 25 cm, $C_1 = 1.5$, the depth of ploughing being over 25 cm with antierosional measures, $C_1 = 1.7$).

Table 1 Possible reduction of the average annual overland runoff (ΔQ_{OV_1}) due to agrotechnical measures in the steppe zone of northern Kazakhstan ($a_1 = 100\%$)

Characteristic	Slope $^0/_{00}$						
	5	10	20	30	40	50	60
	Clay loams						
$\Delta \overline{Q}_{OV_1}$ mm	6.0	6.0	8.0	9.0	9.5	10.0	9.0
$\Delta \overline{Q}_{OV_1}$ %	66	42	40	39	37	36	35

Thus from equation (1),

$$\Delta Q_{OV_1} = -56\%; \quad \Delta Q_{OV_2} = -2.9\%$$

The changes in the depth of the overland runoff (in mm) are computed in the following way. Using the data on the mean weighted slopes of the basin and of Table 3 the mean weighted runoff coefficient K_{QOV_4} is computed conventionally for virgin land (fallow): for open area $K_{QOV_4} = 0.12$, for forest $K_{QOV_4} = 0.17$.

$$Q_{OV_4} = K_{QOV_4} (S + P) \tag{2}$$

where: $(S + P)$ is maximum snow storage and liquid precipitation during the period of overland

Estimation of streamflow changes

Table 2 Possible reduction of the average annual overland runoff ΔQ_{OV_2} due to forest influence in the forest-steppe zone ($a_2 = 100\%$)

Characteristic	Slope $^0/_{00}$									
	10	20	30	40	50	60	80	100	150	200
	Clay loams									
ΔQ_{OV_2} mm	$\frac{12}{13}$	$\frac{14}{16}$	$\frac{30}{32}$	$\frac{40}{44}$	$\frac{44}{47}$	$\frac{48}{51}$	$\frac{54}{58}$	$\frac{59}{63}$	$\frac{60}{63}$	$\frac{56}{58}$
ΔQ_{OV_2} %	98	96	93	92	89	87	82	78	67	56

Note: The figure in the numerator is for spring runoff; in the denominator is for annual runoff (taking into account summer floods).

Table 3 Coefficients of the average annual overland runoff $K_{Q_{OV_4}}$ from fallow land in the steppe zone of Northern Kazakhstan

Runoff Characteristic	Slope $^0/_{00}$						
	5	10	20	30	40	50	60
	Clay loams						
$K_{Q_{OV_4}}$	0.10	0.16	0.23	0.27	0.30	0.32	0.34

runoff, one calculates conventionally the mean value of overland runoff from virgin land (in mm): for the open area $Q_{OV_4} = 8.4$ mm, for forest $Q_{OV_4} = 13.1$ mm.

Multiplying the obtained overland runoff value by the value of its relative reduction (in per cent) one obtains the reduction of overland runoff from the open area, from forest and from the whole of the drainage basin:

$\Delta Q_{OV_1} = -4.7$ mm; $\quad \Delta Q_{OV_2} = -0.4$ mm;

$\Delta Q_{OV_{1,2}} = \Delta Q_{OV_1} + \Delta Q_{OV_2} = (-4.7) + (-0.4) = -5.1$ mm.

The change (in per cent) of the groundwater flow is computed by the following equation

$$\Delta Q_{up_{1,2}} = (\Delta \overline{Q}_{up_{1,2}})_{I,II} \cdot a_{1,2} \cdot C_1, \qquad (3)$$

where: $\Delta \overline{Q}_{up_{1,2}}$ is the average annual groundwater recharge for the whole of the open area and forest ($\Delta \overline{Q}_{up_{1,2}}$) is computed from Table 4; $a_{1,2}$ is the open area (forest) in parts of the total drainage area.

Thus, using equation (3)

$\Delta Q_{up_1} = 31.5\%; \quad \Delta Q_{up_2} = 1.1\%$

Table 4 Possible increase in the average annual groundwater flow due to ploughing and afforestation in the steppe zone of Northern Kazakhstan ($a_{1,2} = 100\%$)

Characteristic	Depth to groundwater table, cm						
	200	300	500	800	1000	1500	2000
Clay loams							
$\Delta \overline{Q}_{up_1}$ mm	4	4	4	4	3	3	
$\Delta \overline{Q}_{up_1}$ %	10	15	17	38	43	50	
$\Delta \overline{Q}_{up_2}$ mm	14	12	12	12	10	7	7
$\Delta \overline{Q}_{up_2}$ %	24	25	26	30	30	38	38

The change in groundwater flow (in mm) is computed in the following way. Using the mean values of the depth to groundwater in the basin and the data in Table 5 one estimates the possible average coefficient of groundwater recharge by precipitation on the virgin land (long fallow).

For the open area $K_{Q_{up_4}} = 0.02$; for forest $K_{Q_{up_4}} = 0.00$.

Using the formula

$$Q_{up_4} = K_{Q_{up_4}} \cdot P, \tag{4}$$

where: P is the average annual precipitation one estimates the average value of groundwater flow within the ploughed area and forest prior to agricultural improvement and forest reclamation. Thus for the open area $Q_{up_4} = 0.02 \cdot 340 = 6.8$ mm; for the forest $Q_{up_4} = 0$.

Table 5 Long-term average coefficients of groundwater recharge $K_{Q_{up_4}}$ on virgin land (long fallow) in the steppe zone of Northern Kazakhstan

Characteristic	Depth to groundwater table, cm								
	50	100	200	300	500	800	1000	1500	2000
Clay loams									
$K_{Q_{up_4}}$	0.19	0.16	0.11	0.10	0.07	0.05	0.04	0.01	0.00

Multiplying the groundwater flow values obtained by the relative value of its reduction (in per cent) one obtains the increase of the groundwater flow from the open area, from the forest and from the whole of the drainage basin:

$$\Delta Q_{up_1} = 6.8 \cdot 0.315 = 2.1 \text{ mm}; \quad \Delta Q_{up_2} = 0;$$

$$\Delta Q_{up_{1,2}} = \Delta Q_{up_1} + \Delta Q_{up_2} = 2.1 \text{ mm}$$

The change in the total streamflow of the Tobol at Kustanai due to agricultural and forest reclamation practices makes

$$\Delta Q = \Delta Q_{ov_{1,2}} + \Delta Q_{up_{1,2}} = -5.1 + 2.1 = -3.0 \text{ mm},$$

or as percentage of the observed runoff

$$\Delta Q = \frac{\Delta Q \cdot 100}{Q} = \frac{(-3.0) \cdot 100}{17.3} = -17\%$$

The streamflow reduction caused by agricultural and forest reclamation practices as compared to the annual streamflow values observed prior to reclamation within the drainage basin is

$$\Delta Q = \frac{\Delta Q \cdot 100}{Q + \Delta Q} = \frac{(-3.0) \cdot 100}{20.3} = -15\%$$

During a wet year (P = 5%) and a dry year (P = 95%) the annual streamflow reduction will be 0.7 mm (2%) and 1.7 mm (100%) respectively. During a dry year (P = 95%) the runoff is insignificant and is entirely retained on the fields, in the forest and forest belts. Subsequently the retained moisture is lost by evaporation. Besides estimating the effect of agricultural and forest reclamation practice during the whole period of land reclamation within the drainage area, an attempt was made to estimate this value for the period of intensive ploughing of virgin and fallow land, ie for the period of 1954-1970.

It appeared that during the period mentioned the streamflow reduction was 2.4 mm, or 14% of the observed runoff.

Bibliography

Bochkov, A.P. 1965. O vlianii agrotechnicheskikh i lesomeliorativnykh meropriatii na stok rek lesostepnykh i stepnykh raionov (On the influence of the agrotechnical and forest reclamation measures on streamflow of forest-steppe and steppe regions). *Trans State Hydr Inst*, 127, 10-81.

Konstantinov, A.P., and Struzer, L.R. 1965. *Lesnye polosy i urozhai* (Forest bells and crop yield). Leningrad, Hydrometeoizdat, 174 pp.

Korzun, V.I. 1968. *Stok i poteri talykh vod na sklonakh polevykh vodosborov* (Runoff and loss of snowmelt water on the slopes of field watersheds). Leningrad, Hydrometeoizdat, 374 pp.

Lvovich, M.I. 1969. *Vodnyi balans SSSR i ego preobrazovanie* (USSR water balance and its transformation). "Nauka", Moscow, 337 pp.

Shiklomanov, I.A. 1973. O metodakh otsenki vliania kompleksa faktorov khoza istvennoi deyatelnosti na vodnye resursy i vodnyi regim vodosborov (On the methods for the estimation of the influence of economic activities on water resources and water regime of drainage basins). *Trans State Hydr Inst*, 206, 3-21.

Sukharev, I.P. 1955. Vlianie obrabotki pochv na stok talykh i livnevykh vod (The influence of soil cultivation on snowmelt and storm runoff). *"Pochvovedenie"*, 4, 48-55.

Vodogretski, V.E. 1968. Opyt izmerenia podruslovogo stoka rek (Measurement of sub-channel flow of rivers). *"Meteorologia i gidrologia"*, 10, 90-92.

Vodogretski, V.E., Zaitseva, E.A., Efimova, L.V. 1972. Sklonovyi stok i ego izmenenie pod vlianiem agrotekhnicheskikh i lesomeliorativnykh meropriatii (Overland runoff and its changes due to agrotechnical and forest reclamation practice). *Trans State Hydr Inst,* 206, 172-207.

Vodogretski, V.E., and Gridasova, T.V. 1973. Otsenka vliania agrolesomeliorativnykh meropriatii na isparenie s vodosbora (Estimation of the influence of agrotechnical and forest reclamation measures on evaporation from watersheds). *Trans State Hydrol Inst,* 221, 160-182.

Voskresenski, K.P. 1962. *Norma, izmenchivost godovogo stoka rek SSSR* (Normal runoff, annual streamflow variability of the USSR rivers). Leningrad, Hydrometeoizdat, 545 pp.

Zavodchikov, A.B. 1966. Stok i vodni balans sklonov v zone nedostatoch nogo uvlazhnenia (Runoff and water balance of slopes in the zone of insufficient moisture). *Trans State Hydr Inst,* 134, 151-205.

3.5.2 THE QUANTITATIVE INFLUENCE OF FORESTS UPON FLOODS
by P Mita[1]

3.5.2.1 Introduction

The studies performed have the following practical objectives: to determine the regulating role of the forest upon runoff and in protecting the soil against erosion and to assess the reduction in runoff due to the forest.

Considering the relative interest in these objectives, the studies performed concentrated either on knowledge of the regulating role of the forest upon runoff and protection of the soil against erosion (USSR, Czechoslovakia, New Zealand, etc) or upon the reduction in runoff by forest (USA, Japan and Finland).

As far as the research activity is Romania is concerned, it encompasses both problems but in the Institut of Meteorology and Hydrology a study was initiated into the influence of forests upon flood formation. This is of utmost importance for practical purposes.

In order to assess the interception of precipitation by different types of trees the data recorded in representative basins No 1 (area: 3.96 km^2, No 2 (area: 2.29 km^2) and No 3 (area: 11.2 km^2) have been used, while for determining the impact of forest on runoff the data recorded in 4 sub-basins of the representative basin No 1 have been considered.

3.5.2.2 Basin characteristics

The physiographic characteristics of these four sub-basins which have different proportions of forest cover (forest coefficient) are given in the table below:

Table 1

No	Sub-basin	Area (km^2)	Mean Altitude (m)	Mean slope of the basin $^0/_{00}$	Forest coefficient C_f%
1	A	0.46	250	153	0.0
2	B	1.78	280	152	47.0
3	C	1.65	270	170	95.4
4	D	3.96	272	159	63.5
5	E	2.17	251	159	63.5

Representative basin No 1 as well as the hydrological network are shown in Figure 1.

---

[1] Institute of Meteorology and Hydrology, Bucharest, Romania

Figure 1 The hydrological network in the representative basin

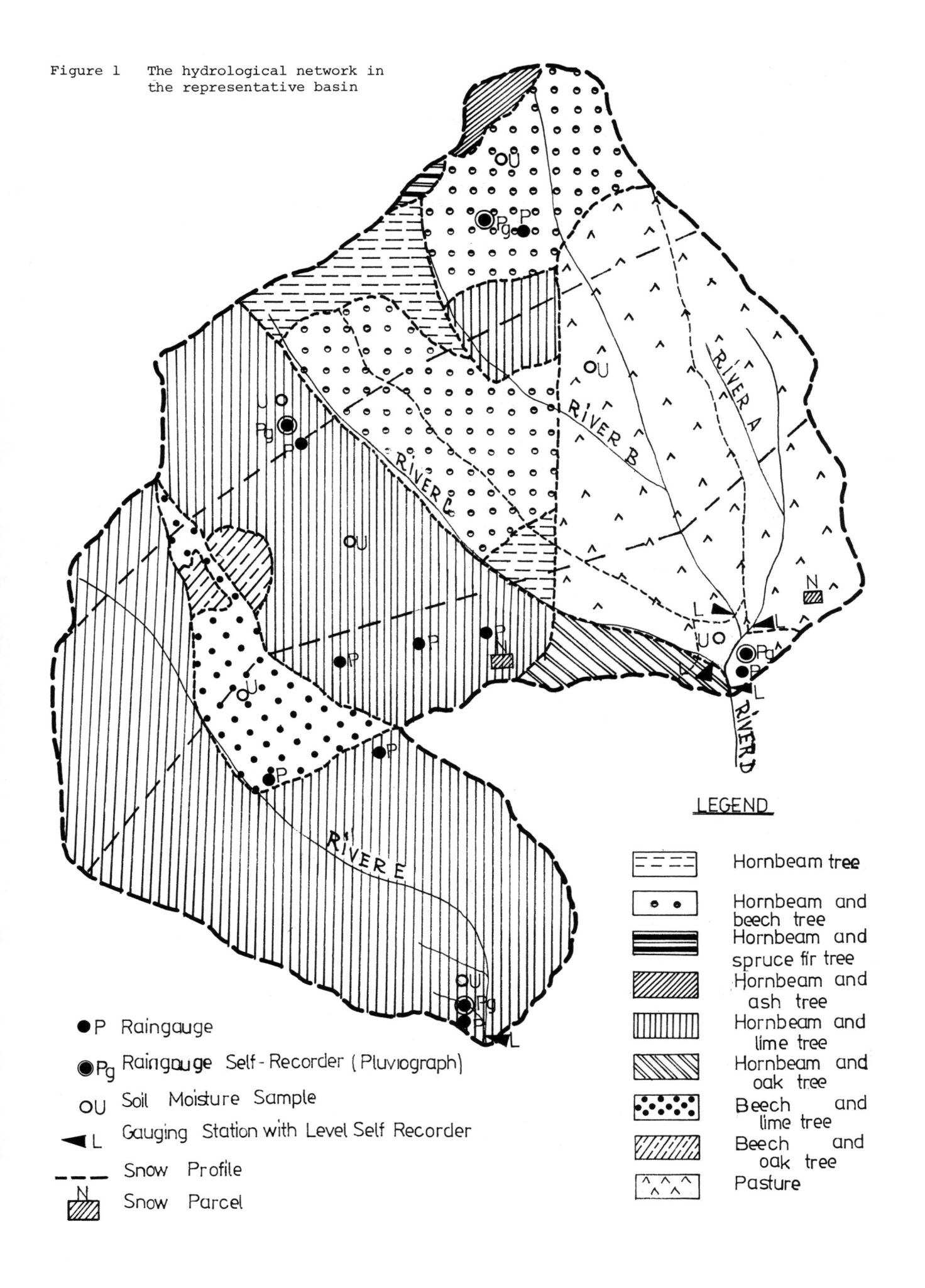

LEGEND

≡≡≡≡	Hornbeam tree
∘ ∘	Hornbeam and beech tree
▬▬▬	Hornbeam and spruce fir tree
▨	Hornbeam and ash tree
‖‖‖	Hornbeam and lime tree
▧	Hornbeam and oak tree
⦁⦁⦁	Beech and lime tree
▨	Beech and oak tree
∧∧∧	Pasture

- ● P   Raingauge
- ⊙ Pg Raingauge Self-Recorder (Pluviograph)
- ∘ U   Soil Moisture Sample
- ◄ L   Gauging Station with Level Self Recorder
- ---   Snow Profile
- ▨ N   Snow Parcel

The quantitative influence of forests upon floods

The selection of sub-basins within a representative basin with similar natural characteristics (precipitation, relief, geology, soil, surface) and essentially different proportions of forest-cover, creates the best possibility for demonstrating the role of the forest in regulating the amount of surface runoff.

The most obvious effect the forest has upon runoff is to regulate runoff, but particularly runoff during floods. Runoff begins later and lower flows take place in the forest covered basin but, at the same time, the runoff is maintained longer in those basins compared to the unforested ones. The volume of runoff is generally smaller with an increasing area of forest. This diminution also depends on the type and age of the trees and sometimes on the season, the diminution being more accentuated in the period of maximum vegetation growth.

3.5.2.3 Results

The diminution of runoff also depends on the rainfall characteristics (amount, intensity), on the characteristics and humidity of the soil, the degree of litter development, and other factors.

Among the factors known to determine the reduction in runoff the most important are the canopy (interception), the litter and the characteristics of the rain. The interception is defined as the difference between the amount of precipitation recorded in open terrain and the amount of precipitation reaching the ground in the forested area.

The amount of precipitation recorded in the representative basins with open areas in relation to the amount reaching the ground in the forest area allows the amount of interception to be determined for different types of trees (Figure 2) as well as the relationship between the average intensity of rain (mm/min) and the amount of precipitation retained by the canopy (Figure 3).

These relationships emphasize the fact that the proportion of precipitation retained by the forest canopy is higher with lower amounts of precipitation. Amounts of 1-1.5 mm/min and below are entirely retained by the canopy. With heavy rains (exceeding 100 mm), the retention is only 3-4% of the amount falling on open terrain, both in the case of coniferous and deciduous forests.

As far as the litter retention is concerned it was not separately analysed as yet, but it can be approximated by comparing the depth of runoff in the forest basins to that in the places lacking litter.

Figure 4 shows the amounts of rainfall that occurred during two storms and the corresponding amounts of runoff in basins A, B and C respectively. While Basin A which has no forest cover lost 29.4% of the rainfall as runoff on 30 June 1969, Basin B lost much smaller proportions as a result of the greater forest cover and litter depth. The results are similar for the storm of 22/23 July 1972.

In order to analyse the ratio of precipitation to runoff, for a certain period with a different forest coefficient C_f, the amounts of precipitation falling were considered. The relationships established between the maximum flow (m^3/s) and the intensity of the rain (mm/min) for various amounts of precipitation (Figure 5) prove on the one hand the dependence of the maximum flows on the amount and intensity of the precipitation and on the other hand on the alternating role of the forest, according to the data recorded in sub-basin B with a 47% forest coefficient and in sub-basin C (95% forest covered). These sub-basins have nearly equal areas: 1.77 km^2, and 1.82 km^2 respectively.

The role of the forest upon maximum runoff is shown by the relationships between maximum flows (m^3/s) recorded in basins with a lower forest coefficient (sub-basin B, for instance, C_f = 47%) and the maximum flows recorded in basins with a high forest coefficient (as is the case with sub-basin C and sub-basin E, with 95% and 100% forest coefficients respectively (Figure 6).

Although these three sub-basins have nearly similar areas and slopes, the maximum flow recorded in B is much higher than the maximum flows in C and E during the same rains as the latter enjoy a higher degree of cover.

The relations established between the maximum specific flows ($l/s/km^2$) (Figure 7a) or between the maximum specific flows and the K% ratio (Figure 7b) (K% - representing the ratio between the maximum specific flows in the sub-basins with different degrees of forest cover and the specific flows in A sub-basin which is entirely uncovered) highlight the low values of the maximum specific discharge in cases of forest cover and the fact that the lower they are, the higher the forest cover coefficient, in spite of the relations being suggested by

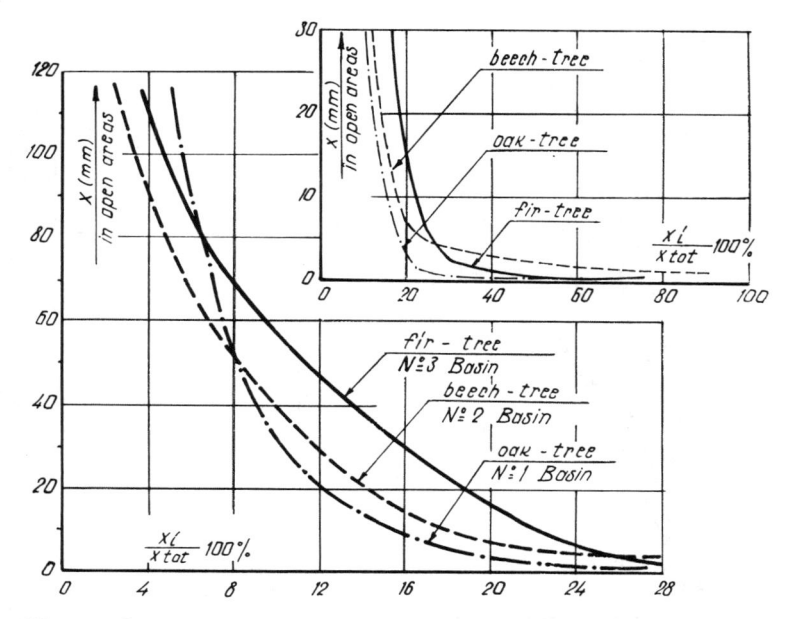

Figure 2 Determination of interception for different trees

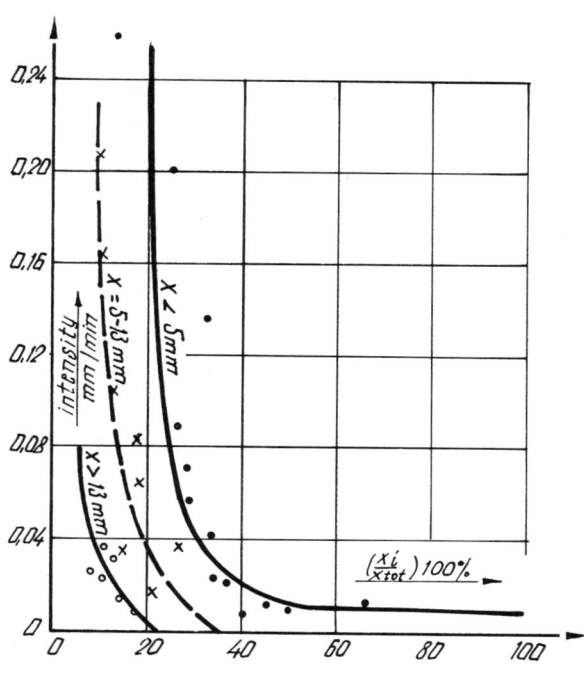

Figure 3 Intensity - canopy retention relations

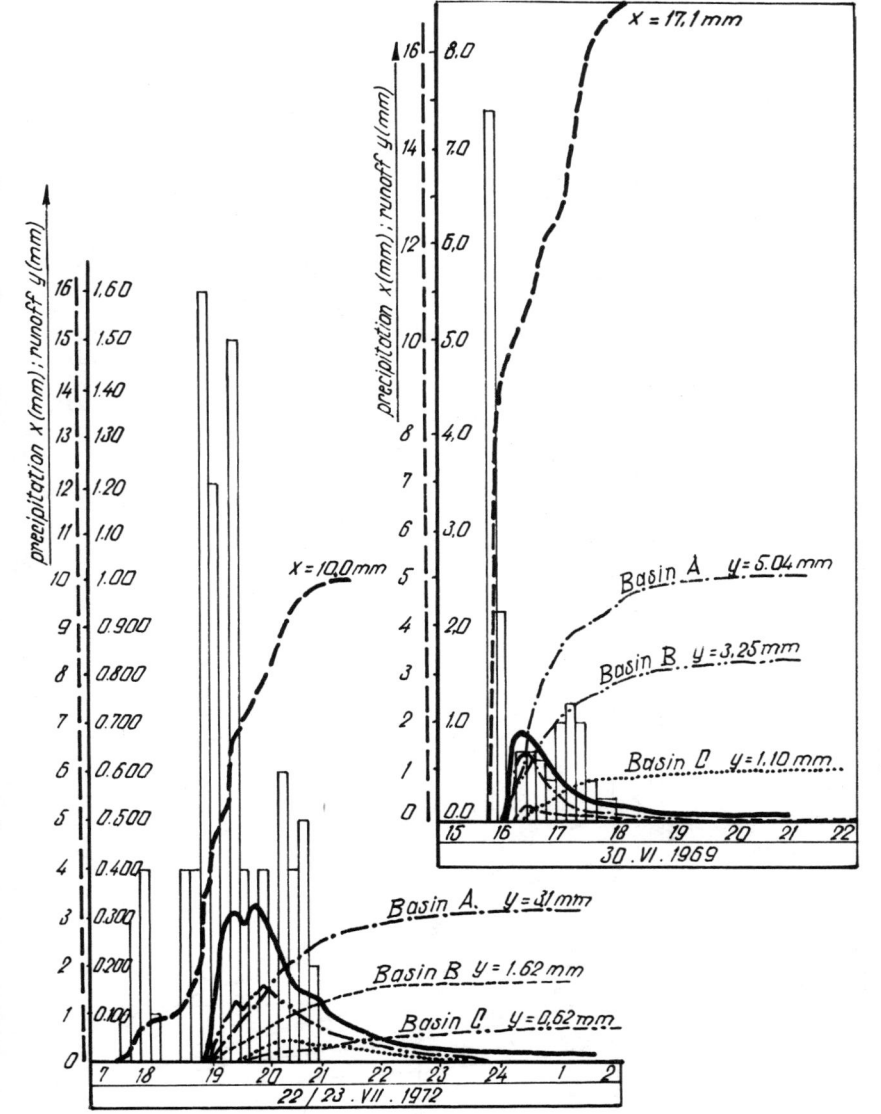

Figure 4 Storm responses of basins A, B and C

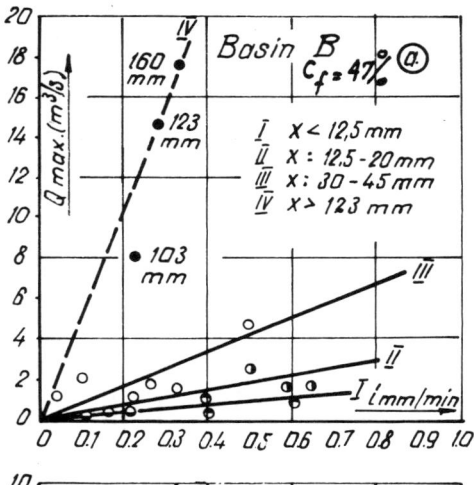

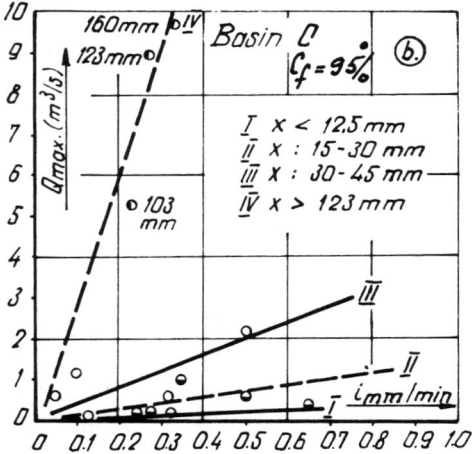

Figure 5 Maximum flow - intensity of rainfall relations

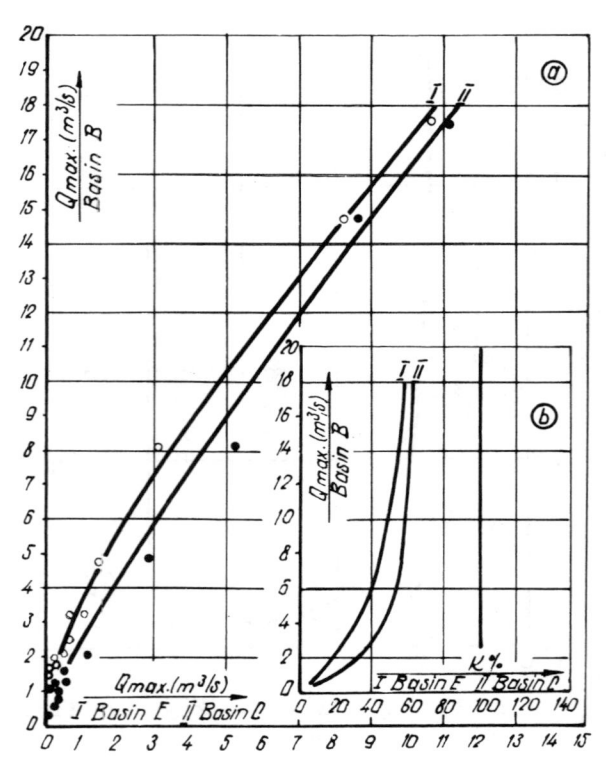

Figure 6 Maximum flows for basins with different proportions of forest

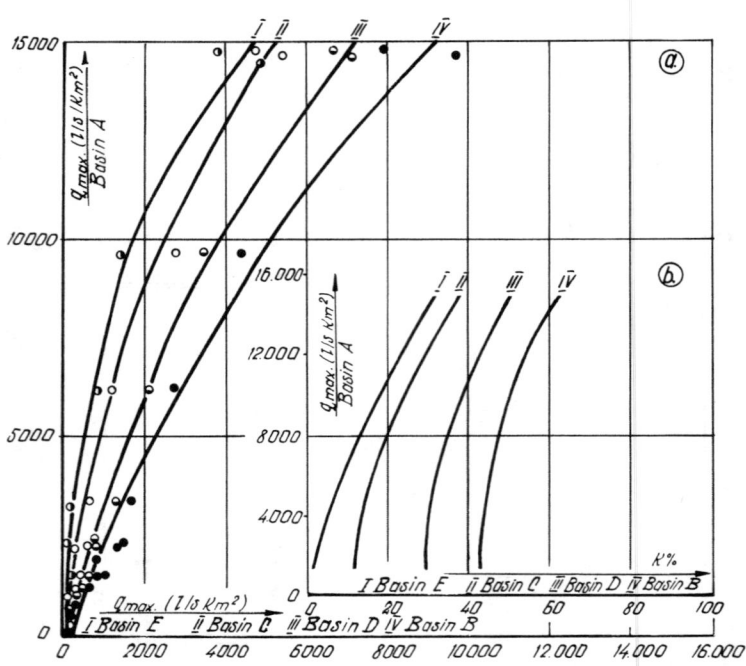

Figure 7 Relations between maximum specific flows in basins with different proportions of forest

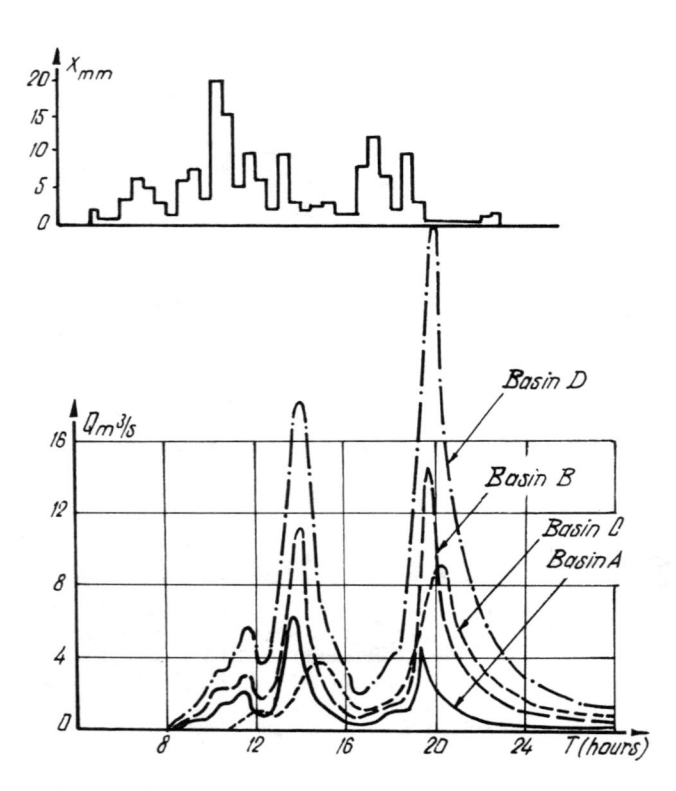

Figure 8 The storm of 25-26 August 1970

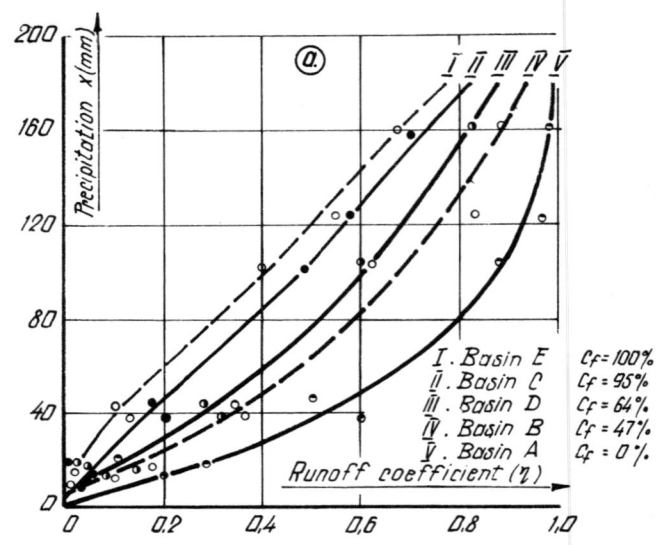

Figure 9a Precipitation-runoff coefficient relations

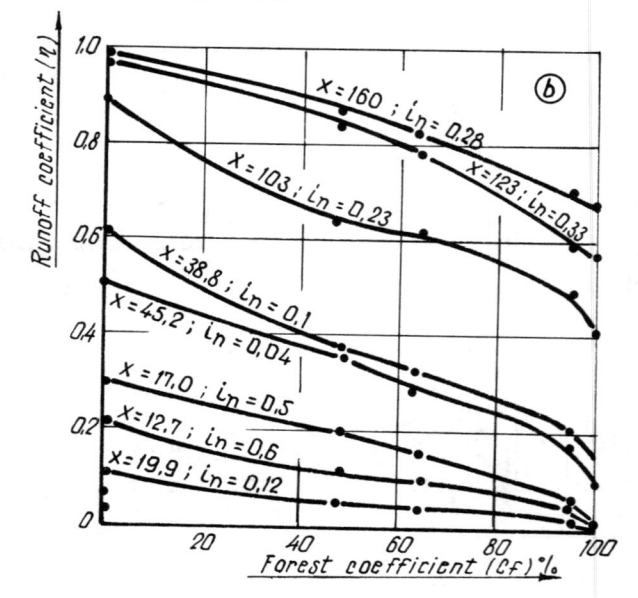

Figure 9b Runoff coefficient-forest coefficient relations

flows from the same amounts of rain.

It is therefore obvious that the influence of the forest is more effective in the case of small amounts of rain when the retention by canopy and litter - expressed in percentage of the total precipitation amount - is also important.

The forest plays a less significant part in cases of heavy rain, when the retention potential of the canopy and litter is reduced as compared to the rainfall and the difference between the maximum specific flows in the forest covered basin compared to those without forest is sensibly reduced. If in the case of some specific flows in sub-basin A (2,000 $l/s/km^2$) for instance), this corresponds to about 40 $l/s/km^2$ in sub-basin E which is entirely forested, that is to say 2% of the discharge recorded in A. Similarly a specific discharge of 15,000 $l/s/km^2$ flow in A corresponds to 4,600 $l/s/km^2$ in E which is 30.6% of the discharge recorded in A. For the other basins having lower forest coefficients, the specific flows are rather similar to the situation in A with the same rainfall. Consequently, with heavier rain, the precipitation contributes effectively to runoff formation after the litter gets saturated and the forest is no longer able to retain water.

An interesting aspect illustrating the way the forest influences runoff formation in the case of exceptionally heavy rains is represented by the flood on 25-26 August 1970 (Figure 8) when the precipitation amount was as large as 160 mm and there was a high runoff coefficient even in basins covered with forests, which proves that the forest loses its retention capacity in such cases.

But this exceptional rain which generated an ample flood in all the sub-basins highlighted another important aspect. Having two distinct peaks these storms had different influences upon the runoff in the different basins. During the first part between 04.00 and 15.30 hours, 110 mm fell and very large floods were recorded in all sub-basins and consequently high runoff coefficients. The influence of the forest was obvious from the runoff coefficients which were characteristized by the lowest values in basins with a large proportion of forest. Only in basin A, which is entirely open did the maximum flow of the flood occur. The maximum flows in the other basins with various forest covers (47%; 100%) occurred in the second interval, from 15.30 onwards, although in this time interval only 50 mm of precipitation fell. This is due to the fact that the forest could retain no more than 110 mm but in the second time interval it released large amounts of water accumulated during the first period and the larger these amounts are the higher the thicker the litter is.

Data concerning precipitation and runoff in the sub-basins show that as the amount of precipitation increases the runoff coefficients in the forested areas get higher and higher so that in the case of outstanding rainstorms the runoff coefficients in the forested basins approach those in unforested areas.

These relationships are proved by the associations shown in Figure 9 between the amount of precipitation and runoff coefficient (Figure 9a), and between the runoff coefficient and forest coefficient (Figure 9b).

3.5.2.4 Conclusions

Knowledge of the influence of forest upon runoff leads to certain conclusions upon the steps to be taken in forest protection in order to regulate runoff and prevent soil erosion, on the other hand it should not hinder the formation of runoff.

It is to be pointed out that the changes induced by man in the forest in a certain area are not immediately reflected in the modification of the runoff regime. In this respect, it has been found in some representative basins that deforestation has not produced an immediate change in runoff owing to the fact that the remaining litter retards runoff. The opposite occurs in sub-basin B which has been recently afforested. Nevertheless, runoff has still continued to be considerable due to the fact that the litter in afforested areas had not yet been developed.

The future studies should be considered in order to assess how long it takes a basin to react to the possible changes in forest cover.

3.5.3 INVENTORY OF FINNISH BASIN CHARACTERISTICS USING LANDSAT DIGITAL DATA, TOPOGRAPHIC MAPS AND AERIAL PHOTOGRAPHS
by Risto Kuittinen[1]

3.5.3.1 Introduction

In Finland drainage basin characteristics have a significant effect on the maximum and minimum runoff. The most important basin characteristic is lake percentage. According to studies made in 1957-1965 by Mustonen (1965) other important basin characteristics especially in medium-sized and small drainage basins, are as follows: mean land slope, amount of coarse mineral soils, peatlands, drained swamps and forests and agricultural land. The timber volume in the drainage basin also has a significant effect on runoff. Of these basin characteristics, man is responsible for draining swamps and forests, and agricultural land. Man is responsible for changing the timber volume of forests. When lake percentage increases differences between maximum and minimum runoffs decrease. Swamp and forest drainage increases mean runoff. Increasing mean land slope increases summer and winter minimum runoffs and decreases spring runoff. When the amount of coarse mineral soils increases, annual runoff increases, whereas increasing timber volume decreases annual runoff. When the area of agricultural land increases minimum runoff increases. Landsat 1, launched in 1972, provided a new way to make an inventory of basin characteristics. The first preliminary studies in Finland were carried out using topographic maps, aerial photos and Landsat images. When it became possible in 1975 to use computers in data analysis an inventory method based on digital Landsat data, topographic maps and aerial photography was studied.

3.5.3.2 Study performance

3.5.3.2.1 The location and characteristics of the study area. The two study areas, the hydrological research basins of Norrskogsdiket and Sulvanjoki, are located between $62°30'N$ and $63°00'N$, and between $21°00'E$ and $22°00'E$. The mean altitude above sea level (Gulf of Bothnia) is 22 metres. Precipitation in this part of Finland is 600 mm per year on average (1931-1960) and runoff 220 mm per year on average (1931-1960) (Mustonen, 1971). The mean temperature in February is $-7°C$ and in July $+16°C$ (1931-1960). The period when the temperature is over $0°C$ lasts, on average, from 10 April to 15 November (1931-1960).

The water equivalent of snow on 16 March is 65 mm, which in general is very close to the maximum of the water equivalent of snow in winter. The study areas are in the humid subboreal region where coniferous forests dominate. The area belongs to a glaciated basement complex with predominantly granitic and gneissic rocks. The surficial deposits, averaging about 8 m in thickness, mainly consist of till, silt and clay with fragments of sand and gravel deposits.

3.5.3.2.2 Data used in the study. The basis for every basin characteristics study in Finland are topographic maps on a 1:20,000 or 1:50,000 scale. Such maps contain a great deal of

---

[1] National Board of Waters, Helsinki, Finland

information for hydrological purposes. Most important of all is that drainage basins areas can be determined very accurately using these maps. In addition to topographic maps, black and white pancromatic aerial photographs on a 1:60,000 scale are available for the whole country. These two sources of material provide a good basis for the interpretation of Landsat data. If possible, colour and colour infrared aerial photos can also be used to obtain basin data for Landsat data interpretation. In this study both of these sources of data were used, too. Landsat-1 has a four-channel multispectral scanner, which measures reflected visible radiation and near-infrared radiation. The channels are 500-600 nm, 600-700 nm, 700-800 nm and 800-1100 nm. The radiation measured is usually stored in digital form on magnetic tapes, which after preprocessing can be used in computers. The Landsat-1 digital data used were from 31 August. The data quality was good but the time of year was not the best possible. Early summer would have been better, because it would have been easier to interpret the vegetation. Because of Finland's northern location the range of radiation intensities was on average from 13 to 35 units, while the whole range is 0-256. This caused some inaccuracies in computer interpretation.

3.5.3.2.3 Method of Landsat data interpretation. The digital Landsat data were interpreted (Andrews, 1972, Fukunaga, 1972) using a computer program based on the LARSYS supervised program. Thus the main parts of the interpretation procedure were:
(1) Processing grey maps from the Landsat magnetic tapes and studying the area to be interpreted.
(2) Selecting training fields and test fields for interpretation. One or more classes whose properties correspond to basin characteristics are selected for every basin characteristic.
(3) Computing statistical parameters for every class to be interpreted.
(4) Computing the optimal channel combination for interpretation.
(5) Interpretation of test fields. If the result is not good, the selection of training fields is improved and new parameters computed.
(6) Interpretation of the whole area.
(7) Printout of interpretation results by a line-printer in the form of symbol, where every basin characteristic has its own symbol.

The decision rule applied is an interpretation of Bayes' decision rule for the minimum error. In this case it was assumed that the observation vectors X_i for every class had a normal distribution. Thus the decision rule was:

$$h(X) = \frac{1}{2}(X-M_a)^T \Sigma_a^{-1}(X-M_a) - \frac{1}{2}(X-M_b)^T \Sigma_b^{-1}(X-M_b) + \frac{1}{2}\ln\left|\frac{\Sigma_a}{\Sigma_b}\right| \lessgtr 0$$

where: M_a and M_b are mean vectors of the classes and Σ_a and Σ_b are covariance matrices of the same classes.

If $h(X_i) > 0$, X_i belongs to class b and if $h(X_i) < 0$, X_i belongs to class a. It was assumed that a priori probabilities for every class were equal.

In computing the optimal channel combination for Landsat data, divergence was used as a measure of class separability.

Divergence D is defined as follows:

$$D = \int |f_a(X) - f_b(X)| \cdot \frac{f_a(X)}{f_b(X)} dX,$$

where: $f_a(X)$ and $f_b(X)$ are the conditional density functions for classes a and b.

When $f_a(X)$ and $f_b(X)$ are normal

$$D = \frac{1}{2}(M_a-M_b)^T (\Sigma_a^{-1}+\Sigma_b^{-1})(M_a-M_b) + \frac{1}{2}tr\left|(\Sigma_a-\Sigma_b)(\Sigma_b^{-1}-\Sigma_a^{-1})\right|$$

The Bhattacharyya distance was also used as a measure of separability. When $f_a(X)$ and $f_b(X)$ are normal B is:

$$B = \frac{1}{8}|M_b-M_a|^T \left|\frac{\Sigma_a+\Sigma_b}{2}\right|^{-1}(M_a-M_b) + \ln\frac{|(\Sigma_a+\Sigma_b)/2|}{|\Sigma_a|^{\frac{1}{2}}|\Sigma_b|^{\frac{1}{2}}}$$

3.5.3.2.4 Landsat data interpretation. In Landsat data interpretation one or more classes whose properties presented those of the basin characteristics were selected for every basin characteristic. For instance, the class "predominantly pine forest" was used in timber volume interpretation and soil type interpretation (see Table 1 and Table 2). Statistical parameters for all classes were computed from data gathered from training fields outside the interpreted areas. The results of basin characteristics interpretation were obtained by combining the interpretation results of all classes.

The following basin characteristics were included in the interpretation:
- amount of coarse mineral soils, A, (%)
- amount of peatland, B, (%)
- amount of agricultural land, C, (%)
- amount of drained forest and peatland, D, (%)
- timber volume, E, $(m^3/10^{-2}km^2)$

Coarse mineral soils include the following soil types: fine sand, sand, gravel, sandy and gravelly till. Areas where the thickness of peat was over 30 cm were included under peatlands. Other soil types were included under fine mineral soils.

After visual interpretation of aerial photos and field studies, the following preliminary classes were selected for the interpretation of basin characteristics, Table 1.

Table 1 Preliminary classes for basin characteristics interpretation. X indicates which basin characteristic is interpreted using the class in the same line

Class	A	B	C	D	E
Predominantly spruce forest					X
Predominantly pine forest	X				X
Hardwood forest		X			X
Pine forest	X				X
Clearcut area					X
Fuscum pine swamp		X			X
Dwarf-shrub pine swamp		X			X
Fuscum bog		X			X
Small sedge bog		X			X
Drained spruce-hardwood swamp		X		X	
Drained fuscum pine swamp		X		X	
Drained fuscum bog		X		X	
Drained small sedge bog		X		X	
Agricultural land			X		

Table 2 Classes used in the interpretation of basin characteristics

Class	Soil type	Terrain type	Timber volume $(m^3/10^{-2}km^2)$
Agricultural land	Fine mineral soil	Agricultural land	0
Predominantly spruce forest	Fine mineral soil	Forest	181
Predominantly pine forest	Coarse mineral soil	Forest	80
Hardwood forest	Peat/fine mineral soil	Forest	111
Clearcut area	Peat/mineral soil	Forest	0
Dwarf-shrub pine swamp	Peat	Peatland	33
Fuscum pine swamp	Peat	Peatland	1
Fuscum bog	Peat	Peatland	0
Small sedge bog	Peat	Peatland	0
Drained ordinary sedge fen	Peat	Peatland	0
Pine forest	Coarse mineral soil	Forest	35

These classes represented all vegetation, soil types, and land use types in the research areas. By computing the B-distance between classes and preliminary classifying test fields, 11 classes were selected for the final interpretation. The criterion was that the expected interpretation error between each pair of classes did not exceed 30%. Table 2 lists these classes and their relationship with the basin characteristics. Soil types, terrain types and timber volumes were determined on the basis of field inventory. The training field areas per class varied from 0.05 to 0.63 km^2. On average it was 0.36 km^2. For some classes several training fields were used to get sufficient observations to compute statistical parameters: the mean vectors M_i and the covariance matrices Σ_i. The average number of observations X_i was 73 per class.

3.5.3.2.5 Interpretation of soil types. Three different soil type groups were interpreted: coarse mineral soils, fine mineral soils and peat soils. Because Finland, and especially the study area, has small differences in elevation, Landsat data cannot be used with sufficient accuracy for the interpretation of topography. Topography is, however, the most important factor when soil types are interpreted in Finnish conditions. In order to use topographic information, soil type interpretation was used with topographic maps and the results of Landsat data interpretation. It was then possible to combine the following four elements in soil type interpretation: topography, vegetation, land use and information which can be obtained on soil from vegetation. The results of this interpretation are given in Tables 3 and 4. Land slope was not interpreted, because it correlates well with the amount of coarse mineral soils.

Table 3 Interpretation results of the Norrskogsdiket drainage basin, A: Landsat data; B: Landsat data, topographic maps and aerial photos; C: field inventory

Basin characteristic	Results A	Results B	Results C	Error %	
Percentage of agricultural land	33		34	3	
Percentage of peatland	28	24	30	20	7*
Percentage of coarse mineral soil	14	25	31	19	55*
Percentage of fine mineral soils	58	51	39	31	49*
Percentage of drained forest and swamp	13	28	28	0	54*
Timber volume (m^3/10^{-2}km^2)	58		48	21	
Area of drainage basin (km^2)			11,6		

* Result of Landsat data interpretation

Table 4 Interpretation results of the Sulvanjoki drainage basin. A: Landsat data; B: Landsat data, topographic maps and aerial photos; C: field inventory

Basin characteristic	Results A	Results B	Results C	Error %	
Percentage of agricultural land	18		23	22	
Percentage of peatland	14	8	11	27	27*
Percentage of coarse mineral soil	32	47	40	18	20*
Percentage of fine mineral soil	54	45	49	8	10*
Timber volume (m^3/10^{-2}km^2)	71		67	6	
Area of drainage basin (km^2)			26.8		

* Result of Landsat data interpretation

3.5.3.2.6 Interpretation of drained swamp and forest areas. Drained swamp and forest areas were interpreted using topographic maps and aerial black and white photographs on a 1:60,000 scale. In this way the drained areas on the topographic map could be updated. Because in general these areas were photographed in late spring or early summer, when the leaves have not yet appeared on the trees, ditches can be seen quite well. As can be seen in Table 2, it is not generally possible in Finland to interpret drained areas using Landsat data. This is due to the very small changes in vegetation many years after draining. In addition, after trees grow in originally treeless drained swamps, these areas are confused with forests and with swamp types where trees are growing. The results of interpretation are presented in Table 3.

3.5.3.3 Results

The interpretation results of the Norrskogsdiket drainage basin are presented in Table 3 and the results of the Sulvanjoki drainage basin in Table 4. These tables contain both the results from Landsat data interpretation and those from Landsat data, topographic map and aerial photography interpretation.

The error of interpretation results is on average 16% compared with the results of a field inventory. The error of the field inventory results is about 5% after accuracy studies of the inventory method. Thus the real error is between 12% and 21%. According to the B-distance studies the interpretation error was between 3% and 30%. The average was 12%. Thus it was expected that an error of between 10% and 20% would occur.

Landsat data in this part of Finland do not give sufficiently good results for a hydrologist to make an interpretation of soil type. The principal reason for this is that the main information content of Landsat data in Finland deals with vegetation, and especially in this part of Finland the correlation between vegetation and soil type is poor in forests. The results are better when topographic maps are used together with the results of Landsat data interpretation.

The interpretation results of agricultural land in the Sulvanjoki drainage basin could be improved if aerial photographs and topographic maps are used. The error of 22% is largely due to the swamp type "small sedge bog", which is partly confused with agricultural lands. The effect of this error is much smaller for the whole of Finland than in the Sulvanjoki drainage basin because these swamp types are less common in other parts of Finland. Sufficiently accurate results can thus be obtained using only Landsat data.

The results of timber volume interpretation can be improved if correction coefficients are determined for timber volume values on the basis of interpreted test areas. As can be seen, Landsat data interpretation gives mostly high values for timber volume. The reason for this is that most of the information on forest timber volume comes from forest density and tree types when Landsat data is used. Thus young, dense forests are given mostly high timber volume values in the interpretation. If correction coefficients are used the error in timber volume interpretation would be about 10% on average.

As is presented in section 2.6, the interpretation of drained swamps and forests is impossible when Landsat data is used. Good results can be obtained when aerial photos and topographic maps are used together. Large areas are interpreted, using systematic sampling, for instance 16 sampling points per square kilometre, instead of direct measurement of the drained area.

3.5.3.4 Conclusions

The interpretation of basin characteristics using Landsat digital multispectral scanner data and a supervised interpretation method together with aerial photographs and topographic maps, gives a practical method for the inventory of large drainage basins in Finnish conditions. Landsat data are useful in the interpretation of soil types and timber volumes although the results obtained in soil interpretation in this study are not the best possible. Other basin characteristics can also be interpretated using topographic maps and aerial photographs. Only aerial photographs and maps are useful in the interpretation of drained swamp and forest areas.

REFERENCES

Andrews, H.C. 1972. *Introduction to Mathematical Techniques in Pattern Recognition*.

References

Fukunaga, K. 1972. *Introduction to Statistical Pattern Recognition*.

Mustonen, Seppo E. 1965. Effects of meteorologic and basin characteristics on runoff. *Soil and Hydrotechnical Investigations,* Engineering Department of the Board of Agriculture, Helsinki.

Mustonen, Seppo E. 1971. Variations in the minimum runoff from small basins. *Publications of the Water Research Institute*, 1, Helsinki.

3.5.4 EFFECT OF THE CULTIVATION OF A TROPICAL BASIN ON ITS HYDROLOGICAL REGIME
(KORHOGO, IVORY COAST, 1962-1972)
by P Chapero[1]

3.5.4.1 Introduction

It is tempting for the hydrologist, whether he is setting up the basic data sample required for a statistical analysis of the regime of a watercourse, or determining the factors involved in the hydrology of an elementary basin, to transplant the drainage network or representative drainage basin into a stable environment in order to eliminate, from amongst all the factors, those which are due to environmental changes caused by man.

This natural inclination is more and more frequently thwarted nowadays by changes in the physical environment produced by the various human activities occurring in those regions where hydrological studies are to an increasing extent being carried out. It is in fact in just those regions where, as a result of the continuous increase in human activity, the problem of the balance between the demand for water and the resources available is beginning to provoke anxiety, that different management projects are being put in hand and the need for studies is making itself felt. However, it is, of course, in these very same regions that environmental changes caused by different soil and resource management practices are most evident.

These changes can be of various kinds. If we concentrate on those which are caused by agricultural activity and which affect the observational data at the outlet (control station), we can distinguish between the following types:
- those which <u>directly</u> affect the details of the hydrological cycle; controlled or natural depletions, which may be permanent or temporary and which vary from one year to another according to the rainfall deficit; redistributions related to various irrigation techniques which graft an artificial cycle on to the natural one;
- those which have an <u>indirect</u> effect by changing the conditional factors involved in the hydrological cycle; agricultural practices, afforestation or deforestation, extension of cultivated land.

The sum-total of the annual hydrological data thus forms a sample which becomes gradually less homogeneous so that it is very difficult or even impossible to carry out a statistical analysis.

Unless the hydrologist is willing to restrict himself to a simple statement of the resources which are still available at a given moment, he must therefore begin to concern himself, not so much with the results of the mechanisms involved in the hydrological cycle, but rather with the actual functioning of this mechanism and with the changes which are produced by alterations in the natural order. From an analysis of these changes, he can hope to extract the elements which he needs to make the observational data samples more homogeneous, or to predict the repercussions that environmental changes will have on the functioning of the cycle.

---

[1] ORSTOM, Paris, France

Let us see what means the hydrologist has at his disposal:

Experimental plot. This is a small region of a drainage basin, of limited size, on which the factors related to soil reactions are modified at will, according to some definite programme. Variations in precipitation can be eliminated by the use of rain simulators. The results are interesting but of limited application. The plot, which is generally a homogeneous unit, is an open system and does not enable a complete water balance to be established. Its area is usually much too small to allow studies to be made of the shape of floods because the surface runoff becomes established in a permanent form and because the discharge is a linear function of the rainstorm hyetograph. Extrapolation to the size of a much more complex complete basin is a difficult or even impossible task. This sort of study is very costly and cannot be carried out in quantity.

Experimental basin. The experimental basin, which is considerably larger, enables the transition to actual dimensions to be made more easily and facilitates the transposition of the results to regional level. Since this is a closed system, it permits the study of complete water balances, provided, of course, that an impermeable substratum crops out at the control point to enable all the flow to be measured. It is clear, however, that rain simulation cannot be used because of the size of the experimental basin. The basin is therefore subject to variations in precipitation and there is a risk that this might obscure the effects produced by deliberate changes in the soil factors. The observation period has to be extended if studies are to be made of the effect of the changes on the mean values. These basins are therefore expensive and this fact limits their wider use.

Representative basin. The environmental changes on a representative basin are not programmed and deliberate. The basin is in a region where agricultural practices are developing naturally. The stages of this development are carefully noted and compared with the hydrological observations. The soil changes are of course non-uniform and made at an uneven pace so that it is difficult to ascribe the changes in the hydrological cycle to any particular transformation occurring in the occupation or utilization of the land. However, if it is well chosen, the basin with all its complex transformations will be highly representative of the development of a whole region.

A better, though more expensive solution is to compare the evolving basin with a control basin where the original conditions prevail. However, it is not always possible to preserve a basin in its natural state in a region where development tends to be all-embracing. There remains the method of studying an evolving basin over a period of many years so as to obtain a sample which is sufficiently representative of the precipitation regime and to allow the cumulative effect of the various transformations which occur to produce quantitatively measurable data.

It is this type of solution that was adopted in the study of the Korhogo representative drainage basin which was undertaken between 1962 and 1972 in the northern part of the Ivory Coast (tropical transition climate). During this period, the region underwent considerable agricultural development featuring an appreciable increase in the area under cultivation and in forestry plantations.

We shall discuss in turn the general, physical and hydrological features of the Korhogo basin and the results of the observations that were made, emphasizing the methodology of the analysis and the changes in the hydrological cycle caused by developments in the use made of the soil. We shall then go on to discuss the conclusions which can be drawn about the effect of agricultural development.

3.5.4.2 Physical environment of the basin and general features of its hydrological regime
The Korhogo basin is representative of the areas situated on the highly cultivated quartz sands of the northern Ivory Coast with a tropical transition climate (mean annual precipitation of 1,400 mm). The presence of a dynamic water table whose boundaries coincide almost exactly with those of the topographic basin and whose external drainage is provided by the water course makes this a closed system in which the complete water balance can be established.

3.5.4.2.1 Topographic features (Figure 1). Situated 5 km from the settlement of Korhogo (near the village of Waraniene), the representative basin involves a small tributary of the Loserigue, itself a tributary of the Lofigue (drainage basin of the Bandama Blanc). The co-ordinates of its outflow situated to the right of a rocky outcrop, are: latitude $9°25'N$, longitude $5°39'W$.

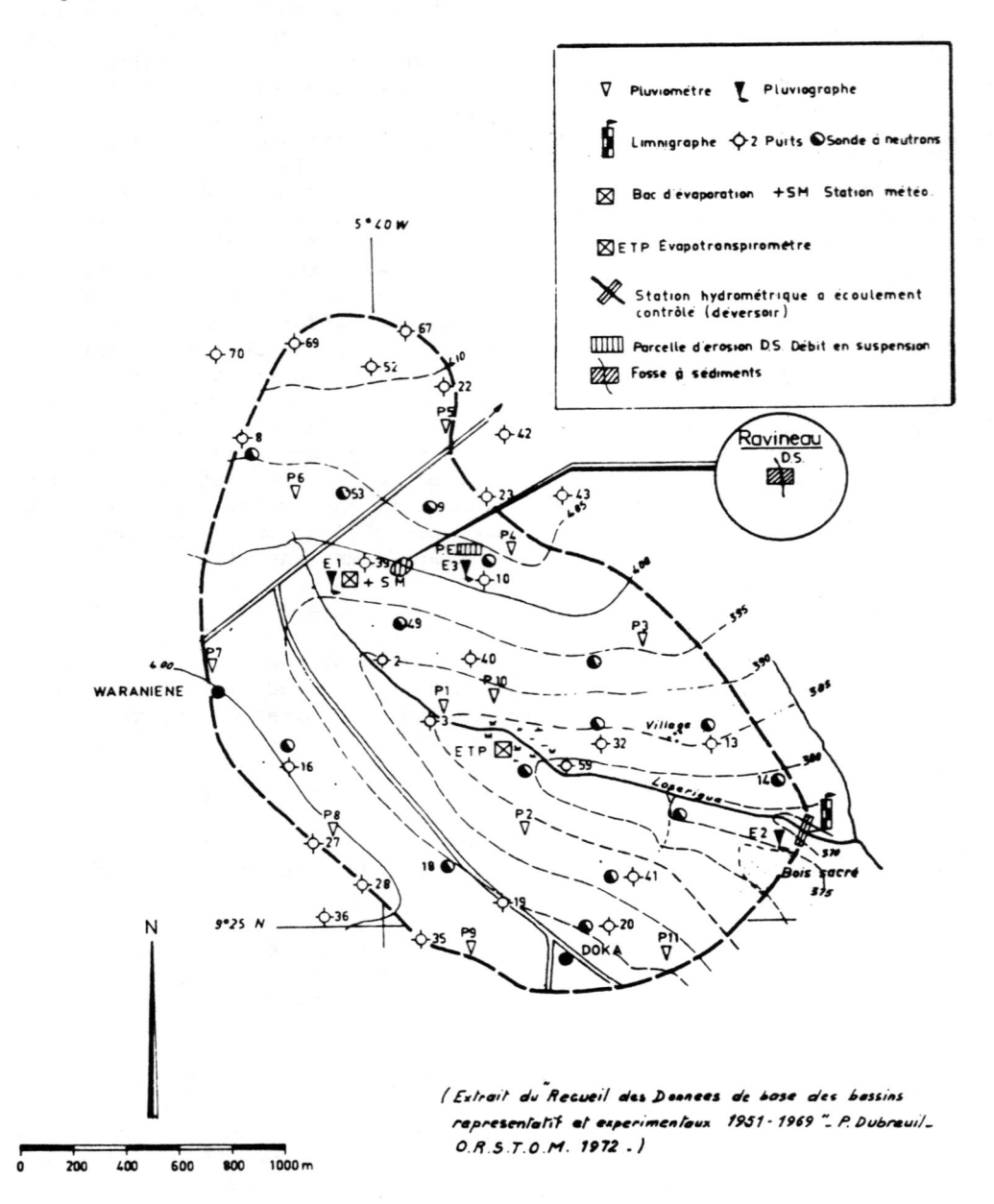

Figure 1   Carte topographique et d'equipement bassin representatif de Korhogo

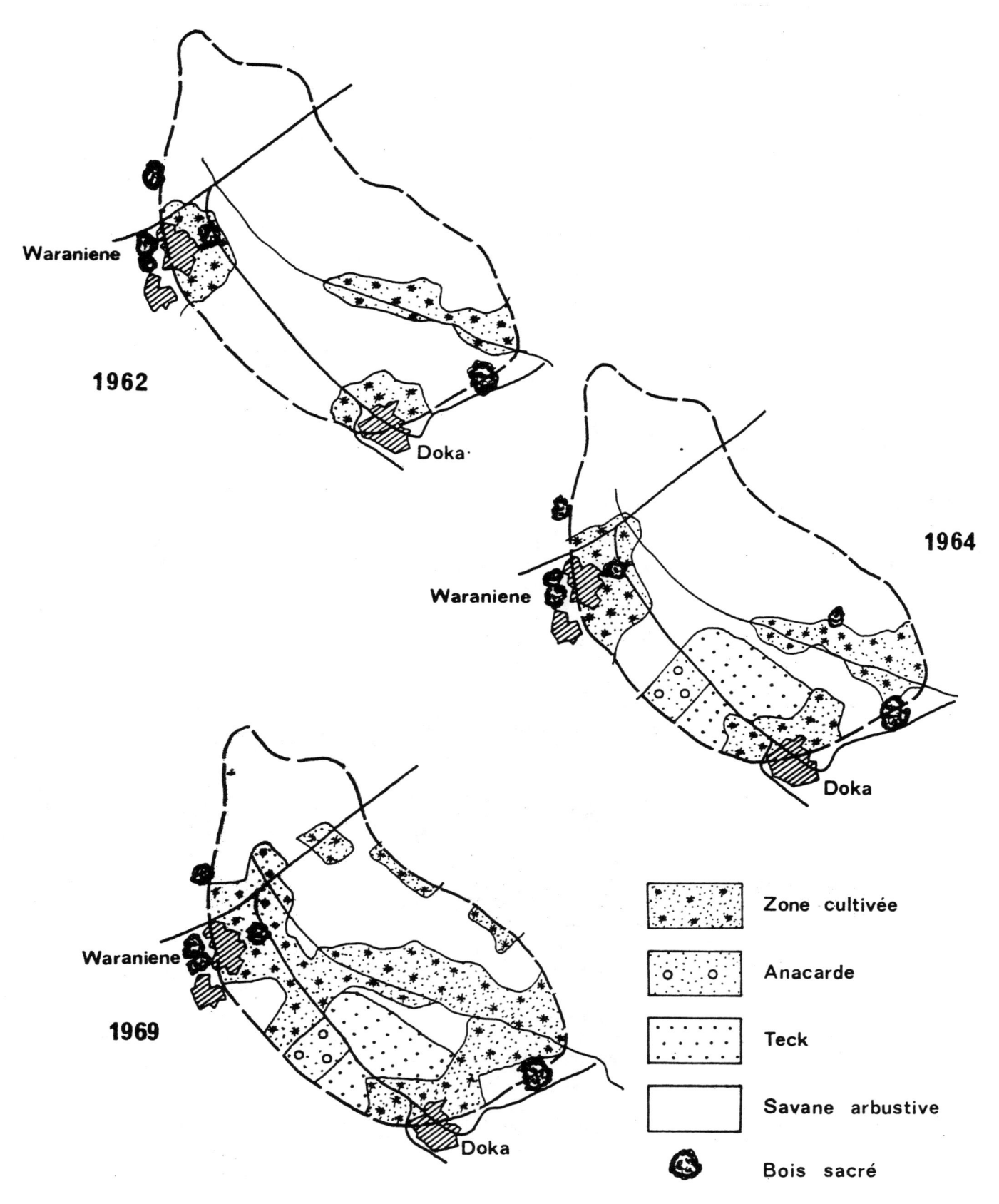

Figure 2   Carte d'occupation des sols   bassin de Waraniene-Doka

Effect of the cultivation of a tropical basin

The basin forms a semi-circle, with the highest point and the outflow at opposite ends of a 2.8 km diameter (running NW-SE).
The characteristics of the basin are as follows:

Area : $S = 3.63$ km^2
Gravelius compactness coefficient : $K_c = 1.13$
Equivalent rectangle : 2.24 by 1.62 km

The maximum height of the basin is 412 m and that of the outflow is 369.25 m.

Slope index $\quad I_p = L^{-\frac{1}{2}} \sum_1^n \sqrt{a_i d_i} = 0.135$

(a_i is the percentage of the area A between two height contours at a distance d_i apart).

Global slope index $\quad I_g = D/L = 15.4$ m/km

D is the difference in level between the H95 altitude (below which 95% of the basin is situated) and H5 (below which 5% of the basin lies); L is the length of the equivalent rectangle).

Specific height difference $\quad D_s = I_g \sqrt{A} = 29.3$

According to the ORSTOM classification, the basin is in class R3 (slight or fairly slight relief).

The channel network is of the ridge type with pools and paddy-fields in the principal bed. The main stream, which becomes sizeable only in the downstream half of the basin, is swollen in the rainy season by small temporary streams. The drainage density is 0.61.

3.5.4.2.2 *Substratum and soils.* The substratum of the basin is formed of a parent rock (calco-alkali granites) which is almost impermeable. This crops out at the basin's mouth, at the side of the outfall. The substratum is topped by a clay-sand zone of weathering of varying thickness (0 to 35 m). Within this zone lies a permanent water table drained by the watercourse.

The pedological study distinguishes the following formations lying in a ring around the central thalweg. From the outside to the inside:

Slightly ferrallitic, red, fine gravel soils on the plateau. These sandy-textured soils, with a predominance of coarse sand (60 per cent), are distinguished by a fine gravel horizon. They occupy 41 per cent of the total area of the land.
The permeability as measured in the laboratory on a modified sample is high (100 to 300 mm/h).

Leached, ferrallitic, colluvial grey soils on the slopes.
These soils containing a high percentage (50 to 60 per cent) of fine gravel, occupy 40 per cent of the area of the basin. The laboratory permeability is from 50 to 100 mm/h.

Grey-yellow feruginous soils on the slopes.
These soils are sandy on the surface but more clayey at depths below 50 cm. They occupy 10 per cent of the basin area. The laboratory permeability varies according to the place from which they are taken (20 to 200 mm/h).

Grey-white, ferruginous leached and hydromorphic soils at the foot of the slopes.
These sandy but gravel-free soils represent 5 per cent of the area. Their permeability is not very high (10 to 70 mm/h).

Grey, hydromorphic gleys in the low-lying ground.
These are clayey-sand soils with a permanent hydromorphy. They occupy 4 per cent of the surface. Their laboratory permeability is small (20 to 50 mm/h).

The permeabilities quoted above were measured on modified soils in the laboratory. Measurements made <u>in situ</u> show great variability, and demonstrate the predominant influence of the vegetation cover and type of cultivation. We shall give the results of these field measurements later.

3.5.4.2.3 *Vegetation and cultivation (Figure 2).* The original vegetation was shrub savanna, but over the ten-year period when observations were being made, the appearance of the basin underwent a profound change. The area under cultivation increased from 20 per cent in 1962 to over 50 per cent in 1971. Various types of agriculture are practised: yams and cassava are grown on mounds; ridges, perpendicular to the slope where it is steep and parallel to the slope where it is gentle, are used for growing rice, maize and millet. Paddy fields and market gardens have been developed on low-lying ground.

Simultaneous with the increase in food crops has been the development of forest plantations. The species include teak and cashew. Since 1964 these plantations have occupied 12 per cent of the area of the basin on the right bank downstream. The average tree density varies: from an average of 500-600 trees/hectare for cashew to 350-400 for teak. The trees have grown rapidly. The average height of the cashews, which was 0.80 m in 1965, reached 3.50 m in 1971. The teaks grew from 0.8-1 m in 1965 to 5-6 m in 1971.

3.5.4.2.4 Climatic features and precipitation. The climate of the Korhogo region is of the tropical transition type (mean annual precipitation of 1,400 mm) and has two distinct seasons:
- A rainy season from April to October, during which rain is frequent and intense (over 100 mm per month, mainly in July and September).
- A dry season from November to March, during which rainfall is low and may even be zero (December and January).

The average year-to-year temperature is $27°C$ ($80.6°F$), with a maximum in April ($29°$) and a minimum in August ($25°$). The diurnal temperatures are highest in February and March ($36°$) and lowest in August ($29°$). The mean year-to-year diurnal value is $33°$. The night-time temperatures are highest in April ($23°$) and lowest in January ($16°$), with a mean value of $20°$. The relative humidity shows a year-to-year mean of 69 per cent. It is greatest in August (84 per cent) and lowest in January (47 per cent). The mean annual evaporation as measured on a Piche apparatus is 1,100 mm, with a daily maximum of 5.3 mm in January and a minimum of 1.4 mm/day in August. From a Colorado pan, the annual evaporation is about 2 m, with a daily maximum (7.8 mm/day) in April and a minimum (3.5 mm/day) in September.

The following figures for the precipitation regime come from the Korhogo meteorological reference station (1909-1926 and 1945-1973):
Mean annual precipitation: 1,351 mm.

Normal distribution, which adapts well to the 1945-1973 data, provides the following values for annual precipitation:
Wet hundred-year period: 1,981 mm
Wet ten-year period: 1,698 mm
Median: 1,351 mm
Dry ten-year period: 1,004 mm
Dry hundred-year period: 722 mm

The year-to-year irregularity can be characterized by the K3 ratio between the rainfall depths recurring every ten years. This ratio gives a value of 1.69 for Korhogo.

Because of the isotropic nature of the rainfall in the Korhogo region, the rainfall regime in the representative basin is very similar to that at the reference station.

Typical values for the hydrological year (May-April) are:
Wet ten-year period: 1,670 mm
Median: 1,330 mm
Dry ten-year period: 990 mm
K3: 1.69

The monthly distribution (mean values in mm) is a follows:

May	Jun	Jul	Aug	Sep	Oct	Nov	Dec	Jan	Feb	Mar	Apr
123	142	196	314	271	114	49	13	6	20	59	82

Rainfall in the rainy season represents 84 per cent of the annual total.
Daily precipitation (in the 24 hours from 7 pm to 7 pm for various intervals of

Effect of the cultivation of a tropical basin

recurrence (average over the basin) is:
1 year   72.7 mm
2 years   86.8 mm
5 years   107.0 mm
10 years 124.0 mm

The ratio of the average precipitation Pm over the basin surface to the precipitation P at a particular point and having the same probability, measured at some point on the basin is nil, which seems normal for a basin of this size.

From the rainfall records, we have been able to show that the probability of having more than one fall of rain per day increases with the depth of the rainfall from 25 per cent for 50 mm to 50 per cent for over 110 mm. There have never been more than three rainstorms per day. When there are two periods of rain, the proportion of the heavier one increases with the daily total from 60 per cent for 20 mm to 80 per cent for 100 mm. The rainstorms have a uniform shape, with an intense concentrated phase called the core, defined as the useful fraction of the rain P (the integrated total of the rainstorm sections above a threshold of 18 mm/h). The following relationships have been found between the rainfall depth C, the duration D of the core and the depth P of the total precipitation.

$C = 0.786 P - 1.6 \quad P < 50$ mm

$C = 0.98 P - 11.2 \quad P > 50$ mm

$D = 0.016 (P - 5)^2 + 1.17 (P - 5) + 15 \quad 5 < P < 90$ mm

Hyetographs for different recurrence periods have been established from a study of the intensities and durations. Using these, we have deduced various models of the real hyetograph of the ten-year rainstorm, all of which are based on the hypothesis of a central core with a single crest segment of maximum intensity.

Assuming two rainstorms per day, the characteristics of the decennial rainstorm are:
Total depth: 105 mm
Core: 90 mm in 110 min
Maximum intensity: 184 mm/h in 5 min

3.5.4.2.5 *General characteristics of the hydrological regime.* Observations were made over a period of 10 years (1962-1971) on the basin which was equipped as follows:
Rain gauges: 9 (1962-1966) and then 11 (1967-1972)
Recording rain gauges: 2
Water-level recorder: 1 OTT X making one revolution per day, situated on the right of a control section (thin-walled spillway) and fixed on a staff gauge.

The details of the water balance are as follows:

	1962 -63	1963 -64	1964 -65	1965 -66	1966 -67	1967 -68	1968 -69	1969 -70	1970 -71	1971 -72	Mean
PM (mm)	1,427	1,489	1,588	1,304	1,637	1,393	1,065	1,606	1,247	1,127	1,388
E (mm)	530	569	676	555	819	528	308	729	429	397	554
Ke (%)	37	38	43	43	50	38	29	45	34	35	40
Hr (mm)	88	86	81	54	156	60	18	109	36	49	74
B (mm)	442	483	595	501	663	468	290	620	393	348	480
DE (mm)	897	920	912	749	818	865	757	877	818	730	834

The observed sample of average rainfall measurements Pm on the basin (mean value of 1,388 mm) is fairly well distributed between a dry year (1968-1969) with a recurrence period of 6.25 years and a wet year (1966-1967) with a ten-year recurrence. The total runoff E represents on average (Ke) 40 per cent of the mean rainfall (minimum of 29 per cent in 1968-1969; maximum of 50 per cent in 1966-1967). The total depth of runoff Hr (direct runoff) represents on average only 5 per cent of the mean rainfall or 1/8 of the total runoff and shows a dispersion of 1 to 5 between 1968-1969 and 1966-1967. The base flow B (delayed runoff) represents on average 35 per cent of the mean rainfall or 7/8 of the total runoff; it has a much smaller dispersion than the direct runoff (minimum of 27 per cent in 1968-1969, maximum of 40 per cent in 1966-1967).

The runoff deficit DE represents on average 60 per cent of the rainfall. It shows a fairly small dispersion about the mean (834 mm) of approximately ±10 per cent, whereas the annual dispersion of the rainfall over the given period is almost double this (+18 per cent to -23 per cent). An analysis of the water balance for each of the hydrological years has made it possible to differentiate three elements in the total runoff viz the surface runoff, the baseflow in the rainy season (May-October) and the baseflow in the dry season (November-April). Each of these elements is related parabolically to a variable which describes the rainfall. As we shall make clear below, only the relationship involving runoff is notably affected by changes in soil usage. By summation of the three systems of equations, we can arrive at an equation which gives the value of the annual flow E_n as a function of the annual rainfall P_n and of the rainfall in the preceding year P_{n-1} (to allow for the delay in the drainage of the groundwater which feeds the baseflow):

$$E_n = 2.63.10^{-4} P_n^2 + 0.125 (P_{n-1} - 1.350)$$

This equation, which describes the average state of the basin, can be used with the long-period rainfall data from the Korhogo station to reconstruct a set of values for the annual flow from which, by applying Galton's law, we can then extract the following remarkable values:

Mean: 500 mm or 15.5 l/s/km^2
Dry ten-year period: 275 mm or 8.7 l/s/km^2
Wet ten-year period: 755 mm or 24 l/s/km^2

The year-to-year variability, as characterized by the ratio of the ten-year values, is 2.75, as against 1.69 for the rainfall.

An analysis of rainstorm-flood events has produced relationships between the rainfall depth of the core C of a given rainstorm and the volume (represented by the depth of runoff Hr) of the resultant flood and also the form of the typical hydrograph of the basis. By a process of combination, the characteristics of the floods for different recurrence periods have been determined:

Median flood:
    Pm = 68 + 12 mm
    C = 56.2 mm
    Hr = 14 mm
    Q_{Max} = 13 m^3/s

Ten year period flood:
    Pm = 104 + 14 mm
    C = 90.3 mm
    Hr = 33 mm
    Q_{Max} = 28.5 m^3/s

These data relate to the average state of the basin from 1962 to 1967. For the subsequent 1968-1971 period, the values must be reduced by 10 to 15 per cent.

All the data given above refer to the average state of the basin. Changes in the vegetation cover and in soil occupation have been responsible for considerable deviations from these mean values, as has been shown by a detailed analysis of the factors and the various terms of the hydrological cycle.

3.5.4.3 Changes in soil occupation and modifications of the hydrological cycle

We shall discuss in turn the observational results and measurements which show the direct effect on the physical parameters of the soil and the repercussions on the water balance caused by the considerable increase in the area under cultivation and in forestry plantations in the Korhogo basin.

3.5.4.3.1 Effect of the vegetation cover on soil permeability. More than 100 permeability measurements were made during 1970 and 1971 on the Korhogo basin. The Muntz infiltrometer method was used. This has the advantage that it enables *in situ* measurements to be made without disturbing the surface structure of the soil too much, and gives the vertical permeability (infiltration) directly. Analysis of the results has shown that permeability values are widely scattered inside each soil unit.

This scatter is related to the type of soil use. We therefore has to superimpose the following eight classes of soil occupations on the 5 types of soil given in 2.2 above:

T1 Natural soils, hard or fine gravel, with dense shrub cover (teak and cashew).
T2 Natural soils with light shrub cover and dense herbaceous cover, or soil with dense to very dense herbaceous cover.
T3 Natural soils with light to dense herbaceous cover.
T4 Natural soils which are bare or have a little vegetation cover.
T5 Soils which are worked annually or biannually, cultivated, with or without vegetation cover; the higher parts of ridges or mounds.
T6 Soils worked annually or biannually, cultivated, with or without vegetation cover; the lower parts between ridges and mounds.
T7 Fairly old worked soils (more than 2 years) with or without vegetation cover.
T8 Very old worked soils (more than 3 years) with or without ridges, with or without vegetation cover.

Four classes of permeability have been distinguished:

(1) Very low to low permeability (K between 4 and 144 mm/h)
In this class we find all soil units, provided only that they are natural and bare or have very little vegetation cover (T4), or that they have been recently worked but lie between the ridges (T6), or again that they have returned to the original state after past working (T8).

All the grey soils from low-lying land, which are only very slightly permeable (K below 10 mm/h), belong to this category.

(2) Low to average permeability (K between 144 and 430 mm/h)
These are the worked soils (T6) between ridges and mounds, the old soils (T7) with vegetation cover and the natural soils with little vegetation cover (T3 and T4).

(3) Average to good permeability (K between 430 and 900 mm/h)
This category corresponds to soils which are worked annually (T5) at the tops of ridges and mounds, to old soils with vegetation cover (T7) and natural soils with a fairly dense vegetation cover (T1 and T3).

(4) Good to very good permeability (K above 900 mm/h)
These are the natural soils with a dense shrub (T1) or grass (T2) cover and recently worked soil at the tops of ridges (T5).

It is clear that with the exception of the clay soils in low-lying areas, which are very clayey and impermeable, the value of K depends not on the pedological unit but on the occupation of the soil. It increases sharply in the forest regions and where the land is cultivated, provided that the land has been recently worked. The gradual spread of cultivated land and forest plantations over the basin has thus had the effect of increasing the average permeability quite significantly and therefore of reducing the response of the basin to precipitation.

3.5.4.3.2 *Effect of the vegetation cover on the response to precipitation: floods.* Every fall of rain which exceeds a certain threshold is accompanied by a flood whose characteristics (volume and shape) are determined by the input factors (rainfall depth, intensity distribution, antecedent moisture conditions) and by the transfer mechanism, governed by the physical properties of the rainfall area (relief, intrinsic permeability of the soils, vegetation, morphology of the drainage network). The "input" in a given region is independent of the physical characteristics of the basin. The preliminary saturation conditions depend mainly on the precipitation regime but they can be influenced by the physical environment. The transfer mechanism involves some elements which are stable over the time scale of an experimental study (the relief and the nature of the soil) and other elements which can change (the vegetation and the working of the soils)

The sample events observed over 10 years on the Korhogo basin is comprised of 446 rain storm floods.

We have made a distinction between:
- 230 floods in which the volume was less than 3,630 m^3 (or a depth of runoff of less than 1 mm). Most of these floods correspond to the runoff over only part of the basin, generally

the wettest central zone and the slopes near the river. The runoff coefficients of these floods are rarely greater than 2-3 per cent. The hydrographs are usually flat except when surface runoff occurs in the region immediately upstream from the outflow, which then gives a flood shape which is peaked and narrow. The delayed part of the surface runoff (interflow) is considerable.
- 216 floods with a volume greater than 3.630 m^3 (or Hr $\geq$ 1 mm). In these cases, we consider that the whole basin, or nearly all of it, is subject to runoff. The proportion of immediate runoff is much greater than the delayed surface part. The volume of these floods can reach quite high values and depends essentially on the average depth of precipitation and the initial moisture content of the soil. In contrast to the small floods, the spatial distribution of the rainfall plays only a very secondary role. These floods represent 90 per cent of the annual runoff.

3.5.4.3.2.1 Study of the runoff depths. The object of this analysis is to determine the relationship which, representing the overall response of the basin to precipitation, establishes a correspondence between the depth of runoff Hr and the average precipitation Pm (principal factor). The aim is also to determine the effect of secondary factors (chief of which is the initial moisture content of the soil) in order to establish a basin response curve for uniform saturation conditions. The position of this homogenized curve is then characteristic of the overall transfer pattern which combines all the physical factors of the rainfall area. <u>If a change is observed in the position of the response curve, this can only be due to the physical elements which are susceptible to variation , ie the vegetation cover and the working of the soil.</u>

(1) Precipitation
A preliminary correction made regarding the properties of the rain storm, is to eliminate its early sections and the tail. Those sections of the rain storm, whose intensity is below the 18 mm/h threshold which we have adopted for the Korhogo basin, have a zero or negligible effect on the depth of runoff. We thus retain only the useful <u>part</u>, or the <u>core</u> C, of the rain storm since it alone can produce runoff.

The intensity limit we have chosen (18 mm/h) is an <u>average</u> threshold which is valid for the majority of rain storms in the effective rainy season. This threshold value may be too high for the monsoon rains, which are long and light, so that the core of these falls of rain is underestimated. Conversely, the threshold may be too low for the exceptional isolated rain storms of May and November, and for these the value of the core is overestimated.

(2) The initial moisture content of the soil
The change in the soil moisture content during the year, apparent in varied reactions to a rainstorm of given depth (total runoff, partial runoff or no runoff), results directly from the sequence of previous rainstorms, ie their depth and distribution in time. In order to allow for the special features of the Korhogo basin, and in particular for the presence of a dynamic water table near the topographic surface, we have adopted two indices for the moisture content of the ground:

(a) <u>A humidity index</u> calculated from the total antecedent precipitation corrected for the interval of time separating earlier rain storms from the one under consideration.

This humidity index (Kohler) corresponds to the equation:

$$I_i^h = I_{i-1}^h \cdot e^{-kT_j}$$

where: I_i^h is the index for the day i under study; I_{i-1}^h is the index relating to the rain storm immediately prior to day i; j is the number of days without rain preceding day i.

Following trials, the value adopted for k was 0.18, or $e^{-k} = 0.835$; T_j was limited to 14 days.

During the rainy season (August to September) the median value of the median values of I^h is equal to 50.

The median value of the maximum values of I^h is 100.

(b) <u>An index</u> relating to the state of the zone of aeration of the soils and consequently to the amount of water required to saturate this part of the ground.

The index adopted was the <u>baseflow</u> Q_o for each day; this corresponds to the position of the dynamic water table and thus shows the size of the zone of aeration.

The baseflow Q_o, being related to the state of the water table, depends on the sum-total of antecedent precipitation.

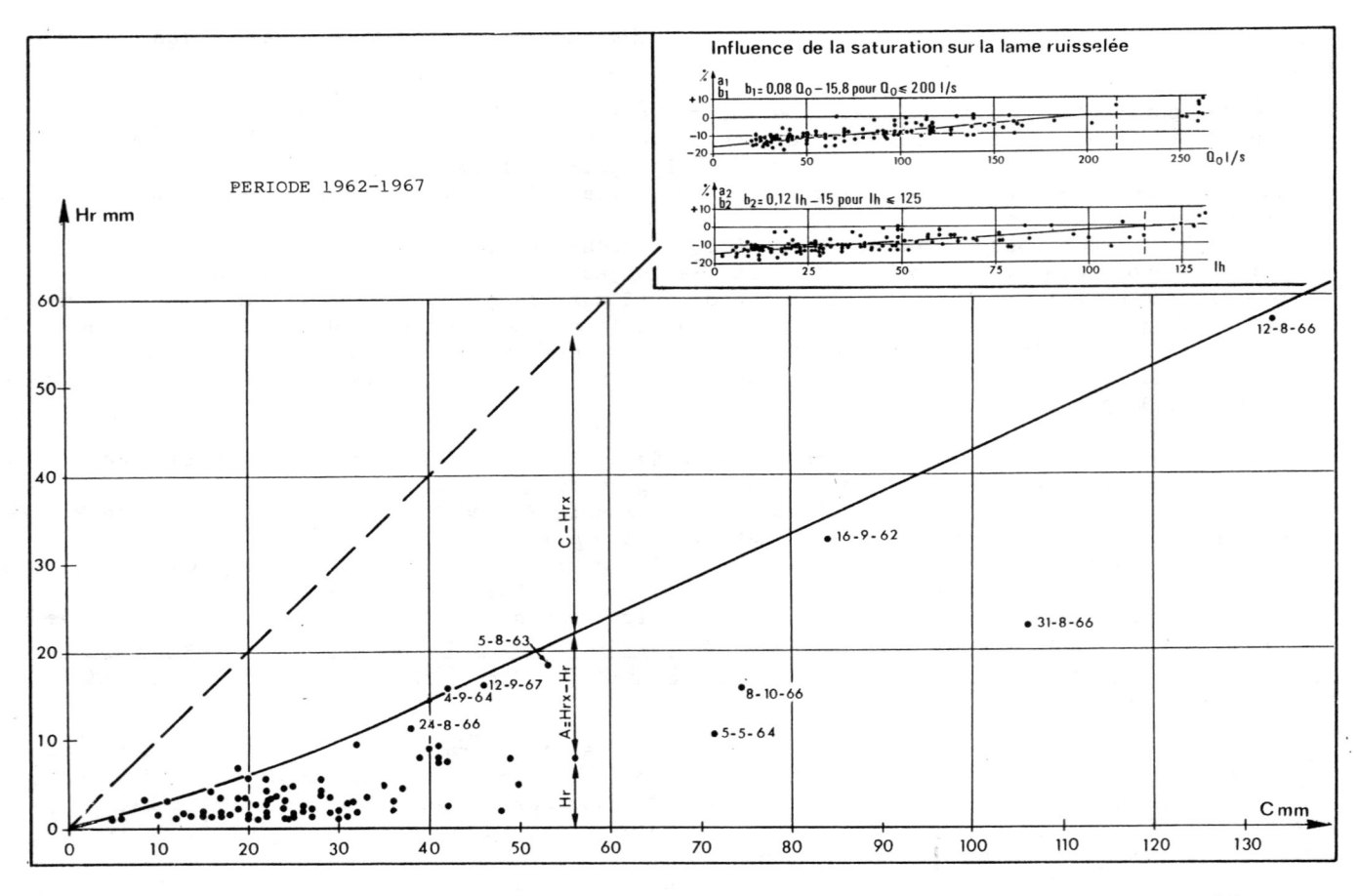

Figure 3   Hauteur de la lame ruisselee en fonction du corps moyen de l'averse responsable

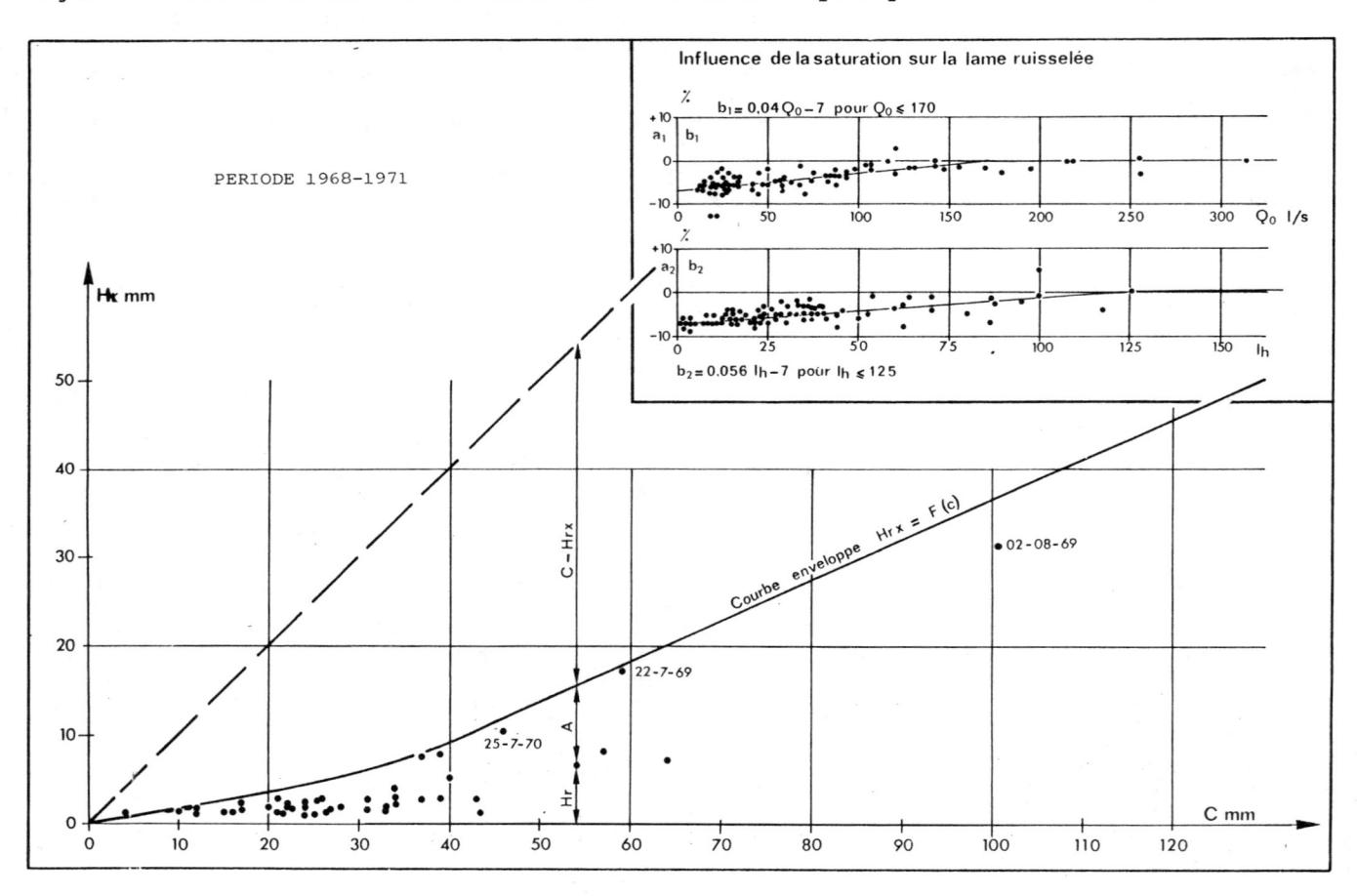

Figure 4   Hauteur de la lame ruisselee en fonction du corps moyen de l'averse responsable

The indices Ih and Qo are thus variables which both depend on the rain but which describe the total antecedent rainfall in different ways.

Ih is a "quick" index of precipitation during the preceding fortnight. Qo is a "slow" index of total precipitation during the preceding months.

At the beginning of the rainy season, Qo thus starts from a low value and increases gradually whereas Ih responds to the successive falls of rain which go to restore the moisture content of the zone of aeration and therefore have only a slight effect on the state of the water table. Conversely, at the end of the rainy season, Ih decreases rapidly whereas Qo falls exponentially and much more slowly.

(3) Precipitation limit

It is possible to calculate the depth which precipitation must attain or exceed, for a given prior moisture content, in order to set up surface runoff over the whole basin. Points are plotted on a graph with the average depths of the rain storms marked on the ordinate axis and the humidity index Ih (or the initial base flows Qo) on the abscissa, representing floods, with different symbols used for surface runoff over most of the basin (Hr > 1 mm), runoff over part of the basin only (Hr < 1 mm), or zero runoff (Hr = 0).

The curve separating the rain storms which cause runoff over most of the basin from those which have very small or zero runoff defines the precipitation limit for a given humidity index.

The conditions required in the Korhogo basin for a rain storm of a given depth of precipitation to be matched by total runoff (Hr < 1 mm) are as follows:

Pm in mm	Ih above	Qo
15	70	125 l/s
20	30	55 l/s
25	15	15 l/s
30	10	25 l/s
40	7	15 l/s

When these graphs were drawn, it became obvious that runoff conditions were tending to become more severe (from 1967 to 1971) so that for the same initial saturation conditions, the precipitation had to be 5 and 10 mm higher than the values in the above table (corresponding to the state of the basin most favourable for surface runoff) in order to set up total runoff.

This fact was confirmed when the global model for the basin was being adjusted to determine the "average theoretical infiltration threshold", a threshold which makes it possible to equalize the surplus runoff depth for each year, calculated from the model, and the observed depth. This threshold is only exceeded for a total of 3-10 hours per year - the total duration of the sections whose intensity is above the selected threshold (useful rain). From 1962 to 1971, this threshold changed from 50 to 53 mm/h.

(4) Response curve of the basin (Figures 3 and 4)

The runoff depths Hr of the floods under study are plotted on a graph as a function of the cores C of the rain storms responsible (Hr as ordinates and C as abscissae). The points corresponding to the rain storm/flood pairs are all plotted beneath the first bisector of the equation Hr = C. For a given storm of core C, the surface runoff deficit Dr = C - Hr is governed by the global characteristics of the basin on the one hand and the initial saturation conditions on the other. By drawing the upper limiting curve Hrx = f(C) which encloses the representative points (a curve which corresponds to the best saturation conditions found on the basin), we can divide the deficit Dr into two parts:

(i) The deficit C - Hrx, which corresponds to the runoff deficit related to the global properties of the basin (physical factors and vegetation) when the best initial saturation conditions are established (maximum possible runoff).

(ii) The deficit A = Hrx - Hr, which corresponds to the supplementary runoff deficit related to the preliminary saturation conditions. The value of A is higher the further the saturation conditions fall below the best found on the basin.

To determine the value of C - Hrx due to the basin's physical factors, the position of the envelope curve Hrx = f(C) should be indicated independently of the secondary factors, the most important of which are the saturation conditions.

At this stage of the analysis we could see that the position of the envelope curve Hrx tended to drop gradually from 1962 to 1971. We had to divide the observations into two groups:
- the floods observed from 1962 to 1967, a period in which the change in the vegetation cover of the basin was most rapid;
- the floods observed from 1968 to 1971, when there was relative stability in the use made of the soil.

(The choice of just two groups is due to the desire to retain samples of sufficient size and must not be understood as indicating a sudden change in the properties of the basin between 1967 and 1968).

Correcting the deviations A = Hrx - Hr to fit the two envelope curves drawn in this way was carried out by the residual deviation method.

For each event, the deviation A (and more accurately in order to restore independence vis-à-vis the principal factor C, the relative deviation a - A/C) is plotted as a function of the two secondary factors related to the initial saturation conditions, Ih and Qo. These two factors are taken simultaneously and not successively into account because of their virtually equivalent effect on runoff conditions. The method used is as follows.

The relative deviations a = A/C are first plotted on graphs as functions of Ih and Qo, as if each of these factors was the only one responsible for them. In this way, we get two clusters of points and two average curves:

$a_{Ih} = f(Ih)$ and $a_{Qo} = f(Qo)$

The deviations are next divided in such a way that:

$$\frac{a1}{a2} = \frac{a_{Qo}}{a_{Ih}}$$

and a1 + a2 = a

The relative deviations a1 and a2 are then plotted on separate graphs and enable the two average curves to be drawn:

b(1) = F(Qo) and b2 = F(Ih)

These curves make it possible to correct the representative points Hr and provide the values

H'r = Hr + (b1 + b2) C

An average curve H'r = F(C) can thus be drawn and this determines the depth of runoff corresponding to a rainstorm core value C for uniform saturation conditions (maximum possible runoff).

The correction has a noticeable effect.

For the first group (1962-1967), the total residual deviation is 168 mm, as against 610 mm before correction, for 125 events (average dispersion ± 0.6 mm). For the second group, it is 57 mm, as against 212 mm before correction, for 91 events (average dispersion ± 0.3 mm).

The residual deviations can be attributed to:
- factors not taken into account; the main factor is probably the spatial distribution of the rain storm (non-uniformity in the rainfall, position of the maximum);
- a change in the catchment conditions inside each group (continuous variation in the vegetation cover from 1962 to 1967 and from 1968 to 1971);
- dispersion factors such as the seasonal growth of vegetation, random errors in the determination of the core C and the rainfall depth Hr.

Comparison of the two response curves (for uniform initial saturation conditions: Ih = 60, Qo = 100 l/s) gives the following values for the runoff deficit Dr = C - Hr (deficit due to the basin characteristics):

C mm	Period 1962-1967		Period 1967-1971	
	Hr mm	Dr mm	Hr mm	Dr mm
20	2.8	17.2	1.9	18.1
40	8.0	32.0	6.2	33.8
60	15.6	44.4	13.6	46.4
80	26.2	53.8	23.2	56.8
100	40.0	60.0	35.2	64.8
120	56.2	63.8	49.0	71.0
140	73	67	65	75

The relative deviation $\frac{Dr\ (68-71) - Dr\ (62-67)}{Dr\ (62-67)}$ increases from 5 to 12 per cent when C rises from 20 to 140 mm. This is clear evidence of the appreciable reduction in the basin's runoff capacity between the basin's average state of 1962-1967 and that of 1968-1971.

In fact, we observed that there was a noticeable variation even inside the 1962-1967 period. Calculated as a moving average, the ratio of the total deviations to the mean response curve for 1962-1967, and the ratio of the points representative of each year to the total runoff depths, we obtain the following results:

$\frac{\Sigma e}{\Sigma He}$ = + 13%   1962-1963
            + 10%   1963-1964
            - 5%   1964-1965
            - 11%   1965-1966
            - 5%   1966-1967

or, on average, a difference of 20 per cent between 1962 runoff (initial state of basin before agricultural development) and 1968 (average state of basin corresponding to fairly stable soil usage.

3.5.4.3.2.2 Shape of the floods. The shape of a flood is represented by a hydrograph which is a graph representing the sequence of flow rates observed at the outflow between the beginning and the end of the runoff. By choosing and analysing the simple floods observed on the basin, ie those which result from a rainfall event which is sufficiently intense to produce surface runoff over the whole basin and brief enough to be able to describe it as unitary, we can derive a mean hydrograph representative of the transfer mechanism in the basin. The shapes of simple floods should all be the same, with an appearance related to the features of the catchment area. In fact, however, they are affected by the changes in the physical characteristics of the basin which occur on an annual scale (contrast between the vegetation cover at the beginning and end of the rainy season) or over many years (changes in soil usage. In the Korhogo basin, we have had to make a distinction between medium-amplitude floods (1 mm < Hr < 5 mm) and of large floods (Hr > 5 mm).
(1) <u>Medium floods</u> are caused by average rain storms which have led to runoff from almost the whole of the basin, or by heavy rain storms occurring during unfavourable saturation conditions (before or after the effective rainy season). The shape of these floods is responsive to the spatial distribution of the rain storm, and the delayed (or interflow) part of the runoff remains considerable. This category includes floods resulting from unitary rain storms.

We were unable to distinguish three periods in the state of the basin: the period 1962-1965 (extension of the area under cultivation); 1966-1967 (turning point); and 1968-1971 (stable soil usage). Graph 5 shows the shapes of the representative median hydrographs.

It can be seen that from 1962 to 1971, the median hydrograph becomes flatter in shape (the ratio of the maximum runoff flow rate to water depth (1 mm) changes from 0.85 m^3/s/mm to 0.63 m^3/s/mm). The concentration time tends to become longer: one half of the total volume

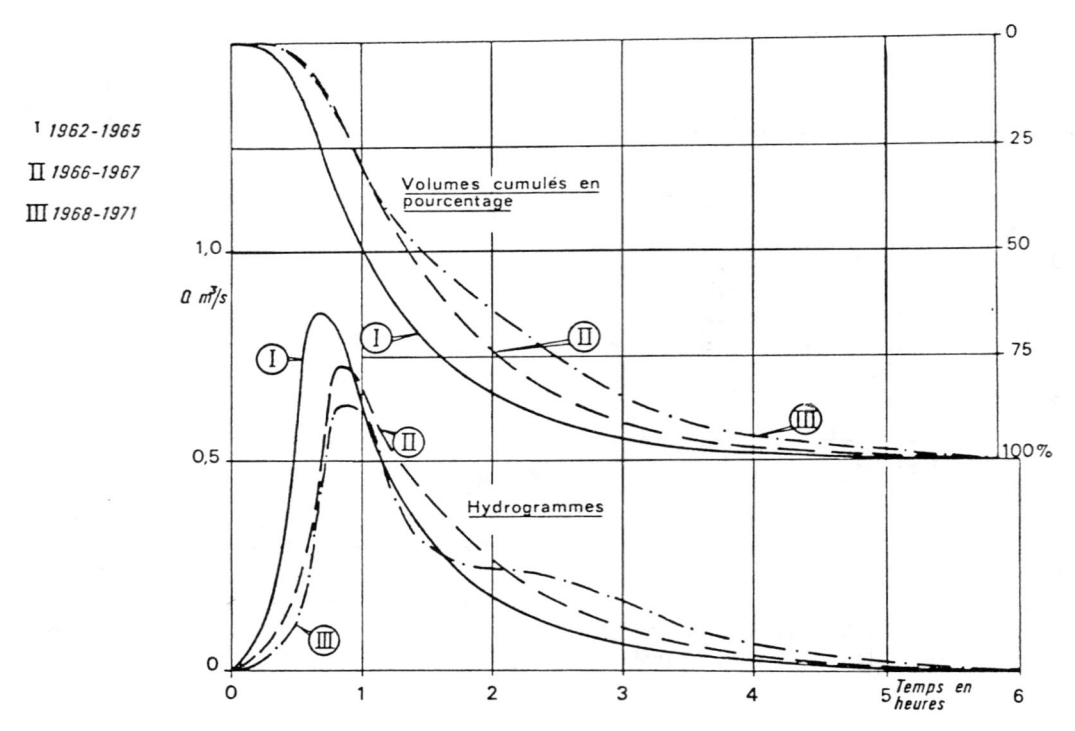

Figure 5   Hydrogrammes representatif des crues moyennes

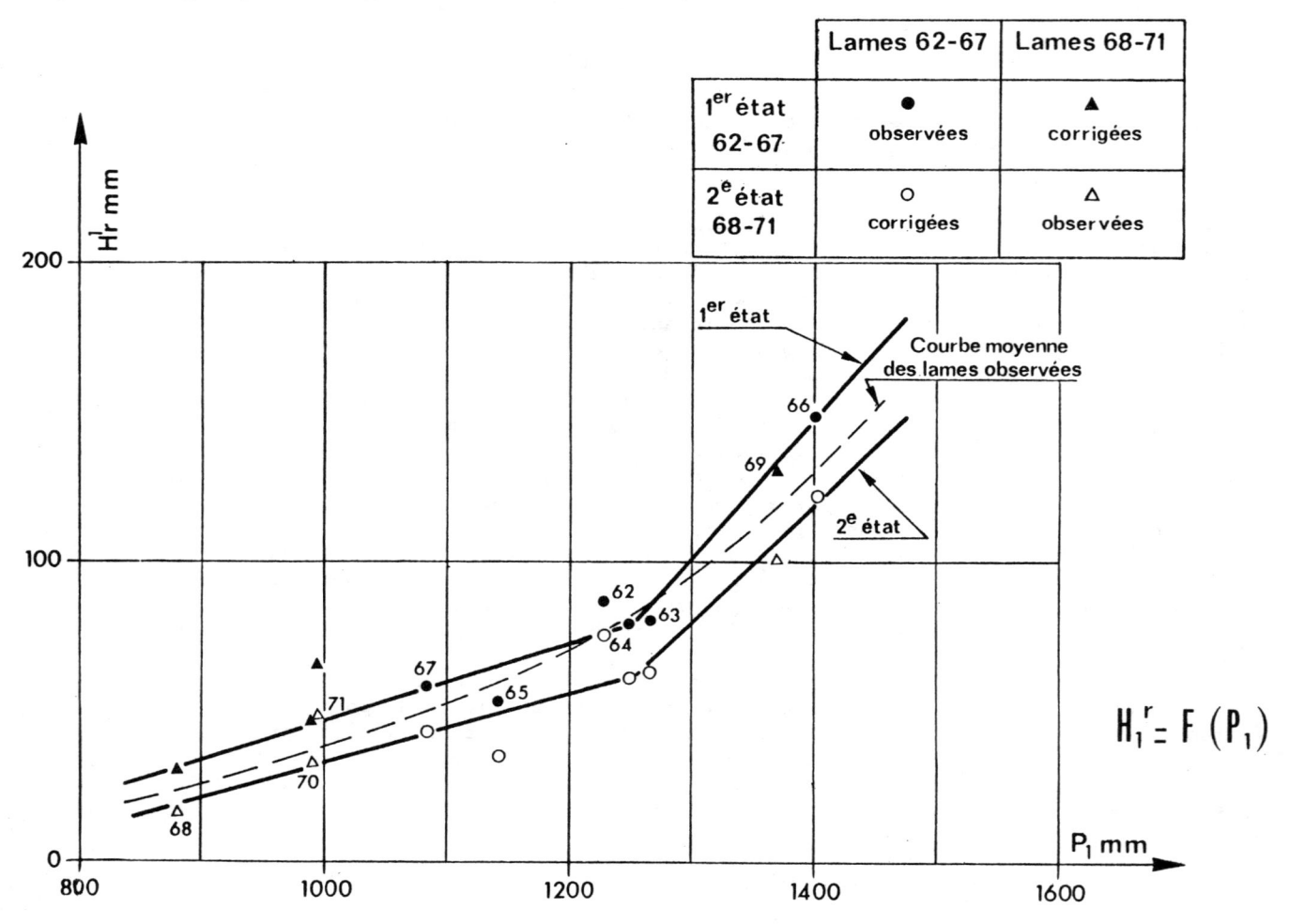

Figure 6   Correspondance entre les lames ruisselees et les hauteurs de pluie sur le bassin en saison des pluies (mai-octobre)

is reached after 60 minutes for the first period, 80 minutes for 1966-1967 and 90 minutes for 1968-1971. The delaying action on the concentration of runoff produced by the development of cultivated land is quite clear. Agricultural practices (the use of ridges parallel to the slope on weak relief and perpendicular on steep gradients) tend to make the runoff more uniform on cultivated sections but accentuate the contrast between the cultivated regions and the waste and fallow savanna. This distortion in the basin's response is further accentuated during the height of the rainy season by the emergence of the water table in the central marshy region and by the presence of paddy-fields in the low-lying parts of the river basin. In certain areas, a rain storm with a single crest segment results in a flood with a complex shape. There is a quick crest due to the immediate runoff from the downstream region, and a flatter crest due to the arrival of the runoff water from the upstream zone.

(2) <u>Intense floods</u> are usually more uniform and less affected by the spatial distribution of the rainfall. Changes in the properties of the soil (infiltration capacity, effect of vegetation) produced by heavy downpours tend to make the hydrographs of intense floods more pointed. Since there were no unitary rain storms for these intense floods, we had to derive the characteristics of the unitary hydrograph by separating out the various elementary floods which make up the observed complex hydrograph. As in the case of medium-amplitude floods, different hydrograph shapes have been established. For simplicity, we have adopted just two unitary hydrographs for intense floods.

The hydrograph for the 1962-1967 period has a 30 minute time of rise and a total surface runoff duration of 250 minutes. The maximum flow rate is 1.05 m^3/s for a runoff depth of 1 mm. For the period 1968-1971, the typical hydrograph has a time of rise of 40 minutes and a total period of 280 minutes. The maximum flow rate is 0.95 m^3/s for a 1 mm depth of runoff.

3.5.4.3.2.3 Exceptional floods. From an analysis of the various terms involved in the runoff (rain storm characteristics, infiltration capacity of the soil and the way it changes during the storm, depth of runoff, typical hydrograph for the basin) we can establish sets of characteristics for floods belonging to rain storms with different recurrence periods.

The following results have been obtained:

<u>Two-year return period flood</u>
    Average precipitation: 68 ± 12 mm
    Core of rain storm: 56.2 mm
    Depth of runoff: 14 mm (1962-1967)   12.2 mm (1968-1971)
    Maximum flow rate: 13 m^3/s (1962-1967)   9 m^3/s (1968-1971)

<u>Ten-year return period flood</u>
    Average precipitation: 104 ± 14 mm
    Core of rain storm: 90.3 mm
    Depth of runoff: 33 mm (1962-1967)   27 mm (1968-1971)
    Maximum flow rate: 28.5 m^3/s (1962-1967)   24.5 m^3/s (1968-1971)

<u>Fifty-year return period flood</u>
    Average precipitation   141 ± 15 mm
    Core of rain storm   127.1 mm
    Depth of runoff: 62 mm (1962-1967)   54.5 mm (1968-1971)
    Maximum flow rate: 41 m^3/s (1962-1967)   35 m^3/s (1968-1971)

The differences of the order of 10 to 15 per cent which can be seen in these results between the depth of runoff and maximum flow rates for floods of the same recurrence period for the two states of the basin, are a direct consequence of the observed diminution in the response of the basin in rainfall and the flattening of the representative hydrograph. These results provide evidence of the fact that changes in soil occupation have a significant effect on direct runoff.

3.5.4.3.3 Effect of the vegetation cover on the annual water balance. The value of the total runoff for each year depends on the total annual rainfall recorded on the basin; we can express this obvious fact in terms of a parabolic curve $E = F(Pm)$. The scatter about this mean runoff curve is caused by secondary factors of which the most important area:
- the distribution of the rainfall over the rainy season;
- the initial state of the groundwater resources;

Effect of the cultivation of a tropical basin

- the changes in soil occupation which occur during the period under study.
The effect of these various factors is best examined by considering separately the different components of the runoff.

3.5.4.3.3.1 Depth of runoff. If we plot the depth of runoff (or more exactly, the corresponding points for the rainy season which accounts on average for 95 per cent of the total runoff depth) as a function of the rainfall in the rainy season Pl (an average of 84 per cent of the total annual mean), we see that the points are scattered about a parabolic curve (Figure 6).

For sum of the deviations is 90 mm or about 13 per cent of the total for the 10 years (702 mm).

The depth of runoff corresponds to the cumulative total depth of the various floods observed and thus reflects the changes in the response of the basin to precipitation. Considering each of the two samples separately, we see that the total cumulative deviation is +22 mm (+4 per cent) for the 1962-1967 sample and -18 (-9 per cent) for the 1968-1971 sample. We can get two uniform samples by correcting the total depth of runoff to take account of the mean deviations of each flood, using the two response curves that we established for the two average states of the basin.

Year	1st state of basin Observed depth	2nd state of basin Corrected depth	Correction
1962-1963	87 mm	(75 mm)	-12
1963-1964	80	(63)	-17
1964-1965	79	(61)	-18
1965-1966	53	(35)	-18
1966-1967	148	(122)	-26
1967-1968	57.5	(43)	-14.5
1968-1969	(30 mm)	16 mm	+14
1969-1970	(131)	101	+30
1970-1971	(47)	33	+14
1971-1972	(65)	48	+17
Total	777.5	597	

We can fit a parabolic curve (or more simply, two straight line segments) to each of these two sets of values. The residual deviations, which are 48 mm (6 per cent) for the first state and 55 mm (9 per cent) for the second, can be attributed mainly to the role played by the distribution of the daily rainfall.

The difference between the two curves, which varies from 12 to 29 mm as the total precipitation in the rainy season changes from 900 to 1,400 mm, represents an average of 23 per cent of the depth of runoff and shows quite clearly the runoff deficit produced by the soil development. This difference, which is related to the two average states of the basin, is probably greater still if one refers to the situation before and after the development of agriculture on the basin.

3.5.4.3.3.2 Baseflow during the rainy season. The baseflow Bl during the rainy season represents $\frac{2}{3}$ of the total baseflow (Figure 7). A parabolic curve can be fitted to the Bl/Pl pairs. The deviations Δ Bl from this average curve can then be replotted on a second graph as a function of the rainfall depth Pn - 1 of the year immediately previous (May-April) and this gives a straight-line correction curve which shows the effect on the baseflow, during the rainy season, of the initial state of the stored water (in April), which itself is a function of the average rainfall for the preceding hydrological year. An average curve Bl = F(Pl) can then be fitted to the corrected points. This correction taking account of the previous year reduces the total deviation from 325 mm (10 per cent) to 150 mm (5 per cent).

The remaining deviations can be largely attributed to the effect of rain storm

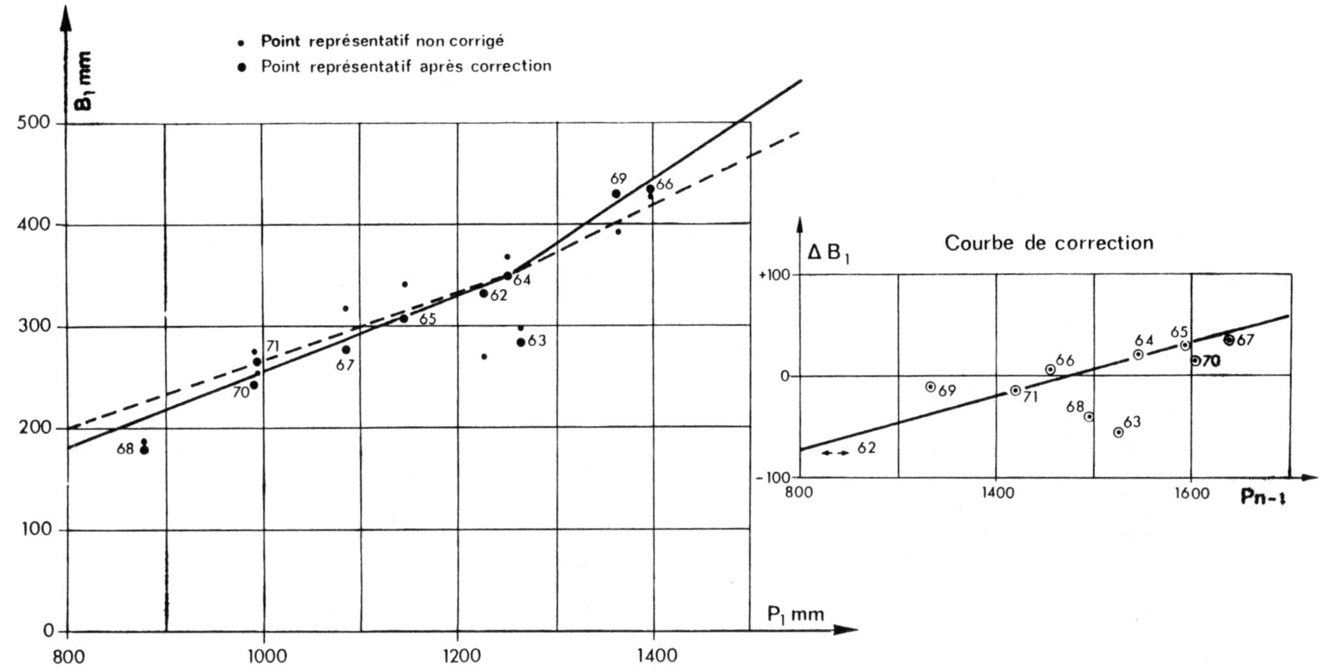

Figure 7 Correspondance entre l'ecoulement de base B, de saison des pluies et la hauteur de pluie P₁ sur le bassin, en saison des pluies (avec correction en fonction de la hauteur de pluie de l'annee anterieure

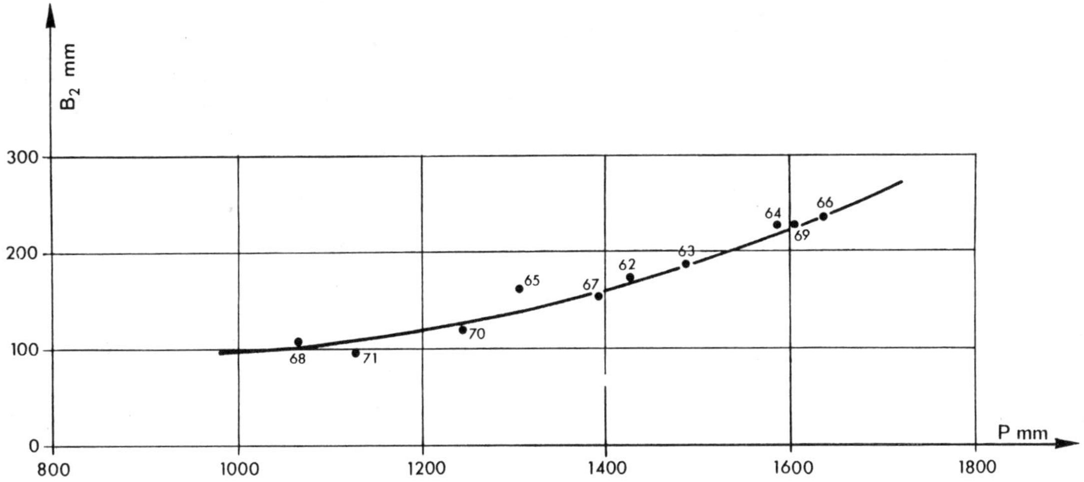

Figure 8 Correspondance entre l'ecoulement de base B₂ de saison seche et la hauteur annvelle de pluie sur le bassin

223

distribution. However, if we take the 1962-1967 and 1968-1971 samples separately (and omit the years 1963 and 1968 since they are well below the average position of the curve, probably owing to inaccuracies in calculating the discharge depths), we see that the cumulative deviation for the first group is -35 mm (-2 per cent) whilst for the second group it is +20 mm (+2 per cent). This suggests that changes in the state of the basin have only a slight effect (increased supply to the baseflow in the rainy season).

3.5.4.3.3.3 *Baseflow in the dry season.* In the same way, we can establish a relationship between the height B2 of the baseflow during the dry season and the depth P1 of the rainfall in the rainy season. A correction can be made which takes account of rainfall in the dry season. This correction comes into play only when the total precipitation in the dry season exceeds a threshold of 300 to 350 mm. If we simplify, it is also possible to establish a relationship (Figure 8) between the runoff depth B2 and the total annual depth P. The scatter about this parabolic curve is quite small (a total deviation of 83 mm or 5 per cent of the sum of the B2 values).

If we consider the two samples separately, we can see a small effect due to the state of the basin. The cumulative deviation for the first period is +33 mm (+3 per cent), whilst for the second it is -15 mm (-3 per cent). This small reduction in the baseflow during the dry season can be attributed to the resumption of evapotranspiration by the forest plantations and the crops. This tendency is confirmed by the changes in the coefficients of the recession curves which follow the equation

$$H_b = H_{bo} e^{-kt} \quad (t \text{ in days})$$

where: H_b is the monthly baseflow depth in the dry season and H_{bo} is the baseflow depth in November. The average value of the coefficient k is 9.5×10^{-3}. From 1963 to 1972, the value of k tended to increase from 8.5×10^{-3} to 10.5×10^{-3}; this means that the time taken for the baseflow to decrease from 10 to 1 changed from 270 to 220 days.

3.5.4.3.3.4 *Characteristic runoffs.* By summation of the curves for the three components in the runoff, we obtain a corresponding curve E = f(P) whose position is more accurately defined that than of the mean curve which could have been fitted to the ten observational values.

The equation of this curve is

$$E = 2.65 \times 10^{-4} P^2$$

A correction term $\Delta E - 0.125 (P_n - 1 - 1350)$ can be used to allow for the effect of the rainfall from the preceding year on the annual water balance.

As we mentioned above (see 2.5), we were able to constitute an extended sample with the following characteristic values (making a distinction this time between the two states of the basin).

	1962-1967 state	1968-1971 state
Average depth	508 mm	492 mm
Dry ten-year period value	269 mm	281 mm
Wet ten-year period value	769 mm	741 mm

The effect on the total annual water balance of the development of the forest plantations and areas under cultivation is thus shown by the average decrease of 4 per cent in the annual depth. The surface runoff, which is essentially affected by the diminution in the response of the basin to precipitation (reduction of from 20 to 25 per cent in the annual runoff depth), constitutes on average only $\frac{1}{8}$ of the total runoff.

3.5.4.4 Effect of cultivation: mechanism and consequences

The mechanism by which cultivation affects the hydrological cycle comes into play at the instant when the rainfall input is distributed over the soil. It is effective at three levels:

<u>Above the soil surface</u>: the extension of the aerial superstructure of the vegetation cover (grasses and especially the foliage of trees) increases by interception the fraction of the rainfall which is stored temporarily in the surface reservoir (pools and puddles) and is taken up by direct evaporation.

<u>On the soil surface</u>: the development of root systems and the destructuring of the soil in cultivated areas by various agricultural practices bring about a significant increase in the natural permeability of the soil (see 3.1) and thus in the fraction of the rainfall which infiltrates into the zone of aeration. This action is intensified by the mechanical braking effect of the vegetation cover, especially in regions planted with graminaea.

Cultivation also has a significant effect on the appearance of the hydrographic network and on the drainage density.

<u>Below the soil surface</u>: the work of the roots and tillage of the soil modify the structure of the superficial layer and change the retention capacity, the vertical permeability and also the horizontal transmissivity and consequently the dynamic fluctuations of the water table.

What becomes of the extra quantity of water which infiltrates into the soil depends on the time of year and the nature of the vegetation cover. The cover can take up all or part of the supplementary water to satisfy the requirements of growth and evapotranspiration. Depending on the season and the water needs of the vegetation cover, the water table may collect part of the infiltrated water (maintenance of the baseflow in the rainy season) or it may, on the other hand, give up part of its reserve (reduction in the baseflow during the dry season).

Applying this mechanism to the Korhogo basin, we find that:

For floods taken individually, we get a reduction of 15 to 20 per cent (up to 30 per cent for small floods) in the depth of runoff for equal storm rainfall depth, although of course we cannot distinguish between what is due to interception and what is due to infiltration. The maximum flow rates are reduced by 10 to 15 per cent under the combined effect of the decrease in the depth of runoff and the flattening of the unit hydrograph for the basin.

Over the year taken as a whole, the runoff depth is reduced by about 25 per cent. The effect on the baseflow is much smaller. The difference between the baseflows during the rainy and dry seasons is accentuated. The baseflow for the rainy season is slightly augmented by the increased infiltration which is not used by the vegetation. The baseflow in the dry season is reduced by the greater quantity used to meet the increased needs of a growing vegetation cover. The exponential decrease in this flow is accelerated by a rise in the transmissivity of the surface formations. The total balance of the baseflow is scarcely changed, however, and this means that the growing vegetation gets what water it requires for its growth and evapotranspiration from the fraction it draws from the runoff. One quarter of the direct runoff depth is thus impounded and used by the vegetation cover, mainly in the rainy season, and the remainder in a delayed way in the dry season.

The amount taken as a result of changes in the soil usage in the Korhogo basin represents about 4 per cent of the total runoff. The importance of this modest figure becomes apparent, however, when one considers the regional context. The region to which the basin belongs is currently an area of intense new cultivation. The area of land used for food and industrial crops (sugar crops) and for forestry plantations is continuously increasing. The need for water is beginning to catch up with the total resource available and so reservoirs are being constructed and irrigation schemes are planned. All this is obviously to the detriment of the downstream region. Even before the associated irrigation schemes had been completed, the major dam at Kossou was not receiving the quantity of water needed for normal operation.

In view of this exhaustive use of the surface water, the changes in input which are observed on the Korhogo basin are therefore of fundamental interest for any planning. Korhogo is, in any case, just an average basin in terms of the use made of the soil (the cultivated land represents 60 per cent of the surface, and 12 per cent of this is used for forestry plantations) and it is easy to imagine that other regions are undergoing even more intense cultivation or are more oriented towards forestry whose water requirements are much greater than those of food crops. The observed reduction in the total runoff could then increase considerably (6 to 8 per cent). We can equally well imagine that basins with a different geological structure would respond differently to changes in soil usage similar to those observed at Korhogo. On a basin which is naturally much less permeable, the surface runoff would be distributed in a different way even if its value remained the same (of the order of 20 to 40 per cent). The baseflow would be smaller and could even, on a very impermeable basin, be negligible compared to the direct runoff. One can presume that the reduction in the global runoff would thus be similar to that at Korhogo (4 to 5 per cent).

On the other hand, on a permeable basin where the infiltrated water could only be recovered by wells or pumps if there was no impermeable substrata close to the surface which happened to crop out, the runoff would represent the entire surface flow. The drainage coefficient (generally much smaller: 5 to 15 per cent) could then be appreciably reduced by agricultural practices.

The changes in the various terms of the water balance for the whole of the northern part of the Ivory Coast could only be determined by studies similar to the one whose results are described here.

The need for this kind of study is obvious at a time when the increasingly pressing need for water demands an ever more precise knowledge of the available resources, and of the mechanisms associated with those human activities which modify the regime of these resources.

3.5.5   THE EFFECT OF LAND USE ON FLOOD FLOW PEAKS FROM SMALL EAST AFRICAN BASINS
by D Fiddes[1]

3.5.5.1   Introduction

In the early 1960s it was generally agreed by engineers in East Africa that improvements in locally available flood estimation methods for small basins were desirable. The UK Transport and Road Research Laboratory (TRRL) had recently completed a major study to develop an urban surface water sewer model for use in the UK (Watkins, 1962) and was actively engaged in a similar study to provide a design method for bridges and culverts where highways crossed small rural basins (Young and Prudhoe, 1973).

In 1966 TRRL and the Kenya and Uganda governments set up a joint research programme to instrument and analyse data from small representative basins within Kenya and Uganda so that similar flood estimation methods could be developed for use in East Africa. Data collection continued until the end of 1973 and the results were first presented at a symposium in Nairobi, Kenya, in October 1975 (Greening, 1977).

This note contains a brief description of the basins and instrumentation the models developed, and discusses the effect of land use on the predicted peak flood flow.

3.5.5.2   Description of basins and instrumentation

3.5.5.2.1 Rural basins. The location of the basins is shown in Figure 1 and details given in Table 1. They were chosen to cover as wide a range as possible of the factors that affect flood runoff: rainfall, land use and topography, the latter being linked to soil type. Most were small (up to 15 km^2) to facilitate accurate measurement of rainfall volumes and flood flow.

Rainfall and streamflow were the only measurements made on site. The density of raingauge coverage was 2.5-5.0 per km^2 for basins up to 10 km^2 in area with lower density for the three largest. Most of the gauges were daily read totalising raingauges. The records from these were used to calculate the mean rainfall for each storm and check on areal variability. Approximately one quarter of the raingauges were autographic and these were used to check the temporal distribution and uniformity of the rainfall.

For economy, wherever possible the flow measuring structures were built into existing road culverts. This meant that each structure had to be individually designed. Various types of structure were used, trapezoidal flumes and crump weirs being the most common, with Plynlimon-type flumes on streams carrying a heavy bedload. On the largest basins, where structures would have been prohibitively expensive, natural, stable controls were used. These were rated in situ. More extensive details of the catchments and instrumentation are given elsewhere (Fiddes and Forsgate, 1970).

3.5.5.2.2 Urban basins. Five basins were instrumented: three in Nairobi, Kenya, and two in Kampala, Uganda. They were chosen to give a range of soil type, slope and type of

---

[1] Transport and Road Research Laboratory, Department of the Environment, Crowthorne, Berks, United Kingdom

Table 1 Summary of rural basin details

Reference	Basin Name	Rainfall zones	Topography	Land use	Area
	Kenya				
K1	Tiwi	750-1250 mm	Undulating	Cultivation alternating with rough grass and scrub	669 ha
K2	Mudanda	250-500 mm	Ridge to gently undulating	Scrub	165 ha
K3	Migwani	500-750 mm	Ridge to gently undulating	Scattered cultivation and rough scrub grazing	83.5 km^2
K4	Kajiado	500-750 mm	Level to depressed	Savannah, rough grazing	359 ha
K5	Eseret	500-750 mm	Ridge to gently undulating	Scrub savannah	322 ha
K6	Kiambu I	750-1250 mm	Highly dissected to broad ridge	Coffee plantations	201 ha
K7	Kiambu II	750-1250 mm	Highly dissected to broad ridge	Intensive small holding cultivation	521 ha
K8	Saosa*	1250 mm+	Highly dissected	Dense forest	680 ha
	Uganda				
U1	Barabili	1250 mm+	Gently undulating to level	Elephant grass and scattered trees with shifting cultivation	392 ha
U2	Munyere sub-catchment	750-1250 mm	Highly dissected to broad ridge	Grass with cultivation on alluvial valley floor	45 ha
U3	Munyere	750-1250 mm	Highly dissected to broad ridge	Grass land and shifting cultivation with significant area of swamp in valley	146 km^2
U4	Rubaare	750-1250 mm	Ridge to gently undulating	Grass with shifting cultivation; no swamps	13.7 km^2
U5	Sezibwa	1250 mm+ (north shore, Lake Victoria)	Redissected	Patches of dense forest permanent and shifting cultivation in woodland savannah; significant area of swamp	171 km^2
U6	Lugula	1250 mm+ (north shore, Lake Victoria)	Redissected	Woodland savannah with permanent and shifting cultivation	307 ha

* Existing basin data supplied by East African Agriculture and Forestry Research Organization

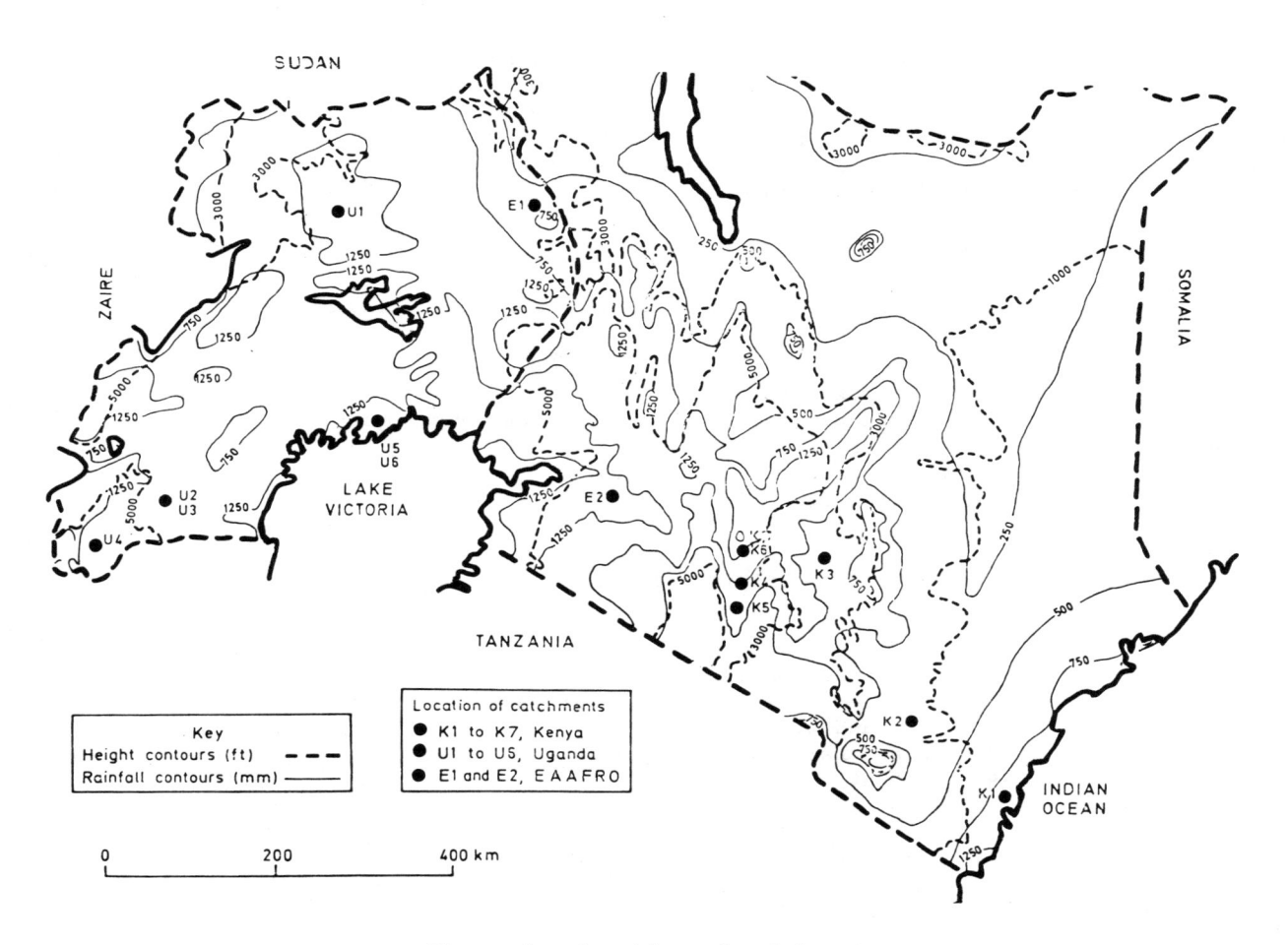

Figure 1   Location of catchments

development. Nairobi and Kampala are also in two very different climatic zones: the rain tending to occur in two distinct rainy seasons in Nairobi and much more evenly spread throughout the year in Kampala. Details of the basins are given in Table 2. It will be noted that they are much smaller than the rural ones.

The instrumentation was similar to the rural basins. The rainfall was measured using autographic raingauges (on average three per basin) and the runoff by trapezoidal or Palmer-Bowlus-type flumes built into the sewer outfalls.

The drainage system was by lined open channel on three of the basins and circular pipe on the remaining two. In two cases (Nairobi, Industrial Area, and Kampala, Kira Road) nearly all paved areas were directly connected to the sewerage system. On two of the other three, the road surfaces were directly connected but roof drainage discharged to lawns. On the Bernhard Estate, Nairobi, even the runoff from the roads had to travel across an unpaved verge before entering the drainage channel.

Table 2   Urban basin details

Bernhard Estate, Nairobi

Area:	36 ha approximately
Density:	2.6 houses per hectare (excluding servants' quarters)
Paved area:	Roofed areas: 5.3%
	Roads and hard shoulders: 7.3%
	Hard murram/stone drives: 3.6%
Drainage density:	53.5 m/ha
Slope:	0.025
Soil type:	Friable clay overlying murram

Industrial area, Nairobi

Area:	63.0 ha approximately
Density:	94 factories or warehouses, average area 0.15 ha each, ranging between 0.065 ha and 0.85 ha
Paved area:	Roofed and hard paved areas: 23.7%
	Roads: 5.6%
Drainage density:	117 m/ha
Slope:	0.0064
Soil type:	Black grumosolic (Black cotton) clay

Ofafa Estate, Nairobi

Area:	44.3 ha approximately
Density:	42.7 house units per hectare
Paved area:	Roofed areas: 8.6%
	Roads and hard shoulders: 6.3%
	Hard murram games pitches: 3.9%
Drainage density:	149 m/ha
Slope:	0.0087
Soil type:	Imported clay overlying murram

Wampewo Avenue, Kampala

Area:	35 ha approximately
Density:	0.5 houses per hectare (blocks of flats taken as one unit)
Paved area:	Roofed areas: 8.5%
	Roads: 7.4%
Drainage density:	142.3 m/ha
Slope:	0.056
Soil type:	Red latasol, outcrops of murram laterite

Table 2 (Continued)

Kira Road, Kampala
    Area: 1.82 ha approximately
    Density: 0.5 houses per hectare (12 blocks of flats taken as one unit)
    Paved area: Roofed areas: 23%
                     Roads and car parks: 13.5%
    Drainage density: 1129 m/ha
    Slope: 0.040
    Soil type: Red latasol

3.5.5.3 Description of models developed

3.5.5.3.1 Rural flood model. At the start of the research programme it was hoped to isolate unit hydrographs and generate a rainfall-runoff correlation for each basin and use these to develop a general flood prediction method. However, it soon became apparent that such an approach was not appropriate because:
(a) An adequate rainfall-runoff correlation requires a large number of storm data including many producing high flows;
(b) Storms that can be used to derive unit hydrographs (ie high intensity storms of unit duration) are rare, particularly on small basins where the unit time is short compared with the typical storm length;
(c) The shape of flood hydrographs on the basins was much more variable than found elsewhere and dimensionless hydrograph techniques found useful in the USA were therefore not applicable.

A method where more effective use could be made of the limited data that could be collected in a few years was therefore required for this study.

Approximately four years of data were available for each basin. A simple model was used to study these. Each basin was divided into a number of sub-basins. The runoff from each sub-basin was simulated using a linear reservoir analogue and the concept of contributing area C_A.

The sub-basin model can be summarised as follows:
(a) Early rain fills the initial retention Y. Runoff at this stage is zero.
(b) Subsequent rain falling on the parts of the basin from which runoff will occur C_A enters the reservoir storage S.
(c) The runoff is then given by $q = S/K$ where K is the reservoir lag time.

The translation of this runoff down the stream system to the outfall was modelled using a modification of the finite difference technique developed by Morgali and Linsley (Morgali and Linsley, 1965). The model was run for each large storm on a basin and for a variety of values of the parameters Y, C_A and K. The recorded and predicted hydrographs were then compared and the optimum values of the parameters arrived at by test of goodness of fit. To develop a general flood model, the difference in response of the basins as shown by the variation in the optimum values of the parameters C_A, Y and K was examined.

When the surface is very dry, runoff is small and occurs only from areas very close to the stream system. For storms following a wet period a larger area contributes and larger volumes of runoff occur. If the basin were sufficiently wet, the whole area would contribute and the value of C_A would approach unity. However, except on very small solid clay or rock basins there is a practical upper limit to C_A which is well below unity. For simplicity it is assumed that the contributing area coefficient varies linearly with soil moisture recharge until the soil reaches field capacity when the limiting value of C_A is attained. Four factors influence the size of the contributing area coefficient. These are soil type, slope, type of vegetation or land use (particularly in the valley bottoms) and basin wetness. The network of basins was selected to cover the range of these factors to be found in East Africa. The results could therefore be used to give indications of their effect on C_A. The effect of slope and soil type was studied by comparing the results of the basins with grass cover and the storms falling on soil at field capacity.

The effect of antecedent wetness was studied by comparing the runoff volumes resulting

from storms occurring at different stages of the rainy season. The reduction in value of C_A was assumed to vary linearly with the soil moisture deficit. For design purposes this has to be related to the probability of the soil being at field capacity when the design storm occurs. Huddart and Woodward have shown that East Africa can be divided into three zones (Greening, 1975):
(a) A semi-arid zone where runoff is not affected by antecedent rainfall;
(b) A wet zone where there is a high probability of the soil being at field capacity;
(c) A dry zone where there is a high probability that the soil will be less than field capacity.

These zones are shown in Figure 2. Using the results appropriate values for the reduction in C_A for design conditions for the various zones were determined.

The effect of land use was calculated by comparing the recorded volumes of runoff with those that would have occurred with a standard grassed basin.

The design value of the contributing area coefficient is therefore given by:

$$C_A = C_S C_W C_L \qquad (1)$$

where: C_S is the standard value of the contributing area coefficient for a grassed basin at field capacity, C_W is the wetness factor and C_L is the land use factor. These factors may be estimated from Tables 3-5. West Uganda has been singled out as an area in which large soil moisture deficits are to be expected frequently. This may be thought surprising considering the relatively high mean annual rainfall but in West Uganda, and to a lesser extent in the other dry zone areas, large rain storms are isolated events which tend to occur in the drier months. In semi-arid areas the initial retention Y has been found to be independent of the soil moisture deficit and a value of 5 mm can be assumed. Elsewhere a zero value can be assumed except for the West Uganda area where 5 mm is appropriate.

The value of lag time K varied widely between basins. Attempts were made to obtain a correlation between K and various basin characteristics such as overland slope, contributing area and drainage density but the only characteristic which showed a strong relationship was vegetation cover.

Table 3 Standard contributing area coefficients (wet zone basin, short grass cover)

Slope	Soil Type		
	Well drained	Slightly impeded drainage	Impeded drainage
Very flat, < 1.0%		0.20	0.40
Moderate, 1-4%	0.10	0.30	0.45
Rolling, 4-10%	0.12	0.40	0.50
Hilly, 10-20%	0.15	0.50	0.60
Mountainous, > 20%	0.20		

Table 4 Basin wetness factor

Rainfall zone	Basin Wetness Factor C_W	
	Perennial streams	Ephemeral streams
Wet zones	1.0	1.0
Semi-arid zone	1.0	1.0
Dry zones (except West Uganda)	0.75	0.50
West Uganda	0.60	0.30

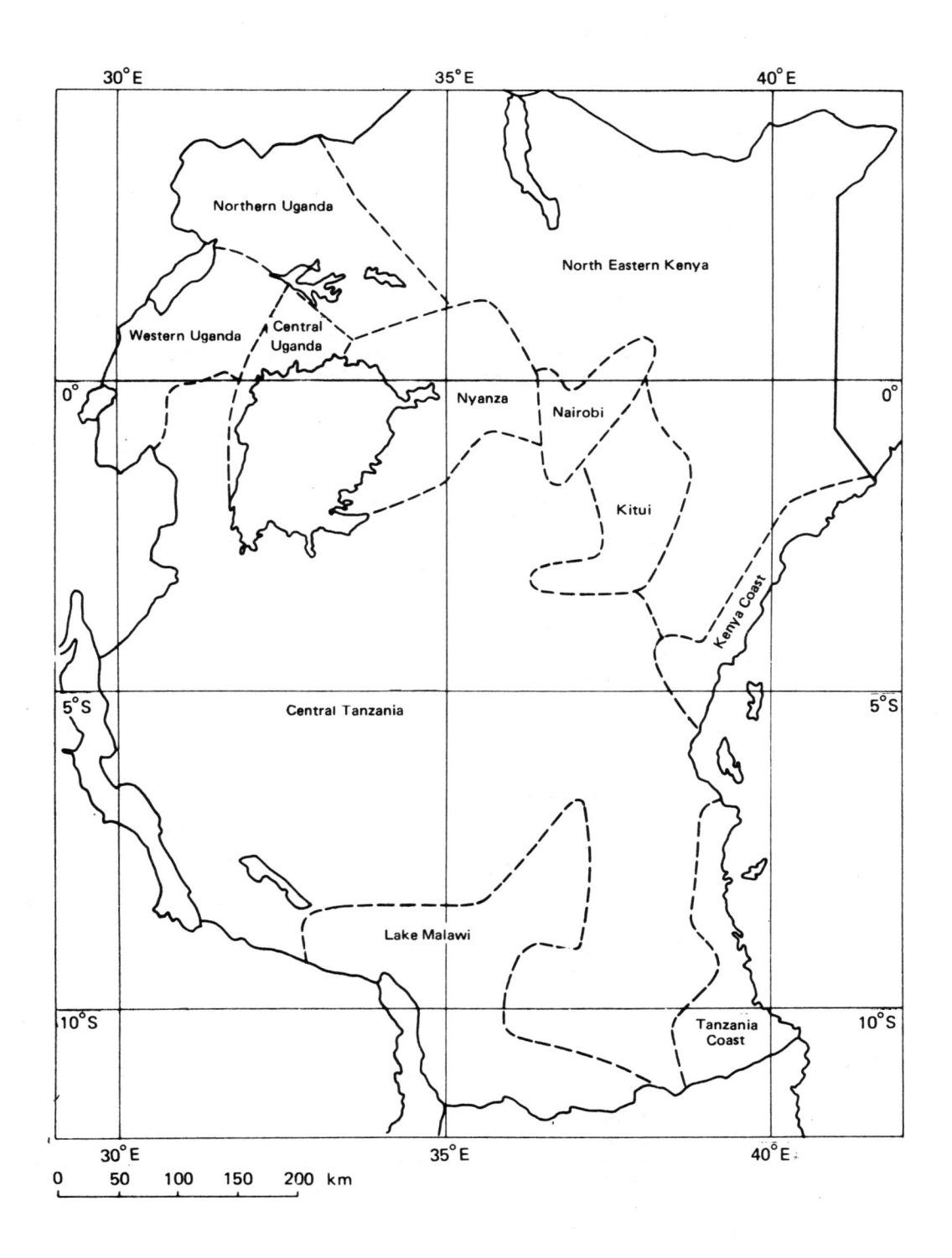

Figure 2   Antecedent wetness zones

Table 5 Land use factors C_L (base assumes short grass cover)

Largely bare soil	1.50
Intense cultivation (particularly in valleys)	1.50
Grass cover	1.00
Dense vegetation (particularly in valleys)	0.50
Ephemeral stream, sand filled valley	0.50
Swamp filled valley	0.33
Forest	0.33

The appropriate value of lag time can be estimated using Table 6. In assessing in which category to place a given basin it should be remembered that generally only small areas either side of the stream are contributing to the flood hydrograph. It is these areas, therefore, which must be assessed.

Table 6 Basin lag times

Basin Type	Lag Time K, h
Arid	0.1
Very steep small grassed or bare catchments (slopes > 15%)	0.1
Semi-arid scrub (large bare soil patches)	0.3
Poor pasture	0.5
Good pasture	1.5
Cultivated land (down to river bank)	3.0
Forest, overgrown valley bottom	8.0
Papyrus swamp in valley bottom	20.0

Once estimates of the parameters Y, C_A and K have been made, a design flood can be estimated by routing a design storm through the computer program. This can be time-consuming and for many purposes a simpler technique is required. From C_A and Y the volume of runoff from any given design storm can be calculated and if the hydrograph shape can be related to the basin lag time K, the peak flow can also be estimated.

Many research workers have published dimensionless hydrographs and it has been shown (Linsley, 1958) that in the USA these approximate closely to:

$$\frac{Q}{Q_m} = \left| \frac{T}{T_m} \exp\left(1 - \frac{T}{T_m}\right) \right|^{4.0} \qquad (2)$$

where: Q is the discharge at time T after the start of rise, Q_m is the peak discharge and T_m is the time to peak.

In all cases the ratios of time to peak to base time are very similar. This was not found to be true for the East African basins studied. For consistency the base time was assumed to be the time from 1% of peak flow on the rising limb to 10% of peak flow on the falling limb of the hydrograph. Defined this way the ratio of base time to time to peak is approximately 3.0 for the US hydrographs. For the East African basins it varied between 2.7 and 11.0. The use of a single hydrograph based on time to peak was therefore not appropriate.

A more stable ratio, peak flow factor F, was found to be the peak flow Q divided by the average flow measured over the base time $\overline{Q}$:

$$F = Q/\overline{Q} \qquad (3)$$

This is the factor used by Rodier and Auvray (1965) in West Africa. For very short lag times ($K \simeq 0.2$ h) F was $2.8 \pm 10\%$. For all lag times longer than one hour, F was $2.3 \pm 10\%$. These figures are valid for the basin results and were confirmed by a similation exercise in which area, slope, lag time and contributing area coefficient were varied systematically. The peak flow can therefore be simply estimated if the average flow during the base time of the hydrograph can be calculated.

The total volume of runoff is given by:

$$RO = (P - Y)C_A A 10^3 \, m^3 \tag{4}$$

where: P is the storm rainfall in mm during time period equal to the base time, Y is the initial retention in mm, C_A is the contributing area coefficient and A is the basin area in km^2.

If the hydrograph base time is measured to a point on the recession curve at which the flow is one tenth of the peak flow then the volume under the hydrograph is approximately 7% less than the total runoff given by equation (4).

The average flow $\overline{Q}$ is therefore given by:

$$\overline{Q} = \frac{0.93 \, RO}{3600 T_B} \tag{5}$$

where T_B is the hydrograph base time in hours.

The method of estimating the base time was derived from the simulation exercise referred to above. It is made up of:
(a) The rainfall time;
(b) The recession time for the surface flow;
(c) The attenuation of the flood wave in the stream system.

The rainfall time T_P is the time during which the rainfall intensity remains at high level. This can be approximated by the time during which 60% of the total storm rainfall occurs. Using the general East African depth duration equation (Greening, 1977):

$$I = \frac{a}{(T + 1/3)^n} \tag{6}$$

where: I is the intensity, T the duration and a and n are constants. The time to give 60% of the total storm rainfall is given by solving the equation:

$$0.6 = \frac{T}{24} \left(\frac{24.33}{T + 0.33}\right)^n \tag{7}$$

Values for the various rainfall zones of East Africa are given in Table 7.

Table 7 Rainfall time T_P for East African ten year storms

	Index n	Rainfall time T_P, h
Inland zone	0.96	0.75
Coastal zone	0.76	4.0
Kenya - Aberdare Uluguru zone	0.85	2.0

The time for the outflow from a linear reservoir to fall to one tenth of its initial value is 2.3K where K is the reservoir lag time. The recession time for surface flow is therefore 2.3K. In the simulation study, values for base time were calculated for various areas, slopes, lag times and contributing area coefficients. Knowing the rainfall time and the surface flow recession time, the additional time for flood wave attenuation T_A can be found by difference. It was found that this could be estimated from the equation:

$$T_A = \frac{0.7nL}{\overline{Q}^{1/4} S^{1/2}} \tag{8}$$

where: L is the length of the main stream in km, n is Manning's n, $\overline{Q}$ is the average flow during base time in m³/s and S is the average slope along the mainstream.

The base time is therefore estimated from the equation:

$$T_B = T_P + 2.3K + T_A \tag{9}$$

The average flow $\overline{Q}$ can then be estimated. It will be noted that $\overline{Q}$ appears in equation (8) so an iterative or trial and error solution is required. If initially T_A is assumed to be zero, two iterations should be adequate

Knowing $\overline{Q}$ and F the peak flow is calculated using equation (3).

3.5.5.3.2 Urban flood model. Previous research in the United Kingdom by TRRL had resulted in a new method for the hydraulic design of urban surface water drainage systems (Watkins, 1962); the TRRL Hydrograph Method. In this method, runoff from paved area sub-basins, directly connected to the sewer system, is routed over the ground surface using a simple triangular time area diagram with base equal to an appropriate time of entry, generally between two and four minutes. The flow from the sub-basins, within the sewer system, is modelled by making appropriate allowance for translation time and hydrograph attenuation through storage within each sewer reach. Runoff from unpaved areas and paved areas not directly connected to the sewer system was found to be negligible or so slow in response that it could be safely neglected in designing for the short, intense summer thunderstorms which are the predominant cause of the critical urban sewer system flood flows in the United Kingdom.

The greater intensity and longer duration of storm rainfall in the tropics made it very unlikely that this latter design assumption would be generally applicable in East Africa. The research programme was therefore primarily aimed at developing a sub-model for runoff from unpaved areas.

The approach adopted was identical to that used for the sub-catchment modelling in the rural flood model: the flow from a contributing area C_A being routed through a linear reservoir with lag time K.

The modified TRRL Hydrograph Method program was then run for all large storms on each of the five basins and optimum values of C_A and K estimated by goodness of fit tests between recorded and predicted hydrographs.

With so few basins, in only two centres, making recommendations for appropriate values for C_A and K for the whole of East Africa would be difficult. However, as the same modelling technique had been used for both the urban and rural basins, the rural results could be used to indicate how the urban values should be extrapolated to cover areas not sampled. Recommendations for C_A are given in Table 8 in which it will be noted that the rural values have been increased by approximately 50% to allow for the much better drainage system found in urban areas.

Table 8 Recommended values for contributory area factor

Slope	Soil Type		
	Well drained	Slightly impeded drainage	Impeded drainage
Very flat, < 1.0%	0.12	0.22	0.45
Moderate, 1-4%	0.14	0.55	0.60
Rolling, 4-10%	0.15	0.65	0.75

Two adjustments are required to these figures for geographic location and land use.
(a) If the basin is in central or northern Uganda, Nyanza or central Tanzania (dry zones in Figure 2) multiply coefficients in Table 10 by 0.50. If it is in western Uganda multiply by

0.30.
(b) If there are many compacted gravel drives or large areas of compacted bare soil (unpaved footpaths) multiply coefficients again by 1.50.

These two adjustments correspond to the basin wetness and land use factors of the rural model.

The lag time K was found, as in the rural study, to be primarily dependant on the roughness of the ground surface and the type of vegetation cover. In urban areas these are closely related to type of development. Overland slope and contributing area C_A were also found to influence these lag times. The form of prediction equation finally adopted was (Watkins and Fiddes, 1978):

$$K = C\left(\frac{C_A}{S}\right)^{0.3} \quad (hrs) \tag{10}$$

where: S is the surface slope, and C a surface type coefficient which takes the values of 0.167, 0.5 and 1.0 for high density housing, low density housing and industrial areas respectively.

3.5.5.4 Discussion of effect of land use on predicted peak flows

The two models described above can be used to estimate the effect on peak flood flows of changes in land use. For rural basins the volume of runoff is directly proportional to the land use factor (Equation 1, Equation 4 and Table 5). The peak flow depends on the volume of runoff, but also the lag time K (Equation 5, Equation 9) which in turn is altered when land use changes (Table 6).

If a rural basin is urbanised the change in peak flow is more difficult to predict. Much of the area will become paved and be directly connected to the sewer system, although the proportion will depend very much on the type of development introduced. Virtually all of the rain falling in such areas during heavy rain storms will very quickly enter the sewer. The drainage density of the sewer network is likely to be much greater than was the case before urbanisation. Runoff from unpaved areas is therefore likely to be greater and occur more quickly (compare Table 8 and Equation 10 with Tables 3 and 6). In addition flow velocities down the sewer system will be greater than in the natural streams due to reduced hydraulic roughness. Thus, as the volume and speed of runoff are both increased, peak flows will tend to be greater.

To give an idea of the effect of changes in land use on peak flows the two models were used to simulate the response of the four larger urban basins to appropriate two-year recurrence interval design storms. Two alternative pre-urbanisation land uses were assumed: pastureland and forest. The storm profiles used are shown in Table 9 and the results of the simulations in Table 10.

Table 9 Two-year rainfall profiles

Time from storm peak (mins)	Nairobi, Kenya (mm/h)	Kampala, Uganda (mm/h)
½	94.4	186.2
2½	70.1	130.6
5	52.5	91.6
10	33.6	51.8
15	23.6	33.6
30	12.3	13.1
45	7.7	6.3
60	5.5	4.2
1 hour total (mm)	32.5	50.2
Daily total (mm)	70.0	70.0

Table 10 Comparison of catchment peak flow response to two-year design storm with different land use

Basin	Grassland (m³/s)	Forest (m³/s)	Urban (m³/s)
Bernhard Estate	0.46	0.05	0.90
Industrial Area	1.59	0.179	3.50
Ofafa Jericho	1.11	0.13	3.04
Wampewo Avenue	0.25	0.02	1.25

The large increase in peak flow resulting from a change in land use from forest to grassland (approximately ten times) will be noted. The further increase resulting from urbanisation of the basin is much more variable, fluctuating from two to five times in the basins studied.

The two basins on relatively well drained soils (Bernhard Estate and Wampewo Avenue) illustrate the effect of water conservation practice most clearly. Both have similar, low density, housing development. On both, roof drainage is discharged on to lawns. The principal difference is that, whereas Wampewo Avenue has conventional road gullies to transmit runoff from the road surfaces directly to the sewer, on the Bernhard Estate all road runoff has to cross a grassed verge approximately two metres wide. High density housing, as at Ofafa Jericho, on a well drained soil would give an even larger percentage increase in peak runoff.

The percentage increase in peak flow on the Industrial Area and Ofafa Jericho resulting from a change from grassland to urban development is relatively small due principally to the relatively impermeable soil giving high pre-development runoffs.

3.5.5.5 Summary and conclusions

Two models have been developed, and are described in this note, for predicting peak flows resulting from storm rainfall on rural and urban basins within East Africa. In both models land use is an important parameter affecting runoff. Thus the models can be used to demonstrate the likely effect of change of land use and of urbanisation.

On rural basins the effect of land use changes on the volume and speed of flood runoff are relatively easy to visualise. The effect of urbanisation is more complex and although generally peak flows will increase the scale of increase is difficult to predict without applying the two models to the particular basin to simulate the flows before and after the urbanisation.

REFERENCES

Fiddes, D. and Forsgate, J.A. 1970. Representative rural catchments in Kenya and Uganda. *Road Research Laboratory Report* LR 318.

Greening, P.A.K. (Ed) 1977. Proceedings of a Symposium on Flood Hydrology held in Nairobi in October 1975. *Transport and Road Research Laboratory Supplementary Report* SR 259.

Linsley, R.K., Kohler, M.A. and Paulhus, J.L.H. 1958. *Hydrology for Engineers*. McGraw Hill Book Co, New York.

Morgali, J.R. and Linsley, R.K. 1965. Computer analysis of overland flow. *J Hydr Div Proc ASCE*. HY3, 91, 81-100.

Watkins, L.H. 1962. The design or urban sewer systems. *Road Research Laboratory Technical Paper* TR 55, HMSO.

Watkins, L.H. and Fiddes, D. 1978. The design of surface water sewer systems in the tropics. *Proc Int Conf Urban Storm Drainage,* University of Southampton.

Young, C.P. and Prudhoe, J. 1973. The estimation of flood flows from natural catchments. *Transport and Road Research Laboratory, Report* LR 565.

Chapter 3.6

3.6 THE EFFECTS OF URBANIZATION AND INDUSTRIALIZATION
by Kokei Uehara[1]

The movement of people from rural to urban areas is growing in all continents, involving changes in land occupancy and use. Half of the world's population will be living in urban areas within a few decades, mainly working in commercial or industrial enterprises.

The concentration of a large urban population in a small space, often of the order of less than 5% of the total land area, changes the hydrological behaviour of a river basin and causes various environmental impacts. These environmental changes are the urbanization and industrialization of areas and these are characterized by intensive migration of people from rural to urban areas, changing the natural environment to a man-made one, involving the quantitative and qualitative aspects of the water cycle.

The following aspects are considered relevant. The water needed for domestic purposes and for industries is rising quickly and often exceeds the natural resource in these areas, so men are forced to import water from distant river basins. The large quantities of waste waters discharged into rivers, lakes and coastal areas endanger the ecosystem. Many river basins were covered by natural forest or prairies in the past but nowadays they are being replaced by buildings or impervious areas reducing the infiltration of rain water, diminishing the base flow of streams - aggravating the pollution problem. When the area of cities is large, there are changes in the local micro-climates. Land subsidence has been observed as a consequence of intensive groundwater withdrawal for human needs. Intrusion of salt water takes place into well fields, in coastal areas, as a consequence of heavy groundwater withdrawal.

The climatic changes which are important are as follows. Air temperature is normally higher for urban areas than for their environs. This is caused by a much smaller latent heat flux; the different physical properties and the different structures of the urban and industrial area; the energy generated by house heating, factories, automobiles, lighting and human metabolic heat; the pall of dust and carbon dioxide that reduces the amount of solar radiation and the net outgoing longwave radiation. The urban heat islands change in sizes and intensities depending on their geographical location, size and peculiar characteristic of the city. The wind velocity is smaller for urban areas than in the country because of the obstacles caused by houses and buildings changing the natural flow and turbulence of the air. The humidity of the air is smaller for urban areas than in the country because the precipitation is quickly discharged through the impervious areas and drainage systems. The amount of fog is higher in a polluted urban area than in the environs of the city, due to an increased amount of condensation nuclei. Rain and snow will not be influenced by the smallest urban areas, but in large ones increasing precipitation amounts have been observed.

The human activities which can modify basin characteristics are due to urbanization and industrialization in most cases, the cities are not planned, so, due to the industrialization,

---

[1] Escola Politecnica, Universidade de Sao Paulo, Brasil.

the movement of people from rural to urban areas has important effects involving change in land occupancy and use, replacing the rural lands with urban and industrialized areas. The following changes take place: increase in the impervious area (houses, streets, avenues, etc); land erosion; construction of drainage systems, reservoirs for flood control, water supply, hydro-electric power; stream canalization and so on.

There are a number of general hydrological characteristics of river basins which are important in relation to human activities. These are: basin area, the natural basin areas are unchangeable, but sometimes they are changed by construction of tunnels to divert flows to other nearby basins. Basin slope is generally modified as a consequence of the streets, avenues, houses, gardens. Basin geology is not affected by urbanization but sometimes mining activities affect urban areas. Soil, due to intensive earth moving work and replacing the natural ground surface with an impervious cover, is affected, causing serious soil erosion or reducing the infiltration of rain water. The vegetative cover is replaced by other types that present a more esthetic aspect but unfortunately the green parts around towns get reduced drastically by urbanization.

The particular physiographic conditions where the changes are relevant are: the increase in the impervious area affects strongly the flood production while infiltration is reduced, decreasing the base flow of streams. The longitudinal profiles of water courses are changed in order to increase the longitudinal slope to decrease the floods in low urbanized areas. The channel cross-sections are enlarged and the channel roughness is diminished in order to increase the flow capacity. Reduction of the time of concentration is observed by increasing the impervious area, construction of drainage systems and so on. Thus, floods will be increased in magnitude. Sediment transport is increased downstream as a result of earth moving works, during construction of urban and industrial areas. Problems of land subsidence are caused by the lowering of the water table level close to lignite and coal mines. The water quantity and quality of streams passing through metropolitan areas are affected because water is derived from that river or imported from a distant one to supply water for needs. Degradation of water quality in rivers is caused mainly by discharge of effluents of domestic and industrial waste water, soil erosion and so on.

Bibliography

McPherson, M.B. 1974. Hydrological effects of urbanization. *UNESCO Studies and Reports in Hydrology,* No 18, 280 pp.

Changes in the physical conditions of aquifers

3.6.1 CHANGES IN THE PHYSICAL CONDITIONS OF AQUIFERS DUE TO WITHDRAWAL OF LARGE VOLUMES OF GROUNDWATER
by L Alföldi[1]

3.6.1.1 Introduction
Changes due to human influences may cause not only the contamination of groundwater since groundwater withdrawal is accompanied by the modification of the flow and pressure conditions of aquifers.

Under the influence of groundwater withdrawal the flow velocity will be changing by an order of magnitude and the flow pattern and the position of the groundwater will be modified, in addition a consolidation of the confined loose aquifers will take place as a result of pressure drop.

The water withdrawals consequent on the mining activities are one of the most important changes in the groundwater regime. Some mineral sources occur in Hungary under the karstic and artesian level. It follows from this that numerous water withdrawal centres are working in the mining districts.

Water withdrawal for mining activities, the water production from the water works based on groundwater reservoirs, crude oil and gas production from the sedimentary basin have the most significant influence on human activity for the physical conditions of aquifers in Hungary (Alföldi and Papp, 1976). This report gives an account of experiences in this field.

3.6.1.2 The location of the area
Hungary is one of the small countries of Central Europe with an area of 93,000 km^2. The country is located in the centre of the Danube basin surrounded by the mountain chains of the Alps, Carpathians and the Dinaric Alps. This area lies on longitude 16'20"-23' east of Greenwich and on longitude 45'40"-48$3^0$ north.

3.6.1.3 The characteristics of the area
Hungary can be divided geographically into mountainous and lowland areas. The mountainous areas consist of karstic formations of Mesozoic age and to a lesser extent of volcanic rocks. The basements of the basin areas are partly karstic Mesozoic carbonate rocks, partly watertight Paleozoic igneous and crystalline formations at a depth of 1200 to 1500 m on average.

The most important water-bearing formations of Hungary are within the young sediments of the basins (Figure 1). The Paleogene and Neogene formations occur only in the forms of insignificant fragments in the great basins along the border zones of the mountains. Most significant are the Pliocene (Pannonian) formations. Their lower part consist of clayey marl and marl series to a thickness of 500 to 700 interbedded by aquifers containing fossil waters. This thick impervious sediment sequence efficiently insulate the basement from the most important, thermal water-bearing Upper Pannonian horizons which consist of alternating sand

---

[1] Institute for Hydrological Research of the Research Centre for Water Resources Development, Budapest, Hungary

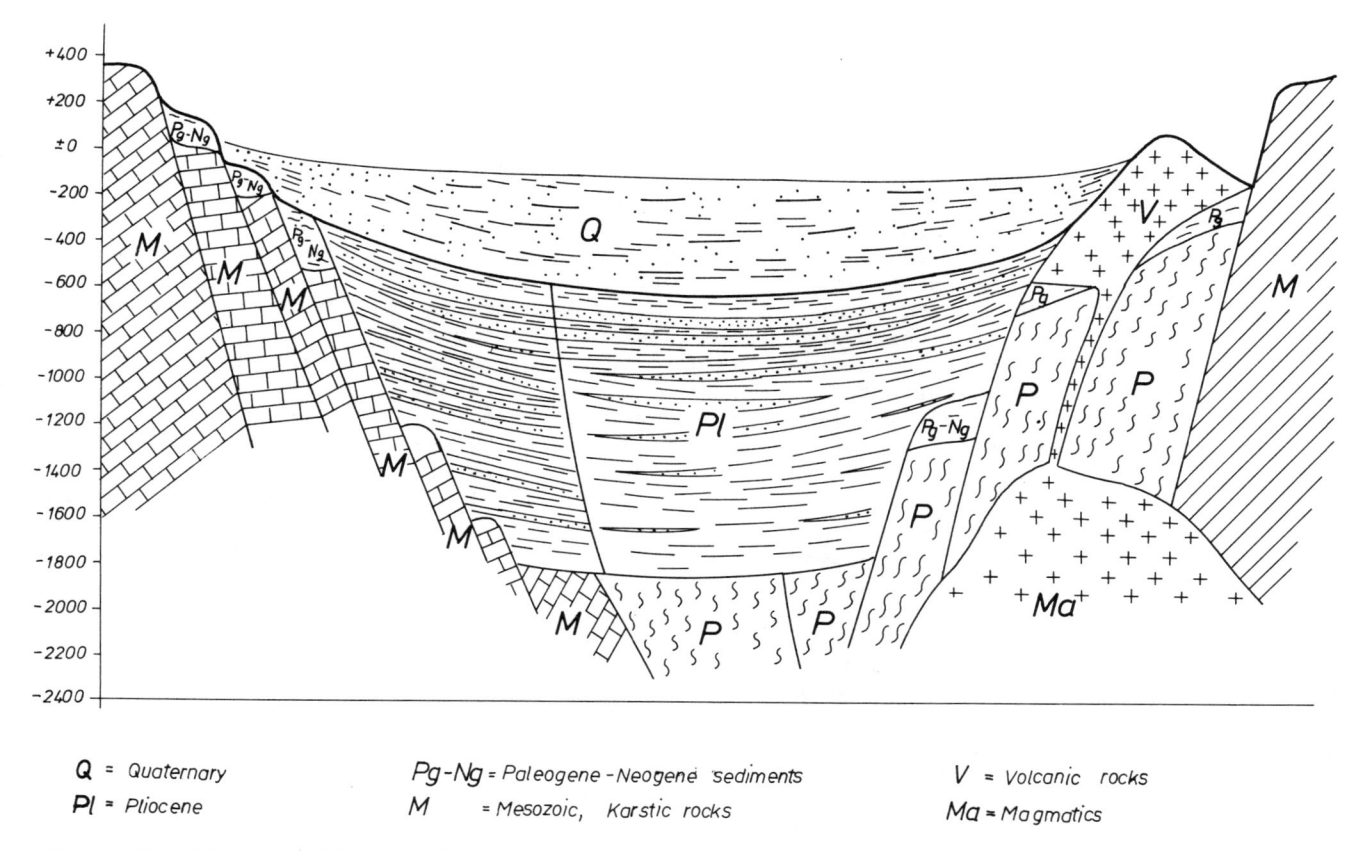

Figure 1 Diagrammatic section showing the geological setting of the Hungarian basin

- Q = Quaternary
- Pl = Pliocene
- Pg-Ng = Paleogene-Neogene sediments
- M = Mesozoic, Karstic rocks
- V = Volcanic rocks
- Ma = Magmatics

Figure 2 Flow patterns of the covered karst

- Mesozoic karstic rocks on the surface or near to surface
- Other karstic rocks on the surface or near to surface
- Direction of karstic water-flow reaching to deep horizons
- Karstic water recharge into the clastic aquifers
- Karstic water recharge from clastic aquifers into the carstic system
- Contour lines of the karstic flow-systems

and clay formations. This sediment sequence of 200 to 800 m thickness include highly favourable water-yielding sand layers and they total some 30 to 40 per cent of the section.

The marine and lacustrine Pannonian formations are overlain by a Quaternary fluviatile sediment sequences of a maximum 700 m thickness in the form of alluvial fans and cones as well as channel fills. This sequence consists of alternating sand, gravel and clay beds. They do not represent continuous beds but lenticular bodies and the entire sediment series form a hydraulically unique and common system. Water exchange is very fast in the border zones but slow in the deeper parts and in the interior of the basin.

These Quaternary formations include the groundwater resources supplying the drinking water for the population. The natural recharge conditions are favourable through the well developed alluvial fans of the streams. The water-bearing series mixed with the alluvial fans extend almost to the ground surface, that is, recharge by vertical infiltration is available. The basement of the basin areas consists of partly karstic mesozoic carbonate rocks directly connected to the ground surface where karstic formations outcrop primarily in the Transdanubian Middle Ranges which transverse the country from southwest to northeast. There are also connected karstic water flow systems in the outcrop and in the basement of the basins covered by the young sediments (Figure 2). The karstic water conditions in the confined aquifer is under pressure. Originally the average karstic water level was situated at an elevation of +105 to 115 m asl. Along the border of the Bakony Mountain in the younger basins important bauxite deposits and further to the north both bauxite and Eocene brown coal deposits can be found which are usually underlain - along with some thin basal sediments - by the karstic basement rock. A considerable part of these very important mineral deposits are situated below the piezometric karstic water level, 100 or even 200 m below sea level in some places. Mining 200 to 300 m below the karstic water level is accompanied by the hazard of water. About 100 to 150 cu m per minute has to be pumped in the mining district of Dorog. To eliminate the uncertainty of the coal mining due to the continuous risk of flooding all the new mines are continuously pumped. A deep and extended cone of depression was formed by pumping in the shafts which cover the entire coal field under development. Nowadays the mining industry pumps about 250 cu m per minute in the bauxite districts and 150 cu m per minute in the coal fields. The total amount of karstic water pumped in the Transdanubian Middle Range is of about 730 cu m per minute (Bocker, 1969).

The water from the bauxite mines which were highly developed after the second world war is utilized for the water supply of the district and storage reservoirs and regional waterworks are provided.

3.6.1.4 The methods applied

The geological circumstances of the karst-systems are well-investigated. Geological and tectonic maps are available for most of the area, at a scale of 1:10,000 or at least at 1:25,000. The frequency of the karstic caverns has been determined, and the distribution of fissure systems and also their frequency was studied on outcrops and cores of boreholes. One figure concerning evaluation of a core-sample is shown (Figure 3). The porosity of karstic rocks varies between 0.5 to 30 per cent. The pore-volume was determined by the investigation of cores, by the investigation of core-samples taken from the tunnels in mines, and by experimental pumping.

In the karstic units unconfined and confined karstwater can be distinguished. The level of the karstwater is determined by observation-boreholes - independently of the fact that the water is unconfined or with a piezometric head. Since 1967 approximately 360 karstwater-level observation boreholes have been installed. The data from about 200 wells, producing water from the confined karst-system are used. In the boreholes the changes of the karstwater table is continuously recorded, or observed frequently. Water temperature and the changes of water-quality are also measured from time to time. For most of the observation-boreholes data are available for 10 to 15 years - giving the possibility of distinguishing between natural influences and the influence of pumping. Curve a in Figure 4 indicates the natural water-table fluctuations, and curve b represents the influence of the dewatering of mines.

The genetics of the karst-systems containing water at high pressure and high temperature in front of the mountains, like the recharge from the unconfined karst, and further flow-mechanism are investigated in detail. The changes of the concentration of dissolved components of the water are systematically investigated. Further the changes of the water-temperature, the processes of the water table, the distribution of oxygen 18 isotope content, duterium, and the C-14 and C-16 isotope-content of the CO_2 of the water are investigated

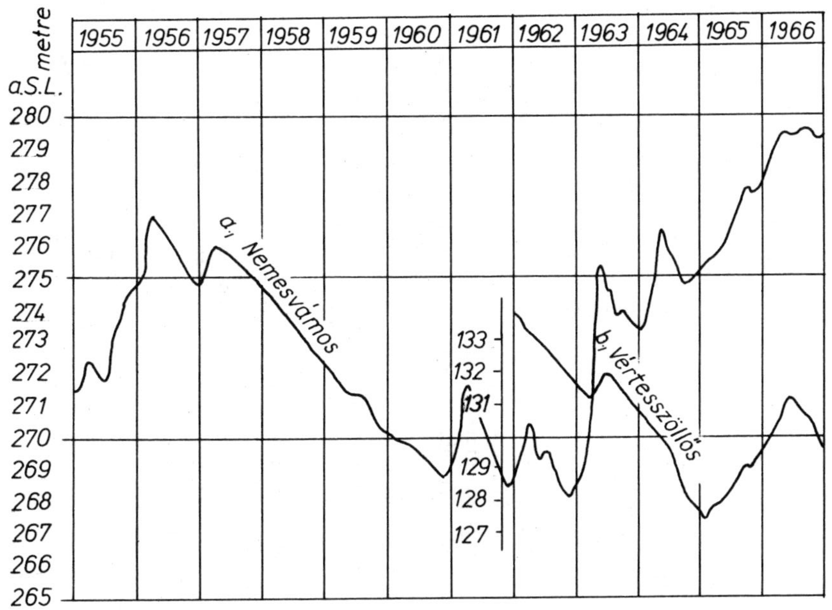

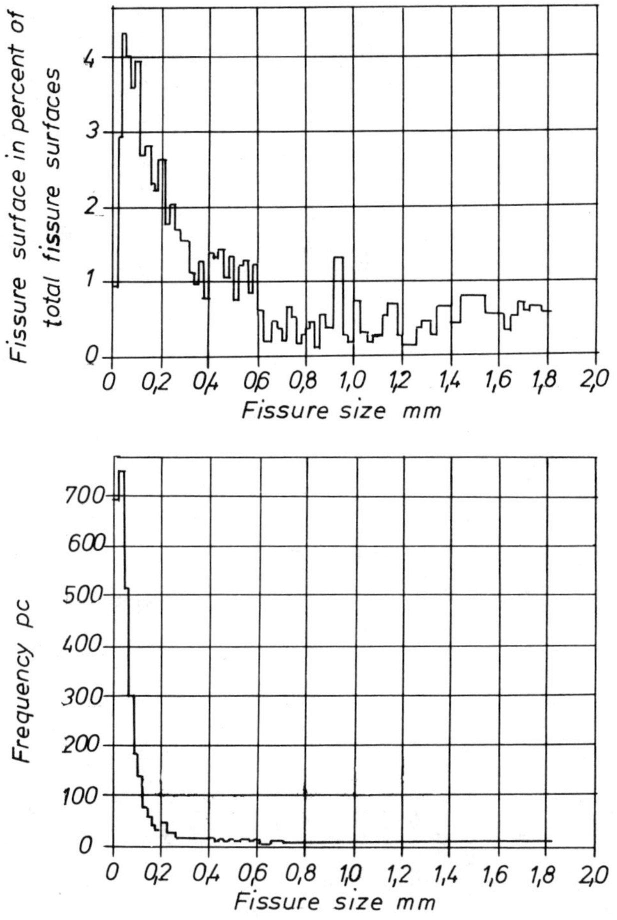

Figure 3 Hystogram of fissure size distribution and frequency after Doleschall

Figure 4 Water level changes in an undisturbed/nemesvamos/and a disturbed/vertesszollos/karstic area after Böcker

Changes in the physical conditions of aquifers

systematically. The time spent by the water under the surface is calculated by isotope-investigations. The water produced from the unconfined and covered karst-systems is systematically recorded and the equations of water- and temperature-regimes are computed. From temperature data and the pressure at the bottom of boreholes and the specific weight of the water: the vertical and horizontal components of the piezometric gradients are calculated and the paths of flow are estimated according to the results obtained.

For mining activities carried out under the artesian water table: the lignite-deposits and the sandy aquifers among them were explored by 250 boreholes drilled on 250 m centres. The grain-size, and all the physical parameters were determined. The maps of water table contours were drawn for the particular aquifers from water table measurements carried out in the boreholes. After this by prolonged water production in the hydrogeological boreholes sunk at 1 km centres, the most important parameters of the aquifers were determined. These parameters are permeability, transmissibility, etc. In order to increase the accuracy of observation every second hydrogeological borehole was surrounded by a group of observation wells.

The main portion of the thermal wells produces water from confined or semi-confined Pliocene-aged porous water-bearing formations, situated at a depth of 1000 to 3500 m. Data from the wells are collected and published every five years in the Register of Thermal Wells. On 1 January 1978 560 thermal wells were registered. It would be too expensive to sink observation boreholes to the depths mentioned and for this reason the thermal wells themselves are controlled without observation wells. Authorities oblige the producers to determine all the most important parameters of the wells every five years - such as: pressure on the bottom, temperature of water, productivity-factor, gas-content, changes of the chemical composition, etc. The yield of the wells has to be recorded continuously during the exploitation. In the most important regions, and in those, where the density of the wells is above the average: VITUKI carries out control investigations at an interval of 2-3 years. By the aid of the measurements the characteristics of the reduction of the head of thermal wells can be determined according to units or regions and the reduction of the head is generally exponential.

3.6.1.5 Description of the cases
The amount of pumping from the karstic systems of the Transdanubian Middle Range exceeds the natural recharge. Under the influence of the continuous pumping carried out in the last decades a regional decrease of the karstic water level has occurred more than 1000 sq km around Dorog and Tatabánya. This decline resulted in a water level subsidence of about 10 to 20 m. Due to this considerable drop in the water level all major karstic springs dried up in the northern part of the Mountain Range and a similar process is taking place in the southern part too (Figure 5). The drying up of springs and half of several karstic swamps has resulted in the drying up of numerous watercourses. At the same time, however, new water courses and creeks were formed due to the water withdrawn during mining (Bocker, 1969).

The ever-increasing withdrawal of karstic water from the hundred year old coal mines simply runs off without utilization and only in recent years has it replaced the dried up springs and lost discharges, eg in Tata.

At a distance of 15 km from the mining site of Tatabánya providing a large spring discharge of warm water were known in Tata which supplied a great lake system while karstic spring holes formed lake springs. In this environment bathing resorts and recreational areas with watersport facilities were developed. Due to the pumping of 120 cu m per minute in Tatabánya (a centre of coal mines) the warm springs of Tata entirely dried up. To replace this loss a 1200 m deep well was drilled into karstic rock formation. By the time the springs were running dry all the spring holes were lined with bentonite and karstic water was introduced from new wells and harmful changes were thus eliminated and the development of this recreational district could be continued.

The production of water can influence water movement within the deeper formations accelerating the movement of groundwater into the cone of depression. Such cases are known in the Transdanubian Middle Range where in a more than ten years old production well exceeding 250 cu m per minute an increase of water temperature from 11 to 20^0C (Nyerges, 1974) was observed. It signifies the stabilization of the deep flow directed from the bottom to the top around the lowest point of the cone of depression (Figure 6). The relation of the karstic aquifers to the condition of the water table is clearly shown simultaneously by the remnant cold branch.

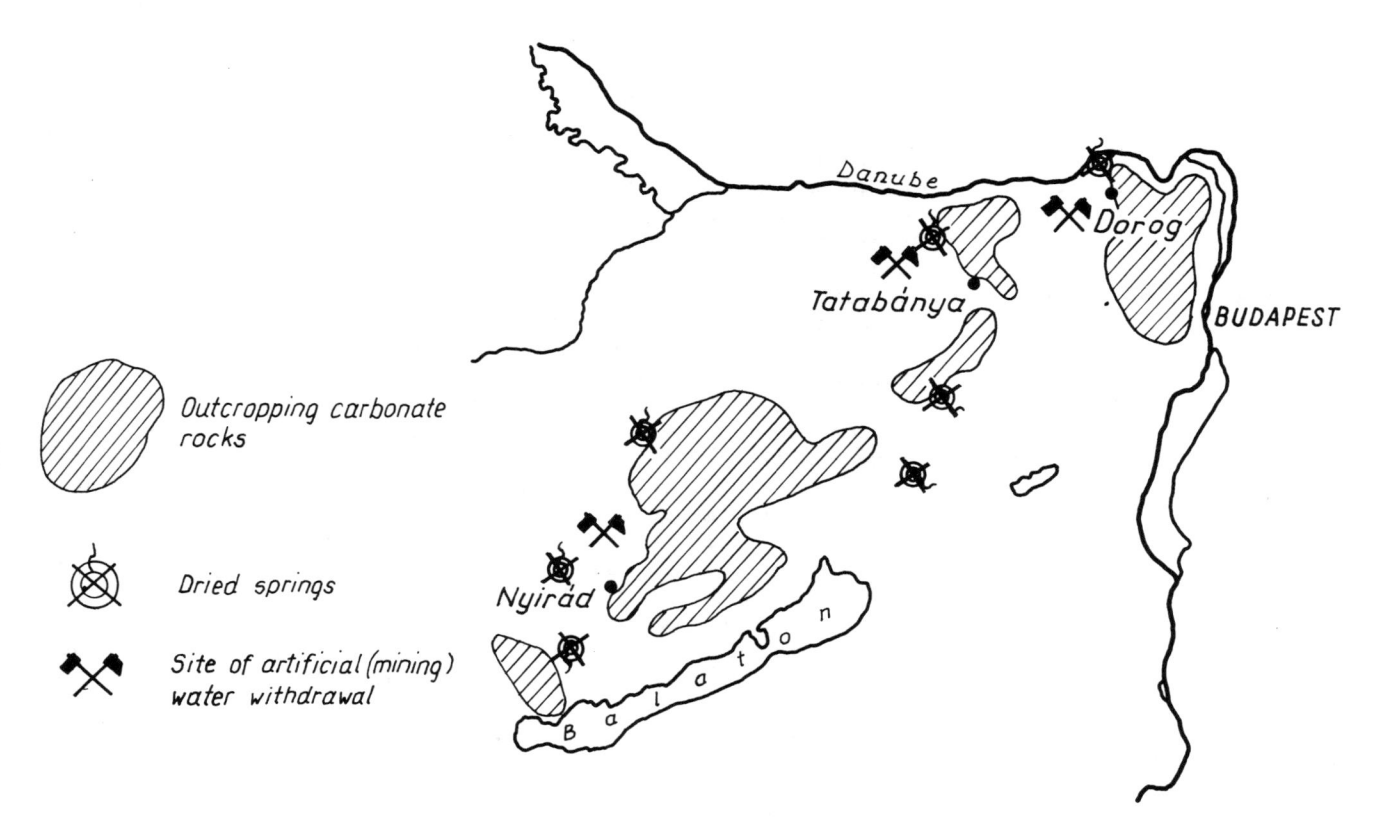

Figure 5 Remarkable dried spring groups due to artificial (mining) water withdrawal

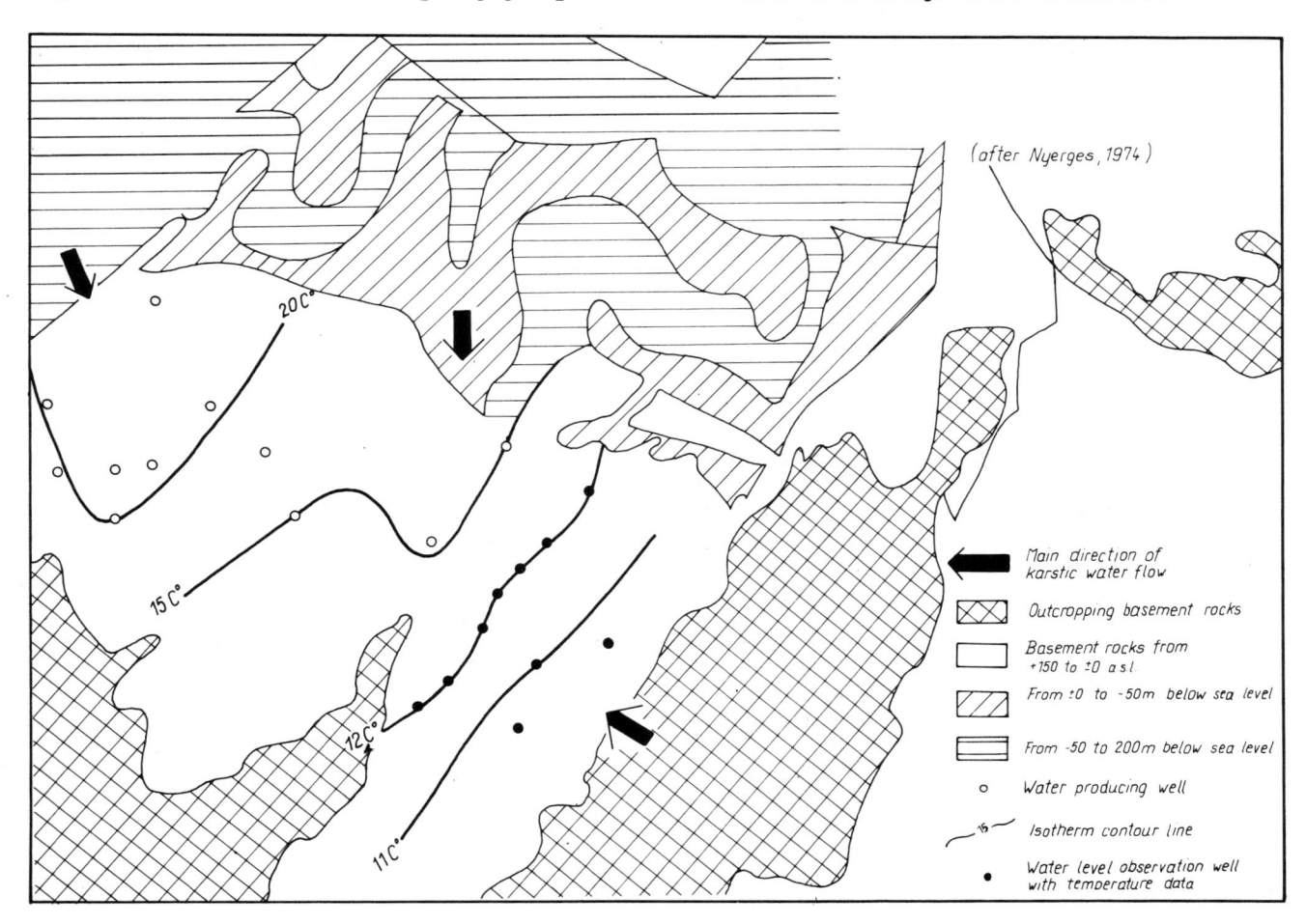

Figure 6 Development of karstic water temperature within the area affected by drawdown in the surrounding of Nyirad

Changes in the physical conditions of aquifers

Along the northern flank of the Transdanubian Middle Range due to the high karstic water production, flow conditions were changed in such a manner that the valley of the Danube which was originally the base level now became - at least periodically - a recharge zone of the karstic water system. The river bed of the Danube was intercepted by the cone of depression.

In the context of the water withdrawal from the mining districts the environmental impact on the natural thermal springs along the border of the Transdanubian Middle Range in Budapest and in Héviz came to light recently. These thermal springs rise to the surface from the deep-seated karstic rock formations and the water is certainly of karstic origin. According to age determinations the residence time of the infiltrated karstic water is about 10,000 to 20,000 years and, therefore, a relationship with the precipitation is not indicated. In the coming years further withdrawal of a great amount of water is planned and the resulting cone of depression will probably intercept the catchment area of the thermal waters of Budapest. The problem is that considering the long period of seepage within this system how long will it be before the effect will be felt in the discharge of the thermal springs and wells? The decline of the thermal spring levels may be hazardous since a part of them is issuing into the bed of the Danube, which means that an excessive decrease of the water level may result in the encroachment of the river water into the conduits of the springs. The risk of depletion of the thermal water in Budapest might be and must be prevented. It is likely that research will not give an unambiguous and satisfying answer about the degree of the hazard and for this reason all precautions must be taken to prevent any extension of the depression in a given direction by increased artificial infiltration (Figure 7) and thus the pressure decline of the thermal waters could be efficiently controlled (Alföldi and Papp, 1976).

Quite another condition prevails within loose sediments in the sandy aquifers. In the southern border area of the Mátra and Bükk Mountain lignite deposits interbedded sand beds forming artesian aquifers which can be stripped by open cast mining. The open cast mining of these lignite deposits requires the dewatering of the mining district as well as the decompression of the sub-surface formations.

It does not need any further explanation that withdrawal of water amounting to a total of 70 to 80 m drawdown and resulting in a water level difference of 100 m will cause a widely extended effect reaching beyond the open cast mine and may lead to wells in some neighbouring villages running dry. The change of the natural flow system will exist only for a few decades.

Ultimately, in this case, considering even longer periods, the amount and areal extent of the pressure decline due to consolidation is governed only by the ratio of the water production to that of the values of horizontal and vertical transmissivities. Due to the constant value of the transmissivity, the land subsidence and the cumulative groundwater production can be well correlated.

Due to the systematic dewatering which proceeds the open cast mining operation the land subsidence can be followed (Figure 8). Land subsidence will occur after a few months and within a period of 20 months, as shown in the figure, will have reached a value of 20 cms. The maximum value of land subsidence under the effect of the dewatering process was 50 cms (Keseru, 1973). The area in question is agricultural land which will later be the target of mining and, therefore, the environmental impact is linked with the mining activity.

The mining pit will be filled with a mixture of rock fragments, rubble, cinders and ashes and it will exert lasting changes upon the groundwater since the one time shallow artesian aquifers extending to a maximum depth of 100 m will be lacking and within this heterogeneous mass of low permeability stagnant water can be formed with a high total solid content (Figure 9). Ultimately, all these filled pits of many tens kilometre in length will form a barrier across the natural flowpath which comes from the mountainous region towards the lowland areas. As a result, the planning of water production projects within this shielded zone must not ignore these altered conditions. Due to the environmental impact of the mining along a wide zone remarkable environmental changes will occur just because of the altered conditions of the groundwater. The rapid organization of the public water supply by a distribution system is required. At the same time, on the border of the mountain a scarcity of water brought about by the dewatering process will be followed by an increase in the water levels and an abundance of groundwater (even some springs) since the filling of the pits by material with low permeability will lead to a possible damming of the groundwater.

The lignite deposits are intercalated by artesian aquifers consisting of fine-grained

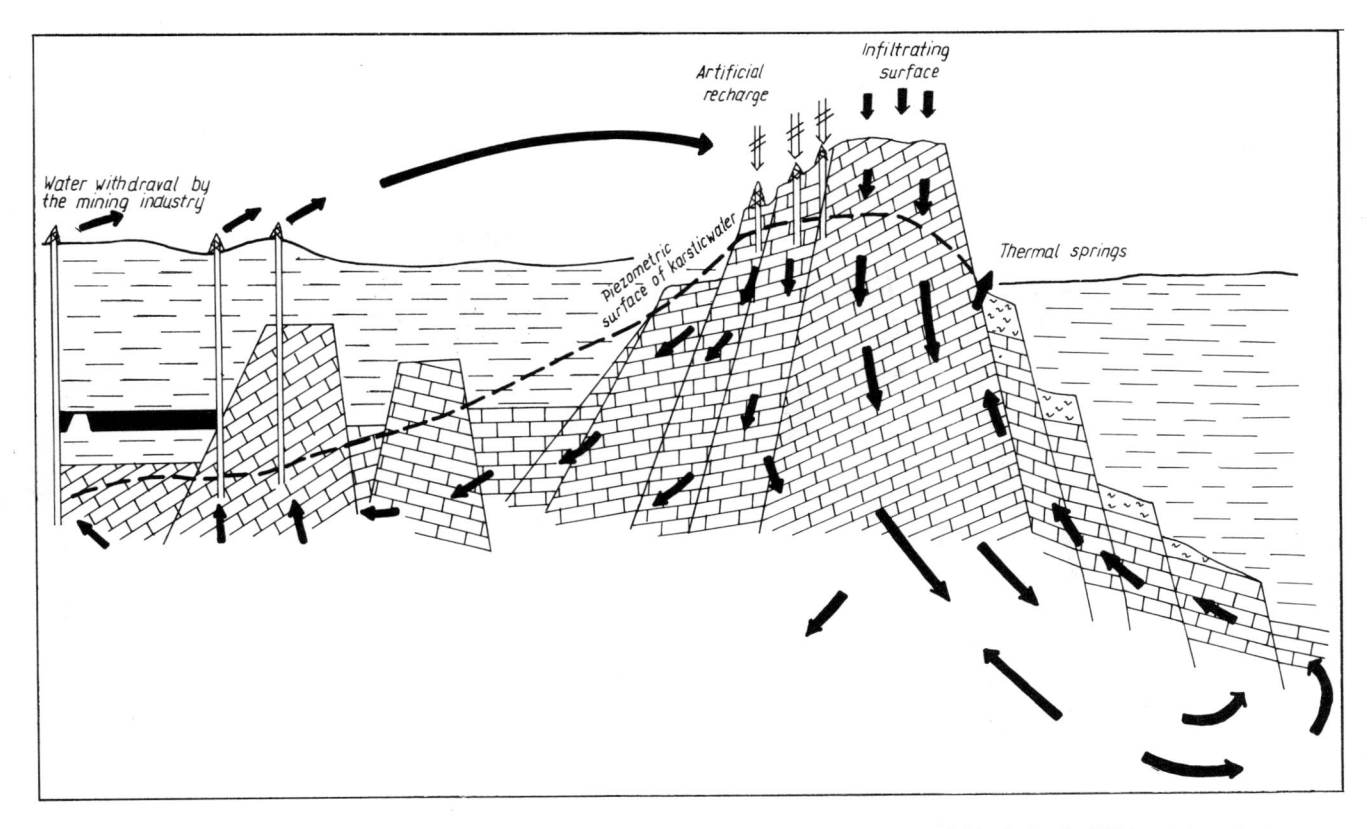

Figure 7 Prevention of the extension of depression applying artificial infiltration

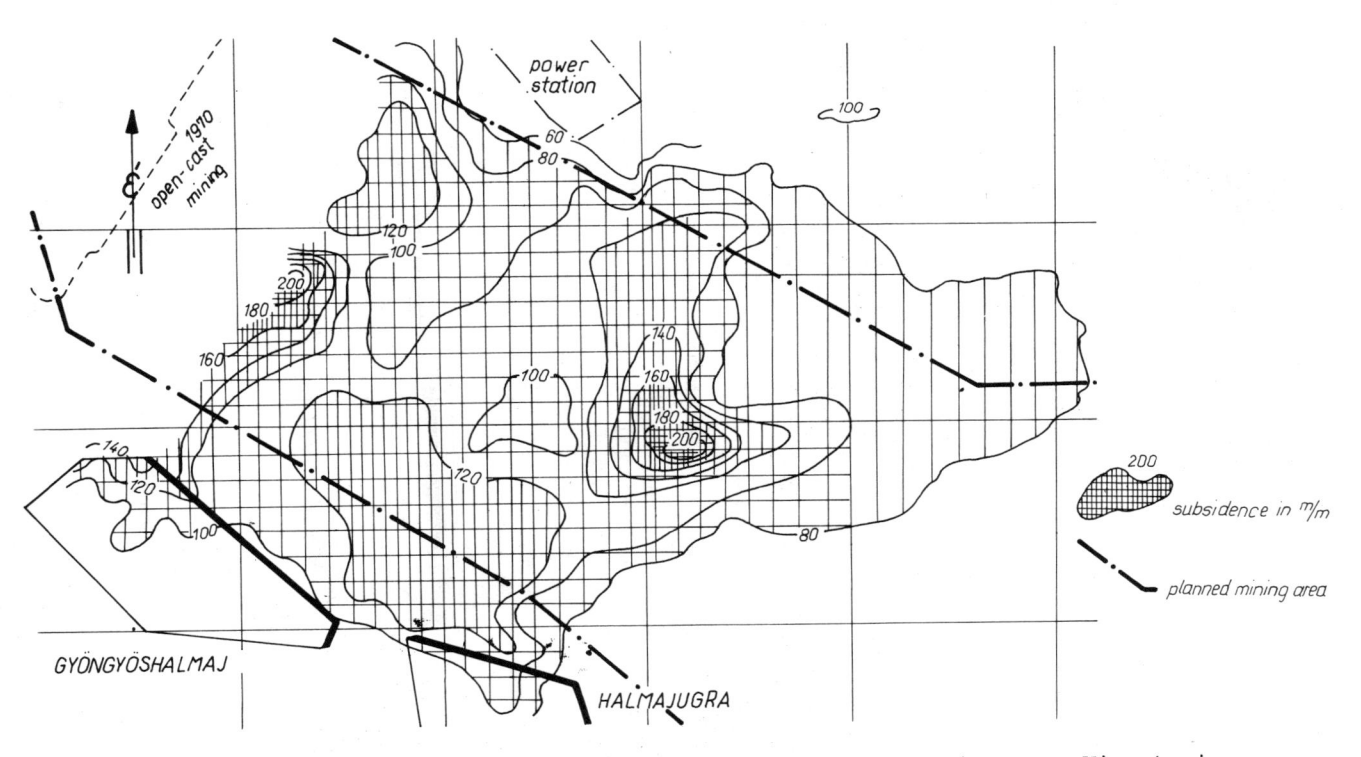

Figure 8 Land subsidence measured in the vicinity of open-cast mine near Visonta in the period from March 1967 to October 1968

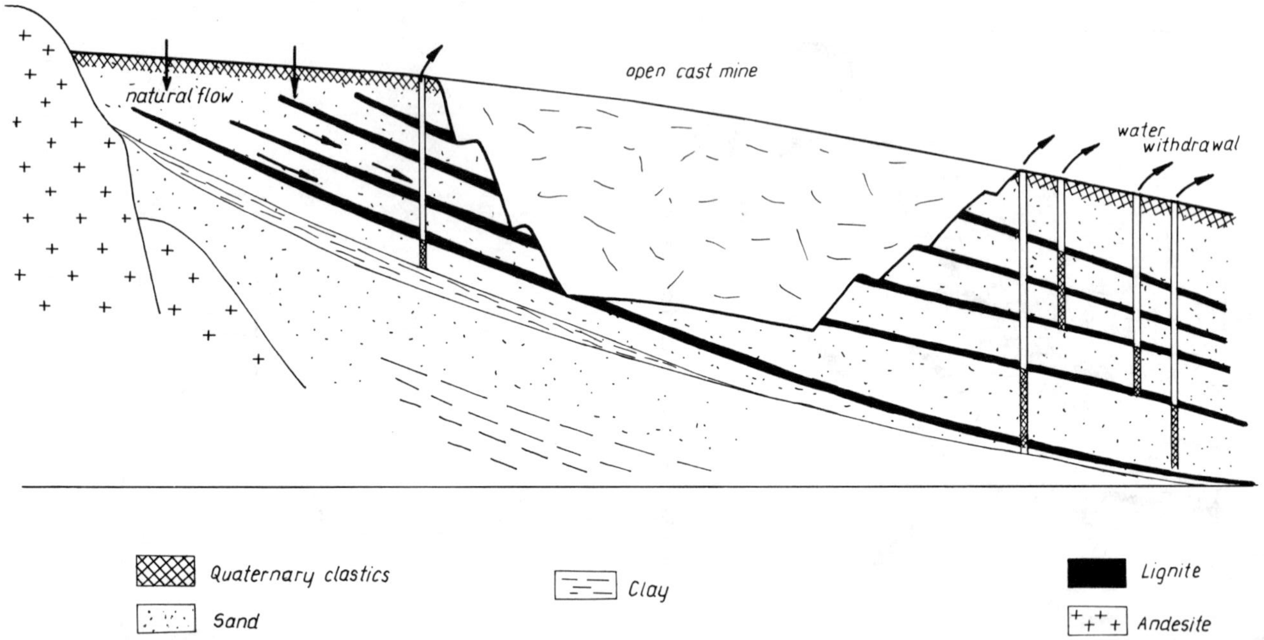

Figure 9 Diagrammatic section of the open-cast lignite mine in the southern border of the Matra mountains

/ after K. Korim 1974 /

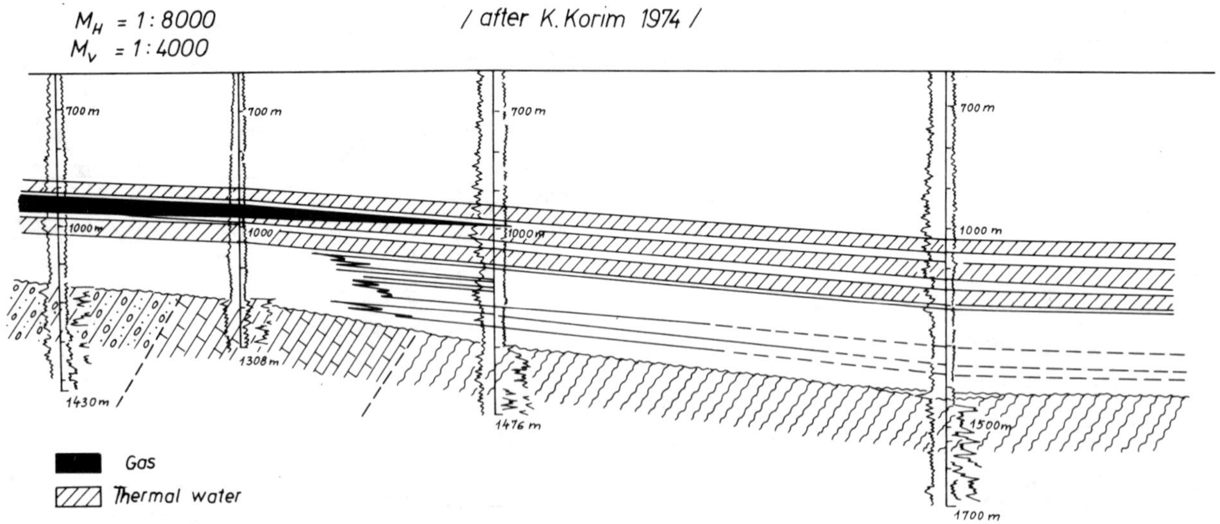

$M_H = 1 : 8000$
$M_V = 1 : 4000$

Quaternary clastics | Clay | Lignite
Sand | | Andesite

Figure 10 Relationship between the gas-field and the thermal water bearing formations around Hajduszoboszló

Gas | Thermal water

sands which are of poor transmissivity. As a consequence, the effective radius of the withdrawal of water is no more than 20 to 25 kms and due to the uniform dip of the strata without any major disturbancies all the effects can be reasonably estimated and the harmful consequences can be eliminated.

Mining is the most drastic interference with underground conditions and the deeper and more intense is this activity the more profound an influence will be exerted upon the groundwaters. Oil and gas production is obtained mostly from formations which contain water and bottom water or edge water will behave like a reservoir fluid belonging to the same system.

In Hungary, the thermal water of Hajduszoboszló is very famous since it was discovered in the 1920s as a byproduct of unsuccessful petroleum exploration. A bathing resort was developed on this valuable, therapeutic thermal water resource and the one time insignificant little town is now prosperous and busy. Later exploration made by modern methods and tools has resulted ultimately in the discovery of the supposed gas-field (Figure 10) at a distance of a few kilometres from the thermal wells. It was revealed that the gas pools and the thermal water reservoirs are situated in the same stratigraphical horizons and due to the considerable volume of gas production the reservoir pressure dropped which inflicted a decline in the well pressures. As a consequence, water no longer flowed from the wells and now a gas-lift operation is under way. In addition, new thermal wells were completed to supply the ever-increasing demand for thermal water. A possible shortage of this medicinal thermal water supply would seriously damage this highly developed bathing resort and recreational area (Korim, 1974).

A similar situation developed in the vicinity of Szeged where due to the abundance of thermal water resources a multi-purpose scheme for the utilization of the geothermal energy was started. The utilization of this geothermal energy brought about favourable changes in the life of this city when, preceding the nearby petroleum exploration, a thermal water well was drilled for an agricultural co-operative which struck and tapped petroleum instead of thermal water indicating the edge of the country's greatest oil field. The identity of the thermal water and hydrocarbon reservoirs raised the question of the possible depletion of the thermal water resources. All these circumstances played an important part in boosting the oil production. The water supply to be repressured is taken from thermal water-bearing formations a few hundred metres above the oil and gas pools and the quality of this repressured water differs only slightly from that of the deeper thermal waters (Figure 11).

Due to the total absence of recharge or a limited recharge the production of thermal water is the result of an elastic reservoir and of consolidation and, therefore, thermal water production is always accompanied by a continuous pressure drop.

Current thermal water production coming from deep sedimentary basins in the lowland areas results in a regional reservoir pressure drop (Figure 12). The rate of pressure drop is directly proportional to the production due to the nature of these confined aquifers: 1 million cu m of thermal water withdrawal causes a pressure drop of 2 m in a unit area of 100 sq kms using a storage coefficient of $S = 5 \times 10^{-4}$.

Within an unconfined aquifer system replenishment will be taking place after the reduction or abandonment of groundwater production and the original conditions can be regained. On the contrary, there is no regeneration of reservoir energy within confined aquifers. The depletion of reservoir energy still does not mean that the available groundwater resources were considerably decreased since the groundwater reserves of elastic origin represent only a minor part of the total groundwater resources stored within deep aquifers. Therefore, reservoir energy may be built up effectively by artificial recharge by means of water repressuring or water injection or the entire groundwater resource can be replaced by water of a somewhat lower quality.

3.6.1.5 Proposal control methods
Exploitation of big volumes of subsurface water requires the investigation of yield capacity and predicting the consequences of drawdown. Aquifer morphology and physical parameters (ie permeability, porosity, transmissibility, grain solidity, etc) of the confined and porous aquifers in question should be determined by the best approach. Bed rock and overlying layers as well as the stratification and connections of the aquifer should be investigated. Replenishing, elastic (compressed) and stored subsurface water resources and the energy, pressure and temperature conditions of the aquifer should be determined. Exploration should begin with drilling and a survey of the geological formations. Further geological surveys with drillings can supply information on the hydrogeological parameters when rotary drilling

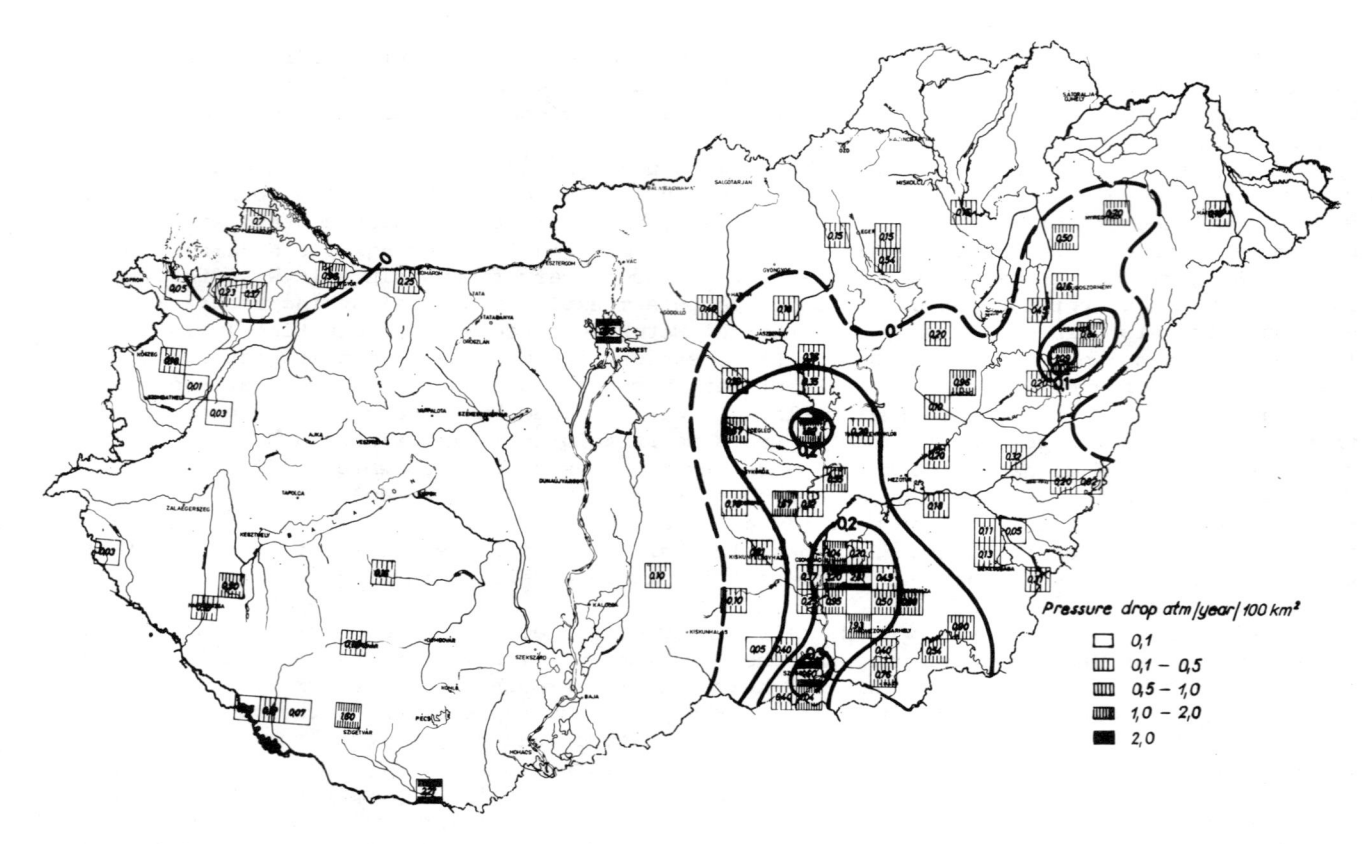

Figure 11   The pressure drop of the thermal water aquifer system due to intense exploitation in the Hungarian basin

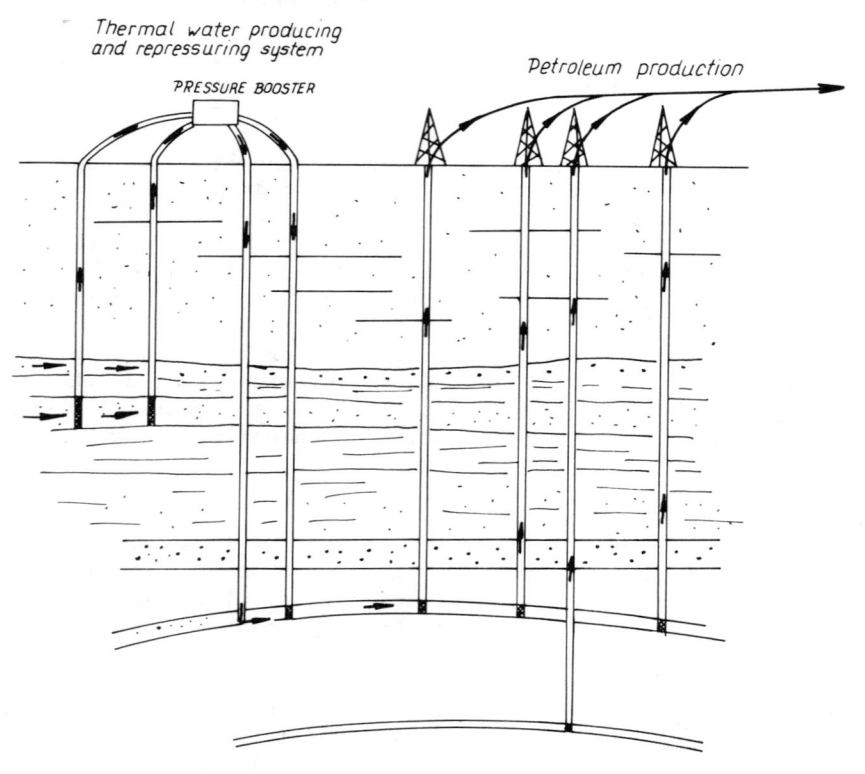

Figure 12   Schematic diagram of the thermal water repressuring applied in the oilfield near Szeged

technology can be applied, however, detailed logging of the wells is necessary. Thorough investigation of the aquifer should be performed. When high accuracy is required the observation wells should be established around the test well in a radial direction. On the basis of these investigations the volume of the water resource to be exploited and the required drawdown, as well as the extension of the depression cone can be estimated.

Hydrogeological exploration of fissured karstic rocks should be executed similarly to the others but a high degree of inhomogeneity makes difficult the location of exploratory wells. Tectonic conditions highly affect inhomogeneity, therefore construction of tectonic maps is required. Aerial or space photos can be used for mapping where the outcropping rock covers large areas. A great number of drills should be located on the structured zones, however, some boreholes should be drilled into zones tectonically less structured.

The discharges of karstic springs and yields of production wells drilled into karstic rocks as well as the discharges of rivers and creeks flowing from the karstic region should be measured at stations established for monitoring and estimates of the different elements of the water balances should be observed with wells in order to predict the fluctuation of the karstic water table in the future, to estimate the value of the regional porosity and the amount of the stored water volume.

A certain portion of the exploratory wells applied for planning the drawdown should be operated as observation wells later on, thereafter the observation of the influence is required by the time when the appropriate network is established.

REFERENCES

Alföldi, L. and Papp, B. 1976. The problems of environmental protection for subsurface waters in Hungary. *Publication in foreign languages,* 12, VITUKI, Budapest.

Böcker, T. 1969. Karstic water research in Hungary. *Bulletin of the International Association of Scientific Hydrology,* 14, 4-12.

Keserü, Zs. 1973. Estimation of the surfacial dislocations damaging building due to reservoir fluid depleting. *Bányászati és Kohászati Lapok-Bányászat,* Vol 103, (in Hungarian).

Korim, K. 1974. Study of the thermal water resources in Debrecen and Hajduszoboszló. *Report of the Research Institute for Water Resources Development,* Budapest (in Hungarian).

Nyerges, L. 1974. Studies and temperature measurements of the warm karstic water in the surrounding of Nagytárkány. Manuscript (in Hungarian).

Bibliography

Bendeffy, L. 1968. Hydrogeological aspects of land subsidence within urban area of Debrecen. *Hidrológiai Közlöny,* 48, 12, 549 (in Hungarian).

Körössy, L. and Kókai, J. 1972. Geological and geomorphological influence of the oil and gas exploitation. Conference held in Budapest (in Hungarian).

3.6.2   APPLICATION OF THE MODEL FOR GROUNDWATER FLOW AND EVAPOTRANSPIRATION TO AN AREA
          AROUND A PUMPING STATION USED FOR PUBLIC WATER SUPPLY
          by R H C M Awater[1]

3.6.2.1 Introduction

The eastern part of the province of Gelderland situated in the east of The Netherlands is supplied with drinking water by the 'Waterleidingmaatschappij Oostelijk Gelderland'. To carry out this task the water company abstracts groundwater at several places in its supply areas. This groundwater is of such a good quality that in most cases aeration followed by rapid filtration (to reduce the high iron-content) is the only treatment needed to yield a high quality drinking-water.

Due to the increasing demand for drinking-water more and more groundwater has to be abstracted by putting into use new pumping-stations. One such a new pumping-station situated near the village of Dinxperlo (Figure 1) is planned to abstract in the near future 2,000,000 m^3 of groundwater a year.

Many areas in the eastern part of the province of Gelderland are in agricultural use and show rather shallow groundwater tables making capillary rise of soil moisture from the groundwater reservoir to the roots of the plants possible. A drawdown of the groundwater table will hamper this capillary rise which may result in a reduction of the evapotranspiration, leading in its turn, to a lower yield of the crop.

Groundwater withdrawal, particularly from unconfined aquifers as exist at the pumping-station 'Dinxperlo', causes a drawdown of the groundwater table and thus may harm the yield. Farmers, when suffering a loss, are nowadays indemnified by the water company.

It would be more satisfactory however if both the farmer and the water company were to prevent the yield-depression or at least to prevent it partly.

Hence an investigation was started to see if it would be possible to recharge the aquifer artificially by infiltrating surface-water, which is available in a nearby brook named 'Keizersbeek' (Figure 1).

It so happens that a re-allotment of the area surrounding the pumping-station is about to be carried out. The plans include a new surface water discharge system which, by adding some connecting-ditches, can be made to transport water from the 'Keizersbeek' to the area in which the drawdown of the groundwater table is to be expected (Figure 2). To force the water to infiltrate the aquifer a certain water level is maintained in the ditches by means of weirs. Any surplus water is discharged to a downstream part of the 'Keizersbeek'.

To study the consequences of these plans, a mathematical model was needed able to handle the hydrological processes involved (evapotranspiration, unsaturated flow, saturated flow) and moreover able to handle these processes on a region-wide scale during a period of at least a few years.

The 'Model for Groundwater flow and Evapotranspirtion' developed by de Laat and van den Akker (1975; 1976) within the framework of the Committee for the Study of Water

---

[1] Committee for the Study of Water Resources Management in Gelderland, Arnhem, Province of Gelderland, The Netherlands

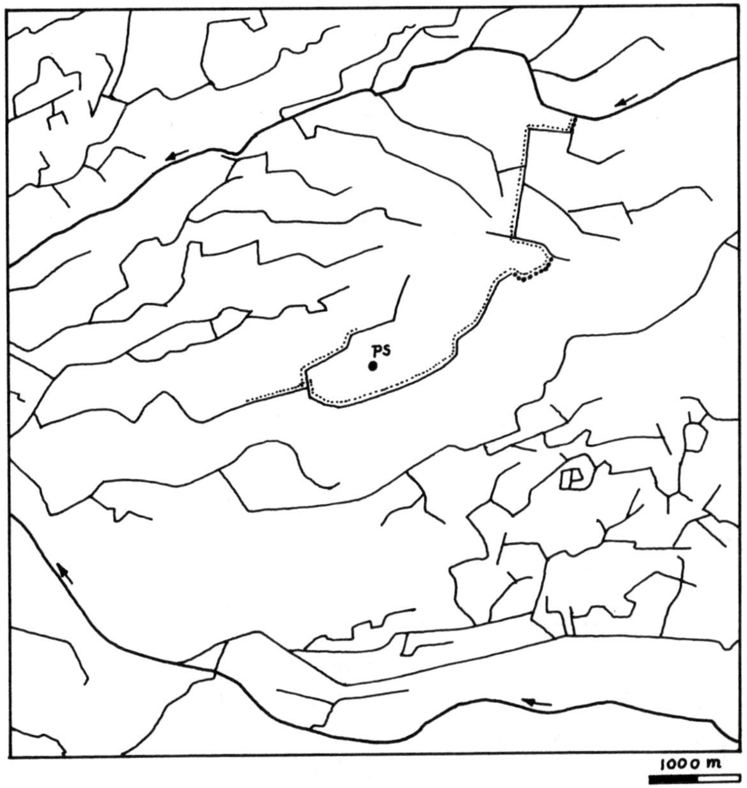

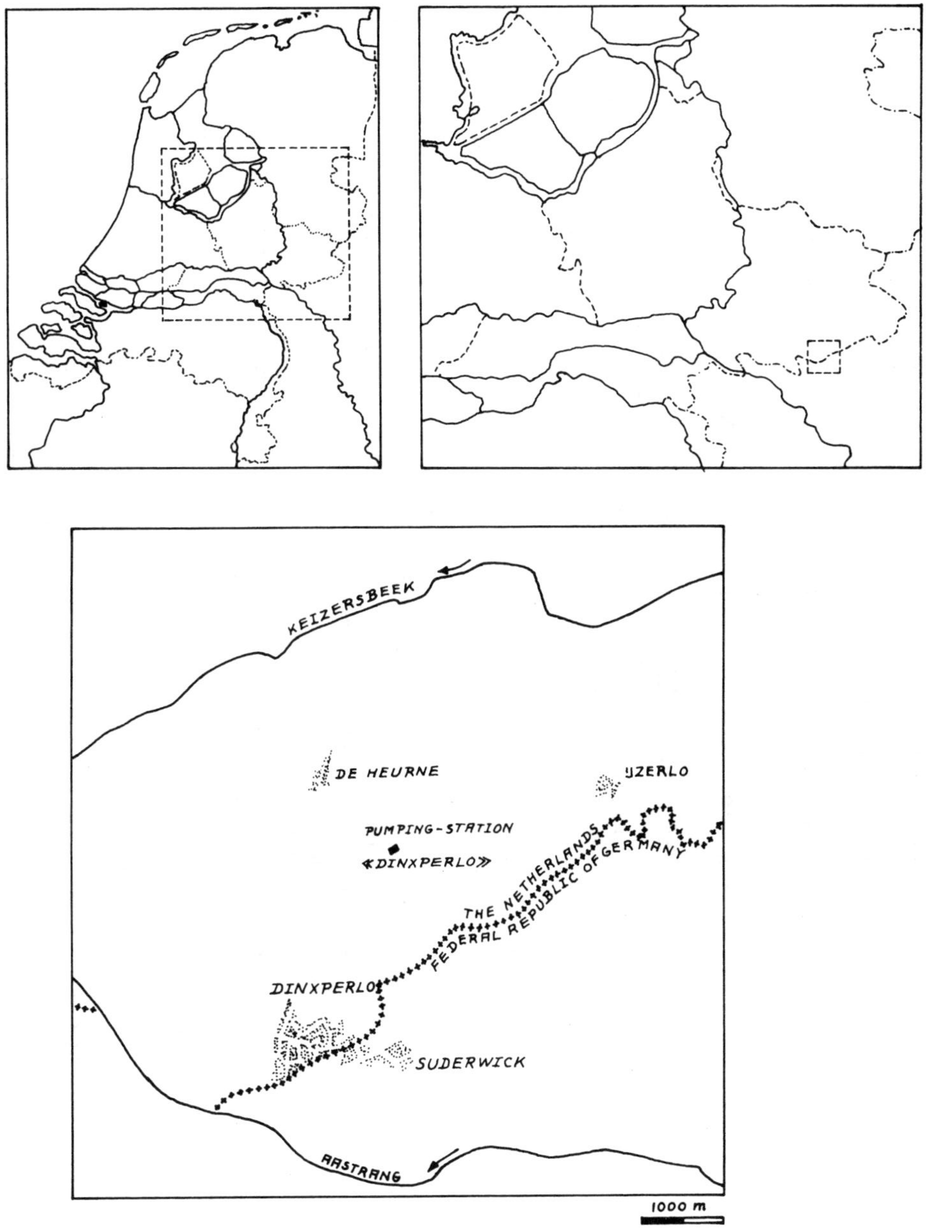

Figure 1 Location of the pumping-station 'Dinxperlo'- water courses after re-allotment

Figure 2 Area of drawdown of water table

Application of the model for groundwater flow and evapotranspiration

Resources Management in Gelderland, was capable of simulating the water movement in the area and predicting the effects of groundwater abstraction as well as artifical groundwater recharge on the components of the hydrological cycle.

During the development of the model, calibration and verification were concentrated on an area around another pumping-station (called 't Klooster), also situated in the eastern part of the province of Gelderland. In the study area 't Klooster, computer water table elevations were extensively verified. To illustrate the capability of the model, some results of this verification are presented in an appendix to this paper.

3.6.2.2 Description of the area around the pumping-station 'Dinxperlo'

3.6.2.2.1 Location. The pumping-station 'Dinxperlo' is situated in the eastern part of the province of Gelderland in The Netherlands near the border with the Federal Republic of Germany, about 2,500 m north-north east of the village of Dinxperlo (Figure 1), latitude 51.53 north, longitude 6.30 east.

3.6.2.2.2 Elevation. The altitude of the pumping station is 18.90 m above mean sea-level. The elevations in the surroundings are shown in Figure 3. The average slope of the land is about 0.6 m per km.

3.6.2.2.3 Geology. The Netherlands are situated in the North Sea basin, a still descending geosyncline. In the course of time this depression was filled up first by the sea-, later on mainly by river sediments. In the Pleistocene epoch, in the centre and south of the country, the rivers Rhine and Maas unloaded thick layers of sand and gravel. Next to this the rivers eroded deep channels in the Pliocene and Miocene sea deposits. Later on these channels were filled up again with sand and gravel. When the final climate improvement did occur large parts of The Netherlands were covered with eolian sands.

A filled-up channel like that described above is situated in the area of Dinxperlo. Some profiles are shown in Figure 4.

3.6.2.2.4 Geomorphology. Although the area is in general relatively flat, at several places elevations appear, looking like platforms, raised to sometimes 1.5 m above the surroundings. These elevations (called 'essen') were built up over several centuries by farmers using sand in their stables and from time to time they manured their land with that sand. It will be clear that the soils developed here, differ strongly from the other soils in the area which are podsols and also from the wet soils in the neighbourhood of brooks.

The main watercourses in the area are the 'Keizersbeek' in the north and the 'Aastrang' in the south (Figure 1), both being brooks fed with water originating from rainfall only. The 'Aastrang' is the largest with a drainage-area of about 300 km^2, the 'Keizersbeek' has a drainage-area of 90 km^2.

Up to and including the first half of this century the whole region was frequently bothered with inundations caused by the rising groundwater table. A dense network of drainage ditches takes care that inundations now belong to the past, while new plans within the framework of a re-allotment of land aim to improve the drainage (Figure 2).

3.6.2.2.5 Climate. The climate is temperate, with mild winters and cool summers. Westerly winds predominate and moderate the climate. July temperatures average about 17 ^{0}C and those of January average 2^{0}C. The average rainfall is highest in summer and autumn and lowest in springtime. The rainfall averages 740 mm a year.

3.6.2.2.6 Land use. Most of the land is in agricultural use. Over time arable land was developed on the eolian sand ridges which rise 1 to 2 m above the surroundings. The elevations were built up on these ridges as discussed in 3.6.2.2.4. Nowadays mostly maize (corn) is grown on these soils. The lower areas are usually covered with grass.

3.6.2.3 Model for groundwater flow and evapotranspiration

3.6.2.3.1 The model for saturated flow. The Jacob-equation for saturated flow is used:

$$\frac{\partial}{\partial x}(T\frac{\partial \phi}{\partial x}) + \frac{\partial}{\partial y}(T\frac{\partial \phi}{\partial y}) = S\frac{\partial \phi}{\partial t}$$

Figure 3 Groundsurface - elevation contour map — geological profiles

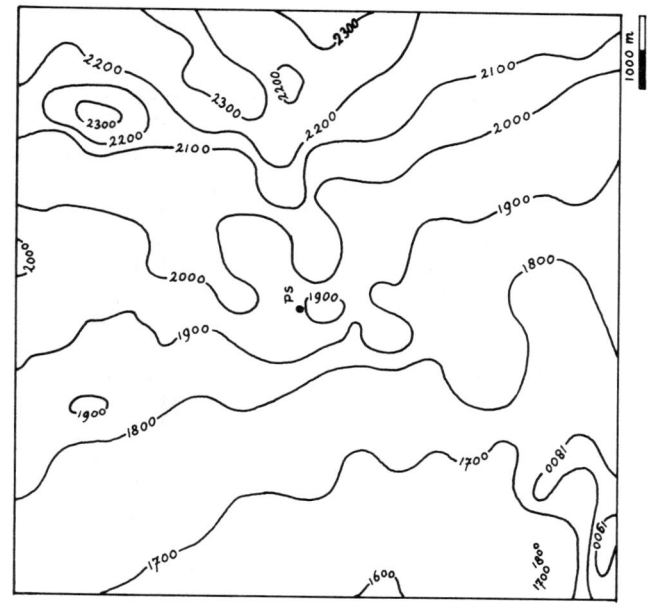

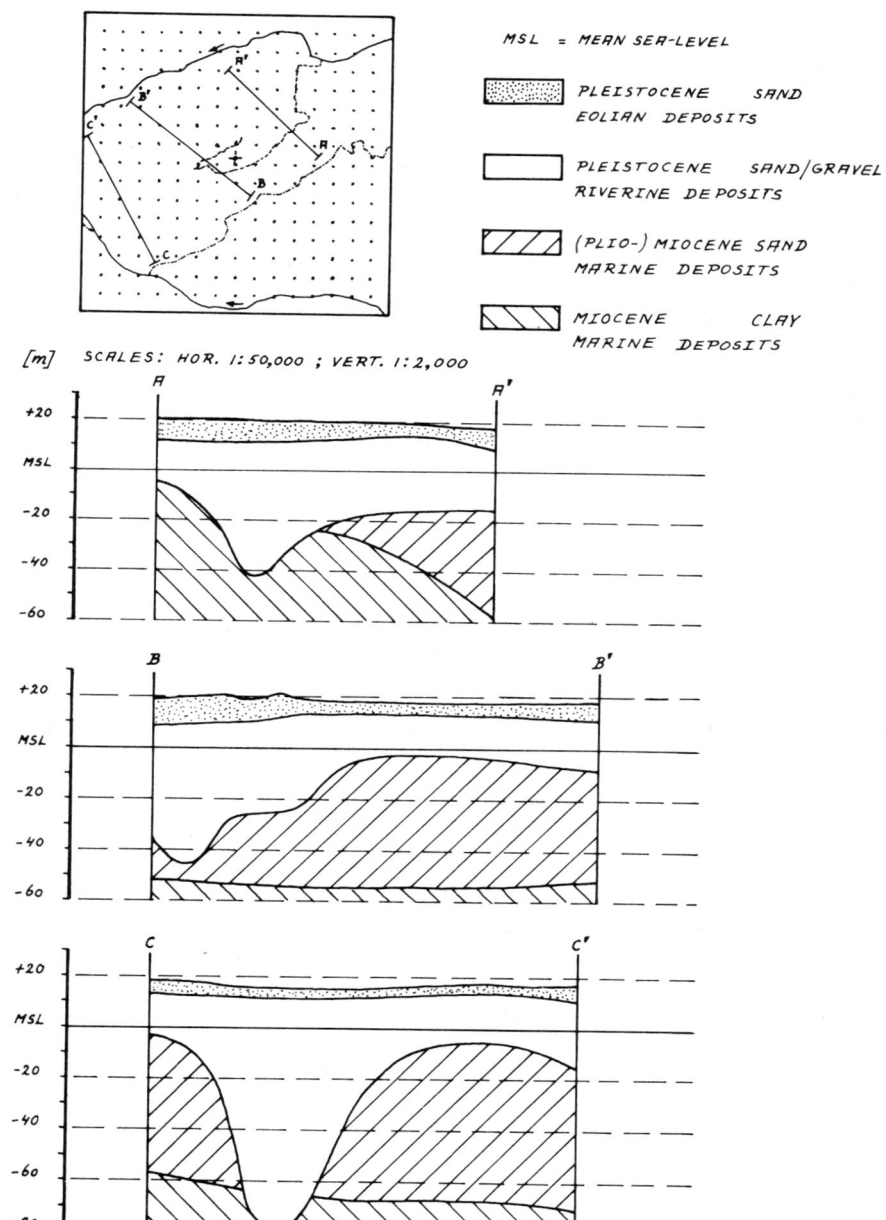

Figure 4 Profiles of filled in channels

in which: x and y are horizontal co-ordinate directions; ϕ is hydraulic head; T is transmissibility; S is specific yield; t is time.

With a generalized function W added to the right, to account for source or sink functions, the equation is solved using a finite element technique. For application to this study, square elements are used, the corners of which are called nodal-points or nodes. To solve, for each time step, the set of simultaneous equations, an iteration procedure (Gauss-Seidel with over-relaxation) is used, resulting in values for the potential ϕ or the discharge Q in each nodal-point.

The flux-functions that are included in W are described as follows:
- q_1 Represents a prescribed flux resulting from artificial recharge or discharge.
- q_2 Represents the discharge to rivers, canals, etc in the nodes in which the channels are schematized. The water-level ϕ_0 has to be prescribed in these nodes. The flux follows from $q_2 = (\phi-\phi_0)/R$, in which R represents the radial- and entrance resistances.
- q_3 Represents the discharge to the surface drainage system (ditches, tile-drains, etc); q_3 is related to the depth of the groundwater level below soil surface according to a linearized empirical relation (the tertiary drainage relation).
- q_w Represents the flux across the phreatic surface. For convenience, the flux resulting from a change in the position of the phreatic level (= $S.\partial\phi/\partial t$) is included in q_w together with the recharge to or the discharge from the saturated system due to flow in the unsaturated zone.

3.6.2.3.2 The model for unsaturated flow. The unsaturated zone is considered to have two layers, the root zone and the subsoil (Figure 5) (de Laat, 1976).

The vertical flow of moisture in the unsaturated zone of the soil is approached by a sequence of solutions of the steady state flow equation (Darcy's law):

$$q_c = -k(\psi)\frac{d\phi}{dz} \qquad (1)$$

where: q_c is flux positive in upward direction; k is hydraulic conductivity (strongly depending on ψ); $-\psi$ is pressure head (negative above the phreatic surface) ψ is commonly referred to as suction; ϕ is hydraulic potential defined as $\phi = z - \psi$ in which z is the elevation above datum level.

3.6.2.3.2.1 Root-zone. It is assumed that flow in the root zone is mainly governed by the water uptake of the roots, making $q_c = 0$, and $d\psi/dz = 1$. The suction at the interface of the root zone and the subsoil is introduced as being ψ_b, yielding $\psi(z) = \psi_b + z$. Given the soil-moisture characteristic for the root zone $\theta_e(\psi)$, θ_e being the volumetric moisture content, the saturation deficit in the root zone, S_e is calculated as follows:

$$S_e = \int_{\psi_b}^{\psi_b+D} \{\theta_{e,s} - \theta_e(\psi)\}d\psi$$

where: $\theta_{e,s}$ is the saturated moisture content for the root zone; D is depth of the root zone.

As an example, a function $S_e(\psi_b)$ is shown in Figure 6.

3.6.2.3.2.2 Subsoil. Taking the datum level at the phreatic surface, where $\psi = 0$; equation (1) is integrated yielding z:

$$z = \int_0^\psi \frac{k(\psi)}{q_c + k(\psi)} d\psi \qquad (2)$$

Given the relation between k and ψ, equation (2) is integrated numerically. It is now possible to calculate the relation between z and ψ for any value of the flux q_c, an example of which is shown in Figure 6. The resulting curves are called moisture-tension curves.

Given the soil-moisture characteristic for the sub-soil $\theta_s(\psi)$, moisture tension curves can be transformed to moisture content curves, ie the relation $\theta_s(z)$, θ_s being the volumetric moisture content, an example of which is also shown in Figure 6. For any value of the flux q_c, the saturation deficit in the subsoil S_s is now calculated as follows:

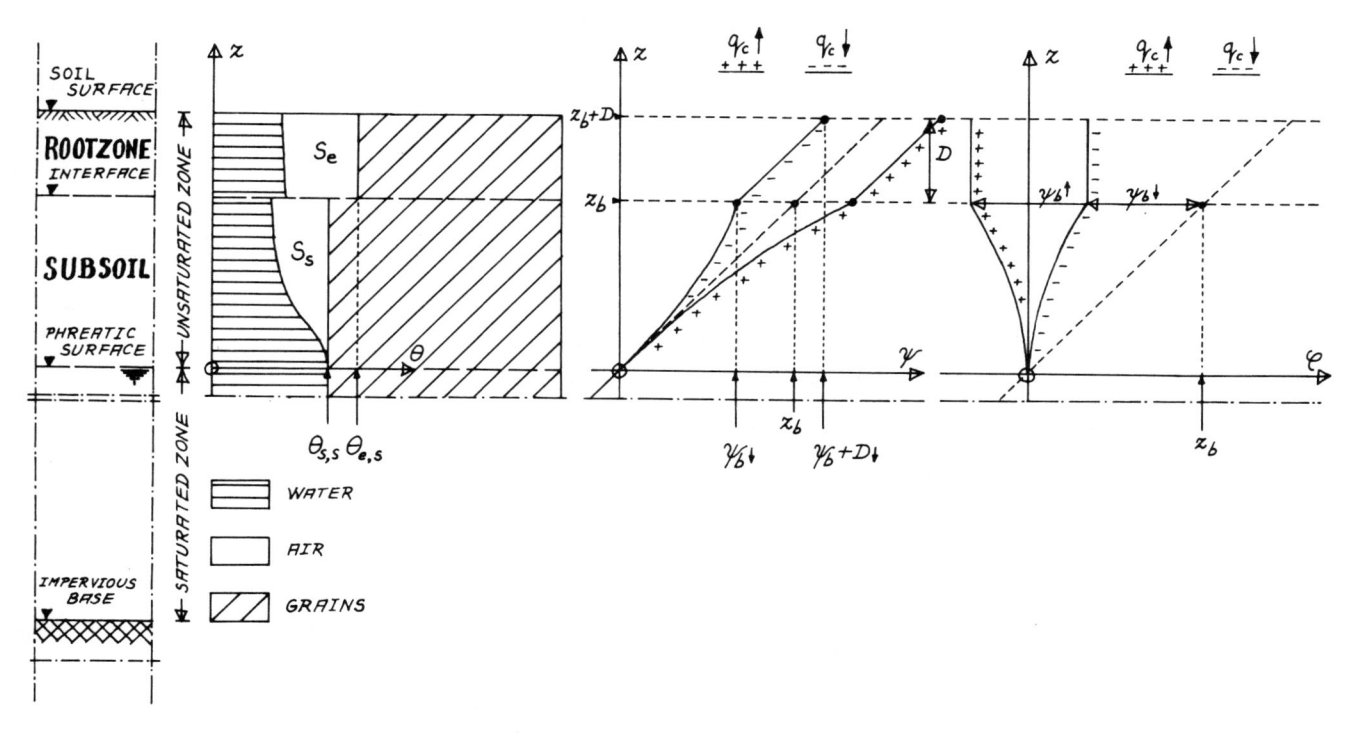

Figure 5 Schematisation of model

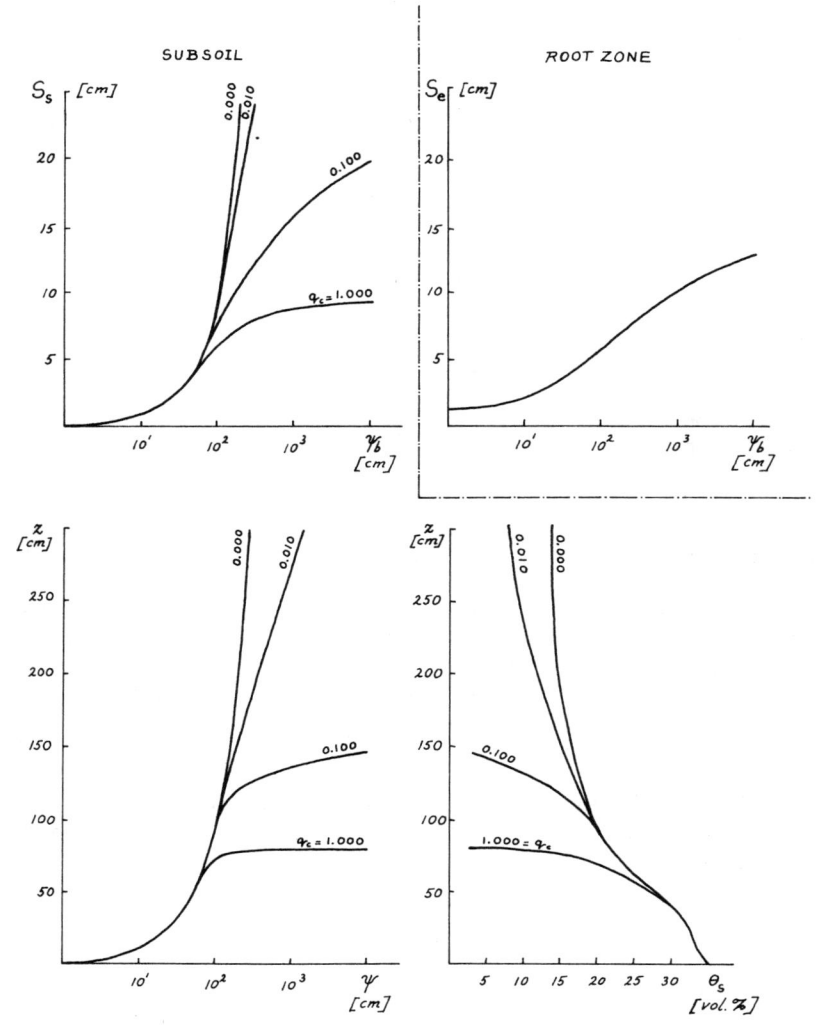

Figure 6 Steady-state flow relations – unsaturated flow

q_c in [cm/day]

Application of the model for groundwater flow and evapotranspiration

$$S_s = \int_0^{z_b} \{\theta_{s,s} - \theta_s(z)\}dx$$

where: $\theta_{s,s}$ is the saturated moisture content for the subsoil; z_b is the depth of the groundwater table below the root zone calculated from equation (2) for a given value ψ_b.

As an example functions $S_s(\psi_b, q_c)$ are also shown in Figure 6.

Solution example: Calculation of the steady state situation at time level n+1 from a given situation at time level n in case of evaporation excess.

given: q_w^{n+1} is flux through the phreatic surface, upward is positive

q_s^{n+1} is flux of evaporation excess (positive)

Iterative procedure:
(1) An initial approach for q_c^{n+1} (capillary flux, upward = positive) may be $q_c^r = q_c^n$, where the superscript r denotes approximate values for time level n+1.
(2) The water balance for the effective root zone yields S_e^r.
(3) From the function $S_e(\psi_b)$, the value ψ_b^r for $S_e = \frac{1}{2}(S_e^r + S_e^n)$ can be calculated.
(4) Calculate S_s^r, for $\psi_b = \psi_b^r$ and $q_c = q_c^r$ from the function $S_s(\psi_b, q_c)$.
(5) If S_s^r satisfies the water balance for the subsoil the calcualtions are stopped; otherwise the scheme is repeated from (2) for a different value of q_c^r.

3.6.2.3.3 The model for evapotranspiration. Actual evapotranspiration is calculated according to Rijtema (1969) using a modified Penman approach, taking into account soil moisture conditions.

3.6.2.3.4 Procedure of solution. The procedure to advance the solution of the combined model from time level n to n+1 can be described as follows (Figure 7):

Step 1 potential evapotranspiration (independent of soil moisture conditions) is calculated in each node and used as a first estimate for the model for unsaturated flow

Step 2 for two assumed values of q_w (flux across the phreatic surface) the model for unsaturated flow is executed, resulting in a linear relation between the change in phreatic level and q_w.

Step 3 the model for saturated flow is executed yielding hydraulic heads in the unconfined aquifer. The change in hydraulic head yields the lower boundary condition q_w for the model for unsaturated flow from the linear relationship established in step 2.

Step 4 with an iterative solution of the models for evapotranspiration and unsaturated flow the upper boundary (= the actual evapotranspiration) is solved in each node.

3.6.2.4 Application of the 'model for groundwater flow and evapotranspiration' to the area around the pumping-station 'Dinxperlo'

3.6.2.4.1 Nodel network. Taking into account the magnitude of the abstraction and the permeability of the water bearing stratum, it is assumed that at a distance of 4 km from the pumping-station drawdowns due to pumping are negligible, leaving an area of 8 x 8 km² to be drawn into the calculations. Furthermore, it is assumed that areas beyond the 'Keizersbeek' and the 'Aastrang' are not influenced either.

With regard to the nodal distance to be applied the available data concerning soil-type-distribution, land use-distribution and elevations of the soil-surface in the area are main factors, besides which watercourses have to be followed properly. The network shown in Figure 8 results when node spacing of 500 m is accepted. The area of an element then becomes 0.25 km². The number of elements is 230 and the total area 57.50 km². There are 264 nodal points.

3.6.2.4.2 Simulated period. The availability of data concerning the groundwater levels inside the area, which are used for verifying purposes, fixes the starting date on 1 January 1971. Taking the length of the time-step to be 10 days, the calculations proceed until 28 July 1975, resulting in 167 time-steps.

FOR CONVENIENCE THE MODEL FOR SATURATED FLOW IS REFERED TO AS SAT,
THE MODEL FOR UNSATURATED FLOW AS UNSAT
AND THE MODEL FOR EVAPOTRANSPIRATION AS EVAP.

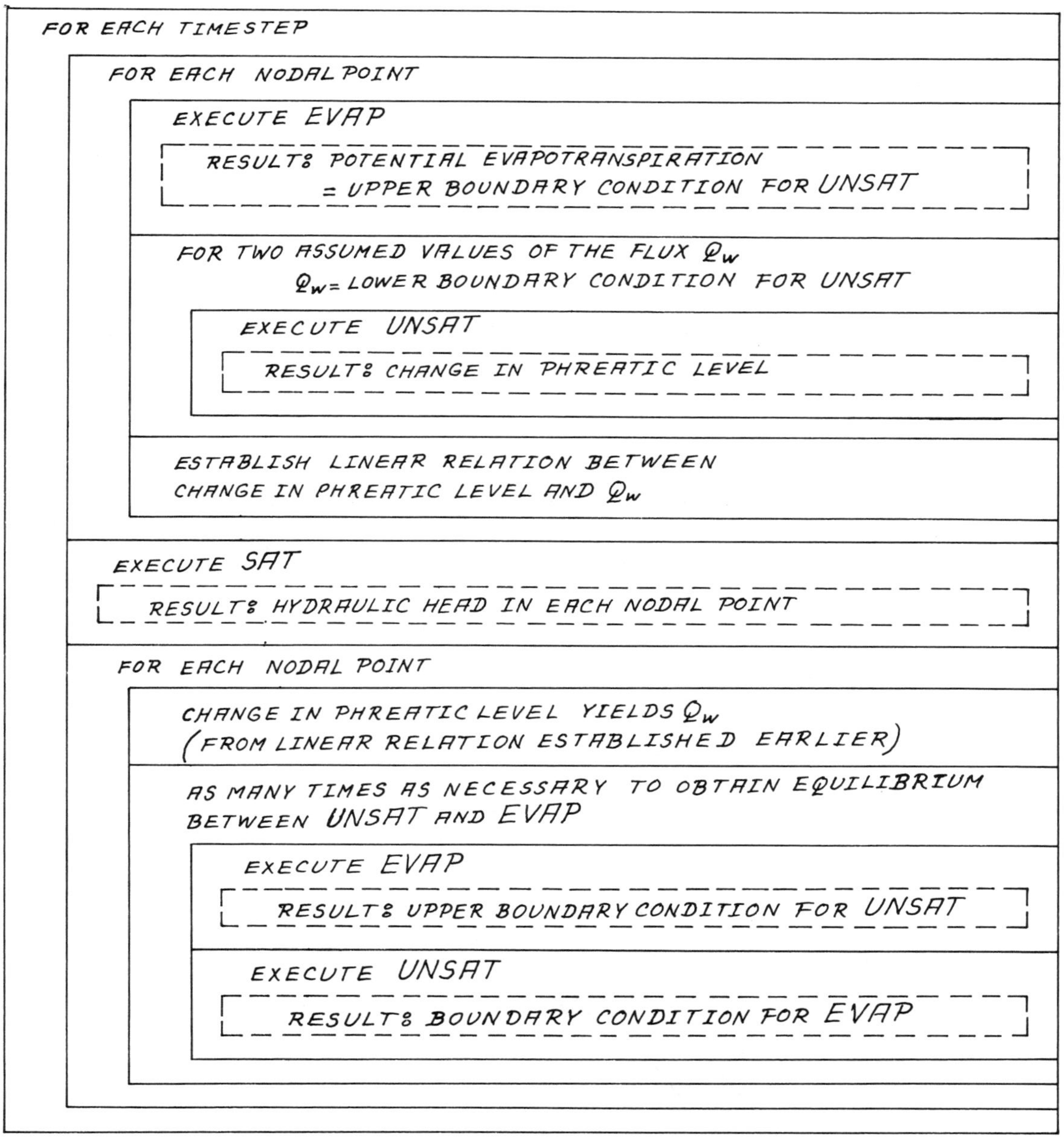

```
FOR EACH TIMESTEP
    FOR EACH NODAL POINT
        EXECUTE EVAP
            RESULT: POTENTIAL EVAPOTRANSPIRATION
                  = UPPER BOUNDARY CONDITION FOR UNSAT

        FOR TWO ASSUMED VALUES OF THE FLUX Q_w
            Q_w = LOWER BOUNDARY CONDITION FOR UNSAT
            EXECUTE UNSAT
                RESULT: CHANGE IN PHREATIC LEVEL

        ESTABLISH LINEAR RELATION BETWEEN
        CHANGE IN PHREATIC LEVEL AND Q_w

    EXECUTE SAT
        RESULT: HYDRAULIC HEAD IN EACH NODAL POINT

    FOR EACH NODAL POINT
        CHANGE IN PHREATIC LEVEL YIELDS Q_w
        (FROM LINEAR RELATION ESTABLISHED EARLIER)

        AS MANY TIMES AS NECESSARY TO OBTAIN EQUILIBRIUM
        BETWEEN UNSAT AND EVAP
            EXECUTE EVAP
                RESULT: UPPER BOUNDARY CONDITION FOR UNSAT
            EXECUTE UNSAT
                RESULT: BOUNDARY CONDITION FOR EVAP
```

Figure 7   Solution procedure

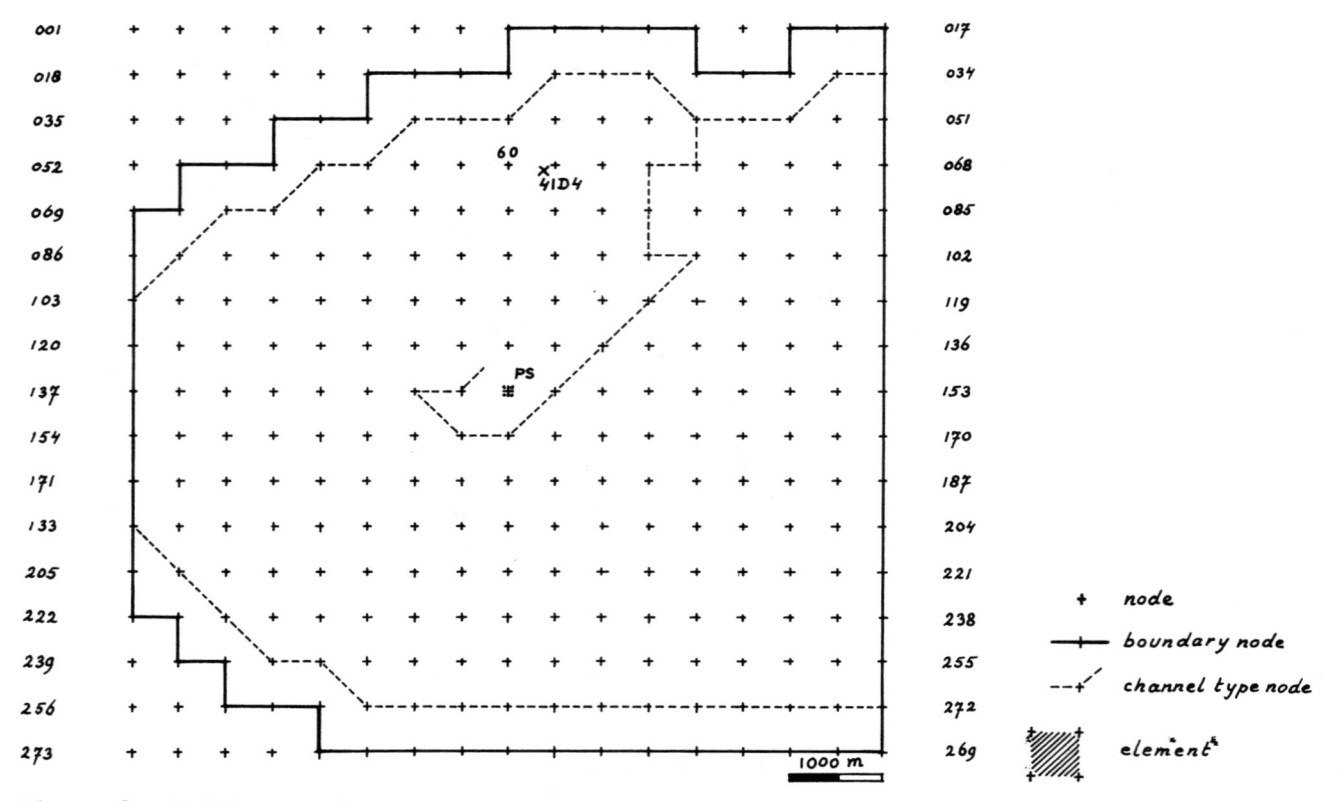

Figure 8   Nodal network

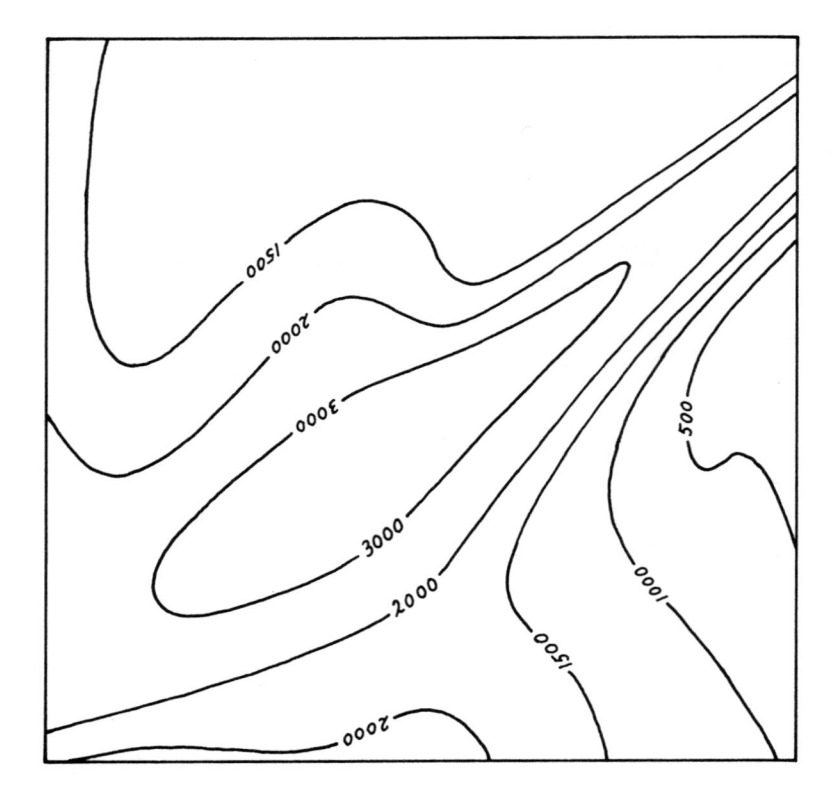

Figure 9   Transmissibility map

3.6.2.4.3 Preparation of data. The area of investigation is situated in two countries, making it often necessary to gather the data from maps with different scales, one showing more detail, besides which there are differences in interpretation, especially in soil-maps. A brief description of the data-preparation is given below.
- Boundary conditions: In the boundary nodes the prescribed heads for each timestep have to be given. A program specially developed for this purpose calculates the Dirichlet conditions in the boundary nodes from piezometric heads observed outside the area of investigation.
- Transmissibility: The transmissibility in every node is obtained from maps prepared from data gathered by geological- and geo-electric-investigations, as well as pumping-tests (Figure 9).
- Ground surface elevation: The average elevation of the area surrounding each nodal-point is calculated from maps showing data for every point in which the elevation is known. A derived contour map is shown in Figure 3.
- Soil physical parameters: In the area, 10 different types of root zone and 11 different types of subsoil are distinguished, the physical parameters of which are used in the model. In Figure 10 only the 4 major soil groups are shown.
- Land use: The land use changes slightly from one year to another. Figure 11 shows the situation in the year 1973.
- Channels: For every channel-type, node data on geometry, entrance resistance and permeability of the substratum as well as water levels for each time-step have to be prescribed.
- Meteorological data: The meteorological data were mainly obtained from a meteorological station at Liedern (Federal Republic of Germany) situated close to the southern boundary of the area. The following data are used: windspeed, relative sunshine amount, relative humidity, temperature and precipitation. They have to be given for each time-step.

3.6.2.4.4 Sequence of the computer-studies. To take into account the influence of both the re-allotment and the groundwater abstraction and the artificial groundwater recharge the following sequence of studies is necessary:
Run 1   Simulation of the present (undisturbed) situation.
Run 2   Calculation of the situation existing when the re-allotment is executed.
Run 3   Calculation of the situation with groundwater abstraction, after the re-allotment.
Run 4   Calculation of the situation with abstraction and artificial groundwater recharge, after the re-allotment.

Following this sequence is unfortunately impossible because of the node-spacing distance chosen, making the modelling of only the main watercourses possible. The discharge to the other water courses (ditches, tile-drains, etc) is in each nodal point related to the groundwater level below the soil-surface according to a linearized empirical relation: the tertiary drainage relation. Changing the dimensions and/or courses of this surface drainage system will change the tertiary drainage relation, making a new calibration of the model unavoidable. Because data on groundwater levels after re-allotment is not executed yet, this calibration is not possible.

A fine network would make the modelling of small ditches and thus the calculation of the situation after a re-allotment possible in principle, but it would increase the computer time and the time required for data preparation (if such refined data were available at all).

For this reason the studies are executed in the following sequence:
Run 1   Simulation of present (undisturbed) situation.
Run 2   Calculation of situation with groundwater abstraction.
Run 3   Calculation of situation with abstraction and artificial groundwater recharge.

This sequence makes it possible to answer the question as to which benefits the projected infiltration-channel would have yielded if it were to exist in the present situation.

3.6.2.4.5 Assumptions. The following assumptions are made:
- in the computer-runs 2 and 3: the groundwater abstraction is constant during the whole period of the calculations.
- in the computer-run 3: the water level in the infiltration-channel is kept constant during time by means of weirs; where possible this level reaches to 60 cm below the

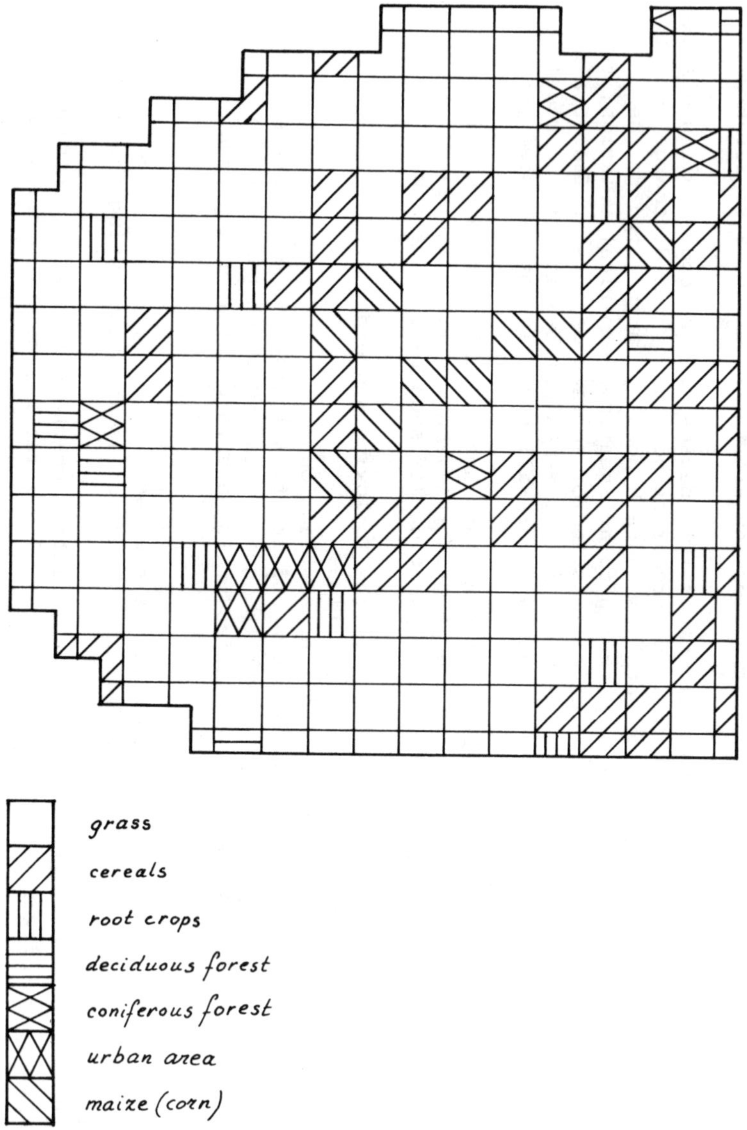

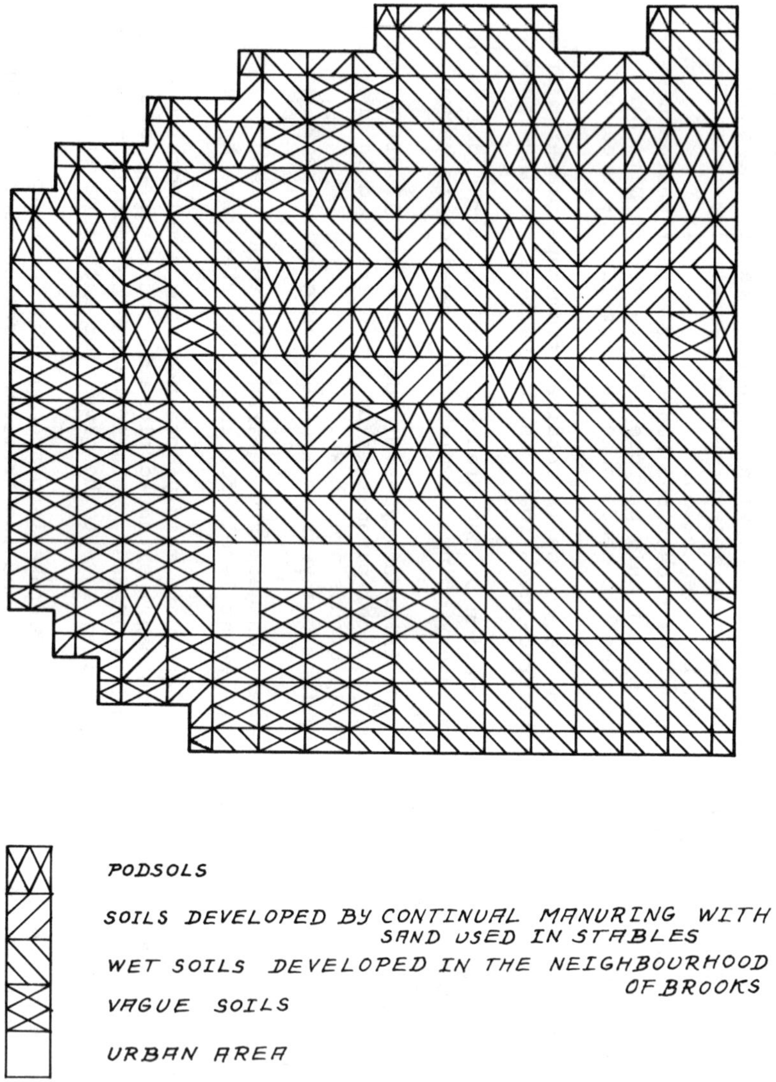

Figure 10 Soil type map

Figure 11 Landuse map

elevation of the banks. The 'Keizersbeek' is always able to supply the quantity of water needed to maintain this water level.

3.6.2.4.6 Calibration of the model and results of Run 1. To calibrate the model, several runs were made to calculate the undisturbed situation during a period of one year.

Deviations between computed and observed values of the hydraulic head occurring in summer were corrected by adjusting (lowering) the pore-volume in the deeper parts of the subsoil and adjusting the tertiary drainage relations.

When computed and observed levels of the groundwater table appeared to match close enough, a run was made calculating the whole period.

An examination of the results showed that no further corrections were needed, so this run was assumed to be run 1.

In Figure 12, the computed head in node 60 and the observed head in a nearby observation well (nr. 41 D 4) are compared. Figure 13a shows the computed water table contour map for the situation at the end of the 98th timestep (summer; date 060973); Figure 13b shows the situation at the end of the 116th timestep (winter; date 050374). In both figures the observed groundwater levels are indicated.

The distribution of the relative evapotranspiration (= real evapotranspiration/potential evapotranspiration) over the area, as calculated for the growing-season of the year 1973, is presented in Figure 14.

The water balance for the year 1973 (expressed in mm) can be found in Table 1.

Table 1 Water balance over 360 days, starting 310373 (terms in mm water depth)

IN:	Precipitation	709	709	709
OUT:	Evapotranspiration	451	446	452
	Surface water discharge	197	170	160
	Groundwater discharge	43	41	45
	Groundwater extraction	1	35	35
	Decreased storage capacity	17	17	17

3.6.2.4.7 Results of run 2. Run 2 calculated the situation with a groundwater abstraction of 2,000,000 m^3 a year for the whole period. The resulting drawdowns at two points in time are shown in Figure 15a (date 060973) and Figure 16a (date 050374).

The reduction in the relative evapotranspiration during the growing-season of the year 1973 is presented in Figure 17a.

The water balance can be found in Table 1 and the consequences of groundwater abstraction on the terms of the water balance are shown in Figure 18a.

3.6.2.4.8 Results of run 3. Run 3 calculated the situation with an abstraction of 2,000,000 m^3 a year, while the aquifer was artificially recharged.

Figure 17b shows the reductions in the relative evapotranspiration during the growing-season of the year 1973.

The water balance is presented in Table 1 while changes in the terms of the water balance due to the abstraction are shown in Figure 18b.

3.6.2.5 Conclusions

The 'Model for groundwater flow and evapotranspiration' makes it possible to predict the consequences of groundwater abstraction on piezometric heads, water balance and actual evapotranspiration (agricultural crop production).

Furthermore, it appeared to be possible to investigate the reduction in drawdown of the water table as well as the reduction in the depression of the yield of agricultural crops due to groundwater abstraction by means of artificial recharge.

The results of the calculations show that the reduction in crop-production caused by a pumping-station is reduced considerably when the groundwater is artificially recharged by means of an infiltration channel.

Figure 12 Comparison of calculated (-) and observed (°) hydraulic head ℓ for position of node and well: figure 8.

node 60
well 41D4

a) summer situation

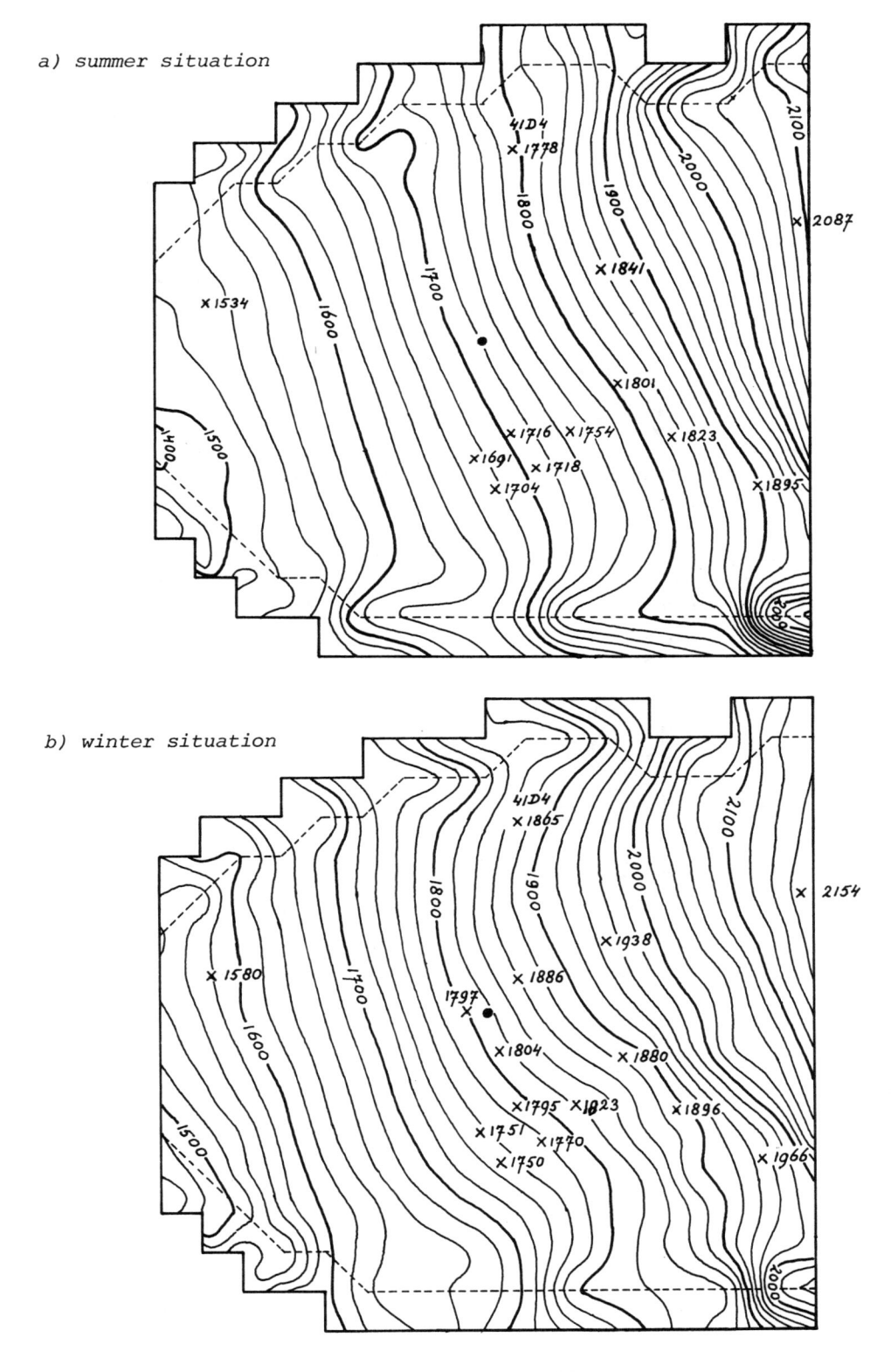

b) winter situation

Figure 13   Computed water table contour map

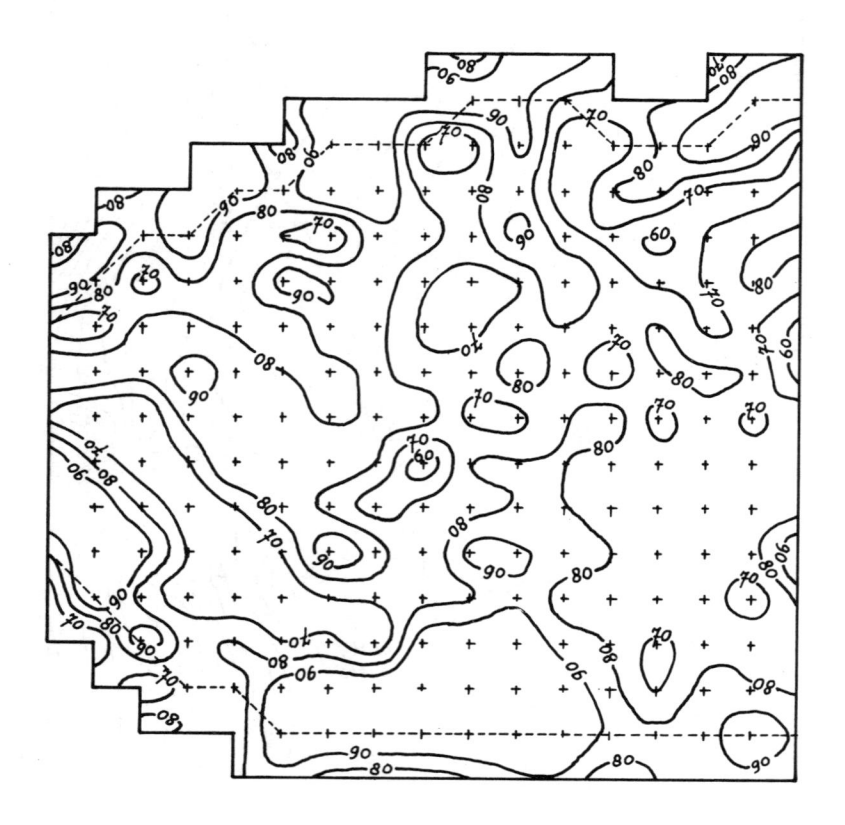

Figure 14   Computed relative evapotranspiration %

a) summer situation

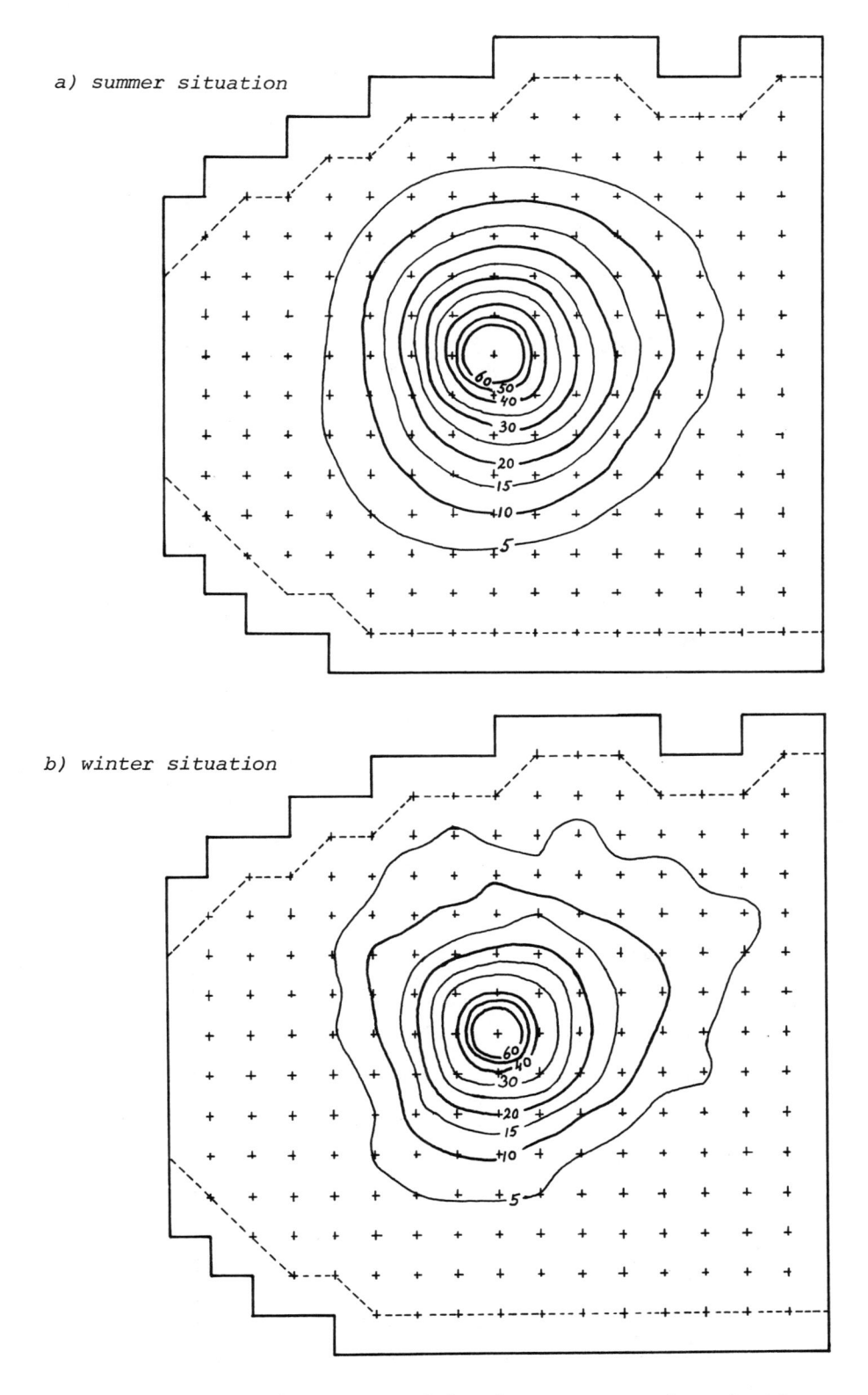

b) winter situation

Figures 15a and 16a   Computed drawdown at two points in time; Run 2

a) summer situation

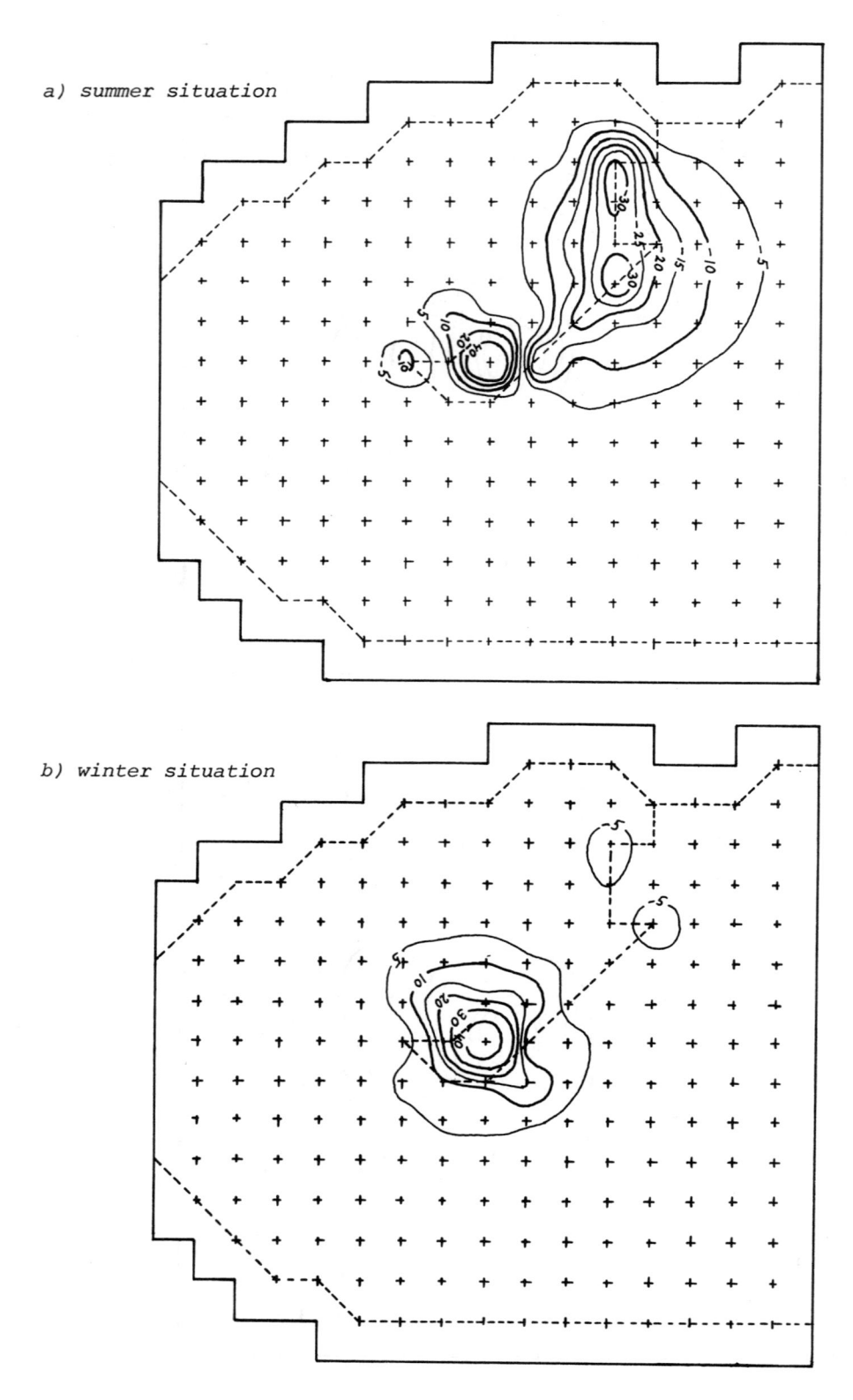

b) winter situation

Figures 15b and 16b   Computed drawdown at two points in time; Run 3

270

a) *without artificial recharge*

b) *with artificial recharge*

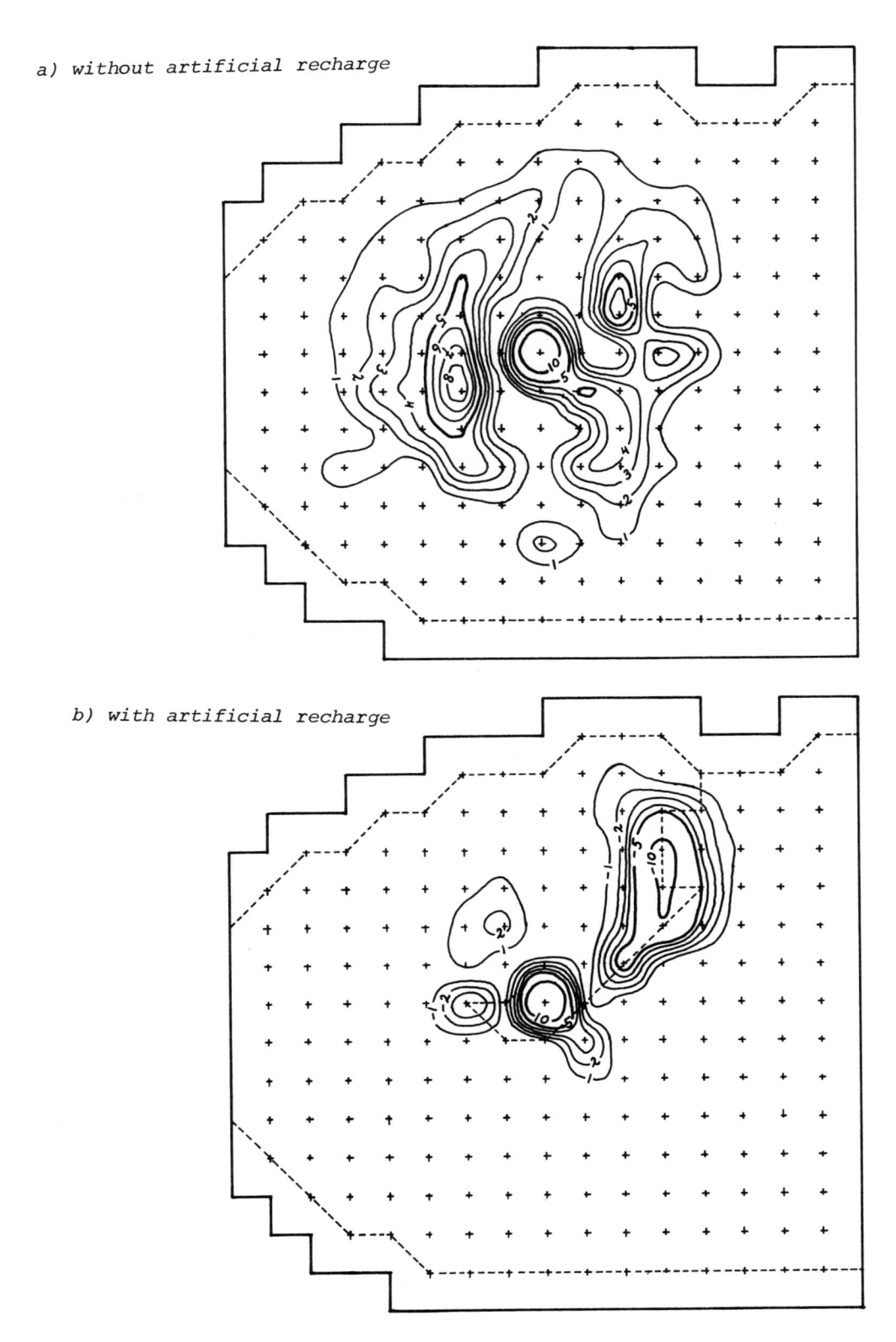

Figure 17   Reduction in relative evapotranspiration due to groundwater abstraction

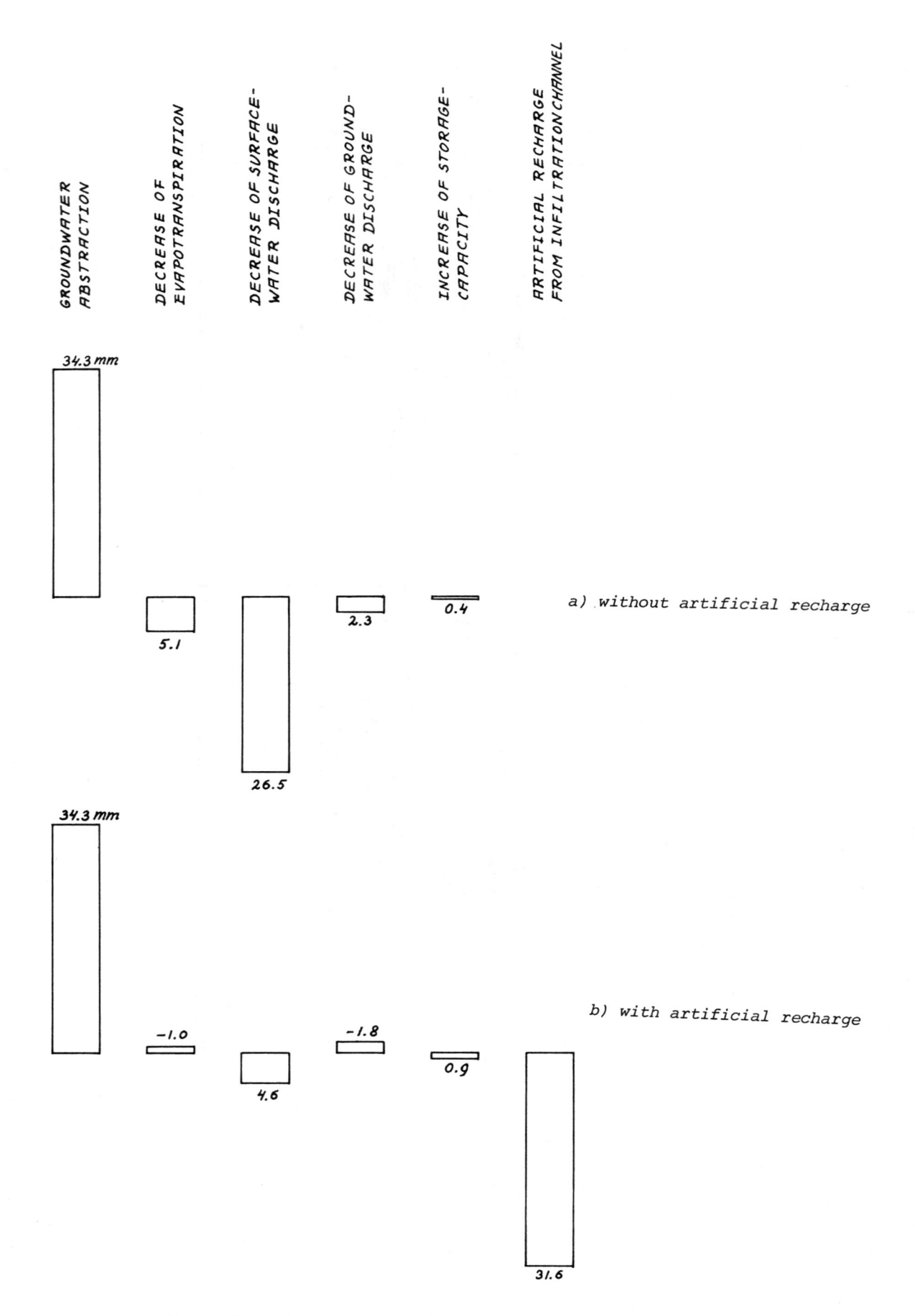

Figure 18 Consequences of groundwater abstraction

APPENDIX

Comparison of computed water table elevations with respect to the observed water table elevations in the area around the pumping station "'t Klooster".

The study area "'t Klooster" is a square area with dimensions 6 x 6 km^2 and is divided into square elements of 500 x 500 m^2 each. The pumping station is located exactly in the middle. Almost 6 years are simulated, starting 1 April 1971, using a time increment of 10 days.

The figure accompanying Table 2 shows the location of 28 observation wells which have been recorded twice a month. Computer water table elevations are interpolated in time and space to be compared with observed values in the 28 locations. If Δh (cm) is the difference between the observed and the simulated water table elevation, the average value $\overline{\Delta h}$ for the total number of observations is presented for each well in the first column of Table 2a. The second column gives the average value of the absolute difference ($\overline{\Delta h}$) and the third column the standard deviation σ of Δh. In column 4 the efficiency factor is presented defined as:

$$R_e = 1 - \Sigma\{(F-F')^2\}/\Sigma\{(F-\overline{F})^2\}$$

where: F represents the observed water table elevations; F' the simulated values and $\overline{F}$ the mean of the observed data. The value $\overline{h}$ is largely governed by the difference between actual and model surface elevation at the observation well. In order to eliminate the effect of $\overline{\Delta h}$ on the comparison of the simulated and observed fluctuation of the phreatic level, values for ($\overline{\Delta h}$) and R_e have been computed for observed data which have been 'corrected' for $\overline{\Delta h}$ (Table 2b). For further details reference is made to De Laat, et al (1978) and Awater, et al (1979).

REFERENCES

Awater, R.H.C.M. 1976. Infiltratie Dinxperlo, *Delft University of Technology*, Dept of Sanitary Eng, Delft (in Dutch).

Awater, R.H.C.M., and De Laat, P.J.M. 1979. Groundwater flow and evapotranspiration. A simulation model. Part 2: Applications. *Basisrapport Commissie Waterhuishouding*, Gelderland, Arnhem (in preparation).

De Laat, P.J.M. 1976. A pseudo steady-state solution of water movement in the unsaturated zone of the soil. *J Hydrol*, 30, 19-27.

De Laat, P.J.M., and Van den Akker, C. 1976. Simulatiemodel voor grondwaterstroming en verdamping. In: *Modelonderzoek 1971-1974*. Commissie Bestudering Waterhuishouding Gelderland, Arnhem, 145-197 (in Dutch).

De Laat, P.J.M., Van den Akker, C., and Van de Nes, Th.J. 1975. Consequences of groundwater extraction on evapotranspiration and saturated-unsaturated flow. Application of Mathematical Models in Hydrology and Water Resources Systems. *IAHS Publication No 115, Proceedings of the Bratislava Symposium*, 67-76.

De Laat, P.J.M., and Awater, R.H.C.M. 1978. Groundwater flow and evapotranspiration. A simulation model. Part I: Theory. *Basisrapport Commissie Waterhuishouding*, Gelderland, Arnhem.

Rijtema, P.E. 1969. On the relation between transpiration, soil physical properties and crop production as a basis for water supply plans. *Techn Bull*, ICW 58, Wageningen.

3.6.3 DEEP OPEN PIT MINING AND GROUNDWATER PROBLEMS IN THE RHENISH LIGNITE DISTRICT
by Dieter Briechle[1] and Rudolph Voigt[2]

3.6.3.1 Introduction

Situated in the northwest of the Federal Republic of Germany, in the southern part of the Lower Rhine Bay between the cities of Aachen, Cologne and Mönchengladbach between latitude 50°40' and 51° north and longitude 6°10' and 6°50' east are Europe's largest lignite deposits, estimated at 55×10^9 tonnes. Since the Old Tertiary, the Lower Rhine Bay has been a depression where marine and lake sediments were deposited. These deposits were divided into horst and trough blocks by several tectonic disturbances running northwest to southeast (Figure 1). Especially during the Miocene, peat beds formed from which the lignite coal originated.

The tertiary sand and gravel layers, several hundred metres thick, and the sands and gravel of the Pleistocene terraces (Figure 2) contain several groundwater bodies. The Old Pleistocene main terrace is thickest and most abundant in water in the Erft block. Its groundwater content in and around the lignite open pit mining area has already been drawn off completely, with only a small part employed for useful purposes.

The drainage of the area is mainly via the Erft river which flows into the Rhine near Düsseldorf (Figure 1). The average precipitation depth in the area is approximately 700 mm/a. The evaporation is approximately 450 mm/a. Information on the monthly distribution (%) of the precipitation and evaporation is contained in Table 1.

Table 1 Mean monthly distribution (%) of precipitation and evaporation

	Jan	Feb	Mar	Apr	May	Jun	Jul	Aug	Sep	Oct	Nov	Dec
Precipitation %	7	7	6	7	9	10	10	13	8	7	8	8
Evaporation %	1	2	4	8	18	19	20	14	8	4	1	1

3.6.3.2 The Rhenish lignite district - a review

The deposit comprises several coal seams. The main seam can locally attain a thickness of 100 metres. Strata between the seams are made up of gravel and sand, or silt and clay beds.

Major and minor normal faults have been active through Tertiary and Quaternary times. Faulting patterns, consequently, are responsible for mining patterns. Mining on an industrial

---

[1] Grosser Erftverband, Paffendorfer Weg 42, D-5010, Bergheir, Federal Republic of Germany
[2] Rheinische Braunkohlenwerke AG, Stuettgenweg 2, D-5000, Koln, Federal Republic of Germany

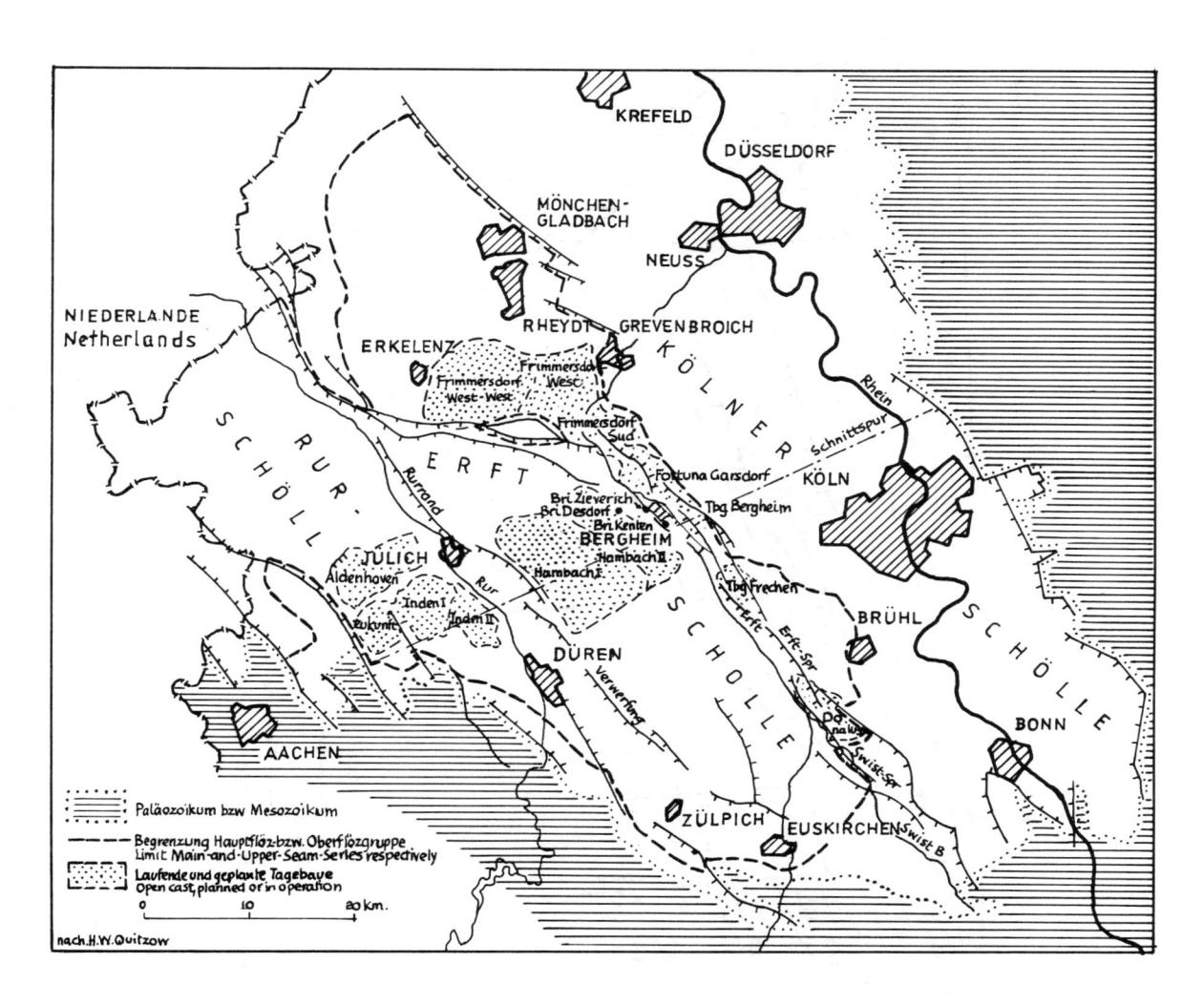

Figure 1   The Rhenish lignite mining district

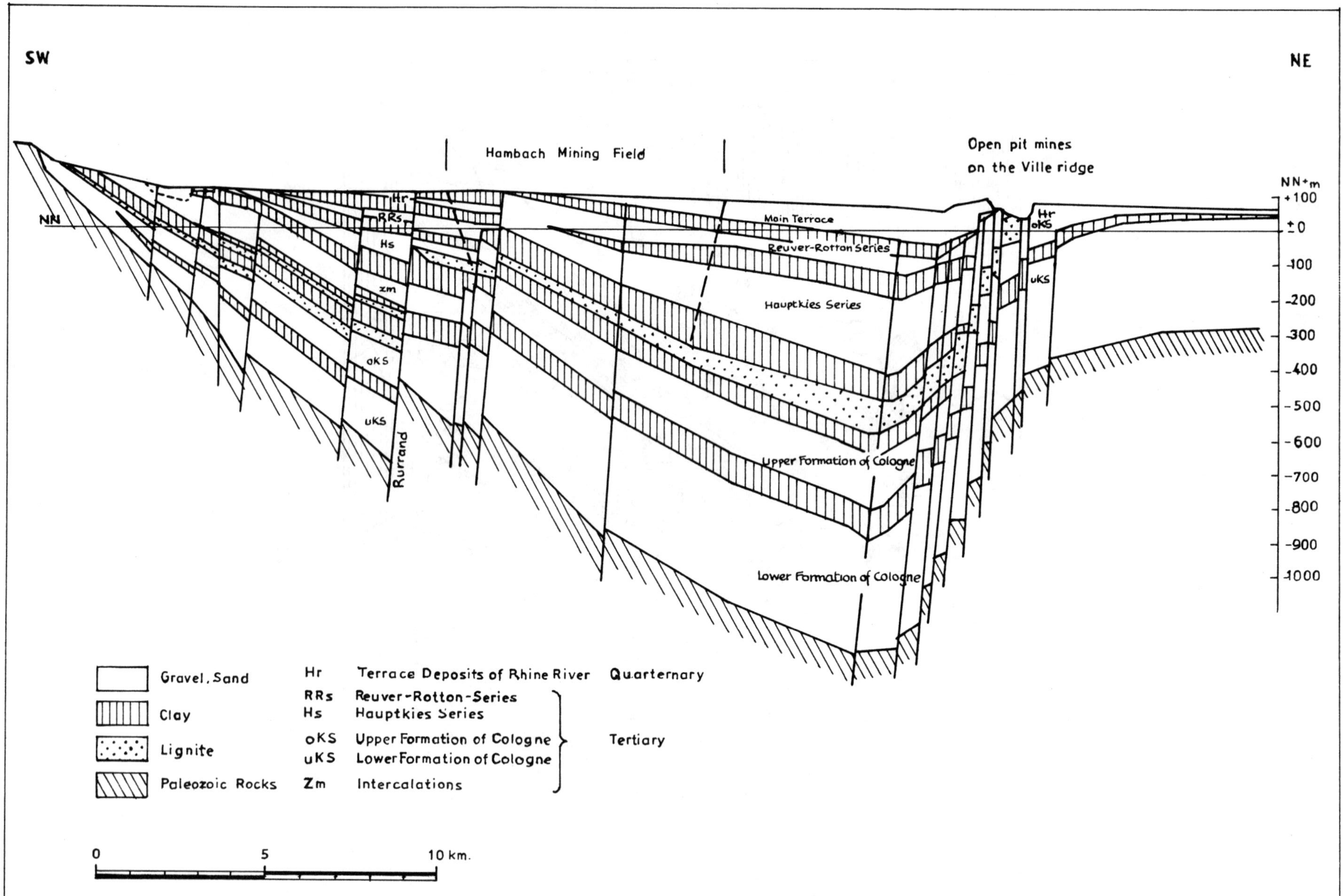

Figure 2 Cross section of the lignite deposit (trace of cross section is indicated in Figure 1)

scale began about 100 years ago in a horst-like structure, named the Ville ridge. There, the main seam was directly exposed or covered only by a thin layer of Quaternary terrace deposits. The ratio of overburden to coal was a favourable 0.3 to 1. Nowadays, these near surface seams have gone (Figure 2).

Mining has moved slowly with the dip of the strata and along the NW-SE-strike faults from southeast to northwest. This means, the thickness of overburden and therefore the total depth of the open pit mines have gradually increased and will also increase in the years ahead. The thickness of the overburden now in the deepest pit, the Fortuna mine (Figure 2), already is 200 metres. With the additional thickness of the main seam of 100 metres, the open pit is 300 metres deep.

The overburden to coal ratio deteriorates in the new Hambach mine, where excavations began in 1978 (Leuschner, 1976). In this mine, the ratio will increase to approximately 6.5 to 1, and the total depth will finally be 500 metres.

All the mines are worked by one company, Rheinische Braunkohlenwerke AG, Cologne (Rheinbraun). The six existing mines produce around 110×10^6 tonnes of lignite per year. 15 per cent of this production is used for making briquettes, a traditional German domestic fuel. But 85 per cent is burned in the nearby thermal power plants, which generate more than one fourth of West Germany's electricity requirements.

A sound estimate is 35×10^9 tonnes of lignite can economically be mined out of the total deposit. This figure is based on the present level of energy prices. So far, 9×10^9 tonnes have been taken out and will be taken out by the mines now in operation.

3.6.3.3 Open pit mining and groundwater

To enable safe mining of lignite in open pits it is necessary to completely dewater the water bearing top strata of the seams, and to reduce the head of the confined aquifers of the footwall beneath the lowermost levels of the mine. Drawing down the water table(s), or potentiometric surface(s), respectively, does not only avoid flooding but also prevents a build-up of pore pressures in the strata behind the slopes and high walls of the mine. The danger of blow-throughs and slope failures is thus reduced.

During the long periods of drawdown, the rate of pumping from storage which accounts for the whole discharge in the beginning decreases steadily, whereas the rate of discharge from recharge to the affected aquifers increases. When the required drawdown around the mine has been achieved, the particular rate of replenishment is pumped. The annual rate of recharge from rainfall in the Rhineland averages 200 mm out of 700 mm.

Since 1955, the year large-scale dewatering began, 23×10^9 m^3 of groundwater have been lifted by, on the average, 900 tube wells. Right now, the total rate of discharge is 1.2×10^9 m^3 per year or nearly 40 m^3 per second. All wells with maximum depths of more than 500 m are equipped with submersible pumps (Blank, 1976). The largest pump discharges 1900 m^3 per hour at a delivery head of 220 m. Cones of depression with drawdowns of several hundred metres at the batteries of wells extend over an area of many square kilometres. Depending on the location of wells, on the hydrological properties of the aquifers, and on the boundary conditions, the individual cones develop differently and may overlay each other. The whole affected area covers approximately 2500 square kilometres.

About 5000 piezometers, up to seven of them in a single observation well but screened in different aquifers at different depths, serve to keep track of the development of dewatering. The deepest piezometer taps a sand nearly 600 m below ground surface.

Readings are taken weekly, monthly or semi-annually and automatically processed at the computer centre. At least once a year these data are used in completing maps with the water table contour lines of the important aquifers, and with the cumulative drawdowns since 1955.

Figure 3 shows the water table contours of the uppermost aquifers in the autumn of 1977. It reveals clearly the steep cones of depression around the producing pits on the Ville ridge. The map also shows the presence of tectonic faults and stratigraphical pinch outs which form barrier boundaries. For comparison, Figure 4 depicts the virgin groundwater surface of the same aquifer system in 1955, just before dewatering started.

The differences, ie the cumulative drawdowns 1955-1977, are shown in Figure 5. Again, the location of the discharging batteries of wells can easily be recognized.

In addition to this principal use, piezometer readings are also used for specific tasks, such as plotting well hydrographs (Figure 6) etc.

In 1958, the Grosser Erftverband (GEV) was established as a corporation under public law to solve all problems connected with dewartering and groundwater drawdowns by common and

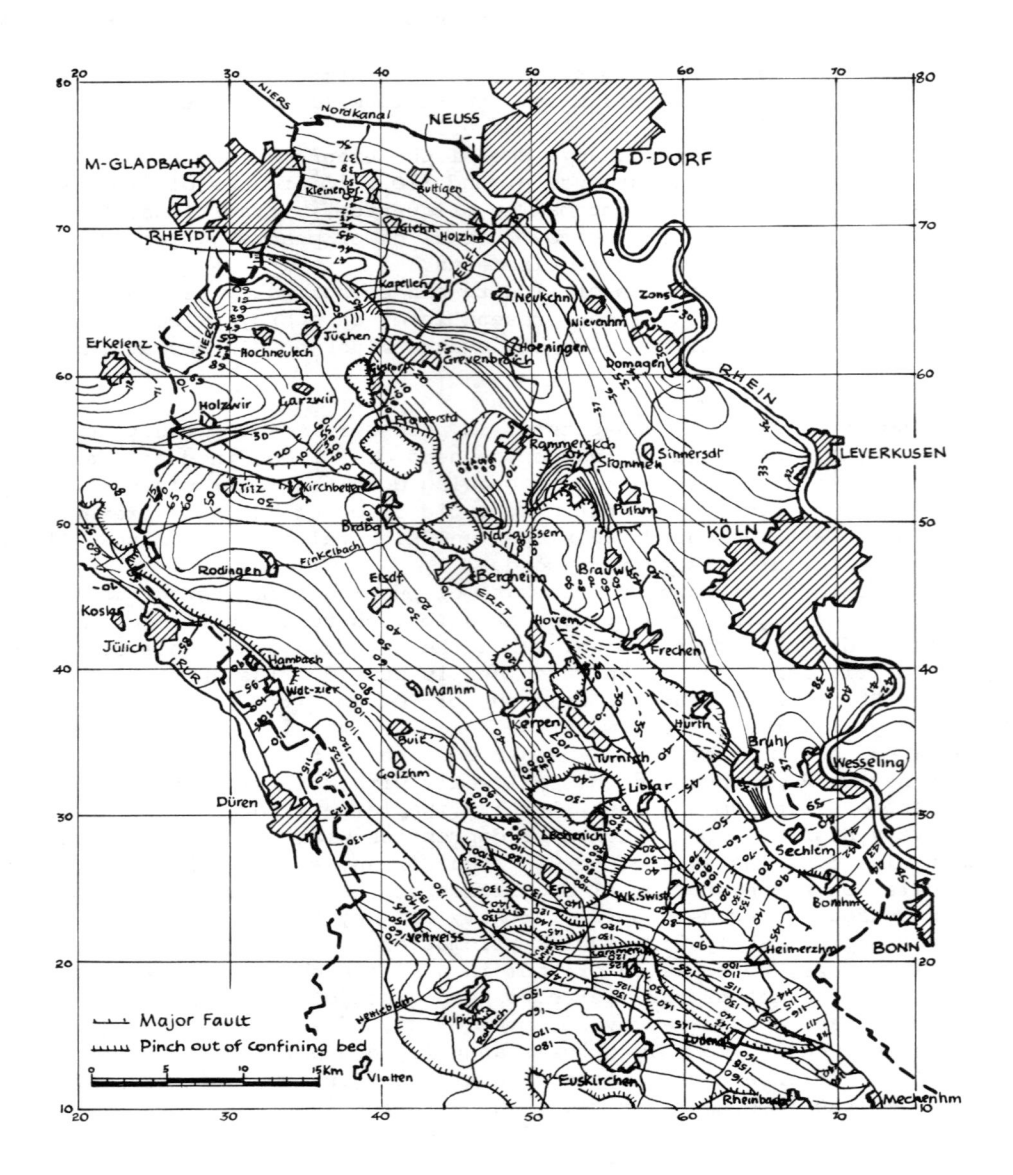

Figure 3   Water table contour lines of the upper aquifers in 1976

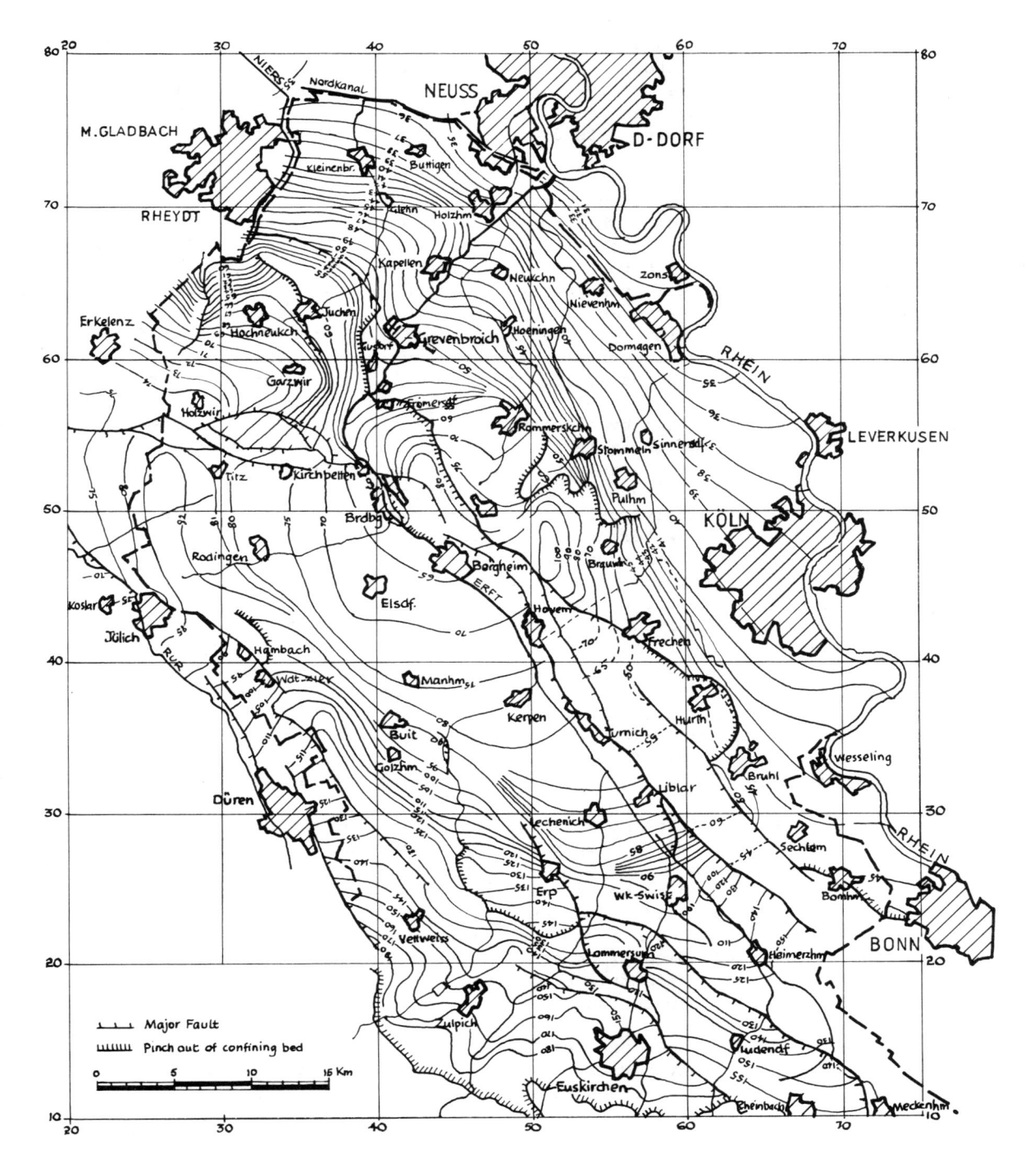

Figure 4   Water table contour lines of the upper aquifers before start of dewatering in 1955

concerted actions. All persons and institutions influencing the water management in the Rhenish lignite district are statutory members of the GEV. Some of the most important functions of the corporation are observations and investigations of the hydrological conditions in connection with planning and execution of projects to guarantee the water supply of people, industry and soil. Figures 3 to 5 of this paper are taken from the annual reports of the GEV.

3.6.3.4 Modelling of the dewatering processes

3.6.3.4.1 Development of methods. When the first huge open pits were started, dewatering began, just by drilling wells and operating them. Theoretical investigations of the cones of depression to be developed and the volumes of water to be lifted did not go far beyond the application of the classical well formulas by Dupuit and Thiem. Considering the planned depths of the mines, it soon became advisable to develop a more accurate knowledge of the expected annual discharges of groundwater through pit lifetimes of more than forty years.

A first thorough investigation of the problems involved was conducted by Siemon (1958). This author tried to approximate the problem of three-dimensional groundwater flow at certain boundary conditions by a one-dimensional (radial) solution. He modelled the continuous unsteady state process of drawdown by a sequence of discrete steady state steps of drawdown. Taking into account the aquifer parameters as well as the boundary conditions, he came up with a procedure to determine the drawdown at any distance r from the battery of wells at any time t after pumping had begun. Because Siemon's method has never been published in English, its principles are more detailedly described in paragraph 3.4.3.4.3. It has been in use to today to design the lines of dewatering wells around the open pits now in operation.

Despite the use of programmable desk computers, the Siemon methods is rather time-consuming. To optimize the number and arrangement of wells and their optimum mode of operation, several runs are necessary and the computations are rather tedious. Such problems are now solved by applying the numerical aquifer model, which is referred to in paragraph 3.4.3.4.4.

Despite the favourable hydrological conditions in this part of Germany - high rates of recharge to extensive sandy-gravely aquifers - it became obvious during recent years that the persistent withdrawal of groundwater can adversely affect the groundwater supply to the public and industry. This mans that future dewatering measures must be designed in a way that also meets the public demand for sufficient groundwater of good quality. The remaining groundwater resources must, therefore, be carefully managed to ensure their maximum conservation. A problem like this requires modelling of whole aquifer systems rather than modelling a single aquifer.

To study the reactions of the multiple-aquifer system of the Erft Basin (Figure 2) to the dewatering measures required to keep the new Hambach mine dry throughout the next 60 years, a hybrid model has been worked out. This was done by a team of modelling experts of Hanover Technical University in close co-operation with the Hydrological Department of the Rheinbraun Company. Paragraph 3.4.3.4.5 describes some details of this model.

Stein (1977) developed and published a special method to calculate the approximate volumes of groundwater to be pumped from storage for dewatering the Hambach mining field. This procedure is based on stereometric computations of the water-filled aquifer comparing the beginning and end of the dewatering process.

3.6.3.4.2 General remarks on open pit dewatering. Any open pit mine in water bearing strata raises the problem of completely dewatering these strata down to a given depth at a given time. Depth and time, as a rule, are specified by the schedule of excavation. The most suited means to remove the groundwater depends on the hydrological properties and the boundary conditions of the aquifers in question. In the Rhineland, hydrological conditions require the operation of submersible motor pumps in large diameter gravel packed wells as the most favourable solution.

The required drawdown in an open pit and around its perimeter can be achieved by measures which are limited by two extreme variants:
(a) A few wells operated over a long time require low investment costs but the operating costs are high because of the long-lasting dewatering process.
(b) Many wells run for a short time require heavy investment but lower operating costs.
 The hydrogeological conditions of the Rhenish Lignite Mining District,
- well developed aquifers of medium to high hydraulic conductivities,
- occurrence of many faults that act as barriers, thus limiting the growth of the cones of

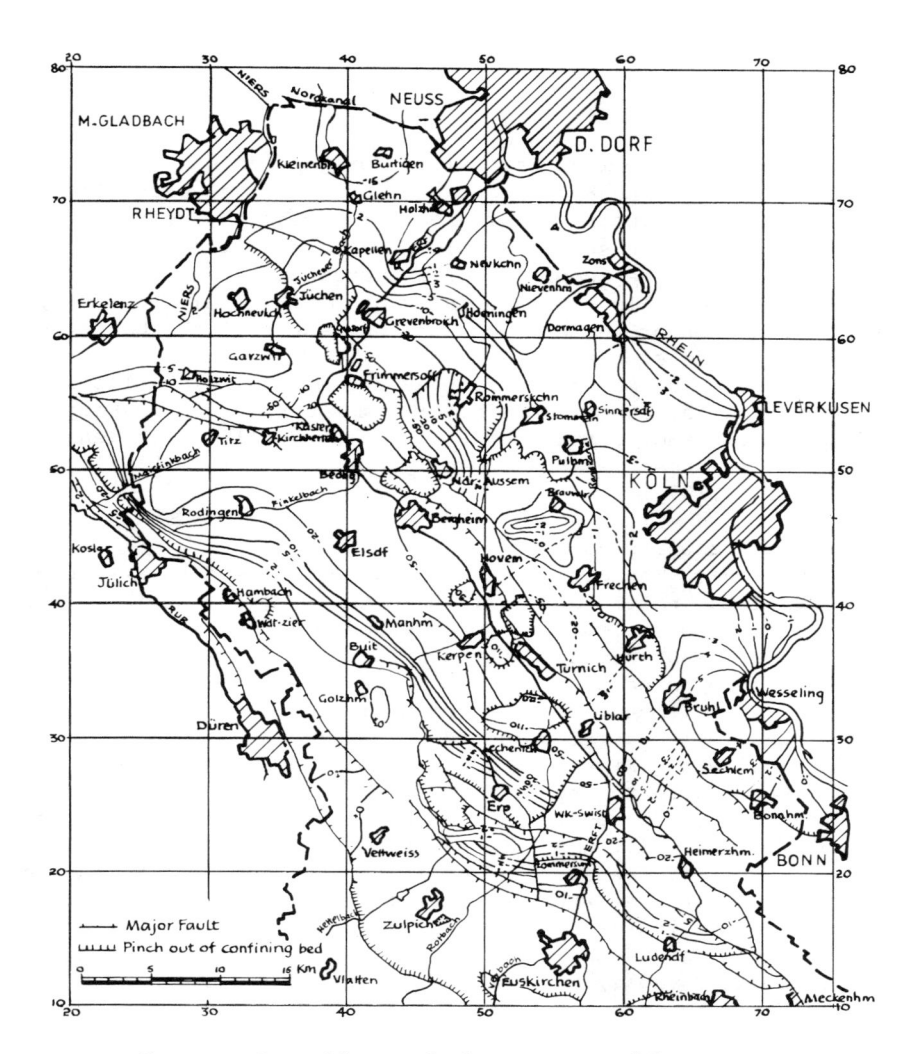

Figure 5   Drawdown lines of the upper aquifers

Figure 6   Groundwater hydrographs of two neighbouring observation wells showing the hydrologic separation by an intermediate fault

depression,
render those variants the most economical that allow for just as many wells that are required to dewater down to the required depth and this takes four to five years (Siemon and Voigt, 1976). This figure cannot be applied to other areas with other hydrological conditions. It is probable, however, that in most cases the optimum variant will be between both abovementioned extremes. Invariably, the modelling of the drawdown will show a decrease of the rate of discharge in time. The wells start normally at maximum pumping rates, which gradually decrease as a function of the drawdown in the centre of the battery and of the maximum (intake) capacity of the single wall.

The enormous drawdowns, which may be as much as 300 m in single wells within a few years, require sequential changes of the submersible motor pumps employed. To keep the costs involved as low as possible, a pump should remain installed in a well for at least half a year. Then, the next pump should be chosen with a capacity curve that smoothly links up with the curve of the old pump (Voigt, 1976).

3.6.3.4.3 Siemon method - sloping aquifer
3.6.3.4.3.1 Basic assumptions. The Siemon method (1958) is based on a step by step determination of the gradient of the water table, or the potentiometric surface in an aquifer where the actual flow of groundwater can be approximated by a radial component. The time interval between steps is at least several months. This allows the assumption of a quasi-steady state flow at each step to be studied. At least, the Dupuit-Forchheimer assumptions are implied to be valid. The Siemon method has been used successfully in the Rhineland to determine the design of the well batteries and to calculate the development of the cones of depression in the major aquifers. Figure 7 shows schematically the geometric patterns of an aquifer which is likely to be affected by the drawdown from a discharging battery of wells on the left side. This aquifer, obviously part of a characteristic tectonic structure of this part of the Rhineland, is subdivided into segments (three in this case).

Each segment in turn is represented by a readial cross section. Boundaries between the segments are supposed to run parallel with the flow paths. The cross-sections again are subdivided by the area elements indicated (Figure 7).

The first step is simple to assume at element O, ie at the centre of the discharging well battery, a height of water table, h_O, that will exist there at an unknown time t after pumping has commenced. The rate of discharge is $Q_D = Q_O$. The following formula applies:

$$Q_D = Q_O = Q_{VO} + Q_{QO} + Q_Z \tag{1}$$

where: Q_O is rate of groundwater flow at element O; Q_{VO} is rate of discharge at element O that is taken from storage; Q_{QO} is rate of discharge at element O that originates from recharge within the cone of depression; Q_Z is rate of discharge at element O that is from recharge outside the cone of depression.

The flow rates at elements O, 1, 2, ..., n are composed equivalently, and

$$Q_O > Q_1 > Q_2 > \ldots > Q_n$$

Rearranging budgetary equation (1) yields

$$Q_{VO} = Q_D - (Q_{QO} + Q_Z) \tag{2}$$

Q_{QO} and Q_Z can be determined by hydrological budgeting; Q_{VO} will then be the difference in the rate of discharge Q_D. It is, however, neither analytically nor numerically possible to split up the rate Q_{VO} as a function of the storage coefficient to the sections between the area elements.

Here the experienced hydrologist must apply the trial and error method in trying to distribute the rate of water taken from storage to the sections between the area elements. Once this distribution is fixed, the gradient of the water table at each element can be calculated.

3.6.3.4.3.2 Determination of the gradient of the water table. In a first approach, the flow rates from storage between the elements are only estimated, thus enabling a calculation of total flow rates $Q_O, Q_1, Q_2, \ldots, Q_n$.

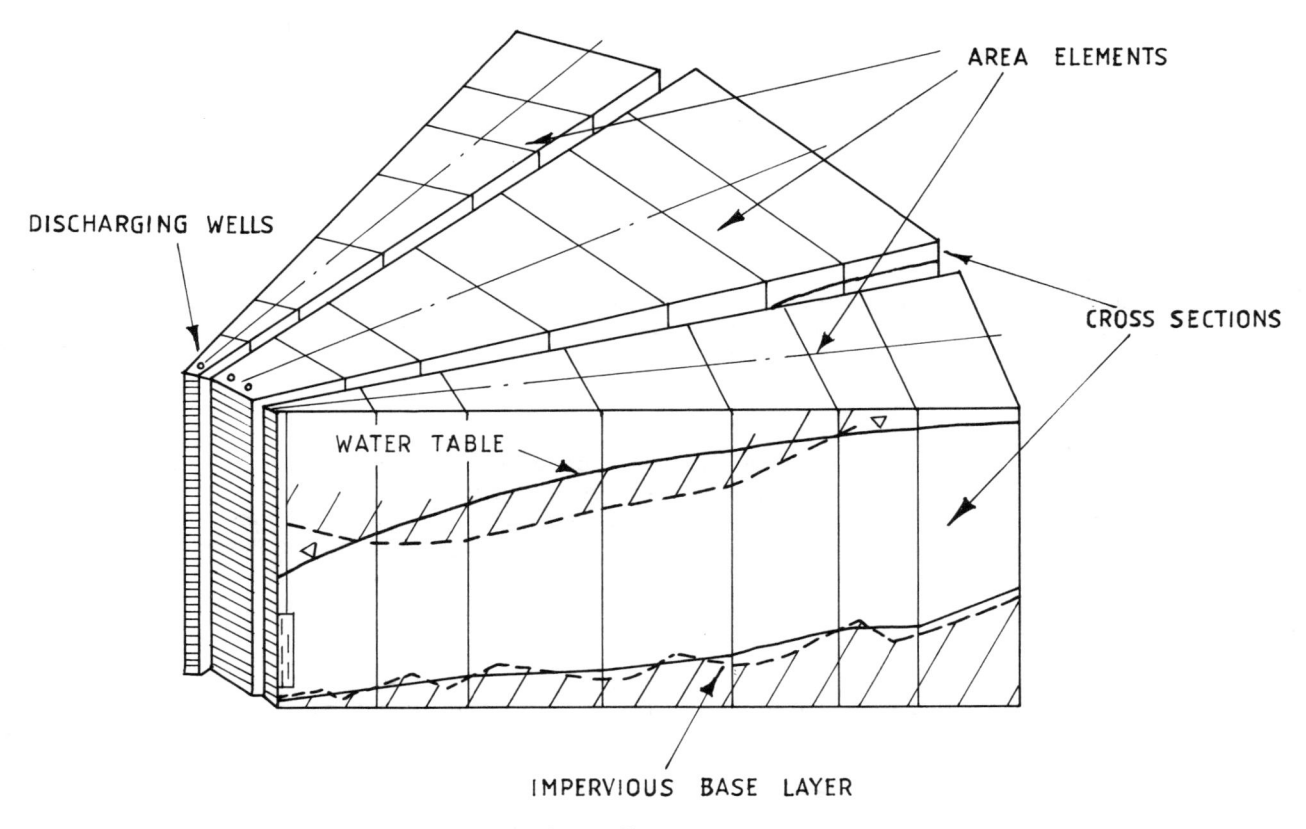

Figure 7   Subdivision of an aquifer into flow segments

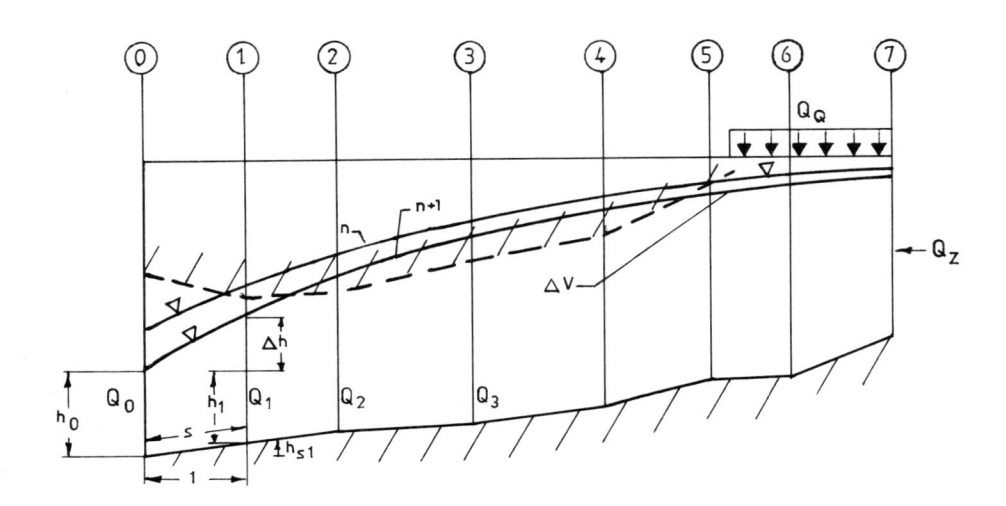

Figure 8   Geometric patterns of a flow element. The water table or the potentiometric surface, respectively, drops from stage n to stage n+1 in time increment Δt_1. Throughout this time, the partial volume, ΔV, of the aquifer is dewatered. Q_0, Q_1, etc indicate the flow of groundwater at area elements, 0, 1, etc

Now, starting from flow element O, it is possible to determine the height of water table h_1 at element 1 (Figure 8).

$$h_O + \Delta h = h_1 + h_{S1}$$

and (3)

$$h_1 = h_O + \Delta h - h_{S1}$$

Δh is still unknown.

Because the flow at the time interval is assumed to be a quasi-steady state, it can be approximated with sufficient accuracy by way of Darcy's law. The hydraulic gradient at the element 1 bis I, which follows from the next line

$$Q = F K I = F K \frac{\Delta h}{s} \approx F K \frac{\Delta h}{l} \qquad (4)$$

In accordance with the assumptions by Dupuit-Forchheimer, s, the actual flow path was replaced in equation (4) by l, the horizontal distance (Figure 8).

To obtain Δh as a good approximation, Q and F in equation (4) must be substituted by the mean of Q_O and Q_1, F_O and F_1 respectively. Rearranging this equation and solving for Δh yields

$$\Delta h = \frac{Q_m}{F_m} \frac{l}{K} \qquad (5)$$

Knowing Δh, one can compute h_1 in equation (3). Then, the values of h_2, h_3, etc can be found by using the same method. The curve which smoothly matches all the points is the water table position at the yet unknown time interval t.

As a matter of fact, the first estimate of the rate of withdrawal from storage between the area elements is usually far from accurate. Then, the water table line, constructed as described, will not be a smoothly running curve but will be jagged. Usually, the smooth line which is also hydraulically logical, will not be obtained until the rate of withdrawal from storage has been split up tentatively three or four times between the area elements of the segment of Figure 8. A jagged curve always indicates a wrong distribution.

Figure 9 shows the real drawdowns and, for comparison, the drawdowns as computed by the Siemon method in the major aquifer of the northern part of the Erft Basin. Figure 10 explains the differences between the calculated and real drawdown in the centre of a discharging battery of wells as a result of differences between computed and actual rates of discharge.

3.6.3.4.3.3 Computation of time of drawdown. Having determined the water table gradient, the hydrologist has now to compute the increment of time, Δt_1, between the old and the new curve.

To achieve a drawdown between steps n-1 and n, the rate of discharge from storage was Q_{VOn}, and to proceed from n to n+1, it was $Q_{VO(n+1)}$. The mean is

$$Q_{VOm} = \frac{Q_{VOn} + Q_{VO(n+1)}}{2}$$

Assuming an average specific yield S_Y for the whole dewatered volume, ΔV, of the aquifer

$$Q_{VOm} \Delta t_1 = S_Y \Delta V$$

and (6)

$$\Delta t_1 = \frac{S_Y \Delta V}{Q_{VOm}}$$

Δt_1 being the time required by the water table to drop from stage n to stage n+1. The rate of withdrawal from storage at the time the aquifer is still confined is comparatively small and can, therefore, be neglected.

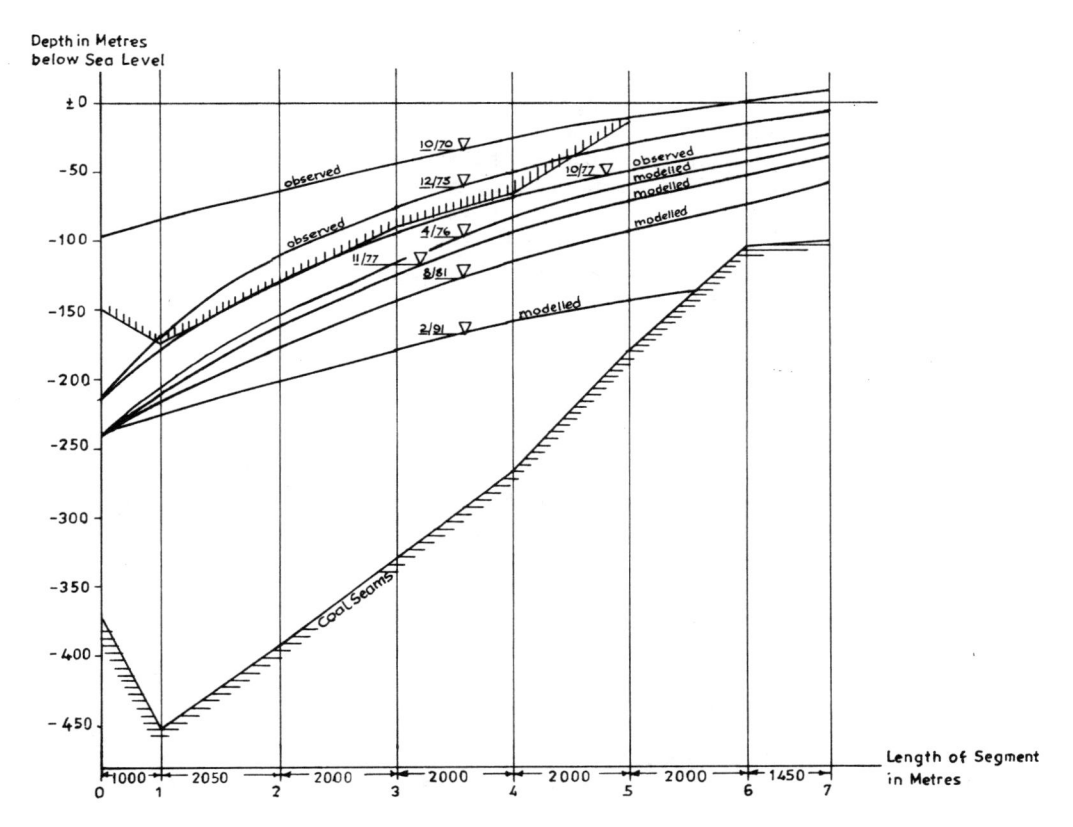

Figure 9 Modelled (computed) and observed drawdowns in the major aquifer of the
Northern Erft basin. The observed drawdown of October 1977 falls remarkably
short of the drawdown as computed for November 1977. The explanation is
given in Figure 10

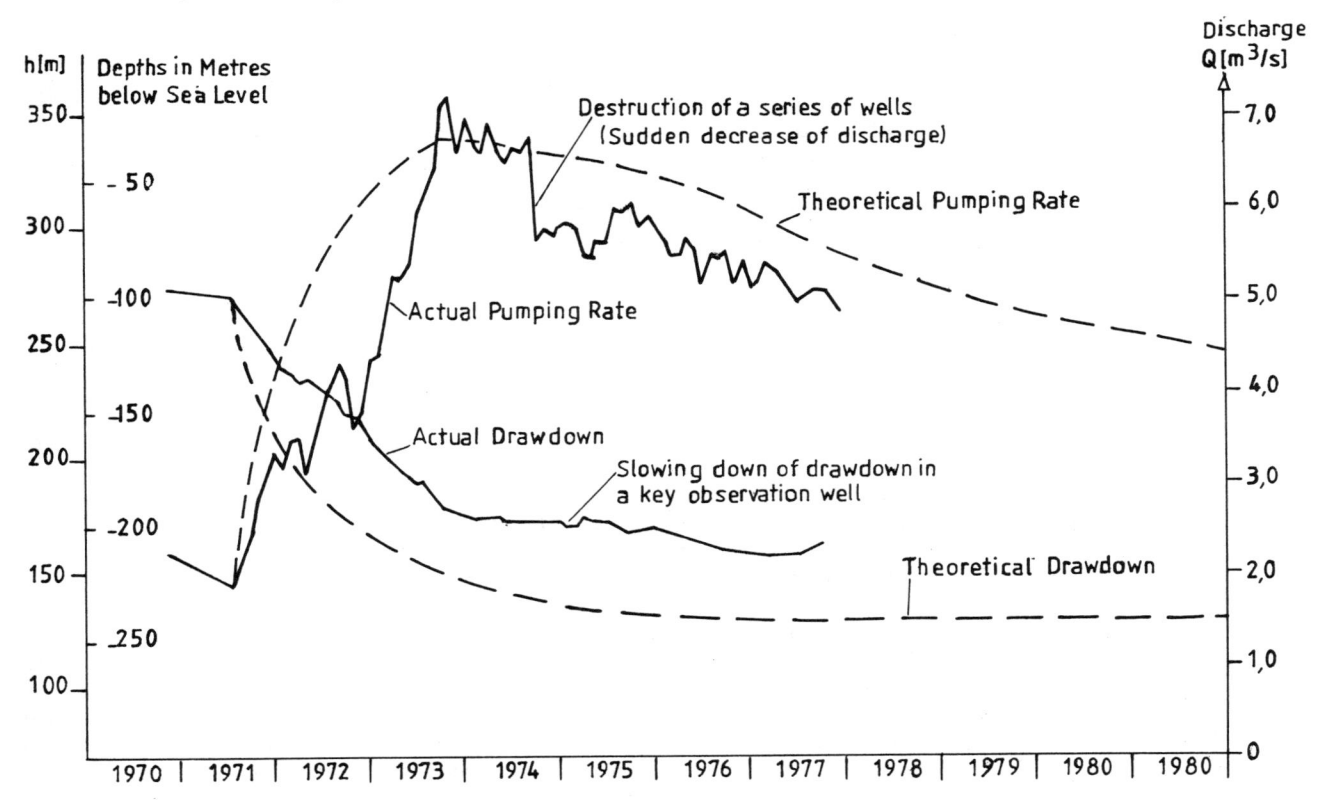

Figure 10 Pumping rates of a battery of discharging wells and drawdown in an
observation well near the centre of the battery. Dotted lines indicate
the computed rates of discharge and drawdown, full lines the actual ones.
Due to the destruction of wells which could not be made up for, the required
drawdown could not be achieved in the given time

3.6.3.4.3.4 Design of batteries of discharging wells and of single wells. Quite contrary to the conditions at some distance from the wells, where the vertical flow components are considered negligible, this is not true in the immediate vicinity of a discharging dewatering well. There, the vertical component of flow must be taken into account to properly design the well.

According to Sichardt (1928), the maximum velocity and, therefore, the maximum flow of groundwater towards a discharging well in a sandy-gravely aquifer will be achieved when the specific flow v_{max} can be described as

$$v_{max} = K\ I_{max} = K\ \frac{1}{\sqrt{15K}} \tag{7}$$

where: K is coefficient of hydraulic conductivity.

This empirically determined equation is dimensionally incorrect, but it can be used as a more or less good approximation to determine the possible maximum discharge of a well against which water flows with a strong vertical component (Siemon, 1958). Then we have:

$$Q_{max} = F\ v_{max} = 2\ \pi\ r_W\ h_W\ \frac{\sqrt{K}}{15} = \phi\ h_W \tag{8}$$

where: Q_{max} is maximum capacity of well at height of water table, h_0, at the effective radius of well, r_W, in m^3/s; ϕ is "coefficient of capacity", in m^2/s.

Equation (8) shows that Q_{max} varies as a function of ϕ and h_W. A prerequisite is, of course, that the aquifer will yield the rate of water the well can discharge.

The discharge of a whole battery of wells totals Q_0, as indicated in paragraph 3.4.3.4.3.1. If Q_0 is the maximum capacity of the battery and h_0 the height of water table in its centre (which is to replace the term effective radius of a single well), then

$$Q_0 = \phi_{Batt}\ h_0$$

and

$$\phi_{Batt} = \frac{Q_0}{h_0} \tag{9}$$

where: ϕ_{Batt} is the coefficient of capacity of the discharging battery, in m^2/s.

This coefficient of capacity, ϕ_{Batt}, is of only limited value. Hydraulic conductivity of the tapped aquifer may vary at short distances, the wells themselves will not be identically developed etc - in fact, the real capacity of any discharging battery of wells will fall short of its theoretical capacity.

Experiences in the Rhenish Lignite Mining District have shown that the real maximum capacity ϕ_{real} is ϕ_{Batt} times a factor $0.7 < \eta < 0.9$.

$$\phi_{real} = \eta\ \phi_{Batt} = \eta\ \frac{Q_0}{h_0}$$

The number of wells, n, that are needed to lift the required total discharge, Q_0, amounts, therefore, to

$$n = \eta\ \frac{Q_0}{\phi\ h_0} = \frac{\phi_{real}}{\phi} \tag{10}$$

where: ϕ is coefficient of capacity of the single well.

The final step of the computation is selection of the proper submersible pumps which will be employed successfully in the wells. This job requires special care because the capacity of the pumps must exceed neither the maximum yield of the aquifer nor the maximum capacity of the well. Both will vary as a function of the drawdown. Long experience in selecting suitable pumps has been proven indispensable (Voigt, 1976).

3.6.3.4.4   Hybrid model, Erft Basin. The Erft Block or Erft Basin (Figure 1) is, with respect to groundwater resources, one of the most important tectonic structures of the Rhenish Lignite Mining District. To enable overall planning of the dewatering measures especially for the new Hambach mine throughout the next 60 years while, at the same time, conserving the remaining groundwater resources as much as possible, this model was ordered by the Rheinbraun Company. Because the work is not yet finished, only general information is given here, which is based mainly on a report given by Billib, Hoffmann, Fredrich, Klenke (1976).

The Erft Basin is a major dip and fault structure which is almost completely bounded by faults (Figures 1 and 2). It forms an irregular triangle with a maximum length of about 50 km in a NW-SE direction and a maximum width of 15 km perpendicular to it. There is a whole sequence of confining and water bearing strata on top of the main seam, the reactions of which to several possible dewatering schemes were to be investigated by means of the multiple-aquifer model.

The hybrid model comprises a digital and an analog part. To simulate the distribution of heads in the aquifers, an active analog computer is employed. The digital computer, on the other hand, executes the numerical computations and controls any run. The results of a run are discrete values of head as a function of time at each node of the discrete multiple-aquifer system.

To obtain a practical model it proved necessary to reduce the diversity of water bearing and confining strata to a system consisting of four water bearing units which are separated from each other by three confining or less permeable units. The flow of groundwater in any of the four aquifer units is assumed to be horizontal. Figure 11 reflects this in a vertical cross section. Any of the four aquifers can analogously be simulated as confined, as partly saturated, and as completely dewatered. There, where the less permeable beds pinch out or are hydraulically not effective, the lattice-points A through H are also kept (right side of Figure 11).

The whole Erft Basin was represented by approximately 600 nodes, which form a grid consisting of triangles. The vertical line beneath each node intersects all strata at the points A to H. These discrete points characterize finite elements of the strata involved. Figure 12 depicts such an element characterized by point B. A special identification is used to make the volume element as being confined, as being partly confined or as being fully depleted.

The following data were used to calibrate the model:
- recharge and discharge boundaries of the Erft Basin,
- precipitation and runoff,
- blocking factors of tectonic faults,
- discharge rates of wells,
- thicknesses of water bearing and confining strata
- values of hydraulic conductivity of all strata
- values of storage coefficients, and of specific yields, respectively.
- contour line maps of water tables and potentiometric surfaces of the four aquifer units since 1955.

The model now aims at the following points of interest:
- determination of the optimum mode of operation of the already existing batteries of wells in the Erft Basin,
- localization of sites, where, and determination of time, when, new wells will be sunk,
- evaluation of the effects that will show in the multiple aquifer system when drawdowns continue in some aquifers and partial recoveries occur in others. (This will be the case when the centres of pumping move along with the centres of mining.)

A series of papers will be published later which focus on the problems arising during calibration and modelling of future flow conditions.

3.6.3.5 Use of discharging groundwater

The total discharge of groundwater throughout the coming decades will, in all probability, greatly exceed the water demands of the public, the industry, and agriculture in the region affected. Despite the expected decrease of discharge in the late eighties of this century, the water supply is not likely to fail by the end of this century.

Right now, it is impossible to use consumptively more than fifteen per cent of the pumped water. Out of the total annual pumping rate of 1.2×10^9 m^3, about 60×10^6 m^3/a is delivered to customers whose groundwater resources were depleted by the drawdown. 90×10^6 m^3/a are pumped to industrial users, such as thermal power plants which need cooling water. Since 1975, a 30 km long aqueduct links the major cities of Düsseldorf and Neuss with the mining district and provides the people there with 30×10^6 m^3/a top quality groundwater.

Irrigation of agricultural areas has been of no importance in this part of Germany in the

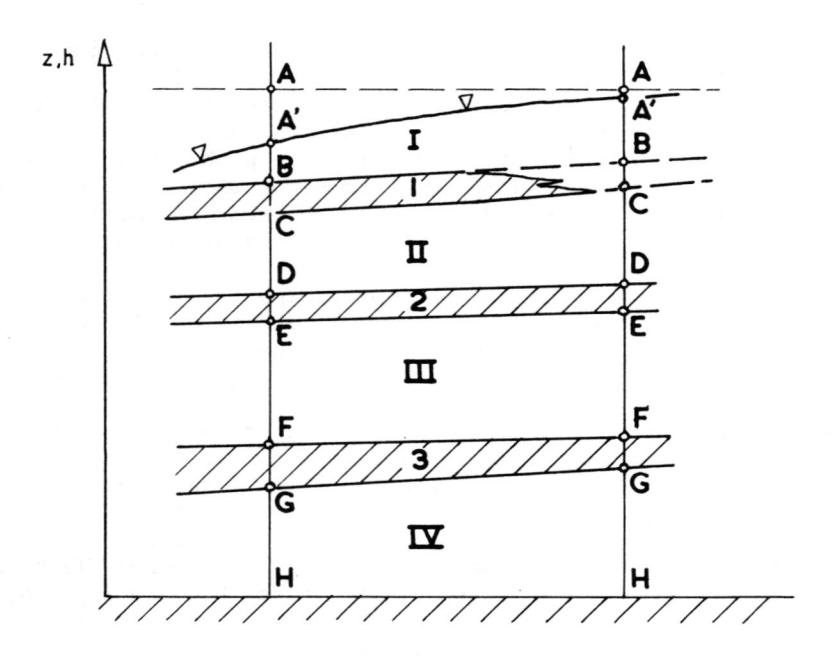

Figure 11 Schematic cross-section of the four aquifers and three confining units of the hybrid model of the Erft basin

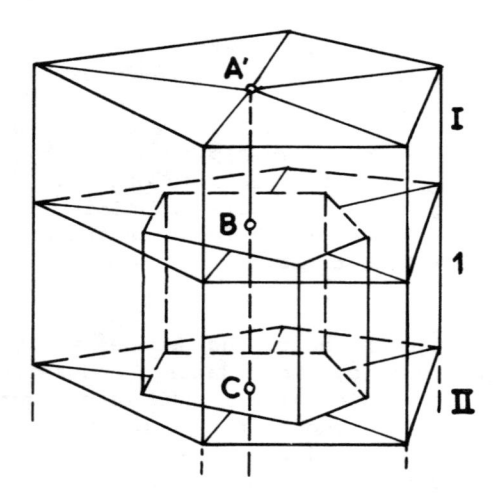

Figure 12 Diagram showing the volumetric element of confining unit 1, as characterized by lattice point B

past. High moisture capacities of the prevailing loess top soils and medium to high rates of precipitation render farming independent of additionally applied water.

So far, quality of the pumped water has been satisfactory. Temperatures and the contents of iron, manganese, and carbon dioxide have increased, to be sure, but remain within tolerable limits. In the years to come, water temperatures will become higher because the portion of water lifted from greater depths will rise. This means that in future a separation of water of significantly different temperatures will be required to preserve the cold water for domestic and industrial supplies.

All surplus water from the wells is piped to receiving water courses, most of it directly or via its tributaries into the Erft River, which flows into the River Rhine. This stream with an average flow of 6 m^3/s had to be sealed against water losses and widened for handling an average flow of 30 m^3/s in its lower reaches. Because even this proved not sufficient to safely discharge temporary peak pumping rates and natural floods, a 22 km canal links the Erft directly with the River Rhine just north of Cologne. This Cologne Perimeter Canal carries a flow of up to 18 m^3/s.

At the end of lignite mining in the distant future, some open holes will remain which will account for the cumulative losses of the volume of coal and overburden, the latter having been stacked at outside dumps. The largest of these holes will be that of the Hamback mine. There is already a definite plan for turning this hole into an artificial lake by piping treated water from the Rhine River through a tunnel (Gärtner, 1968). The new lake, which will eventually contain 2.5×10^9 cubic metres of water, will also recharge the depleted aquifers of the Erft Basin. The careful management of this new water body will secure the water supply for future generations.

3.6.3.6 Conclusions

Mining of lignite in deep open pits results in a thorough, mostly long-lasting disturbance of groundwater conditions in and around the Rhenish Mining District. The experience that has been gained through more than twenty years show clearly, however, that by co-operation between a mining company and all state agencies involved all problems can be mastered and the inevitable damage can at least be eased.

REFERENCES

Billib, H., Hoffmann, B., Fredrich, K.J., and Klenke, M. 1976. Hybridmodell zur Prognose von Grundwasserabsenkungen im Braunkohlentagebau (Hybrid model for the prognosis of groundwater recession in lignite strip pits). *Proc IWRA Symp Wasserwirtschaft und Gewinnung Fossiler Energieträger*, Düsseldorf, 20 pp.

Blank, R. 1976. Tagebauentwässerung im Rheinischen Braunkohlenrevier mit grosskalibrigen Tiefbrunnenbohrungen und entsprechenden Tauchmotorpumpen (Strip pit drainage with deep wells of large diameter and submersible motor pump). *bbr*, Köln, 27, 87-92.

Gärtner, E. 1968. Die Ausbildung des Erftbeckens als obser- und unterirdischer Grosswasserspeicher zur zukünftigen Wasserversorgung (Development of the Erft Basin as a regional surface and subsurface water reservoir for future water supply). *Braunkohle, Wärme und Energie*, Düsseldorf, 20, 2, 37-43.

GEV (1958 onwards) Grosser Erftverband. *Annual Reports*, Bergheim.

Leuschner, H.J. 1976. The Opencast Mine of Hambach - a synthesis of mining and landscaping. *Braunkohle, Tagebautechnik, Energieversorgung*, Düsseldorf, 28, 5, 4-18.

Sichardt, W. 1928. *Das Fassungsvermögen von Rohrbrunnen und seine Bedeutung fur die Grundwasserabsenkung, insbesondere fur grössere Absenkungstiefen* (Capacity of tube wells and its significance for groundwater recession, in particular for large recession depths). Julius Springer Verlag, Berlin.

Siemon, H. 1958. *Berechnung von Grundwasserabsenkungen unter Berücksichtigung des Grundwasserhaushaltes* (Computation of groundwater recession depth, taking into account the groundwater budget). Min f Ernährung, Landwirtschaft und Forsten des Landes Nordrhein-

References

Westfalen, Düsseldorf, 72 pp.

Siemon, H. and Voigt, R. 1976. Planung und Berechnung der grossräumigen Grundwasser-Absenkungsmassnahmen im Rheinischen Braunkohlenrevier (Planning and computation of regional groundwater recession measures in the Rhenanian lignite mining district). *Proc IWRA Symp Wasserwirtschaft und Gewinnung Fossiler Energieträger*, Düsseldorf, 20 pp.

Stein, A. 1977. Tagebau Hambach und Umwelt - Wasserwirtschaft (Strip mining at Hambach, and the environment). *Geolog Landesamt Nordrhein-Westfalen,* Krefeld, 85-125.

Voigt, R. 1976. Evaluation of geologic, hydrologic, and geomechanic properties controlling future open pit mining. *Proc first Int Coal Exploration Symp,* London, 1976, Miller-Freeman, San Francisco, Calif, 296-323.

Bibliography

Lindner, W., and Stein, A. 1976. Wasserwirtschaft und Braunkohlenbergbau im Erftgebiet (Water management and lignite mining in the Erft Basin). *Proc IWRA Symp Wasserwirtschaft und Gewinnung Fossiler Energieträger*, Düsseldorf, 20 pp.

3.6.4 A PARALLEL CASCADES MODEL TO PREDICT THE EFFECTS OF URBANIZATION ON WATERSHED RESPONSE
by Hartmut Wittenberg[1]

3.6.4.1 Introduction

When natural or agricultural basins are urbanized and covered with buildings, roads, or parking areas, infiltration of rainfall is decreased while its concentration to runoff is accelerated. The path of surface flow to the stream is shortened by sewer systems. Thereby, the part of rainfall which is converted to direct runoff increases, resulting in flood hydrographs of steeper and shorter shape.

This fact has formed the basis of all design methods for urban storm drainage structures. Increasing urbanization in the densely populated areas of the world, however, make it more and more necessary to consider these influences on river runoff.

It was therefore the aim of a research study at the Institut Wasserbau III at the University of Karlsruhe in Germany to analyse the effects of growth of urban areas and to develop a suitable model for predicting the change in basin responses (Wittenberg, 1974).

3.6.4.2 Choice of a suitable rainfall-runoff model

Reliable conclusions about catchment behaviour can only be obtained by the analysis of measured rainfall and runoff data with a hydrological model. Changes in model parameters found for a catchment at different stages of urbanization, for example, may be explored and compared with statistical data.

As a matter of principle, linear and time invariant models or model components were used in this study. Besides favourable conditions for mathematical treatment and computation, these methods make it possible directly to compare the behaviour of a system as expressed in the response functions and to identify influences simply by assuming superposition of different components.

Linear models with a single response function have been applied by a number of investigations (Crippen, 1965, Rao, Delleur and Sarma, 1972, Hall, 1973) to detect changes in runoff due to urbanization.

Thus as a preliminary investigation, the most general linear unit-hydrograph model was applied to rainfall-runoff data from urbanizing basins to be described later. In all linear time invariant systems, the relation between input $I(t)$ and output $Q(t)$ is given by the convolution integral:

$$Q(t) = \int_0^t I(\tau) \cdot h(t-\tau) \, d\tau \tag{1}$$

in which h is the unit-response function characterizing the system's behaviour.

---

[1] Salzgitter Consult GmbH, Consulting Engineers, 3320 Salzgitter 41, Federal Republic of Germany

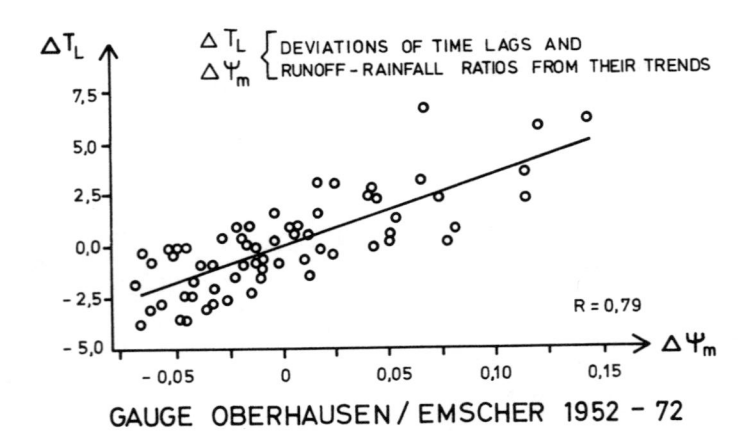

Figure 1   Effect of urbanization on the average unit hydrograph

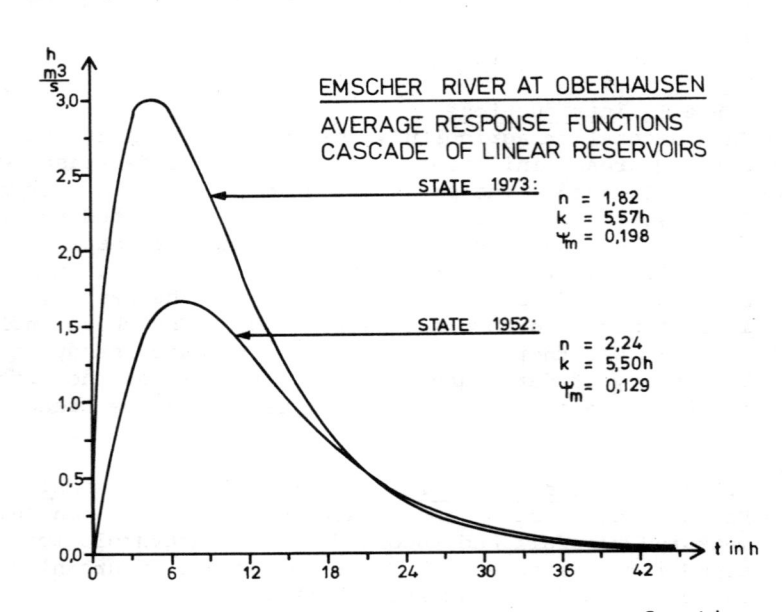

Figure 2   Effect of urbanization on average response function

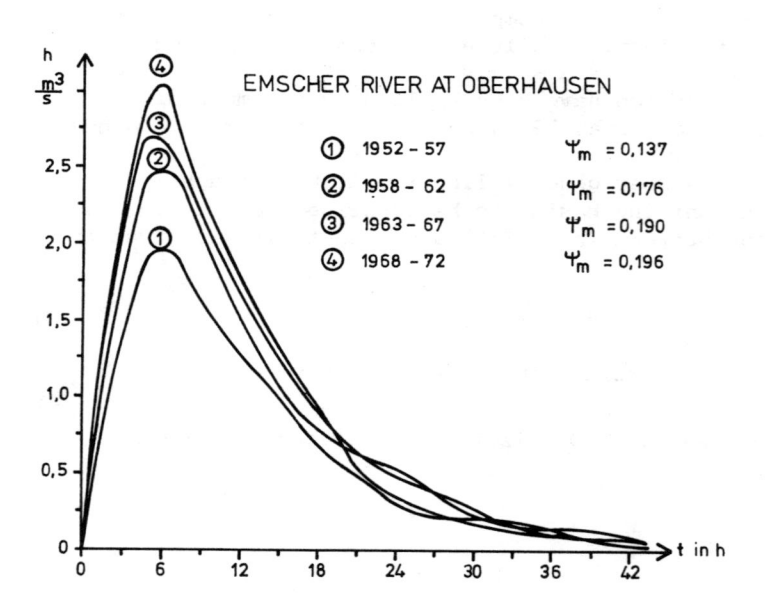

Figure 3   Relation between time lag and runoff-rainfall ratio

For practical computations, the functions Q, I and h are expressed in discrete values. Given rainfall and runoff data, unit hydrographs can be computed by the least squares method. This was done here also with an algorithm including an optimized baseflow separation and rainfall loss. The details of this data treatment are discussed elsewhere (Wittenberg, 1974).

The unit hydrographs computed for the individual events show considerable differences mainly in their falling limbs, while differences in peak-time are not important. The latter effect results because the runoff from impervious areas, which is relatively quick and stable in its characteristics, mainly shapes the rising limbs of the hydrographs. The falling limbs, however, essentially characterize the behaviour of the natural areas. The differences occurring here are caused mainly by large variations of rainfall excess rate due to soil conditions.

To get a general picture of the temporal development of catchment behaviour, 76 unitgraphs obtained for the Emscher River at Oberhausen were averaged for 4 time intervals as illustrated in Figure 1. Falling limbs of the average unitgraphs are indicative of the mean runoff behaviour of pervious areas, which essentially remains unchanged. The peak value, however, increases with time, while peak-time does not change significantly. Thus, while runoff from impervious areas is increasing, it does not change its characteristics. As stated in Figure 1, the average ratio m between total storm runoff and total rainfall is increasing systematically.

Although yielding the best possible response of a linear system, the discrete unit hydrograph is hardly suitable for physical interpretation. For this reason, it has to be replaced by a mathematical model function. As a first approximation, the cascade of identical linear reservoirs (Nash, 1957) was applied. Its response function is given by:

$$h(t) = \frac{t^{(n-1)}}{k^n \Gamma(n)} \cdot e^{-t/k} \tag{2}$$

in which n is the number of reservoirs with the identical reservoir constant k. Parameters were fitted for the runoff events used in Figure 1 by a least-squares method, which is described below. The results are equivalent to those obtained by the general unitgraph analysis. Figure 2 shows the mean response functions, one corresponding to the beginning, the other to the end of the observed time interval, the parameters of which were obtained by trend analysis of the fitted values.

Corresponding to the unitgraph shapes, individual parameter values show very large variations. Other investigators obtained very similar results and tried to relate variations, such as with time lag, to physiographic and storm characteristics (Rao, Delleur and Sarma, 1972). It can be concluded, however, that they are the result of a varying combination of two separate runoff components, one from pervious and one from impervious areas. This conclusion is in agreement with observations of the Emscher Water Authority (Annen and Schoss, 1972), and is confirmed by the regression shown in Figure 3. For the rainfall-runoff events mentioned above, deviations of lag-time values ΔT_L from their temporal mean calculated by trend analysis were related to corresponding deviations of runoff-rainfall ratio $\Delta \psi m$. The relatively high correlation coefficient $r = 0.79$ indicates the strong relation between values of $\Delta \psi m$ and the contribution of pervious, slower reacting areas to runoff which results in increasing time lag.

The consequence of the observations made during these preliminary investigations was to apply a two-component model for urban runoff simulation. As the cascade of linear reservoirs has proved its value in modelling homogeneous runoff behaviour, two cascades were combined to describe the present situation. Such a model was first used to divide direct runoff into surface and sub-surface flow (Diskin, 1964). Effective rainfall was split proportionally to enter the two subsystems. In contrast to this concept a modification was required for urban runoff simulation because the hydrological system is not subdivided vertically, but horizontally. Both subsystems, corresponding to pervious and impervious areas, receive the same total rainfall, but release it in different quantities and rates. The different loss rates of the subsystems are of special importance. Impervious sewered areas show only small initial losses for wetting and depression storage. For the catchments investigated, an average value of 1 mm can be assumed (Annen and Schoss, 1972). After that, almost all the rainfall is transformed into runoff. The determination

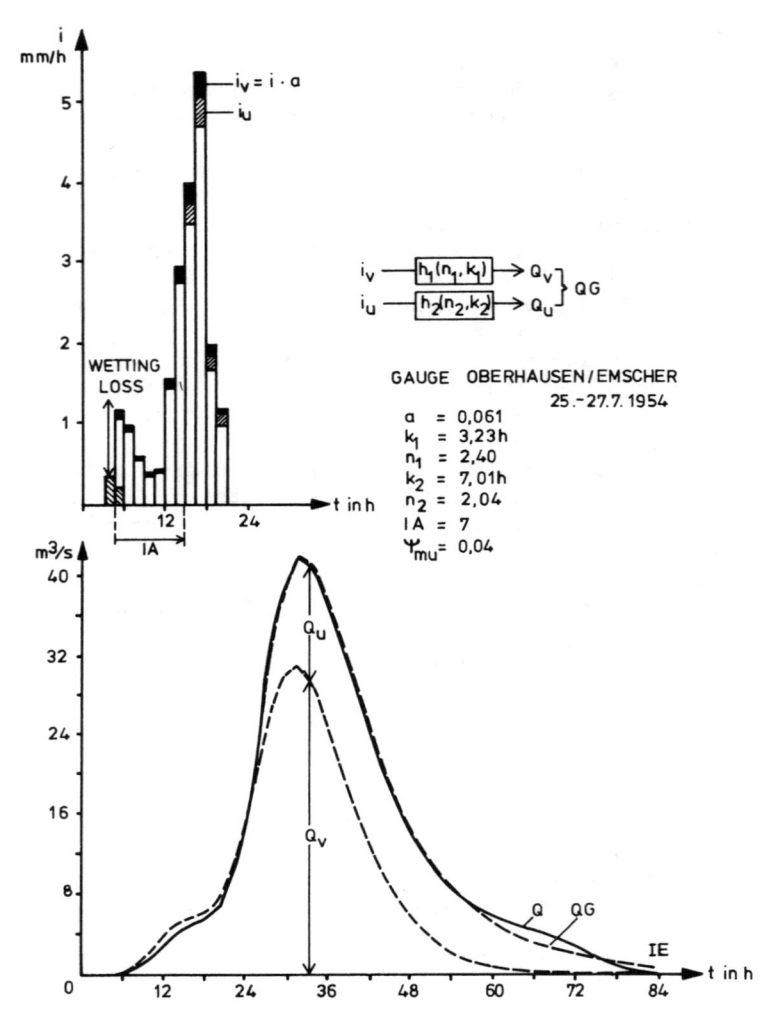

Figure 4 Application of the modified double-cascade model

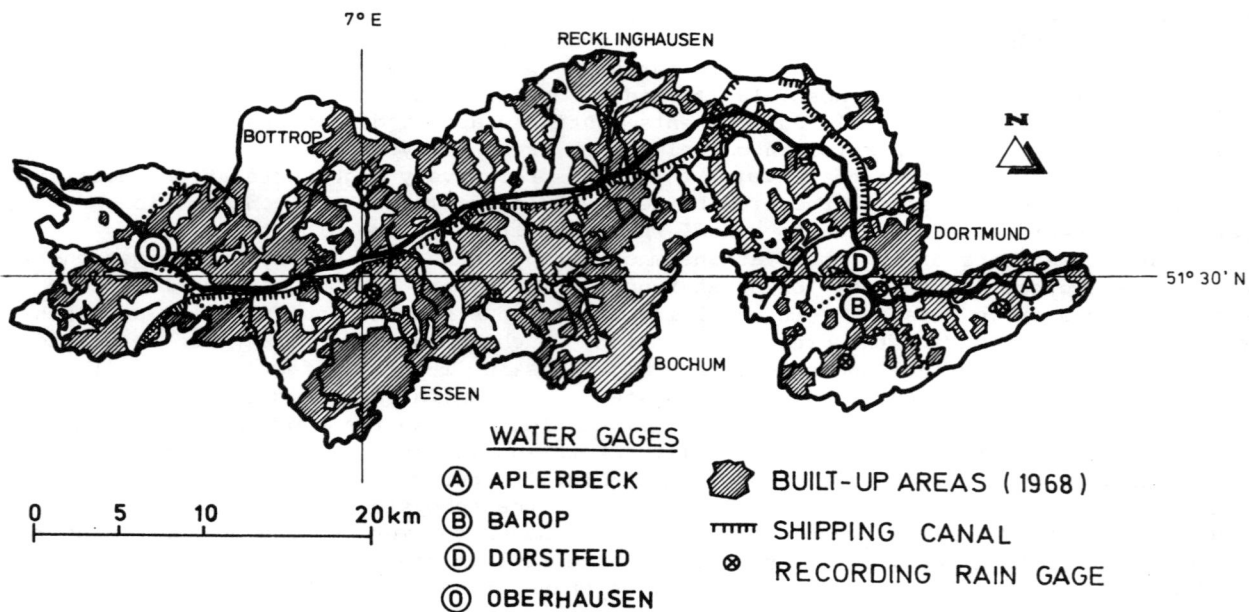

Figure 5 The Emscher basin

of loss rates on pervious areas is more complicated. Good results were obtained by using the following procedure: All rain up to a certain time is lost by infiltration and saturation of soil, depending on its initial conditions. After this, a certain fixed percentage of the rainfall will become direct runoff. The appropriate model is illustrated in Figure 4.

After separation of wetting loss, a percentage, a, of the total hyetograph, i, corresponding to the impervious portion of the catchment, is transformed by the first cascade, h_1. Parameter IA expresses the number of time steps until the beginning of effective rainfall on pervious areas. This excess rain, i_u, is proportional to the total intensity, satisfies the continuity equation and is transformed by the second cascade, h_2. Although the transforming model is completely linear, nonlinear effects in the runoff process can be described by the derivation of different loss rates for the two subsystems. The mathematical formulation of the model is given by the following equations in which I(t) is i(t), transformed into m^3/s.

3.6.4.2.1 Effective rainfall. Impervious areas:

$$I_v(t) = I(t) \cdot a \tag{3}$$

Pervious areas:

$$t < IA : I_u(t) = 0 \tag{4a}$$

$$t \geq IA : I_u(t) = I(t) \cdot \frac{\int_{IA}^{IE} Q(t)dt}{\int_{IA}^{IE} I(t)dt} - I_v(t) \tag{4b}$$

3.6.4.2.2 Direct runoff. Impervious areas:

$$Q_v(t) = \int_0^t I_v(t) \cdot h_1(t-\tau) \, d\tau \tag{5}$$

Pervious areas:

$$Q_u(t) = \int_0^t I_u(t) \cdot h_2(t-\tau) \, d\tau \tag{6}$$

Computed runoff:

$$QG(t) = Q_v(t) + Q_u(t) \tag{7}$$

Each response function h_1 and h_2 is one cascade of linear reservoirs as given in Equation (2). Thus, there are 6 free parameters to be determined for every event, namely a, k_1, n_1 k_2, n_2 and IA. ψμ denotes the ratio between runoff from pervious areas and total rainfall.

3.6.4.3 <u>Method of parameter fitting</u>
After trying some other methods, a computer program was written using nonlinear least-squares optimization to estimate model parameters. As underlying principles are described, elsewhere (McCuen, 1973; Snyder, 1972), only the main details of the present application are given here.

The difference between corresponding values of a given function Y and the model function YG depending on its parameters $P_1....m$ at the location k can be expressed

$$\Delta Y_k = Y_k - YG_k = \frac{\delta YG_k}{\delta P_1} \Delta P_1 + \frac{\delta YG_k}{\delta P_2} \Delta P_2 + \ldots \frac{\delta YG_k}{\delta P_m} \Delta P_m \tag{8}$$

The partial derivatives $\delta YG_k / P_i$, called sensitivities, are given for the cascade of linear reservoirs by:

$$\frac{\delta h(t)}{\delta k} = \frac{t^{n-1} e^{-t/k}(t - n \cdot k)}{k^n \Gamma(n) k^2} = \frac{h(t)(t - n \cdot k)}{k^2} \tag{9}$$

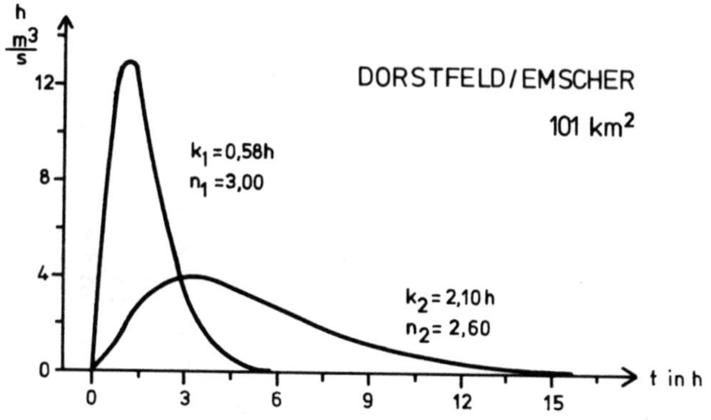

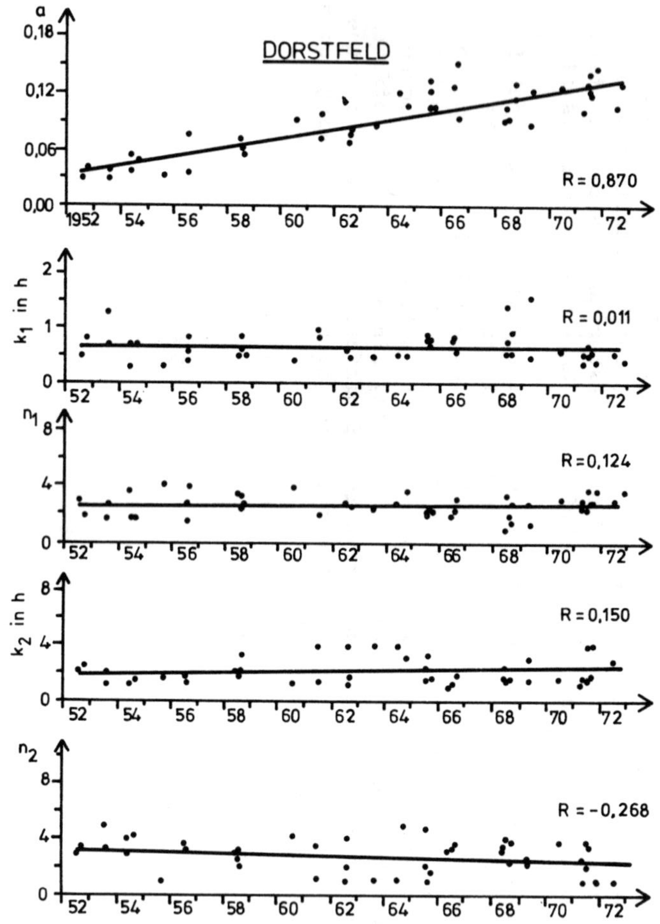

Figure 7 Responses to 1 mm effective rainfall of catchment in impervious and pervious state

Figure 6 Optimized parameters

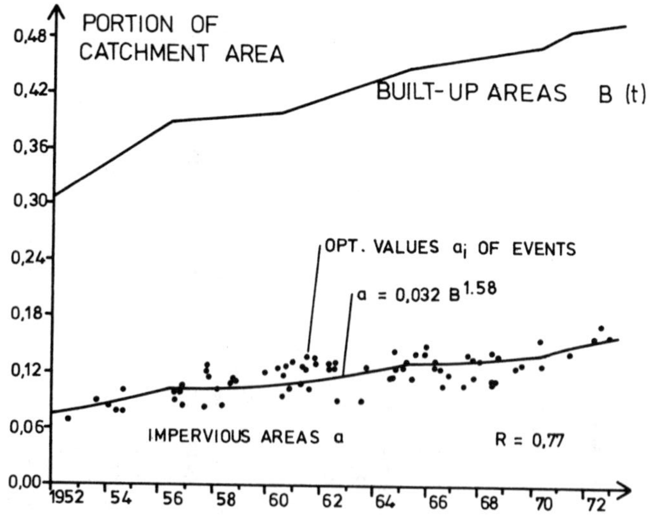

Figure 8 Temporal changing of built-up and impervious areas, Emscher catchment

$$\frac{\delta h(t)}{\delta n} = \frac{t^{n-1}e^{-t/k}(\ln(t/k) - \Gamma'(n)/\Gamma(n))}{k^n \Gamma(n)} = h(t)(\ln(t/k) - \frac{\Gamma'(n)}{\Gamma(n)}) \qquad (10)$$

Hence, for the double cascade model:

for $t < IA$:

$$\frac{\delta QG(t)}{\delta a} = \int_0^t I(t) h_1(t-\tau) \, d\tau \qquad (11)$$

for $t \geq IA$:

$$\frac{\delta QG(t)}{\delta a} = \int_0^t I(t) h_1(t-\tau) \, d\tau - \int_0^t I(t) h_2(t-\tau) \, d\tau \qquad (12)$$

for $t > 0$:

$$\frac{\delta QG(t)}{\delta k_1} = \int_0^t I_v(t) \frac{\delta h_1(t-\tau)}{\delta k_1} \, d\tau \qquad (13)$$

$$\frac{\delta QG(t)}{\delta n_1} = \int_0^t I_v(t) \frac{\delta h_1(t-\tau)}{\delta n_1} \, d\tau \qquad (14)$$

$$\frac{\delta QG(t)}{\delta k_2} = \int_0^t I_u(t) \frac{\delta h_2(t-\tau)}{\delta k_2} \, d\tau \qquad (15)$$

$$\frac{\delta QG(t)}{\delta n_2} = \int_0^t I_u(t) \frac{\delta h_2(t-\tau)}{\delta n_2} \, d\tau \qquad (16)$$

Equation 8 is given for every digital value of the hydrograph to be fitted. As it is in linear form, multiple regression can be used to obtain values of ΔP. Starting from an initial assumed set of P_i, new estimates of the parameters are given by $P_i + \Delta P_i$. The process is repeated and continued until an arbitrary test level is reached. The parameter IA, which can only have integral values is not determined by this approach, but varied in an adequate range. For each value IA an optimal set of the other 5 parameters is computed. The set yielding the best fit to the given hydrograph is considered to be representative. Besides this principal procedure a number of subroutines was necessary to manage optimization problems.

3.6.4.4 Data used and watersheds

The model was first tested by using rainfall-runoff data from 4 water level recorders and 6 raingauges of the Emscher river system, a tributary of the Rhine. This basin, shown in Figure 5, is situated in the densely populated and industrialized Ruhr district in West Germany. Its altitude is some 200 m above msl and the average annual precipitation about 800 mm. While during dry weather periods a big portion of runoff in the canalized river beds consists of waste water, critical floods are caused by intense rainfalls normally occurring in summer. During the period of observations, from 1952-1972, the proportion of built-up areas increased from about 30 to 50% (s. Figure 8). Some further details such as catchment area A (km), length L (km) and slope S, the average slope of the main channel from the watershed border to the gauging site in parts per 1000 are given in Table 1.

In column Δt digitization intervals of the data are given. Rainfall events were tested by trend analysis and found to be stationary.

A parallel cascades model

TABLE 1   Details of data analysed

Gauge	River	A km²	L km	S %	Events used	Δt h
Oberhausen	Emscher	773	74	0.96	80	1.5
Dorstfeld	Emscher	101	18	2.64	47	0.5
Barop	Rüpingsbach	36	9	6.92	37	0.5
Aplerbeck	Emscher	11.8	7.1	8.21	31	0.5

3.6.4.5   Results

Optimal parameters of the double-cascade model were evaluated for all rainfall-runoff events as demonstrated in Figure 4. For each watershed, the values were checked by linear regression to determine whether there was a temporal trend or not. As a criterion of the significance, the correlation coefficient r was used. Figure 6 shows parameters for the events of one catchment plotted against time with best fit straight lines determined by linear regression. The results are identical for all 4 catchments: The two response functions determined by the parameters k_1, n_1, k_2 and n_2 do not change significantly. However, the parameter, a, which determines the portion of impervious areas increases systematically in all cases.

An additional analysis for parameter dependences was made. As parameter sensitivities are correlated, parameter deviations from the trend, due to random noise, are often intensified considerably. The response parameters k_1, n_1, k_2 and n_2 were therefore set constant and the remaining free parameters, a and IA, optimized again. The excellent reproductions of measured hydrographs indicate that the parameters obtained are characteristic for their respective hydrological systems. They are listed in Table 2. Using the response parameters, it is possible to construct theoretical responses both for natural and for fully impervious conditions (Figure 7). Thus, with the present model influences of urbanization on catchment behaviour can be related to only one parameter, namely a. The values obtained for this factor were now compared with statistical data from built-up areas, B. This is illustrated in Figure 8. The function found to represent the best relation between a and B leads to the curved line.

TABLE 2   Parameters of double-cascade model.

Gauge	a 1952	a 1973	k_1 (h)	n_1	k_2 (h)	n_2	r a/Time
Oberhausen	0.08	0.15	3.29	2.46	5.58	3.69	0.74
Dorstfeld	0.04	0.13	0.58	3.00	2.10	2.60	0.81
Barop	0.03	0.16	0.62	2.41	1.90	2.70	0.86
Aplerbeck	0.03	0.13	0.52	1.95	1.90	2.50	0.85

An intensive study was carried out recently for a number of sub-catchments of the Emscher River (Schoss, 1977) to determine the proportion of directly sewered impervious areas by examination of 1:25,000 survey maps. For purposes of comparison, the computer program described above was used to evaluate the parameter a of the parallel cascades model for at least 10 measured floods for six catchments. The results are given in Table 3 and they demonstrate that the parameter a represents indeed the degree of imperviousness.

TABLE 3   Comparison of values a

Basin	Area in km²	Values of parameter a Survey maps	Cascade model
Körne km 1.5	109.0	0.125	0.150
Körne km 9.9	29.0	0.261	0.269
Hüller Mühlenbach	31.7	0.336	0.321
Berne	18.6	0.439	0.390
Landwehrbach	12.3	0.142	0.137
Luserbach	8.6	0.078	0.086

3.6.4.6   Applications

The appropriateness of the present model to identify the two main components of storm runoff from urbanized basins was confirmed by the present investigations as well as by recent applications in the same region (Schoss, 1977; Anderl and Stalmann, 1979), in South-West Germany (Schmidt and Plate, 1977) and Arizona, USA (Diskin, Ince and Oben-Nyarko, 1978). In addition, the model can be used for forecasting and prediction of floods. For direct forecasting it is necessary to know the individual conditions of natural areas, here expressed by IA and $\psi\mu$ for every event. This is a general problem in modelling of natural catchments and is only mentioned here in passing.

For the design of water resources or flood protection projects, prediction, ie information about probability of hydrological events is of special interest. The model makes it possible to transpose all historical events to a chosen degree of imperviousness as expressed by the factor a. Figure 9 illustrates this.

How the historical event would have happened at other states of imperviousness has been calculated, under the same soil conditions as given by IA and $\psi\mu$. As all events for a catchment computed for the same conditions are stationary in a statistical sense, flood characteristics can be submitted to statistical analysis. This is demonstrated in Figure 10, where frequency distributions (Pearson type III) of maximum annual floods were estimated for different states. In this manner, an impression is given of the magnitude of changes in maximum floods caused by urbanization.

3.6.4.7   Parameter derivation by regional analysis

Model parameters can be fitted by the program described above for all basins for which adequate rainfall and runoff data are available and which have already a certain degree of urbanization.

Frequently, it will be necessary, however, to calibrate the model for ungauged cross-sections of rivers and to estimate the respective parameters from catchment characteristics. As already mentioned, the portion, a, of impervious areas can be evaluated from survey maps (Schoss, 1977).

Anderl and Stalmann (1979) used runoff data from 10 stations in the Emscher and Lippe basins to establish regional relationships between the cascades' parameters and watershed properties.

After testing various equations by least squares regression, the following relations were found to yield the best fit for the data:

1. Cascade: $m_{I,1} = 0.20 \cdot A^{0.57}$ (17)

   $m'_{II,1} = k_1 = 0.38 + 0.0037 \cdot A$ (18)

2. Cascade: $m_{I,2} = 2.0 + 0.42 \cdot A^{0.57} = 2.0 + 2.1 \cdot m_{I,1}$ (19)

   $m'_{II,2} = k_2 = 3.60 \cdot A^{0.14} \cdot S^{-0.47}$ (20)

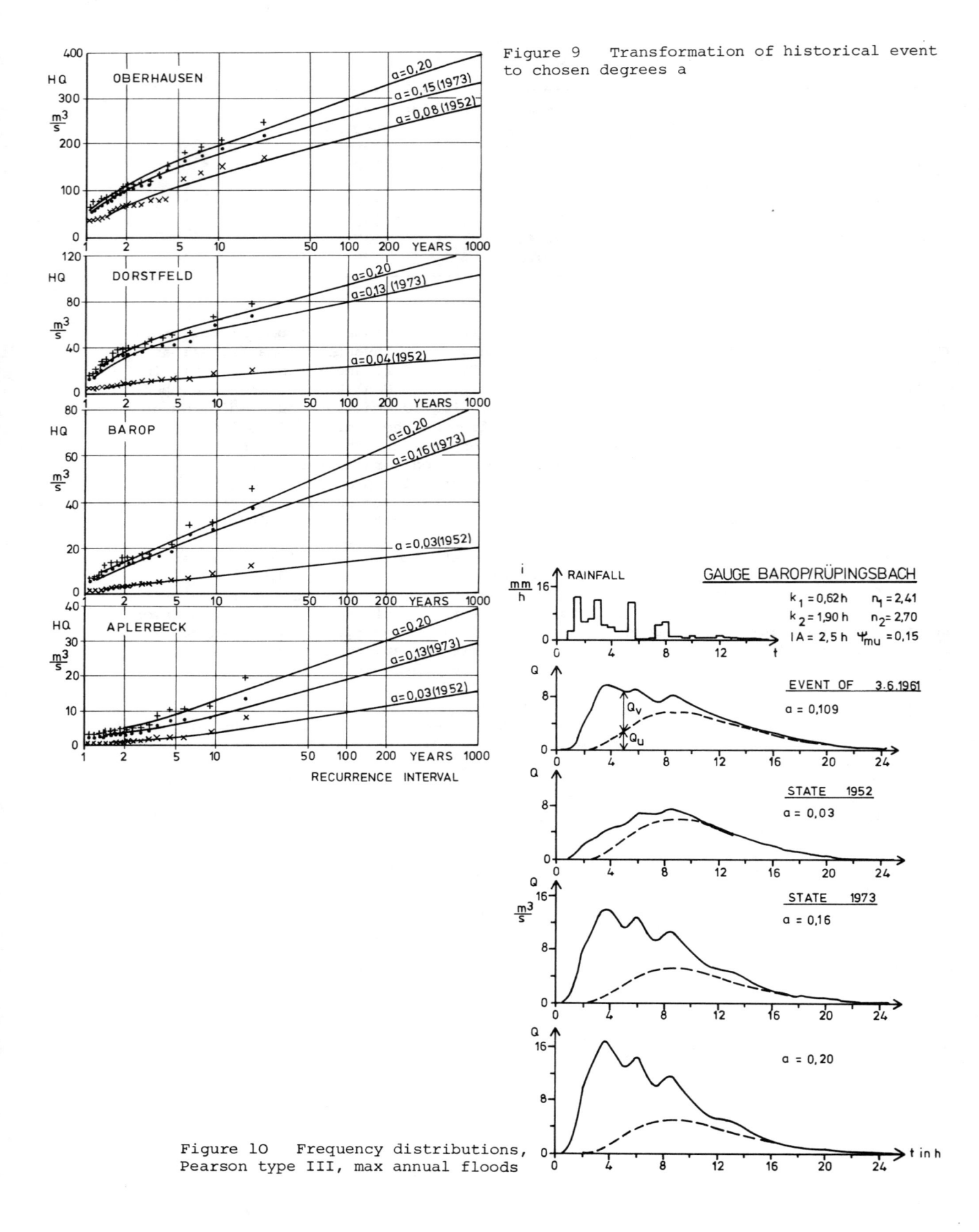

Figure 9 Transformation of historical event to chosen degrees a

Figure 10 Frequency distributions, Pearson type III, max annual floods

in which m_I and m_{II} are the first two statistical moments of the cascades which can be related to the parameters n and k as follows:

$$m_{I,i} = k \cdot n \qquad \text{in h} \tag{21}$$

$$m_{II,i} = k^2 \cdot n \qquad \text{in h} \tag{22}$$

$$m'_{II,i} = m_{II,i}/m_{I,i} = k \qquad \text{in h} \tag{23}$$

The small influence of slope S on the cascade parameters is astonishing but can be explained by the canalization of the river beds which produces a similar velocity profile along all channels independent of their actual slope.

Due to the good results the Emscher and Lippe River Authorities have adopted the Parallel Cascades Model using parameter values derived either from rainfall-runoff data or from the regional equations as a standardized method for the computation of design floods in the two basins (Anderl and Stalmann, 1979).

3.6.4.8 Conclusions

Urban runoff systems with two main subsystems corresponding to pervious and impervious areas are well simulated by a two-component model of two parallel cascades of linear reservoirs receiving different rates of effective rainfall. Increasing of urbanization in a catchment can be related to one parameter only, the portion of impervious area, while the two response functions were found to retain their appropriate parameter values. These parameter values can be determined from measured rainfall-runoff data or for ungauged rivers by regional regression equations using watershed characteristics.

3.6.4.9 Acknowledgements

This paper is a revised and extended version of an earlier publication (Wittenberg, 1975) The investigation was sponsored by the German Research Association (Deutsche Forschungsgemeinschaft). The author thanks the Emscher Water Authority (Emschergenossenschaft) for their support in data collection and useful information.

REFERENCES

Anderl, B., and Stalmann, V. 1979. Niederschlag-Abfluß-Modell zur Hochwasserabfluß-Berechnung mit Gebietsmerkmalen im Emscher- und Lippegebiet (Rainfall-Runoff-Model for the Computation of Flood-Runoff using Regional Parameters in the Emscher and Lippe Watersheds). *Proceedings of the Emschergenossenschaft und Lippeverband,* Essen, Germany.

Annen, G., and Schoss, H.D. 1972. Das Einheitsganglinienverfahren bei stark bebauten Gebieten (The Unit Hydrograph Method on Highly Built up Areas). *gwf - wasser/abwasser,* München, 2, 78-81.

Crippen, J.R. 1965. Changes in Character of Unit Hydrograph after Suburban Development. *US Geol. Survey Prof. Paper* 525D, 196-198.

Diskin, M.H. 1969. *A Basic Study of the Linearity of the Rainfall-Runoff Process in Watersheds.* Ph.D. thesis, University of Illinois, Urbana.

Diskin, M.H., Ince, S., and Oben-Nyarko, K. 1978. Parallel Cascades Model for Urban Watersheds. *Journal of the Hydraulics Division, ASCE,* New York, 104, No HY2.

Hall, M.J. 1973. Synthetic Unit Hydrograph Technique for the Design of Flood Alleviation Works in Urban Areas. *Proceedings of Symposium on the Design of Water Resources Projects with Inadequate Data,* Madrid, 145-161.

McCuen, R.H. 1973. The Role of Sensitivity Analysis in Hydrologic Modelling. *Journal of Hydrology,* Amsterdam, 18, 37-53.

References

Nash, J.E. 1957. The Form of the Instantaneous Unit Hydrograph. *Proceedings of the General Assembly of Toronto, IASH, Publication No. 45,* 3, 114-121.

Rao, R.A., Delleur, J.E., Sarma, P.B. 1972. Conceptual Hydrologic Models for Urbanizing Basins. *Journal of the Hydraulics Division, ASCE,* New York, 98, No. HY7, 1205-1220.

Schmidt, O., Plate, E. 1977. Einfluß anthropogener Veränderungen auf den Hochwasserabluß am Beispiel der Körsch (Man-made Effects on Flood-Runoff of the River Körsch). Report to the *Kuratorium für Wasser und Kulturbauwesen,* Hamburg, 50 pp.

Schoss, H.D. 1977 Die Bestimmung des Versiegelungsfaktors nach Meßtischblatt-Signaturen (Sealing Coefficient Determinations from Survey-Map Signatures). *Wasser und Boden,* Hamburg, No. 5, 138-140.

Snyder, W.M. 1972. Fitting of Distribution Functions by Nonlinear Least Squares. *Water Resources Research.* 8, No. 6, 1423-1432.

Wittenberg, H. 1974 Der Einfluß zunehmender Bebauung auf den Hochwasserabfluß (The Influence of Increasing Urbanization on Flood Runoff). *Mitteilungen Institut Wasserbau III, Universität Karlsruhe,* Karlsruhe, Germany, 4, 113 pp.

Wittenberg, H. 1975. A Model to Predict the Effects of Urbanization on Watershed Response. Proceedings of *National Symposium on Urban Hydrology and Sediment Control.* Lexington, Ky, USA, 161-167.

Chapter 3.7

3.7 THE INTEGRATED INFLUENCE OF VARIOUS HUMAN ACTIVITIES
by Kokei Uehara[1]

The integrated impacts may be observed, on the one hand, as the result of the complex effects discussed in the preceeding sections, on the other hand as the direct or secondary effects of a number of other human activities not mentioned here, which may be superimposed on the effects of some principal human activity.

The combined objective of irrigation and drainage is to increase crop yields in agriculture, or to make agricultural production altogether possible. In advanced agricultural water management these two kinds of activity are complementary. Their overall impact is generally to increase runoff and to moderate slightly the seasonal extremes. As a consequence of irrigation losses, runoff may occur in dry periods as well. Since soil moisture is increased by irrigation, the specific runoff and consequently the need for drainage may increase in the irrigation season. The contingency of soil deterioration may be counteracted by drainage design to supplement irrigation.

For providing adequate irrigation supplies runoff control, water storage may often be necessary. The balanced flow regime created by reservoir releases may be greatly influenced by irrigation diversions. Irrigation in the vicinity of reservoirs may result in raising the groundwater table considerably. Intensive irrigation practised close to large water surfaces of reservoir systems may produce significant changes in evaporation conditions as well.

By controlling the pattern of land use, specifically that of agricultural production, surface runoff is greatly influenced by irrigation. The arrangement of irrigated plots may results in runoff retention depending on the topography of the particular area, so that plant evapotranspiration is controlled by the combination of land use and irrigation.

The changeover to irrigated farming is prompted substantially by urbanisation and industrialisation partly by the market thus created, partly by the increase in property values which entails more intensive farming practices. The general effect of these two processes is to increase abstractions and water use and potentially the runoff as well.

The areas made arable by reclamation-drainage need flood protection, which can be attained by the diverse means of runoff control. The waters reaching the streams under natural conditions in an irregular pattern are collected and discharged by the canals into the channel, or are pumped into it. In this way runoff is controlled to a certain extent by drainage itself.

A positive interrelation exists between drainage and land use, in that the pattern of the latter is changed radically by drainage in marsh areas, in lowlands subject to periodic inundations and where the groundwater table is high. This, in turn has inevitable consequences on runoff conditions. The impact is an indirect one, in that in the wake of drainage new types of farming equipment and methods may find wider application, such as use of fertilizers, deep cultivation, etc, so that the texture and water regime of the soil may undergo fundamental changes.

---

[1] Escola Politecnica, Universidade de Sao Paula, Brazil

The integrated influence of various human activities

Drainage and urbanization are inevitably interrelated as the former is a prerequisite of the latter. The urban storm sewer systems or the sewage treatment plants may discharge into the drainage canal. Thus a drainage system is created, the catchment of which is partly urban, where the accumulation processes are controlled by parameters other than those in the drained farm areas. In urban areas protected by flood levees appreciable volumes of underseepage water may rise to the surface; these must be returned by pumping into the stream carrying a flood discharge. Underground structures, such as underground railways may produce radical changes in groundwater conditions causing the water table to rise in some locations and to decrease at others. Urbanization tends to create large concentrated demands for water supply and concentrated groundwater withdrawal may contribute substantially to lowering the groundwater table. In some areas this may obviate partly or completely the need for drainage

The impacts of runoff control and of land use pattern may be considerable in major regions. The principal factors affecting land uses are flood control and river regulation, specifically the construction of levees in the flood plains. In the latter, land use must be subject to the interests of flood control. Nevertheless, the influence on the passage of flood waves may be an important one. The retention effect of forests in the flood plain may be appreciable, particularly on the falling branch of the flood hydrograph. Much sediment is deposited in the reservoirs constructed for runoff control and the resulting decrease in the fertilization effect downstream may also prompt a change of land use.

The large reservoirs created for runoff control and hydro-electric development attract urbanization and industry. Large reservoirs are used as a rule for recreation, so that the hydro-electric power projects often become multi-purpose developments, to meet the growing water demands of the industries utilizing the cheap power. In other instances, urbanization and industrial settlement call for water supply-oriented storage. Runoff is inevitably reduced by such diversions.

Agricultural land use and urbanization including industrialization are logically interrelated, in that the towns and industrial plants are constructed mostly on farmland while in their influence area they usually cause agricultural production to increase considerably. Towns and industrial plants developing in forest areas result in the removal of the plant cover and in the rapid spreading of paved areas, so that runoff is increased and interception minimised.

All these interactions occur in even more complex forms in major catchment areas. In general, the smaller the catchment, the more readily can the impacts be discerned and the greater the probability of a particular impact becoming predominant. In catchments covering several ten, or hundred thousand square kilometres the impacts may be interwomen to such an extent that their discrimination becomes virtually impossible.

The process can take the form of a chain reaction. A change in land use, such as deforestation in the catchment of a reservoir, may multiply the amount of sediment transported into, and accumulated in, the storage space. Soon the live storage volume is reduced so that the regulating capacity of the reservoir is diminished. Hence discharges which could be diverted formerly over the downstream section will decrease and irrigation must be restricted. As the area of irrigation shrinks, farming practices must be modified initiating a return to dry farming or the spreading of desert areas. Subsequently the sand starts migrating and filling the canals. The sequence of events could be continued even further.

Water plays an important socio-economic role, controlling development in some climates. It is for this reason the influence of human activities on hydrological conditions must be studied carefully, to avoid detrimental impacts which may be retroactive on socio-economic evolution and detrimental to the fundamental conditions of human life.

Owing to the interplay of forces the need for a complex approach is unquestionable. Where the impacts are different in nature, an optimum should be attempted in multi-purpose projects. Optimal solutions involve invariably some sort of compromise, to maximize the benefits and to minimize the undesirable consequences. In this manner multi-variable target functions are obtained in which the optimum solution is sought by maximizing some factors while minimizing others. The solution of similar problems has become possible by the advanced methods of mathematical economics.

In examining complex impacts it is essential to distinguish between those which are cumulative and those which tend to offset each other. For instance, in one part of a catchment runoff is reduced by a change in land use, while in other parts unco-ordinated development of new large irrigation projects gives rise to growing diversions. Over downstream sections the channel may become dry for part of the year. On the other hand, a changeover to a kind of land use increasing the dry weather runoff in the upstream part of the catchment might have retained adequate dry weather flow in the channel in spite of the increased irrigation demand.

It follows therefrom that although nature itself tends towards a beneficial balance in major catchment areas, the co-ordination of human activities is also essential.

The impact of human activities on runoff conditions may take a wide variety of forms; the resultant effect is registered in the hydrological observation network. Whereas some deliberate (planned) influences can be traced, the causes of others are difficult to detect. Some effects are realized only indirectly, over several links and in such cases the quantitative description of cause and effect may defy all attempts.

The component influences reflected by the integrated impacts observed have been dealt with in the foregoing chapters, which have also demonstrated methods for their determination and prediction. The analysis of integrated impacts may be tackled by this approach, namely where the relationship

$$E(t) = f \left| C_i(t) \right|$$

exists between the time series of the impact $E(t)$ and that of the cause $C(t)$, the causes can be distinguished in the form

$$E(t) - E'(t) = f \left| C_i(t) - C'_i(t) \right|$$

where $E'(t)$ is the effect of the known cause $C'(t)$. The relationship holds true if t is constant within the period of time considered, ie the time series are uniform, and there are no interactions so that the causes C_i are independent of each other.

Consider for example the simple case where the effects of urbanization (u) and irrigation (i) appear simultaneously in a particular catchment and result in the time series for the effect $E(t)$ (eg change in runoff).

Accordingly

$$E(t) = f \left| C_I(t) + C_u(t) \right|$$

Where it is possible to produce the effect time series $E_I(t)$ resulting from the cause time series $C_I(t)$, no particular difficulty should be encountered in writing the time series of urbanization.

$$E_u(t) = E(t) - E_I(t) = f_u \left| C_u(t) \right|$$

Difficulties are encountered where interactions exist between urbanization and irrigation, since then the time series $E_u(t)$ thus determined holds true exclusively at the given rate $C_I(t)$, thus

$$E_u(t) = F \{ f_u \left| C_u(t) \right| + f_I \left| C_I(t) \right| \}$$

so that the relationship determined must not be generalized.

Whereas in small catchments the interactions are easy to detect and identify, this is hardly the case in large ones.

The identification of effects is thus strongly influenced by the size of the catchment and presents a very difficult problem in large river basins. In such cases we are often limited to considering the effect (response) time series $E(t)$ relative to a certain datum, examining no more than the trends of effects, or the gradient of their variation.

Since the causes triggering integrated effects are extremely difficult to identify, great importance must be attributed to the efforts at exploring the numerical relationship between a particular cause and its effect by an experimental, or empirical approach.

Integrated effects may have different time scales. The effects may be superimposed on, or may extinguish each other. The examination of averages is thus less relevant in the case of integrated effects than in that of a single case. The extreme values and periodicities detectable in the time series may then be adopted for any more pertinent description of the effects.

Under such conditions an additional difficulty, namely that due to coincidence probability is encountered.

Consider, for instance, a river diversion supplying irrigation plots, as well as water for domestic and industrial purposes. The streamflow time series is modified thereby downstream of the diversion. The direct effect appears in the periodic fluctuation over the day in the streamflow time series and is evidently strongest at low stages, while the influences on sediment transport in the channel, or on the power demand of pumping at other diversions from the stream will be secondary ones. The effect will appear conspicuously where the peak demands for the three different purposes coincide, but will be less pronounced where the peaks are displaced relative to each other in time. The average reduction in streamflow will be the same whatever the diversion schedule, but the extreme values may differ greatly from each other.

Development entails the superimposement of various human activities, the increase in diversions and consumption, the growing efforts of agriculture to retain as much water as possible for its own purposes, which lead logically to a decrease in runoff. This phenomenon is demonstrated by long records. Deforestation at the same time triggers an opposite process resulting in higher average and peak runoff values.

The integrated effects may thus be distinguished according to the shift and frequency of average, highest and lowest values. The change in average and extreme values can be detected by advanced methods of mathematical analysis for time series. Modern hydrology has made considerable advances in this very direction in recent decades by the application of these methods.

In the papers aimed at the demonstration of integrated effects attempts have been made
- to examine integrated effects and the changes thereof in catchments of different sizes and levels of development,
- to distinguish the component effects and to analyse numerically the effects only without the triggering causes, owing to the complexity of the phenomenon,
- to identify the dominant cause, by control of which the effects are also subject to at least a certain amount of control,
- to analyse cases, where the cause is either deliberate, or spontaneous in triggering the response.

For the more distant future of mankind the predictability of the influences of various human activities is important. By studying the integrated effects, systems can be developed permitting optimal effects to be attained and the growing water, food and power problems of mankind to be solved.

Bibliography

Bogárdi, J. 1974. The impact of human activities on hydrological processes, *Hungary and the International Hydrological Decade,* 203-214, Budapest.

International Commission on Irrigation and Drainage, 1969. *Irrigation and Drainage in the World - A Global Review,* ICID, New Delhi.

International Commission on Irrigation and Drainage, 1976. *Irrigation and Salinity - A World-wide Survey,* ICID, New Delhi.

Shiklomanov, I.A. 1976. Impact of economic activities on water resources and hydrological regime (In Russian), *Obzor VNIIGMN-MID,* Obnunsk.

Starosolszky, Ö. 1973. Complex canalization of rivers. *Water Power,* 9.

Starosolszky, Ö. 1974. Environmental aspects of water power development. *Water Power,* 10.

USSR National Committee for the International Hydrological Decade, 1974. *World Water Balance and Water Resources of the Earth* (in Russian), Gidrometeoizdat, Leningrad.

3.7.1   STREAMFLOW CHANGES DUE TO MAN'S ACTIVITY
         by I A Shiklomanov[1]

3.7.1.1 Introduction

The Volga drainage basin, 1,360,000 sq km in area occupies a vast territory in Eastern
Europe including various physiographic zones from taiga-forest to semi-deserts. The basin
area where almost one fourth of the population of the USSR lives is influenced by various
economic factors among which the most important in terms of runoff changes are the following:
reservoir construction and operation, irrigation agrotechnical measures, and water
consumption for industrial and municipal needs.

During the latest 15-20 years economic activities in the Volga basin have developed
intensively. The largest reservoirs of the Volga-Kama cascade, which radically transformed
the hydrological regime of the river, have been put into operation. This period witnesses
high rates of industrial development including those branches of industry that demand
water, and the growth of municipal water supply. Advanced agricultural practices, such as
deep autumn ploughing and snow detention, have been introduced to increase crop yields;
numerous small ponds and storage basins fed by local runoff have been constructed; irrigated
farming has developed intensively.

All the above could not but strongly influence the hydrological regime of the Volga and
the volume of the total runoff discharged into the Caspian sea.

Up to 1930, however, water management was not practised in the drainage basin, there
were no large reservoirs on the Volga and on the tributaries, water consumption was
insignificant. During this period there was no influence of economic activities upon the
streamflow at the outlet. Hydrometric observations at the main gauging sites on the Volga
have been conducted since the end of the nineteenth century and cover the various stages of
economic development of the basin.

A reliable quantitative estimation of the streamflow changes due to economic activities
is most important not only for planning utilization of water resources but also for computing
and forecasting Caspian sea levels and salinity, the Volga being the main contributor to the
water balance of the endorheic Caspian sea. The major portion of the streamflow of the Volga
is formed in the forest zone with sufficient moisture where the anthropogenic factors do not
alter substantially the hydrological regime of the surface water, while irretrievable water
losses are observed as a rule in the southern forest-steppe and steppe zones of the basin.
Also there are long (75-90 years) series of observations on streamflow of the main river and
its tributaries covering various stages of economic development.

3.7.1.2 Methodology

The changes in the annual, seasonal and maximum monthly runoff at the outlets (the towns of
Kuibyshev and Volgograd) were estimated from relationships with the streamflow of index
rivers in the undisturbed forest zone for the whole long-term observational period and the

---

[1] State Hydrological Institute, 2 Linija 23, Leningrad V-53, USSR

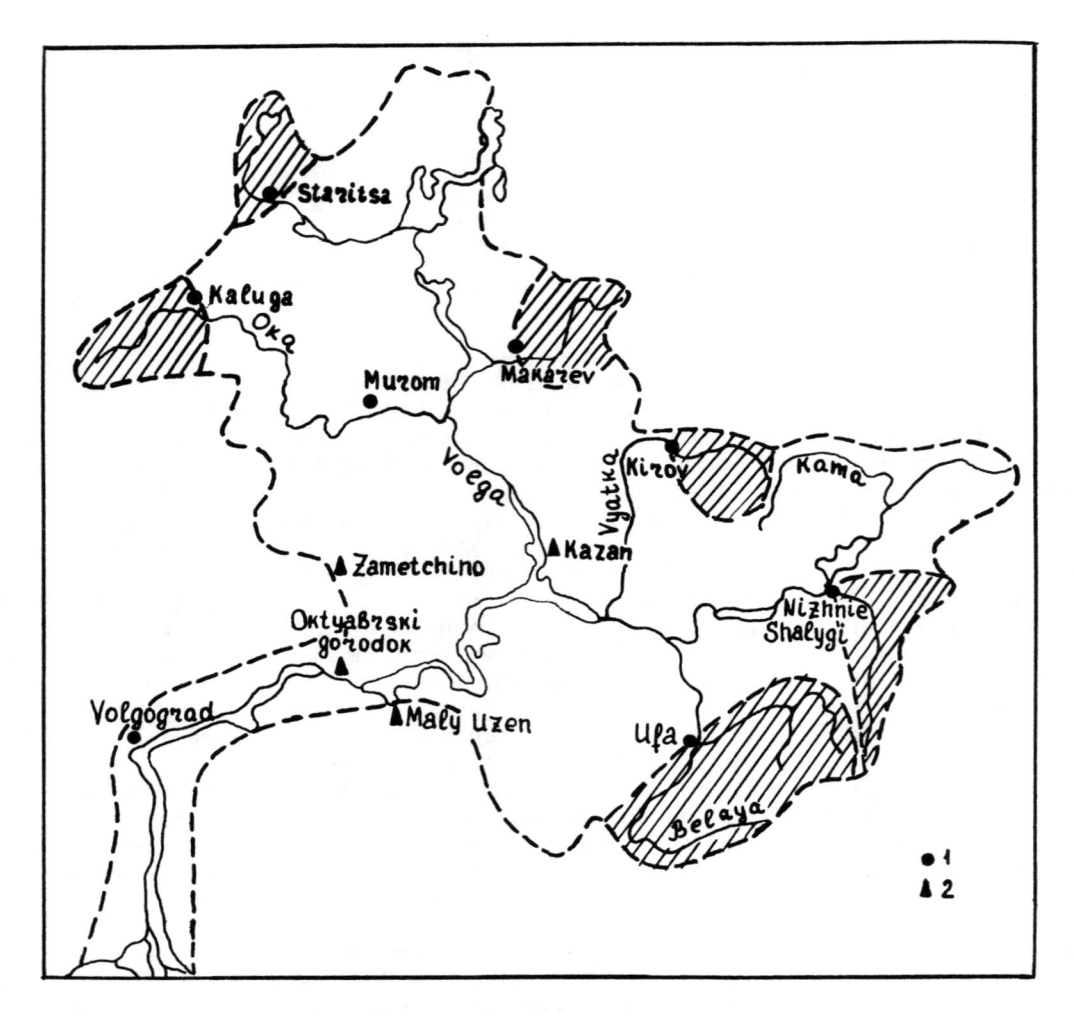

Figure 1 Diagram of location of index basins and meteostations in the Volga basin at Volgograd

1. Hydrological stations
2. Meteorological stations

meteorological factors of precipitation and air temperature in the southern parts of the basin in the zone of runoff use:

$$Q = f(Q_1, Q_2 \ldots Q_n, P, \theta) \qquad (1)$$

where: $Q_1, Q_2, \ldots Q_n$ are the streamflow of the index rivers with natural regime; P and θ are mean precipitation and mean air temperature from four meteorological stations (Shiklomanov, 1975) located in the zone of runoff use.

Six basins, tens of thousands of square kilometres in area, with runoff observation series from 1882, were adopted as index basins. The location of the basins and meteorological stations is shown in Figure 1.

Computations of the relationships in equation (1) were carried out by multiple linear correlation. For each group of initial data the computer program foresees the assessment of the significance of each factor and computation of several variants of regression equations with different number of parameters, to allow for the selection of the most reliable equations with a minimum number of stable coefficients. Thus significant factors carrying a small amount of new information but considerably deteriorating the stability of the solution obtained are excluded and do not participate in the design regression equation.

Numerous regression equations on the basis of relationship (1) were calculated for periods of various duration with different numbers of predictors for annual, spring and maximum runoff. For all the periods when the economic activities in the Volga basin were insignificant sufficiently reliable regressions of runoff on the main factors determining the runoff formation resulted with multiple correlation coefficients being: R = 0.92 to 0.96 for the average annual runoff; R = 0.88 to 0.96 for the spring flood runoff volume (April-June); R = 0.86 to 0.93 for the maximum mean monthly discharges.

With the help of these equations the values of natural runoff at the outlet can be estimated for subsequent years; the effect of man's activities can be calculated as the difference between the restored and observed runoff values.

The accuracy of such restored values for the Volga, however, will not be very high since the error in restored runoff values may be comparable in magnitude with the changes caused by the economic activites (especially for annual runoff).

Therefore to obtain a more reliable quantitative estimate of runoff changes their values were computed for the periods during which the river regime was natural, and then they were compared to the equivalent values obtained for the periods of intensive economic activities in the basin. Such a comparison gives possibilities not only for the assessment of runoff changes during the latest years but also allows for the determination of the period starting from which these changes tend to influence the hydrological regime of the river at the outlet. Regression equations of type (I) have been developed in the first variant for the periods starting from 1896 up to 1920, to 1925 and so on adding each five years up to 1955; in the second variant starting from 1882 by the same periods. Using several equations obtained for each period, annual values of the restored runoff were computed some 15 to 30 years ahead. After this, in view of a greater reliability, the restored runoff values were averaged for 5-year and 10-year periods. Then, the averaged values of the changes were evaluated for such 5-year period from 1921 to 1973 included, covering the periods of both natural and modified runoff of the Volga (Shiklomanov, 1975). Analysis of the values obtained led to the following conclusions:

(1) Up to 1935 the streamflow regime of the Volga at Volgograd may be regarded as natural, the economic activities were insignificant and had no sensible effect upon the annual runoff values, spring flood volumes and maximum water discharges.

(2) After 1936 man's economic activities started to exert a substantial influence upon the hydrological regime of the river at the outlet; spring flood volumes, maximum discharges and average annual runoff changed, the changes being particularly substantial during the latest 15-20 years. From 1956 to 1970 the annual streamflow of the Volga at Volgograd has decreased on average by 23 km^3 per year as compared to the natural period, or by 9% relative to the normal annual natural runoff. The spring flood volume during the same period has decreased on average by 50 km^3 per year, and maximum discharge value by 6,000 m^3/s, which makes 29% and 18% respectively relative to the norm of these characteristics under the natural regime.

(3) The period from 1936 to 1955 in the Volga drainage basin is the period of transition from the natural regime to the disturbed one. The reduction of the runoff characteristics was significant; average annual runoff decreased by 6 to 8 km^3 per year (2 to 3% of the norm),

spring flood volumes and maximum water discharges by 7 to 8 km^3/year (4-5%) and 700-800 m^3/s (2-2.5%) respectively.

(4) The annual streamflow reduction caused by anthropogenic factors is most evident during the low water periods; this can be explained by a particularly intensive irretrievable loss of water over the basin area for all kinds of economic activities.

During a particularly dry period from 1936 to 1940 the annual streamflow of the Volga fell due to man's activities by about 12 km^3/year (5% of the norm), mainly at the expense of the spring flood reduction of 10 km^3/year. During the low water period of 1971-1973 the average annual river runoff decreased on the average by 34 km^3/year (13% of the norm).

However, in view of a large random error of the computations, the above values of runoff reduction during dry periods may be regarded as approximate only.

(5) The random error of computed annual and maximum streamflow of the Volga averaged for the period 1956-1970 is 15 to 20%, while that of the spring flood value is 8-10% (relatively the value of the changes).

The computations based on standard observational data, (Table 1), provide only an integrated estimate of the influence of the total number of anthropogenic factors in the basin, and does not allow for the determination of each factor separately. Thus, there is no ground for scientifically substantiated forecasts of the future water regime. In view of this, differential estimates of the influence of the individual anthropogenic factors upon the streamflow have been sought.

The main economic activities in the Volga basin are channel storage, irrigation, industrial, municipal and rural water supply and agrotechnical measures. The role of these factors in the modifications of the annual streamflow will be discussed below.

3.7.1.3 Reservoirs

At present in the Volga basin there exist about 300 reservoirs, the live storage (V) of each being over 1 mln m^3. Among them there are 9 larger reservoirs of the Volga-Kama cascade, 29 reservoirs with live storage (V) over 50 mln m^3; all the rest are of local importance (V = 1 to 50 mln m^3). Besides there are more than 40,000 small storage basins and ponds with V < 1 mln m^3.

It is planned to put into operation three more reservoirs of the Volga-Kama cascade as well as over 20 other reservoirs with V > 50 mln m^3. Of all the reservoirs of the Volga basin 95% of the live storage and 94% of the areas submerged are in the reservoirs of the Volga-Kama cascade. Therefore, to estimate the influence of reservoirs on the streamflow of the Volga means in practice to estimate the role of the largest reservoirs of the Volga-Kama cascade.

The influence of reservoirs upon the Volga streamflow was estimated as described in section 2.3; the change in streamflow volume at the river outlet is estimated taking into account both the changes in evapotranspiration over the basin and the accumulation of water in the reservoirs and increased groundwater storage. Computations have been made for all existing and planned reservoirs, up to the year 2000. For the period from 1936 to 1973 annual computations were carried out on the basis of the available hydrometeorologial and hydrological data and project specifications for each large reservoir (Shiklomanov and Veretennikova, 1973, Shiklomanov, 1975).

The main characteristics of the largest reservoirs in the Volga basin and the additional evaporation from each reservoir averaged over 15 years are given in Table 2. This shows that annual losses are of typical zonal character and range from 90-100 mm for the reservoirs in the north to 350-400 mm for the reservoirs in the zone of insufficient moisture.

The mean volume of additional water losses by evaporation from all nine reservoirs of the cascade is 3.7 km^3/year or 1.5% of the total annual river runoff. The greatest portion of losses (2.1 km^3) occurs from the Kuibyshevskoe and Volgogradskoe reservoirs. During the warm period the average reduction of the streamflow of the Volga due to runoff losses (F_1) is 5.4 km^3 (about 5%), while during the cold season the streamflow increases by 1.7 km^3 (about 3%).

Table 3 demonstrates the influence of reservoirs and ponds on the streamflow of the Volga averaged for each 5 or 10 year period from 1936 to 2000 (Shiklomanov, 1975).

The effect of small storage basins and ponds has been evaluated from data on their number, aggregate storage volume and water surface area available for various administrative regions and different years, using also the maps of mean evaporation from water and land surfaces.

Table 1 Results of the integrated evaluation of the changes in the Volga streamflow at Volgograd under the effect of the economic activities

| Period | Streamflow reduction ||||| Random error of computations ||||
| | Annual || Spring flood volume || Maximum | Annual | Spring flood | Maximum |
	km³	%	km³	%	m³/s	%	km³	km³	m³/s
1956-1970	23	9	50	29	6,000	18	3-5	3-5	900-1,200
1936-1955	6-8	2-3	7-8	4-5	700-800	2-2.5	3-4	3-5	800-1,000
1936-1940	12	5	10	6	–	–	6-8	6-8	1,500-2,000
1971-1973	34	13	50	29	1,000	3	8-10	8-10	1,800-2,400

Table 2 Characteristics of the Volga-Kama cascade reservoirs and water losses by evaporation from their surface (averaged for 1959-1973)

Reservoir	$\bar{A}_1$ km²	$\bar{A}_2$ km²	$\bar{A}l$ km²	Runoff losses Warm period F_1 km³	Cold period	year F_1 km³	mm
Ivankovskoye	327	273	235	0.056	-0.029	0.027	100
Uglichskoye	250	226	186	0.058	-0.029	0.029	140
Rybinskoye	4580	4030	4030	1.16	-0.46	0.70	130
Gorkovskoye	1570	1570	1220	0.43	-0.18	0.25	220
Kamskoye	1920	1540	1320	0.35	-0.19	0.16	120
Votkinskoye	1120	900	650	0.16	-0.10	0.06	90
Kuibyshevskoye	6450	5490	4010	1.62	-0.41	1.21	290
Saratovskoye	1830	1830	1250	0.52	-0.08	0.44	350
Volgogradskoye	3120	3010	2070	1.06	-0.21	0.85	410
Total	21160	18870	14970	5.41	-1.69	3.72	

The analysis of the data in Table 3 has shown that at present the reduction of the Volga streamflow due to the reservoirs was caused mainly by the temporary losses due to the accumulation of water in reservoirs and groundwater replenishment. These losses were particularly substantial during 1956 to 1970 and amounted to about 173 km³ or 11.5 km³ per year. In the foreseeable future, up to 2000, the major reservoirs in the Volga basin being already in operation, water losses by accumulation and groundwater recharge will decrease sharply to average 2.5 km³/year between 1976 to 2000.

The losses by additional evaporation from ponds and reservoirs are at present 4.6 km³ annually, of which 4.0 km³ evaporated from the Volga-Kama reservoirs. It is expected that during 1990-2000 these values will become somewhat greater, ie 5.9 and 4.6 km³ per year respectively.

Additional evaporation from the areas with shallow groundwater tables is not high and is estimated as 0.5 km³/year at present and 0.6 km³/year in future.

The total reduction in the streamflow of the Volga discharged into the Caspian sea was about 0.7 km³/year up to 1940 and 15.7 km³/year during 1956-1970. It is expected that by 2000 the value will be much less and during 1975-2000 it will be on average 9 km³/year (Shiklomanov, 1976).

3.7.1.4 Irrigation

Until recently irrigation has not been widely practised in the Volga basin. Before 1940 the total irrigated area was only 4 thousand hectares, mainly in the Volga-Akhtuba flood plain and the delta. In 1965 the irrigated area in the basin was already 163 thousand hectares, in 1970 - 260 thousand hectares, and in 1974 - 493 thousand hectares (Table 4).

At present the Volga basin is regarded as the main region of future irrigation development in the country. It is planned to irrigate 2.4 to 2.5 million hectares during the next 8-10 years, and 3.7 million hectares by the end of the century. The scheme of future irrigation development showing the major irrigation systems in the basin and the volumes of water abstracted is given in Shiklomanov (1976).

In view of the potential effect of irrigation upon the streamflow of the Volga the irrigated areas of the basin can be sub-divided into three irrigation zones according to the type of the irrigation system, the types of crops, the system of distribution and use of the river water:
(1) Littoral zone - hydrographically connected with the Volga and its tributaries;
(2) Outlying zone - located in endorheic depressions deprived of outlets or beyond the boundaries of the basin;
(3) Flood plain - delta zone - located in the Volga-Akhtuba flood plain and in the Volga

Table 3 Streamflow reduction of the Volga due to ponds and reservoirs during 1936-2000 (km³/year)

Characteristics of streamflow losses		1936-1940	1941-1950	1951-1955	1956-1960	1961-1965	1966-1970	1971-1975	1976-1980	1981-1985	1986-1990	1991-2000
Reservoirs of the Volga-Kama cascade	F_1	0.2	0.6	0.9	2.0	3.0	3.6	4.0	3.7	4.6	4.6	4.6
	F_2	0.0	0.0	0.0	0.3	0.4	0.5	0.5	0.6	0.6	0.6	0.6
	F_3	0.0	0.0	0.0	-1.2	-1.4	-1.4	-1.4	-1.4	-1.5	-1.5	-1.5
	ΔS_L	0.1	2.2	-1.6	16.5	4.7	1.7	5.0	0.0	6.0	0.0	0.2
	G_1	0.0	0.6	0.6	2.1	0.2	0.4	0.0	0.0	0.9	0.0	0.0
	G_2	0.0	0.3	0.1	1.8	1.6	1.3	0.3	0.1	0.7	0.1	0.0
Reservoirs with V > 50 mln m³	F_1	0.0	0.0	0.0	0.1	0.2	0.2	0.2	0.3	0.3	0.4	0.6
	ΔS_L	0.0	0.0	0.2	0.3	0.3	0.4	0.5	1.5	0.4	1.0	0.8
Ponds and storage basins with V < 50 mln m³	$F_1+\Delta S_L$	0.7	0.3	0.4	0.5	0.6	0.8	0.9	1.0	1.1	1.2	1.5
Total		1.0	4.0	0.6	22.4	9.6	7.5	10.0	5.8	13.1	6.4	6.8

Note: For symbols see Section 2.3

delta.

Each zone has its own special features of the water balance, hydrological and irrigation regime which depend on the climate, hydrology, the lack or availability or two-way hydrographic communication between a given area and the Volga, agricultural technology and crop pattern.

The distribution of irrigated areas by the zones is shown in Table 4. The littoral irrigation systems have two-way hydrographic communication. Water is pumped from the Volga or its tributaries into the irrigation systems and the return water is discharged back into the main river or its tributaries through a system of collectors and drains or a sewage system with a certain lag time due to the partial accumulation of water in the aeration zone. Irrigation is mainly aimed at grain-crop and vegetable production.

Table 4 Irrigated areas (thousand hectares) in different irrigated zones of the Volga region and the Volga streamflow reduction due to irrigation (km^3/year)

Irrigation zone		1971	1975	1980	1985	1990	2000
I. Littoral	Irrigated area	95	400	1000	1700	2000	2300
	Streamflow reduction	0.3	1.7	4.3	7.2	8.8	9.7
II. Outlying							
(a) Sarpinskaya Lowland	Irrigated area	9	34	62	90	210	260
	Streamflow reduction	0.0	0.7	1.3	1.8	3.9	4.9
	Water disposal into the Kuma river (approx)	-	-	-	-	(0.3)	(0.3)
(b) Volga-Ural Interfluve	Irrigated area	15	35	280	520	640	720
	Streamflow reduction	0.2	0.7	2.1	2.4	3.1	3.5
	Water diverted into the Volga-Ural Canal (besides irrigation)	-	-	-	1.2	2.5	4.5
	Water disposal into the Ural river	-	-	-	0.9	0.9	1.5
III. Flood plain - delta	Irrigated area	112	190	250	300	380	470
	Streamflow reduction	0.9	1.5	2.0	2.4	3.0	3.7
Total (approx)	Irrigated area	230	660	1600	2600	3200	3700
	Streamflow reduction	1.4	4.6	9.7	14	19	22

The outlying zone consists of the two regions: the Volga-Ural endorheic region and the Sarspinskaya lowland. For this zone there is no return hydrographic communication with the Volga, ie all water supplied into the irrigation systems is either evaporated entirely in the endorheic depressions or diverted beyond the boundaries of the Volga basin. In this particular case one may neglect the flow of irrigation groundwater. Thus, water withdrawal from the Volga for these irrigation systems may be regarded as an absolute loss of streamflow to the Volga.

The irrigation systems mainly for vegetables and rice in the flood plain dela region with high groundwater tables have a distinct two-way hydrographic communication. All excess water returns almost immediately into the river via surface or underground routes. The amount of water accumulated in the aeration zone is very small.

As only approximate data on future irrigation projects are available and as there are practically no integrated experimental studies, the effect of irrigation on the streamflow of the Volga was estimated from the main project specifications and the main factors influencing the amounts of irretrievable losses and of return water in the basin.

In the outlying zone the change in the streamflow due to irrigation is practically equal to the amount of water withdrawn since no water is returned. In the littoral and flood plain delta zones that have two-way hydrographic communication with the Volga, the change of the streamflow ΔQ subsequent to irrigation was computed from the following equations.

$$\begin{aligned} \Delta Q &= Q_d + Q_\beta \\ Q_\beta &= N + P - E - \Delta M + \Delta Q_S \\ \Delta Q_S &= (S_{sn} + P_s)(K_2 - K_1) \end{aligned} \quad (2)$$

where: Q_d is total amount of water withdrawn from the river; Q_β is excessive (return) water; N is average application; P is precipitation from April to October inclusive; E is evapotranspiration during the warm period; ΔM is the change in groundwater storage and moisture stored in the zone of aeration; ΔQ_S is the change in the volume of local spring runoff subsequent to irrigation; $(S_{sn} + P_s)$ is snow storage plus precipitation in spring; K_1 and K_2 are averaged runoff coefficients for non-irrigated and irrigated lands.

The influence of the present-day and future irrigation projects on the streamflow of the Volga was computed by equations (2) separately for various zones and regions of the Volga basin.

As a first stage actual data on irrigated land areas, water intakes and field application rates for the period from 1963 to 1974 were analysed. The irrigation zones to which given irrigated areas belong, sewerage canals and drains discharging water into the rivers were determined from maps of irrigation systems. Precipitation totals and snow storage for the period were taken from the data of meteorological stations. Evapotranspiration during the warm period was computed by A R Konstantinov's (1968) method. K_1 and K_2 values were computed from the relationship between spring runoff volume and autumn precipitation developed for the rivers of the steppe zone of the Volga basin (Appolov, 1960) on the assumption that irrigated areas receive most moisture in autumn.

Water losses by accumulation in the aeration zone were estimated from data on groundwater table dynamics and soil moisture storage available for some irrigation systems of the Trans-Volga region.

When computing the effect of future irrigation projects values of P, E, $(S_{sn} + P_s)$, averaged for a long-term period were used; $K_1 = 0.40$, $K_2 = 0.80$; Q_α, N and the area of irrigated land were taken from the project specifications of the future irrigation systems.

The M values for the littoral zone were estimated from average values of the rise of the groundwater tables at the existing irrigation systems and hydrogeological maps.

For the flood plain zone M was assumed to be zero.

The computed values of the changes in the Volga streamflow due to irrigation in different irrigation zones for the period of 1971-2000 are given in Table 4. The streamflow reduction due to irrigation was 2.8 km^3 in 1974, the major reason for this being the flood plain delta and littoral irrigation zones. In 1985 the total reduction of the streamflow will be $\approx$ 14 km^3 per year of which 7.2 km^3/year (49%) will be lost in the littoral zone; 4.2 km^3/year (38%) in the outlying zone and 2.4 km^3/year (13%) in the flood plain delta zone. By the end of the century the reduction in streamflow may reach 22 km^3/year, the distribution by the irrigation zones being 9.7; 8.4 and 3.7 km^3/year respectively. The values of the return water in the flood plain delta zone are 50 to 60% of the total amount of water withdrawn and for the littoral zone 15 to 20%.

3.7.1.5 Agricultural practices

The influence of agricultural practices on the streamflow of the Volga basin and in Kazakhstan was evaluated by the technique developed by V E Vodogretsky in 1973 (Vodogretsky, 1974) and briefly described earlier. This method is based on the use of wide experimental data and is most reliable from the physical point of view.

The resultant estimates coincide closely with the results obtained from the analysis of observations of streamflow and the main factors for a long-term period.

In the forest and northern forest-steppe zones of the Volga basin the influence of agricultural technology is negligible while in the steppe zone it amounts to 7 to 20%. Since the water content of the tributaries in the forest-steppe and steppe zones is respectively

15% and 5% of the total streamflow of the Volga, the overall streamflow reduction of the Volga due to agricultural practices is insignificant at present as it is only 2.7 km^3/year, or about 1% of the normal runoff. It is expected that the values will be practically the same in future.

3.7.1.6 Industrial, municipal and rural water supply

An approximate assessment of the role of industrial, municipal and rural water supply on the average annual streamflow of the Volga basin within which there exists a wide variety of populated communities and industrial enterprises, was obtained using the following computation scheme:

(1) Overall water consumption volumes were determined from different departments of industry and municipal services for the present and for the future and averaged by river basins and regions.

(2) It was accepted that the present day irretrievable losses expressed as a percentage of the water intake and from 10% (northern regions) to 25% (southern regions) in industry and from 1% to 3% in heat-and-power engineering. In future the wide use of closed water supply systems and re-use of water are expected to increase the irretrievable losses to 30-40% in industry and to 2-4% in heat and power engineering respectively.

(3) Irretrievable water losses in municipal water supply were evaluated as 10% to 25%, in water supply for rural areas and for irrigation as 70% to 90% in the northern and southern regions respectively. With the proposed wide development of centralized water conduits and canals the above values are expected to go down to 5-10% in the urban and to 50-70% in the rural areas.

(4) During dry and hot years with low precipitation the above values of irretrievable losses increase approximately by 15% to 25%, while during the wet years they decrease by the same percentage.

In 1940 the reduction of the annual streamflow of the Volga due to industrial, municipal and rural water supply was roughly 0.8 km^3/year, currently it is 3.5 km^3/year and by 1985 and 2000 it is expected to be 5.0 km^3/year and 7.3 km^3/year respectively.

The streamflow changes in the Volga due to various kinds of man's economic activities from 1940 to 2000 estimated as described above are given in Table 5.

Table 5 Annual streamflow reduction of the Volga due to economic activities (km^3/year)

Type of economic activites	Year						
	1940	1950	1960	1965	1973	1985	2000
Total streamflow reduction including:	5.0	7.3	26	14	19	36	42
Reservoir effect	0.4	4.0	23	11	11	15	8
Irrigation effect	0.2	0.3	0.8	0.9	2.4	14	22
The effects of agricultural practices	2.5	1.5	2.0	2.3	3.2	2.8	2.8

The values of the streamflow changes (km^3/year) due to a certain anthropogenic factor corresponding to a given year represent the changes averaged for a 5 or 10 year antecedent period. The comparison of Tables 1 and 5 shows that these data fit well though they have been computed by different methods using different sets of initial data (ie network long-term hydrometeorological data in the former case, and experimental water balance data, information on the economic development of the regions, water withdrawals and return water volumes, etc in the latter). Thus, for the period of 1956 to 1973 according to Table 1 the streamflow reduction due to the integrated influence of the anthropogenic factors was 23 km^3/year. Assessment of the influence of the anthropogenic factors provided a figure of about 20 km^3/year. The agreement between the two figures is satisfactory bearing in mind the errors in the initial data and the approximate nature of the methods. On the whole these figures testify to the reliability of the estimates.

By 1940 the streamflow reduction of the Volga (Table 5) had reached 5.0 km^3/year, at present it is about 20 km^3/year, by 1985 the reduction may have reached 36 km^3/year and by 2000 - 42 km^3/year (Taking into account the planned water diversions into the Volga-Ural Canal and water disposals into the Ural River, which amount to 1.5 km^3/year). Until recently (1956-1970) reservoirs and ponds caused the major portion, 75%, of the reduction in streamflow; by 2000 it is expected that intensive growth of irrigated farming will cause 52% of the streamflow reduction, while the role of reservoirs will go down to 20%.

All the above data on the streamflow changes of the Volga correspond to the conditions of normal moisture content in the basin and normal water volumes at the outlets of the rivers. Meanwhile, there occur extremely dry and hot periods with scarce precipitation in the forest-steppe and steppe zones of the Volga basin, where the main use of the water resources is observed. Consequently, the absolute water losses through man's economic activities increase substantially. Very often such dry periods cover the whole of the basin and coincide with the low water period of the main river.

This happened, for instance, in some very dry years from 1936 to 1940 and in 1972 when an extraordinarily low water content of the Volga coincided with a very hot and dry summer over almost all of the basin; these resulted in a very substantial streamflow reduction at the outlet under the influence of economic activities. In 1972, for instance, additional evaporation from the reservoirs of the Volga-Kama cascade amounted to 7.5 km^3/year which was more than twice as great as the long-term average value. Usually during such years water losses caused by other anthropogenic factors (agriculture, irrigation, ponds, industrial, urban and rural water supply) increase also.

The reverse phenomena are usually observed during the years with extremely wet and cold summer-autumn periods when irretrievable water losses from the basin caused by anthropogenic factors decrease sharply. Thus, the minimum water losses by evaporation from the areas inundated by the reservoirs of the Volga-Kama cascade are only 1.8 km^3/year which is only half the average value. It is most probable that such years coincide with periods of high water content in the Volga at the outlet.

Approximate estimates for the Volga drainage basin show that during very dry years when the annual streamflow is 180 to 190 km^3/year, the streamflow reduction due to the integrated influence of anthropogenic factors may reach 22 to 24 km^3/year, or 12 to 14% of the total streamflow at the outlet. During wet years, on the other hand, the absolute value of streamflow reduction becomes less and is only 3 to 5%.

REFERENCES

Apollov, B.A. Kalinin, G.P., and Komarov, V.D. 1960. *Gidrologicheskie prognozy* (Hydrological forecasts). Leningrad, Hidrometeoizdat, 406 pp.

Konstantinov, A.R. 1968. *Isparenie v prirode* (Evaporation in nature). Leningrad, Hidrometeoizdat, 588 pp.

Shiklomanov, I.A., and Veretennikova, G.M. 1973. Bezvozvratnye poteri stoka r. Volgi za schet isparenia s vodokhranilisch Volzksko-Kamskogo Kaskada (Irretrievable losses of the Volga streamflow by evaporation from the reservoirs of the Volga-Kama Cascade). *Trans GGI*, 206, 22-51.

Shiklomanov, I.A. 1975. Otsenka izmeneii stoka r. Volgi u Volgograda pod vlianiem khozaistvennoi deyatelnosti (Evaluation of the streamflow changes of the Volga at Volgagrad under the effect of economic activities). *Trans GGI*, 229, 3-35.

Shiklomanov, I.A. 1976. *Gidrologischeskie aspecty problemy Kaspiiskogo morya* (Hydrological aspects of the Caspian Sea problem). Leningrad, Hidrometeoizdat, 78 pp.

Vodogretsky, V.E. 1974. Vlianie agrolesomeliorativnykh meropriatii na stok rek i metodika ego rascheta (The influence of agrotechnical and forest reclamation practice upon river runoff and methods for its computation). *Trans GGI*, 221, 47-104.

3.7.2 INTEGRATED HUMAN ACTIVITIES IN THE UPPER BASIN OF THE PARAIBA DO SUL RIVER, BRAZIL
by Kokei Uehara[1]

3.7.2.1 General characteristics
The Paraiba do Sul River basin is located between 41°W and 46°30 W longitude and between 20°26'S and 23°38'S latitude. Its drainage area is 57,000 km². It is a very important river basin due to its proximity to two big urban centres, São Paulo and Rio de Janeiro, with populations of 8 million and 6 million respectively. These two cities with their satellites will have populations greater than 20 million and 10 million by the year 2000 (Figure 1).

About 1.2 million people live today in the basin, both in urban centres and rural areas, practising agriculture and cattle-breeding, industrial, commercial and other terciary activities, causing changes in the characteristics of the basin. A number of civil engineering works have been built such as:
- dams for flow regulation for various multi-purposes such as irrigation, drainage, flood control, recreation, supply of drinking water and for industries, dilution of sewage, transference of water to other basins, power production etc.
- water intakes for providing water to cities and also for irrigation.
- sewage treatment plants - for domestic and industrial sewage.
- elimination of meanders to improve the drainage.
- construction of dams for the insertion of 'polders' (drainage and irrigation).
- establishment of new urban and industrial areas.
- construction of roads.
- establishment of new areas with mechanized agriculture.

The Paraiba do Sul River basin was initially settled by the Portuguese from 1560. However, after the beginning of the 19th century, the original forests were cut down, gradually for coffee cultivation, thus bringing an intense influence of human activities into the local ecology. In 1888, with the liberation of the slaves who worked in the plantations, coffee cultivation begin to decrease.

The European immigrants who came to Brazil to replace the labourers in the plantation went to other regions of the country. So the coffee plantations were little by little abandoned due to the lack of labour and so they were substituted by pastures for cattle-breeding for both milk and beef. This activity is in process today in the hills of the Paraiba do Sul valley. As far as erosion is concerned, the substitution of coffee by pasture was a great benefit.

The plain areas surrounding the river were used for rice plantations and horticulture.

In this report, only the upper basin of the Paraiba do Sul River will be considered as this segment is mostly affected by the human action. Moreover, in this region there are more records for studying the trend of the modifications introduced in the physical characteristics of the basin. This basin corresponds to the Paraiba do Sul River basin that is located at the Estado de São Paulo, with a drainage area of 13,500 km² (23,7% of the

---

[1] Escola Politecnica Universidade de São Paulo, São Paulo, Brazil

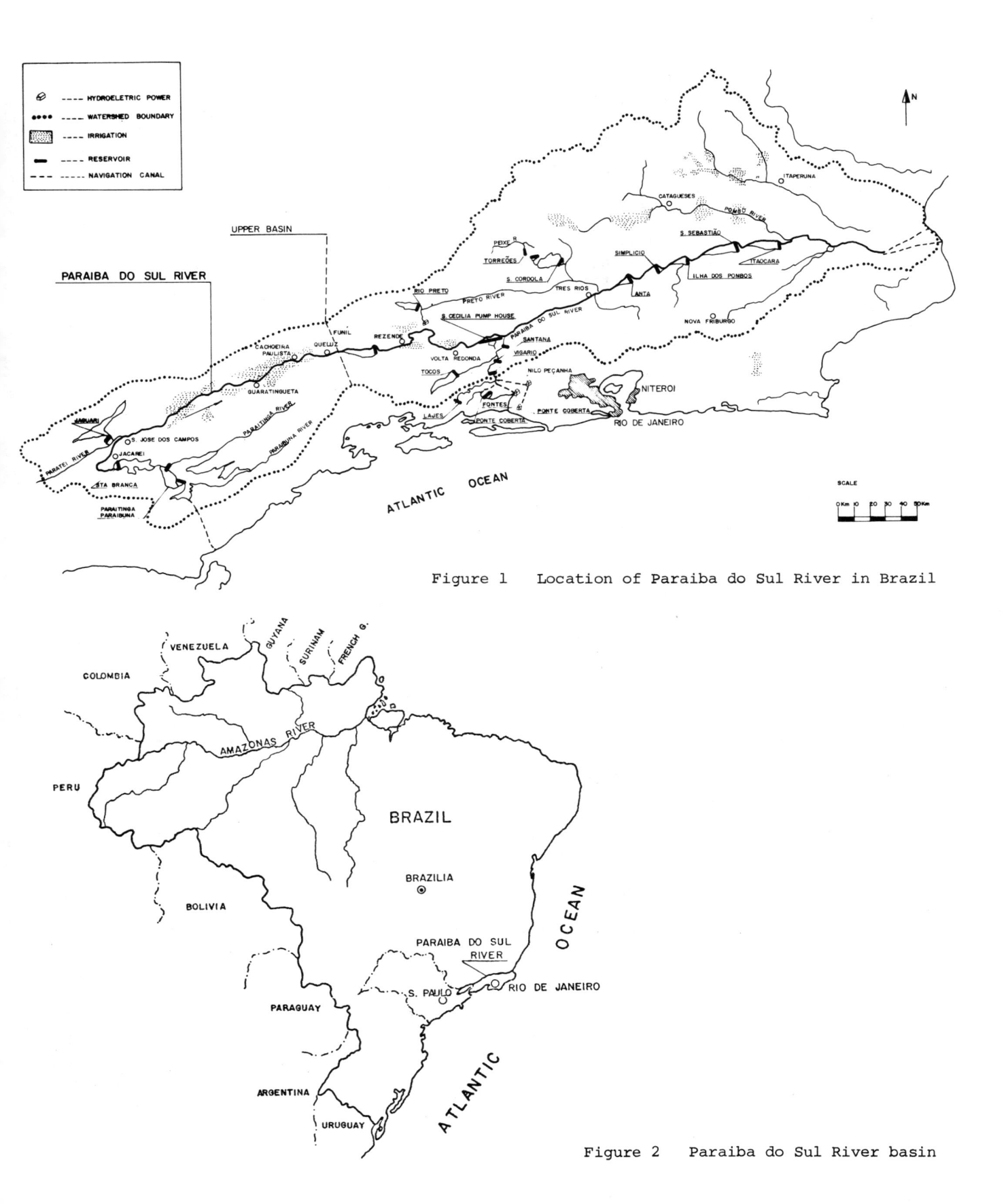

Figure 1 Location of Paraiba do Sul River in Brazil

Figure 2 Paraiba do Sul River basin

Integrated human activities in the upper basin

whole basin) (Figure 2).

3.7.2.2 Physical environment of the upper basin of Paraiba do Sul River

3.7.2.2.1 Topographic features. The Paraiba do Sul River is formed by the joining of two rivers: Paraitinga and Paraibuna. Their upper reaches are at an elevation of 1,800 m and 1,600 m respectively. The level of this river, in the segment being considered is at an altitude of 465 m, at the city of Queluz.

The upstream course has an average slope of 4.9 m/km along a reach of 250 km from the spring of Paraitinga River to the city Guararema (570 m).

On the following segment, the average slope is 0.19 m/km, along a reach of 300 km, until the city Cachoeira Paulista (513 m). This is the most important segment for the study, since the Paraiba do Sul goes through a fertile alluvial plain, where rice plantations and horticulture are intensively developed. Along the plains, on the higher areas, several cities are located, where developing industrial activities modify the topography and the soil utilization, while polluting the river water.

At this segment, the Paraiba do Sul River meanders; since 1953 these have been eliminated by increasing the longitudinal slope, for easy passage of flood waves. This elimination of meanders was beneficial in increasing the capacity for flood flows, but it brought problems that will be considered later.

Percentage distribution of relief:

Sloping: 23.4
Mountainous: 34.9
Undulating: 31.3
Plain: 10.4

Slope of the basin:

Slope (%)	% of area
0 - 2	3.69
2 - 20	6.75
more than 20	89.56

3.7.2.2.2 Soils and substratum. The predominant geological formations are acid, crystalline gneiss with frequent outcrops of granite. They show, also, lenticular formations of crystalline-limestone and quartz. Basic rocks such as diorite, diabase and gabbro are seldom found.

The predominant soil is the ortho-yellow-red latosol which covers 51% of the area while the yellow-red podzoilic covers 22.5%.

3.7.2.2.3 Vegetation and cultivation. On the high areas of the basin, where the land is too steep or in deep valleys, tropical forests are found but without important commercial species.

On the hills are pastures and fruit cultivation.

On the plains, agriculture is practised with rice plantations and horticulture.

3.7.2.2.4 Precipitation and climatic features. The Paraiba do Sul basin is located in the tropical zone, with a hot to medium climate, depending on the topography. There are more than 114 river gauging stations operating in the upper basin of this river. Some meteorological stations have been maintained since 1930.

Table 1 Temperature in ^{0}C (mean annual temperature: 21.1^{0}C)

	Jan	Feb	Mar	Apr	May	Jun	Jul	Aug	Sep	Oct	Nov	Dec
Average	23.2	23.1	22.5	20.3	18.6	18.9	16.4	17.9	19.5	20.3	21.4	22.3
Maximum	29.9	29.7	29.1	27.3	26.2	24.7	24.3	26.4	27.2	27.3	26.3	28.8
Minimum	18.9	18.9	18.2	15.6	13.2	11.3	10.6	11.8	13.8	15.5	16.7	17.4

Table 2 Precipitation in mm (mean annual precipitation is 1245 mm)

	Jan	Feb	Mar	Apr	May	Jun	Jul	Aug	Sep	Oct	Nov	Dec
Average	222	205	171	67	36	40	22	28	36	107	123	186

Table 3 Relative humidity in %

	Jan	Feb	Mar	Apr	May	Jun	Jul	Aug	Sep	Oct	Nov	Dec
Average	77.0	78.9	79.3	78.6	79.1	78.5	74.8	71.0	71.2	75.3	74.9	76.4
Maximum	83.9	84.7	82.9	82.9	84.0	82.9	80.4	78.1	78.9	81.2	79.8	81.6
Minimum	65.5	71.5	74.5	75.6	74.2	74.2	70.3	82.4	65.0	70.6	68.5	71.5

Table 4 Evaporation in mm (mean annual evaporation is 884 mm)

	Jan	Feb	Mar	Apr	May	Jun	Jul	Aug	Sep	Oct	Nov	Dec
Average	74	61	67	61	60	53	76	94	93	83	80	82
Maximum	119	86	91	74	80	76	91	117	125	118	104	98

3.7.2.2.5 Hydrological regime of Paraiba do Sul River. At some river gauging stations, discharges have been measured since 1920. During 1961, the construction of the Santa Branca Dam was completed with a drainage area of 5,026.0 km^2 and with a volume of 419 x 10^6 m^3. The operation of this reservoir has modified the behaviour of the discharges with the time. Table 5 shows mean monthly discharge for the period before 1961.

Table 5 Mean monthly discharges in m^3/s

City - Period	Jan	Feb	Mar	Apr	May	Jun	Jul	Aug	Sep	Oct	Nov	Dec	Average
Cacapava 1923/1956	200	240	239	172	127	108	92	81	85	97	108	152	142
Tremembé 1934/1956	197	243	245	179	125	108	92	81	80	94	106	143	141
Pindamonhagaba 1928/1956	203	264	263	184	134	114	97	86	81	102	111	158	149
Guaratinguetá 1933/1956	246	292	303	208	139	117	103	88	89	106	121	172	165
Cachoeira Paulista 1923/1954	288	349	349	243	161	137	113	93	105	123	240	205	193
Rezenda 1923/1957	397	464	465	321	212	176	145	123	128	152	192	292	256

Integrated human activities in the upper basin

3.7.2.3 River regulation
On the upper basin of the Paraiba do Sul River there are three dams being operated:

Dams	Capacity (m^3)
Paraibuna-Paraitinga	$2,633 \times 10^6$
Santa Branca	419×10^6
Jaguari	625×10^6

Due to the construction of the dams, some minor deltas have been formed at the entrances to the lakes, caused by deposits of sediments. Upstream of the dams the bed of the river is being eroded, causing degradation. Hence, many intakes for water supply and irrigation were either not usable or had to be modified for the new situation.

Bathymetric records at intervals downstream of the dams, sampling of solid materials, and analysis of changes in stage-discharge relationships are being used to study the degradation problem. These data will be used in the application of the mathematical model that will be explained.

For the dams operations, synthetic series of mean monthly discharges were generated by using Markovian-type Flow Models. All the records, however, were also analysed by methods of autocorrelation, lag cross correlation, spectral and cross spectral analysis, and so on prior to the application of the Markovian Model.

Evaporation from the lakes is being studied through the analysis of correlations of discharges before and after construction of dams.

Mathematical models of rainfall/runoff such as the Stanford IV or Tank Model are being applied to the study of basins which are not controlled by dams. Bathymetric records are being made in small dams for the study of the phenomenon of aggradation.

3.7.2.4 Flood control by levees
The upper basin of the Paraibe do Sul River extends over 300 km across a plain with a gentle slope of 0.19 m/km, causing the occurrence of meanders. Since 1953, the work of elimination of meanders and the construction of levees has increased the capacity for flood flow as well as creating polders for rice plantation and horticulture.

Short-cutting of meanders increased the flow, but also increased the degradation of the river bed; many intakes for water supply and irrigation could not be utilized due to the lowering of the levels of the water, as occurred just downstream of the dams. Periodically, bathymetric records are made to evaluate the degradation.

The construction of levees reduces the attenuation of flood waves caused by storage in swampy areas; however, the flood waves upstream are attenuated by the three upstream dams. So, a study is in progress to establish whether the construction of dams and levees increases or decreases the flood peaks on the lower parts of this basin. Therefore, mathematical models were applied to the determination of the flood waves that enter the dams, of the attenuation of these waves by storage and of the effect of the streamflow routing by the application of the method of characteristics. The great difficulty is collecting data on topography, channel roughness, and the contribution of discharges from areas not controlled by dams.

3.7.2.5 Mathematical model for predicting the effects of aggradation and degradation
A mathematical model was applied to study the behaviour of the river bed following the short-cutting of meanders and the construction of dams. It has the following equations:

Continuity equation of the liquid phase:

$$\frac{\partial h}{\partial t} + \frac{\partial h}{\partial x} + \frac{A}{b}\frac{\partial u}{\partial x} = 0$$

Dynamical equation of the liquide phase

$$\frac{\partial u}{\partial t} + u\frac{\partial u}{\partial x} + g\frac{\partial u}{\partial x} + g\frac{\partial z}{\partial x} + \frac{g}{k^2} Q/Q/ = 0$$

Continuity equation of the solid phase

$$b' \frac{\partial z}{\partial t} + \frac{\partial q_s}{\partial x} = 0$$

Dynamical equation of the solid phase

$$q_s(x,t) = f(u,h)$$

where: $h(x,t)$ is depth of the flow; $u(x,t)$ is average velocity in a cross section of the flow; $z(x,t)$ is quota of the bottom of the river bed; $q_s(x,t)$ is bed load transport; A is area of the cross section of the flow; b is surface width of the cross section; g is gravity acceleration; K is capacity of conveyance of flow; b' is part of the wet perimeter that interfere with the solid conveyance by drawling; Q is discharge at the cross section of the flow.

This model is not satisfactorily calibrated because of the lack of direct measurements of the bed load transportation, on the country. This approach is being carried out but complete success has still to be attained.

3.7.2.6 Afforestation and deforestation

Some areas of the basin are being devastated and even the forests are being eliminated. But, the government is intensifying the fiscalization with the support of public opinion. Other areas are being reforested with eucalyptus and pines with the aid of government allowances. The agriculture on the hills is being modernized with the development of appropriate methods of irrigation and with ploughing on the contours.

Works to combat the erosion are being executed little by little. Aerial photographs to a scale 1:24,000 are being used in the preservation of vegetation and in the location of areas with erosion.

3.7.2.7 Water quality and pollution

Due to the increased urban population, with the establishment of big industries for cellulose, petrochemicals and for manufacturing as well as the indescriminate use of insecticides for agriculture, the water of Paraiba do Sul River is suffering the effects of pollution. So, state and federal departments are monitoring the quality of the water across the river. Many mathematical models were applied to predict the trends in pollution.

Fortnightly measurements of temperature, colour, turbidity, bacteriological characteristics, total residue, pests, sulphates, chlorates and mercury are taken. The preservation of the quality of the water is important for the survival of the population that lives in the basin and to the population of the city of Rio de Janeiro which gets this water by transfer just downstream of the considered interval in this work. Studies of quality of the water in the dams are being undertaken to test the eutrofication rate.

Bibliography

Chow, Ven Te. 1959. *Open channel hydraulics*. McGraw Hill.

Chow, Ven Te. 1964. *Handbook of Applied Hydrology*. McGrawHill.

DAEE, 1975. *Sondotécnica-Hydraulics Study of Paraiba do Sul River*. Report, São Paulo.

IBRA-ITALCONSULT, 1967. *Development of Paraiba do Sul River Basin, Repport,* Roma.

IPPOLITO, Claudio, J.M. 1967. The plan of Paraiba Valley, *Tau baté*, DAEE

Yevjevich, Vujica, 1972. *Stochastic Processes in Hydrology,* Water Resources Publications, Fort Collins, Colorado, USA.

Part 3 Conclusions

Chapter 4 Conclusions

From the material contained in the previous chapters, the following conclusions can be drawn:

(1) Regretfully, very few case studies have become available from arid and tropical zones, notwithstanding the great efforts that have been made there. Because most of the developing countries are located in these zones, more attention should be paid to these regions in future studies. The experience gained in the developed nations can be exploited to avoid the harmful effects of human activities on the hydrological regime.

(2) The effect of the various human activities on the hydrological regime can be clearly detected as has been demonstrated in the various case studies. In order to determine or predict these effects, the experiences and results of the selected case studies can be utilized.

(3) The interrelationship between human activities and changes in the hydrological regime are basically of a "cause and effect" type, and are often complex and sequential in character. For example, the type of human activity with respect to time, whether it is gradual or sudden, will have a different effect on the hydrological regime.
   The human causes are either "direct" or "indirect". Water management activities, such as irrigation, drainage and streamflow control have a direct influence on the hydrological regime while, the other activities such as changes in land use, industrialization and urban activities influence the cycle less directly.

(4) With regard to the use of river water, the following human activities and their different effects have to be distinguished:
   - Consumptive use of water (definite extraction, eg for agricultural purposes);
   - Non-consumptive water use (a temporary extraction, eg for cooling).
   The consumptive use of water will mainly influence the water volume transported by the river (constantly or seasonally) while the non-consumptive uses of water can influence the distribution of flow in time and water quality.

(5) The methods used for the detection or prediction of the effect or effects depend partly on the character of the change (eg for gradual changes trend analysis can be applied; for sudden changes homogeneity tests).

(6) Methods for the detection or forecasting of the changes are in principal available, and, with certain improvements, they will give satisfactory results.
   The most applicable methods are introduced in Chapter 2 briefly and are demonstrated in Chapter 3 by case studies of methodological importance.

(7) The assessment of the quantitative changes in the hydrological regime can be performed

Conclusions

to different levels of accuracy.

If we write the general equation:

$$M = N \pm \Delta$$

where: M is the modified and N is the natural regime, and Δ is the impact (change), two methods can be followed to assess the Δ value.

With the first method Δ can be determined directly by direct computation or measurement. In this case the ε_Δ accuracy of Δ depends on the accuracy of the method of assessment.

With the second method M and N are either measured or evaluated and the difference between them is computed. While assessing the human impact, the result should be considered reliable provided the value of Δ substantially exceeds either the errors of the measurements or of the computation, or both.

(8) To derive any relationship between human activities and the hydrological regime, observations of both are necessary, otherwise the quantification of the cause is impossible and an interrelationship cannot be derived by any statistical method.

The data on the human activities should also be collected and stored within the framework of the environmental monitoring - and their availability enables the appropriate bodies to study their effect on the hydrological data collected at the same time and stored in the same place.

(9) On a global scale, the components of the water budget may change as a consequence of the various human activities. It is foreseen that the water demands will increase and thus the natural water supply (runoff) of the streams will decrease, due to intakes and water use. Especially in arid zones, water losses by evaporation and evapotranspiration will increase, due to the improvement of irrigation and storage. Moreover, while considering the effect of streamflow changes due to human activity, particularly on large basins, it may be noted that there is a possibility of additional precipitation being produced.

These tendencies might be considered in large-scale water resources planning.

(10) The need for data collection and analysis related to human activities should be recognized by everybody concerned.

For large projects, future human activities with a possible impact on the water regime should be studied in the planning phase of the projects and then the change in the hydrological regime may be predicted.

In environmental impact studies, adequate attention should be given to this type of study and not only to effects on water quality. The legal measures concerning the protection of the water resources should also follow the technical improvement.

Chapter 5 Selected bibliography

Anon 1975. *Metodicheskie rekomendatsii po otsenke i uchetu vliania agrolescomeliorativnykh meropriatiy no stok rek (Methodological recommendations on the evaluation and account of the effect of agricultural afforestation on streamflow)*, Girdrometeoizdat, 110 pp.

Dooge, J.C.I., Costin, A.B., and Finkel, H.J. 1973. 'Man's influence on the hydrological cycle'. *FAO Irrigation and Drainage Paper*, No 17, 71 pp.

IAHS 1975. The hydrological characteristics of river basins and the effects of these characteristics on better water management. *IAHS Publication No 117, Symposium of Tokyo*, 882 pp.

IAHS/UNESCO 1968. The use of analogy and digital computer in hydrology, *Proceedings of the Tucson Symposium, IAHS Publication Nos 80 and 81*, Tucson, 755 pp.

IAHS/UNESCO 1969. Floods and their comparison, *IAHS Publication Nos 84 and 85, Proceedings of the Leningrad Symposium*, 985 pp.

IAHS/UNESCO 1974. Mathematical models in hydrology, *IAHS Publication Nos 100, 101 and 102, Proceedings of the Warsaw Symposium*, 1357 pp.

ICID 1969. Irrigation and Drainage in the World - a global review. *International Commission on Irrigation and Drainage*, New Delhi.

ICID 1976. Irrigation and Salinity - a World Survey. *International Commission on Irrigation and Drainage*, New Delhi.

Kharchenko, S.I. 1975. *Hydrologia oroshaemykh zemel (Hydrology of irrigated areas)*. Gidrometeoizdat, Leningrad, 373 pp.

Klibashev, K.P., and Goroshkov, I.F. 1970. *Hydrologichaskie reachety (Hydrological computations)*, Leningrad, 460 pp.

Lvovich, M.I. 1969. *Vodnyi balans SSSR i ego preobrazovanic (USSR water balance and its transformation)*, Nauka, Moscow, 337 pp.

McPherson, M.B. 1974. Hydrological effects of urbanization. *UNESCO Studies and Reports in Hydrology*, No 18, 280 pp.

ORSTOM 1976. *Travaux et documents de l'Orstom*, No 52, Vol 1, ORSTOM, Paris.

Pereira, H.C. 1972. The influence of man on the hydrological cycle - Guide lines to policies

Selected bibliography

for the safe development of land and water resources in Status and Trends of Research in Hydrology, *UNESCO Studies and Reports in Hydrology,* No 10.

Roche, M. 1963. *Hidrologie de Surface,* Gauthier-Villars, Paris.

Romanov, V.V. 1962. *Isparenie s bolot Evropeiskoi territorii SSSR (Evaporation from swamps in the European territory of the USSR).* Gidrometeoizdat, Leningrad, 288 pp.

Shebeko, V.F. 1965. *Isparenie s bolot i balans pochvennoi vlagi (Evaporation from swamps and soil moisture balance).* Urozhai Press, Minsk, 394 pp.

Shklomanov, I.A. 1976. *Vlianie khoziaistvennoi deatelnosti na vodnye resursy i hydrologicheski rezhim (Impact of man's activity on water resources and hydrological regime).* Survey, VNIIGMI - Obninsk, 111 pp.

Sokolov, A.A., and Chapman, T.G. (Eds) 1974. *Methods of water balance computations: An international guide for research and practice.* Studies and Reports in Hydrology 17, The UNESCO Press, 127 pp.

Toebes, C., and Ouryvaev, V. (Eds) 1970. *Representative and experimental basins: An international guide for research and practice.* Studies and Reports in Hydrology 4, The UNESCO Press, 348 pp.

UNESCO 1976. Workshop on the balance on Europe, Varna, 178 pp.

UNESCO/WMO/IAHS 1973. *Proceedings of the Symposium on the design of water resources projects with inadequate data,* Madrid 1, 442 and 2, 643.

USSR IHP Committee 1978. World water balance and water resources of the earth. *UNESCO Studies and Reports in Hydrology,* No 25.

Ven Te Chow 1964. *Handbook of Applied Hydrology.* McGraw Hill, Book Comp Inc, New York.

World Meteorological Organisation 1974. *Guide to Hydrological Practices,* Third Ed, WMO Geneva.

Yevjevich, Vujica 1972. *Probability and Statistics in Hydrology.* Water Resources Publications, Fort Collins, Colorado.

Titles in this series

1. The use of analog and digital computers in hydrology. Proceedings of the Tucson Symposium, June 1966 / L'utilisation des calculatrices analogiques et des ordinateurs en hydrologie: Actes du colloque de Tucson, juin 1966. Vol. 1 & 2. *Co-edition IASH-Unesco / Coédition AIHS-Unesco.*
2. Water in the unsaturated zone. Proceedings of the Wageningen Symposium, August 1967 / L'eau dans la zone non saturée: Actes du symposium de Wageningen, août 1967. Edited by/Édité par P. E. Rijtema & H. Wassink. Vol. 1 & 2. *Co-edition IASH-Unesco / Coédition AIHS-Unesco.*
3. Floods and their computation. Proceedings of the Leningrad Symposium, August 1967 / Les crues et leur évaluation: Actes du colloque de Leningrad, août 1967. Vol. 1 & 2. *Co-edition IASH-Unesco-WMO / Coédition AIHS-Unesco-OMM.*
4. Representative and experimental basins. An international guide for research and practice. Edited by C. Toebes and V. Ouryvaev. *Published by Unesco.* (Will also appear in Russian and Spanish.)
4. Les bassins représentatifs et expérimentaux: Guide international des pratiques en matière de recherche. Publié sous la direction de C. Toebes et V. Ouryvaev. *Publié par l'Unesco.* (A paraître également en espagnol et en russe.)
5. Discharge of selected rivers of the world / Débit de certains cours d'eau du monde / Caudal de algunos ríos del mundo / Расходы воды избранных рек мира. *Published by Unesco / Publié par l'Unesco.*
    Vol. I: General and régime characteristics of stations selected / Vol. I: Caractéristiques générales et caractéristiques du régime des stations choisies / Vol. I: Caracteristicas generales y caracteristicas del régimen de las estaciones seleccionadas / Том I: Общие и режимные характеристики избранных станций.
    Vol. II: Monthly and annual discharges recorded at various selected stations (from start of observations up to 1964) / Vol. II: Débits mensuels et annuels enregistrés en diverses stations sélectionnées (de l'origine des observations à l'année 1964) / Vol. II: Caudales mensuales y anuales registrados en diversas estaciones seleccionadas (desde el comienzo de las observaciones hasta el año 1964) / Том II: Месячные и годовые расходы воды, зарегистрированные различными избранными станциями (с начала наблюдений до 1964 года).
    Vol. III: Mean monthly and extreme discharges (1965-1969) / Vol. III: Débits mensuels moyens et débits extrêmes (1965-1969) / Vol. III: Caudales mensuales medianos y caudales extremos (1965-1969) / Том III: Средне-месячные и экстремальные расходы (1965—1969 гг.).
    Vol. III (part II): Mean monthly and extreme discharges (1969-1972) / Vol. III (partie II): Débits mensuels moyens et débits extrêmes (1969-1972) / Vol. III (parte II): Caudales mensuales medianos y caudales extremos (1969-1972) / Том III (часть II); Средне-месячные и экстремальные расходы (1969—1972 гг.).
    Vol. III (part III): Mean monthly and extreme discharges (1972-1975) (English, French, Spanish, Russian).
6. List of International Hydrological Decade Stations of the world / Liste des stations de la Décennie hydrologique internationale existant dans le monde / Lista de las estaciones del Decenio Hidrológico Internacional del mundo / Список станций международного гидрологического десятилетия земного шара. / *Published by Unesco / Publié par l'Unesco.*
7. Ground-water studies. An international guide for practice. Edited by R. Brown, J. Ineson, V. Konoplyantzev and V. Kovalevski. (Will also appear in French, Russian and Spanish / Paraîtra également en espagnol, en français et en russe.)
8. Land subsidence. Proceedings of the Tokyo Symposium, September 1969 / Affaissement du sol: Actes du colloque de Tokyo, septembre 1969. Vol. 1 & 2. *Co-edition IASH-Unesco / Coédition AIHS-Unesco.*
9. Hydrology of deltas. Proceedings of the Bucharest Symposium, May 1969 / Hydrologie des deltas: Actes du colloque de Bucarest, mai 1969. Vol. 1 & 2. *Co-edition IASH-Unesco / Coédition AIHS-Unesco.*
10. Status and trends of research in hydrology / Bilan et tendances de la recherche en hydrologie. *Published by Unesco / Publié par l'Unesco.*
11. World water balance. Proceedings of the Reading Symposium, July 1970 / Bilan hydrique mondial: Actes du colloque de Reading, juillet 1970. Vol. 1-3. *Co-edition IAHS-Unesco-WMO / Coédition AIHS-Unesco-OMM.*
12. Research on representative and experimental basins. Proceedings of the Wellington (New Zealand) Symposium, December 1970 / Recherches sur les bassins représentatifs et expérimentaux: Actes du colloque de Wellington (N.Z.), décembre 1970. *Co-edition IASH-Unesco / Coédition AIHS-Unesco.*
13. Hydrometry: Proceedings of the Koblenz Symposium, September 1970 / Hydrométrie : Actes du colloque de Coblence, september 1970. *Co-edition IAHS-Unesco-WMO.*
14. Hydrologic information systems. *Co-edition Unesco-WNO,*
15. Mathematical models in hydrology: Proceedings of the Warsaw Symposium, July 1971 / Les modèles mathématiques en hydrologie: Actes du colloque de Varsovie, juillet 1971. Vol. 1-3. *Co-edition IAHS-Unesco-WMO.*
16. Design of water resources projects with inadequate data: Proceedings of the Madrid Symposium, June 1973 / Elaboration des projets d'utilisation des resources en eau sans données suffisantes: Actes du colloque de Madrid, juin 1973. Vol. 1-3. *Co-edition Unesco-WMO-IAHS.*
17. Methods for water balance computations. An international guide for research and practice.
18. Hydrological effects of urbanization. Report of the Sub-group on the Effects of Urbanization on the Hydrological Environment.
19. Hydrology of marsh-ridden areas. Proceedings of the Minsk Symposium, June 1972.
20. Hydrological maps. *Co-edition Unesco-WMO.*

21. World catalogue of very large floods/Répertoire mondial des très fortes crues/Catalogo mundial de grandes crecidas/ Всемирный каталог больших наводков.
22. Floodflow computation. Methods compiled from world experience.
23. Guidebook on water quality surveys. (In press.)
24. Effects of urbanization and industrialization on the hydrological regime and on water quality. Proceedings of the Amsterdam Symposium, October 1977, convened by Unesco and organized by Unesco and the Netherlands National Committee for the IHP in co-operation with IAHS / Effets de l'urbanisation et de l'industrialisation sur le régime hydrologique et sur la qualité de l'eau. Actes du Colloque d'Amsterdam, Octobre 1977, convoqué par l'Unesco et organisé par l'Unesco et le Comité national des Pays-Bas pour le PHI en coopération avec l'AISH. (In press / Sous presse).
25. World water balance and water resources of the earth.
26. Impact of urbanization and industrialization on water resources planning and management.
27. Socio-economic aspects of urban hydrology.
28. Casebook of methods of computation of quantitative changes in the hydrological régime of river basins due to human activities

FUNDERBURG LIBRARY
MANCHESTER COLLEGE

**WITHDRAWN
from
Funderburg Library**

(A) SC 80/XX-28/A